MEASUREMENT AND EVALUATION IN TEACHING
THIRD EDITION

MEASUREMENT AND EVALUATION IN TEACHING
THIRD EDITION

Norman E. Gronlund

Professor of Educational Psychology
University of Illinois

Macmillan Publishing Co., Inc.
New York

Collier Macmillan Publishers
London

MACMILLAN PUBLISHING CO., INC.
866 Third Avenue, New York, New York 10022
COLLIER MACMILLAN CANADA, LTD.

Library of Congress Cataloging in Publication Data

Gronlund, Norman Edward, (date)
    Measurement and evaluation in teaching.

    Bibliography: p.
    Includes index.
    1. Educational tests and measurements.   I. Title.
LB3051.G74   1976   371.2'6   75-4848
ISBN 0-02-348050-5

Printing: 3 4 5 6 7 8   Year: 7 8 9 0 1 2

To My Parents

PREFACE

This third edition retains the same organization as the earlier editions, but it gives increased attention to two important areas. First, greater emphasis is given to the use of tests and other evaluation instruments in the improvement of learning and instruction. Second, new material has been added throughout the book on the preparation, use, and evaluation of *criterion-referenced* tests (i.e., tests used to describe the learning tasks pupils can and cannot perform). The need for such instruments has been stimulated by the increased use of mastery learning and individualized instruction in the schools, and by the new trend toward making teachers accountable for the learning of their pupils. For these purposes, it is more important to know *what* the pupil is learning than to know how he compares with others (*norm-referenced* measurement). Thus, criterion-referenced tests provide a useful adjunct to the traditional tests and evaluation instruments used by teachers, and they are given this emphasis in the book.

To incorporate the desired changes in this edition, a number of chapters have been extensively revised (1, 2, 3, 6, 18) and minor revisions made in others. Chapter 18 has been expanded to include sections on mastery learning and individualized instruction, and a new Chapter 19 has been added on marking and reporting. Material on criterion-referenced measurement has been included in Chapters 1 through 6, 11, 12, 15, 18, and 19. In addition, new suggested readings are listed for all chapters, and the standardized tests referred to in the text and listed in the appendix have been updated. The new material on criterion-referenced testing and the increased attention given to the use of tests in improving learning, along with the various other changes, should make this edition of the book even more useful to teachers and prospective teachers than the two previous editions.

The basic theme of the book remains the same: classroom evaluation is viewed as an integral part of the teaching-learning process. It involves three fundamental steps: (1) identifying and defining the intended learning outcomes, (2) constructing or selecting tests and other evaluation instruments that are relevant to the specified outcomes, and (3) using the results to improve learning and instruction. Major sections of the book are devoted to each of these areas.

The special emphases in the book are probably best indicated by a listing of the learning outcomes that should result from its use. In general terms, these expected outcomes are

1. An understanding of the interrelated nature of teaching, learning, and evaluation.
2. The ability to clearly define instructional objectives in behavioral terms.
3. An understanding of the concepts of validity and reliability and their role in the construction, the selection, and the use of evaluation instruments.
4. The ability to construct classroom tests that measure specific learning outcomes (from simple to complex).
5. The ability to select the standardized tests that are most appropriate for a particular situation.
6. The ability to administer tests properly and to use test results effectively (with due regard to the necessary precautions).
7. The ability to interpret test scores (with full awareness of the ever-present error of measurement).
8. The ability to construct, select, and use nontest evaluation instruments.
9. An appreciation of both the potentialities and the limitations of the various tests and evaluation procedures used in teaching.
10. An understanding of how evaluation procedures can contribute to the teaching-learning processs.

The book was originally designed for both elementary and secondary school teachers, at both the undergraduate and beginning graduate levels, and the examples and illustrations used in the text reflect this orientation. Special efforts have been made to keep the book interesting and understandable without slighting basic concepts, such as validity and reliability, or sacrificing technical accuracy. The writing style is direct, and practical examples are used to clarify difficult points. Liberal use is made of sample test items and excerpts from evaluation devices to illustrate principles and techniques.

In keeping with the focus of the book, statistical procedures receive minor attention in the main body of the text. Statistical concepts are introduced only when essential for understanding the discussion and then the emphasis is on interpretation rather than on computation. For those who want to acquire a minimum level of computational skill in statistics, a special section is provided in the appendices.

Special appreciation is expressed to Jean C. Angley, Lee J. Cronbach, and Tom Hastings for their assistance on the first edition of this book. My appreciation is also expressed to the publishers and individuals who permitted the use of copyrighted materials in the current edition. In addition, the efficient typing services of Marian Brinkerhoff are gratefully acknowledged.

N. E. G.

CONTENTS

PART IV
Evaluating Procedures,
Products, and Typical Behavior

PART V
Using Evaluation Results in Teaching

APPENDICES

PART I

The
Evaluation Process

CHAPTER 1
The Role of Evaluation in Teaching

Evaluation includes a number of techniques that are indispensable to the teacher. . . . However, evaluation is not merely a collection of techniques—evaluation is a process—it is a continuous process which underlies all good teaching and learning.

Some form of evaluation is inevitable in teaching. It is as inevitable in classroom teaching as it is in all fields of activity when judgments need to be made, however simple or complex the consideration involved—whether a matter of deciding what to wear today or what profession to follow through the ensuing years. Unfortunately, evaluation in the classroom is all too often done as though it were extraneous to the main purpose of teaching.

When crossing a little-used country lane, we normally decide when it is safe to cross with little awareness of having made a judgment. On the other hand, a test pilot is quite aware of making a judgment when he decides to fly a new airplane. His life depends upon meticulous inspection of all tabulations of laboratory tests, reports from the weather station, medical reports about his own physical condition and capabilities and, finally, upon his judgment based on past experience and on every bit of reliable information which it has been possible to gather about test-flying in general and about test-flying this new plane in particular. A test pilot who failed to make such a carefully considered judgment and relied instead on his "feeling" of how the plane looked or the motors sounded, would obviously be accepting a greater risk than most of us would care to incur.

The possible aftermath of haphazard, or wholly subjective, evaluation in a teaching-learning situation is not likely to be quite so dire as in the case of a foolhardy test pilot. But since the evaluations teachers make can have a tremendous influence on the lives of their pupils, they should not be lightly made, and certainly never casually made. The role of evaluation is so intrinsic to the teaching-learning situation that even hasty consideration seems to indicate the advantages of a systematic use of planned evaluation procedures. Carefully collected evaluation data help teachers understand the learner, plan learning experiences for him, and determine the extent to which the instructional objectives are being achieved. It is not intended that the use of evaluation techniques replace the thoughtful judgments of teachers, but rather that they provide a more dependable basis for making such judgments. Instructional decisions are more likely to be sound when they are based on information that is *accurate, relevant,* and *comprehensive.*

The purpose, then, of a book on measurement and evaluation is to help teachers and other school personnel make better evaluative judgments. You should be warned at the outset, however, that you will find no magic solutions to your educational problems in test scores or the results of other evaluation techniques. There is no more magic in these than there is an absolute guarantee in laboratory findings that a test pilot will survive. What you will find is exactly what a pilot finds in his specialized tabulations and reports—more *objective* information on which to base decisions.

As we guide pupils toward the achievement of instructional objectives, diagnose their learning difficulties, determine their readiness for new learning experiences, place them in classroom groups for special activities, assist them with their problems of adjustment, and prepare reports of pupil progress for parents, we cannot escape making evaluative judgments. Decisions must be made and action must be taken. The more accurately we judge our pupils, the more effective we will be in directing their learning. An understanding of the principles and procedures of evaluation, then, should aid us in making more intelligent decisions in directing pupil progress toward worthwhile educational outcomes.

INSTRUCTIONAL DECISIONS REQUIRING EVALUATION DATA

There are numerous day-to-day decisions that teachers must make that require some knowledge of their pupils' aptitudes, achievements, and personal development. Although it would be infeasible to make an exhaustive list of all such decisions, it is possible to identify some of the common ones. The following list of questions illustrates some of the major instructional decisions teachers are likely to encounter during the course of their teaching. Examples of the types of evaluation information that might be most helpful in answering the questions are included in the parentheses.

1. How realistic are my teaching plans for this particular group of pupils? (mental ability tests, past record of achievement).
2. How should the pupils be grouped for more effective learning? (range of mental ability scores, past record of achievement).
3. To what extent are these pupils ready for the next learning experience? (readiness tests, pretests covering needed skills, past record of achievement).
4. To what extent are pupils attaining the minimum essentials of the course? (mastery tests, observation).
5. To what extent are pupils progressing beyond the minimum essentials? (periodic quizzes, general achievement tests, observation).
6. At what point would a review be most beneficial? (periodic quizzes, observation.)
7. What types of learning difficulties are the pupils encountering? (diagnostic tests, observation, pupil conferences).
8. Which pupils are underachievers? (mental ability tests, achievement tests).
9. Which pupils should be referred to counseling, special classes, or remedial programs? (mental ability tests, achievement tests, diagnostic tests, observation).
10. Which pupils have poor self-understanding? (self-ratings, pupil conferences).
11. Which school mark should be assigned to each pupil? (review of all evaluation data).
12. How effective was my teaching? (achievement tests, pupils' ratings, supervisors' ratings).

Although this list of questions provides a good overview of the need for evaluation information in teaching, instructional decisions are, of course, not that neatly ordered. Within any decision area there are numerous subquestions to be answered, there is a functional overlap among the various areas, and a wide array of different types of evaluation data might be useful in any particular situation. Thus, the teaching-learning process involves a continuous and interrelated series of instructional decisions concerning ways to enhance pupil learning. Our main contention here, however, is that the effectiveness of the instruction depends to a large extent on the quality of the evaluation information on which the decisions are based.

THE MEANING OF EVALUATION

As is common with terms which are part of our general vocabulary, there is some confusion concerning the meaning of the term *evaluation* as it applies especially to education. In some instances, it is used as a synonym for the term *measurement*. Thus, a teacher who administers an achieve-ment test might say either that he is "measuring" achievement or that he is "evaluating" achievement, with little regard for the specific meaning of the two terms. In other cases, "evaluation" is used as a collective term for those appraisal methods which do not depend on "measurement." This use of the two terms distinguishes "evaluations as qualitative descriptions of pupil behavior" (e.g., anecdotal records of behavior) as opposed to "measurements," which are quantitative descriptions (e.g., test *scores*). When the meaning of the term evaluation is analyzed, it is easy to under-stand how these misconceptions came about.

From an instructional standpoint, *evaluation* may be defined as a *systematic process of determining the extent to which instructional ob-jectives are achieved by pupils.* There are two important aspects of this definition. First, note that evaluation implies a *systematic process,* which omits casual, uncontrolled observation of pupils. Second, evaluation always assumes that *instructional objectives* have been previously identified. With-out previously determined objectives, it is patently impossible to judge the nature and extent of pupil learning.

This definition indicates that *evaluation* is a much more comprehensive and inclusive term than *measurement.* Evaluation includes both qualitative and quantitative descriptions of pupil behavior *plus* value judgments con-cerning the desirability of that behavior. Measurement is limited to quanti-tative descriptions of pupil behavior. It does not include qualitative descrip-tions nor does it imply judgments concerning the worth or value of the behavior measured. The following diagrams clearly show the relationship between measurement and evaluation:

Evaluation = Quantitative description of pupils (measurement)
+ Value judgments
Evaluation = Qualitative description of pupils (nonmeasurement)
+ Value judgments

As noted in the diagrams, evaluation may or may not be based on measure-ment, but when it is, it goes beyond the simple quantitative description.

The main emphasis in classroom evaluation is on the extent to which learning outcomes are achieved. How much more accurately and quickly can a pupil do multiplication problems? How much greater is his under-standing of the number system? Has he made any improvement in working with other pupils in small groups without constant supervision? If so, how much? Has he made any improvement in using his time effectively? If so, how much? Is his handwriting more legible? If so, how much more? These questions are typical of those which we must be prepared to ask ourselves and to answer about each of our pupils. A variety of methods are therefore necessary, and a sound evaluation program will include both measurement and nonmeasurement techniques, each to be used as ap-propriate.

EVALUATION IN THE SCHOOL PROGRAM

Evaluation plays an important role in many facets of the school program. It contributes directly to the teaching-learning process used in classroom instruction, and it is useful in programed instruction, curriculum development, accountability programs, marking and reporting, guidance and counseling, school administration, and school research programs. Each of these uses will be discussed in turn.

Evaluation and the Instructional Process

Broadly conceived, the main purpose of classroom instruction is to change pupil behavior in desired directions. The term *behavior* is used here in a broad sense to include all changes in the intellectual, emotional, and physical spheres. When classroom instruction is viewed in this light, evaluation becomes an important part of the teaching-learning process. The "desired directions" are established by the instructional objectives, the changes in behavior are brought about by the planned learning activities, and the pupils' learning progress is periodically evaluated by tests and other evaluation devices. While the interdependent nature of teaching and learning is beyond dispute, the interdependent nature of teaching, learning, *and* evaluation is less often recognized. The interdependence of these three facets of education can be clearly seen, however, in the following steps involved in the instructional process.

Preparing Instructional Objectives in Terms of Desired Learning Outcomes. The first step in both teaching and evaluation is that of determining the learning outcomes to be expected from classroom instruction. What should pupils be like at the end of the learning experience? In other words, what kind of learning product is being sought? What knowledges and understandings should the pupils possess? What skills should they be able to display? What interests and attitudes should they have developed? What changes in habits of thinking, feeling, and doing should have taken place? In short, what specific behavior changes are we striving for, and what are pupils like when we have succeeded in bringing about those changes?

Only by identifying instructional objectives and stating them clearly in terms of specific behavior can we provide direction to the teaching process and set the stage for ready evaluation of learning outcomes. This step is so vital to the total role of evaluation that the next chapter is entirely devoted to the process of identifying and defining instructional objectives.

Preassessing the Learners' Needs. When the instructional objectives have been clearly specified, it is usually desirable to make some assessment of the learners' needs in relation to the learning outcomes to be achieved. Do the pupils possess the abilities and skills needed to proceed with the instruction? Have the pupils already mastered some of the intended learning outcomes? Evaluating pupils' knowledge and skill at the beginning of instruction enables us to answer such questions. This information is useful in planning remedial work for pupils who lack the prerequisite skills, in revising our list of instructional objectives, and in modifying our instructional plans to fit the needs of the learners.

Providing Relevant Instruction. It is in the provision of relevant instruction that course content and teaching methods are integrated into planned instructional activities designed to help pupils achieve the desired learning outcomes. During this instructional phase, testing and evaluation provide a means of (1) monitoring learning progress, and (2) diagnosing learning difficulties. Thus, periodic evaluation during instruction provides a type of feedback-corrective procedure that aids in continuously adapting instruction to group and individual needs.

Evaluating Intended Outcomes. The final step in the instructional process is to determine the extent to which the instructional objectives have been achieved by the pupils. This is accomplished by using tests and other evaluation instruments that are specifically designed to measure the intended learning outcomes. Ideally, the instructional objectives will clearly specify the desired changes in pupil behavior, and the evaluation instruments will provide a relevant measure, or description, of the same behavior. Matching evaluation instruments to instructional objectives is basic to effective classroom evaluation, and will receive considerable attention in later chapters.

Using the Evaluation Results. Pupil evaluation is often regarded as being essentially for the benefit of teachers and administrators. This attitude overlooks the direct contribution evaluation can make to pupils. Properly used, evaluation procedures can contribute directly to improved pupil learning by (1) clarifying the nature of the intended learning outcomes, (2) providing short-term goals to work toward, (3) providing feedback concerning learning progress, and (4) providing information for overcoming learning difficulties and for selecting future learning experiences. Although these purposes are probably best served by the periodic evaluation during instruction, the final evaluation of intended outcomes should also contribute to these ends.

Information from carefully developed evaluation techniques can also be used to evaluate and improve instruction. Such information can aid in judging (1) the appropriateness and attainability of the instructional objectives, (2) the usefulness of the instructional materials, and (3) the effectiveness of the instructional methods. Thus, evaluation procedures can contribute to improvements in the teaching-learning process itself, as well as contributing directly to improved pupil learning.

Evaluation results are, of course, also used for assigning marks and reporting pupil progress to parents. Unfortunately, too many teachers focus on these functions of evaluation rather than on its use in improving learning and instruction. In addition to marking and reporting, evaluation results are also used for various administrative and guidance functions. These will be described shortly. Here, we are simply presenting an overview of the instructional process and the vital role that evaluation plays in it. The simplified instructional model shown in Figure 1.1 summarizes the basic steps involved in instruction and illustrates the interrelated nature of teaching and evaluation.

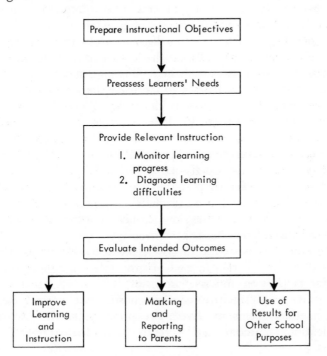

FIGURE 1.1. Simplified instructional model.

The few brief remarks in this section about the role of evaluation in instruction will be expanded upon throughout this book. In addition, two chapters are specifically devoted to the use of evaluation in teaching. Chapter 18 is concerned with the use of evaluation results in improving learning and instruction, and Chapter 19 is devoted to using evaluation results in marking and reporting.

Evaluation and Programed Instruction

There is no place in education where testing has played a more central role than it has in programed instruction. Essentially, programed instruction consists of a continuous series of learning sequences, each containing the following elements: (1) the presentation of a limited amount of instructional material (called a *step* or *frame*); (2) a test item, question, or problem, requiring a response to the instructional material; (3) immediate knowledge of results, or feedback, concerning the correctness of the response made in step two. This basic learning sequence is repeated over and over again in a program. The instructional materials, on which the learning sequences are based, are carefully ordered to guide the learner toward a specific set of instructional objectives.

There are two basic types of programs: linear programs and branching programs. The *linear* program consists of a carefully graded set of materials, in continuous order, that the learner works through step by step. Typically, the steps are so small that the learner has a high rate of success in answering the questions at each step. This high success rate is designed to reinforce correct responses and to motivate the learner to continue. In contrast, the *branching* program is designed to permit each learner to follow the most efficient route for him. After each instructional segment the learner is asked a question, and his answer determines where he goes next. If he answers correctly, he proceeds to the next instructional sequence. If he answers incorrectly, he is referred back to the material he misunderstood or to specially prepared remedial material. Branching permits the rapid learner to proceed through the program with the minimum number of steps and enables the slow learner to obtain as much repetition and remedial instruction as he is apt to need.

Although the test question is the key element in both types of programs, it serves a different function in each. In the linear program, the question provides for motivation and reinforcement of learning. In the branching program, it is used primarily as a diagnostic and referral device. The branching method seems to have more promise for the programing of complex learning material, and it tends to be increasingly favored by programers.

Programed instruction has been presented in many different forms. In some cases teaching machines have been used. In other cases, the programed materials have been put into workbook or textbook form. More recently, computer-assisted instruction has come into being, at least on an experimental basis. All of these procedures have been designed to serve as supplementary methods of individualizing instruction, primarily by providing for different rates of learning among pupils. In addition to its direct use, however, the rapid growth of programed instruction has also had a number of indirect effects on classroom teaching—some positive and some negative. Among the positive effects are the following:

1. There has been greater emphasis on the stating of instructional objectives in specific behavioral terms. (Programing has stressed the need to specify the desired changes in pupil behavior before effective programs can be developed.)

2. There has been greater emphasis on the need to organize learning experiences into more orderly sequences. (Programing has focused on the logical order and the hierarchical nature of instructional content.)
3. There has been greater emphasis on the use of tests for improving learning. (Programing has directed attention to the interrelated nature of instruction, testing, and learning.)

Among the *possible* negative effects are the following:

1. Stress on specific behavioral objectives may cause some teachers to focus on the more simple and relatively unimportant learning outcomes. (These are, of course, the easiest to identify and define.)
2. Adopting the relatively simple "instruction-test-feedback" model used in most programing may cause some teachers to reduce all instruction to the training level. (Programing frequently does not provide for transfer of learning or other aspects of complex achievement.)
3. Emphasis on mastery in programed instruction may cause some teachers to overemphasize the mastery of simple knowledges and skills. (Pupils also need to be encouraged to develop intellectual skills and abilities that go beyond the minimum essentials.)

The possible negative effects can, of course, all be avoided by careful planning. It is largely a matter of not fitting classroom instruction too closely to the typical model used for programed instruction. The model is especially good for the mastery of minimum essentials and for learning at the training level, but it is less useful as a guide for the development of complex achievement. A desirable procedure might be to turn over as many routine tasks as possible to programed instruction and to give greater emphasis to the teaching and testing of complex learning outcomes (e.g., understanding, application, interpretation) during regular classroom instruction. When computer-assisted instruction becomes more widely used in schools, this recommendation may, of course, have to be radically modified.

Evaluation and Curriculum Development

Essentially the same steps as those already described for the teaching-learning process have been adopted as a frame of reference for curriculum building. A common procedure is to appoint committees of teachers in each major content area and to have them develop units of work in their respective areas. Lindvall has listed the following steps as those a committee should follow in developing a unit for a curriculum guide:[1]

---

[1] C. M. Lindvall, S. Nardozza, and M. Felton, "The Importance of Specific Objectives in Curriculum Development," in C. M. Lindvall (ed.), *Defining Educational Objectives* (Pittsburgh: University of Pittsburgh Press, 1964), p. 13.

1. *Defining Desired Outcomes or Specific Objectives in Behavioral Terms.* A first task of a team working on the development of a specific unit is to define exactly what pupils are to be expected to be able to do after they have mastered the unit. The emphasis here is on stating these objectives in terms of definite *pupil behaviors.* They are not to be stated in terms of what the teacher is going to do. They are not to describe learning activities. Each statement is to describe something that the pupil will be able to do after he has had the learning experience. . . .

2. *Identifying Suggested Activities.* For each unit the responsible committee is to develop a list or brief description of learning activities that should be effective in helping pupils to achieve the specific objectives. Note that this list is intended to be suggestive only. It is not intended as a strait jacket which will prevent the teacher from employing those instructional procedures which seem most effective for him with his particular students.

3. *Developing a List of Suggested Materials.* Each particular unit is to be developed further through the identification of text books, supplementary reading books, other reading materials, audiovisual aids, and any other materials which should be helpful in teaching the unit.

4. *Suggesting Evaluation Procedures.* A final step that must be taken in the development of a unit is to suggest some appropriate procedures that a teacher might use in determining the extent to which pupils have mastered the stated specific objectives. Naturally, these suggested evaluation procedures must be related directly to the previously developed objectives. That is, the objectives tell what the pupil is to be able to do, and the evaluation procedures provide a means of determining the extent to which he is able to do it.

If all curriculum guides were patterned along this line, the work of the classroom teacher would be greatly simplified. Unfortunately, most contain only very general statements of objectives and many neglect to include suggestions of appropriate evaluation procedures. These two steps, of course, go hand in hand. Unless objectives are stated in specific terms, it is difficult to determine which evaluation procedures are most relevant.

On a broader scale, evaluation of the curriculum itself also plays an important role in curriculum development. During the early stages, when new methods and materials are being tried, evaluation data enable the curriculum developer to determine the effectiveness of the new procedures and to identify areas where revision is needed. When the new curriculum program has been fully developed, evaluation data make it possible to determine the degree to which the new curriculum is effective in meeting the instructional objectives for which it was designed. The first type of curriculum evaluation has been called *formative evaluation* and the second *summative evaluation.*[2] The main purpose of formative evaluation is to im-

---

[2] M. Scriven, "The Methodology of Evaluation," in *Perspectives of Curriculum Evaluation,* AERA Monograph Series on Curriculum Evaluation, No. 1 (Chicago: Rand McNally, 1967).

prove the instructional methods and materials so that greater student learning will result. The main purpose of summative evaluation is to appraise the overall effectiveness of a curriculum program. In this case, the data are not intended to serve as a basis for modifying the procedures, but rather as a basis for selecting the most appropriate curriculum for school use.

Evaluation and School Accountability Programs

During the past several years a number of states have passed laws making teachers and other school personnel accountable (i.e., answerable) for the learning and development of students. Although the specific nature of these educational accountability laws vary from state to state, they typically include provisions for specifying and evaluating the intended outcomes of the school program. The following brief excerpt from the California Stull Act (Assembly Bill 293), passed in 1971 and put into effect in the fall of 1972, illustrates the nature of such accountability requirements:[3]

> 13487. The governing board of each school district shall develop and adopt specific evaluation and assessment guidelines which shall include but shall not necessarily be limited in content to the following elements:
>
> (a) The establishment of standards of expected student progress in each area of study and of techniques for the assessment of that progress.
>
> (b) Assessment of certificated personnel competence as it relates to the established standards.
>
> (c) Assessment of other duties normally required to be performed by certificated employees as an adjunct to their regular assignments.
>
> (d) The establishment of procedures and techniques for ascertaining that the certificated employee is maintaining proper control and is preserving a suitable learning environment.

Accountability laws, such as the Stull Act, create special needs for knowledge and skill in the evaluation area. Teachers are typically expected to prepare instructional objectives for each course they teach and to prepare tests and other evaluation instruments for measuring and reporting on pupil progress.[4]

Other Uses of Evaluation Results

As we have seen in the preceding sections, the main purpose of evaluation is to improve learning and instruction. All other uses are secondary

---

[3] Statutes of California (1971), p. 727.
[4] N. E. Gronlund, *Determining Accountability for Classroom Instruction* (New York: Macmillan, 1974).

or supplementary to this major purpose. At this point, however, some of the more important supplementary uses do merit brief discussion.

Use in Reporting Pupil Progress to Parents. The systematic use of evaluation procedures in the classroom provides the teacher with an objective and comprehensive picture of each pupil's learning progress. Whether this report is presented to parents in writing, or orally in teacher-parent conferences, the objectivity apparent in planned measurement and evaluation procedures enables the teacher to focus on the pupil's actual school achievement instead of resorting to unsubstantiated generalities. The comprehensive nature of the evaluation process also equips the teacher to report on the total development of the pupil rather than on a limited area of it. This kind of overall objective information about pupils provides the foundation for the most effective cooperation between parents and teachers.

Use in Guidance and Counseling. The results of evaluation procedures are especially useful for guidance and counseling. Assisting a pupil with educational and vocational decisions, guiding him in the selection of curricular and extracurricular activities, and helping him solve personal and social adjustment problems, all require an objective knowledge of the pupil's abilities, interests, attitudes, and other personal characteristics. The more comprehensive the picture of the pupil's strengths and limitations in various areas, the greater the likelihood of effective guidance and counseling.

Use in School Administration. Just as planned appraisal methods help the teacher determine the effectiveness of course content and teaching methods, a comprehensive continuous evaluation program in the school aids the administrator. From the collected data, he is able to judge the extent to which the objectives of the school are being achieved, to identify strengths and weaknesses in the curriculum, and to appraise special programs in the school. Evaluation also provides the information on which to base administrative decisions concerning the placement, grouping, and promotion of pupils. In the public relations area, an evaluation program is indispensable for gathering the objective data to be used in explaining to the community the goals and accomplishments of the school.

Use in School Research. Evaluation data can also play an important role in the school research program. Carefully controlled studies of such things as the comparative effectiveness of different curricula, different teaching methods, and different organizational plans require objective measures of pupil performance.

TYPES OF EVALUATION PROCEDURES

One of the distinctive features of the evaluation process is the use of a wide variety of procedures. These may be classified and described in many different ways, depending on the frame of reference used. What we shall do here is present those bases for classification that are most useful for understanding and using evaluation techniques in teaching. Although the categories are not discrete, they provide a good general overview of evaluation procedures and a useful introduction to some of the basic terminology in the area. The specific techniques used in classroom evaluation will be described and illustrated in later chapters.

Maximum Performance Versus Typical Performance

Evaluation procedures may be placed in two broad categories on the basis of the nature of the measurement. These have been labeled by Cronbach as measures of *maximum* performance and measures of *typical* performance.[5] In the first category are those procedures used to determine a person's *abilities*. Procedures of this type are concerned with how well an individual performs when he is motivated to put forth his best effort. In short, the evaluation results indicate what an individual *can* do. *Aptitude* and *achievement* tests are included in this category. These two types of tests are commonly distinguished by the use made of the results rather than by the qualities of the tests themselves. An aptitude test is primarily designed to predict success in some *future learning activity*, while an achievement test is designed to indicate degree of success in some *past learning activity*. Since some tests may be used for both purposes, however, it is obvious that the difference is mainly a matter of emphasis. For example, an algebra test designed to measure achievement at the end of the course may also be used to predict success in future mathematics courses. Such overlapping of function prevents a distinct classification, but the terms aptitude and achievement provide useful designations for discussions of measures of ability.

The second subdivision in this classification of procedures includes those designed to reflect a person's *typical behavior*. How does the individual *usually* behave in normal or routine situations? Results in this area, then, tend to indicate what an individual *will* do rather than what he can do. The importance of this distinction between ability and typical behavior is easily illustrated. An individual with the ability to drive an automobile safely may typically drive in an unsafe manner. A student with considerable aptitude for mathematics may show little interest in the pursuit of mathematics. A pupil who knows the rules of good sportsmanship may refuse to abide by them. Observation of the daily behavior of children and adults alike will provide numerous illustrations of the difference between ability and typical behavior.

Evaluations of typical behavior fall in the general area of personality appraisal. Methods designed to evaluate *interests, attitudes,* and various

---

[5] L. J. Cronbach, *Essentials of Psychological Testing*, 3rd ed. (New York: Harper and Row, 1970).

aspects of *personal-social adjustment* are included in this category. While this is an extremely important area in which to appraise pupil behavior, evaluations of typical behavior are fraught with difficulties. Inadequacy of testing instruments in this field has led to wide use of interviews, questionnaires, anecdotal records, ratings, and various other self-report and observational techniques. None of these techniques when used alone provides an adequate appraisal of typical behavior, but the combined results of a number of them enables the teacher to make fairly accurate judgments concerning pupil progress and change in these areas.

Placement, Formative, Diagnostic, and Summative Evaluation

The way evaluation techniques are used in classroom instruction also provides a convenient framework for describing evaluation procedures. One such classification system follows the sequence in which evaluation procedures are likely to be used in classroom instruction.[6] These categories are related to their role in teaching in the following manner:

1. Evaluation of pupil entry behavior in a sequence of instruction (*placement* evaluation).
2. Evaluation of pupil learning progress during instruction (*formative* evaluation).
3. Evaluation of pupil learning difficulties during instruction (*diagnostic* evaluation).
4. Evaluation of pupil achievement at the end of instruction (*summative* evaluation).

The functions of each of these types of classroom evaluation are unique enough to require instruments specifically designed for the intended use.

Placement Evaluation. Placement evaluation is concerned with the pupil's entry behavior and typically focuses on questions such as the following: (1) Does the pupil possess the knowledge and skills needed to begin the planned instruction? For example, does the beginning algebra student have a sufficient command of computational skills? (2) To what extent has the pupil already mastered the objectives of the planned instruction? Sufficient mastery might indicate the desirability of the pupil's skipping certain units or of his being placed in a more advanced course. (3) To what extent do the pupil's interests, work habits, and personality characteristics indicate that one mode of instruction might be better than another (e.g., group instruction versus independent study)? Answers to questions like these require the use of a variety of techniques: readiness tests, aptitude tests, pretests on course objectives, self-report inventories,

---

[6] P. W. Airasian and G. J. Madaus, "Functional Types of Student Evaluation," *Measurement and Evaluation in Guidance*, 4, 221–233, 1972.

observational techniques, and so on. The goal of placement evaluation is to determine the position in the instructional sequence and the mode of instruction that are most likely to provide optimum achievement for each pupil.

Formative Evaluation. As noted earlier, formative evaluation is used to monitor learning progress during instruction. Its purpose is to provide continuous feedback to both pupil and teacher concerning learning successes and failures. Feedback to students provides reinforcement of successful learning and identifies the specific learning errors that need correction. Feedback to the teacher provides information for modifying instruction and for prescribing group and individual remedial work. Formative evaluation depends heavily on specially prepared tests for each segment of instruction (e.g., unit, chapter). These are usually mastery tests that provide direct measures of all the intended learning outcomes of the segment. Prescriptions for alternative or remedial instruction are typically keyed to each item in the test or to each set of items measuring a separate skill. Tests used for formative evaluation are most frequently teacher-made, but customized tests (tests made to order by publishers) can also serve this function. Observational techniques are, of course, also useful in monitoring pupil progress and identifying learning errors. Since formative evaluation is directed toward improving learning and instruction, the results are typically *not* used for assigning course grades.

Diagnostic Evaluation. Diagnostic evaluation is concerned with the pupils' persistent or recurring learning difficulties that are left unresolved by the standard corrective prescriptions of formative evaluation. If a pupil continues to experience failure in reading, mathematics, or other subjects, despite the use of prescribed alternate methods of instruction (e.g., programmed materials, visual aids), then a more detailed diagnosis is indicated. To use a medical analogy, formative evaluation provides first aid treatment for simple learning problems, and diagnostic evaluation searches for the underlying causes of those problems that do not respond to first aid treatment. Thus, diagnostic evaluation is much more comprehensive and detailed. It involves the use of specially prepared diagnostic tests as well as various observational techniques. Serious learning problems are also likely to require the services of remedial, psychological, and medical specialists. The primary aim of diagnostic evaluation is to determine the causes of learning problems and to formulate a plan for remedial action.

Summative Evaluation. Summative evaluation typically comes at the end of a course (or unit) of instruction. It is designed to determine the extent to which the instructional objectives have been achieved and is used primarily for assigning course grades or for certifying pupil mastery of the intended learning outcomes. The techniques used in summative evaluation are determined by the instructional objectives, but they typically include teacher-made achievement tests, ratings on various types of performance (e.g., laboratory, oral report), and evaluations of products (e.g., themes, drawings, research reports). Although the main purpose of summative evaluation is grading, or the certification of pupil mastery, it also provides information for judging the appropriateness of the course objectives and the effectiveness of the instruction.

Criterion Referenced Versus Norm Referenced

A fairly recent method of describing evaluation procedures is in terms of how the results are interpreted. There are two basic ways of interpreting pupil performance on tests and other evaluation instruments. One is to describe his performance in terms of the specific behavior he can demonstrate (e.g., He can type 40 words per minute without error). The other is to describe his performance in terms of the relative position he holds in some known group (e.g., He can type better than 90 per cent of his classmates). The first type of interpretation is called *criterion referenced;* the second is *norm referenced.*[7] Both types of interpretation are useful. Criterion-referenced interpretations enable us to describe what an individual can do, without reference to the performance of others. For example, we can judge pupil performance by comparing it to some absolute standard that has been set (e.g., He can define at least 80 percent of the terms in the unit). Norm-referenced interpretations enable us to determine how an individual's performance compares to that of others. This might be a classroom group, or some local, state, or national group, depending on the use to be made of the results. Using national norms, for example, we might describe a pupil's performance on a vocabulary test as exceeding that of 76 per cent of a national sample of sixth-graders. It should be noted that with norm-referenced interpretation we are *not* describing what percentage of the vocabulary items the pupil answered correctly, but simply what per cent of the pupils in the norm group he surpassed.

Strictly speaking, *criterion reference* and *norm reference* refer only to the method of interpreting evaluation results. These distinct types of interpretation are likely to be most meaningful and useful, however, when the evaluation instruments are specifically designed for the type of interpretation to be made. Thus, it is legitimate to use the terms criterion referenced and norm referenced as broad categories for classifying tests and other evaluation techniques. Differences in the preparation of the two types of instruments can be most easily described in the area of achievement testing.

Norm-referenced achievement tests are familiar to all of us, since most teacher-made and standardized tests of achievement used in the past have

---

[7] R. Glaser, "Instructional Technology and the Measurement of Learning Outcomes," *American Psychologist,* 18, 510–522, 1963. Some authors have used the terms *objective referenced, domain referenced,* or *universe referenced* with somewhat the same meaning as *criterion referenced.*

been norm referenced. These tests are designed to rank students in order of achievement, from high to low, so that decisions based on relative achievement (e.g., selection, grouping, grading) can be made with greater confidence. Thus, a key feature in constructing norm-referenced tests is the selection of test items that provide a wide range of scores. This is done by eliminating those items that all pupils are likely to answer correctly and by favoring items at the 50 per cent level of difficulty. Such items tend to maximize differences in performance and thus provide the most reliable ranking of pupils.

Since criterion-referenced tests are not concerned with the relative achievement of pupils, item difficulty and the power of items to discriminate among pupils are not used as criteria in item selection. Instead, the items are selected on the basis of how well they reflect the specific learning tasks being measured. If the learning tasks are easy, the test items will be easy. If the learning tasks are difficult, the test items will be difficult. No attempt is made to eliminate easy items or to arbitrarily alter item difficulty to obtain a range of scores. Here the purpose is to prepare a test that can be interpreted directly in terms of the specific knowledges and skills that pupils are able to demonstrate. Within the context of classroom instruction, then, *a criterion-referenced test is one that is deliberately constructed to yield measurements that are directly interpretable in terms of a specified domain of instructionally relevant tasks.*[8]

Both criterion-referenced and norm-referenced measurement can serve the four basic uses of evaluation in classroom instruction. However, the functions of formative and diagnostic evaluation are likely to be best served by criterion-referenced instruments and those of summative evaluation by instruments that are norm referenced. Placement evaluation is likely to require both criterion-referenced measurement (e.g., to describe possession of prerequisite skills) and norm-referenced measurement (e.g., to determine level of performance for advanced placement).

A summary of these basic ways of describing classroom evaluation procedures is presented in Table 1.1. Further discussion of these evaluation categories will be encountered in later chapters.

Other Descriptive Terms

The following terms are most frequently used in describing tests, but they have similar meaning when applied to other evaluation instruments.

Informal Versus Standardized. Informal tests are those constructed by classroom teachers, while those designed by test specialists and administered, scored, and interpreted under standard conditions are called standardized tests.

---

[8] R. Glaser and A. J. Nitko, "Measurement in Learning and Instruction," in R. L. Thorndike (ed.), *Educational Measurement,* 2nd ed. (Washington, D.C.: American Council on Education, 1971).

TABLE 1.1

Basis for Classification	Type of Evaluation	Function of the Evaluation	Illustrative Instruments
Nature of the Measurement	Maximum performance	Determine what a person *can do* when performing at his best.	Aptitude tests; Achievement tests
	Typical performance	Determine what a person *will do* under natural conditions.	Attitude scales; Interest inventories; Personality inventories; Observational techniques; Peer appraisal
Use in Classroom Instruction	Placement	Determine possession of prerequisite skills, degree of mastery of course objectives, and/or best mode of learning.	Readiness tests; Aptitude tests; Pretests on course objectives; Self-report inventories; Observational techniques
	Formative	Determine learning progress, provide feedback for reinforcement of learning, and identify and correct learning errors.	Teacher-made mastery tests; Custom-made tests from test publishers; Observational techniques
	Diagnostic	Determine causes (intellectual, physical, emotional, environmental) of persistent learning difficulties.	Published diagnostic tests; Teacher-made diagnostic tests; Observational techniques
	Summative	Determine end-of-course achievement for assigning grades or certifying mastery of objectives.	Teacher-made survey tests; Performance rating scales; Product scales
Method of Interpreting the Results	Criterion-referenced	Describe pupil performance in terms of a specified domain of instructionally relevant tasks (e.g., He can add single-digit whole numbers).	Teacher-made mastery tests; Custom-made tests from test publishers; Observational techniques
	Norm-referenced	Describe pupil performance in terms of the relative position held in some known group (e.g., He ranks tenth in a classroom group of 30).	Standardized aptitude tests; Standardized achievement tests; Teacher-made survey tests; Interest inventories; Adjustment inventories

Individual Versus Group. Some tests are administered on a one-to-one basis using careful oral questioning (e.g., individual intelligence test), while others can be administered to a group of individuals.

Mastery Versus Survey. Some achievement tests measure the degree of mastery of a limited set of specific learning outcomes, while others measure a pupil's general level of achievement over a broad range of outcomes. Mastery tests are typically criterion referenced, and survey tests tend to be norm referenced, but some criterion-referenced interpretations are also possible with carefully prepared survey tests.[9]

Supply Versus Selection. Some tests require examinees to recall and supply the answers (e.g., essay test), while others require them to select the correct responses (e.g., multiple-choice test).

Speed Versus Power. A speed test is designed to measure the number of items an individual can complete in a given time, while a power test is designed to measure level of performance under ample time conditions. Power tests typically have the items arranged in order of increasing difficulty.

Objective Versus Subjective. An objective test is one on which equally competent scorers will obtain the same scores (e.g., multiple-choice test), while a subjective test is one where the scores are influenced by the opinion or judgment of the person doing the scoring (e.g., oral test, essay test).

GENERAL PRINCIPLES OF EVALUATION

A wide array of evaluation procedures are used in the schools. As you study these evaluation procedures, it is easy to become so concerned with the *methods* of appraising pupil behavior that evaluation is viewed merely as a collection of techniques. However, evaluation is a *process*. It is a process of determining the extent to which instructional objectives are achieved by pupils. This process, like the process of teaching, of counseling, and of administration, is most effective when it is based on sound operational principles. These principles, or guiding ideas, provide direction to the process and serve as criteria for appraising the effectiveness of specific procedures and practices. The following principles provide a general framework within which the ongoing process of evaluation may be viewed:

1. *Determining and clarifying what is to be evaluated always has priority in the evaluation process.* No evaluation device should be selected or developed until the purposes of evaluation have been carefully defined. In terms of evaluating pupil progress, this means that the identification and definition of instructional objectives, to which reference has already been made, is always the first order of business. As we shall see later in the text,

9 N. E. Gronlund, *Preparing Criterion-Referenced Tests for Classroom Instruction.* (New York: Macmillan, 1973).

the effectiveness of the evaluation process depends as much upon a careful description of *what to evaluate* as it does upon the technical qualities of the evaluation instruments used.

One of the factors which has retarded development in the measurement of human behavior generally has been the concentration upon *techniques* rather than *process*. All too frequently, tests and other evaluation instruments have been developed and used without a clear notion of the characteristics being measured. Even the concept of intelligence has been only vaguely defined by those developing intelligence tests. Recent efforts to describe the components of the intellect more clearly[10] and to define educational outcomes more precisely[11] indicate a desirable trend toward greater concern with a careful definition of the aspects of human behavior to be measured. Future progress in the area of educational measurement and evaluation depends heavily upon our ability to define in precise terms those aspects of pupil behavior which are regarded as significant for the educative process.

2. Evaluation techniques should be selected in terms of the purposes to be served. When the aspect of pupil behavior to be evaluated has been precisely defined, the evaluation technique which is most appropriate for evaluating that aspect of pupil behavior should be selected for use. All too frequently evaluation techniques are selected on the basis of how accurately they measure, how objective the results are, or how convenient they are to use. All of these criteria are important but secondary to the main criterion—is this evaluation technique the most effective method for determining what we want to know about the pupil? Each evaluation technique is appropriate for some purposes and inappropriate for others. The appropriateness of the technique for the intended purpose should be the first consideration in its selection.

Fruitless discussions concerning the relative merits of various types of evaluation procedures are avoided, if this principle is followed. A question which frequently leads to much heated debate is: *Should* teachers use objective tests or essay tests? It is obvious—in light of this principle— that both should be used. Objective tests are most effective for measuring some educational objectives, and essay tests are most effective for others. Similarly with other evaluation techniques. The question is not: *Should* this technique be used?, but rather: *When* should this technique be used?

3. Comprehensive evaluation requires a variety of evaluation techniques. No single evaluation technique is adequate for appraising pupil progress toward all of the important outcomes of instruction. In fact, most evaluation techniques are rather limited in scope. An objective test of factual knowledge provides important evidence concerning a pupil's achievement, but the results tell us little or nothing about how well he

---

[10] J. P. Guilford, *The Nature of Intelligence* (New York: McGraw-Hill, 1967).
[11] See Appendix E.

understands the material, the extent to which he is developing thinking skills, how his attitudes are changing, how he would perform in an actual situation requiring application of the knowledge, or what influence the knowledge might have on his personal adjustment. Such outcomes require evidence beyond that which can be obtained by an objective test. Essay tests, self-report techniques, and various observational methods would all be needed to evaluate such a diverse array of instructional outcomes.

One reason we have so many different types of evaluation procedures is that each provides unique, but limited, evidence on some aspect of pupil behavior. To get a more complete picture of a pupil's achievement, we need to combine the results from a variety of techniques. If the techniques are selected in terms of the specific purposes they can best serve— as suggested previously—then our composite picture of the pupil will be as adequate as we can obtain with our present evaluation instruments.

4. *Proper use of evaluation techniques requires an awareness of their limitations as well as their strengths.* Evaluation techniques vary from fairly well-developed measuring instruments (e.g., scholastic aptitude tests) to rather crude observational methods. Even our very best educational measuring instruments, however, fall far short of the precision we would like them to have. All are subject to one or more types of error.

First, there is sampling error. Since we can only measure a small sample of a pupil's behavior at any one time, there is always a question of the adequacy of the sample. Is this spelling test of twenty words a good sample of the pupils' spelling ability? Is this test of social studies a representative sample of what the pupils should know about social studies? Are these observations of a pupil's social behavior typical of his general social adjustment? Such questions make clear the problem of obtaining an adequate sample and the possibility of sampling error being present in our measurements of pupil behavior.

A second source of error is found in the evaluation instrument itself or in the process of using the instrument. For example, scores on objective tests are influenced by chance factors such as guessing; scores on essay tests are modified by the subjective judgment of the person doing the scoring; the results of self-report techniques are distorted by the individual's desire to present himself in a favorable light; and observations of behavior are subject to all of the biases of human judgment. These and other errors inherent in the use of evaluation techniques must be recognized if the techniques are to be used wisely.

A major source of error arises from improper interpretation of evaluation results. Persons unwilling to recognize the limitations in measurement and evaluation instruments attribute to them a precision they do not possess. It is not uncommon for teachers to distinguish between two pupils on the basis of one or two test-score points when such differences can be accounted for by chance errors alone. At best, our evaluation instruments provide only approximate results and should be interpreted accordingly.

This brief introduction to some of the limitations of evaluation techniques should not be viewed as support for the position held by those who are overly skeptical of evaluation procedures. A healthy awareness of the limitations of evaluation instruments makes it possible to use them most effectively. Many of the errors that commonly occur in the evaluation process can be eliminated by using care in constructing and selecting evaluation techniques. Others can be controlled by developing skill in the use of these techniques. The remainder can be allowed for in the interpretation of results. Much of what is written in the following chapters is directed toward helping you minimize errors and use evaluation techniques skillfully. As a guiding principle, it will be helpful to keep in mind that the cruder the instrument, the greater the limitations and, consequently, the more skill needed in its use.

5. *Evaluation is a means to an end not an end in itself.* The use of evaluation techniques implies that some useful purpose will be served and that the teacher is clearly aware of the purpose. To blindly gather data about pupils and then to file the information away in the hope that it will some day prove useful is a waste of both time and effort. If standardized tests are used, it is also a waste of money. Unfortunately, in some schools there is still a tendency to administer and score batteries of standardized tests with little regard for the use to be made of the results. Such practices are of no value to the school program and may actually be harmful if the motives for testing are misinterpreted by pupils, teachers, or parents.

Most of the misuses of tests and other evaluation techniques can be avoided by viewing evaluation as a process of obtaining information upon which to base educational decisions. This would imply that the types of decisions to be made would be identified before the evaluation procedures were selected; that the evaluation procedures would be selected in terms of the decisions to be made; and that no evaluation procedure would be used unless it contributed to improved decisions of an instructional, guidance, or administrative nature.

SUMMARY

Evaluation plays an important role in the school. It is an integral part of the instructional program and it provides information which serves as a basis for a variety of educational decisions. The main emphasis in educational evaluation, however, is on the pupil and his learning progress.

Evaluation may be defined as a systematic process of determining the extent to which instructional objectives are achieved by pupils. The evaluation process includes both measurement and nonmeasurement techniques for describing changes in pupil behavior as well as value judgments concerning the desirability of the behavioral changes.

The interrelated nature of teaching, learning, and evaluation can be seen in the following sequence of steps in the instructional process: (1) preparing instructional objectives, (2) preassessing learners' needs, (3) providing relevant instruction (monitoring learning progress and diagnosing difficulties), (4) evaluating intended outcomes, and (5) using the evaluation results to improve learning and instruction. In addition to the direct contribution testing and evaluation make to classroom instruction, they also play an important role in programed instruction, curriculum development, school accountability programs, marking and reporting, guidance and counseling, school administration, and school research.

The vast array of evaluation procedures used in the school can be classified and described in many different ways. The following are especially useful designations for describing classroom evaluation procedures:

Nature of the Measurement:

1. Maximum performance (what a person *can* do).
2. Typical performance (what a person *will* do).

Use in Classroom Instruction:

1. Placement evaluation (determine entry behavior).
2. Formative evaluation (determine learning progress).
3. Diagnostic evaluation (determine causes of learning problems).
4. Summative evaluation (determine end-of-course achievement).

Method of Interpreting the Results:

1. Criterion-referenced (describe pupil performance in terms of a specified domain of instructionally relevant tasks).
2. Norm-referenced (describe pupil performance in terms of the relative position held in some known group).

Other terms used to describe tests, and other evaluation instruments, include the following contrasting types:

- Informal and standardized.
- Individual and group.
- Mastery and survey.
- Supply and selection.
- Speed and power.
- Objective and subjective.

Evaluation should not be viewed as a collection of techniques, but rather as a *process* that is guided by a number of general principles. These principles emphasize the importance of the following: (1) identifying the purposes of evaluation, (2) selecting evaluation techniques in terms of these purposes, (3) using a variety of evaluation techniques, (4) being aware of the limitations of the evaluation techniques used, and (5) regarding evaluation as a process of obtaining information upon which to base educational decisions.

LEARNING EXERCISES

1. Why should classroom evaluation be considered an integral part of the teaching-learning process?
2. Describe the role of instructional objectives in the teaching-learning process.
3. It has often been said that "pupils will learn whatever they expect will show up in the tests." What implications does this have for teaching and testing?
4. Which of the following would be considered *measurement* and which *evaluation?* Why?
   a. Bill had a score of 70 on the arithmetic test.
   b. Mary got 90 per cent correct on the spelling test.
   c. Joe has shown good progress in reading.
   d. John's study habits are ineffective.
5. Indicate which of the following represent an evaluation of *maximum performance* and which represent an evaluation of *typical performance.*
   a. Determine a pupil's skill in arithmetic.
   b. Determine a pupil's attitude toward science.
   c. Determine a pupil's study habits.
   d. Determine a pupil's laboratory performance.
   e. Determine a pupil's understanding of social studies.
6. Classify each of the following by indicating whether it refers to placement evaluation, formative evaluation, diagnostic evaluation, or summative evaluation.
   a. A social studies test used to assign grades.
   b. A pretest in arithmetic.
   c. A unit test in science used to measure mastery.
   d. A device for observing and recording reading errors.
7. Indicate which of the following refers to *criterion-referenced* testing and which to *norm-referenced* testing.
   a. Mary's reading score placed her near the top of the class.
   b. John defined 90 per cent of the science terms correctly.
   c. Bill can identify all of the parts of a sentence.
   d. Betty surpassed 85 per cent of the sixth graders on the arithmetic test.
8. How would you distinguish between each of the following?
   a. Informal test and standardized test.
   b. Individual test and group test.
   c. Mastery test and survey test.
   d. Supply test and selection test.
   e. Speed test and power test.
9. To what does the term *objective* refer in the designation *objective test?*
10. Why is it desirable to use a variety of evaluation techniques when evaluating learning outcomes?

SUGGESTIONS FOR FURTHER READING

ANDERSON, S. B., S. BALL, R. T. MURPHY, and ASSOCIATES. *Encyclopedia of Educational Evaluation.* San Francisco: Jossey-Bass, 1975. Provides brief descriptions of the concepts and techniques used in educational evaluation. Good place to look up the meaning of a concept that is not fully understood.

BLOOM, B. S., J. T. HASTINGS, and G. F. MADAUS. *Handbook on Formative and Summative Evaluation of Student Learning.* New York: McGraw-Hill Book Company, 1971. A handbook on evaluation of student learning which relates testing and observational procedures to instructional acts. Part one covers general material on teaching and testing. Part two contains a series of chapters on the evaluation of student learning in various subject areas.

CRONBACH, L. J. *Essentials of Psychological Testing,* 3rd ed. New York: Harper and Row, Publishers, 1970. Chapter 2, "Purposes and Types of Tests." Describes the types of decisions for which tests are used and the major classes of tests.

DuBOIS, P. H. *The History of Psychological Testing.* Boston: Allyn and Bacon, 1970. An interesting history of the development of educational and psychological tests. Provides a good introduction to important men and events that influenced the testing movement.

GRONLUND, N. E. *Determining Accountability for Classroom Instruction.* New York: Macmillan Publishing Co., Inc., 1974. A brief book (57 pages) describing the nature of educational accountability, some of the problems involved, and the role of instructional objectives and measurement in an accountability program.

GRONLUND, N. E. *Preparing Criterion-Referenced Tests for Classroom Instruction.* New York: Macmillan Publishing Co., Inc., 1973. A brief book (55 pages) describing the nature of criterion-referenced testing and the steps in test preparation.

MEHRENS, W. A., and I. J. LEHMANN. *Measurement and Evaluation in Education and Psychology.* New York: Holt, Rinehart & Winston, Inc., 1973. Chapter 3, "General Considerations and Issues in Evaluation." A discussion of curriculum evaluation and student evaluation, cognitive and affective evaluation, and norm-referenced and criterion-referenced measurement.

Test Bulletins*

A Glossary of Measurement Terms. Monterey, Calif.: California Test Bureau.

LENNON, R. T. "A Glossary of 100 Measurement Terms," *Test Service Notebook,* No. 13. New York: Harcourt Brace Jovanovich, Inc.

---

* These and other test bulletins cited in this book may be obtained free (or at small cost) from the test publishers. See Appendix C for publishers' addresses.

CHAPTER 2
Preparing
Instructional Objectives

What types of learning outcomes do you expect from your teaching—knowledges—understandings—applications—thinking skills—performance skills—attitudes? . . . Clearly defining the desired learning outcomes is the first step in good teaching—it is also essential in the evaluation of pupil learning.

As noted in the last chapter, instructional objectives play a key role in the instructional process. If properly stated, they serve as guides for both teaching and evaluation. When we clearly define the intended outcomes of our instruction, we are better able to select relevant materials and methods of instruction, monitor pupil learning progress, and select or construct appropriate evaluation procedures.

All too frequently, little attention is paid to determining precisely and specifically what pupils should be like at the end of an instructional sequence. As a result, one of two extreme situations typically exists. In the one case, our objectives are limited to the learning of material covered in a textbook, and our teaching and evaluation procedures are primarily concerned with the retention of textbook content. At the other extreme, overly ambitious goals are set for a course—goals so general and so idealistic that their attainment is impossible either to achieve or to evaluate. The reason these two situations are so common is probably because the task of clearly defining instructional objectives appears Gargantuan and, therefore, overwhelming. It need not be, despite some admitted complexities. Furthermore, the rewards in terms of more effective teaching, learning, and evaluation are great.

The purpose of this chapter is to help you learn how to reduce the task to manageable proportions and thus avoid the equally undesirable extremes already discussed. It is designed to help you learn how to prepare statements of instructional objectives that go beyond a listing of course content and yet are realistic in terms of pupil attainment. The logical first step in this direction is to analyze the nature of the task. Just what kinds of things, precisely, are we talking about when we talk about *instructional objectives?*

INSTRUCTIONAL OBJECTIVES AS LEARNING OUTCOMES

Instructional objectives are intended learning outcomes toward which pupils progress. They are the end results of learning stated in terms of *changes in pupil behavior.* The term behavior, as used here, refers to mental and emotional, as well as physical, reactions. Thus an increase in knowledge, a broadening of understanding, an improvement in a physical skill, a shifting of attitude, and a deepening of appreciation are all classified as changes in behavior.

When viewing instructional objectives in terms of learning outcomes, it is important to keep in mind that we are concerned with the *products* of learning rather than with the *process* of learning. The relation of instructional objectives (product) to learning experiences (process) designed to develop desired changes in behavior is shown by the following diagram:

	Learning Experience (Process)		Learning Outcomes (Product)
Pupil $\longrightarrow$	Study of cell structure of plants in laboratory	$\longrightarrow$	Knowledge of parts of cell Skill in using microscope Ability to write accurate reports of scientific observations

This diagram should help make clear a number of pertinent points regarding the role of instructional objectives in teaching-learning situations. First, note that objectives establish direction, and that when they are stated in terms of learning outcomes, they consist of more than a list of content. Note also the distinction between "study of" and "knowledge of" cell structure. The content (study of cell structure) is more aptly listed under process because it is the vehicle through which objectives (knowledge of parts of cell, and so on) are attained.

Second, consider the varying degrees of dependence that the products, "knowledge," "skill," and "ability," have on the course content. "Knowledge of parts of cell" is the most closely related, even though other specific content (i.e., cell structure of animals) could serve the same purpose equally well. In the case of "skill in using microscope" and "ability to write accurate reports of scientific observations," a still greater variety of course content could be used to achieve the same objectives. This discussion should by no means be construed as an attempt to deemphasize the importance of course content. Course content is extremely important. However, content serves its most useful purpose when viewed as a means of obtaining instructional objectives rather than as an end in itself.

Another point illustrated by the diagram is the degree to which objectives vary in complexity. The first learning outcome, "knowledge of parts of cell," is specific, easily attained, and can be measured directly by a paper-and-pencil test. The last learning outcome, "ability to write accurate reports of scientific observations" is rather general, cannot be attained completely in a single course, and can be evaluated only by subjective means. Since this variation in the complexity of learning outcomes causes considerable difficulty in the process of identifying and defining instructional objectives, the various dimensions of objectives need to be considered before we proceed further (see "Some Basic Terminology" in box).

SOME BASIC TERMINOLOGY

Educational Goal	General aim or purpose of education that is stated as a broad, long-range outcome to work toward. Goals are used primarily in policy making and general program planning (e.g., Develop proficiency in the basic skills of reading, writing, and arithmetic).
Instructional Objective	An intended outcome of a period of instruction (also called Learning Objective, Learning Outcome, and Course Objective).
General Instructional Objective	An intended outcome of instruction that has been stated in general enough terms to encompass a *class of behavior* (e.g., Comprehends the literal meaning of written material). A general instructional objective is, typically, further defined by a set of specific learning outcomes.
Specific Learning Outcome	An intended outcome of instruction that has been stated in specific *behavioral* (*performance* or *measurable*) *terms* (e.g., Identifies details that are explicitly stated in a passage). Specific learning outcomes describe the observable behavior learners will be able to exhibit when they have achieved a general instructional objective (specific learning outcomes are also called Behavioral Objectives, Performance Objectives, and Measurable Objectives).
Behavioral Term	An action verb that indicates specific and directly observable behavior (e.g., Identifies, describes, constructs).

DIMENSIONS OF INSTRUCTIONAL OBJECTIVES

When instructional objectives are viewed as learning outcomes, they can be described in terms of a number of dimensions. Although such descriptions do not provide discrete categories, discussion of the various dimensions will help clarify the process of stating objectives for instructional purposes. It will also point out some of the complexities mentioned earlier.

Mastery Versus Developmental Outcomes[1]

Learning outcomes can generally be divided into those that should be mastered by all students and those that provide for maximum individual development. The mastery outcomes are typically concerned with the minimum essentials of a course, that is, with those learning tasks that must be mastered if the pupil is to be successful at the next level of instruction. The developmental outcomes are concerned with those objectives that can never be fully achieved. Here, we can expect varying degrees of pupil progress along a continuum of development. In arithmetic, for example, we might expect all pupils to demonstrate mastery of certain computational skills, but expect considerable variation in the development of arithmetical reasoning ability. Similarly, in social studies we might require all pupils to master certain terms, concepts, and skills that are basic to further study in the area, but we would encourage each pupil to go as far as he can in developing application, interpretation, and critical thinking skills. Thus, the instructional emphasis with mastery outcomes is to bring all pupils to a uniform level of performance on the minimum essentials of the course, while the emphasis with developmental outcomes is to assist each pupil to achieve the maximum development of which he is capable. Both emphases are important in classroom instruction, and this has implications for the specification and use of instructional objectives.

Mastery objectives are typically concerned with relatively simple knowledge and skill outcomes. This makes it possible to analyze each intended learning outcome in considerable detail and to describe the expected pupil performance in very specific terms. The objective to "add whole numbers," for example, might be further defined by a list of specific tasks such as the following:[2]

Adds two single-digit numbers with sums of ten or less $(2 + 5)$.
Adds two single-digit numbers with sums greater than ten $(6 + 8)$.

---

[1] It also has been suggested that the designations *mastery objectives* and *transfer objectives* be used. See Krathwohl and Payne (1971) in the "Suggestions for Further Reading" at the end of this chapter.
[2] N. E. Gronlund, *Preparing Criterion-Referenced Tests for Classroom Instruction* (New York: Macmillan, 1973).

Adds three single-digit numbers with sums of ten or less $(2 + 4 + 3)$.
Adds three single-digit numbers with sums greater than ten $(7 + 5 + 9)$.
Adds two two-digit numbers without carrying $(21 + 34)$.
Adds two two-digit numbers with simple carrying $(36 + 27)$.
Adds two two-digit numbers with carrying into 9 $(57 + 48)$.
Adds two or more three-digit numbers with repeated carrying $(687 + 839)$.

Thus, with mastery outcomes it is frequently possible to specify all, or nearly all, of the specific responses the pupils are expected to demonstrate at the end of instruction. This type of detailed specification makes it possible to place the learning tasks in sequential order and to teach and test each specific task on a one-to-one basis as follows:

State the task. (e.g., Adds single-digit whole numbers.)	→	Teach the task. (e.g., Practice in adding single-digit numbers.)	→	Test the task. (e.g., Problems in adding single-digit numbers.)

This procedure of stating specific tasks and then teaching and testing them on a one-to-one basis, is used in programed instruction, in training programs, and in those areas of classroom instruction where simple learning outcomes are stressed (e.g., basic skills). The limited nature of the objectives and the detailed specification of the learning tasks enhance the use of criterion-referenced testing, since such tests are used to describe specifically what a pupil can and cannot do in a particular area of learning.

Instructional objectives at the developmental level are typically concerned with the more complex learning outcomes (e.g., understanding, application, thinking skills). Thus, each general instructional objective tends to encompass many more specific learning outcomes than could possibly be listed for it. All we can reasonably expect to do in defining an objective at this level is to list a *representative sample* of the specific outcomes to be expected. An objective concerned with one aspect of reading comprehension, for example, might be defined by a sample of specific learning outcomes as follows:

Comprehends the literal meaning of written material.

1. Identifies *details* that are explicitly stated in a passage.
2. Identifies the *main thought* that is explicitly stated in a passage.
3. Identifies the *order* in which events are described in a passage.
4. Identifies *relationships*, between persons or events, that are explicitly stated in a passage.

Although other specific learning outcomes could be listed for this instructional objective, this sample of outcomes provides a fairly good notion of what pupils should be able to do to demonstrate "literal comprehension of written material." It is not expected, of course, that these specific learning outcomes will be taught and tested on a one-to-one basis, as is done with mastery outcomes. Instead, a variety of teaching-learning experiences will need to be directed toward the development of literal comprehension skills, and the testing will need to be done with various passages of written material that are new to the pupils. Thus, instruction at the developmental level emphasizes complex learning outcomes that result from the cumulative effect of many specific learning experiences and that are expected to *transfer* to a variety of situations. Since continuous development rather than mastery is intended, norm-referenced testing (i.e., comparing the relative performance of pupils) is an appropriate means of describing pupil progress. Some descriptions of the types of learning tasks pupils can perform (criterion-referenced interpretations) are, of course, also useful at the developmental level, but the infinite number of possible outcomes makes such behavior descriptions rather sketchy, cumbersome, and difficult to interpret.

In summary, mastery objectives are typically concerned with simple learning tasks on which pupils are expected to demonstrate a uniformly high level of performance. These objectives tend to be limited enough in scope that all, or nearly all, intended outcomes can be specified for each objective. The learning tasks are typically taught and tested on a one-to-one basis and criterion-referenced testing is especially appropriate for measuring achievement. Developmental objectives are concerned with complex outcomes toward which pupils can be expected to show varying degrees of progress. Since these objectives emphasize higher order learnings, that stress the *transfer* of knowledges and skills to new situations, only a sample of the infinite number of possible learning outcomes can be specified for each objective. Achievement at the developmental level depends on a variety of learning experiences and is typically tested with items containing some novelty (to measure transfer). Norm-referenced interpretations of pupil achievement are especially appropriate at this level, but these can be supplemented with some criterion-referenced descriptions of pupil performance.[3]

Ultimate Versus Immediate Objectives

Another useful way of viewing educational objectives is in terms of the extent to which they are ultimate or immediate.[4] Ultimate objectives are those concerned with typical performance of individuals in the actual situations they will face in the future. For example, good citizenship is reflected in adult life through voting behavior, interest in community affairs, and the like; safety consciousness shows up in safe driving and safe work habits and in obeying safety rules in other areas of daily activity; critical

---

[3] N. E. Gronlund, *Preparing Criterion-Referenced Tests for Classroom Instruction* (New York: Macmillan, 1973).
[4] R. L. Thorndike (ed.), *Educational Measurement* (Washington, D.C.: American Council on Education, 1971).

thinking is apparent in an individual's resistance to propaganda, his evaluation of arguments, and his general approach to life's problems. Although these ultimate objectives are the important goals of education, they generally cannot be evaluated directly for obvious reasons of complexity and the fact that most of us are teaching children and adolescents rather than adults.

We must therefore usually be content with more immediate objectives. In identifying the immediate objectives of instruction, however, it is possible to move closer to the ultimate objectives than has been the practice in the past. One way to do this is to include objectives of typical performance, wherever possible, which are closely related to the ultimate situations.

Evaluation in driver training classes serves as a good illustration of how immediate objectives can closely parallel the ultimate goal being sought. The ultimate objective of driver training is "the operation of an automobile in a safe manner."[5] The immediate objectives include "knowledge of the rules of the road," "knowledge of how to operate an automobile," and "ability to operate an automobile safely." It should be noted that although the first two objectives (pertaining to knowledge) are more easily and accurately evaluated, the last objective is the one most pertinent to the ultimate goal. Consequently, an evaluation of how safely a student actually operates the automobile, even though it be by use of subjective devices such as a rating scale or a checklist, is more significant to the ultimate purpose of the course than are precise measures of the student's knowledge.

The illustration of ultimate versus immediate objectives in driver training is rather obvious, since most people recognize that an individual may know the rules of the road and know how to operate an automobile and still not drive an automobile skillfully or safely. Parallel situations exist in many other areas of evaluation, however. Knowledge of subject matter is frequently accepted as evidence of an understanding of subject matter, even though there is typically a relatively low relationship between the two types of learning outcomes. Knowledge of study skills is commonly the only objective evaluated at the end of a unit designed to improve study habits, even though teachers all too often must deal with the discrepancy between knowledge and application.[6] Likewise, knowledge of safety rules is sometimes taken as evidence of a predisposition to behave in a safe manner, knowledge of procedures for maintaining good health as evidence of effective health habits, and knowledge of good literature as evidence of appreciation of good literature.

Knowledge is, of course, an important outcome, the foundation for all

---

[5] It is interesting to note that the lower accident rate among persons completing driver training indicates this ultimate objective is being achieved, at least in part. If we could obtain similar evidence concerning achievement of other ultimate objectives, both teaching and evaluation could be improved more rapidly.

[6] We are all familiar with the pupil who habitually gets perfect scores on spelling tests but misspells every fifth word in all his written assignments.

other learning, and an outcome which should be evaluated for its own sake. Knowledge alone, however, cannot be used as evidence of having acquired understanding, skills, habits, attitudes, or appreciations, since there may be little or no relationship between the acquisition of these outcomes and the acquisition of knowledge. The most effective procedure for assuring that all important learning outcomes are being evaluated properly is to state the immediate objectives of instruction in a manner to reflect most clearly the ultimate objectives to be achieved, and then to develop, or select, the evaluation procedures best suited to each of the various types of objectives.

Single-Course Versus Multiple-Course Objectives

Still another means of classifying objectives is on the basis of the number of courses contributing to the stated outcomes. Some instructional objectives are unique to a particular course so that other educational experiences make little or no direct contribution to their attainment. Knowledge of subject matter, for example, is usually concerned with separate and distinct content for each course. In fact, special efforts are usually made to prevent an overlapping of content from one course to another. A similar situation commonly exists for such learning outcomes as understandings, laboratory skills, and performance skills. In such instances, the instructional objectives are limited to those learning outcomes that can be derived from the specific course.

On the other hand, a number of instructional objectives are dependent on a wide variety of courses and a number of years for their attainment. A good illustration of this is found in the development of thinking skills. Certain courses may well make greater contributions than others to the development of thinking skills, but learning outcomes in this area can logically be included in the objectives stated by every teacher. This is based on the assumption that a single learning experience, or a single series of learning experiences, will make little change in a pupil's methods of thinking. The cumulative effect, however, of many learning experiences over a period of years, in a variety of subject-matter areas, is apt to make an appreciable difference in the development of thinking skills. Other objectives, such as those pertaining to communication skills, study skills, attitudes, appreciations, and the development of various character traits, can also be considered within the province of every teacher and, therefore, are multiple-course objectives. It appears, in fact, that the more complex the objective, the more desirable is the use of a multiple approach toward its attainment.

The fact that some instructional objectives are common to a number of courses requires consideration of more factors than would be the case if all objectives were unique to one particular course or another. In addition to identifying, selecting, and clarifying for evaluation purposes the more obvious learning outcomes of his course, the teacher must also consider the contribution his course can make to the more general development of the pupil. This requires a knowledge of the general objectives of the school, an understanding of the potentialities of his subject with regard to these objectives, and the ability to state the learning outcomes of his course in such a manner that they clearly indicate degrees of progress toward the more general objectives.

Stated Versus Functional Objectives

Instructional objectives may also be classified in terms of the degree to which they are operative in the instructional program. There is, frequently and unfortunately, a wide discrepancy between the objectives which are stated for a course and those which are implicit in the teaching-learning process. This discrepancy may be due partly to a tendency to state educational objectives in such vague and general terms that they are difficult to translate into classroom practice. Even when that error is avoided and objectives are more clearly and specifically stated, however, the stated objectives commonly fail to contribute to the instructional process because of inadequate attention to, or improper choice of, the evaluative techniques used. An objective test of terminology and specific facts will do more to determine the type of learning pupils engage in than any number of impressive statements concerning the importance of critical thinking, scientific methods, and the like. This does not mean to imply that pupils regard as significant only those experiences on which they are to be evaluated, but "things that count" certainly have a major influence on how and what they learn. Even college students frequently ask what will be included in examinations and what types of questions will be used.

Recognizing and removing the discrepancy between the stated objectives for a course and the functional objectives arising from the teaching-learning situation is therefore extremely important if we are to improve instruction and provide optimal learning conditions for pupils. In fact, this is one of the primary ways in which improved evaluation procedures contribute to improved learning. By stating instructional objectives clearly, in terms of expected learning outcomes, and by selecting or constructing evaluation instruments that actually evaluate these outcomes, it is possible to translate the stated objectives of instruction into functional goals which guide and direct the learning of pupils. This is one of the main purposes of a sound evaluation program and is a major thesis of this book.

PREPARING INSTRUCTIONAL OBJECTIVES: GENERAL CONSIDERATIONS

In identifying instructional objectives, it is easy to become confused by the seemingly endless array of learning outcomes that might be considered and by the lack of authoritative information concerning which objectives are most valuable for a given course, or area of learning. There is no simple method for identifying and selecting instructional objectives, but a systematic approach reduces the confusion and provides greater assurance that important learning outcomes will not be overlooked.

A systematic approach involves proceeding from the general to the specific. This section, then, is devoted to the general factors, and the following section illustrates a specific procedure for preparing instructional objectives for a particular course.

Types of Learning Outcomes to Consider

Although the specific learning outcomes resulting from a course of study may run into the hundreds, most of them can be classified under a relatively small number of headings. Any such classification is of necessity arbitrary, but it serves a number of useful purposes. It indicates types of learning outcomes that should be considered; it provides a framework for classifying those outcomes; and it directs attention toward changes in pupil behavior in a variety of areas.

The following list of types of outcomes delineates the major areas in which instructional objectives might be classified. The more specific areas under each type should not be regarded as exclusive; they are merely suggestive of categories to be considered.

1. Knowledge.
    1.1 Terminology.
    1.2 Specific facts.
    1.3 Concepts and principles.
    1.4 Methods and procedures.
2. Understanding.
    2.1 Concepts and principles.
    2.2 Methods and procedures.
    2.3 Written material, graphs, maps, and numerical data.
    2.4 Problem situations.
3. Application.
    3.1 Factual information.
    3.2 Concepts and principles.
    3.3 Methods and procedures.
    3.4 Problem-solving skills.
4. Thinking skills.
    4.1 Critical thinking.
    4.2 Scientific thinking.
5. General skills.
    5.1 Laboratory skills.
    5.2 Performance skills.
    5.3 Communication skills.
    5.4 Computational skills.
    5.5 Social skills.
6. Attitudes.
    6.1 Social attitudes.
    6.2 Scientific attitudes.
7. Interests.
    7.1 Personal interests.
    7.2 Educational and vocational interests.
8. Appreciations.
    8.1 Literature, art, and music.
    8.2 Social and scientific achievements.
9. Adjustments.
    9.1 Social adjustments.
    9.2 Emotional adjustments.[7]

---

[7] This list is not meant to be exhaustive. For more detailed lists of outcomes, see the taxonomies by Bloom (1956), Krathwohl, Bloom, and Masia (1964), and Harrow (1972) in the "Suggestions for Further Reading" at the end of this chapter.

Even a cursory glance at this list reveals the wide variety of learning outcomes that can be considered when one is developing a list of instructional objectives for a particular course. Not every teacher, of course, will identify objectives in all of these areas. The age level of the pupils, the subject-matter area, and the philosophy of the school will determine the nature of the learning outcomes to be emphasized in a particular set of instructional objectives. In general, however, we need to expand our view of expected learning outcomes so that all logical outcomes of a course are included in the final list of objectives.

Using the *Taxonomy of Educational Objectives*

One extremely useful guide for developing a comprehensive list of instructional objectives is the *Taxonomy of Educational Objectives.*[8] This is a detailed classification of objectives that is similar in form to the classification system used for plants and animals. It first divides objectives into three major areas: (1) the cognitive domain, which is concerned with knowledge outcomes and intellectual abilities and skills; (2) the affective domain, which is concerned with attitudes, interests, appreciations, and modes of adjustment; and (3) the psychomotor domain, which is concerned with motor skills. Each of these three domains is further divided into categories and subcategories. The major categories of the cognitive domain, for example, include knowledge, comprehension, application, analysis, synthesis, and evaluation. It should be noted that these categories for classifying objectives in the cognitive domain start with the relatively simple knowledge outcomes and proceed through increasingly complex levels of intellectual ability. This hierarchical pattern of classification is characteristic of all three domains of the taxonomy.

As an aid for use of the taxonomy, tables are included in Appendix E that describe the major categories of each domain and present illustrative objectives and relevant behavioral terms for each category.

Other Sources of Suggestions for Instructional Objectives

A classroom teacher who desires to consult lists of instructional objectives developed by others will find it relatively easy to obtain such information. There are numerous published lists of objectives covering all grade levels and all subject-matter areas. These various lists of objectives are generally most helpful after a tentative list of objectives has been developed by the teacher. At this point, they assist him in evaluating the comprehensiveness and validity of his own list of objectives.

Two fairly old but still useful lists of objectives are found in *Ele-*

---

[8] See Bloom (1956) Krathwohl, Bloom, and Masia (1964), and Harrow (1972) in the list of references at the end of this chapter.

mentary School Objectives[9] and *Behavioral Goals of General Education in High School.*[10] Both lists were developed by committees of teachers, administrators, and consultants representing several professional organizations, the United States Office of Education, the Educational Testing Service, and the Russell Sage Foundation. An important feature of these objectives, in addition to their comprehensive coverage of all grade levels, is the fact that they are stated as learning outcomes.

There are several good sources for locating objectives in specific subject-matter areas. The *Encyclopedia of Educational Research*[11] includes an article on each teaching area. These articles include references to recent statements of instructional objectives as well as other aspects of the subject-matter area. The *Review of Educational Research,* published quarterly by the American Educational Research Association, occasionally summarizes the literature on various teaching fields and provides references to journal articles concerning educational objectives. The yearbooks of the National Society for the Study of Education frequently provide suggested lists of objectives in the various subject-matter fields. Special reports by the National Council of Teachers of English, the National Council of Teachers of Mathematics, the National Council for the Social Studies, and the National Science Teachers Association also include suggested statements of objectives in these particular areas.

Another source of ideas for instructional objectives is found in the various pools of objectives and test items that have been prepared for national distribution. Typical of these collections are those maintained by the Instructional Objectives Exchange and the Westinghouse Learning Corporation. Both collections contain thousands of instructional objectives and related test items designed to measure the behavior specified in the objectives. Most subject areas and grade levels are covered, and the lists of objectives are continuously being expanded. Information concerning how to purchase objectives from these, and other objective-item pools, may be obtained by writing to the addresses listed in Appendix C.

When using these various sources to obtain ideas for instructional objectives, there are two basic problems. First, no published list of objectives is likely to be completely appropriate for any particular local instructional program. Most lists will contain some objectives that are not relevant to the local situation and at the same time neglect areas that are of vital interest to the local curriculum. Second, the objectives will vary from one list to another in the manner in which they are stated. Some will be stated as very general objectives, and others will be specified in great detail.

---

[9] Nolan C. Kearney, *Elementary School Objectives* (New York: Russell Sage Foundation, 1953).
[10] Will French and Associates, *Behavioral Goals of General Education in High School* (New York: Russell Sage Foundation, 1957).
[11] R. L. Ebel (ed.), *Encyclopedia of Educational Research,* 3rd ed. (New York: Macmillan, 1969).

Some will be stated in terms of what the teacher is expected to do, and others will be stated in terms of pupil performance. Some will be stated in behavioral terms, and others will be stated in nonbehavioral terms. This variation in content and form of statement from one set of objectives to another simply means that great care must be taken in adopting and adapting any list of objectives for local use. As suggested earlier, it is generally wise for teachers to develop their own tentative lists of instructional objectives for their courses before consulting outside sources. This will increase the likelihood that appropriate objectives will be selected from these sources and, thus, help prevent any undesirable influence that external collections of objectives might have on the local curriculum.

Stating the Objectives as Learning Outcomes

A list of objectives for a course, or unit of study, should be detailed enough to clearly convey the intent of the instruction and yet general enough to serve as an effective overall guide in planning for teaching and testing. This can be most easily accomplished by the defining of objectives in two steps: (1) stating the general objectives of instruction as *expected learning outcomes;* (2) listing under each objective a *sample of the specific types of behavior* that pupils are to demonstrate when they have achieved the objective.[12] This procedure would result in statements of general instructional objectives and specific learning outcomes like the following:

Understands scientific principles.
1. Describes the principle in his own words.
2. Identifies examples of the principle.
3. States tenable hypotheses based on the principle.
4. Lists the differences between two given principles.
5. Explains the relationship between two given principles.

Note that the expected learning outcome is concerned with *understanding* and that the general instructional objective starts right off with the verb *understands.* There is no need to add such repetitious material as "the pupil should be able to demonstrate that he understands." Keeping the statement free of unnecessary wording and starting with a verb helps focus attention directly on the nature of the expected outcome.

There are several important things to note about the *specific learning outcomes* listed beneath the general objective. First is the fact that, like the general objective, each statement begins with a verb. Here, however, the verbs are specific and indicate definite observable behavior—behavior

---

[12] N. E. Gronlund, *Stating Behavioral Objectives for Classroom Instruction* (New York: Macmillan, 1970).

that can be seen and evaluated by an outside observer. These verbs are listed here to illustrate what is meant by stating the specific learning outcomes in *behavioral terms*.[13]

- Describes.
- Identifies.
- States.
- Lists.
- Explains.

Terms such as these make clear precisely what the pupils will do to demonstrate their *understanding*. Such nonbehavioral terms as *realizes, sees,* and *believes* are less useful in defining objectives because they describe internal states that can be expressed by many different types of overt behavior.

Second, it should be noted that the list of specific learning outcomes is merely a sample of the many specific ways that *understanding of scientific principles* might be shown. Because it would be impractical to list all of the specific behaviors that denote understanding, an attempt is made to obtain a *representative sample*. This procedure provides for a behavioral definition of each general objective and still keeps the overall list of objectives and specific learning outcomes within manageable proportions.

Finally, it should be noted that the specific learning outcomes are free of specific subject-matter content. Rather than containing a list of scientific principles the pupils are to understand, they specify the types of pupil behavior we are willing to accept as evidence of understanding. Keeping the statements free of specific subject-matter content in this manner makes it possible to use the same list of learning outcomes with different units of study. Each particular unit of study indicates the principles to be understood, and the list of specific learning outcomes indicates how the pupils are expected to demonstrate their understanding. As we shall see in the next chapter, a table of specifications provides a convenient means of relating the learning outcomes to the various content areas for evaluation purposes.

In the planning of a unit of instruction for programed learning, or for some limited area of training, it may be possible to list *all* of the specific learning outcomes to be achieved. In such cases, the expected outcomes are frequently stated as specific tasks to be performed, rather than goals to work toward. Thus, the final list consists of a series of separate, specific statements describing the terminal behavior of pupils who have successfully completed the unit. In addition, it has been suggested that such statements should also include the conditions under which the be-

---

[13] See Appendix E for lists of illustrative behavioral terms.

havior is to be shown and the standards of performance that are to be accepted.[14] The following statement illustrates this method of describing learning outcomes:

> When given a list of ten historical events, the pupil should be able to supply the dates for at least nine of them.

In this statement, the *condition* is "when given a list of historical events," the *behavior* is "to supply the dates," and the *standard of performance* is "for at least nine of them." Statements such as these are especially useful where the area of instruction is limited in scope, where simple knowledge outcomes and specific skills are stressed, and where direct training is emphasized. When used for regular classroom instruction, however, such statements result in a long, cumbersome list that tends to overemphasize the memorization of factual information. In the more complex areas of achievement (e.g., understanding, application, thinking skills), the specific learning outcomes are so numerous that all we can reasonably expect to do is state a *sample* of them. Thus, stating the general instructional objectives first and then defining each with a representative sample of specific learning outcomes provides a more effective procedure for most classroom instruction.

PREPARING INSTRUCTIONAL OBJECTIVES: SPECIFIC PROCEDURES

As pointed out previously, the process of identifying and defining instructional objectives for evaluation purposes is a complex one. There is no simple, or single, procedure which is best for all teachers. Some prefer starting with course content, some with the general objectives of the school, and some with lists of objectives suggested by curriculum experts in the area. Although the same end results may accrue from various approaches to the problem, the following procedures have been found useful to teachers in a variety of teaching fields.

Orientation

The task of preparing instructional objectives is simplified if we constantly keep in mind that we are making a list of expected outcomes of teaching-learning situations. We are *not* identifying subject-matter content but the reaction pupils are to make to this content. We are *not* listing the learning experiences of the pupils but the changes in pupils' behavior resulting from these experiences. We are *not* describing what we intend to

---

[14] R. F. Mager, *Preparing Instructional Objectives* (San Francisco: Fearon, 1962).

do during instruction but are making a list of the expected results of this instruction. The point of orientation, then, is the *pupil* and what he is like at the end of the teaching-learning process.

Stating objectives in terms of *learning outcomes* rather than the learning process admittedly is easier said than done. Most of us are so concerned with the content of the course and the ongoing process in the classroom that we find it difficult to concentrate our attention on the changes in pupil behavior which are really our reason for teaching. The very nature of teaching conditions us to focus our attention on the immediate learning process. We can successfully shift this focus, however, if we continually ask ourselves: What should the pupils be able to do at the end of the course that they could not do at the beginning? As we attempt to answer this question, always in terms of knowledge, understandings, skills, attitudes, and so on, we find that the pupils' end-of-course performance has almost automatically become the center of focus. We are then in a much better position to define our instructional objectives in terms of *learning outcomes*.

Identifying and Stating General Instructional Objectives

In developing a list of objectives for a course of study, we have two immediate goals in mind. One is to obtain as complete a list of instructional objectives as possible. The other is to state these objectives so that they clearly indicate the learning outcomes that we expect from the course. A typical approach, likely to result in a comprehensive and well-stated list of instructional objectives, is illustrated in the attempts of Mr. Brown to develop a list of objectives for his tenth-grade biology class. Other attacks on the problem may be equally effective, but his procedure includes the major steps involved.

Although Mr. Brown had been teaching biology for six years, he started at the same point where a teacher-in-training might start: he examined the major purposes of the biology course he was teaching. He asked himself questions such as: What are the main reasons for teaching this course? What should students be like, in terms of behavior, when they complete this course? After considerable deliberation, he concluded that at the end of the course pupils should *know certain biological facts, be able to perform certain laboratory operations, and have a scientific attitude toward biological phenomena.* Mr. Brown recognized that these general purposes needed to be analyzed and subdivided into more definite statements of objectives and that other outcomes might be added later, but he felt he had achieved a good starting point.

He began his analysis of the general purposes of his course with *knowledge of biological facts.* His first impulse was to list all of the biological facts he thought pupils should know by the end of the course. When he recalled, however, that the pupil and his behavior is the proper point of orientation, he quickly subdued that impulse, and asked himself another question: What will students be able to do that will indicate they "know biological facts"? In answering this question, he soon realized that his original concept was too narrowly conceived and that other aspects of knowledge needed to be included. After several unproductive attempts, he finally listed the following general instructional objectives, properly stated in terms of expected learning outcomes:

- Knows common terms used in biology.
- Knows specific biological facts.
- Understands general biological principles.
- Applies biological facts and principles to new situations.

Since his list of knowledge outcomes was as complete as he could make it, at least for the present, Mr. Brown decided to analyze the outcomes pertinent to *laboratory performance*. He concluded that at the end of their laboratory experiences, pupils should have attained these objectives (stated in terms of expected learning outcomes):

- Knows common laboratory procedures.
- Uses the microscope skillfully.
- Performs basic operations of dissection skillfully.
- Writes clear and accurate reports of laboratory experiences.

This list seemed inadequate to Mr. Brown, but he decided to go ahead with the area of *scientific attitude* since this could also be considered one of the outcomes of laboratory work. As he attempted to analyze this area, he realized that he could describe behaviors which indicated a scientific attitude, but he could not identify separate objectives in this area. He therefore kept as his instructional objective the original statement:

- Displays a scientific attitude toward biological phenomena.

Although he considered all of the general objectives so far identified by analyzing the major purposes of the course important. Mr. Brown still felt his list incomplete. To check for missing objectives, he analyzed the course content, topic by topic, asking himself the same question about each topic: Why is this topic included in the course? When he finished this analysis, he could add the following instructional objectives:

- Appreciates the achievements of scientists.
- Interprets diagrams, charts, and graphs.

Mr. Brown's next step was to study his classroom and laboratory procedures to see if there were any objectives based primarily on his teaching methods. Implicit in his assignment of library work was the hope that pupils would learn a systematic procedure for locating information. In directing laboratory work he frequently stressed the importance of working cooperatively on laboratory projects. These reflections led to the identification of two more instructional objectives.

- Locates biological information.
- Works cooperatively with others.

By this time, Mr. Brown had exhausted his own resources in identifying objectives, so he turned to the experts to find out what they could offer him. Consultation of the *Encyclopedia of Educational Research* and recent issues of the *Review of Educational Research* led to a number of lists of objectives in biology. He found the lists a bit confusing because some included both process and product objectives, some were concerned mainly with course content, and all seemed to use somewhat different terminology. Despite these shortcomings, Mr. Brown was able to determine that his own list covered the main outcomes of biology, with one exception. There seemed to be an area related to such abilities as drawing valid conclusions from data, justifying conclusions, weighing evidence, and using other similar mental processes. These learning outcomes were variously categorized under headings such as reasoning ability, scientific method, critical thinking, and problem-solving ability.[15] For his own purposes, Mr. Brown decided to use the phrase "critical thinking" and added to his list:

- Demonstrates skill in critical thinking.

For clearness and greater usefulness, Mr. Brown then grouped his general instructional objectives according to the major types of learning outcomes indicated by each objective. His complete list of general objectives is shown in Table 2.1.

From General Instructional Objectives to Specific Learning Outcomes

Now that Mr. Brown had an acceptably clear idea of what he wanted his pupils to be able to do at the end of the course that they could not do at the beginning, he turned his attention to the problem of determining how he could find out how much and how well these changes had taken place. In looking over his list of general instructional objectives, he saw that, for evaluation purposes, he needed more specific statements of learning outcomes. Thus he decided to describe each objective in greater detail.

He started at the top with "Knows common terms used in biology," and his question was: What specific behaviors should be accepted as evidence

---

[15] This illustrates one of the problems in stating and evaluating a list of instructional objectives. The same aspects of behavior may be categorized and labeled in many different ways.

TABLE 2.1

GENERAL INSTRUCTIONAL OBJECTIVES FOR TENTH-GRADE BIOLOGY COURSE

Types of Learning Outcomes	General Instructional Objectives
Knowledge	1. Knows common terms used in biology
	2. Knows specific biological facts
	3. Knows common laboratory procedures
Understanding	4. Understands general biological principles
Application	5. Applies biological facts and principles to new situations
Thinking Skills	6. Demonstrates skill in critical thinking
Laboratory Skills	7. Uses the microscope skillfully
	8. Performs basic operations of dissection skillfully
Communication Skills	9. Writes clear and accurate reports of laboratory experiences
Study Skills	10. Locates biological information
	11. Interprets diagrams, graphs, and charts
Attitudes	12. Displays a scientific attitude toward biological phenomena
Appreciation	13. Appreciates the achievements of scientists
Adjustments	14. Works cooperatively with others

that a pupil *knows* the common terms? He finally settled on three specific behaviors, which he listed beneath the general objective:

1. Knows common terms used in biology.
   1.1 Defines common terms.
   1.2 Differentiates between common terms on basis of meaning.
   1.3 Identifies the meaning of common terms when used in context.

As he reviewed his "breakdown" of the first objective, Mr. Brown could not help but notice that these specific learning outcomes almost told him how to evaluate "knowledge of common terms." They indicated precisely what a pupil could do when he had achieved this general objective. Encouraged by this immediate success, he continued to "break down" the other objectives in the areas of knowledge, understanding, and application. He encountered no difficulty in identifying specific pupil behaviors for each general objective until he started on "Demonstrates skill in critical thinking." This objective sent him hurriedly back to the professional literature for suggestions concerning types of pupil behavior which reflected critical thinking in biology.

A review of the literature led him to a yearbook of the National Society for the Study of Education entitled *Rethinking Science Education*.[16] Sug-

---

[16] J. Darrell Barnard, *Rethinking Science Education,* Fifty-ninth Yearbook of the National Society for the Study of Education, Part I (Chicago: University of Chicago Press, 1960).

gestions from this source, as well as from the *Encyclopedia of Educational Research* and the *Review of Educational Research* consulted earlier, provided Mr. Brown with a fairly comprehensive list of specific behaviors which reflected critical thinking. He discarded some of the suggestions (e.g., "Identifies and defines a problem," "Collects and organizes pertinent information," and "Formulates possible hypotheses") because they did not appear relevant to his classroom and laboratory procedures.[17] After sifting through the remaining suggestions he decided that, for the purpose of his course, the critical thinking objective should be limited to four specific behaviors:

6. Demonstrates skill in critical thinking.
    6.1 Distinguishes between facts and opinions.
    6.2 Draws valid conclusions from given data.
    6.3 Identifies assumptions underlying conclusions.
    6.4 Identifies the limitations of given data.

We can appreciate Mr. Brown's relief when he finished "breaking down" this objective. He had felt that the objective concerning critical thinking was one of the most difficult objectives to analyze. He was a bit abashed to recall he had frequently told parents at PTA meetings that he believed science courses developed critical thinking, when he had never before systematically determined what biology students could do when they thought "critically"! His sense of accomplishment was not erased by this embarrassing recollection, however, because he felt that his analysis would not only be of aid in his evaluation of pupil progress but would also improve his teaching in this area.

So, with this difficult objective behind him, Mr. Brown continued to analyze each of the other general instructional objectives into more specific learning outcomes. The following samples of his work have been selected because each represents a slightly different problem in identifying specific behaviors which indicate attainment of the general objective:

10. Locates biological information.
    10.1 Locates references using the library card catalogue.
    10.2 Identifies common sources of biological information.
    10.3 Uses the table of contents and index when seeking information in books.
    10.4 Identifies the relevancy of information for a particular problem.
12. Displays a scientific attitude toward biological phenomena.
    12.1 Suspends judgment until all of the facts are available.
    12.2 Identifies cause-and-effect relationships in biological data.

---

[17] It should be noted that it is not always necessary, nor desirable, to discard suggested learning outcomes that do not fit classroom practice. It may be more desirable to modify the classroom practice. In either case, however, classroom practice and learning outcomes must be in harmony.

12.3 Demonstrates willingness to consider new interpretations of biological data.

12.4 States interpretations of biological data which are free from bias.

12.5 Indicates confidence in biological data obtained by scientific procedures.

13. Appreciates the achievements of scientists.

13.1 Identifies the main contributions of selected scientists.

13.2 Describes the influence of scientific achievements on modern life.

13.3 Reads supplementary materials regarding scientific achievements.

It should be noted that Mr. Brown did not confine his list of intended outcomes to those that could be evaluated by written tests. Instead he identified all important instructional objectives of the course and then defined these with a sample of specific learning outcomes that characterized attainment of the general objectives. Many of the specific behavioral outcomes could, of course, be evaluated with paper-and-pencil tests. Others, however, would require the use of such techniques as controlled observation, rating scales, checklists, and product evaluation.

Summary of Steps for Preparing Instructional Objectives

Although we have used a biology course for a tenth-grade class to illustrate the process of identifying and defining instructional objectives, it is possible to separate out the procedural steps that would apply to any subject-matter area and any grade level. The following outline summarizes the general procedure for defining instructional objectives:

I. Identifying the general instructional objectives.
   1. Identify the general purposes of the course.
   2. Analyze each purpose of the course into definite statements of general instructional objectives.
   3. Analyze the content of the course, topic by topic, and add the instructional objectives suggested by content analysis.
   4. Examine the teaching methods used and add the instructional objectives resulting primarily from methods of instruction.
   5. Consult lists of objectives published by experts and add those instructional objectives that are appropriate.
   6. Check the list of objectives against the various types of learning outcomes to be sure all important outcomes have been included.

II. Stating the general instructional objectives.
   1. State the general instructional objectives as intended learning outcomes.
   2. Include only one objective in each statement.
   3. State the general instructional objectives so that each encompasses a class of behavior that can be further defined by a set of behaviorally stated learning outcomes.

4. Group the objectives in terms of type of learning outcome indicated by each objective.

III. Defining the general instructional objectives.

1. List a representative sample of the specific learning outcomes that characterize the attainment of each objective.
2. State the specific learning outcomes in terms of observable pupil behavior (start each statement with an action verb).
3. Consult the professional literature for behavioral components of those concepts that lack common meaning (e.g., critical thinking, creativity, social sensitivity, and so on).

In defining instructional objectives, it is, of course, impossible to list all specific learning outcomes that characterize the attainment of each general instructional objective. However, enough should be listed for each objective to clarify the typical behavior of pupils who have satisfactorily achieved the objective.

OTHER EXAMPLES OF INSTRUCTIONAL OBJECTIVES

The following examples further illustrate the process of identifying and stating instructional objectives for evaluation purposes. In each example, the analysis has been limited to only one, fairly complex, area, since it is our purpose to illustrate the procedure for identifying and stating objectives rather than to suggest specific objectives teachers should use.

Reading Comprehension at the Second-Grade Level

A universal objective of second-grade teachers is that pupils should comprehend what they are able to read. Mrs. Jackson had already developed satisfactory descriptions of pupil behaviors which display possession of the knowledge and skills necessary for reading, but she experienced some difficulty in describing those which are evidence of comprehension. She knew that most of her students did comprehend what they read because they were able to produce written answers to written questions, and some were even able to write story "reports," but these indications were limited in two important ways. Written work involved ability to spell and write with ease, as well as ability to comprehend, and daily written work did not provide a systematic way of determining varying levels of comprehension. She was particularly interested, also, in developing evaluative techniques which would clearly indicate the difference between comprehension achieved through the printed word alone, unaccompanied by picture clues, and comprehension achieved with the help of pictures. Standardized achievement tests and unit tests published by the textbook publishers were not very helpful in this respect.

A study of the teacher's guidebook, inspection of workbook pages, and an analysis of her teaching methods did give her some clues as to the nature and level of second-grade reading comprehension, but she felt the need of still more information. She decided to consult the *Taxonomy of Educational Objectives*[18] and found there that comprehension was divided into three levels: translation, interpretation, and extrapolation. Her only problem, then, was to translate those terms into second-grade behavior terms! As she started to work, however, she was much encouraged, for the clues she had found in the analysis of her own materials and methods fell into place quite nicely.

Here, in outline, is her solution to the problem of identifying specific behaviors which reflect reading comprehension at the second-grade level.

Comprehension	*Characterized by*	*Specific Behavior*
1. Translation	Ability to define, paraphrase, demonstrate by example	1.1 Follows written or printed directions 1.2 Responds to written questions, either orally or in writing 1.3 Tells "what happened" in a story*
2. Interpretation	Ability to explain, summarize	2.1 Indicates sequence of events 2.2 Chooses most appropriate title for a story 2.3 Tells why that title is most appropriate
3. Extrapolation	Ability to see implications, consequences, effects, corollaries, make predictions	3.1 Reacts emotionally to story 3.2 Chooses most probable reason for particular action of a character 3.3 Chooses most probable ensuing action implied by the story 3.4 Chooses most probable emotional attitude of a particular character

* In each instance the story is not illustrated.

Arithmetic Reasoning at the Fourth-Grade Level

Mr. Whiteside encountered a problem similar to Mrs. Jackson's when he attempted to identify specific objectives which would exemplify arithmetic reasoning on a fourth-grade level. He recognized that ability to reason arithmetically depends upon knowledge of arithmetic facts, knowledge of the number system, and familiarity with the variety and frequency of the use of quantitative statements and processes in a number of other

---

[18] Benjamin S. Bloom (ed.), *Taxonomy of Educational Objectives: Handbook I, Cognitive Domain* (New York: McKay, 1956).

subject-matter areas. It was also clear to him that reasoning goes beyond understanding and can rightfully be considered a thinking skill. Since "arithmetic reasoning" so often is used to designate everything except computation, however, Mr. Whiteside resolved to scrutinize especially those behaviors which typify understanding and those which typify reasoning with the purpose of distinguishing between the two. He realized that both are developed slowly and in conjunction with increasing knowledge, and that he must keep his objectives in tune with the amount of knowledge expected. He therefore limited his general objectives, typical of *understanding*, to the following, with specific learning outcomes for each, as shown:

1. Recognizes relationships between arithmetic processes.
    1.1 Illustrates relationship between addition and multiplication.
    1.2 Illustrates relationship between subtraction and division.
    1.3 Solves problems by more than one process.
2. Understands place values of notation.
    2.1 Uses place values as guides in estimating.
3. Recognizes quantitative meanings illustrated in diagrams, graphs, and charts.
    3.1 Identifies main point illustrated in diagrams, graphs, and charts.
    3.2 Constructs simple diagrams, graphs, or charts to illustrate quantitative concepts.
4. Uses "language" of arithmetic.
    4.1 Translates arithmetic expressions to verbal statements.
    4.2 Translates simple verbal statements to arithmetic expressions.
    4.3 Uses quantitative terms accurately when appropriate in other subject areas.

After considerable thought, Mr. Whiteside concluded that the traditional "ability to solve story problems" was quite applicable as a statement identifying his general objective under *arithmetic reasoning* and went on to answer: What do pupils who can solve story problems do to achieve their solutions? He thought of four specific behaviors:

1.1 Identifies the problem (what is unknown).
1.2 Identifies the relevant known facts.
1.3 Identifies arithmetic process which relates known to the unknown.
1.4 Solves quantitative problems by using steps 1.1, 1.2, and 1.3.

Since arithmetic reasoning contributes to reasoning in general, and since both are obviously multiple-course objectives, Mr. Whiteside was not yet satisfied that he had identified all of the pertinent specific behaviors. However, he felt that he had made a good start in arithmetic, and that other learning outcomes in the area of reasoning would become more apparent as he developed objectives in other subject-matter areas. (See Figure 12.1, Chapter 12, for mathematics objectives.)

Effectiveness of Communication at the Eighth-Grade Level

An eighth-grade language arts teacher, Mrs. Parsons, had a somewhat different situation confronting her. As she was making a list of objectives for composition, she found herself entangled in the varying complexities of the number of different skills which are used in organizing and presenting a composition. She knew that eighth graders often are not yet able to pursue detailed analysis of sentence structures, but that most are capable of using language and organizing their ideas for presentation. She wanted her objectives to be applicable to all kinds of verbal compositions; she wanted to include both written and oral composition; and she wanted to include those behaviors which, if absent, can detract from the effectiveness of any communication even though they do not contribute directly to skillful compositional structure.

Rather than classify objectives by degree of complexity, she decided to list all the important objectives relating to all forms of composition and to use, for evaluation, those which applied to the particular case at hand. She would not consider the ability to outline, for instance, in evaluating a short poem. Since the point of composition is communication, Mrs. Parsons started by stating her general goal as that of "communicating ideas clearly and concisely." She then listed her objectives and more specific learning outcomes as follows:

1. Uses language skillfully.
   1.1 Uses correct grammatical forms.
   1.2 Uses correct punctuation and capitalization.
   1.3 Uses words recently added to vocabulary.
   1.4 Uses complete sentences.
   1.5 Varies type, length, and structure of sentences.
   1.6 In written composition:
       1.61 Spells correctly.
       1.62 Writes legibly.
       1.63 Prepares written work which is neat and attractive to the eye.
   1.7 In oral composition:
       1.71 Uses correct pronunciations.
       1.72 Speaks clearly.
       1.73 Uses inflection to emphasize and "point up" ideas.
       1.74 Presents a neat and clean appearance.
2. Organizes material logically for unity and coherence.
   2.1 Prepares outlines clearly showing a beginning, middle, and end.
   2.2 Writes finished composition that follows outline.
   2.3 Writes paragraphs based on topic sentences.
   2.4 Limits paragraphs to one central idea.
   2.5 Limits composition to issues and ideas relevant to main theme.

Social Understanding at the High School Level

Mr. Morris, who teaches social studies at the high school level, assigned himself a task he knew would be difficult to complete. As a matter of fact, he realized he could never regard the task as finally complete, for the nature of it required continuing refinement and continuing modifications in his teaching methods.

For some time he had been concerned with a particular aspect of learning which was common to all his courses. He was interested in the contribution his courses could make toward developing the *social understanding* he hoped his pupils would ultimately achieve. A search through the literature and discussions with several other social studies teachers led to the following tentative list of general objectives and specific learning outcomes:

1. Displays awareness of social phenomena.
   1.1 Identifies common social problems and their related issues.
   1.2 Identifies motivating forces behind social movements.
   1.3 Identifies the roles of social institutions in society.
   1.4 Describes the behavior of individuals in terms of social phenomena.
2. Analyzes social problems, issues, and phenomena objectively.
   2.1 Identifies the significant aspects in social problems.
   2.2 Distinguishes facts from opinions.
   2.3 Identifies bias, prejudice, and other distortions in social statements.
   2.4 Discriminates between issues in terms of their relevance to particular social problems.
   2.5 Identifies cause-and-effect relationships in social problems.
3. Displays interest in solving social problems and resolving social issues.
   3.1 Describes the need for social action.
   3.2 Obtains information regarding social problems from a variety of source materials.
   3.3 Presents sound theoretical solutions to social problems.
   3.4 Participates in school groups engaged in social action.
4. Maintains a scientific attitude toward social phenomena.
   4.1 Suspends judgment until the information is complete enough to permit conclusions.
   4.2 Listens carefully to ideas that are contrary to his own.
   4.3 Revises conclusions when additional reliable information is obtained.
   4.4 Identifies cause-and-effect relationships in social data.
   4.5 Judges all ideas, opinions, and conclusions in terms of the authoritativeness of the information supporting them.

Although Mr. Morris was far from satisfied with his completed list of objectives and learning outcomes, he felt that he had made great progress in translating a previously intangible goal into identifiable pupil behaviors.

With this list as a guide, he was certain that his teaching in this area would be more effective and that evaluation of these specific learning outcomes would lead to further modification and refinement of the *social understanding* objectives.

APPRAISING THE FINAL LIST OF OBJECTIVES

Throughout this chapter, we have emphasized the role of the classroom teacher in the *process* of preparing instructional objectives. We have deliberately avoided discussions concerning which objectives should receive priority at various grade levels and in various subject-matter areas. This is a decision for school boards, administrators, curriculum committees, and individual teachers. Our aim has been to clarify how to identify and state instructional objectives so that they will be most useful for teaching and evaluation purposes.

In developing statements of objectives for a particular course, however, the teacher is still faced with the problem of determining the adequacy of his final list of objectives. The following questions will serve as criteria for this purpose:

1. *Do the objectives include all important outcomes of the course?* Knowledge objectives are seldom neglected. However, objectives in the area of understandings, thinking skills, performance skills, attitudes, and the like tend to be slighted unless special efforts are made to consider them. . Objectives derived mainly from the methods of instruction and the social experiences of the pupils are also easily overlooked.

A safe procedure in appraising a final list of objectives is to compare it with lists published by curriculum experts. This will bring to attention any flagrant omissions in the teacher's list. Care should be taken, however, not to indiscriminately adopt the stated objectives of experts. Their lists tend to reflect the common goals or outcomes of a subject. A list of objectives for a specific course must also take into account the philosophy of the school, the abilities and needs of the pupils, the available facilities in the school and community, the teaching methods used, and a host of other factors unique to that particular course.

2. *Are the objectives in harmony with the general goals of the school?* The objectives developed by individual teachers must be consistent with the general goals of the school in which they are used. If independent thought, self-direction, and effectiveness of communication are highly valued in the school, these outcomes should be reflected in the teachers' objectives. Similarly, objectives inconsistent with these valued outcomes should be omitted from the list. Part of the difficulties of applying this criterion is that the goals of the school are seldom explicitly stated and therefore must be inferred from the course of study and the educational practices in the school. Nevertheless, the teacher must make some judgment

concerning the appropriateness of his objectives as teaching aims in his particular school.

3. Are the objectives in harmony with sound principles of learning? Since objectives indicate the desired outcomes of a series of learning experiences, they should be consistent with sound principles of learning, that is, they should (1) be appropriate to the age level and experiential background of the pupils (principle of readiness), (2) be related to the needs and interests of the pupils (principle of motivation), (3) reflect learning outcomes which are most permanent (principle of retention), and (4) include learning outcomes which are most generally applicable to various specific situations (principle of transfer). A knowledge of child and adolescent development and the psychology of learning is needed to apply such criteria effectively. It can be pointed out here, however, that understandings, thinking skills, applications of knowledge, and other complex learning outcomes tend to be retained longer and to have greater transfer value than the more simple learning outcomes such as knowledge of specific facts. Consequently, special efforts should be made to include such learning outcomes in the final list of objectives.

4. Are the objectives realistic in terms of the abilities of the pupils and the time and facilities available? First attempts at identifying objectives for a particular course frequently result in an impressive but unattainable list of goals. Thus, the final list of objectives should be reviewed in light of the abilities of the group members, the time available for achieving the objectives, and the adequacy of the facilities and equipment available It is usually better to have several clearly defined attainable objectives than a long list of nonfunctional goals.

This should not discourage the inclusion of multiple-course objectives. Although such objectives are not completely attainable in a particular course, realistic degrees of progress toward their attainment can be indicated.

5. Are the objectives defined in terms of changes in pupil behavior? Although this criterion has been stressed in earlier sections of this chapter, it is included here so that it will not be overlooked in appraising the final list of objectives. The objectives should be stated as expected learning outcomes, clearly indicating what the pupil is like who has satisfactorily completed the learning experience. They should *not* include what the teacher is going to do, the subject-matter content to be used, or other aspects of the teaching process. Rather the objectives should provide a precise description of the intended learning outcomes in terms of desired changes in pupil behavior.

UNANTICIPATED LEARNING OUTCOMES

No matter how carefully a set of instructional objectives has been prepared for a course, there are likely to be some unanticipated effects of the instruction. These effects may be desirable or undesirable, and the majority of them are likely to fall into the affective area. For example, as a result of instruction, pupils may become more dependent or more independent, more conforming or more creative, more critical of printed material or more uncritical, more positive in their self-concept or more negative, and more interested in the subject or more disinterested. Outcomes of this nature are easily overlooked because they are more likely to result from the method of instruction than from the content of instruction.

In addition to these more global changes in behavior, specific class-room activities may create a need for focusing on outcomes that were not prespecified. An accident in the chemistry laboratory, for example, may indicate a need for special instruction in safety. Similarly, an unanticipated pupil interest in the metric system may create a need to modify instruc-tion in a mathematics class, or an unforeseen international crisis may alter social studies instruction. Thus, although instructional objectives provide a useful guide for instruction, teachers need to be flexible enough in their teaching and testing to allow for unplanned events and unanticipated learning outcomes.

In many cases it may be possible, and desirable, to incorporate into a set of instructional objectives some of the unanticipated outcomes that occurred during previous instruction. If observation in a mathematics class seemed to indicate that pupils might be developing a poor attitude toward mathematics, for example, an objective on attitudes could be added to the list of outcomes for future use. This would provide greater assurance that more direct attention would be focused on attitudes during both teaching and evaluation. Although we can never expect to anticipate all possible outcomes of instruction, we can reduce the proportion of unanticipated outcomes by being alert to their presence, by up-dating our list of objec-tives periodically, and by striving for as comprehensive a list of instructional objectives as is feasible to maintain. Those unplanned effects that do occur, despite our careful planning, should, of course, be taken into con-sideration when evaluating the outcomes of instruction.

SUMMARY

Instructional objectives make clear what learning outcomes we expect from our teaching. They describe our instructional intent in terms of the types of behavioral changes pupils are expected to exhibit as a result of instruc-tion. A convenient means of preparing instructional objectives is to follow a two-step process. (1) State the *general instructional objectives* as in-tended learning outcomes. (2) Define each general objective with a list of *specific learning outcomes* that describes the specific observable behavior learners will be able to demonstrate when they have achieved the general objective.

The process of clearly defining instructional objectives is enhanced by a consideration of the various dimensions of objectives. For most classroom instruction, we need to consider both mastery and developmental outcomes, ultimate and immediate outcomes, and single-course and multiple-course outcomes. We also need to state the intended outcomes of instruction in such a manner that they become functional objectives that direct the learning of pupils and provide guidelines for evaluating learning progress.

When instructional objectives are viewed as learning outcomes and are defined in behavioral terms, numerous types of behavioral changes might be included. In addition to the more obvious knowledge outcomes, those in the areas of understanding, application, thinking skills, performance skills, attitudes, interests, appreciation, and adjustment should also be considered. Suggestions for objectives in these and other areas may be obtained from the *Taxonomy of Educational Objectives* (see Appendix E), from various published sources, and from objective-item pools that have been prepared for national distribution. These external sources should be used as aids only. Teachers should first develop their own lists of instructional objectives that take into account the unique features of the local school and community.

The procedure for preparing instructional objectives for a particular course includes the following steps:

1. Identifying the general instructional objectives by analyzing the purposes and content of the course, the teaching methods used, and lists of objectives prepared by curriculum specialists.
2. Stating each general instructional objective in broad enough terms that it encompasses a class of specific behavioral outcomes.
3. Defining each general instructional objective by listing a representative sample of the behaviorally stated specific learning outcomes that indicate achievement of the general objective. Throughout this process, it is helpful to keep in mind that the pupil—and changes in his behavior— is the point of orientation.

Although our emphasis has been on the *process* of preparing instructional objectives, the adequacy of the final list of objectives can be appraised in terms of the extent to which it: (1) includes all important outcomes of the course, (2) is in harmony with the general goals of the school, (3) is in harmony with sound principles of learning, (4) is realistic in terms of the abilities of the pupils and the time and facilities available, and (5) clearly indicates the intended learning outcomes in terms of changes in pupil behavior.

No matter how comprehensive a set of instructional objectives may be, however, there are likely to be some unanticipated outcomes of instruction. Thus, teachers, alert to this possibility, should take these unplanned effects into account when evaluating the learning outcomes of a course.

LEARNING EXERCISES

1. Make a list of general instructional objectives for a course or unit of instruction in your teaching area. Next, list beneath each general objective a set of specific learning outcomes.
2. State one general instructional objective and several specific learning outcomes for each of the major categories in the *Taxonomy of Educational Objectives* (see Appendix E).
3. Using the suggestions given in this chapter, restate the following as general instructional objectives.
   a. Improves his reading ability.
   b. To teach the use of square root.
   c. Realizes the value of effective study habits.
   d. The pupil will study the basic vocabulary.
   e. Develops an appreciation of literature.
4. Define each of the following general objectives with a list of specific learning outcomes.
   a. Interprets line graphs.
   b. Applies principles to new situations.
   c. Constructs weather maps.
   d. Demonstrates how to use measuring devices.
   e. Evaluates poetry.
5. Which of the following can be classified as *behavioral terms?*
   a. Identifies.
   b. Sees.
   c. Realizes
   d. Describes.
   e. Enjoys.
   f. Awareness of.
6. Describe how teaching and testing at the *developmental* level differ from teaching and testing at the *mastery* level. What are the implications for stating the instructional objectives at each level?
7. Why is pupil progress toward the ultimate goals of education so seldom evaluated? What can be done to give ultimate goals greater emphasis in our instructional objectives?
8. Why is it important in teaching to attempt to evaluate all important instructional objectives? What would be the advantages and limitations of focusing on just a few of the most important ones?
9. List as many examples of unanticipated learning outcomes as you can think of that might occur in a particular course in your teaching area.
10. How can a teacher allow for unanticipated learning outcomes during teaching and classroom evaluation?

SUGGESTIONS FOR FURTHER READING

Bloom, B. S. (ed.) *Taxonomy of Educational Objectives: Handbook I, Cognitive Domain.* New York: David McKay Co., Inc., 1956. Describes the intellectual outcomes of education in detail and presents sample objectives and test items for each area.

GRONLUND, N. E. *Stating Behavioral Objectives for Classroom Instruction.* New York: Macmillan Publishing Co., Inc., 1970. A brief guide (58 pages) describing the step-by-step procedure for stating instructional objectives and for using them in teaching, testing, and marking and reporting. Presents illustrations of instructional objectives, lists of behavioral terms, and a checklist for evaluating instructional objectives.

HARROW, A. J. *A Taxonomy of the Psychomotor Domain.* New York: David Mc-Kay Co., Inc., 1972. Provides a model for classifying learning outcomes in the psychomotor domain and presents sample objectives and methods of evaluation for the major areas.

KRATHWOHL, D. R., B. S. BLOOM, and B. B. MASIA. *Taxonomy of Educational Objectives: Handbook II, Affective Domain.* New York: David McKay Co., Inc., 1964. Describes the affective outcomes of education in detail and presents sample objectives and test items for each area.

KRATHWOHL, D. R., and D. A. PAYNE. "The Nature and Definition of Educational Objectives, and Strategies for Their Assessment," Chapter 2 in R. L. Thorndike (ed.), *Educational Measurement.* Washington, D.C.: American Council on Education, 1971. An extended treatment of objectives and their use in evaluation.

PAYNE, D. A. (ed.). *Curriculum Evaluation.* Lexington, Mass.: D. C. Heath & Company, 1974. See Section 2, "Identifying and Specifying Relevant Educational Goals and Curriculum Objectives," for a series of articles on educational objectives and their role in evaluation.

CHAPTER 3
Relating Evaluation Procedures to Instructional Objectives

Instructional objectives encompass a variety of learning outcomes. . . .
Evaluation includes a variety of procedures. . . . The key to sound evaluation is to relate the evaluation procedures as directly as possible to the
specific learning outcomes being evaluated.

By now it should be clear that evaluation is an integral part of the teaching-
learning process. It is *not* something tacked on at the end of a course; it is
not limited to the measurement of the amount of factual material retained;
it is *not* limited to paper-and-pencil examinations. Evaluation is a continuous comprehensive process which utilizes a variety of procedures and
which is inescapably related to the objectives of the instructional program.

In the last chapter, we were concerned with the process of preparing
instructional objectives for evaluation purposes. This process included
identifying the general instructional objectives and then defining each of
those objectives with a list of specific learning outcomes. The final step in
the evaluation process is to *select or develop evaluation instruments that
provide the most direct evidence concerning the attainment of each specific
learning outcome.*

The sequence of steps shown in Figure 3.1 summarizes this general procedure for relating evaluation techniques to objectives.

These procedural steps clarify the importance of relating the evaluation
techniques directly to the specific learning outcomes being evaluated. This
is the only way we can have any certainty that we are evaluating pupil
progress toward the outcomes we have selected as our instructional objectives.

The process of relating evaluation techniques to specific learning outcomes is essentially one of logical analysis and judgment. This process can
be greatly facilitated, however, by the use of some systematic evaluation
plan.

GENERAL INSTRUCTIONAL OBJECTIVES
(Intended outcomes directing our teaching)

SPECIFIC LEARNING OUTCOMES
(Pupil behaviors we are willing to accept as
evidence of the attainment of objectives)

EVALUATION TECHNIQUES
(Procedures for obtaining samples of pupil
behavior described in the specific learning
outcomes)

FIGURE 3.1. Relation of evaluation techniques to objectives.

GENERAL EVALUATION PLAN

Whether a teacher is deciding on evaluation procedures for a unit of work, a semester's work, or a sequence of courses, some general evaluation plan is desirable. As a minimum, this plan should include a list of the desired learning outcomes and the techniques to be used in evaluating progress toward them. The following chart, based on several of the objectives developed by Mr. Brown, our tenth-grade biology teacher, illustrates the procedure for developing a general plan. The numbering system is that used by Mr. Brown and helps identify each objective in his original list (see Table 2.1). The complete evaluation chart would, of course, include all of the objectives and specific learning outcomes identified by Mr. Brown.

Mr. Brown's chart for a general evaluation plan clarifies a number of important points concerning the relationship between instructional objectives and evaluation procedures. For one thing, it makes clear the fact that the specific learning outcomes, stated in terms of pupil behavior, are so numerous and varied that no single evaluation technique could possibly provide adequate evidence concerning their achievement. Although objective tests are indicated for many of the learning outcomes, checklists, anecdotal records, and other observational techniques are also frequently mentioned. The chart also highlights the importance of a clear statement of the objectives and learning outcomes in selecting the evaluation technique. In fact, when the learning outcomes are clearly stated in terms of pupil behavior, they not only indicate *what* is to be evaluated but they also suggest *how* to evaluate. For example, the phrase "1.1 Defines common terms" provides an indication of the type of evaluation technique that should be used. It indicates that *the pupil must provide the definitions himself.* Therefore, the short-answer test, in which the pupil is given selected terms and asked to define them, is the most appropriate technique of evaluation. An objective test item, such as a multiple-choice question, where the pupil must merely identify the definition, would be inadequate for evaluating this learning outcome, as stated. Of course, the specific learning outcome could be restated to read "Identifies the meaning of common

Objectives and Specific Learning Outcomes	*Evaluation Techniques*°
1. Pupil *knows common terms used in biology* when he:	
1.1 Defines common terms.	1.1 Short-answer test.
1.2 Differentiates between common terms on basis of meaning.	1.2 Objective test.
1.3 Identifies the meaning of common terms when used in context.	1.3 Objective test.
6. Pupil *demonstrates skill in critical thinking* when he:	
6.1 Distinguishes between facts and opinions.	6.1 Objective test.
6.2 Draws valid conclusions from given data.	6.2 Short-answer test.
6.3 Identifies assumptions underlying conclusions.	6.3 Objective test.
6.4 Identifies the limitations of given data.	6.4 Objective test.
8. Pupil *performs basic operations of dissection skillfully* when he:	
8.1 Places specimen in proper position.	8.1 Checklist or rating scale.
8.2 Cuts skillfully without damaging the structure to be studied.	8.2 Checklist or rating scale.
8.3 Separates the structural parts of the specimen without damaging them.	8.3 Checklist or rating scale.
8.4 Completes dissection in allotted time.	8.4 Checklist or rating scale.
10. Pupil *locates biological information* when he:	
10.1 Locates references using the library card catalogue.	10.1 Research report. Observation.
10.2 Identifies common sources of biological information.	10.2 Objective test.
10.3 Uses the table of contents and index when seeking information in books.	10.3 Observation.
10.4 Identifies the relevancy of information for a particular problem.	10.4 Research report. Observation.
12. Pupil *displays a scientific attitude toward biological phenomena* when he:	
12.1 Suspends judgment until all of the facts are available.	12.1 Anecdotal records. Objective test.
12.2 Identifies cause-and-effect relationships in biological data.	12.2 Anecdotal records. Objective test.
12.3 Demonstrates willingness to consider new interpretations of biological data.	12.3 Anecdotal records. Objective test.
12.4 States interpretations of biological data which are free from bias.	12.4 Anecdotal records. Essay test.
12.5 Indicates confidence in biological data obtained by scientific procedures.	12.5 Anecdotal records. Objective test.

° Evaluation technique relates to learning outcome with corresponding number.

terms" so that objective test items could be used. However, this would be a change in the specific behavior Mr. Brown is willing to accept as evidence that the pupil knows the common terms used in biology. If he believes that knowing terms requires that a pupil be able to define the terms in his own words, the only adequate procedure of evaluation is to ask the pupil to thus define the terms. The ability to *identify* the correct definition could not be accepted as proof of the pupil's ability to *provide* a correct definition.

Although our discussion has focused on one specific learning outcome, *the basic principle of appraising each learning outcome as directly as possible* is one that characterizes the entire chart. For example, "6.1 Distinguishes between facts and opinions" can be evaluated by objective tests. It is simply a matter of presenting the pupil with a number of statements and asking him to indicate which are the facts and which are opinions. On the other hand, however, "6.2 Draws valid conclusions from given data" requires a short-answer test because the outcome indicates that the pupil will draw his own conclusions and not merely identify conclusions drawn by others. Similarly, all of the outcomes pertinent to "8. Pupil *performs basic operations of dissection skillfully*" must be evaluated by some observation device such as a checklist or rating scale. Knowledge of dissection procedure *cannot* be accepted as evidence of dissection skill. *Knowledge* of procedure can and should be measured for its own sake, but *skill* can be evaluated only by directly observing and judging the pupil's dissection procedure and the resulting product. In the area of scientific attitude, such learning outcomes as "12.1 Suspends judgment until all of the facts are available" require more than one type of evidence because of the difficulty of the evaluation. Anecdotal records based on daily observation in the classroom and laboratory will provide evidence concerning the pupil's typical behavior in dealing with scientific problems. But because of the lack of opportunity to observe all pupils in situations requiring this behavior and because of the subjective nature of such observations, it is also desirable to use objective test items. Such test items merely supplement the anecdotal records, however, because responses to objective test items do not indicate how the pupil will typically behave when confronted with problems of a scientific nature. In short, both methods are inadequate but together they complement' each other and provide more adequate evidence than either would alone. For each instructional objective, then, the evaluation chart indicates the evaluation techniques which provide the most direct and adequate evidence concerning the extent to which the pupil's behavior corresponds to the desired learning outcomes.

An evaluation chart, such as Mr. Brown's, also makes clear the necessity for planning the evaluation program at the beginning of the unit, or course, of instruction. If evaluative data are to be obtained by means of anecdotal records, rating scales, and other observational devices, the nature of the observations must be specified early in the instructional process. Ideally, the planning for evaluation should occur at the same time as other plans are made for the course. When this is done, teachers sometimes include the *objectives* of instruction, the *methods* of instruction, and the *evaluation* techniques all together in one plan. The following chart illustrates a simplified version of a plan for Mr. Whiteside's objective in arithmetic reasoning at the fourth-grade level:

Objectives	*Teaching Methods*	*Evaluation Techniques*
1. Pupil *demonstrates arithmetic reasoning ability* when he:		
1.1 Identifies the problem (what is unknown).	Presents the pupils with a variety of story prob-	Observation and anecdotal rec-
1.2 Identifies the relevant known facts.	lems which contain more facts than are	ords
1.3 Identifies the arithmetic process which relates known to the unknown.	needed so that the pupils obtain practice in identifying the prob-	Objective tests.
1.4 Solves quantitative problems using the above steps.	lem, and selecting the relevant facts as well as in computing the answers.	

Including the objectives, teaching methods, and evaluation techniques in one general plan highlights the interrelationships among these facets of classroom teaching and assures that planning for evaluation will be done at the beginning of the course. In using this procedure, however, one must be careful not to try to relate the teaching methods too closely to instructional objectives. One method (e.g., class discussion) may relate to a variety of objectives, such as knowledge, understanding, communication skills, and social adjustment. Similarly, one objective (e.g., appreciation) may be the end result of a series of learning experiences requiring a multitude of methods. Within this limitation, a plan such as that developed by Mr. Whiteside can add general direction to both the teaching and evaluation process.

USING A TABLE OF SPECIFICATIONS

Another type of evaluation plan is that provided by a two-way chart called a table of specifications. Such a chart relates the instructional objectives to the course content and specifies the emphasis to be given to each type of learning outcome. Where the table is to serve as a general evaluation plan, all of the general instructional objectives for a unit or course of instruction are listed across the top of the table, and all of the major areas of content are listed down the side of the table. The cells within the table are used to indicate the number of test items to be prepared for each outcome of instruction and for describing how the nontest outcomes will be evaluated. A simplified version of such a table, for a weather unit in junior high school science, is presented in Table 3.1.

It will be noted in Table 3.1 that of the fifty items in the test, twelve will measure "knowledge of symbols and terms." Two of these twelve items will be concerned with "air pressure," four with "wind," two with "tempera-ture," two with "humidity and precipitation," and two with "clouds." The numbers in the other columns are to be read in the same manner. Since the skill outcomes require performance evaluation, those columns contain brief descriptions of the evaluation procedures to be used.

The relative emphasis given to each objective and each area of con-tent in the table of specifications should, of course, reflect the emphasis given during instruction. Those learning outcomes that are stressed as being more important, and to which more instructional time is devoted, should be given greater weight in the evaluation plan. In our illustrative table, for example, the two skill outcomes are assigned 50 per cent of the total evaluation (25 per cent each) and the four objectives to be evaluated by paper-and-pencil tests are assigned the other 50 per cent (10 to 16 per cent each).

Tables of specifications frequently include only those objectives that can be measured by paper-and-pencil tests (see Table 6.2 in Chapter 6), however, there is some advantage to including all instructional objectives in the table. Including all objectives makes clear what is, and what is not, being measured by classroom tests. This clarifies the important role of test-ing in the total evaluation process but, at the same time, prevents an over-emphasis on testing procedures. Each evaluation technique is viewed in proper perspective.

Some teachers prefer to expand the table of specifications by including the specific learning outcomes for each general instructional objective and by listing a more detailed outline of course content. This is a desirable approach as long as the number of specifics does not become unmanage-able. It is more feasible where a table of specifications is based on a unit of instruction (as in formative evaluation) than where the table is based on the intended outcomes of an entire course (as in summative evaluation).

RELATING TEST ITEMS TO SPECIFIC LEARNING OUTCOMES

The table of specifications indicates the number of test items to be devoted to each general instructional objective. This is the first step in relating testing procedures to objectives and a significant one since it provides some

TABLE 3.1

TABLE OF SPECIFICATIONS FOR A WEATHER UNIT IN JUNIOR HIGH SCHOOL SCIENCE

Content	Objectives						Total number of items
	Knows		Understands	Interprets	Skill in		
	symbols and terms	specific facts	influence of each factor on weather formation	weather maps	use of measuring devices	constructing weather maps	
Air pressure	2	3	3	3	Observe pupils using measuring devices (rating scale)	Evaluate maps constructed by pupils (checklist)	11
Wind	4	2	8	2			16
Temperature	2	2	2	2			8
Humidity and precipitation	2	1	2	5			10
Clouds	2	2	1				5
Total number of items	12	10	16	12			50
Per cent of evaluation	12%	10%	16%	12%	25%	25%	100%

assurance that each objective will be represented in the test according to its relative importance. The ultimate question, however, in relating testing procedures to objectives, is this: *Are the pupil responses called forth by the test items directly relevant to the behaviors defined by the specific learning outcomes?*

Clarifying the Expected Pupil Responses

We can increase the certainty that our test items call forth relevant pupil behavior by further clarifying the expected pupil responses for each specific learning outcome. This might be done in one of the following ways:

1. Add a third level of specificity to the list of objectives.
2. Define the *action verbs* used in the specific learning outcomes.
3. Use sample test items to illustrate the intended outcomes.

Each of these methods will be discussed in turn.

The meaning of each specific learning outcome can be further clarified by listing some, or all, of the specific tasks pupils are expected to perform in demonstrating achievement of the outcome. This would provide three levels for each instructional objective, as follows:

1. *Knows* the parts of speech in English.
   1.1 *Identifies* nouns in sentences.
       1.11 *Underlines* each proper noun.
       1.12 *Encircles* each common noun.

Adding a third level of specificity such as this might be useful for clarifying some learning outcomes. The specific tasks describe precisely what pupils will do to indicate that they can identify nouns. It should be noted, however, that our intended outcome is still the *identification* of nouns. The processes of *underlining* and *encircling* are simply behaviors we are willing to use as *indicators* of the *ability to identify*. Thus, the third level provides a transition between specific learning outcomes and test items, but these specific behaviors are not instructional outcomes in their own right (i.e., In our example, we are not interested in teaching students how to *underline* and *encircle*, but rather how to *identify*. We assume they already can do the former.) This third level of specificity highlights one of the advantages of using levels of objectives, rather than a list of specific tasks only, to describe the intended outcomes of instruction. With levels, we are less likely to confuse the intended *outcomes* of instruction with the *indicators* of those outcomes.

Another way of clarifying the expected pupil responses is to define, or

TABLE 3.2

ILLUSTRATIONS OF HOW TO CLARIFY EXPECTED PUPIL RESPONSES FOR SELECTED ACTION VERBS

Action Verb	Types of Response	Sample Test Task
Identify[*] Name[*]	Point to, touch, mark, encircle, match, pick up. Supply verbal label (orally or in writing).	"Put an X under the right triangle." "What is this type of angle called?"
Distinguish between	Identify as separate or different by marking, separating into classes, or selecting out a common kind.	"Which of the following statements are *facts* (encircle *F*) and which are opinions (encircle *O*)?"
Define	Supply a verbal description (orally or in writing) that gives the precise meaning or essential qualities.	"Define each of the following terms."
Describe[*]	Supply a verbal account (orally or in writing) that gives the essential categories, properties, and relationships.	"Describe a procedure for measuring relative humidity in the atmosphere."
Classify	Place into groups having common characteristics, assign to a particular category.	"Write the name of the type of pronoun used in each of the following sentences."
Order[*]	List in order, place in sequence, arrange, rearrange.	"Arrange the following historical events in chronological order."
Construct[*]	Draw, make, design, assemble, prepare, build.	"Draw a bar graph using the following data."
Demonstrate[*]	Perform a set of procedures with, or without, a verbal explanation.	"Set up the laboratory equipment for this experiment."

[*] Sullivan states that these six action verbs (and their synonyms) encompass nearly all cognitive learning outcomes in the school. See H. J. Sullivan, "Objectives, Evaluation, and Improved Learner Achievement," in *Instructional Objectives*, AERA Monograph Series on Curriculum Evaluation, No. 3 (Chicago: Rand McNally, 1969).

describe, each *action verb* used in the list of specific learning outcomes, as illustrated in Table 3.2. (Note the Types of Responses and Sample Test Tasks.) This procedure is especially useful where the teachers in a department, or an entire school, are developing instructional objectives for each course in the curriculum. Describing the types of responses associated with each action verb provides uniform meaning from one set of objectives to another and, at the same time, eliminates the need for adding a third level of specificity to each set of objectives. Including examples of specific tasks, as illustrated in Table 3.2, also helps to clarify the meaning of each action verb.

In some cases, for instance where the test items are to be constructed by others, it is desirable to illustrate each specific learning outcome with one or more model test items. The examples presented in the following section provide numerous illustrations of how this might be done. In communicating your instructional intent to others, nothing can convey the intended outcomes as clearly as illustrative test items. This assumes, of course, that each sample test item is directly relevant to the specific learning outcome that it represents.

Matching Test Items to Intended Outcomes

Preparing test items that are directly relevant to the specific learning outcomes to be measured is primarily a matter of matching the behavior specified by the intended outcome and the behavior measured by the test item. Stating the outcomes as specifically as possible and defining the action verbs in greater detail are both useful in this regard, but the process is still a matter of analysis and judgment. If the specific learning outcome calls for *supplying* an answer (e.g., name, define), the test item should also require that the answer be supplied (rather than selected). If the specific learning outcome calls for *identifying* a procedure, the test item should be concerned only with the process of identifying (rather than with more complex outcomes). If the specific learning outcome calls for *performing* a procedure, the test item should require actual performance (rather than a verbal description of how to do it). Issues such as these highlight the care needed in determining whether there is a good match between the behaviorally stated outcome and the expected response to the test item.

The procedure for constructing test items will be considered in later chapters. Here, we are simply focusing on the importance of matching each test item, as closely as possible, to the specific learning outcome it is intended to measure. The following examples, from various content areas, illustrate reasonably good matches between intended outcomes and test items. In each example, note how the specific learning outcome describes the behavior the pupil is to exhibit and how the test item presents a task that calls forth that particular behavior.

EXAMPLES

Specific Learning Outcome: Defines common terms. (Elementary Mathematics)
Directions: In a sentence or two, define each of the following words.
1. Interest
2. Premium
3. Dividend
4. Collateral
5. Profit

Specific Learning Outcome: Identifies procedure for converting from one measure to another. (Elementary Mathematics)
1. The area of a rug is given in square yards. How should you determine the number of square feet?
   A Multiply by 3
   Ⓑ Multiply by 9
   C Divide by 3
   D Divide by 9
2. The amount of milk a family drinks in one month is expressed in pints. How should you change it to gallons?
   A Multiply by 4
   B Multiply by 8
   C Divide by 4
   Ⓓ Divide by 8
3. The air space in a room is expressed in terms of cubic feet. How should you change it to cubic yards?
   A Multiply by 9
   B Multiply by 27
   C Divide by 9
   Ⓓ Divide by 27

Specific Learning Outcome: Differentiates between relative values expressed in fractions. (Elementary Mathematics)
1. Which of the following fractions is smaller than one half?
   A 2/4
   B 4/6
   Ⓒ 3/8
   D 9/16
2. Which of the following fractions indicates the greatest value?
   Ⓐ 2/3
   B 4/7
   C 5/9
   D 9/16
3. Which of the following fractions has the same value as one fifth?
   A 2/20
   B 5/50
   C 25/75
   Ⓓ 20/100

Specific Learning Outcome: Distinguishes fact from opinion. (Elementary Social Studies)

Directions: Read each of the following statements carefully. If you think the statement is a *fact,* circle the "F." If you think the statement is an *opinion,* circle the "O."

Ⓕ O 1. George Washington was the first President of the United States.

F Ⓞ 2. Abraham Lincoln was our greatest President.

Ⓕ O 3. Franklin Roosevelt was the only President elected to that office three times.

Ⓕ O 4. Alaska is the biggest state in the United States.

F Ⓞ 5. Hawaii is the most beautiful state in the United States.

Specific Learning Outcome: Identifies common uses of weather instruments. (Elementary Science)

1. Which one of the following instruments is used to determine the speed of the wind?

    A Wind vane

    Ⓑ Anemometer

    C Altimeter

    D Radar

2. Which one of the following instruments is used to determine the amount of moisture in the air?

    A Altimeter

    B Barometer

    Ⓒ Hygrometer

    D Radiosonde

Specific Learning Outcome: Identifies cause-and-effect relationships. (Elementary Science)

Directions: In each of the following statements, both parts of the statement are true. You are to decide if the second part explains *why* the first part is true. If it does, circle the "Yes." If it does not, circle the "No."

Examples:

Ⓨⓔⓢ No 1. People can see   *because*   they have eyes.

Yes Ⓝⓞ 2. People can walk   *because*   they have arms.

In the first example, the second part of the statement explains *why* "people can see" so the "yes" was circled. In the second example, the second part of the statement does *not* explain *why* "people can walk" so the "no" was circled. Read each of the following statements and answer the same way.

Yes Ⓝⓞ 1. Some desert snakes are hatched from eggs   *because*   the weather is hot in the desert.

Ⓨⓔⓢ No 2. Spiders are very useful   *because*   they eat harmful insects.

Ⓨⓔⓢ No 3. Some plants do not need sunlight   *because*   they get their food from other plants.

Yes Ⓝⓞ 4. Water in the ocean evaporates   *because*   it contains salt.

Ⓨⓔⓢ No 5. Fish can get oxygen from the water   *because*   they have gills.

Specific Learning Outcome: Identifies reasons for an action or event. (Biology)

1. Which one of the following best explains why green algae give off bubbles of oxygen on a bright, sunny day?

    A Transpiration

      B Plasmolysis
      Ⓒ Photosynthesis
      D Osmosis

2. Which one of the following best explains why bread mold can be grown in a dark room?

      Ⓐ Some plants do not produce their own food.
      B Photosynthesis can take place in the dark.
      C Chlorophyll aids the growth of plants in the darkness.
      D Bread mold takes in carbon dioxide and gives off oxygen in both darkness and light.

Specific Learning Outcome: Identifies the relevance of arguments. (Social Studies)

   Directions: The items in this part of the test are to be based on the following resolution:

      RESOLVED: *The legal voting age in the United States should be lowered to eighteen.* Some of the following statements are arguments *for* the resolution, some are arguments *against* it, and some are *neither* for nor against the resolution. Read each of the following statements and circle:

      F if it is an argument *for* the resolution.
      A if it is an argument *against* the resolution.
      N if it is *neither* for nor against the resolution.

Ⓕ A   N   1. Most persons are physically, emotionally, and intellectually mature by the age of eighteen.

F   A   Ⓝ   2. Many persons are still in school at the age of eighteen.

F   A   Ⓝ   3. In most states it is legal to drive an automobile by the age of eighteen.

F   Ⓐ   N   4. The ability to vote intelligently increases with age.

F   A   Ⓝ   5. The number of eighteen-year-old citizens in the United States is increasing each year.

These examples are sufficient to show how test items should be related to specific learning outcomes. Although all subject-matter areas and all types of learning outcomes are not represented, the basic principle is the same. *State the desired learning outcomes in behavioral terms and select or develop test items which call forth that specific behavior.*

RELATING NONTESTING PROCEDURES
TO SPECIFIC LEARNING OUTCOMES

There are many areas in which testing procedures are not useful. In evaluating some performance skills (e.g., singing, dancing, speaking), it is necessary to observe the pupil as he performs and to make judgments concerning the effectiveness of the performance. In other instances, it is possible to evaluate a pupil's skill by judging the quality of the product resulting from his performance (e.g., a theme, a painting, a typed letter, a baked cake, and so on). In evaluating a pupil's social adjustment, it may be necessary to observe the pupil in formal and informal situations in order to judge his tendencies toward aggression or withdrawal, his relations with his peers, and the like. In fact, whenever we are interested in evaluating how a pupil will typically behave in a situation, some type of observational procedure is usually called for.

As with testing procedures, the selection or development of an observational technique should evolve from the objectives and the specific learning outcomes. In the case of rating scales or checklists, the specific learning outcomes become the dimensions of behavior to be observed. In the following examples, note how the specific learning outcomes require only a slight modification to become items in a rating scale:

Speech

Specific Learning Outcome: Maintains good eye contact with audience.
  Rating Scale Item:
  How effective is the speaker in maintaining eye contact with the audience?

1	2	3	4	5
Ineffective	Below Average	Average	Above Average	Very Effective

Theme Writing

Specific Learning Outcome: Organizes ideas in a coherent manner.
  Rating Scale Item:
  Organization of ideas

1	2	3	4	5
Poor organization		Fair organization		Clear, coherent organization

Group Work

Specific Learning Outcome: Contributes worthwhile ideas to group discussion.
  Rating Scale Item:
  How often does the pupil contribute worthwhile ideas to group discussion?

1	2	3	4	5
Never	Seldom	Occasionally	Fairly Often	Frequently

More complete rating scales and checklists are presented in later chapters. It is our purpose here merely to illustrate how nontesting procedures can be related to the specific outcomes we wish to evaluate. The specific learning outcomes specify the behavior to be observed and the rating scale provides a convenient method of recording our judgments. Such judgments are, of course, still subjective, but we have made them as objective as possible by clearly defining the samples of pupil behavior we wished to observe and then deliberately observing those behaviors in pupils.

RELATING STANDARDIZED TESTS
TO LOCAL OBJECTIVES

The importance of relating evaluation techniques as directly as possible to the instructional objectives and specific learning outcomes to be measured is not limited to teacher-made devices. This type of relevance is also a major consideration when selecting standardized achievement tests for instructional purposes. Ideally, a standardized test should measure the subject-matter content and the behavioral changes which have been emphasized in the instructional program. The degree to which a test meets this ideal can be determined only by a careful and systematic examination of the test.

In judging the relevance of a standardized test to the instructional program, it is desirable to analyze the test item by item. As each item is studied, a record should be made of the subject-matter content and the behavioral changes it seems to measure. This tabulation can later be compared to the areas covered in the instructional program to determine the degree to which the coverage and emphasis are adequate. If a table of specifications has been prepared for a course, the test analysis can be compared directly to the table.

We seldom expect to find a standardized test in perfect agreement with the objectives and subject-matter content emphasized in a particular course or curriculum. However, an analysis of the test items will help determine how well the test actually does measure what we want to measure, which instructional areas are neglected, and which areas receive too much stress. This information is useful in interpreting the test results and in developing supplementary evaluation devices.

USING CUSTOM-MADE PUBLISHED TESTS

Some test publishers have built up banks of instructional objectives and matching test items for the various school subjects. This makes it possible to provide tests that are custom-made to fit a particular local instructional program. A typical procedure for obtaining a custom-made test is as follows: (1) teachers, and other school personnel, select from lists of objectives those that reflect the intended outcomes of the local program, and (2) the publisher selects the corresponding test items and assembles them into one or more forms of the test. In addition, the publisher might also provide special scoring and reporting services.

Custom-made tests are especially useful for criterion-referenced testing because they can be designed to yield descriptions of the specific knowledges and skills that pupils have acquired. They are also useful for norm-referenced testing (relative ranking of pupils), however, since they can provide evidence of pupil progress toward the more complex objectives of the local program. In either case, it is important to examine the custom-made test carefully, to make certain that the individual items, and the test as a whole, satisfactorily measure the pupil behaviors specified in the instructional objectives.

EVALUATION ON A BROADER SCALE

The major theme running throughout this book is that evaluation is an integral part of the teaching-learning process and that it involves two basic steps: (1) identifying and defining the objectives of instruction, and (2) constructing or selecting evaluation instruments which best appraise these objectives. Thus, our primary emphasis is on the extent to which the *specified* learning outcomes for a *particular* course or curriculum have been achieved. In an article concerning evaluation and course improvement, Cronbach has pointed out that there are times when it may be desirable to evaluate outcomes beyond those which have been set for a given course or curriculum. Note these provocative comments.[1]

> In course evaluation, we need not be much concerned about making measuring instruments fit the curriculum. However startling this declaration may seem, and however contrary to the principles of evaluation for other purposes, this must be our position if we want to know what changes a course produces in the pupil. An ideal evaluation would include measures of all the types of proficiency that might reasonably be desired in the area in question, not just the selected outcomes to which *this* curriculum directs substantial attention. If you wish only to know how well a curriculum is achieving *its* objectives, you fit the test to the curriculum; but if you wish to know how well the curriculum is serving the national interest, you measure all outcomes that might be worth striving for. One of the new mathematics courses might disavow any attempt to teach numerical trigonometry, and indeed, might discard nearly all computational work. It is still perfectly reasonable to ask how well graduates of the course can compute and can solve right triangles. Even if the course developers went so far as to contend that computational skill is no proper objective of secondary instruction, they will encounter educators and laymen who do not share their view. If it can be shown that students who come through the new course are fairly proficient in computation despite the lack of direct teaching, the doubters will be reassured. If not, the evidence makes clear how much is being sacrificed.

Although these comments are directly concerned with the evaluation of large-scale curriculum improvement projects, the basic idea is generally

---

[1] L. J. Cronbach, "Course Improvement through Evaluation," *Teachers College Record,* 64, 680, 1963. [Reprinted in N. E. Gronlund (ed.), *Readings in Measurement and Evaluation* (New York: Macmillan, 1968).]

applicable. For some purposes, it may be appropriate to determine pupil progress toward objectives other than those specified for a course or curriculum. An English teacher, for example, might do no direct teaching of grammar, but still be interested in measuring pupils' proficiency in grammar. Similarly, a science teacher might not consider spelling an intended outcome of science, but still be interested in determining how well pupils can spell the more complex scientific terms. It is always legitimate to ask how much incidental learning is taking place, or as Cronbach has indicated, how much is being sacrificed in those areas receiving no direct teaching.

When evaluating on a broader scale, the process of relating evaluation procedures to learning outcomes is basically the same. However, in this case it is, of course, necessary to relate the evaluation instruments as directly as possible to *all* of the outcomes to be measured; not just those that have been identified as the intended outcomes of instruction.

SUMMARY

Instructional objectives will function most effectively in classroom evaluation if a conscious effort is made to relate the evaluation procedures to the specific learning outcomes encompassed by each objective. This endeavor can be facilitated by (1) a general evaluation plan, (2) a table of specifications, and (3) a selection of evaluation techniques that measure each learning outcome most closely.

A general evaluation plan consists of a list of all general instructional objectives and specific learning outcomes with an indication of the type of evaluation technique to be used for each intended outcome. For teaching purposes, the methods to be used in achieving the objectives may also be included. The development of a general evaluation plan assures that provision has been made for evaluating all instructional objectives and alerts the teacher to types of evaluative information that must be gathered periodically during the semester.

A table of specifications is especially useful in planning for classroom evaluation. This is a two-way chart that relates the instructional objectives of a course to the subject-matter content used to achieve the objectives. It guides the teacher in constructing tests and other evaluation instruments that measure the intended outcomes of instruction in a balanced manner.

The most crucial step in relating evaluation procedures to instructional objectives is in the selection, or construction, of the specific evaluation technique to be used. In the case of both test items and nontest evaluation instruments, a concerted effort must be made to obtain samples of pupil behavior that are similar to the behavior described in the specific learning outcomes. Matching test behavior to intended outcome can be enhanced by further defining the action verbs used in the specific learning outcomes and by taking special care when judging the correspondence between an expected test response and the behaviorally stated outcome it is designed to measure.

In some instances, we might be interested in determining the extent to which a course or curriculum is modifying pupil behavior in areas other than those toward which our teaching is directed. This requires evaluation procedures that go beyond the intended outcomes of instruction, but the basic principle of relating the evaluation instruments as closely as possible to the outcomes to be measured is still pertinent.

LEARNING EXERCISES

1. What are the advantages and limitations of including teaching methods in a general evaluation plan (as Mr. Whiteside did)?
2. What are the advantages of including all general instructional objectives in a table of specifications, rather than just those that can be measured by paper-and-pencil tests? Are there any disadvantages?
3. Describe the factors to be considered when determining how many test items to devote to each instructional objective, and to each area of content, during the preparation of a table of specifications.
4. What steps can be taken to further assure that the items in a classroom test will call forth the appropriate responses? Can we ever be certain that we have a perfect match between test item and intended outcome?
5. Select a chapter in a textbook in your teaching area and do the following:
   a. List the major areas of content covered in the chapter.
   b. List several general learning outcomes (e.g., Knows terms).
   c. Construct a table of specifications for a twenty-item test on the material in the chapter (include other evaluation methods, if appropriate).
6. What are the relative advantages of using custom-made published tests instead of standardized tests for measuring pupil learning? What are the disadvantages?
7. How could a table of specifications be used in selecting a standardized test?
8. In your own teaching area, cite instances where you might want to measure learning outcomes beyond those specified for a particular course.
9. What type of test or evaluation method would be best for each of the following outcomes? Why?
   a. Demonstrates good study habits.
   b. Interprets a selection of poetry.
   c. Draws inferences from written material.
   d. Identifies the main idea in a paragraph.
   e. Relates well to his peers.
   f. Explains how to set up laboratory equipment.
10. What types of problems would be encountered in your teaching area if you were unable to use paper-and-pencil tests of any kind? What evaluation procedures would you use? How would you relate these procedures to your intended learning outcomes?

SUGGESTIONS FOR FURTHER READING

BLOOM, B. S., J. T. HASTINGS, and G. F. MADAUS. *Handbook on Formative and Summative Evaluation of Student Learning.* New York: McGraw-Hill Book Company, 1971. Part two contains eleven chapters that illustrate how test items and various evaluation instruments are related to learning outcomes in a variety of subject areas.

GRONLUND, N. E. *Stating Behavioral Objectives for Classroom Instruction.* New York: Macmillan Publishing Co., Inc., 1970. Chapter 7, "Using Instructional Objectives in Test Preparation." Includes a list of objectives, a table of specifications, and sample items keyed to the objectives for a unit in economics.

MORSE, H. T., and G. H. MCCUNE. *Selected Items for the Testing of Study Skills and Critical Thinking.* Washington, D.C.: National Council for the Social Studies, 1971. Contains numerous illustrations of test items keyed to learning outcomes in the study skills and critical thinking areas.

NOLL, V. H., and D. P. SCANNELL. *Introduction to Educational Measurement,* 3rd ed. Boston: Houghton Mifflin Company, 1972. Chapter 6, "Objectives As the Basis of All Good Measurement." See especially the last section of this chapter, where a variety of types of test items are keyed to specific objectives.

SYND, R. B., and A. J. PICARD. *Behavioral Objectives and Evaluation Measures: Science and Mathematics.* Columbus, Ohio: Charles E. Merrill Publishers, 1972. Chapter 10, "Sample Cognitive Objectives and Achievement Measures." This chapter presents fifty pages of sample test items keyed to objectives in science and mathematics at the elementary school, junior high school, and high school levels.

See also the *taxonomy* books by BLOOM (1956), HARROW (1972), and KRATHWOHL, BLOOM, and MASIA (1964), in the list of readings at the end of Chapter 2, for illustrations of how evaluation procedures are related to the various outcomes of education.

CHAPTER 4
Validity

In selecting or constructing an evaluation instrument the most important question is: To what extent will the results serve the particular uses for which they are intended? This is the essence of validity.

Many aspects of pupil behavior are evaluated in the school, and the results are expected to serve a variety of uses. For example, achievement may be evaluated in order to diagnose learning difficulties or to determine progress toward instructional objectives; scholastic aptitude may be measured in order to predict success in future learning activities or to group pupils for instructional purposes; and appraisals of personal-social development may be obtained in order to better understand pupils or to screen them for referral to a guidance counselor. Regardless of the area of behavior being evaluated, however, or the use to be made of the results, all of the various procedures used in an evaluation program should possess certain common characteristics. The most essential of these characteristics can be classified under the headings of *validity, reliability,* and *usability.*

Validity refers to the extent to which the results of an evaluation procedure serve the particular uses for which they are intended. If the results are to be used to describe pupil achievement, we should like them to represent the specific achievement we wish to describe, to represent all aspects of the achievement we wish to describe, and to represent nothing else. Our desires in this regard are similar to the defense attorney in the courtroom who wants the truth, the whole truth, and nothing but the truth. If the results are to be used to predict pupil success in some future activity, we should like them to provide as accurate an estimate of future success as possible. Basically, then, validity is always concerned with the specific use to be made of evaluation results and with the soundness of our proposed interpretations.

Reliability refers to the consistency of evaluation results. If we obtain quite similar scores when the same test is administered to the same group on two different occasions, we can conclude that our results have a high degree of reliability from one occasion to another. Similarly, if different teachers independently rate the same pupils on the same instrument and obtain similar ratings, we can conclude that the results have a high degree of reliability from one rater to another. As with validity, reliability is intimately related to the type of interpretation to be made. For some uses, we may be interested in asking how reliable our evaluation results are over a given period of time, and for others, how reliable they are over samples of the same behavior. In all instances in which reliability is being determined, however, we are concerned with the *consistency* of the results, rather than with the extent to which they serve the specific use under consideration.

Although reliability is a highly desired quality, it should be noted that reliability provides no assurance that evaluation results will yield the desired information. As with a witness testifying in a courtroom trial—the fact that he consistently tells the same story does not guarantee that he is telling the truth. The truthfulness of his statements can be determined only by comparing them with some other evidence. Similarly, with evaluation results consistency is an important quality but only if it is accompanied by evidence of validity, and that must be determined independently. Little is accomplished if evaluation results consistently provide the wrong information. In short, reliability is a necessary but not a sufficient condition for validity.

In addition to providing results which possess a satisfactory degree of validity and reliability, an evaluation procedure must meet certain practical requirements. It should be economical from the viewpoint of both time and money, it should be easily administered and scored, and it should provide results that can be accurately interpreted and applied by the school personnel available. These practical aspects of an evaluation procedure can all be included under the heading of usability. The term *usability*, then, refers only to the *practicality* of the procedure and implies nothing about the other qualities present.

In this chapter we shall consider the validity of evaluation results, and in the following chapter we shall turn our attention to reliability and usability.

NATURE OF VALIDITY

When using the term *validity*, in relation to testing and evaluation, there are a number of cautions to be borne in mind.

1. Validity pertains to the *results* of a test, or evaluation instrument, and *not* to the instrument itself. We sometimes speak of the validity of a test for the sake of convenience, but it is more appropriate to speak of the validity of the test results, or more specifically, of the validity of the interpretation to be made from the results.
2. Validity is *a matter of degree*. It does not exist on an all-or-none basis. Consequently, we should avoid thinking of evaluation results as valid or invalid. Validity is best considered in terms of categories that specify degree, such as high validity, moderate validity, and low validity.
3. Validity is always *specific to some particular use*. It should never be considered a general quality. For example, the results of an arithmetic test may have a high degree of validity for indicating computational skill, a low degree of validity for indicating arithmetical reasoning, a moderate degree of validity for predicting success in future mathematics courses, and no validity for predicting success in art or music. Thus, when appraising or describing validity, it is necessary to consider the use to be made of the results. Evaluation results are never just valid; they have a different degree of validity for each particular interpretation to be made.

TYPES OF VALIDITY

Three basic types of validity have been identified and are now commonly used in educational and psychological measurement.[1] They are: *content* validity, *criterion-related* validity, and *construct* validity. The general meaning of these types of validity is indicated in Table 4.1. Each type will be explained more fully as the chapter proceeds. For the sake of clarity, the discussion will be limited to validity as it relates to testing procedures. It should be recognized, however, that these three types of validity are also applicable to all of the various kinds of evaluation instruments used in the school.

Content Validity

The content of a course or curriculum may be broadly defined to include both subject-matter content and instructional objectives. The former is concerned with the topics, or subject-matter areas, to be covered, and the latter with the behavioral changes sought in pupils. Both of these aspects of content are of concern in determining content validity. We should like any achievement test we construct, or select, to provide results which are representative of the topics and behaviors we wish to measure. This is the essence of content validity. More formally, *content validity may be defined as the extent to which a test measures a representative sample*

---

[1] American Psychological Association, *Standards for Educational and Psychological Tests* (Washington, D.C.: APA, 1974).

TABLE 4.1
THREE TYPES OF VALIDITY

Type	Meaning	Procedure
Content validity	How well the test measures the subject-matter content and behaviors under consideration	Compare test content to the universe of content and behaviors to be measured
Criterion-Related validity	How well test performance predicts future performance or estimates current performance on some valued measure other than the test itself	Compare test scores with another measure of performance obtained at a later date (for prediction) or with another measure of performance obtained concurrently (for estimating present status)
Construct validity	How test performance can be described psychologically	Experimentally determine what factors influence scores on the test

of the subject-matter content and the behavioral changes under consideration.

The focus of content validity, then, is on the adequacy of the *sample* and not simply on the appearance of the test. A test that appears to be a relevant measure, based on superficial examination, is said to have *face* validity. Although a test should look like an appropriate measure to obtain the cooperation of those taking the test, face validity should not be considered a substitute for content validity.

As might be expected, content validity is of primary concern in achievement testing. The procedures used are those of logical analysis and comparison. The test is examined to determine the subject-matter content covered and the responses pupils are intended to make to the content, and this is compared with the domain of achievement to be measured. Although this is sometimes done in a rather haphazard manner, greater assurance of content validity is obtained by observing the following steps:

1. The major topics of subject-matter content and the major types of behavioral changes to be measured by the test are separately listed. These lists are usually derived from the topical content and the objectives emphasized in the instructional program. If the test is to measure achievement in a specific course, the teacher involved might develop the lists. If the test is to be used on a school-wide basis, the preparation of the lists might best be handled by a committee of teachers.
2. The various subject-matter topics and types of behavioral changes are weighted in terms of their relative importance. There is no simple procedure for determining appropriate relative weights for the various topics and behaviors. It depends on personal judgment as guided by the

amount of time devoted to each area during instruction, the philosophy of the school, the opinion of experts in the area, and similar criteria.

3. A table of specifications, like the one presented in Chapter 3, is built from the weighted lists of subject-matter topics and expected behavioral changes. This table, then, specifies the relative emphasis the test should give to each subject-matter topic and each type of behavioral change.

4. The achievement test is constructed, or selected, in accordance with the table of specifications. The closer the test corresponds to the specifications indicated in the table, the greater the likelihood that the pupils' responses to the test will have a high degree of content validity.

A table of specifications, in a very simple form, is presented in Table 4.2 to illustrate how such a table is used to check on content validity. The percentages in the table indicate the relative degree of emphasis each subject-matter area and each type of behavioral change is to be given in the test. Thus, if the test is to measure a representative sample of *subject-matter content*, 15 per cent of the test items should be concerned with plants, 15 per cent with animals, 30 per cent with weather, 15 per cent

TABLE 4.2

TABLE SHOWING THE RELATIVE EMPHASIS TO BE GIVEN TO THE
VARIOUS SUBJECT-MATTER AREAS AND TO THE CHANGES IN
BEHAVIOR FOR A TEST IN ELEMENTARY SCHOOL SCIENCE

Subject-matter Areas	Changes in Behavior (in Percentage)		
	Understands Concepts	Applies Concepts	Total
Plants	10	5	15
Animals	10	5	15
Weather	15	15	30
Earth	5	10	15
Sky	10	15	25
Total	50	50	100

with the earth, and 25 per cent with the sky. If the test is to measure a representative sample of *behavioral changes,* 50 per cent of the items should measure the "understanding of concepts," and 50 per cent should measure the "application of concepts." This, of course, implies that the specific emphasis on "understanding" and "application" for each subject-matter area will follow that indicated by the percentages in the table of specifications. For example, 10 per cent of the test items concerned with plants should measure "understanding of concepts," and 5 per cent of the test items should measure "application of concepts."

It should be noted that this procedure merely provides a rough check on content validity. Such an analysis reveals the *apparent* relevance of the test items to the subject-matter areas and behavioral changes to be measured. Content validity is concerned with the extent to which the test items actually do call forth the responses represented in the table of specifications. Test items may appear to measure "understanding" but not function as intended because of defects in the items, unclear directions, inappropriate vocabulary, or poorly controlled testing conditions. Thus, content validity is dependent on a host of factors other than the apparent relevance of the test items. Most of what is written in this book concerning the construction and selection of achievement tests is directed toward improving the content validity of the obtained results.

Although our discussion of content validity has been limited to achievement testing, content validity is also of some concern in the measurement of aptitudes, interests, attitudes, and personal-social adjustment. For example, if we are selecting an interest inventory we should like it to cover those aspects of interest with which we are concerned. Similarly, an attitude scale should include those attitudinal topics that are in accord with the objectives we wish to measure. The procedure here is essentially the same as that in achievement testing. It is a matter of analyzing the test materials and the outcomes to be measured and judging the degree of correspondence between them.

Criterion-Related Validity

Whenever test scores are to be used to predict future performance or to estimate current performance on some valued measure other than the test itself, we are concerned with criterion-related validity. For example, reading readiness test scores might be used to predict pupils' future achievement in reading, or a test of dictionary skills might be used to estimate pupils' current skill in the actual use of the dictionary (as determined by observation). In the first example, we are interested in *prediction* and thus in the relationship between the two measures over an extended period of time. This type of validity is called *predictive* validity. In the second example, we are interested in *estimating present status* and thus in the relationship between the two measures obtained concurrently. A high relationship in this case would show that the test of dictionary skills is a good indicator of actual skill in use of the dictionary. This procedure for determining validity is called *concurrent* validity. In the new test *Standards*,[2] the designations of predictive validity and concurrent validity have been subsumed under the more general category—*criterion-related* validity. This appears to be a desirable arrangement because the method of determining and expressing validity is the same in both cases. The major difference resides in the time period between the two obtained measures.

---

[2] American Psychological Association, *Standards for Educational and Psychological Tests* (Washington, D.C.: APA, 1974).

Criterion-related validity may be defined as the extent to which test performance is related to some other valued measure of performance. As noted earlier, the second measure of performance may be obtained at some future date (when we are interested in predicting future performance), or concurrently (when we are interested in estimating present performance). First let us examine the use of criterion-related validity from the standpoint of predicting success in some future activity. Then we shall return to its second use.

Predicting Future Performance. Suppose that Mr. Young, a junior high school teacher, wants to determine how well scores from a certain scholastic aptitude test predict success in his seventh-grade arithmetic class. Since the scholastic aptitude test is administered to all pupils when they enter junior high school, these scores are readily available to Mr. Young. His biggest problem is deciding on a *criterion* of successful achievement in arithmetic. For lack of a better criterion, Mr. Young decides to use a comprehensive departmental examination that is administered to the various seventh-grade arithmetic sections at the end of the school year. It is now possible for Mr. Young to determine how well the scholastic aptitude test scores predict success in his arithmetic class by comparing the pupils' scholastic aptitude test scores with their scores on the departmental examination. Do those pupils who have high scholastic aptitude test scores also tend to have high scores on the departmental examination? Do those who have low scholastic aptitude test scores also tend to have low scores on the departmental examination? If this is the case, Mr. Young is inclined to agree that the scholastic aptitude test scores tend to be accurate in predicting achievement in this arithmetic class. In short, he recognizes that the test results possess criterion-related validity.

In our illustration, Mr. Young merely inspected the scholastic aptitude test scores and the achievement test scores to determine the agreement between them. Although this may be a desirable preliminary step, it is seldom sufficient for indicating criterion-related validity. The usual procedure is to correlate statistically the two sets of scores and to report the degree of relationship between them by means of a correlation coefficient. This enables validity to be presented in precise and universally understood terms. They are, of course, "universally understood" only by those who understand and can interpret correlation coefficients. This should pose no great problem, however, since the meaning of correlation coefficient can be easily grasped by persons whose computational skill goes no further than that of simple arithmetic.

Rank-Difference Correlation. To clarify the calculation and interpretation of correlation coefficients, let's consider the exact scores Mr. Young's pupils received on both the scholastic aptitude test and the departmental examination in arithmetic. This information is provided in the first two columns of Table 4.3. By inspecting these two columns of scores, as Mr. Young did, it is possible to note that high scores in Column 1 tend to go

TABLE 4.3
TEST SCORES AND TEST-SCORE RANKS FOR TWENTY
JUNIOR HIGH SCHOOL PUPILS

	1	2	3	4	5	6
Pupil	Fall Aptitude Scores	Spring Arithmetic Scores	Aptitude Rank	Arithmetic Rank	(D) Difference in Rank	(D²) Difference Squared
John	119	77	1	3	−2	4
Henry	118	76	2	4	−2	4
Mary	116	72	3	6	−3	9
Susan	115	67	4	8	−4	16
Bill	112	82	5	1	4	16
Carl	109	63	6	10	−4	16
Grace	108	60	7	12	−5	25
Ralph	106	78	8	2	6	36
Jane	105	69	9	7	2	4
Karl	104	49	10	18	−8	64
Jim	102	48	11	19	−8	64
Frank	100	58	12	14	−2	4
Karen	98	56	13	16	−3	9
Joan	97	57	14	15	−1	1
Ruby	95	74	15	5	10	100
June	94	62	16	11	5	25
Helen	93	46	17	20	−3	9
George	91	65	18	9	9	81
Alice	90	59	19	13	6	36
Martin	89	54	20	17	3	9
						$\Sigma D^2 = 532$

with high scores in Column 2. This comparison is difficult to make, however, since the sizes of the test scores in the two columns are different.

The agreement of the two sets of scores can be more easily made if the test scores are converted to ranks. This has been done in Columns 3 and 4 of Table 4.3. Note that the pupil who was first on the aptitude test ranked third on the arithmetic test; the pupil who was second on the aptitude test ranked fourth on the arithmetic test; the pupil who was third on the aptitude test ranked sixth on the arithmetic test; and so on. Comparing the rank order of the pupils on the two tests, as indicated in Columns 3 and 4 of Table 4.3, gives us a fairly good picture of the relationship between the two sets of scores. From this inspection we know that pupils who had a high standing on the aptitude test also had a high standing on the arithmetic test, and pupils who had a low standing on the aptitude test also had a low standing on the arithmetic test. Our inspection of Columns 3 and 4 also shows us, however, that the relationship between the pupils' ranks on the two tests is not perfect. There is some shifting in rank order from one test to another. Our problem now is—How can we express the degree of relationship between these two sets of ranks in meaningful terms? This is where the correlation coefficient becomes useful.

The rank-difference correlation is simply a method of expressing the degree of relationship between two sets of ranks. The steps in determining a rank-difference correlation coefficient are presented in the following computing guide.[3] Mr. Young's data, in Table 4.3, are used to illustrate the

COMPUTING GUIDE: RANK-DIFFERENCE CORRELATION

Steps	Results in Table 4.3
1. Arrange pairs of scores, for each pupil, in columns.	Columns 1 and 2
2. Rank pupils from 1 to N (number in group) for each set of scores.	Columns 3 and 4
3. Find the difference (D) in ranks by subtracting the rank in the right-hand column (Column 4) from the rank in the left-hand column (Column 3).	Column 5
4. Square each difference in rank (Column 5) to obtain difference squared (D^2).	Column 6
5. Sum the squared differences in Column 6 to obtain ΣD^2.	Bottom of Column 6
6. Apply the following formula: $$\rho \text{ (rho)} = 1 - \frac{6 \times \Sigma D^2}{N(N^2 - 1)}$$ Σ = Sum of D = Difference in rank N = Number in group	$$\rho = 1 - \frac{6 \times 532}{20(20^2 - 1)}$$ $$= 1 - \frac{3192}{7980}$$ $$= 1 - .40$$ $$= .60$$

procedure. It will be noted that the Greek letter rho (ρ) is used to identify a rank-order correlation coefficient. From our computations for Mr. Young's data we find that $\rho = .60$. This correlation coefficient is a statistical summary of the degree of relationship between the two sets of scores in Mr. Young's data. In this particular instance, it indicates the extent to which the fall aptitude test scores (predictor) are predictive of the spring arithmetic test scores (criterion). In short, it refers to the criterion-related validity of the aptitude test scores.

How good is Mr. Young's validity coefficient of .60? Should Mr. Young be happy with this finding or should he be disappointed? Does this particular aptitude test provide a good prediction of future performance in arithmetic?

Unfortunately, simple and straightforward answers cannot be given to such questions. The interpretation of correlation coefficients is dependent

---

[3] Correlation coefficients may also be determined by the product-moment technique which is easier to apply to large groups. See the computing guide in Appendix A.

upon information from a variety of sources. First, we know that the following correlation coefficients indicate the extreme degrees of relationship that it is possible to obtain between variables:

$$1.00 = \text{perfect positive relationship}$$
$$.00 = \text{no relationship}$$
$$-1.00 = \text{perfect negative relationship}$$

Since Mr. Young's validity coefficient is .60, we know that the relationship is positive but somewhat less than perfect. Obviously, the nearer a validity coefficient approaches 1.00 the happier we are with it because larger validity coefficients indicate greater accuracy in predicting from one variable to another.[4]

Another way of evaluating Mr. Young's validity coefficient of .60 is to compare it to the validity coefficients obtained with other methods of predicting performance in arithmetic. If this validity coefficient is larger than those obtained with other prediction procedures, Mr. Young will continue to use the scholastic aptitude test as the best means available to him for predicting the arithmetic performance of his pupils. Thus, validity coefficients are large or small only in relation to each other. Where criterion-related validity is an important consideration, we shall always consider more favorable the test with the largest validity coefficient. In this regard, even aptitude tests with rather low validity may be useful, however, if they are the best predictors available, and the predictions they provide are better than chance.[5]

Probably the easiest way of grasping the practical meaning of a correlation coefficient is to note how the accuracy of prediction increases as the correlation coefficient becomes larger. This is shown in the various charts presented in Table 4.4. The rows in each chart represent the fourths of a group on some predictor (such as a scholastic aptitude test) and the columns indicate the percentage of persons falling in each fourth on the criterion measure (such as an achievement test). First note that for a correlation coefficient of .00, being in the top quarter on the predictor provides no basis for predicting where a person might fall on the criterion measure. His chances of falling in each quarter are equally good. Now turn to the chart for a correlation coefficient of .60. Note, here, that if a person falls in the top quarter on the predictor, he has 54 chances out of a 100 of falling in the top quarter on the criterion measure, 28 chances out of 100 of falling in the second quarter, 14 chances out of 100 of falling in the third quarter, and only 4 chances out of 100 of falling in the bottom quarter. The remainder of the chart is read in a similar manner.

---

[4] A coefficient of -1.00 would also give us perfect prediction from one variable to another but in educational measurement we are most commonly concerned with positive relationships.

[5] L. J. Cronbach, *Essentials of Psychological Testing*, 3rd ed. (New York: Harper and Row, 1970).

TABLE 4.4
PREDICTION EFFICIENCY FOR DIFFERENT-SIZE CORRELATION COEFFICIENTS[*]

		Quarter on Criterion							*Quarter on Criterion*			
		4	*3*	*2*	*1*				*4*	*3*	*2*	*1*
Quarter	*1*	25	25	25	25	*Quarter*		*1*	4	14	28	54
on	*2*	25	25	25	25	*on*		*2*	14	26	32	28
Predictor	*3*	25	25	25	25	*Predictor*		*3*	28	32	26	14
	4	25	25	25	25			*4*	54	28	14	4

$r = .00$ 　　　　　　　　　　　　　$r = .60$

		Quarter on Criterion							*Quarter on Criterion*			
		4	*3*	*2*	*1*				*4*	*3*	*2*	*1*
Quarter	*1*	10	19	28	43	*Quarter*		*1*	1	7	25	67
on	*2*	19	25	28	28	*on*		*2*	7	27	41	25
Predictor	*3*	28	28	25	19	*Predictor*		*3*	25	41	27	7
	4	43	28	19	10			*4*	67	25	7	1

$r = .40$ 　　　　　　　　　　　　　$r = .80$

[*] Adapted from tables in R. L. Thorndike and E. Hagen, *Measurement and Evaluation in Psychology and Education*, 3rd ed. (New York: John Wiley & Sons, 1969), p. 173. Numbers in each cell were adjusted to nearest whole number to provide 100 cases in each row and each column.

By comparing the charts for the different-size correlation coefficients, it is possible to get some feel for the meaning of correlation coefficient in terms of prediction efficiency. As the correlation coefficient becomes larger, a person's chances of being in the same quarter on the criterion measure as he is on the predictor are increased. This can be seen by looking at the entries in the diagonal cells. With a correlation coefficient of 1.00, each diagonal cell would, of course, contain 100 per cent of the cases—indicating perfect prediction from one measure to another.

Estimating Present Performance. Up to this point we have emphasized the role of criterion-related validity in predicting future performance. Although this is probably its major use, there are times when we are interested in the relation of test performance to some other current measure of performance. In this case, we would obtain both measures at approximately the same time and correlate the results. This is commonly done when a test is being considered as a replacement for a more time-consuming method of obtaining information. For example, Mr. Brown, the biology teacher, wondered if an objective test of study skills could be used in place of the elaborate observation and rating procedures he was currently using. He felt that if a test could be substituted for the more complex procedures, he would have much more time to devote to individual pupils during the supervised study period. An analysis of the specific pupil behaviors on which he rated the pupils' study skills indicated that many of the procedures could be stated in the form of objective test questions. Consequently, he developed an objective test of study skills that he administered to his pupils. To determine how adequately his test measured study skills he correlated the test results with his ratings of the pupils' study skills. A resulting correlation coefficient of .75 indicated considerable agreement between the test results and the criterion measure. This correlation coefficient represents the criterion-related validity of Mr. Brown's test of study skills.

We might also correlate test performance with some other current measure of performance to determine if a predictive study is worth doing. For example, if a set of scholastic aptitude test scores correlated to a sufficiently high degree (e.g., .60) with a set of achievement test scores obtained at the same time, it would indicate that the scholastic aptitude test had enough potential as a predictor to make a predictive study worthwhile. On the other hand, a low correlation would discourage us from carrying out the predictive study, because we know that the correlation would become still lower when the time period between measures was extended. Other things being equal, the larger the time span between two measures the smaller the correlation coefficient.

Expectancy Table. How well a test predicts future performance or estimates current performance on some criterion measure can also be shown by directly plotting the data in a twofold chart like the one shown in Figure 4.1. Here, Mr. Young's data (from Table 4.3) have been tabulated by placing a tally showing each individual's standing on both the fall aptitude scores and the spring arithmetic scores. For example, John scored 119 on the fall aptitude test and 77 on the spring arithmetic test, so a tally, representing his performance, was placed in the upper right-hand cell. The performance of all other pupils on the two tests was tallied in the same manner. Thus, each tally mark in Figure 4.1 represents how well each of Mr. Young's twenty pupils performed on the fall and spring tests. The total number of pupils in each cell, and in each column and row, have also been indicated.

The expectancy grid shown in Figure 4.1 can be used directly as an expectancy table, simply by using the frequencies in each cell. The interpretation of such information is simple and direct. For example, of those pupils who scored above average on the fall aptitude test, none scored below 65 on the spring arithmetic test, 2 out of 5 scored between 65 and 74, and 3 out of 5 scored between 75 and 84. Of those who scored below average on the fall aptitude test, none scored in the top category on the spring arithmetic test and 4 out of 5 scored below 65. These interpretations are limited to the group tested but from such results one might make predictions concerning future pupils. We can say, for example, that pupils who score above average on the fall aptitude test will probably score

Fall Aptitude Scores	Spring Arithmetic Scores				Totals
	45—54	55—64	65—74	75—84	
Above Average (over 110)			// 2	/// 3	5
Average (95-110)	// 2	𝟀𝟀𝟀 5	// 2	/ 1	10
Below Average (below 95)	// 2	// 2	/ 1		5
Totals	4	7	5	4	20

FIGURE 4.1. Expectancy grid showing how scores on the fall aptitude test and spring arithmetic test are tallied in appropriate cells. (From data in Table 4.3.)

above average on the spring arithmetic test. Other predictions can be made in the same way by noting the frequencies in each cell of the grid in Figure 4.1.

More commonly, the figures in an expectancy table are expressed in percentages. This is readily obtained from the grid by converting each cell frequency to a percentage of the total number of tallies in its row. This has been done for the data in Figure 4.1 and the results are presented in Table 4.5. The first row of the table shows that of the 5 pupils who scored above average on the fall aptitude test, 40 per cent (2 pupils) scored between 65 and 74 on the spring arithmetic test, and 60 per cent (3 pupils) scored between 75 and 84. The remaining rows are read in a similar manner. The use of percentage makes the figures in each row and column comparable. Our predictions can then be made in standard terms (that is, chances out of 100) for all score levels. Our interpretation is apt to be a little clearer

TABLE 4.5

EXPECTANCY TABLE SHOWING THE RELATION BETWEEN FALL
APTITUDE SCORES AND SPRING ARITHMETIC SCORES[*]

Fall Aptitude Scores	Percentage in Each Score Group on Spring Arithmetic Test			
	45–54	55–64	65–74	75–84
Above average (Over 110)			40	60
Average (95–110)	20	50	20	10
Below average (Below 95)	40	40	20	

[*] From data in Figure 4.1.

if we say Henry's chances of being in the top group on the criterion measure are 60 out of 100 and Ralph's are only 10 out of 100, than if we say Henry's chances are 3 out of 5 and Ralph's are 1 out of 10.

Expectancy tables take many different forms and may be used to show the relation between various types of measures. The number of categories used with the predictor, or criterion, may be as few as two or as many as seem desirable. Also, the predictor may be any set of measures for which we wish to establish criterion-related validity and the criterion may be course grades, ratings, test scores, or whatever other measure of success is relevant.[6]

When interpreting expectancy tables based on a small number of cases, like Mr. Young's class of twenty pupils, our predictions should be regarded as highly tentative. Each percentage is based on so few pupils that we can expect large fluctuations in these figures from one group of pupils to another. It is frequently possible to increase the number of pupils represented in the table by combining test results from several classes. Where this is done, our percentages are, of course, much more stable, and our predictions can be made with greater confidence. In any event, expectancy tables provide a simple and direct means of indicating the validity of test results.

The "Criterion" Problem. In the determination of criterion-related validity, a major problem is that of obtaining a satisfactory *criterion* of success. It will be recalled that Mr. Young used a comprehensive departmental examination as the criterion of success in his seventh-grade arithmetic class. Mr. Brown used his own ratings of the pupils' study skills. In each instance the criterion of success was only partially suitable as a basis for test validation. Mr. Young recognized that the departmental examination did not measure all of the important learning outcomes that he aimed at in teaching arithmetic. There was not nearly enough emphasis on arithmetic reasoning; the interpretation of graphs and charts was sadly neglected; and, of course, the test did not evaluate the pupils' attitudes toward arithmetic (which Mr. Young considered to be extremely important). Likewise, Mr. Brown was well aware of the shortcomings of his rating of pupils' study skills. He sensed that some pupils "put on a show" when they knew they were being observed. In other instances he felt that some of the pupils were probably overrated on study skills because of their high achievement in class work. Despite these recognized shortcomings, both Mr. Young and Mr. Brown found it necessary to use these criterion measures because they were the best criterion measures available.

The plights of Mr. Young and Mr. Brown in locating a suitable criterion of success for the purpose of test validation are not unusual. The selection of a satisfactory criterion is one of the most difficult problems in validating

---

[6] A. G. Wesman, *Expectancy Tables—A Way of Interpreting Test Validity,* Test Service Bulletin No. 38 (New York: The Psychological Corporation, 1949).

a test. For most educational purposes, no adequate criterion of success exists. Those which are used tend to be lacking in comprehensiveness and in most cases provide results that are less stable than those of the test being validated.

The lack of a suitable criterion for validating achievement tests has important implications for the classroom teacher. Since statistical types of validity will usually not be available, teachers will have to depend on procedures of logical analysis to assure test validity. This means carefully identifying the objectives of instruction, stating these objectives in terms of specific changes in pupil behavior, and constructing or selecting evaluation instruments which satisfactorily measure the behavioral changes sought in pupils. Thus, content validity will assume a role of major importance in the teacher's evaluation of pupil progress.

Construct Validity

The two types of validity thus far described are both concerned with some specific practical use of test results. They help us determine how well test scores represent the achievement of certain learning outcomes (content validity), or how well they predict or estimate a particular performance (criterion-related validity). In addition to these more specific and immediately practical uses, we may wish to interpret test scores in terms of some general psychological quality. For instance, rather than speak about a pupil's score on a particular arithmetic test, or how well it predicts success in mathematics, we might want to infer that the pupil possesses a certain degree of *reasoning ability*. This provides a broad general description of pupil behavior which has implications for many different uses.

Whenever we wish to interpret test performance in terms of some psychological trait or quality, we are concerned with construct validity. A *construct* is a psychological quality which we assume exists in order to explain some aspect of behavior. Reasoning ability is a construct. When we interpret test scores as measures of reasoning ability, we are implying that there is a quality that can be properly called reasoning ability and that it can account to some degree for performance on the test. Verifying such implications is the task of construct validation.

Common examples of constructs are intelligence, scientific attitude, critical thinking, reading comprehension, study skills, and mathematical aptitude. There is an obvious advantage in being able to interpret test performance in terms of such psychological constructs. Each construct has an underlying theory which can be brought to bear in describing and predicting a person's behavior. If we say a person is highly intelligent, for example, we know what behaviors might be expected of him in various specific situations.

Construct validity may be defined as the extent to which test performance can be interpreted in terms of certain psychological constructs. The process of determining construct validity involves the following steps: (1) identifying the constructs presumed to account for test performance; (2) deriving hypotheses regarding test performance from the theory underlying the construct; (3) verifying the hypothesis by logical and empirical means. For example, let us suppose that we wish to check the claim that a newly constructed test measures intelligence. From what is known about "intelligence," we might make the following predictions:

1. The test scores will increase with age (intelligence is assumed to increase with age until approximately age sixteen).
2. The test scores will predict success in school achievement.
3. The test scores will be positively related to teachers' ratings of intelligence.
4. The test scores will be positively related to scores on other so-called intelligence tests.
5. The test scores will discriminate between groups which are known to differ, such as "gifted" and "mentally handicapped."
6. The test scores will be little influenced by direct teaching.

Each of these predictions, and others, would then be tested, one by one. If positive results are obtained for each prediction, the combined evidence lends support to the claim that the test measures intelligence. If a prediction is not confirmed, say the scores do not increase with age, we must conclude that either the test is not a valid measure of intelligence, or there is something wrong with our theory. As Cronbach and Meehl[7] have indicated, with construct validation both the theory and the test are being validated at the same time.

Methods Used in Obtaining Evidence for Construct Validation. As noted in our illustration, there is no adequate single method of establishing construct validity. It is a matter of accumulating evidence from many different sources. We may use both content validity and criterion-related validity as partial evidence to support construct validity, but neither of them alone is sufficient. Construct validation depends on logical inferences drawn from a variety of types of data. The following procedures illustrate the broad range of methods that might be used in obtaining evidence for construct validity:[8]

1. *Analysis of the mental process required by the test items.* One may analyze the mental processes involved by examining the test items to determine what factors they appear to measure and/or by administering the test to individual pupils and having them "think aloud" as they answer. Thus, examination of a science test may indicate that the test scores are likely to be influenced by knowledge, comprehension, and quantitative

---

[7] L. J. Cronbach and P. E. Meehl, "Construct Validity in Psychological Tests," *Psychological Bulletin*, **52**, 281–302, 1955.
[8] G. C. Helmstadter, *Principle of Psychological Measurement* (New York: Appleton-Century-Crofts, 1964).

ability. Similarly, "thinking aloud" on an arithmetic reasoning test may verify that the items call for the intended reasoning process, or it may reveal that most problems can be solved by a simple trial-and-error procedure.

2. *Comparison of the scores of known groups.* In some cases, it is possible to predict that scores will differ from one group to another. These may be age groups, boys and girls, trained and untrained, adjusted and maladjusted, and the like. For example, most abilities increase with age (at least during childhood and adolescence), and boys obtain higher scores than girls on certain tests (e.g., mechanical comprehension). Also, it is reasonable to expect that achievement test scores will discriminate between groups with different amounts of training and that scores on adjustment inventories will discriminate between groups of adjusted and maladjusted individuals. Thus, a prediction of differences for a particular test can be checked against groups that are known to differ and the results used as partial support for construct validation.

3. *Comparison of scores before and after some particular treatment.* Some test scores can be expected to be fairly resistant to specific training (e.g., intelligence), whereas others can be expected to increase (e.g., achievement). Similarly, some test scores can be expected to change as certain types of experimental treatment are introduced. For example, we would expect the scores on an anxiety test to change when individuals are subjected to an anxiety-producing experience. Thus, from the theory underlying the trait being measured, we can make predictions that the scores of a particular test will change (or remain stable) under various conditions. If our predictions are verified, the results provide further support for construct validation.

4. *Correlations with other tests.* The scores of any particular test can be expected to correlate substantially with the scores of other tests that presumably measure the same thing. By the same token, the test scores can be expected to have lower correlations with tests that were designed to measure a different ability or trait. For example, we would expect a set of scholastic aptitude test scores to correlate rather highly with those of another scholastic aptitude test, but much lower with the scores of a musical aptitude test. Thus, for any given test, we would predict higher correlations with like tests and lower correlations with unlike tests. In addition, we might also predict that the test scores would correlate with various practical criteria. Scholastic aptitude scores, for example, should correlate satisfactorily with school grades, achievement test scores, and other measures of achievement. This latter type of evidence is, of course, criterion-related validity. Our interest here, however, is not in the immediate problem of prediction, but rather in using these correlations to support the claim that the test is a measure of scholastic aptitude. As indicated earlier, construct validation depends on a wide array of evidence, including that provided by the other types of validity.

In examining construct validity, our interest is not limited to the psychological construct the test was designed to measure. Any factor which might influence the test scores is of legitimate concern. For example, although a test author claims his test measures arithmetic reasoning, we might rightfully ask to what extent the test scores are influenced by computational skill, reading ability, and similar factors. Broadly conceived, construct validity is an attempt to account for the differences in test scores. Instead of asking, "Does this test measure what the author claims it measures?" we are asking, "Precisely what does this test measure? How can we most meaningfully interpret the scores in psychological terms?" The aim of construct validation is to identify the nature and strength of all factors influencing performance on the test.

Construct validity is of importance in all types of testing—achievement, aptitude, and personal-social development. When selecting any standardized test, we should note what interpretations are suggested for the test and then review the test manual to determine the total available evidence supporting these interpretations. The confidence with which we can make the proposed interpretations is directly dependent on the type of evidence presented. Also, if we suspect that test scores are influenced by factors other than those described in the manual (such as speed and reading ability), we should check these hunches with a suitable experiment of our own.

VALIDITY OF CRITERION-REFERENCED
MASTERY TESTS

As noted in Chapter 1, norm-referenced tests are designed to emphasize differences among individuals. An individual's performance on a norm-referenced test has little meaning by itself. To be meaningful, the test performance must be compared to the performance of others who have taken the test. We judge whether a norm-referenced score is high or low by noting its relative position in a set of scores. Basic to this measurement approach is a wide spread of test scores so that dependable discriminations can be made among individuals. We can speak of differences between Tom and Bill and Mary and Jane with greater confidence if the score differences are large. This variability among scores, that is essential to norm-referenced testing, is also necessary for computing validity coefficients. In fact, most of the traditional statistical measures for estimating validity and reliability use formulas based on the variability among scores. Thus, although all of the various estimates of validity discussed earlier are appropriate for norm-referenced testing, they are not completely appropriate for judging the validity of criterion-referenced mastery tests.[9]

Whereas variability among scores is essential for norm-referenced tests,

---

[9] Do not confuse *criterion-referenced* testing and *criterion-related* validity. *Criterion* in the former refers to the type of behavior (as described in instructional objectives) that the test scores represent. *Criterion* in the latter refers to some second measure of performance that the test scores are to predict or estimate.

it is irrelevant for criterion-referenced mastery tests. These tests are designed to describe the types of tasks an individual can perform. If all pupils can perform a given set of tasks (e.g., identify the measuring instruments included in a weather unit) at the end of instruction, and thus all get perfect scores (zero variability), so much the better. From a mastery learning standpoint, both the test and the instruction would appear to be effective. Since variability among scores is not a necessary condition for a good criterion-referenced mastery test, the conventional statistical measures for determining validity are inappropriate.[10]

The type of validity that is of greatest importance for criterion-referenced mastery tests is content validity. The procedures for obtaining content validity described earlier in this chapter are as applicable here as they are with norm-referenced tests. The fact that criterion-referenced mastery tests are typically confined to a more delimited domain of learning tasks (e.g., unit or chapter), even simplifies the process of defining and selecting a representative sample of tasks. In some cases, the domain of tasks is so limited (e.g., addition of single-digit whole numbers) that a representative sample can be obtained without the use of a table of specifications.

Although content validity is of primary concern with criterion-referenced mastery tests, we might also be interested in using the test results to make predictions about pupils. We might, for example, use a criterion-referenced pretest to predict which pupils are likely to master the material in a unit of instruction, or use an end-of-unit mastery test to determine which pupils should proceed to the next unit of instruction. Such instructional decisions require some evidence (criterion-related validity) that our decisions are soundly based. This evidence can be obtained by means of an expectancy table, like the one shown in Table 4.6. It will be noted in this table that the majority of pupils with pretest scores of 20 or lower failed to achieve mastery at the end of the unit. In such a case, a test score of 20 would provide a good cutoff score for determining which pupils should proceed with the unit and which should receive remedial help before proceeding. We would, of course, prefer a larger number of pupils than thirty when selecting such cutoff scores, but this represents a realistic classroom situation. As noted earlier, it is frequently possible to increase the number of pupils used in an expectancy table by combining test results from several classes.

There is nothing in the nature of criterion-referenced mastery testing to rule out construct validity. So much of the supporting evidence for construct validity is dependent on correlations and other statistical measures, however, that the construct validity of a criterion-referenced test would, of necessity, be based on rather meager evidence (i.e., only that evidence not dependent on variability among scores).

---

[10] W. J. Popham and T. R. Husek, "Implications of Criterion-Referenced Measurement," in W. J. Popham (ed.), *Criterion-Referenced Measurement* (Englewood Cliffs, N.J.: Educational Technology Publications, 1971).

TABLE 4.6

EXPECTANCY TABLE SHOWING THE RELATION BETWEEN
PRETEST SCORES AND THE NUMBER OF STUDENTS
ATTAINING MASTERY AT THE END OF THE UNIT
$(N = 30)$*

| | Number of Students | |
Pretest Scores	Nonmastery	Mastery
41–50	0	3
31–40	1	6
21–30	2	8
11–20	7	1
1–10	2	0

* From N. E. Gronlund, *Preparing Criterion-Referenced Tests for Classroom Instruction*. New York: Macmillan, 1973. Used by permission.

FACTORS INFLUENCING VALIDITY

Numerous factors tend to make test results invalid for their intended use. Some are rather obvious and easily avoided. No teacher would think of measuring knowledge of social studies with an English test. Nor would a teacher consider measuring problem-solving skill in third-grade arithmetic with a test designed for sixth graders. In both instances the test results would be obviously invalid. The factors influencing validity are of this same general nature but much more subtle in character. For example, a teacher may overload a social studies test with items concerning historical facts and thus it is less valid as a measure of achievement in social studies. Or a third-grade teacher may select appropriate arithmetic problems for his pupils but write directions that only the better readers are able to understand clearly. The arithmetic test then becomes a reading test which invalidates the results for their intended use. This is the nature of some of the more subtle factors influencing validity. These are the factors for which the teacher should be alert, whether constructing classroom tests or selecting standardized tests.

Factors in the Test Itself

A careful examination of test items will indicate whether the test seems to measure the subject-matter content and the mental functions that the teacher is interested in testing. However, any of the following factors can prevent the test items from functioning as intended and thereby lower the validity of the test results:

1. *Unclear directions.* Directions which do not clearly indicate to the pupil how to respond to the items, whether it is permissible to guess, and how to record the answers will tend to reduce validity.

2. *Reading vocabulary and sentence structure too difficult.* Vocabulary and sentence structure which is too complicated for the pupils taking the test will result in the test measuring reading comprehension and aspects of intelligence rather than the aspects of pupil behavior that the test is intended to measure.

3. *Inappropriate level of difficulty of the test items.* In norm-referenced tests, items which are too easy or too difficult will not provide reliable discriminations among pupils and will therefore lower validity. In criterion-referenced tests, failure to match the difficulty of the test items with the difficulty specified in the instructional objectives will lower validity.

4. *Poorly constructed test items.* Test items which unintentionally provide clues to the answer will tend to measure the pupils' alertness in detecting clues as well as the aspects of pupil behavior that the test is intended to measure.

5. *Ambiguity.* Ambiguous statements in test items contribute to misinterpretations and confusion. Ambiguity sometimes confuses the better pupils more than the poorer pupils, causing the items to function even less effectively for them.

6. *Test items inappropriate for the outcomes being measured.* Attempting to measure understandings, thinking skills, and other complex types of achievement with test forms that are appropriate only for measuring factual knowledge will invalidate the results.

7. *Test too short.* A test is only a sample of the many questions that might be asked. If a test is too short to provide a representative sample of the behavior we are interested in, validity will suffer accordingly.

8. *Improper arrangement of items.* Test items are typically arranged in order of difficulty with the easiest items first. Placing difficult items early in the test may cause pupils to spend too much time on these and prevent them from reaching items they could easily answer. Improper arrangement may also influence validity by having a detrimental effect on pupil motivation.

9. *Identifiable pattern of answers.* Placing answers in some systematic pattern (e.g., T, T, F, F, or A, B, C, D, A, B, C, D) will enable students to guess the answers to some items more easily and this will lower validity.

In short, any defect in the construction of the test which prevents the test items from functioning in harmony with their intended use will contribute to the invalidity of the measurement. Much of what is written in the following chapters is directed toward improving the validity of the results obtained with classroom tests and other evaluation instruments.

Functioning Content and Teaching Procedures

In the case of achievement testing, the functioning content of test items cannot be determined merely by examining the form and content of the test. For example, the following item may appear to measure arithmetical reasoning if examined without reference to what the pupils have already been taught:

> If a 40′ pipe is cut so that the shorter piece is 2/3 as long as the longer piece, what is the length of the shorter piece?

However, if the teacher has taught the solution to this particular problem before giving the test, the test item now measures no more than memorized knowledge. Similarly, tests of understanding, critical thinking, and other complex learning outcomes are valid measures in these areas only if the test items function as intended. If the pupils have previously been taught the solutions to the particular problems included in the test, or have been taught mechanical steps for obtaining the solutions, such tests can no longer be considered valid instruments for measuring the more complex mental processes.

Factors in Test Administration and Scoring

The administration and scoring of a test may also introduce factors that have a detrimental effect on the validity of the results. In the case of teacher-made tests, such factors as insufficient time to complete the test, unfair aid to individual pupils who ask for help, cheating during the examination, and the unreliable scoring of essay answers would tend to lower validity. In the case of standardized tests, failure to follow the standard directions and time limits, giving pupils unauthorized assistance, and errors in scoring would similarly contribute to lower validity. For all types of tests, adverse physical and psychological conditions at the time of testing may also have a detrimental effect.

Factors in Pupils' Responses

In some instances, invalid test results are due to personal factors influencing the pupil's response to the test situation rather than to any shortcomings in the test instrument. Pupils may be hampered by emotional disturbances which interfere with their test performance. Some pupils are frightened by the test situation and thereby unable to respond normally. Still others are not motivated to put forth their best effort. These and other factors which restrict and modify pupils' responses in the test situation will obviously lower the validity of the test results.

A less obvious factor which influences test results is that of *response set*.[11] A response set is a consistent tendency to follow a certain pattern in responding to test items. For example, some persons will respond "true" when they do not know the answer to a true-false item, while other persons will tend to mark "false." A test with a large number of true statements will consequently be to the advantage of the first type of person and to the disadvantage of the second type. Although some response sets,

---

[11] L. J. Cronbach, *Essentials of Psychological Testing*, 3rd ed. (New York: Harper and Row, 1970).

such as the one illustrated, can be offset by careful test construction procedures (e.g., including an equal number of true and false statements in the test) other response sets are more difficult to control. Typical of response sets in this latter category are the tendency to work for speed rather than accuracy, the tendency to gamble when in doubt, and the use of a particular style in responding to essay tests. These response sets reduce the validity of the test results by introducing into the test score factors which are not pertinent to the purpose of the measurement.[12]

Nature of the Group and the Criterion

Validity is always specific to a particular group. An arithmetic test based on story problems, for example, may measure reasoning ability in a slow group, and a combination of simple recall of information and computational skill in a more advanced group. Similarly, scores on a science test may be accounted for largely by reading comprehension in one group and by knowledge of facts in another. What a test measures is influenced by such factors as age, sex, ability level, educational background, and cultural background. Thus, in appraising reports of test validity included in test manuals, or other sources, it is important to note the nature of the validation group. How closely it compares in significant characteristics to the group of pupils we wish to test determines how applicable the information is to our particular group.

In evaluating validity coefficients, it is also necessary to consider the nature of the criterion used. For example, scores on a mathematics aptitude test are likely to provide a more accurate prediction of achievement in a physics course in which quantitative problems are stressed than in one where they play only a minor role. Likewise, we can expect scores on a critical thinking test to correlate more highly with grades in social studies courses which emphasize critical thinking than in those which depend largely on the memorization of factual information. Other things being equal, the greater the similarity between the behaviors measured by the test and the behaviors represented in the criterion, the higher the validity coefficient.

Since validity information varies with the nature of the group tested and with the composition of the criterion measures used, published validation data should be considered as highly tentative. Whenever possible, the validity of the test results should be checked in the specific local situation.

This discussion of factors influencing the validity of test results should make clear the pervasive and functional nature of the concept validity. In the final analysis the validity of test results is based on the extent to which the behavior elicited in the testing situation is a true representation of

---

[12] L. J. Cronbach, *Essentials of Psychological Testing*, 3rd ed. (New York: Harper and Row, 1970).

the behavior being evaluated. Thus, anything in the construction or the administration of the test which causes the test results to be unrepresentative of the characteristics of the person tested contributes to lower validity. In a very real sense, then, it is the user of the test who must make the final judgment concerning the validity of the test results. He is the only one who knows how well the test fits his particular use, how well the testing conditions were controlled, and how typical the responses were to the testing situation.

SUMMARY

The most important quality to consider when selecting or constructing an evaluation instrument is validity. This refers to the extent to which the evaluation results serve the particular uses for which they are intended. In interpreting validity information, it is important to keep in mind that validity refers to the *results* rather than to the instrument, that its presence is a matter of *degree*, and that it is always *specific* to some particular use.

There are three basic types of validity. *Content* validity refers to the extent to which a test measures a representative sample of the subject-matter content and the behavioral changes under consideration. It is especially important in achievement testing and is determined by logical analysis of test content. *Criterion-related* validity is concerned with the extent to which test performance is accurate in predicting some future performance or estimating some current performance. This type of validity can be reported by means of a correlation coefficient called a validity coefficient or by means of an expectancy table. It is of special significance in all types of aptitude testing, but is pertinent whenever test results are used to make specific predictions, or whenever a test is being considered as a substitute for a more time-consuming procedure. *Construct* validity refers to the extent to which test performance can be interpreted in terms of certain psychological constructs. The process of construct validation involves identifying and clarifying the factors which influence test scores so that the test performance can be interpreted most meaningfully. This involves the accumulation of evidence from a variety of different studies. Both of the other types of validity may be used as partial support for construct validity, but it is the combined evidence from all sources that is important. The more complete the evidence, the more confident we are concerning the psychological qualities measured by the test.

Because *criterion-referenced* mastery tests are not designed to discriminate among individuals, statistical types of validity are inappropriate. For this type of test, we must depend primarily on content validity. Where the test scores are to be used for prediction (e.g., mastery-nonmastery), an expectancy table can be effectively used.

A number of factors tend to influence the validity of test results. Some of these influences can be found in the test instrument itself, some in the relation of teaching to testing, some in the administration and scoring of the test, some in the atypical responses of pupils to the test situation, and still others in the nature of the group tested and in the composition of the criterion measures used. A major aim in the construction, selection, and use of tests, and other evaluation instruments, is to control those factors which have an adverse effect on validity and to interpret evaluation results in accordance with what validity information is available.

LEARNING EXERCISES

1. In what way does a table of specifications contribute to content validity? What aspects of content validity are most apt to suffer if a table of specifications is *not* used?
2. Compare the relative difficulty of determining content validity for a spelling test and a social studies test. For which area would a table of specifications be most useful? Why?
3. If you wanted to determine the content validity of a standardized achievement test, what procedure would you follow? Describe your procedure step by step and give reasons for each step.
4. If a fellow teacher told you that a particular standardized achievement test had high validity, what types of questions would you ask him?
5. Which type of validity is illustrated by each of the following statements?
   a. Test scores are correlated with course grades.
   b. A test is analyzed to see how adequately it samples what has been taught.
   c. A teacher constructs an expectancy table.
   d. High scorers and low scorers on a test are compared to see how they differ.
   e. Validity is determined by logical analysis only.
6. What is the advantage of an expectancy table over a validity coefficient for expressing the predictive effectiveness of a scholastic aptitude test? What are some limitations?
7. What specific types of evidence might be useful in evaluating the construct validity of each of the following?
   a. Test of critical thinking.
   b. Test of creativity.
   c. Test of anxiety.
8. Study the validity sections of test manuals for a few standardized achievement tests and scholastic aptitude tests. How does the information differ for these two types of test? Why?
9. Consult the validity section of the *Standards for Educational and Psychological Tests* (see the reading list for this chapter) and review the types of information that test manuals should contain. Compare a recent test manual against the *Standards*.
10. List and briefly describe as many factors as you can think of that might lower the validity of a *norm-referenced* classroom test. Do the same for a *criterion-referenced* test. Which factors differ?

SUGGESTIONS FOR FURTHER READING

AMERICAN PSYCHOLOGICAL ASSOCIATION. *Standards for Educational and Psychological Tests*. Washington, D.C.: APA, 1974. See section on validity (pages 25–48) for descriptions of the basic types and for the nature of validity information to be sought in test manuals.

ANASTASI, A. *Psychological Testing*, 4th ed. New York: Macmillan Publishing Co., Inc., 1976. Chapter 6, "Validity: Basic Concepts." Describes the standard types of validity and methods of determining them.

CRONBACH, L. J. "Test Validation," Ch. 14 in R. L. Thorndike (ed.), *Educational Measurement*. Washington, D.C.: American Council on Education, 1971. A comprehensive discussion of validity, with special emphasis on educational tests.

POPHAM, W. J., and T. R. HUSEK. "Implications of Criterion-Referenced Measurement," in W. J. Popham (ed.), *Criterion-Referenced Measurement*. Englewood Cliffs, N.J.: Educational Technology Publications, 1971. Describes the characteristics of criterion-referenced measurement and the difficulties of obtaining meaningful measures of validity and reliability.

Test Bulletin

WESMAN, A. G. *Double-Entry Expectancy Tables*. Test Service Bulletin, No. 45. New York: The Psychological Corporation, 1966. This bulletin describes and illustrates how to prepare expectancy tables using two predictors.

CHAPTER 5

Reliability and Other Desired Characteristics

Next to validity, reliability is the most important characteristic of evaluation results. . . . Reliability (1) provides the consistency which makes validity possible, and (2) indicates how much confidence we can place in our results. . . . The practicality of the evaluation procedure is, of course, also of concern to the busy classroom teacher.

In Chapter 4 it was emphasized that validity is the most important consideration in the selection and construction of evaluation procedures. First and foremost we want evaluation results to serve the specific uses for which they are intended. Next in importance is *reliability,* and following that is a host of practical features which can best be classified under the heading of *usability.*

RELIABILITY

Reliability refers to the *consistency* of measurement. That is, to how consistent test scores or other evaluation results are from one measurement to another. Suppose, for instance, that Miss Jones had just given an achievement test to her pupils. How similar would the pupils' scores have been had she tested them yesterday or tomorrow or next week? How would the scores have varied had she selected a different sample of equivalent items? If it was an essay test, how much would the scores have been changed had a different teacher scored it? These are the types of questions with which reliability is concerned. Test scores merely provide a limited measure of behavior obtained at a particular time. Unless the measurement can be shown to be reasonably consistent (that is, generalizable) over different occasions or over different samples of the same behavior, little confidence can be placed in the results.

On the other hand, we cannot expect test results to be perfectly consistent. There are numerous factors other than the quality being measured which may influence test scores. If a single test is administered to the same group twice in close succession, some variation in scores can be expected due to temporary fluctuations in memory, attention, effort, fatigue, emotional strain, guessing, and similar factors. With a longer time period between tests, additional variation in scores may be caused by intervening learning experiences, changes in health, forgetting, and less comparable testing conditions. If we use a different sample of items in the second test, still another factor is likely to influence the results. Individuals may find one test easier than the other because it happens to contain more items on specific topics with which they are familiar.[1] Such extraneous factors as these introduce a certain amount of error into *all* test scores. Methods of determining reliability are essentially means of determining how much error is present under different conditions. In general, the more consistent our test results are from one measurement to another, the less error present and, consequently, the greater the reliability.

The meaning of reliability, as applied to testing and evaluation, can be further clarified by noting the following general points:

1. Reliability refers to the *results* obtained with an evaluation instrument and not to the instrument itself. Any particular instrument may have a number of different reliabilities, depending on the group involved and the situation in which it is used. Thus it is more appropriate to speak of the reliability of "the test scores," or of "the measurement," than of "the test," or "the instrument."
2. A closely related point is that an estimate of reliability always refers to a particular type of consistency. Test scores are not reliable in general. They are reliable (or generalizable) over different periods of time, over different samples of questions, over different raters, and the like. It is possible for test scores to be consistent in one of these respects and not in another. The appropriate type of consistency in a particular case is dictated by the use to be made of the results. For example, if we wish to know what individuals will be like at some future time, constancy of scores is highly important. On the other hand, if we want to measure an individual's shifts in anxiety from moment to moment, we shall need a measure which lacks constancy over occasions in order to obtain the information we desire. Thus, for different interpretations we need different analyses of consistency. Treating reliability as a general characteristic can only lead to erroneous interpretations.
3. Reliability is a necessary but not a sufficient condition for validity. A

---

[1] L. J. Cronbach, *Essentials of Psychological Testing*, 3rd ed. (New York: Harper and Row, 1970).

test which provides totally inconsistent results cannot possibly provide valid information about the behavior being measured. On the other hand, highly consistent test results may be measuring the wrong thing or may be used in ways that are inappropriate. Thus, low reliability can be expected to restrict the degree of validity that is obtained, but high reliability provides no assurance that a satisfactory degree of validity will be present. In short, *reliability merely provides the consistency which makes validity possible.*

Although a highly reliable measure may have little or no validity, a measure which has been shown to have a satisfactory degree of predictive validity must of necessity possess sufficient reliability. Thus, where we are interested only in predicting a specific criterion, reliability will be of little concern if predictive validity is satisfactory.[2]

4. Unlike validity, reliability is primarily statistical in nature. Logical analysis of a test will provide little evidence concerning the reliability of the scores. The test must be administered, one or more times, to an appropriate group of persons and the consistency of the results determined. This consistency may be expressed in terms of shifts in the relative standing of persons in the group or in terms of the amount of variation to be expected in a specific individual's score. Consistency of the first type is reported by means of a correlation coefficient called a *reliability coefficient.* Consistency of the second type is reported by means of the *standard error of measurement.* Both methods of expressing reliability are widely used and should be understood by persons responsible for interpreting test results.[3] Since both methods require variability in scores, these procedures for estimating reliability are primarily useful with *norm-referenced* measures.

Determining Reliability by Correlation Methods

In determining reliability it would be desirable to obtain two sets of measures under identical conditions and then to compare the results. This procedure is impossible, of course, since the conditions under which evaluation data are obtained can never be identical. As a substitute for this ideal procedure several methods of estimating reliability have been introduced. The methods are similar in that all of them involve correlating two sets of data, obtained either from the same evaluation instrument or from equivalent forms of the same procedure. The correlation coefficient used to determine reliability is calculated and interpreted in the same manner as that used in determining the statistical estimates of validity. The only difference between a validity coefficient and a reliability coefficient is that

---

[2] L. J. Cronbach, *Essentials of Psychological Testing*, 3rd ed. (New York: Harper and Row, 1970).

[3] American Psychological Association, *Standards for Educational and Psychological Tests* (Washington, D.C.: APA, 1974).

the former is based on agreement with an outside criterion, and the latter is based on agreement between two sets of results from the same procedure.

The chief methods of estimating reliability are shown in Table 5.1. Note that different types of consistency are determined by the different methods—consistency over a period of time, consistency over different forms of the instrument, and consistency within the instrument itself. The reliability coefficient resulting from each method must be interpreted in terms of the type of consistency being investigated. Each of these methods of estimating reliability will be considered in further detail as we proceed. Although the methods will be discussed mainly with reference to testing procedures, they are also applicable to other types of evaluation techniques.

TABLE 5.1
METHODS OF ESTIMATING RELIABILITY

	Type of Reliability Measure	Procedure
Test-retest method	Measure of stability	Give the same test twice to the same group with any time interval between tests from several minutes to several years
Equivalent-forms method	Measure of equivalence	Give two forms of the test to the same group in close succession
(Test-retest with equivalent forms)	Measure of stability and equivalence	Give two forms of the test to the same group with increased time interval between forms
Split-half method	Measure of internal consistency	Give test once. Score two equivalent halves of test (e.g., odd items and even items); correct reliability coefficient to fit whole test by Spearman-Brown formula
Kuder-Richardson method	Measure of internal consistency	Give test once. Score total test and apply Kuder-Richardson formula

Test-Retest Method. To estimate reliability by means of the test-retest method the same test is administered twice to the same group of pupils with a given time interval between the two administrations of the test. The resulting test scores are correlated, and this correlation coefficient provides a measure of stability; that is, it indicates how stable the test results are over the given period of time. If the results are highly stable, those pupils who are high on one administration of the test will tend to be high on the other administration of the test, and the remaining pupils will tend to stay in their same relative positions on both administrations of the test. Such stability would be indicated by a large correlation coefficient.

It will be recalled from our previous discussion of correlation coefficients that a perfect positive relationship is indicated by 1.00 and a zero relationship by .00. Measures of stability in the .80's and .90's are commonly reported for standardized tests of aptitude and achievement over occasions within the same year.

One important factor to keep in mind in interpreting measures of stability is the time interval between tests. If this time interval is short, say a day or two, the constancy of the results will be inflated by the fact that pupils will remember some of their answers from the first test to the second. If the time interval is long, say about a year, the results will not only be influenced by the instability of the testing procedure but also by actual changes in the pupils over that period of time. In general, the longer the time interval between test and retest the more the results are influenced by changes in the pupil characteristic being measured, and the smaller the reliability coefficient.

What time interval between tests is most preferable will depend largely on the use to be made of the results. If we are trying to predict from ninth-grade test scores whether a boy is likely to succeed in college, stability over a several year period is quite important. If we are trying to predict whether he will succeed in this year's algebra course, stability over any period longer than a few months is quite unimportant. Thus, for some decisions we are interested in reliability coefficients based on a long interval between test and retest and, for others, reliability coefficients based on a short interval may be sufficient. The important thing is to seek evidence of stability which fits the particular interpretation to be made.

Most teachers will not find it possible to compute test-retest reliability coefficients for their own classroom tests. However, in choosing standardized tests the stability of the scores serves as one important criterion. The test manual should provide evidence of stability, indicating the time interval between tests and any unusual experiences the group members might have had between testings. Other things being equal (such as validity), we shall favor the test whose scores have been shown to possess the type of stability we need to make sound decisions.

Information concerning the stability of test scores also has implications for the use of test results from school records and for the frequency with which retesting is needed. We know, for example, that first-grade scholastic aptitude test scores are fairly stable over occasions within the same year, but relatively unstable over a period of several years. Thus, we can expect to use such results in determining readiness for first-grade work, but should not rely on them for estimates of learning ability in the later elementary grades. For this use, a second test will need to be administered at the beginning of the later elementary period. Similarly, when using *any* test score from permanent records, one should check the date of testing and the stability data available to determine if the results are still dependable. Where doubt exists and the decision is important, retesting is in order.

Equivalent-Forms Method. Estimating reliability by means of the equivalent-forms method involves the use of two different but equivalent forms of the test (also called parallel or alternate forms).[4] The two forms of the test are administered to the same group of pupils in close succession and the resulting test scores are correlated. This correlation coefficient provides a measure of *equivalence*. Thus, it indicates the degree to which both forms of the test are measuring the same aspects of behavior.

It should be noted that the equivalent-forms method tells us nothing about the stability of the pupil characteristic being measured. This reliability coefficient reflects the extent to which the test represents an adequate sample of the characteristic being measured. In achievement testing, for example, there are thousands of questions that might be asked in a particular test. However, due to time limits and other restricting factors, only a limited number of the possible questions can be used. The questions included in the test should provide an adequate sample of the possible questions in the area. The easiest way to estimate if a test measures an adequate sample of the content is to construct two forms of the test and correlate the results. A high correlation indicates that both forms are measuring the same content and therefore are probably reliable samples of the general area of content being measured.

The equivalent-forms method of estimating reliability does away with the troublesome problem of selecting a proper time interval between tests as is necessary with the test-retest method. However, the need for two equivalent forms of the test restricts its use almost entirely to standardized testing. Here it is widely used, since most standardized tests have two or more forms available. In fact, a teacher should look with suspicion upon any standardized test which has two forms available and does not report information concerning their equivalence. The comparability of the results of the two forms cannot be assumed unless such evidence is presented.

The equivalent-forms method is sometimes used with a time interval between the administration of the two forms of the test. Under these conditions, the resulting reliability coefficient provides a measure of *stability and equivalence*. This is the most rigorous test of reliability because it includes all possible sources of variation in the test scores. The stability of the testing procedures, the constancy of the pupil characteristic being measured, and the representativeness of the sample of tasks included in the test are all taken into account. Consequently, this is generally recommended as the soundest procedure for estimating the reliability of test scores. As with the ordinary test-retest method, the reliability coefficient must be interpreted in light of the time interval between the two forms of the test. For longer time periods, we should ordinarily expect smaller reliability coefficients.

---

[4] Equivalent forms are built to the same set of specifications (e.g., test content, difficulty, and so on) but are constructed independently.

Split-Half Method. The reliability of test scores can also be estimated from a single administration of a single form of a test. The test is administered to a group of pupils in the usual manner and then is divided in half for scoring purposes. To split the test into halves which are most equivalent, the usual procedure is to score the even-numbered items and the odd-numbered items separately. This provides two scores for each pupil which, when correlated, provides a measure of *internal consistency*. This coefficient indicates the degree to which the two halves of the test are equivalent.

As noted, the above reliability coefficient is determined by correlating the scores of two half-tests. To estimate the reliability of the scores based on the full-length test the Spearman-Brown formula is usually applied. This formula is as follows:

$$\text{Reliability on full test} = \frac{2 \times \text{Reliability on } \frac{1}{2} \text{ test}}{1 + \text{Reliability on } \frac{1}{2} \text{ test}}$$

The simplicity of the formula can be seen in the following example where the correlation coefficient between the two halves of a test is .60:

$$\text{Reliability on full test} = \frac{2 \times .60}{1 + .60} = \frac{1.20}{1.60} = .75$$

This correlation coefficient of .75, then, provides an estimate of reliability of a full test where the half-tests correlated .60.

The split-half method is similar to the equivalent-forms method in that it indicates the extent to which the sample of test items is an adequate sample of the content being measured. A high correlation between scores on the two halves of a test denote the equivalence of the two halves and consequently the adequacy of the sampling. However, like the equivalent-forms method, it tells nothing about changes in the individual from one time to another.

Kuder-Richardson Method. Another method of estimating the reliability of test scores from a single administration of a single form of a test is by means of formulas such as those developed by Kuder and Richardson.[5] These formulas also provide a measure of *internal consistency* but they do not require splitting the test in half for scoring purposes. One of the formulas, called the Kuder-Richardson Formula 20, is based on the proportion of persons passing each item and the standard deviation of the total scores.[6] The computation is rather cumbersome, unless information is already available concerning the proportion passing each item, but the

---

[5] J. C. Stanley, "Reliability," in R. L. Thorndike (ed.), *Educational Measurement* (Washington, D.C.: American Council on Education, 1971).
[6] Standard deviation is a measure of the spread of scores. See Appendix A for method of computing.

result is equal to the average of all possible split-half coefficients for the group tested.

A less accurate but simpler formula to compute is the Kuder-Richardson Formula 21. This formula can be applied to the results of any test which has been scored on the basis of the number of correct answers. A modified version of the formula[7] is

$$\text{Reliability Estimate (KR21)} = \frac{K}{K-1}\left(1 - \frac{M(K-M)}{Ks^2}\right)$$

where $K =$ the number of items in the test
$\quad\ M =$ the mean (arithmetic average) of the test scores
$\quad\ \ s =$ the standard deviation of the test scores

This formula will yield approximately the same results as Kuder-Richardson Formula 20, but in most cases the reliability estimate will be smaller.[8] Its chief advantage is the ease with which it can be applied.

Kuder-Richardson estimates of reliability assume that the items in the test are homogeneous. That is, that each test item measures the same quality or characteristic as every other. Where this assumption is justified, the reliability estimate will be similar to that provided by the split-half method. If homogeneity is lacking, as in an achievement test which measures different types of learning outcomes, an underestimate of split-half reliability will result.[9]

The simplicity of applying the split-half method and the Kuder-Richardson method has led to their widespread use in estimating reliability. However, such internal consistency procedures have limitations which restrict their value. First, they are not appropriate for speeded tests—for tests with time limits which prevent pupils from attempting every item. Where speed is a significant factor in the testing, the reliability estimates will be inflated to an unknown degree. This poses no great problem in estimating the reliability of test scores from teacher-made tests, since these are usually power tests. In the case of standardized tests, however, time limits are seldom so liberal that all pupils complete the test. Thus, measures of internal consistency reported in test manuals should be generally disregarded *unless* evidence is also presented that speed of work is a negligible factor. For speeded tests, reliability obtained by the test-retest or equivalent-forms method should be sought.

A second limitation of internal consistency procedures is that they do not indicate the constancy of pupil response from day to day. In this

---

[7] L. J. Cronbach, *Essentials of Psychological Testing*, 3rd ed. (New York: Harper and Row, 1970).
[8] L. J. Cronbach, *Essentials of Psychological Testing*, 3rd ed. (New York: Harper and Row, 1970).
[9] Internal consistency can also be determined by *coefficient alpha* and *analysis of variance* procedures. See J. C. Stanley (footnote 5) and L. J. Cronbach (footnote 7).

regard, they are similar to the equivalent-forms method without a time interval. Only test-retest procedures indicate the extent to which test results are generalizable over different periods of time.

Comparing Correlation Methods. As noted in our previous discussion, each of the methods of estimating reliability provides different information concerning the consistency of test results. A summary of this information is presented in Table 5.2. This table makes clear the fact that most methods are

TABLE 5.2

TYPE OF CONSISTENCY INDICATED BY EACH OF THE
METHODS FOR ESTIMATING RELIABILITY

Method of Estimating Reliability	Type of Consistency		
	Consistency of Testing Procedure	Constancy of Pupil Characteristics	Consistency Over Different Samples of Items
Test-retest (immediate)	X	*	
Test-retest (time interval)	X	X	
Equivalent-forms (immediate)	X	*	X
Equivalent-forms (time interval)	X	X	X
Split-half	X		X
Kuder-Richardson	X		X

* Short-term constancy of response is reflected in immediate retest, but day-to-day stability is not shown.

concerned with only one or two types of consistency sought in test results. The test-retest method, without a time interval, takes into account only the consistency of the testing procedure and short-term constancy of response. If a time interval is introduced between the tests, the constancy of the characteristics of the pupil from day to day is also included. However, neither of the test-retest procedures provides information concerning the consistency of results over different samples of items, since both sets of scores are based on the same test.

The equivalent-forms method without a time interval, the split-half method, and the Kuder-Richardson method all take into account the consistency of testing procedures and the consistency of results over different samples of items.

Only the equivalent-forms method with an intervening time period between tests takes into account all three types of consistency. This is the reason that this measure of stability and equivalence is generally regarded as the most useful estimate of test reliability.

The Standard Error of Measurement

If it were possible to test a pupil over and over again on the same test, we would find that his scores would vary somewhat. The amount of variation in his test scores would be directly related to the reliability of the testing procedures. Low reliability would be indicated by large variations in the pupil's test scores. High reliability would be indicated by little variation from one testing to another. Although it is impractical to administer a test many times to the same pupils, it is possible to *estimate* the amount of variation to be expected in test scores. This estimate is called the *standard error* of measurement.

Test manuals usually give the standard error of measurement. Thus all we need to do is to take it into account when interpreting individual test scores. For example, let us assume that we have just administered an intelligence test to a class and the results indicate that Mary Smith has an IQ of 97. We note in the test manual that the standard error of measurement is 5. What does this 5 mean with regard to Mary Smith's IQ? In general, it indicates the amount of error that must be taken into consideration in interpreting Mary Smith's IQ score. More specifically, it provides the limits within which we can reasonably expect to find Mary Smith's "true" IQ score. A "true" score is one that would be obtained if the test were perfectly reliable.[10] If Mary Smith were tested repeatedly under identical conditions 68 per cent of her obtained scores would fall within 1 standard error of her "true" score, 95 per cent would fall within 2 standard errors, and 99 per cent would fall within 3 standard errors.[11] For practical purposes, these limits may be applied to Mary Smith's obtained score of 97 to give us the following ranges within which we could be reasonably sure to find her "true" score:

Number of Standard Errors	Level of Confidence	Score Units to Apply to Mary's IQ Score of 97	Range of Scores
1	68%	5	92–102
2	95%	10	87–107
3	99%	15	82–112

On this basis, we can be nearly certain that Mary Smith's "true" IQ score is somewhere between 82 and 112 (within 3 standard errors). In interpreting individual test scores, however, the use of one standard error of measurement is more common. Thus, a range of scores from 92 to 102

[10] The "true score" has been called a "universe score" by Cronbach, because it is the hypothetical average of many measurements within a particular universe. See L. J. Cronbach, *Essentials of Psychological Testing*, 3rd ed. (New York: Harper and Row, 1970), p. 153.
[11] These percentages are based on the normal curve. See Chapter 15 for a description of the normal curve.

would typically be used to describe Mary Smith's test performance. Recognizing this amount of error in Mary Smith's score, we would not be surprised if on a later intelligence test she received a score of 92, a score of 102, or even scores beyond this range. Such variations can be accounted for by errors of measurement alone. The standard error makes us wary of attributing significance to minor fluctuations in test scores.

The standard error of measurement makes it clear that a test score should be interpreted as a "band of scores" rather than as a specific score. With a large standard error the band of scores is large and we have less confidence in our obtained score. If the standard error is small the band of scores is small and we have greater confidence that our obtained score is a dependable measure of the characteristic. Viewing a test score as a "band of scores" makes it possible to interpret and use test results more intelligently. Apparent differences in test scores, between individuals and for the same individual over a period of time, frequently disappear when the standard error of measurement is considered. A teacher or counselor who has an acute awareness of the standard error of measurement finds it impossible to be dogmatic in interpreting minor differences in test scores.

The relationship between the reliability coefficient and the standard error of measurement can be seen in Table 5.3 This table presents the standard errors of measurement for various reliability coefficients and

TABLE 5.3

STANDARD ERRORS OF MEASUREMENT FOR GIVEN VALUES OF
RELIABILITY COEFFICIENT AND STANDARD DEVIATION*

	Reliability Coefficient					
SD	.95	.90	.85	.80	.75	.70
30	6.7	9.5	11.6	13.4	15.0	16.4
28	6.3	8.9	10.8	12.5	14.0	15.3
26	5.8	8.2	10.1	11.6	13.0	14.2
24	5.4	7.6	9.3	10.7	12.0	13.1
22	4.9	7.0	8.5	9.8	11.0	12.0
20	4.5	6.3	7.7	8.9	10.0	11.0
18	4.0	5.7	7.0	8.0	9.0	9.9
16	3.6	5.1	6.2	7.2	8.0	8.8
14	3.1	4.4	5.4	6.3	7.0	7.7
12	2.7	3.8	4.6	5.4	6.0	6.6
10	2.2	3.2	3.9	4.5	5.0	5.5
8	1.8	2.5	3.1	3.6	4.0	4.4
6	1.3	1.9	2.3	2.7	3.0	3.3
4	.9	1.3	1.5	1.8	2.0	2.2
2	.4	.6	.8	.9	1.0	1.1

* This table is based on the formula: SE (Measurement) $= SD \sqrt{1-r}$ where SD is the standard deviation of the test scores and r is the reliability coefficient. Reprinted from J. E. Doppelt, *How Accurate Is a Test Score?* Test Service Bulletin, No. 50 (New York: The Psychological Corporation, 1956).

standard deviations.[12] It will be noted that as the reliability coefficient increases, for any given standard deviation, the standard error of measurement decreases. Thus, high reliability coefficients are associated with small errors in specific test scores and low reliability coefficients are associated with large errors.

If a test manual does not report the standard error of measurement, Table 5.3 can be used to estimate the standard error. In fact this is the purpose for which the table was developed. All one needs to do to obtain an estimate of the standard error for a given test is to enter the column and the row nearest to the reliability coefficient and standard deviation reported in the test manual. For example, a reliability coefficient of .92 and a standard deviation of 16 would result in a standard error of 5.1. This is obtained by going down the second column (.90) until you come to the row in which the standard deviation is 16. Our example is similar to data commonly reported for group intelligence tests. The resulting standard error is approximately the same as that used in our earlier illustration with Mary Smith and would, of course, be interpreted in the same manner.

There are several precautions to be kept in mind when using Table 5.3 to estimate the standard error of measurement. First, the reliability coefficient and standard deviation must be based on the same group of persons. Second, entering the table with the reliability coefficient and standard deviation nearest to those in the manual gives you only an approximation of the standard error of measurement. Third, the table does not take into account the fact that the standard error of measurement varies slightly at different score levels. Within these limitations, however, Table 5.3 provides a simple and quick method for estimating the standard error of measurement and an approximation accurate enough for most practical applications of test results.

The standard error of measurement has two special advantages as a means of estimating reliability. First, the estimates are in the same units as the test scores. This makes it possible to directly indicate the margin of error to allow for when interpreting individual scores. Second, the standard error is likely to remain fairly constant as you go from group to group. This is not true of the reliability coefficient which is highly dependent on the spread of scores in the group tested. Since the groups on which reliabilities are reported in test manuals will always differ somewhat from the group to be given the test, the greater constancy of the standard error of measurement has obvious practical value. The main difficulty encountered with the standard error occurs when we want to compare two tests which use different types of scores. Here the reliability coefficient is the only suitable measure.

---

[12] Standard deviation is a measure of the spread of scores. See Appendix A for method of computing.

Factors Influencing Reliability Measures

A number of factors have been shown to affect the conventional measures of reliability.[13] If sound conclusions are to be drawn, these factors must be considered when interpreting reliability coefficients. We have already seen, for example, that speeded tests will provide a spuriously high reliability coefficient with the internal consistency methods of estimating reliability. We have also noted that test-retest reliability coefficients are influenced by the time interval between testings, with shorter time intervals resulting in higher reliability coefficients. Thus, in comparing the reliability coefficients of two or more tests we must take such factors into account. Although we might want to favor the test with the highest reliability coefficient, we would not do so if we recognized that the reported coefficient was inflated by factors irrelevant to the consistency of the measurement procedure. Similarly, we might discount the difference between reliability coefficients reported for two different tests if the conditions under which they were obtained favored the test with the highest reliabiliy coefficient.

Consideration of the factors influencing reliability will not only help us interpret the reliability coefficients of standardized tests more wisely, but should also aid us in constructing more reliable norm-referenced classroom tests. Though teachers seldom find it profitable to calculate reliability coefficients for the tests they construct, they can and should take cognizance of the factors influencing reliability to maximize the reliability of their own classroom tests.

Length of Test. In general, the longer the test the higher the reliability. This is due to the fact that a longer test will provide a more adequate sample of the behavior being measured and the scores are apt to be less distorted by chance factors such as guessing. Suppose, to measure spelling ability, we asked pupils to spell *one* word. The results would be patently unreliable. Pupils who were able to spell the word would be *perfect spellers* and pupils who could not would be *complete failures.* If we happened to select a difficult word most pupils would fail; if the word was an easy one most pupils would appear to be perfect spellers. The fact that *one* word provides an unreliable estimate of a pupil's spelling ability is obvious. It should be equally apparent that as we add spelling words to the list, we come closer and closer to a good estimate of each child's spelling ability. Scores based on a large number of spelling words are more apt to reflect real differences in spelling ability and therefore to be more stable. Thus, by increasing the size of the sample of spelling behavior we increase the consistency of our measurement.

A longer test also tends to lessen the influence of chance factors such as guessing. For example, on a ten-item true-and-false test a pupil might know seven of the items and guess at the other three. He could guess

---

[13] As noted earlier, these measures are primarily useful with *norm-referenced* tests, where the purpose is to discriminate among individuals.

right on all three items and have a perfect score or he could guess wrong on all three items and end up with only seven correct. This would represent considerable variation in his test score due to guessing alone. However, if this same pupil were taking a test with a hundred true and false items his correct guesses would tend to be cancelled by his incorrect guesses, and the score would be a more dependable indication of his actual knowledge.

The fact that a longer test tends to provide more reliable results was implied earlier in our discussion of the split-half method. It will be recalled that when scores from two halves of a test correlated .60 the Spearman-Brown formula estimated the reliability of the scores for the full-length test to be .75. This, of course, is equivalent to estimating the increase in reliability to be expected when the length of the test is doubled.

There is one important reservation in evaluating the influence of test length on the reliability of the scores, which is that the statements we have been making assume that the test will be lengthened by adding test items of the same quality as those already in the test. Adding ten spelling words that are so easy that everyone will get them correct or adding ten spelling words that are so difficult that no one will get them correct will not increase the reliability of the scores on a norm-referenced spelling test. In fact there would be no influence on the reliability coefficient since such additions would not influence the relative standing of the pupils in the group.

In constructing classroom tests it is important to keep in mind the influence of test length on reliability and strive for longer tests. Where short tests are necessary because of time limits or the age of the pupils, more frequent testing may be used to obtain a dependable measure of achievement.

In using standardized tests, we should be wary of part scores based on relatively few items. Such scores are usually low in reliability and of little or no practical value. Before using such scores the test manual should be carefully checked for their reported reliabilities. If these are not reported, or are very low, the part scores should be ignored and only the total test score should be used.

Spread of Scores. As noted earlier reliability coefficients are directly influenced by the spread of scores in the group tested. Other things being equal, the larger the spread of scores, the higher the estimate of reliability. Since larger reliability coefficients result when individuals tend to stay in the same relative position in a group, from one testing to another, it naturally follows that anything which reduces the possibility of shifting positions in the group also contributes to larger reliability coefficients. In this case greater differences between the scores of individuals reduce the possibility of shifting positions. Stated another way, errors of measurement have less influence on the relative position of individuals where the differences among group members are large—that is, where there is a wide spread of scores.

This can be easily illustrated without recourse to statistics. Compare the following two sets of scores in terms of the probability that the individuals will remain in the same relative position on a second administration of the test. Even a cursory inspection of these scores will make it clear that the persons in Group B are more likely to shift positions on a second administration of the test. With only a spread of ten points from the top score to the bottom score, radical shifts in position can result from changes of just a few points in the test scores of these individuals.

However, in Group A the test scores of individuals could vary by several points, on a second administration of the test, with very little shifting in the relative position of the group members. The large spread of test scores in Group A makes shifts in relative position unlikely, and thus gives us greater confidence that these differences among group members are real differences.

Group A	Group B
95	95
90	94
86	93
82	93
76	92
65	91
60	89
56	88
53	86
47	85

When constructing criterion-referenced mastery tests, a spread of scores is irrelevant since we would hope that all, or nearly all, pupils would get perfect scores. When measuring the degree to which pupils have progressed beyond the minimum essentials of a course, however, we should attempt to construct norm-referenced classroom tests that result in a wide spread of scores. In this way we can have greater assurance that the differences in pupil development (beyond the mastery level) reflect dependable differences in achievement and not differences due to chance factors such as guessing. To obtain a wider spread of test scores, most teachers need to construct more difficult norm-referenced tests. This should typically be done by stressing the measurement of more complex learning outcomes (e.g., transfer, problem solving). Such a procedure will tend to increase the reliability of the test scores and at the same time have a favorable influence on validity. Arbitrarily manipulating the wording of test items, simply to make them more difficult, is likely to result in increased reliability at the expense of validity.

In selecting standardized tests, the influence of the spread of test scores on reliability coefficients should also be considered. For example, many test publishers report reliability coefficients calculated on test scores over several grade levels. Since the combined scores of pupils from several grade levels have a much larger spread of scores than that found at a single grade level, such reliability coefficients are spuriously high. These reliability coefficients should be disregarded when selecting a test for a particular grade level. Every effort should be made to obtain reliability evidence on a group of pupils similar to the one to which we plan to administer the test. Only in this way can we have some assurance that the reliability coefficients reported in the test manual provide a satisfactory estimate of the test's reliability for our particular group of pupils.

Difficulty of Test. Norm-referenced tests which are too easy or too difficult for the group members taking it will tend to provide scores of low reliability. This is due to the fact that both easy and difficult tests result in a restricted spread of scores. In the case of the easy test, the scores are close together at the top end of the scale. With the difficult test, the scores are grouped together at the bottom end of the scale. For both, however, the differences among individuals are small and tend to be unreliable. A norm-referenced test of ideal difficulty will permit the scores to spread out over the full range of the scale, as shown in Figure 5.1.

The implications for classroom testing are obvious and were touched upon in the previous section. Classroom achievement tests designed to

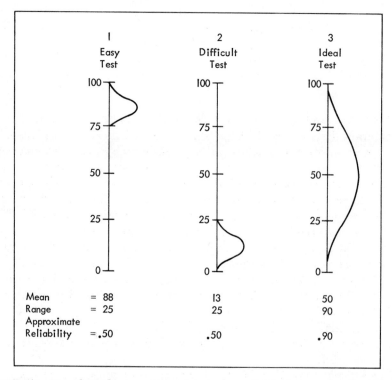

FIGURE 5.1. Hypothetical comparison of test score distributions and estimated reliability coefficients for a 100 item norm-referenced test. (Reliability was estimated by KR21 formula assuming reasonable standard deviations.)

measure differences among pupils (norm-referenced) should be so constructed that the average score is 50 per cent correct and that the scores range from near zero to near perfect. Actually, the 50 per cent correct applies only to the short-answer type item. For selection-type items, the ideal average score would be higher, since a proportion of the items could be answered correctly by guessing. On a true-false test, for example, pupils could be expected to get 50 per cent of the items correct by guessing (chance score), and on a five-choice multiple-choice test the expected chance score would be 20 per cent correct (one out of five). We can estimate the ideal average difficulty for a selection-type test by taking the point midway between the expected chance score and the maximum possible score. Thus, for a 100 item true-false test the ideal average difficulty would be 75 (midway between 50 and 100), and for a 100 item five-choice multiple-choice test the ideal average difficulty would be 60 (midway between 20 and 100). Constructing tests that match these ideal levels of difficulty enable the full range of possible scores to be used in measuring differences among individuals. As noted earlier, the bigger the spread of scores, the greater the likelihood that the measured differences are reliable.

The difficulty of test items in standardized tests should also be carefully evaluated. Where a test has been designed for several grade levels the difficulty level is usually most appropriate for the grades in the middle of the range. The test may be a bit too difficult for the lowest grade level and a bit too easy for the highest grade level. Thus, at the extreme grade levels one can typically expect the differences between individuals to be less reliable. Information concerning the difficulty of a test, at each of the grade levels for which it was designed, can usually be obtained from the test manual.

In evaluating the difficulty of a standardized test the teacher must also take into account the level of ability of his pupils. A test that is of appropriate difficulty for average fifth graders may be inappropriate for a fifth-grade class containing a disproportionate number of slow learners or of gifted pupils. More appropriate difficulty for a particular group can frequently be obtained by using the test designed for the next lowest or the next highest grade.

Objectivity. The objectivity of a test refers to the degree to which equally competent scorers obtain the same results. Most standardized tests of aptitude and achievement are high in objectivity. The test items are of the objective type (e.g., multiple-choice), and the resulting scores are not influenced by the judgment or opinion of the scorers. In fact, such tests are usually constructed so that they can be accurately scored by trained clerks and scoring machines. Where such highly objective procedures are used the reliability of the test results are not affected by the scoring procedures.

In the case of classroom tests constructed by teachers, however, objectivity may play an important role in obtaining reliable measures of achievement. In essay testing, as well as in the use of various observational procedures, the results depend to a large extent upon the person doing the scoring. Different persons get different results, and even the same person may get different results at different times. Such inconsistency in scoring has an adverse affect on the reliability of the measures obtained, for the test scores now reflect the opinions and biases of the scorer as well as the differences among pupils in the characteristic being measured.

The solution is *not* to use only objective tests and abandon all subjective methods of evaluation. This would have an adverse effect on validity and, as we noted earlier, validity is the most important quality of evaluation results. A more desirable solution is to select the evaluation procedure most appropriate for the behavior being evaluated and then to make the evaluation procedure as objective as possible. In the use of essay tests, for example, objectivity can be increased by careful phrasing of the questions and by using a standard set of rules for scoring. Such increased objectivity will contribute to greater reliability without sacrificing validity.

Methods of Estimating. When examining the reliability coefficients of standardized tests it is important to consider the methods that were used to obtain the reliability estimates. In general, the size of the reliability coefficient is related to the method of estimating reliability in the following manner:

(1) Test-retest method	Typically provides *medium to large* reliability coefficients for a given test. May be larger than split-half method if time interval is short. Coefficients become smaller as time interval between tests is increased.
(2) Equivalent-forms method (without time interval)	Typically provides *medium to large* reliability coefficients for a given test. Tend to be lower than test-retest method using short time interval.
(3) Equivalent-forms method (with time interval)	Typically provides *smallest* reliability coefficients for a given test. Coefficients become smaller as time interval between tests is increased.
(4) Split-half method	Typically provides *largest* reliability coefficients for a given test. Spuriously high estimates are produced for speeded tests.
(5) Kuder-Richardson methods	Typically provides reliability estimates that are *smaller* than those obtained by split-half method. These estimates are also inflated by speed.

The variation in the size of the reliability coefficient due to the method of estimating reliability is directly attributable to the type of consistency included in each method. It will be recalled that the equivalent-forms method with an intervening time interval took into account all possible sources of variation in the test scores and consequently is the most rigorous method of estimating reliability. Thus, smaller reliability coefficients can be expected with this method, and it is grossly unfair to make a direct comparison of such reliability coefficients with those obtained by less stringent methods.

At the other extreme, the larger reliability coefficients typically reported for the split-half method must be accepted cautiously. If speed is an important factor in the testing, split-half reliability coefficients should be disregarded entirely and other evidence of reliability should be sought.

Reliability of Criterion-Referenced Mastery Tests

When using criterion-referenced mastery tests, our desire for consistency of measurement is similar to that for norm-referenced tests. Thus, we would like an individual's performance to be (1) consistent from one item to another, where all items are measuring the same learning outcome (internal consistency); (2) consistent from one time to another, where the learning outcomes are expected to have a reasonable degree of constancy (stability); and (3) consistent from one form of the test to another, where the forms are intended to measure the same sample of learning tasks (equivalence). Unfortunately, our means for estimating these types of consistency do not match our need for such information. Since criterion-referenced mastery tests are not designed to discriminate among individuals, and thus variability need not be present in the scores, the traditional correlational estimates of reliability are inappropriate. There have been various attempts to develop statistical measures for estimating the reliability of criterion-referenced mastery tests, but a satisfactory solution has not yet been achieved.[14]

When using criterion-referenced mastery tests in classroom instruction, we can increase the likelihood of reliable results by using a sufficiently large sample of test items for each learning outcome to be measured. If the outcome is very specific and highly structured (e.g., adds two single-digit numbers), a relatively small number of items (say five) may be sufficient for a dependable judgment concerning mastery. For most mastery-nonmastery decisions, however, ten items for each specific learning outcome would provide a more desirable minimum. Where instructional decisions are based on fewer than ten items, we should make only tentative judgments

---

[14] R. K. Hambleton and M. R. Novick, "Toward an Integration of Theory and Method for Criterion-Referenced Tests," *Journal of Educational Measurement*, **10**, 159–170, Fall 1973.

and seek verification from other available data and from classroom observation.

How High Should Reliability Be?

The degree of reliability we demand in our educational measures depends largely on the nature of the decision to be made. If we are going to use test results as a basis for deciding whether to review certain areas of subject matter, we might be willing to use a teacher-made test of unknown reliability. Our decision will be based on the scores of the total group, and inconsistency in individual scores will not distort our decision too much. Even if we do err in our decision, no major catastrophe will result. The worst that can happen is that the pupils will get an unnecessary review of material, or they will be deprived of a review that might be beneficial to them. On the other hand, if we are going to use test results as a basis for deciding which pupils should be placed in special classes for the mentally handicapped we shall demand the most reliable measurement available. We would not be satisfied with group tests of intelligence for this purpose but would want to use one of the more reliable individual measures of intelligence. We probably would also want to obtain the most reliable evidence available concerning the pupil's learning, social development, and adjustment before a final decision is made. This decision is so important and the consequences so significant that we are willing to devote considerable time and expense to increase the reliability of our data even if the increase is slight. We want to be as confident as possible that we are making the right decision when we place a pupil in a special class for the mentally handicapped.

It is not only the importance of a decision that matters, but also whether it is possible to confirm or reverse the judgment at a later time.[15] Decision making in education is seldom a single, final act. It tends to be sequential in nature, starting with rather crude judgments and proceeding through a series of more refined judgments. In the early stages of decision making low reliability might be quite tolerable, because test results are used primarily as a guide to further information gathering. For example, on the basis of classroom tests of questionable reliability we might decide that some of our pupils are having learning difficulties of such a serious nature that they are in need of special help. This decision provides a useful hunch that can be confirmed or refuted by further testing with more dependable measures. Similarly, a personality inventory of low reliability may be useful as a first step in detecting maladjusted pupils, providing those with scores indicating *possible* maladjustment are followed up by more intensive study. Also, group scholastic aptitude scores of only mod-

---

[15] L. J. Cronbach, *Essentials of Psychological Testing*, 3rd ed. (New York: Harper and Row, 1970).

erate stability may be useful in grouping elementary pupils, since those who are misclassified can be easily shifted as new evidence becomes available. Opportunities for confirmation and reversal of judgments without serious consequences are almost always present in the early stages of educational decision making.

The important thing when reliability is low, or unknown, is not to treat the scores as if they were highly accurate. Make tentative judgments, seek confirming data, and be willing to reverse decisions when wrong. Some modification in school policy may also be required. If, for example, mental ability proves to be unstable until age sixteen, one should not adopt a classification policy which makes the decision about who shall plan to go to college at age eleven. In summary, test scores of low reliability can be useful if they are interpreted with caution and used only for tentative reversible decisions.[16]

Where final irreversible decisions are being made, we shall be, of course, compelled to seek the most reliable information available. We would not want to award scholarships, reject college applicants, or commit a person to a mental institution on the basis of measures with low or questionable reliability.

Thus, when we ask the question—How high should reliability be?—several considerations must be taken into account. How important is the decision? Is it one that can be confirmed or reversed at a later time? How far reaching are the consequences of the action taken? For important decisions which are irreversible and apt to have great influence on the lives of individual pupils, we shall make stringent demands on the reliability of the measures we use. For lesser decisions, and especially for those that can be later confirmed or reversed without serious consequences, we shall be willing to settle for less reliable measures. Thus, it depends largely on how confident we need to be about the decision being made. Greater confidence requires higher reliability.

USABILITY

In selecting evaluation instruments, practical considerations cannot be neglected. Tests are usually administered and interpreted by teachers with only a minimum amount of training in measurement. The time available for testing is almost always limited and is in constant competition with other important activities for its allotted time in the school schedule. Likewise, the cost of testing, though a minor consideration, is as carefully scrutinized by budget-conscious administrators as are other expenditures of school funds. These and other factors pertinent to the *usability* of tests

---

[16] Teacher-made tests commonly have reliabilities somewhere between .60 and .85, for example, but these are useful for the types of instructional decisions typically made by teachers.

and evaluation procedures must be taken into account when selecting evaluation instruments. Such practical considerations are especially pertinent in selecting standardized tests for a school-wide testing program.

Ease of Administration

Where tests are to be administered by teachers or others with limited training, ease of administration is an especially important quality to seek in a test. For this purpose the directions should be simple and clear, the subtests should be relatively few, and the timing of the test should not be too difficult. Administering a test with complicated directions and a number of subtests lasting but a few minutes each is a taxing chore for even an experienced examiner. For a person with little training and experience, such a situation is fraught with possibilities for errors in giving directions, timing, and other aspects of the administration which are likely to affect the results. Such errors of administration have, of course, an adverse effect on the validity and reliability of the resulting test scores.

Time Required for Administration

With time for testing at a premium, we shall always favor the shorter test, other things being equal. In this case other things are seldom equal, however, since reliability is directly related to the length of the test. If we attempt to cut down too much on the time allotted to testing we are apt to reduce drastically the reliability of our scores. For example, tests designed to fit a normal class period usually provide total test scores of satisfactory reliability, but their part scores, obtained from the subtests, tend to be unreliable. If we want reliable measures in the areas covered by the subtests, we need to increase our testing time in each area. On the other hand, if we want a general measure in some area, such as verbal intelligence, we can obtain reliable results in 30 or 40 minutes and there is little advantage in extending the testing time. A safe procedure is to allot as much time as is necessary to obtain valid and reliable results and no more. Somewhere between 20 and 60 minutes of testing time for each individual score yielded by a standardized test is probably a fairly good guide.

Ease of Scoring

Traditionally, one of the most tedious and troublesome aspects of a school testing program has been the scoring of the tests. In the past, many an overworked teacher has spent hours upon hours at this task. To make the procedure even more burdensome than it needed to be, scoring directions were frequently complicated, the tests contained numerous subtests and some subjective test items, and the scoring keys were cumbersome. Although the scoring of tests is still a problem to be reckoned with, recent developments in testing have eased the burden considerably. These developments include (1) the trend toward completely objective standardized tests, (2) improved clarity in the directions for scoring and increased simplicity in the scoring key, (3) the use of separate answer sheets, and (4) machine scoring.

In selecting standardized tests, those which require a minimum amount of time, skill, and expense for the scoring should be given preference. The use of separate answer sheets, for example, will not only contribute to ease of scoring but will also reduce the cost of testing due to the fact that the same test booklets can be used over again a number of times. In addition, if machine scoring is available at a reasonable cost, separate answer sheets could relieve teachers of an irksome clerical task. Such factors should be taken into account at the time the test is being evaluated, and no test should be selected until the provisions for scoring have been given careful thought. Other things being equal, we shall favor the test which provides for ease and economy of scoring without sacrificing scoring accuracy.

Ease of Interpretation and Application

In the final analysis, the success or failure of a testing program is determined by the use made of the test results. If they are interpreted correctly and applied effectively they will contribute to more intelligent educational decisions. On the other hand, if the test results are misinterpreted or misapplied or not applied at all they will be of little value and may actually be harmful to some individual or group.

Information concerning the interpretation and use of test results is usually obtained directly from the test manual or related guides. Attention should be directed toward the ease with which the raw scores can be converted into meaningful derived scores, the clarity with which the tables of norms are presented, and the comprehensiveness of the suggestions for applying the results to educational problems. Where the test results are to be presented to the pupils, or to their parents, ease of interpretation and application should be given special consideration.

Availability of Equivalent or Comparable Forms

For many educational purposes *equivalent* forms of the same test are often desirable. Equivalent forms of a test measure the same aspect of behavior by using test items which are alike in content, level of difficulty, and other significant characteristics. Thus, one form of the test can substitute for the other. This makes it possible to test pupils twice in rather close succession without their answers on the first testing influencing their performance on the second testing. The advantage of equivalent forms is readily seen in studies of achievement gain. Here we want to eliminate the factor of memory while testing the pupils twice in the same area of achievement. Equivalent forms of a test may also be used to verify a questionable test score. For example, a teacher may feel that a scholastic aptitude or achievement test score is too low for a given pupil. This may be easily checked by administering an equivalent form of the test.

Many tests also provide *comparable* forms. Achievement tests, for example, are commonly arranged in a series which cover different grade levels. Although the content and level of difficulty varies, the tests at the different levels are made comparable through a common score scale. Thus, it is possible to compare measurements in grade four with measurements in grade six on a more advanced form of the test. Comparable forms are especially useful in long-range studies of educational growth.

Cost

The factor of cost has been left to the last because it is relatively unimportant in selecting tests. The reason for discussing it at all is that it is sometimes given far more weight than it deserves. Testing is relatively inexpensive, and cost should not be a major consideration. In large-scale testing programs where small savings per pupil add up, using separate answer sheets, machine scoring, and reusable booklets will reduce the cost appreciably. To select one test instead of another, however, because the test booklets are a few cents cheaper is false economy. After all, validity and reliability are the important characteristics to look for, and a test lacking in these qualities is too expensive at any price. On the other hand, the contribution that valid and reliable test scores can make to educational decisions seems to indicate that such tests are always economical in the long run.

SUMMARY

Next to validity, reliability is the most important quality to seek in evaluation results. Reliability refers to how consistent test scores and other evaluation results are from one measurement to another. In interpreting and using reliability information, it is important to remember that reliability estimates refer to the *results* of measurement, that different ways of estimating reliability indicate different types of consistency, that a reliable measure is *not* necessarily valid, and that reliability is primarily a statistical concept. Reliability estimates may be reported in terms of a *reliability coefficient* or the *standard error of measurement*.

Reliability coefficients are determined by several different methods and each method provides a different measure of consistency. The test-retest method involves giving the same test twice to the same group with an intervening time interval, and the resulting coefficient provides a measure of *stability*. How long the time interval should be between tests is determined largely by the use to be made of the results. We shall be primarily interested in reliability coefficients based on intervals comparable to the periods of time covered in our predictions. The equivalent-forms method involves giving two forms of a test to the same group in close succession or with an intervening time interval. The first results in a measure of *equivalence*, and the second, in a measure of *stability and equivalence*. The latter procedure provides the most rigorous test of reliability, since it includes all possible sources of variation in the test score. Reliability can also be estimated from a single administration of a single form of a test, either by correlating the scores on two halves of the test or by applying one of the Kuder-Richardson formulas. Both methods provide a measure of *internal consistency* and are easy to apply. However, they are not applicable to speeded tests, and they provide no information concerning the stability of test scores from day to day.

The standard error of measurement indicates reliability in terms of the amount of variation to be expected in individual test scores. It can be computed from the reliability coefficient and the standard deviation, but it is frequently reported directly in test manuals. The standard error is especially useful in interpreting test scores, since it indicates the "band of error" surrounding each score. It also has the advantage of remaining fairly constant from group to group.

Reliability estimates may vary in accordance with the length of the test, the spread of scores in the group tested, the difficulty of the test, the objectivity of the scoring, and the method of estimating reliability. These factors should be taken into account when appraising reliability information. The degree and type of reliability to be sought in a particular instance depends primarily on the decision being made. For tentative reversible decisions low reliability may be tolerable. However, for final irreversible decisions we must make stringent demands on the reliability of our measures.

The conventional measures of reliability are based on variability among scores. Since score variability is irrelevant for criterion-referenced tests (i.e., all may get perfect scores), the conventional means for estimating reliability are inappropriate. Unfortunately, however, techniques specifically adapted to criterion-referenced mastery tests have not been adequately developed. When used in classroom testing, the reliability of such tests can be enhanced by using a sufficiently large number of test items (ten or more) for each specific learning outcome to be measured.

In addition to their validity and reliability, it is also important to consider the usability of tests and other evaluation instruments. This includes such practical features as ease of administration, time required, ease of scoring, ease of interpretation and application, availability of equivalent or comparable forms, and cost.

LEARNING EXERCISES

1. Compare validity and reliability with regard to (a) the meaning of each concept, (b) the relative importance of each in the evaluation process, and (c) the extent to which each one depends on the presence of the other.
2. Which specific method of estimating reliability would provide the most useful information for each of the following? Why?
   a. Selecting a scholastic aptitude test.
   b. Selecting an achievement test.
   c. Using aptitude scores obtained two years earlier.
   d. Determining if a test is measuring a homogeneous trait.
3. What influence would the following most likely have on the reliability of a norm-referenced test?
   a. Removing items that were too difficult for pupils.
   b. Removing items that were so simple all pupils could answer them correctly.
   c. Removing items that are ambiguous.
   d. Changing from a multiple-choice test to an essay test covering the same material.
4. What is the relative value of using the standard error of measurement or the reliability coefficient for expressing the reliability of test scores? For which purpose is each most useful?
5. Using Table 5.3, determine the standard error of measurement for a set of test scores with a standard deviation of 16 and a reliability of .83.
6. Study the reliability sections of test manuals for a few scholastic aptitude tests. What type of reliability data is reported? Of what value is this type of data in deciding whether to choose the tests?
7. Consult the reliability section of the *Standards for Educational and Psychological Tests* (see the reading list for this chapter) and review the types of information that test manuals should contain. Compare a recent test manual against the *Standards*.
8. In reviewing the reliability data in a test manual a teacher noted the following reliability coefficients:
   a. Correlation of Form A test scores over a one-month interval = .90.
   b. Correlation of Form A with Form B test scores over a one-month interval = .85
   c. Correlation of test scores based on two halves (odd-even) of Form A = .95.
   How would you account for these differences in reliability coefficients (assume that the groups tested were the same)? Which estimate of reliability provides the most useful information? Why?
9. List and briefly describe as many things as you can think of that a classroom teacher might do to increase the reliability of his norm-referenced classroom tests. How would the list differ for criterion-referenced mastery tests?
10. Assume you are selecting a standardized achievement test battery to be administered annually from grades four through twelve. List in *order of importance* all of the test characteristics that should be considered and give reasons for the particular placement of each characteristic in your list.

SUGGESTIONS FOR FURTHER READING

AMERICAN PSYCHOLOGICAL ASSOCIATION. *Standards for Educational and Psychological Tests.* Washington, D.C.: APA, 1974. See section on reliability (pages 48–55) for descriptions of the basic types and for the nature of reliability information to be sought in test manuals.

ANASTASI, A. *Psychological Testing,* 4th ed. New York: Macmillan Publishing Co., Inc., 1976. Chapter 5, "Reliability." Describes the various types of reliability coefficients, the standard error of measurement, and the factors influencing reliability. Includes material on the reliability of criterion-referenced tests.

BAUERNFEIND, R. H. *Building a School Testing Program,* 2nd ed. Boston: Houghton Mifflin Company, 1969. Chapter 6, "The Concept of Reliability." A simple, clear discussion of the basic types of reliability.

CRONBACH, L. J. *Essentials of Psychological Testing,* 3rd ed. New York: Harper and Row, Publishers, 1970. Chapter 6, "Other Characteristics Desired in Tests." An advanced treatment of reliability with emphasis on the "generalizability" of test results and the use of analysis of variance methods.

STANLEY, J. C. "Reliability," Chapter 13 in R. L. Thorndike (ed.), *Educational Measurement.* Washington, D.C.: American Council on Education, 1971. An advanced treatment of reliability that is rather technical.

Test Bulletins

DIEDERICH, P. *Short-Cut Statistics for Teacher-Made Tests.* Princeton, N.J.: Educational Testing Service, 1973. Presents simple methods of estimating the standard error and the reliability coefficient.

DOPPELT, J. E. *How Accurate Is a Test Score?* Test Service Bulletin, No. 50. New York: The Psychological Corporation, 1956. Describes the standard error of measurement.

PART II

Constructing Classroom Tests

CHAPTER 6

Planning the Classroom Test

Classroom tests play a central role in the evaluation of pupil learning. . . . They provide relevant measures of many important learning outcomes and indirect evidence concerning others. . . . The validity of the information they provide, however, depends on the care with which the tests are planned and prepared.

The likelihood of preparing valid and useful classroom tests is greatly enhanced if a series of basic steps is followed, as shown in Figure 6.1. In this chapter, we shall discuss those factors concerned with the planning of classroom tests. This includes considerations in each of the following areas:

1. Determining the purpose of testing.
2. Building a table of specifications.
3. Selecting appropriate item types.
4. Preparing a set of relevant test items.

Specific procedures for constructing each of the various types of test items will be described in Chapters 7 through 10, and Chapter 11 will be concerned with assembling, administering, and appraising classroom tests.

DETERMINING THE PURPOSE OF TESTING

Classroom tests can be used for a variety of instructional purposes. As noted in Chapter 1, however, the various uses of tests and other evaluation instruments can be classified under four basic types of classroom evaluation. These types are (1) placement evaluation, (2) formative evaluation,

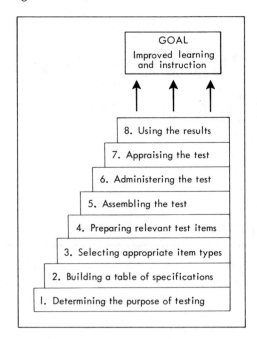

FIGURE 6.1. Basic Steps in Classroom Testing

(3) diagnostic evaluation, and (4) summative evaluation. Since teacher-made tests are useful in all four areas, this classification system provides a convenient basis for considering the role of test purpose in planning the classroom test.

Placement Testing

Most placement tests constructed by classroom teachers are *pretests* designed to measure (1) whether pupils possess the prerequisite skills needed to succeed in a unit or course, or (2) the extent to which pupils have already achieved the objectives of the planned instruction. In the first instance we are concerned with the pupils' readiness to begin the instruction. In the second, we are concerned with the appropriateness of our planned instruction for the group and with the proper placement of each pupil in the instructional sequence.

Pretests for determining prerequisite skills are typically rather limited in scope. For example, a pretest in algebra might be confined to computational skill in arithmetic, a pretest in science might consist solely of science terms, and a pretest in beginning German might be limited to knowledge of English grammar. In addition to being confined to a limited area of knowledge or skill, the readiness pretest also tends to have a relatively low level of difficulty. This is due to the fact that this type of pretest is used to determine whether pupils have the minimum essentials needed to proceed with the course or unit of work. Pretests of this type are typically criterion-referenced tests (i.e., tests designed to describe the learning tasks pupils can perform) since their major function is to identify the presence or absence of prerequisite skills.

Pretests for determining the extent to which pupils have already achieved the objectives of the planned instruction are no different from the tests used to measure the outcomes of instruction. Thus, a test designed to measure final achievement in a course could be given at the beginning of the course to measure entry performance on the course objectives. Since this type of test is broad in scope, and measures instructional objectives at various levels of complexity, it is typically a norm-referenced test (i.e., test designed to rank pupils in order of achievement) using items with a wide range of difficulty. If the purpose of the test is to measure the achievement of a limited set of objectives for a unit of instruction, however, this pretest might be designed as a criterion-referenced test. This would be the case where mastery was the goal and the end-of-unit test was criterion-referenced, as in individualized instruction and in some types of classroom instruction (e.g., Bloom's Mastery Approach).[1]

Formative Testing

Formative tests are given periodically during instruction to monitor pupil learning progress and to provide ongoing feedback to pupils and teacher.[2] Formative testing provides reinforcement of successful learning and reveals learning weaknesses in need of correction. A formative test typically covers some predefined segment of instruction (e.g., unit, chapter, or particular set of skills), and thus encompasses a rather limited sample of learning tasks. The test items may be easy or difficult, depending on the learning tasks in the segment of instruction being tested. Formative tests are typically criterion-referenced mastery tests, but norm-referenced survey tests could also serve this function. Ideally, the test will be constructed in such a way that corrective prescriptions can be given for missed test items, or sets of test items. Since the main purpose of the test is to improve learning, the results are seldom used for assigning grades.

Diagnostic Testing

Diagnosis of persistent learning difficulties involves much more than diagnostic testing, but such tests are useful in the total process. The diagnostic test takes up where the formative test leaves off. If pupils do not respond to the feedback-corrective prescriptions of formative testing, a more detailed search for the source of learning errors is indicated. For this

---

[1] See N. E. Gronlund, *Individualizing Classroom Instruction* (New York: Macmillan, 1974).
[2] Such tests are also commonly called learning tests, quizzes, unit tests, and the like.

type of testing, we will need to include a number of test items in each specific area with some slight variation from item to item. In diagnosing pupils' difficulties in adding whole numbers, for example, we would want to include addition problems containing various number combinations, with some *not* requiring carrying and some requiring carrying, to pinpoint the specific types of error each pupil is making. Since our focus is on the pupils' learning difficulties, diagnostic tests must be constructed in light of the most common sources of error encountered by pupils. Such tests are typically confined to a limited area of instruction, and the test items tend to have a relatively low level of difficulty.

Summative Testing

The summative test is given at the end of a course or unit of instruction and the results are used primarily for assigning grades, or for certifying pupil mastery of the instructional objectives. The results can also be used, of course, for evaluating the effectiveness of the instruction. The *end-of-course* test (final examination) is typically a norm-referenced survey test that is broad in coverage and that includes test items with a wide range of difficulty. The more restricted *end-of-unit* summative test might be norm-referenced or criterion-referenced, depending on whether mastery or developmental outcomes are the focus of instruction.

As a guide for test planning, a summary comparison of the basic types of classroom testing is presented in Table 6.1. Although classroom testing frequently requires tailoring a test to fit a unique instructional situation, these four basic test types provide a good general framework for test planning.

BUILDING THE TABLE OF SPECIFICATIONS

The only assurance we have that a classroom test is a valid measure of the instructional objectives and course content we are interested in testing is to use some systematic procedure for obtaining a representative sample of pupil behavior in each of the areas to be measured. The table of specifications is one device that provides such a systematic approach. In Chapter 3, we described how a table of specifications could be used for all phases of classroom evaluation. Here, we shall limit its use to planning a classroom test.

Obtaining the List of Instructional Objectives

Many of the changes in pupil behavior can be measured by means of paper-and-pencil tests. In fact, a novice in the area of measurement is frequently surprised at the variety of learning outcomes that can be measured

TABLE 6.1

SUMMARY COMPARISON OF THE BASIC TYPES OF CLASSROOM TESTING*

	Placement Testing		Formative Testing	Diagnostic Testing	Summative Testing
	Readiness Pretest	Placement Pretest			
Focus of measurement	Prerequisite entry skills	Course or unit objectives	Predefined segment of instruction	Most common learning errors	Course or unit objectives
Nature of sample	Limited sample of selected skills	Broad sample of all objectives	Limited sample of learning tasks	Limited sample of specific errors	Broad sample of all objectives
Item difficulty	Typically has low level of difficulty	Typically has wide range of difficulty	Varies with the segment of instruction	Typically has low level of difficulty	Typically has wide range of difficulty
When test administered	Beginning of course or unit	Beginning of course or unit	Periodically during instruction	As needed during instruction	End of course or unit
Type of instrument	Typically is criterion-referenced mastery test	Typically is norm-referenced survey test	Typically is criterion-referenced mastery test	Specially designed test to identify learning errors	Typically is norm-referenced survey test
Use of results	Remedy entry deficiencies or assignment to learning group	Instructional planning and advance placement	Improve and direct learning through on-going feedback	Remedy errors related to persistent learning difficulties	Assign grades, certify mastery, or evaluate teaching

* Adapted from P. W. Airasian and G. F. Madaus, "Functional Types of Student Evaluation," *Measurement and Evaluation in Guidance*, 4, 221–233, 1972.

in this manner. Thus, all of the intended outcomes of instruction should be considered when planning a classroom test. If a comprehensive list of instructional objectives and specific learning outcomes has been prepared, as described in Chapter 2, it is simply a matter of selecting those outcomes that can be measured by paper-and-pencil tests. If such a list is not available, a set of instructional objectives can be prepared for a classroom test by following the suggestions in Chapter 2.

Outlining the Course Content

The list of objectives describes the behavioral changes we are attempting to bring about in pupils, and the course content provides the means through which the objectives are to be achieved. Thus, the second step in planning a classroom test is to make an outline of course content. This might be simply a list of major topics to be covered during the instruction, or a more detailed list of topics and subtopics. The amount of detail in the content outline depends on the purpose of the test, the segment of the course covered, and the type of test interpretation to be used. A criterion-referenced test (used to describe the learning tasks pupils can perform), for example, will require a much more detailed description of both objectives and content than will a norm-referenced test (used to rank pupils in order of achievement).

Preparing the Table of Specifications

As noted earlier, a table of specifications is a two-way chart that relates the instructional objectives to the course content and specifies the nature of the desired test sample. The use of such a chart serves the test maker in much the same way that a blueprint serves the carpenter (It is frequently called a *test blueprint*). It specifies the characteristics desired in the finished product. In the case of the test maker, it provides greater assurance that the test will measure the instructional objectives and course content in a balanced manner.

An example of a table of specifications for the preparation of a summative (end-of-course) test in third-grade social studies is presented in Table 6.2. This table was prepared by listing the general instructional objectives across the top, listing the major areas of content down the left side, and indicating what proportion of the test items should be devoted to each objective and each area of content. It will be noted in the bottom row of the table, for example, that 20 per cent of the items are to be devoted to "knowledge of common terms," 20 per cent to "knowledge of specific facts," and so on across the bottom row. Similarly, the right-hand column shows that 10 per cent of the items are to be concerned with the topic of "food," 10 per cent with "clothing," 15 per cent with "transportation," and so on down the column. Each cell within the table indicates the percentage of test items

TABLE 6.2

TABLE OF SPECIFICATIONS FOR A SUMMATIVE THIRD-GRADE SOCIAL STUDIES TEST
(IN PERCENTAGE)

Content Area	Objectives					Total
	Knows Common Terms	Knows Specific Facts	Understands Principles and Generalizations	Applies Principles and Generalizations	Interprets Charts and Graphs	
Food	2	6	2			10
Clothing	2	6	2			10
Transportation	4	2	2	2	5	15
Communications	4	2	2	2	5	15
Shelter			5	5		10
City life	4	2	6	8		20
Farm life	4	2	6	8		20
Total	20	20	25	25	10	100

to be devoted to the objective and the content area that are opposite the cell. The number 2 in the cell in the upper left-hand corner, for example, indicates that 2 per cent of the test items should be concerned with "knowledge of common terms" in the "food" area. The numbers in the other cells within the table are to be read in the same manner. The empty cells indicate areas where no test items are to be allotted. Although the relative emphasis in Table 6.2 is expressed in terms of the *percentage* of test items, it is equally satisfactory to put the *number* of test items in each cell. In some cases, it may be desirable to include both.

The relative emphasis to be given to each instructional objective and each content area should, of course, reflect the emphasis given during the instruction. In assigning relative weights, both the importance the teacher attaches to the learning outcome and the amount of instructional time devoted to it can serve as guidelines. Typically, the weighting is done by first assigning percentages across the bottom row (for each objective), then assigning percentages down the right-hand column (for each content area), and finally allotting the percentage, or number, of test items to each of the two-way cells within the table. Proper weighting will make it possible to construct a test which measures a representative sample of the intended outcomes of instruction that can be evaluated by paper-and-pencil tests. (See Figure 12.1 in Chapter 12 for a table of specifications in mathematics.)

Tables of Specifications and Criterion-Referenced Testing

As noted earlier, norm-referenced tests (i.e., tests designed to rank pupils in order of achievement) tend to be broad in coverage. Typically, such tests are used for summative testing (i.e., end-of-course testing), and for other types of testing concerned with a relatively large and diverse domain of learning tasks. In contrast, criterion-referenced tests (i.e., tests designed to describe the learning tasks pupils can perform) tend to focus on a more restricted range of learning outcomes. Such tests are most widely used in placement testing, formative testing, and in other types of testing where the domain of learning tasks is rather limited.

Because of its broad coverage, a table of specifications is especially useful in constructing a norm-referenced test. Here, the table provides some assurance that each of the diverse learning tasks will receive appropriate emphasis in the test. Whether a table of specifications is useful in constructing a criterion-referenced test, however, depends on the scope of learning tasks to be covered by the test. If the domain of tasks is very limited, such as "adds fractions with the same denominator," a table of specifications might be unnecessary. We could simply list all, or nearly all, of the specific tasks encompassed by the limited domain of behavior, as follows:

Adds two fractions with same denominator where the answer is less than one ($\frac{1}{6} + \frac{2}{6}$).

Adds two fractions with same denominator where the answer equals one
($\frac{1}{3} + \frac{2}{3}$).

Adds two fractions with same denominator where the answer is greater
than one ($\frac{3}{5} + \frac{4}{5}$).

Adds two fractions with same denominator and reduces answer to lowest
terms ($\frac{4}{6} + \frac{4}{6}$).

Adds more than two fractions with same denominator and reduces answer
($\frac{3}{8} + \frac{5}{8} + \frac{6}{8}$).

A list of learning tasks, such as this, specifies quite clearly what pupil behaviors are involved in "adding fractions with the same denominator." We
could obtain a representative sample of such tasks simply by constructing
four or five items for each task, using various number combinations.

If our criterion-referenced test were to cover a slightly larger domain
of behavior, say "addition of fractions," we might now find a table of
specifications quite useful. An illustration of such a table for a forty-item
test is shown in Table 6.3. The use of such a table does not mean, of course,

TABLE 6.3
TABLE OF SPECIFICATIONS FOR A FORTY-ITEM TEST
ON ADDITION OF FRACTIONS*

Content Area \\ Instructional Objectives	Adds Fractions	Adds Fractions and Mixed Numbers	Adds Mixed Numbers	Total Items
Denominators are alike	5	4	4	13
Denominators are unlike (with common factor)	5	4	4	13
Denominators are unlike (without common factor)	6	4	4	14
Total items	16	12	12	40

* From N. E. Gronlund, *Preparing Criterion-Referenced Tests for Classroom Instruction*,
New York: Macmillan, 1973. Used by permission.

that we should not make the type of detailed breakdown illustrated for
"adding fractions with the same denominator." Such a detailed listing of
tasks aids in teaching, in detecting learning errors, and in constructing
test items. The table of specifications, however, supplements such lists by
specifying the sample of tasks to be included in the test. As noted earlier,
this provides greater assurance that the intended outcomes will be measured
in a balanced manner.

SELECTING APPROPRIATE ITEM TYPES

The items used in classroom tests are typically divided into two general categories: (1) the objective item which is highly structured and requires the pupil to supply a word or two or to select the correct answer from among a limited number of alternatives, and (2) the essay question which permits the pupil to select, organize, and present his answer in essay form. There is no conflict between these two item types. For some instructional purposes the objective item may be most efficient while for others the essay question may prove most satisfactory. Each type should be used where most appropriate, with appropriateness determined by the learning outcomes to be measured and by the unique advantages and limitations of each item type.

The Objective Test Item

The objective item includes a variety of different types, but they can be classified into those which require the pupil to *supply* the answer and those which require him to *select* the answer from a given number of alternatives. These two general classes are commonly further divided into the following basic types of objective test items:

Supply types:
  1. Short answer.

EXAMPLES

What is the name of the author of *Moby-Dick?*   (Herman Melville)
What is the formula for hydrochloric acid?   (HCl)
What is the value of X in the equation $2X + 5 = 9$?   ($\underline{2}$)

  2. Completion.

EXAMPLES

Lines on a weather map joining points with the same barometric pressure are called (isobars).
The formula for ordinary table salt is (NaCl).
In the equation $2X + 5 = 9$; $X = $ ($\underline{2}$).

Selection types:
  1. True-false or alternative response.

EXAMPLES

(T) F   A virus is the smallest known organism.
T (F)   An atom is the smallest particle of matter.
Yes (No)   In the equation $2X + 5 = 9$, X equals 3.
(Yes) No   Acid turns litmus paper red.

2. Matching.

EXAMPLES

(C)	1. And	A	Adjective
(D)	2. Dog	B	Adverb
(G)	3. Jump	C	Conjunction
(F)	4. She	D	Noun
(B)	5. Quickly	E	Preposition
		F	Pronoun
		G	Verb

3. Multiple-choice.

EXAMPLES

Why is the inhaling of carbon monoxide harmful to man?
   A   It causes increased blood pressure.
   B   It damages lung tissue.
  (C)   It destroys red blood cells.
   D   It prevents oxygen from entering the lungs.

In the equation $2X + 5 = 9$, the $2X$ means
   A   2 plus X.
   B   2 minus X.
   C   2 divided by X.
  (D)   2 multiplied by X.

Which of the following sentences has a disagreement between subject and verb?
   A   When they win, they are happy.
  (B)   Politics are hard to understand.
   C   The majority is always right.
   D   One or the other is to be elected.

In addition to these basic types of objective test items, there are num-
ous modifications and combinations of types. However, there is little to be
ined from a listing of all the possible variations, since many are unique
 particular objectives or to specific subject-matter areas. Some of the
ore common variations used to measure understanding, thinking skills,

and other complex learning outcomes will be illustrated later. These, plus an understanding of the general principles of test construction and of the principles that apply to each of the specific types of objective test items, should enable the teacher to make adaptations which best fit his particular purposes.

The different types of objective test items have one feature in common which distinguishes them from the essay test. They present the pupil with a highly structured task that limits the kind of response he can make. To obtain the correct answer, the pupil must demonstrate the specific knowledge, understanding, or skill called for in the item. He is not free to redefine the problem or to organize and present the answer in his own words. He must select one of several alternative answers or supply the correct word, number, or symbol. This structuring of the problem and restriction on the method of responding contribute to objective scoring which is quick, easy, and accurate. On the negative side, this same structuring makes the objective test item inappropriate for measuring the ability to select, organize, and integrate ideas. To measure such outcomes we must depend on the essay question.

The Essay Question

The essay question is commonly viewed as a single item type. A useful classification, however, is one based on the amount of freedom of response allowed the pupil. This includes the *extended response* type where the pupil is given almost complete freedom in making his response, and the *restricted response* type where limitations are placed on the nature, length, or organization of his response. These types are illustrated as follows:

1. Extended response type:

    Describe what you think should be the role of the Federal Government in maintaining a stable economy in the United States. Include specific policies and programs and give reasons for your proposals.

2. Restricted response type:

    State two advantages and two disadvantages of maintaining high tariffs on goods from other countries.

It will be noted, in these examples, that the *extended response* type question permits the pupil to decide which facts he thinks are most pertinent, to select his own method of organization, and to write what he deems necessary to provide a comprehensive answer. Thus, such questions tend to reveal the ability to evaluate ideas, to relate them in a coherent manner, and to express them succinctly. To a lesser extent, they also reflect individual differences in attitudes, values, and creative ability.

Despite the apparent virtues of the extended response type of question, it has two weaknesses which impose rather severe limitations on its use: (1) It is inefficient for measuring knowledge of factual material, since the questions are so broad that only a limited area of content can be covered in any one test; and (2) The scoring is difficult and apt to be unreliable because the answers include an array of factual information of varying degrees of correctness, organized with varying degrees of coherence, and expressed with varying degrees of legibility and conciseness.

The *restricted response* type of question minimizes some of the weaknesses of the extended response type. Restricting the type of response called for makes it more efficient for measuring knowledge of factual material and reduces somewhat the difficulty of the scoring. On the other hand, the more highly structured task presented by the restricted response type question makes it less effective as a measure of the ability to select, organize, and integrate ideas, which is one of the unique purposes to be served by the essay test.

As with the various forms of objective test items, neither the extended response type question nor the restricted response type question can serve all purposes equally well. The type to use in a particular situation depends mainly on the learning outcomes to be measured and to a lesser extent on such practical considerations as the difficulty of scoring.

Comparative Advantages of Objective and Essay Questions

From our previous discussion, it is apparent that both the objective item and the essay question can provide valuable evidence concerning pupil achievement. Each has unique qualities which make it more appropriate for some purposes than for others. A comparison of the relative merits of tests based on these two item types, with regard to a number of important characteristics, is presented in Table 6.4.

In considering the comparative advantages of these two main item types as a basis for building a classroom test, we must be careful not to fall into the "either or" type of thinking in which we use either objective items or essay questions. It is frequently more valid to use both types in a single test, with each measuring the particular learning outcomes for which it is best suited. This should also have a desirable influence on the pupil's learning, since in preparing for such tests he has to devote attention both to the specific types of learning outcomes measured by objective items and to the synthesis type outcomes measured by essay questions.

Selecting the Most Appropriate Item Types

In constructing a classroom test one of our major concerns is that the test items call forth the particular behaviors (e.g., define terms, state facts, apply knowledge, identify cause-effect relations, and so on) indicated by the specific learning outcomes pertinent to each of our instructional objectives.

TABLE 6.4

COMPARATIVE ADVANTAGES OF OBJECTIVE AND ESSAY TESTS

	Objective Test	*Essay Test*
Learning outcomes measured	Efficient for measuring knowledge of facts. Some types (e.g., multiple-choice) can also measure understandings, thinking skills, and other complex outcomes. Inefficient or inappropriate for measuring ability to select and organize ideas, writing abilities, and some types of problem-solving skills.	Inefficient for measuring knowledge of facts. Can measure understandings, thinking skills and other complex learning outcomes (especially useful where originality of response is desired). Appropriate for measuring ability to select and organize ideas, writing abilities, and problem-solving skills requiring originality.
Preparation of questions	A relatively large number of questions needed for a test. Preparation is difficult and time consuming.	Only a few questions are needed for a test. Preparation is relatively easy (but more difficult than generally assumed).
Sampling of course content	Provides an extensive sampling of course content, due to the large number of questions that can be included in a test.	Sampling of course content is usually limited, due to the small number of questions that can be included in a test.
Control of pupil's response	Complete structuring of task limits pupil to type of response called for. Prevents bluffing and avoids influence of writing skill. However, selection-type items are subject to guessing.	Freedom to respond in own words enables bluffing and writing skill to influence the score. However, guessing is minimized.
Scoring	Objective scoring which is quick, easy, and consistent.	Subjective scoring which is slow, difficult, and inconsistent.
Influence on learning	Usually encourages pupil to develop a comprehensive knowledge of specific facts and the ability to make fine discriminations among them. Can encourage the development of understandings, thinking skills and other complex outcomes, if properly constructed.	Encourages pupils to concentrate on larger units of subject matter, with special emphasis on the ability to organize, integrate, and express ideas effectively.

This is necessary if we are to accept the pupils' responses to the test items as evidence that the specific learning outcomes, and consequently the instructional objectives, have been achieved. As noted earlier, this process of relating the test items as directly as possible to the specific outcomes provides us with the greatest assurance that our test is a *valid* measure of our instructional objectives. Therefore, the nature of the test items selected should depend chiefly on the nature of the outcomes to be measured.

Each type of test item is efficient for measuring some learning outcomes and inefficient, or inappropriate, for measuring others. The *short-answer* type, for example, effectively measures the recall of specific facts but is generally inappropriate for measuring understanding, application, interpretation, and other complex learning outcomes. The *true-false* or *alternative-response* type of item is most useful where the desired outcomes are either determining the truth or falsity of a statement, distinguishing between fact and opinion, or discriminating between appropriate and inappropriate responses. As with the short-answer type, the true-false item is generally inadequate for measuring the more complex learning outcomes. The *matching* type of item is similarly restricted. It is limited almost entirely to learning outcomes that call for the identification of simple relationships and the ability to classify things into given categories. The *multiple-choice* item is the most generally adaptable type of objective test item. It can be used effectively in measuring a variety of learning outcomes, from simple to complex. Even the multiple-choice type of item is restricted, however, in that it is inefficient or inappropriate for measuring some of the more complex outcomes. The *essay* and other *supply* types are the most effective for measuring the ability to organize data, the ability to present original ideas, and for some types of problem-solving activity.

Whether a test item actually measures the particular behavior called for a specific learning outcome depends, of course, to a large extent on the skill with which the test item is constructed. No amount of skill, however, will enable us to develop a valid test of achievement if the test items selected for use are inappropriate for measuring the intended outcomes.

CONSIDERATIONS IN PREPARING RELEVANT TEST ITEMS

As noted earlier, the construction of items for a classroom test should be preceded by a series of preliminary steps. First, the purpose of the test should be determined. Second, a table of specifications should be prepared. Third, the most appropriate item types should be selected for use. Finally, specific test items should be constructed in accordance with the specifications developed during the preceding steps. The rules for constructing each item type will be discussed in Chapters 7 through 10. Here, we shall focus on some of the general considerations involved in preparing relevant items for a classroom test.

Matching Items to Intended Outcomes

A classroom test is most likely to provide a valid measure of the instructional objectives, if the test items are specifically designed to measure the behavior defined by the specific learning outcomes. The process of matching test items to the learning outcomes to be measured was described and illustrated in Chapter 3. Essentially, it involves fitting each test item as directly as possible to the intended outcome, as follows:

Specific Learning Outcome: Identifies the function of a given body structure.
    Relevant Test Item:
      What is the function of the kidneys?
        (A) Eliminate waste products
        B   Improve the circulation of blood
        C   Maintain respiration
        D   Stimulate digestion

Thus, the preparation of relevant test items involves a careful analysis of the behavior described in the specific learning outcome (i.e., Identifies the function of . . .) and the construction of a test item that calls forth that behavior (i.e., What is the function of . . . ?). It should be noted, in our example, that the specific learning outcome defines the *behavioral response* the pupil is expected to make, but it does not indicate the *specific* body structure (i.e., kidney) the pupil is to identify. Keeping the learning outcome free of specific course content, as in this case, makes it possible to key the behavioral response to various areas of content. For example, pupils could be asked to identify the function of the heart, the lungs, the muscles, or any other body structure that was pertinent to the content of the course. The desired behavioral response is keyed to each specific area of content by means of the table of specifications.

In some cases, it may be desirable to prepare a general *item pattern* as an intermediate step between the specific learning outcome and the test item. A general item pattern for our illustrative test item, for example, would be as follows:

    What is the function of . . . ?

An item pattern, such as this, could be completed by adding the name of any body structure and using it as a short-answer question, or, in addition, by listing appropriate alternatives and using it as a multiple-choice question. Thus, using the item pattern as a guide, we could generate large numbers of relevant test items for this particular learning outcome. This procedure is especially useful where a file of test items is being prepared, or where more than one form of the test is needed (e.g., pretesting-posttesting, retesting in mastery learning or in individualized instruction).

Where item patterns are used as a guide to test construction, they could be arranged by type of learning outcome as follows:

    Knowledge Outcomes:
      1. What is the name of . . . ?
      2. What is the location of . . . ?

   3. What are the characteristics of . . . ?
   4. What is the function of . . . ?
Understanding Outcomes:
   1. What is the reason for . . . ?
   2. What is the relationship between . . . ?
   3. Which of the following is an example of . . . ?
   4. Which of the following best summarizes . . . ?
Application Outcomes:
   1. What method would be best for . . . ?
   2. What steps should be followed to construct . . . ?
   3. Which of the following indicates correct application of . . . ?
   4. Which of the following solutions is correct for . . . ?

Item patterns such as these should not, of course, be developed haphazardly. Rather, they should be derived from the specific learning outcomes they represent. Although it typically will not be possible to develop item patterns for all outcomes, the preparation of a basic list will aid in generating pools of relevant test items. Hopefully, the test construction time saved by using such a list can be profitably applied in constructing more effective items in those areas where general item patterns are infeasible.

Obtaining a Representative Sample

A test, no matter how extensive, is always a sample of the many possible test items that could be included. For example, we expect pupils to know thousands of specific facts but we can test for only a limited number of them; we expect pupils to develop understandings which are applicable to innumerable situations, but we can test for application to only a limited number of situations; and we expect pupils to develop thinking skills which will enable them to solve a variety of problems but we can test their problem-solving ability with only a limited number of problems. In each area of content and for each specific learning outcome, then, we merely select a sample of pupil behavior and accept it as evidence of achievement in that area. We assume that a pupil's responses to our selected set of test items are typical of what his responses would be to other test items drawn from the same area. This means, of course, that our limited samples must be selected so as to provide a representative sample in each of the areas for which the test is being developed.

The problem of obtaining a representative sample, as noted earlier, is greater with norm-referenced testing than with criterion-referenced testing because of its broader coverage. For both types of tests, however, our sampling is most likely to be representative when test preparation is guided by a table of specifications. Unless a table of specifications, or some similar device, is used as a guide in test construction, there is a tendency to overload the test with items measuring knowledge of isolated facts and to neglect the more complex learning outcomes. In the social studies area, for example, it is not uncommon to include a disproportionately large number of items which measure knowledge of names, dates, places, and the like. In science, the defining of terms and the naming of structures and functions is commonly overemphasized. In mathematics, computational skill is frequently the only learning outcome measured. In language arts and literature, the identification of parts of speech, literary characters, authors, and the like, are frequently all too prominent. These learning outcomes are, generally, *not* stressed because the teacher thinks knowledge of isolated facts is more important than understandings, applications, interpretations, and various thinking skills. Rather, they usually receive undue prominence because the teacher finds it easier to construct such test items. *Without a carefully developed test plan, ease of construction all too frequently becomes the dominant criterion in constructing test items. As a consequence, the test measures a limited and biased sample of pupil behavior and neglects many of the learning outcomes considered most important by the teacher. In short, without a carefully developed test plan, the test tends to lack content validity.*

Test Length. The length of a test is, of course, also an important factor in obtaining a representative sample. Test length is determined at the time the table of specifications is built, and depends on such factors as the purpose of testing, the types of test items used, the age of the pupils, and the level of reliability needed for effective test use. Thus, a criterion-referenced mastery test for a brief third-grade social studies *unit* might contain 20 objective items, whereas a norm-referenced survey test covering a tenth-grade social studies *course* might contain more than 100 objective items and several essay questions. Although there are no hard and fast rules for determining test length, an important consideration from a sampling standpoint is the number of test items devoted to each specific area being measured. We want our classroom tests to be long enough to provide an adequate sampling of each objective and each content area. As a rule of thumb, it would be desirable to use several objective test items for measuring each specific learning outcome and ten or more for measuring each general instructional objective.

Special problems of sampling arise when complex learning outcomes are being measured, because here we must typically turn to more elaborate objective-type items and to essay questions. Both item types require considerable testing time, but a single test item is still inadequate for measuring an intended outcome. One test item calling for the interpretation of graphs, for instance, is not sufficient to adequately measure the pupil's ability to interpret graphs. The nature of the data or the type of graph may be the most influential factor in determining whether the pupil responds correctly to a single test item. Where several items are used, however, the influence of such specific factors are minimized, and we obtain a more representative sample of the pupil's ability to interpret graphs. A similar situation occurs with the use of essay questions. The answer to any single question depends too heavily upon the particular sample of information called for by the question. The only feasible solution we seem to have, here, is to confine each test of complex outcomes to a more limited area (e.g., graph interpretation, problem solving) and to test more frequently. In any event, our major aim should be to obtain as representative a sample of pupil behavior as possible in each area to be tested. Other things being equal, the greater the number of test items the more adequate the sample and the more reliable the results.

Selecting the Proper Item Difficulty

The difficulty of the items to be included in a classroom test depends largely on whether the test is being designed to describe the specific learning tasks pupils can perform (i.e., criterion-referenced test), or to rank the pupils in order of their achievement (i.e., norm-referenced test). As noted previously, these two basic approaches to measurement place quite different emphasis on the role of item difficulty in classroom testing.

Item Difficulty and Criterion-Referenced Testing. The difficulty of the test items in a criterion-referenced *mastery* test is determined by the nature of the specific learning tasks to be measured. If the learning tasks are easy, the test items should be easy. If the learning tasks are of moderate difficulty, the test items should be of moderate difficulty. No attempt should be made to modify item difficulty, or to eliminate easy items from the test, in order to obtain a range of test scores. On a criterion-referenced mastery test we would expect all, or nearly all, pupils to obtain perfect scores when the instruction has been effective.

When constructing criterion-referenced mastery tests, great care must be taken to match item difficulty to the difficulty of the learning task described in the intended outcome. This also involves special precautions to avoid irrelevant barriers to the answer (e.g., ambiguity), unintended clues to the correct response, or any other factor that might alter the level of difficulty of the test task. In the final analysis, we want the pupil's performance on each test item to serve as a valid indicator of the presence or absence of the specific behavior defined in the intended learning outcome.

For criterion-referenced tests at the *developmental level of learning,* we need test items of varying difficulty for each instructional objective. Since the developmental level is concerned with how much pupils have learned beyond the minimum essentials of a course, a wide range of item difficulty is necessary to adequately describe pupil performance. Ideally, the difficulty of the test tasks would be derived directly from the instructional content, however, rather than from some arbitrary attempt to manipulate item difficulty. In measuring reading comprehension, for example, a series of graded paragraphs ranging from easy to difficult could be used to measure the level of reading a pupil has attained. Similarly, a series of test tasks could require the pupil to demonstrate an understanding of increasingly complex concepts, or the application of principles to a series of increasingly difficult problems. Here, in contrast to criterion-referenced mastery testing, we expect to obtain a range of scores. In contrast to the typical norm-referenced test, however, these tests are being designed to describe the types of learning tasks pupils can perform, rather than to simply indicate the relative standing of pupils in some known group.

Item Difficulty and Norm-Referenced Testing. Since norm-referenced tests are designed to rank pupils in order of achievement, deliberate attempts are made to obtain a wide spread of test scores. This involves eliminating the easy items that all pupils are likely to answer correctly and by favoring items that maximize the differences in test performance among pupils. Our aim is to obtain as reliable a ranking of pupils as possible, so that the decisions based on relative achievement (e.g., classroom grouping, grading) can be made with a high degree of confidence.

Maximum differentiation among pupils in terms of achievement is obtained when the average score is near the midpoint of the possible scores, and the scores range from "near zero" to "near perfect." With a 100-item short-answer test, for example, an average score of 50 and a range of scores from 5 to 95 would be ideal. The ideal average score for selection-type items falls midway between the expected chance score (proportion of items marked correctly by guessing) and the maximum possible score (total number of items in the test). Thus, ideal average difficulty on a 100-item test for various choice-type items would be as follows:

	Chance Score	Ideal Average
Two-choice item (e.g., true-false)	50	75
Three-choice multiple-choice item	33	67
Four-choice multiple-choice item	25	63
Five-choice multiple-choice item	20	60

Except for a few items at the beginning of the test, for motivational purposes, none of our items should be so easy that everyone answers them correctly. Similarly, none of our test items should be so difficult that everyone misses them. Neither type of item discriminates among pupils, and therefore neither contributes to the intended function of a norm-referenced test. As we shall see in Chapter 11, maximum discrimination among levels of achievement is made possible by using items of average difficulty (approximately 50 per cent answer the item correctly).

In attempting to construct test items of average difficulty, we should avoid resorting to undesirable methods for obtaining difficulty. It is not uncommon, for example, to use more obscure, less important factual information to increase the difficulty of test items. This generally leads to a lessening of content validity and may also be undesirable from a learning standpoint. Pupils are likely to concentrate their efforts on the learning of the less important material and to neglect the more important learning outcomes. A closely related method of achieving difficulty at the expense of validity is to require pupils to make difficult but unimportant discriminations. In the following test items, for example, note how the significance of the information decreases as the difficulty increases:

> The Government of the United States was declared in effect under the Constitution in
> A   1787.
> C   1789.
> B   1788.
> D   1790.
>
> The Government of the United States was declared in effect under the Constitution in
> A   January.
> B   February.
> C   March.
> D   April.
>
> The Government of the United States was declared in effect under the Constitution on
> A   Monday.
> B   Tuesday.
> C   Wednesday.
> D   Thursday.

Asking pupils to make fine discriminations, of course, does not always lead to learning outcomes of less significance. However, we need to be on guard against such dangers when increasing the difficulty of our test items. Other things being equal, the best way to increase the difficulty of test items is to move toward the measurement of learning outcomes of a more complex nature, such as the understanding of concepts and principles or the application of principles to new situations.

Eliminating Irrelevant Barriers to the Answer

During the construction of the items for a classroom test, care must be taken to eliminate any extraneous factors that might prevent the pupil from responding. If a pupil has achieved a particular learning outcome (e.g., knowledge of terms), we would want him to obtain correct answers to those test items that measure the attainment of that learning outcome. We would be very unhappy (and so would he), if he answered such test items incorrectly merely because the sentence structure was too complex, the vocabulary too difficult, or the type of response called for too vague. These factors, which are extraneous to the central purpose of the measurement, limit and modify the pupil's responses and prevent him from showing his true level of achievement. Such factors are as unfair as determining a person's running ability when he has a sprained ankle. Although a measure of running ability would be obtained, the performance would be restricted by a factor we did not intend to include in our measurement.

One way to eliminate factors which are extraneous to the purpose of measurement is to be certain that all pupils have the prerequisite skills and abilities needed to make the response. These have been called "enabling behaviors" because they enable the pupil to make the response but are not meant to be critical factors in the measurement.[3] That is, they are a necessary but not a sufficient condition for responding correctly. Probably the most important "enabling behavior" in objective testing is reading skill. In essay testing, skill in written expression is an additional factor to be considered. In measuring understandings, thinking skills, and other complex learning outcomes, knowledge of certain specific facts and simple computational skills might also be necessary prerequisites.

In constructing test items, then, we need to strive for items which measure achievement of the specific learning outcomes and not differences in "enabling behaviors." Differences in reading ability, computational skill, communication skills, and the like, should not influence the pupils' responses unless such outcomes are specifically being measured. The only functional difference between those pupils who get an item correct and those who miss it should be the possession of the knowledge, understanding, or other learning outcome being measured by the item. All other differences are extraneous to the purpose of the item, and their influence should be eliminated or controlled for valid test results.

A special problem in preventing extraneous factors from distorting our test results is that of avoiding ambiguity. Objective test items are especially subject to misinterpretation where long complex sentences are used, where the vocabulary is unnecessarily difficult, and where words which lack precise meaning are used. Thus, the antidote for ambiguity seems to be a

---

Some Common *Barriers* in Test Items

    Ambiguous statements
    Excessive wordiness
    Difficult vocabulary
    Complex sentence structure
    Unclear instructions

Some Common *Clues* in Test Items

    Grammatical inconsistencies
    Verbal associations
    Specific determiners (e.g., always)
    Length of correct responses
    Location of correct responses

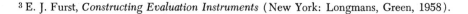

[3] E. J. Furst, *Constructing Evaluation Instruments* (New York: Longmans, Green, 1958).

careful choice of words, from the viewpoint of both level of reading difficulty and preciseness of meaning, and the use of brief, concise sentences.

Preventing Unintended Clues to the Answer

Test items should be so constructed that the pupil obtains the correct answer *only* if he has attained the desired learning outcome. This is the counterpart of the preceding principle where we were concerned with those factors which prevent a pupil from responding correctly even though he has attained the desired learning outcome. Here, we are concerned with those factors which make it possible for the pupil to respond correctly even though he *lacks* the necessary achievement. These are the clues, some rather obvious and some very subtle, which inadvertently creep into test items during their construction. They lead the nonachiever to the correct answer and thereby prevent the items from functioning as intended. When test items are short-circuited in this manner, they of course provide invalid evidence concerning achievement.

Some of the most obvious clues in test items are those due to grammatical structure, as illustrated by the article *an* in the following item.

> A porpoise is an
>   A   plant.
>   B   reptile.
>   Ⓒ animal.
>   D   bird.

Such clues are not limited to selection-type items. They also appear in supply-type items, as indicated in the following illustration:

> A piece of land that is completely surrounded by water is known as an
>
> _____.

The clue is much less obvious, to the person constructing this test item, than it was in our first illustration. To the pupil taking the test, however, it becomes readily apparent. The two most plausible answers are "island" and "peninsula." Since peninsula begins with a consonant sound and does not follow the article *an*, it is ruled out as a possibility. This does not imply, of course, that pupils need to know the rules for good grammatical structure in order to use such clues. Most clues are not analyzed and evaluated, as above. Rather they are responded to in terms of partial knowledge and hunches. "An peninsula" just does not sound right to the pupil so he responds with the word "island" and obtains the correct answer.

Leads to the correct answer may also be provided by simple verbal associations. Note how the word "wind," in the following items, provides a clue to the answer:

Which one of the following instruments is used to determine the *direction* of the wind?

A Anemometer
B Barometer
C Hygrometer
Ⓓ Wind vane.

Rather than lead the uninformed to the correct answer, such clues should lead the nonachiever away from it. In the following item, the same clue makes "wind vane" a plausible (but incorrect) answer for those pupils who have not learned the uses of the various weather instruments.

Which one of the following instruments is used to determine the *speed* of the wind?

Ⓐ Anemometer
B Barometer
C Hygrometer
D Wind vane

Verbal clues need not be as obvious as those illustrated earlier. In fact, the clues which appear in the final version of a test are usually rather subtle. They are based on partial knowledge and verbal associations not readily apparent to the casual observer. For example, at first glance the following item appears to be free from clues:

Which one of the following is used to prevent polio?

A Gamma globulin
B Penicillin
Ⓒ Salk vaccine
D Sulpha

A careful examination of this item, however, will indicate that the word "vaccine" provides a clue to the answer. All the pupil needs to know to answer the item correctly is that "vaccine" is used to "prevent" disease. Since most pupils have been vaccinated at one time or another, they probably possess this partial knowledge needed to make the clue apparent to them. Some pupils may also have developed a verbal association between "Salk" and "polio" and respond correctly on that basis. In either case, partial knowledge can lead to the correct answer and prevent the item from functioning as intended.

Another type of subtle clue is that based on the words used to qualify statements. For example, true-false statements that include qualifiers such as "sometimes," "usually," "generally," and the like are most frequently true, whereas statements containing absolutes such as "always," "never," "none," "only," are most frequently false. Such words have been called *specific determiners.* They are difficult to remove from true-false items because true statements generally must be qualified, and false statements frequently must be stated in terms of absolutes to make them clearly false.

Clues, which prevent test items from functioning as intended, can usually be eliminated during test construction. In fact, many of the suggestions for constructing each of the specific types of test items are aimed directly at removing such clues. It is also helpful to analyze each completed test item in terms of the mental process a pupil must use to obtain the correct answer and to compare this with the intended purpose of the item. Only when these two are in harmony, can we be fairly certain that irrelevant factors are *not* operating, and that correct answers to the test items indicate attainment of the desired learning outcomes.

Focusing on Improving Learning and Instruction

The ultimate purpose of testing, as with all classroom procedures, is to improve pupil learning. Thus, any classroom test we construct should be evaluated in terms of the extent to which it contributes, directly or indirectly, toward this end. A well-constructed classroom test should increase both the quantity and quality of learning, should lead to more effective teaching procedures, and should enhance teacher-pupil relations.

One way we can assure that tests have a desirable influence on pupil learning is to pay particular attention to the breadth of content and learning outcomes measured by our tests. As we select a representative sample of content from *all* of the areas covered in our instruction, we are emphasizing to the pupil that he must devote his attention to *all* areas. He cannot neglect some aspects of the course and do well on the tests. Similarly, when our tests measure a variety of types of learning outcomes, the pupil soon learns that a mass of memorized factual information is not sufficient. He must also learn to interpret and apply facts, develop conceptual understandings, draw conclusions, recognize assumptions, identify cause-and-effect relations, and the like. This discourages the pupil from placing sole dependence on memorization as a basis for learning and encourages him to develop the use of more complex mental processes.

The practice of constructing tests which measure a variety of learning outcomes should also lead to improved teaching procedures. As we translate the different learning outcomes into test items, we develop a better notion of the mental processes involved. Thus, the functional nature of understandings, thinking skills, and other complex learning outcomes becomes increasingly clear to us. This clarification of how achievement is reflected in terms of mental processes enables us to plan the learning experiences of our pupils more effectively. Furthermore, we are more likely to emphasize complex learning outcomes in our teaching when we include them in our testing. This may seem a case of the cart pulling the horse, but a well-constructed test frequently leads to a review of teaching procedures and to the abandonment of those which encourage rote learning.

Finally, a test will contribute to improved teacher-pupil relations if pupils view the test as a *fair* and *useful* measure of their achievement. We can make fairness apparent by including a representative sample of the subject-matter content and the outcomes we have emphasized during instruction, by writing clear directions, by making certain that the intent of each test item is clear and can be answered correctly by any pupil who has achieved the desired outcome, and by providing adequate time for the test. Pupil recognition of usefulness, however, depends as much on what we do with the results of the test as on the characteristics of the test itself. We make the usefulness apparent by using the results as a basis for guiding and improving learning.

SUMMARY

The planning for a classroom test involves (1) determining the purpose of testing, (2) building a table of specifications, (3) selecting appropriate item types, and (4) preparing a set of relevant test items.

Classroom tests can be used for a number of instructional purposes. The various specific uses can be classified under the four basic types of classroom evaluation. Thus, we have (1) placement testing that is used at the beginning of a course or unit to determine learning readiness, to aid in instructional planning, and to make advanced placements; (2) formative testing that is used periodically during instruction to improve and direct pupil learning; (3) diagnostic testing that is used as needed during instruction to identify and remedy errors related to persistent learning difficulties; and (4) summative testing that is used at the end of a course or unit to assign grades, certify mastery, or evaluate teaching. Each of these types of classroom testing places different demands on item sampling, item difficulty, and the nature of the instrument used (i.e., criterion-referenced or norm-referenced).

A representative sample of pupil behavior is more likely to result if a table of specifications is used in planning the test. Building the table involves (1) obtaining the list of instructional objectives, (2) outlining the course content, and (3) preparing a two-way chart that relates the instructional objectives to the course content and specifies the nature of the desired test sample. Although a table of specifications is especially useful in preparing norm-referenced tests (because of its broad coverage), it is also of use in preparing most criterion-referenced tests.

The tests constructed by classroom teachers may be classified as objective tests or essay tests. These may be further subdivided into the following basic types of test items:

Objective Test:

  A. Supply type.
    1. Short answer.
    2. Completion.
  B. Selection type.
    1. True-false or alternative-response.
    2. Matching.
    3. Multiple-choice.

Essay Test:

  A. Extended response.
  B. Restricted response.

The objective test provides the pupil with a highly structured task which limits the pupil's response to supplying a word, number, or symbol, or to selecting the answer from among a given number of alternatives. The essay test permits the pupil to respond by selecting, organizing, and presenting those facts he considers appropriate. Both types of tests serve useful purposes in measuring pupil achievement. The type to use in a particular situation is best determined by the learning outcomes to be measured, and by the unique advantages and limitations of each type. A common practice is to include both objective test items and essay questions in a single test.

The preparation of a set of relevant test items involves (1) matching the items to the learning outcomes as directly as possible, (2) obtaining a representative sample of all intended outcomes, (3) selecting the proper level of item difficulty, (4) eliminating irrelevant barriers to the answer, (5) preventing unintended clues to the answer, and (6) focusing on improving learning and instruction. The specific rules for constructing each item type will be described in the chapters that follow.

LEARNING EXERCISES

1. Describe the major differences between each of the following:
  a. Readiness pretest and placement pretest.
  b. Formative test and summative test.
  c. Criterion-referenced mastery test and norm-referenced survey test.
2. Describe how the purpose of testing might influence the preparation of a set of relevant test items.
3. What types of information should be considered during each of the following steps in test construction?
  a. Building the table of specifications.
  b. Selecting the types of test items to use.
  c. Preparing the test items.
4. A classroom teacher recently said, "You have a good objective test, if you can point to the answer for each question on a particular page in the textbook." Do you agree or disagree with this statement? Why?

5. What are the advantages of using "item patterns" as a guide to test construction? What are some of the possible disadvantages?
6. List as many factors as you can think of that might prevent a pupil from getting an item correct even though he possesses the knowledge the item was designed to measure. What steps can be taken to remove such barriers?
7. List as many factors as you can think of that would enable a pupil to answer an item correctly even though he lacks the knowledge the item was designed to measure. How can such clues be prevented?
8. Describe the various ways that classroom tests might be used to facilitate learning. How might they interfere with learning?
9. Assume that you are going to prepare a pretest for a course in your major teaching area. How would you proceed?
10. Assume that you are on a committee of teachers with the responsibility for developing a departmental final examination for a course in your major teaching area. What steps would you recommend to the committee for developing a test that has good content validity? Justify each step.

SUGGESTIONS FOR FURTHER READING

BLOOM, B. S., J. T. HASTINGS, and G. F. MADAUS. *Handbook on Formative and Summative Evaluation of Student Learning.* New York: McGraw-Hill Book Company, 1971. See Chapters 4–5 for comprehensive descriptions of summative evaluation, formative evaluation, and evaluation for placement and diagnosis.

GRONLUND, N. E. *Preparing Criterion-Referenced Tests for Classroom Instruction.* New York: Macmillan Publishing Co., Inc., 1973. A brief book describing the planning and preparation of criterion-referenced tests.

MEHRENS, W. A. and I. J. LEHMANN. *Measurement and Evaluation in Education and Psychology.* New York: Holt, Rinehart & Winston, Inc., 1973. Chapter 7, "Classroom Testing: The Planning stage." Describes the factors to consider in planning teacher-made achievement tests.

TINKLEMAN, S. N. "Planning the Objective Test," Chapter 3 in R. L. Thorndike (ed.), *Educational Measurement.* Washington, D.C.: American Council on Education, 1971. A comprehensive discussion of the steps in test planning.

Classroom Testing in Special Areas

AHMANN, J. S., M. D. GLOCK, and H. L. WARDEBERG. *Evaluating Elementary School Pupils.* Boston: Allyn & Bacon, Inc., 1960. Chapters 11–13. Cover evaluation in language arts, mathematics, and content areas.

ARNY, B. *Evaluation in Home Economics.* New York: Appleton-Century-Crofts, 1953.

AUSTIN, M. *Reading Evaluation: Appraisal Techniques for Schools and Classrooms.* New York: Ronald Press, 1971.

BERG, H. D. (ed.). *Evaluation in Social Studies.* Thirty-fifth Yearbook, National Council for the Social Studies. Washington, D.C.: National Council for the Social Studies, 1965.

COLWELL, R., *The Evaluation of Music Teaching and Learning.* Englewood Cliffs, N.J.: Prentice-Hall, Inc., 1970.

DRESSEL, P. L. (ed.). *Evaluation in Higher Education.* Boston: Houghton Mifflin Company, 1961. Chapters 4–7. Cover evaluation in social science, natural science, humanities, and communication areas.

DUTTON, W. H. *Evaluating Pupils' Understanding in Arithmetic.* Englewood Cliffs, N.J.: Prentice-Hall, Inc., 1964.

HARDAWAY, M. *Testing and Evaluation in Business Education,* 3rd ed. Cincinnati: South-Western Publishing Co., 1966.

HARRIS, D. P. *Testing English as a Second Language.* New York: McGraw-Hill Book Company, Inc., 1969.

HEDGES, W. D. *Testing and Evaluation for the Sciences in the Secondary School.* Belmont, Calif.: Wadsworth Publishing Company, 1966.

LADO, R. *Language Testing: The Construction and Use of Foreign Language Tests.* New York: Longmans, Green & Company, 1961.

MATHEWS, D. K. *Measurement in Physical Education,* 3rd ed. Philadelphia: W. B. Saunders Company, 1968.

NATIONAL COUNCIL OF TEACHERS OF MATHEMATICS. *Evaluation in Mathematics.* Twenty-sixth Yearbook. Washington, D. C.: The National Council, 1961.

NEDELSKY, L. *Science Teaching and Testing.* New York: Harcourt Brace Jovanovich, Inc., 1965.

SYND, R. B., and A. J. PICARD. *Behavioral Objectives and Evaluation Measures: Science and Mathematics.* Columbus, Ohio: Charles E. Merrill Publishers, 1972.

Test Bulletin

Educational Testing Service. *Making the Classroom Test: A Guide for Teachers.* Princeton, N.J.: ETS, 1973. Describes and illustrates simple tables of specifications and various types of test items.

CHAPTER 7

Constructing Objective
Test Items: Simple Forms

Each type of test item has its own unique characteristics . . . uses . . .
advantages . . . limitations . . . and rules for construction. . . . Here, these
are considered for the objective-test forms which measure relatively
simple learning outcomes: (1) the short-answer item, (2) the true-false
item, and (3) the matching exercise.

The preliminary test planning described in the last chapter provides a
sound basis for developing classroom tests that can be used for a variety
of instructional purposes. The table of specifications clarifies the sample of
behavior to be measured, and the various considerations in test planning
provide a general framework within which to proceed. The next step is the
actual construction of test items. This step is crucial, because ultimately
the validity of a classroom test is determined by the extent to which the
behaviors to be measured are actually called forth by the test items. Selecting item types that are inappropriate for the learning outcomes to be
measured, constructing items with technical defects, or unwittingly including irrelevant clues in the items can undermine all of the careful planning that has gone on before.

The construction of good test items is an art. The skills it requires,
however, are the same as those found in effective teaching. Needed are a
thorough grasp of subject matter, a clear conception of the desired learning
outcomes, a psychological understanding of pupils, sound judgment, persistence, and a touch of creativity. The only additional requisite for constructing good test items is the skillful application of an array of simple
but important rules and suggestions.[1] These techniques of test construc-

---

[1] A. G. Wesman, "Writing the Test Item," Chapter 4 in R. L. Thorndike (ed.), *Educational Measurement* (Washington, D.C.: American Council on Education, 1971).

tion are the topic of this and the next several chapters. The rules for constructing test items, described in these chapters, are applicable to all of the various types of classroom tests.

In this chapter we shall limit our discussion to the simpler forms of objective test items, namely, the (1) short-answer item, (2) true-false or alternative-response item, and (3) matching exercise. These item types are treated together since their use in classroom testing is restricted, almost exclusively, to the measurement of simple learning outcomes in the knowledge area. The multiple-choice item and other methods of measuring more complex achievement will be considered in the following chapters.

SHORT-ANSWER ITEMS

The short-answer item and the completion item are both supply-type test items which can be answered by a word, phrase, number, or symbol. They are essentially the same, differing only in the method of presenting the problem. In the case of the short-answer item a direct question is used, whereas the completion item consists of an incomplete statement.

EXAMPLES

Short answer: What is the name of the man who invented the steamboat? (Robert Fulton)

Completion: The name of the man who invented the steamboat is (Robert Fulton).

(or)

The (steamboat) was invented by Robert Fulton.

Also included in this category are problems in arithmetic, mathematics, science, and other areas, where the solution must be supplied by the pupil.

Uses of Short-Answer Items

The short-answer type of test item is suitable for measuring a wide variety of relatively simple learning outcomes. The following outcomes and test items illustrate some of the common uses of this type of item:

EXAMPLES

Knowledge of terminology
  Lines on a weather map which join points of the same barometric pressure are called (isobars).
Knowledge of specific facts
  A member of the United States Senate is elected to a term of (6) years.

Knowledge of principles
    If the temperature of a gas is held constant while the pressure applied to it is increased, what will happen to its volume? (It will decrease.)
Knowledge of method or procedure
    What device is used to detect whether an electric charge is positive or negative? (*electroscope*)
Simple interpretations of data
    How many syllables are there in the word *Argentina*? (4)
    In the number 612, what value does the 6 represent? (600)
    In the triangle below, what is the number of degrees in each angle? (60)

If an airplane flying northwest made a 180 degree turn, what direction would it be heading? (southeast)

Interpretations of a more complex nature are obtained where the short-answer item is used to measure the ability to interpret diagrams, charts, graphs, and various types of pictorial data.

There are even more notable exceptions to the general rule that short-answer items are limited to measuring simple learning outcomes. These are in areas of mathematics and science where the solutions to problems can be indicated by numbers or symbols. The following examples illustrate this use:

EXAMPLES

Ability to solve numerical problems
    Milk sells for $.26 a quart and $.88 a gallon. How many cents would you save on each quart of milk, if you bought it by the gallon? (4)

Skill in manipulating mathematical symbols

If $\dfrac{x}{b} = \dfrac{3}{b-1}$, then $x = \dfrac{(3b)}{(b-1)}$.

Ability to complete and balance chemical equations

$\underline{}\ Mg + \underline{(2)}\ HCl \to \underline{(MgCl_2 + H_2)}$
$\underline{(2)}\ Al + \underline{(6)}\ HCl \to \underline{(2AlCl_3 + 3H_2)}$

For outcomes similar to those indicated in these last examples, there is no adequate substitute for the short-answer item. The behavior described in the learning outcomes is identical to the behavior called forth by the test items. To obtain correct answers, pupils must actually solve problems, manipulate mathematical symbols, and complete and balance equations.

Attempts are sometimes made to measure such problem-solving activities with selection-type test items. This commonly results in test items which do not function as intended or which measure quite different learning outcomes. In the following multiple-choice items, for example, note how the division problem can be solved by working it backwards (multiplying 2×43, or merely 2×3), and how in the second problem the value of x can be determined by substituting each of the alternative answers in the equation on a trial-and-error basis. Such problems obviously do not call forth the problem-solving behavior we are attempting to measure.

EXAMPLES

$2\overline{)86} =$

A   41
B   42
Ⓒ   43
D   44

If $\dfrac{x}{4} + \dfrac{x}{16} = 10$, then x equals

A   16
B   24
Ⓒ   32
D   48

Similar difficulties are encountered when we substitute selection items measuring the ability to "recognize balanced chemical equations" for short-answer items measuring the ability to "complete and balance chemical equations." The former task is a simple one requiring little more than a knowledge of arithmetic, while the latter one requires rather extensive knowledge of chemical reactions and their resulting products.

In summary, if the short-answer test item is most effective for measuring a specific learning outcome, it should be used. We should not discard it for items of the selection type unless we are fairly certain that the same learning outcomes will be measured. For many of the simpler learning outcomes, such as knowledge of factual information, changing to some form of selection item will *not* decrease the validity of the measurement and *will* result in increased objectivity and ease of scoring. For some of the more complex learning outcomes such as in mathematics and science, however, discarding the short-answer test item may mean a change in the learning outcomes being measured. In deciding whether to use short-answer items or some other item type, our best guide is the following general principle: *Each learning outcome should be measured as directly as possible and the test item type which is most appropriate for that purpose should be selected for use.*

Advantages and Limitations of Short-Answer Items

The short-answer test item is one of the easiest to construct. This is partly due to the relatively simple learning outcomes usually measured with this type of item. Except for the problem-solving outcomes measured in mathematics and science, the short-answer item is used almost exclusively to measure the recall of memorized information.

A more important advantage of the short-answer item arises out of the fact that the pupil must supply the answer. This reduces the possibility that the pupil will get the correct answer by guessing. He must either recall the information requested or make the necessary computations to solve the problem presented to him. Partial knowledge, which might enable him to choose the correct answer on a selection item, is insufficient for answering a short-answer test item correctly.

There are two major limitations which restrict the use of the short-answer test item. One—unsuitability for measuring complex learning outcomes—has already been mentioned. The other has to do with the difficulty of scoring. Unless the question is very carefully phrased, a variety of answers of varying degrees of correctness must be considered for total or partial credit. For example, a question such as "Where was George Washington born?" could result in the name of the city, county, state, region, or continent. Although the teacher had the name of the state in mind when he wrote the question, he could not dismiss the other answers as incorrect. Even when this problem is avoided, the scoring is contaminated by the pupil's spelling ability. If full or partial credit is taken off for misspelled words, the pupils' test scores reflect varying degrees of knowledge and spelling skill. If spelling is not counted in the scoring, the teacher must still decide whether misspelled words actually represent the correct answer. We are all familiar with misspellings that are so bad that it is difficult to determine what the pupil had in mind. These complications make scoring more time consuming and less objective than that obtained with selection-type items.

The limitations discussed above are less troublesome when the answer is to be expressed in numbers or symbols, as in problem solving in physical science and mathematics. Here, more complex learning outcomes can be measured, spelling is not a problem, and it is usually easier to write test items to which there is only one correct response.

Suggestions for Constructing Short-Answer Items

The short-answer item is subject to a variety of defects, despite the fact that it is considered one of the easiest to construct. The following suggestions will aid in avoiding possible pitfalls and will provide greater assurance that the items will function as intended.

1. *Word the item so that the required answer is both brief and definite.* As indicated earlier the answer to an item should be a word, phrase, num-

ber, or symbol. This can be easily conveyed to the pupils through the directions at the beginning of the test and by proper phrasing of the question. More difficult is the stating of the question so that only one answer is correct.

EXAMPLES

Poor: An animal that eats the flesh of other animals is (carnivorous).
Better: An animal that eats the flesh of other animals is classified as (carnivorous).

The first version of this test item is so indefinite that it could be completed with answers such as "the wolf," "a meat eater," or even "hungry." Asking the pupils to classify this type of animal, as called for in the improved version, provides a more definite structure to the problem and makes clear the type of response required.

2. *Do not take statements directly from textbooks to use as a basis for short-answer items.* When taken out of context, textbook statements are frequently too general and ambiguous to serve as good short-answer items. Note the vagueness of the first version of the following test item, which was taken verbatim from a chemistry textbook:

EXAMPLES

Poor: Chlorine is a (halogen).
Better: Chlorine belongs to a group of elements that combine with metals to form salt. It is therefore called a (halogen).

Pupils would most-likely respond to the first version of this test item with the word "gas," since that is the natural state of chlorine and there is nothing in the statement to imply that the word "halogen" is wanted. The only pupils who would be apt to supply the intended answer would be those who had memorized textbook statements. The revised version measures an important knowledge which does not depend on the specific phraseology of any particular textbook. Such items tend to discourage the pupils from developing little understood verbal associations based on textbook language and encourages them to achieve the learning outcomes being measured.

3. *A direct question is generally more desirable than an incomplete statement.* There are two advantages to the direct-question form. First, it is more natural to the pupils, since this is the usual method of phrasing questions in daily classroom discussions. This is especially important to elementary pupils when first exposed to short-answer tests. Second, the direct question usually provides greater structure to the situation and prevents much of the ambiguity that creeps into items based on incomplete statements. Just the phrasing of a question seems to require us to clarify what it is we precisely want to know.

Poor: John Glenn made his first orbital flight around the earth in (1962).

Better: When did John Glenn make his first orbital flight around the earth? (1962).

Best: In what year did John Glenn make his first orbital flight around the earth? (1962).

The first version of the item could, of course, be completed with "a space capsule," "Friendship Seven," "space," and similar answers. Putting it in question form forces us to indicate whether it is the time, place, or method we are interested in knowing. The last version is merely a refinement which makes the question even more specific and which naturally evolves from a consideration of the "when" aspect of the previous question.

4. *Where the answer is to be expressed in numerical units, indicate the type of answer wanted.* For computational problems, it is usually preferable to indicate the units in which the answer is to be expressed. This will clarify the problem to the pupil and will simplify the scoring.

Poor: If oranges weigh 5⅔ oz. each, how much would a dozen oranges weigh? Answer: (4 lb. 4 oz.)

Better: If oranges weigh 5⅔ oz. each, how much would a dozen oranges weigh? Answer (4) lb. (4) oz.

Unless the type of unit is specified, as in the revised version, correct answers will include 68 oz., 4¼ lbs., 4.25 lbs., and 4 lbs. and 4 oz. This adds unnecessary confusion to the scoring.

Where problems do not come out even, it is also usually desirable to indicate the degree of precision expected in the answers. For example, specifying that the answers should be "carried out to two decimal places" or "rounded off to the nearest tenth of a per cent" makes clear to the pupil how far to carry his calculations. This will provide assurance that he reaches the degree of precision desired and by the same token it will prevent him from wasting valuable testing time attempting to achieve a degree of precision that is not expected.

There are some instances, especially in the area of science, when knowing the proper unit in which the answer is to be expressed and knowing the degree of precision to be expected are important aspects of the learning outcome to be measured. In such cases, the previous suggestions must, of course, be modified.

5. *Blanks for answers should be equal in length and in a column to the right of the question.* If blanks for answers are kept equal in length, the length of the blank space does not supply a clue to the answer. In the

poor version of the following items, note how the length of the blank restricts the possible answers a pupil need consider. For the first item he needs a long word and for the second item a short one.

EXAMPLES

Poor: What is the name of the part of speech that connects words, clauses, and sentences? (conjunction)
What is the name of the part of speech that declares, asserts, or predicts something? (verb)

Better: What is the name of the part of speech that
connects words, clauses, and sentences?   (conjunction)
What is the name of the part of speech that
declares, asserts, or predicts something?   (verb)

Placing the blanks in a column to the right of the question, as shown in the improved version, makes scoring quicker and more accurate.

6. Where completion items are used do not use too many blanks. If a statement is overmutilated the meaning will be lost, and the pupil usually must resort to guessing what the teacher had in mind. Although some mutilated statements seem to measure rather complex reasoning abilities, such responses are more appropriate as measures of intelligence than achievement.

EXAMPLES

Poor: (Warm-blooded) animals that are born (alive) and (suckle) their young are called (mammals).

Better: Warm-blooded animals that are born alive
and suckle their young are called   (mammals).

In the revised version of the above item, note also that the blank is at the end of the statement. This is a desirable practice, since the pupil is presented with a clearly defined problem before he comes to the blank.

TRUE-FALSE OR ALTERNATIVE-RESPONSE ITEMS

The alternative-response test item consists of a declarative statement that the pupil is asked to mark true or false, right or wrong, correct or incorrect, yes or no, fact or opinion, agree or disagree, and the like. In each case there are only two possible answers. Since the true-false option is the most common, this item type is frequently referred to as simply the true-false test item. Some of the variations, however, deviate considerably from the simple true-false pattern and have their own distinct characteristics. For this reason, the more general category, *alternative-response* item, is preferred.

Uses of Alternative-Response Items

Probably the most common use of the alternative-response item is in measuring the *ability to identify the correctness of statements of fact, definitions of terms, statements of principles, and the like.* For measuring such relatively simple learning outcomes, a single declarative statement is used with any one of several methods of responding.

EXAMPLES

Directions: Read each of the following statements. If the statement is true, circle the "T." If the statement is false, circle the "F."

Ⓣ F   1. The green coloring material in a plant leaf is called chlorophyll.
T Ⓕ   2. The corolla of a flower includes petals and sepals.
Ⓣ F   3. Photosynthesis is the process by which leaves make the food for a plant.

Directions: Read each of the following questions. If the answer is yes, circle the "Y." If the answer is no, circle the "N."

Ⓨ N   1. Is 51% of 38 more than 19?
Y Ⓝ   2. Is 50% of 4/10 equal to 2/5?
Y Ⓝ   3. If 60% of a number is 9, is the number smaller than 9?
Ⓨ N   4. Is 25% of 44 less than 12?

One of the most useful functions of the alternative-response item is in measuring the pupil's *ability to distinguish fact from opinion.* The following examples illustrate this use:

EXAMPLES

Directions: Read each of the following statements. If the statement is a fact, circle the "F." If the statement is an opinion, circle the "O."

Ⓕ O   1. The Constitution of the United States is the highest law of our country.
F Ⓞ   2. The first amendment to the Constitution is the most important amendment.
Ⓕ O   3. The fifth amendment to the Constitution protects an individual from testifying against himself.
F Ⓞ   4. Other countries should adopt a constitution like that of the United States.

Directions: Read each of the following statements. If the statement is true, circle the "T." If the statement is false, circle the "F." If the statement is an opinion, circle "O."

Ⓣ F O   1. The earth is a planet.
T Ⓕ O   2. The earth revolves around the moon.
T F Ⓞ   3. There are *no* plants or animals on Mars.

The above items measure a learning outcome which is of importance in all subject-matter areas. If a person is to think critically about a topic, he must first be able to distinguish fact from opinion.

All too frequently true-false tests include numerous opinion statements to which the pupil is asked to respond merely true or false. This is extremely frustrating, since there is no objective basis for determining whether a statement of opinion is true or false. The pupil must usually guess what opinion the teacher holds and mark his answers accordingly. This, of curse, is undesirable from all standpoints—testing, teaching and learning. It is much better to have the pupil identify the statements of opinion as such. An alternative procedure is to attribute the opinion to some source. This makes it possible to mark the statements true or false and provides a good measure of *knowledge concerning the beliefs held by an individual, or the values supported by an organization or institution.*

EXAMPLES

Directions: Read each of the following statements. If the statement is true, circle the "T." If the statement is false, circle the "F."

T (F) 1. Franklin D. Roosevelt believed that labor unions interfered with the free enterprise system in the United States.

(T) F 2. The American Federation of Labor favors the closed shop.

T (F) 3. The Supreme Court of the United States would support the principle of equal but separate facilities for the education of different racial groups.

Items such as the preceding can become measures of aspects of *understanding*, if the opinion statements attributed to an individual, or group, are new to the pupil. The task then becomes one of interpreting the beliefs held by the individual, or group, and applying them to the new situation.

Another aspect of understanding that can be measured by the simple alternative-response item is the *ability to recognize cause-and-effect relationships*. This type of item usually contains two true propositions in one statement, and the pupil is to judge whether the relationship between them is true or false.

EXAMPLES

Directions: In each of the following statements, both parts of the statement are true. You are to decide if the second part explains *why* the first part is true. If it does, circle the "Yes." If it does not, circle the "No."

Yes (No) 1. Leaves are essential *because* parts of a tree   they shade the trunk of the tree.

Yes (No) 2. Whales are mammals *because*   they are large.

(Yes) No 3. Some plants do *not*   *because*   they get their food from other need sunlight   plants.

The alternative-response item can also be used to measure some *simple aspects of logic,* as illustrated by the following items:

Directions: Read each of the following statements. If the statement is true, circle the "T"; if it is false circle the "F." *Also,* if the converse of the statement is true, circle the "CT"; if the converse is false, circle the "CF." Be sure to give two answers for each statement.

Ⓣ   F   CT   ⊂ＣＦ⊃   1. All trees are plants.
T   Ⓕ   CT   ⊂ＣＦ⊃   2. All parasites are animals.
T   Ⓕ   ⊂ＣＴ⊃   CF   3. All eight-legged animals are spiders.
Ⓣ   F   ⊂ＣＴ⊃   CF   4. No spiders are insects.

A common criticism of the simple alternative-response type item is that a pupil may be able to recognize a false statement as incorrect but still not know what *is* correct. For example, when a pupil answers the following item as false, it does not indicate that he knows what negatively charged particles of electricity are called. All his answer tells us is that he knows they are *not* called neutrons. This is a rather crude measure of knowledge,

T Ⓕ Negatively charged particles of electricity are called neutrons.

because there is an inestimable number of things that negatively charged particles of electricity are *not* called. To overcome such difficulties, some teachers prefer to have the pupils change all false statements to true. When this is done, the part of the statement it is permissible to change should be indicated.

Directions: Read each of the following statements. If a statement is true, circle the "T." If a statement is false, circle the "F" *and* change the underlined word to make the statement true. Place the new word in the blank space after the "F."

T Ⓕ (electrons) ___ 1. Particles of negatively charged electricity are called neutrons.
Ⓣ F ___ 2. Mechanical energy is turned into electrical energy by means of the generator.
T Ⓕ (store) ___ 3. An electric condenser is used to generate electricity.

Unless the key words to be changed are indicated in the correction-type true-false item, pupils are liable to rewrite the entire statement. In addition to the increase in scoring difficulty, this frequently leads to true statements which deviate considerably from the original intent of the item.

Advantages and Limitations of Alternative-Response Items

The advantages attributed to alternative-response items are not, unfortunately, very valid. One advantage cited most frequently is ease of construction. This has probably resulted from the all-too-common practice of taking statements from textbooks, changing half of them to false statements, and submitting the product to pupils as a true-false test. Such test items are frequently so obvious that everyone gets them correct or so ambiguous that even the better pupils are confused by them. In short, it is easy to construct *poor* alternative-response items. To construct unambiguous alternative-response items, which measure significant learning outcomes, however, requires an extremely high degree of skill.

A second advantage attributed to the alternative-response item, which is also more apparent than real, is that a wide sampling of course material can be obtained. Since a pupil can respond to many test items in a short period of time, it seems obvious that a large number of areas can be covered. Less obvious, however, is the fact that many types of subject matter do not lend themselves to alternative-response type items. True-false statements require course material that can be phrased in such a manner that the statements are true or false without qualification or exception. In all subject-matter fields there are areas in which such absolutely true or false statements cannot be made. In some fields, such as the social sciences, practically all significant statements require some qualification. Only the most trivial statements can be reduced to absolute terms.

One of the most serious limitations of the simple alternative-response item is in the types of learning outcomes that can be measured. As with the short-answer item, it is limited to the more elementary learning outcomes in the knowledge area. The main exceptions to this seem to be in distinguishing between fact and opinion, and in identifying cause-and-effect relationships. These two outcomes are probably the most important measured by this type of item. Most of the knowledge outcomes measured by the alternative-response item can be measured more effectively by other forms of selected items, especially the multiple-choice form.

Another factor which limits the usefulness of the alternative-response is its susceptibility to guessing. With only two alternatives, a pupil has a 50–50 opportunity of selecting the correct answer on the basis of chance alone. Due to the difficulty of constructing items which do *not* contain clues to the answer, the pupil's chances of guessing correctly are usually much greater than 50 per cent. With a typical 100-item true-false test, it is not unusual to have the lowest score somewhere above 80. Although an indeterminate amount of knowledge is reflected in such a score, many of the correct answers, beyond chance, can be accounted for by correct guesses guided by various clues that have been overlooked in constructing the items. A scoring formula utilizing a correction for guessing is frequently suggested as a solution for this problem. This formula takes into account only chance guesses, however, and does not include those guided by clues. In addition, such a scoring formula favors the aggressive individual willing to take a chance. When warned that there will be a penalty for guessing, he will continue to guess, using any clues available, and will do better than chance. The cautious student, on the other hand, will mark only those answers he is certain are correct and will omit many of the items he could mark correctly on the basis of clues and partial information. Thus, the scores tend to reflect personality differences as well as knowledge of the subject.

The high likelihood of successful guessing on the alternative-response item has a number of deleterious effects. (1) The reliability of each item is low, making it necessary to include a large number of items to obtain a reliable measure of achievement. (2) The diagnostic value of such a test is practically nil, since analyzing a pupil's response to each item is meaningless. (3) The validity of pupils' responses is questionable because of response sets. As noted earlier, a response set is a consistent tendency to follow a certain pattern in responding to test items. In taking a true-false test, for example, some pupils will consistently mark "true" those items they don't know while others will consistently mark them "false." Thus, any given test will favor one response set over another and introduce an element into the test score which is irrelevant to the purpose of the test.

The limitations of the simple alternative-response item are so serious that it would seem wise to use this item type only when other items are inappropriate for measuring the desired learning outcomes. This would include situations where there are only two possible alternatives (e.g., "right," "left"; "more," "less"; "who," "whom"; and so on) and special uses such as distinguishing fact from opinion, cause from effect, superstition from scientific belief, relevant from nonrelevant information, valid from invalid conclusions, and the like.

Suggestions for Constructing Alternative-Response Items

The main task in constructing alternative-response items, such as the true-false type, is that of formulating statements which are free from ambiguity and irrelevant clues. This is an extremely difficult task and the only guidance that can be given is of a negative sort—that is, a list of things to avoid when phrasing the statements.

1. *Avoid broad general statements, if they are to be judged true or false.* Most broad generalizations are false unless qualified, and the use of qualifiers provides clues to the answer.

Poor: T   (F)   The President of the United States is elected to that office.
Poor: (T)   F   The President of the United States is usually elected to that office.

In this example, the first version is generally true but must be marked false because there are exceptions, such as the Vice-President taking office in event of the President's death. In the second version, the qualifier "usually" makes the statement true but provides a definite clue. Words such as "usually," "generally," "often," and "sometimes," are most likely to appear in true statements, and absolute terms such as "always," "never," "all," "none," and "only" are more apt to appear in false statements. Although the influence of such clues sometimes can be offset by balancing their use in true-false statements, the simplest solution seems to be to avoid the use of broad generalizations which are obviously false or must be qualified by the use of these specific determiners.

2. *Avoid trivial statements.* In an attempt to obtain statements which are unequivocally true or false, we sometimes inadvertently turn to specific statements of fact which fit this criterion beautifully but which have little significance from a learning standpoint.

Poor: (T)   F   Harry S. Truman was the 33rd President of the United States.
Poor: T   (F)   The United States declared war on Japan, December 7, 1941.

The first item calls for a relatively unimportant fact concerning Truman's tenure as President. The second item expects the student to remember that the United States did not declare war until December 8. Such items cause students to direct their attention toward the memorization of minutiae at the expense of more general knowledge and understanding.

3. *Avoid the use of negative statements, and especially double negatives.* Negative words, such as "no" or "not," tend to be overlooked by pupils and double negatives contribute to the ambiguity of the statement. Note the ambiguity in the relatively simple statement, using two negatives, which follows:

Poor: (T)   F   None of the steps in the experiment was unnecessary.
Better: (T)   F   All of the steps in the experiment were necessary.

Where it is imperative that a negative word be used, it should be underlined or put in italics so that pupils do *not* overlook it.

4. *Avoid long, complex sentences.* As noted earlier, a test item should indicate whether a pupil has achieved the knowledge or understanding

being measured. Long, complex sentences tend to also measure the extraneous factor of reading comprehension and therefore should be avoided in tests to measure achievement.

Poor: Ⓣ F   Despite the theoretical and experimental difficulties of determining the exact *pH* value of a solution, it is possible to determine if a solution is acid by the red color formed on litmus paper when it is inserted into the solution.

Better: Ⓣ F   Litmus paper turns red in an acid solution.

As in the preceding example, it is frequently possible to shorten and simplify a statement by eliminating nonfunctional material and restating the main idea. Where this is not possible, it might be necessary to change to another item form in order to avoid complex sentence structure.

5. *Avoid including two ideas in one statement, unless cause-effect relationships are being measured.* Some difficulties arising from the inclusion of two ideas in one statement are apparent in the following example. This is one of many items of similar type a teacher actually used in a biology examination. In each instance, he asked the pupils to merely judge whether the statement was true or false.

Poor: T Ⓕ   A worm cannot see because it has simple eyes.

This item is keyed "false" because a worm does *not* have simple eyes. However, when this teacher asked one of his slow learners why he marked it false, the pupil said, "Worms can too see." This of course highlights the fact that pupils can get such items correct with misinformation of the most erroneous sort. This is so because the first proposition can be true or false, the second proposition can be true or false, and the relationship between them can be true or false. Thus, when a pupil marks the item false, there is no way of determining which of the three elements he is responding to. The best solution to this dilemma seems to be to use only true propositions and to ask the pupils to judge the truth or falsity of the relationship between them. Such items might, of course, also be divided into two simple statements, each containing a single idea.

6. *If opinion is used, attribute it to some source, unless the ability to identify opinion is being specifically measured.* As pointed out earlier, statements of opinion cannot be marked true or false, and it is unfair to expect pupils to guess how the teacher will score such items. It is, of course, also poor teaching practice to expect pupils to respond to opinion statements as statements of fact. Knowing whether some significant individual or group supports or refutes a certain opinion, however, can have significance from a learning standpoint.

Poor: T   F   Adequate medical care can best be provided through socialized medicine.

Better: T   Ⓕ   The American Medical Association favors socialized medicine as the best means of providing adequate medical care.

The first version, in this example, may serve a useful purpose in an attitude test, but there is no factual basis on which to decide the truth or falsity of the statement. The second version is clearly false.

7. *True statements and false statements should be approximately equal in length.* There is a natural tendency for true statements to be longer because such statements must be precisely phrased to meet the criterion of absolute truth. This can be overcome by lengthening the false statements through the use of qualifying phrases similar to those found in true statements. This will eliminate length of statement as a possible clue to the correct answer.

8. *The number of true statements and false statements should be approximately equal.* Constructing a test with the number of true statements and false statements approximately equal will prevent response sets from unduly inflating or deflating the pupils' scores. You will recall that some pupils have a consistent tendency to mark "true" when in doubt about an answer, while others have a consistent tendency to mark "false." Neither response set should be favored by overloading the test with items of one type.

In honoring this suggestion the words "approximately equal" should be given special attention. If a teacher consistently uses "exactly" the same number, this will provide a clue to the pupil who is unable to answer some of the test items. The best procedure seems to be to vary the percentage of true statements somewhere between 40 and 60 per cent. Under no circumstance should the statements be all true or all false. Pupils who detect this as a possibility can obtain perfect scores on the basis of one guess.

MATCHING EXERCISES

In its traditional form, the matching exercise consists of two parallel columns with each word, number, or symbol in one column being matched to a word, sentence, or phrase in the other column. The items in the column for which a match is sought are called *premises* and the items in the column from which the selection is made are called *responses*. The basis for matching responses to premises is sometimes self-evident but more frequently must be explained in the directions. In any event, the pupil's task is to identify the pairs of items that are to be associated on the basis indicated. For example, the pupil may be asked to identify important historical events, as in the following illustration:

EXAMPLES

Directions: On the line to the left of each United States space event in *Column A,* write the letter of the astronaut in *Column B* who achieved that honor. Each name in Column B may be used once, more than once, or not at all.

	Column A		*Column B*
(G)	1. First United States astronaut to ride in a space capsule	A	Edwin Aldrin
(E)	2. First United States astronaut to orbit the earth	B	Neil Armstrong
(H)	3. First United States astronaut to walk in space	C	Frank Borman
(B)	4. First United States astronaut to step on the moon	D	Scott Carpenter
		E	John Glenn
		F	Wally Schirra
		G	Alan Shepard
		H	Edward White

This matching exercise illustrates an *imperfect match,* that is, there are more terms in *Column B* than are needed to match each phrase in *Column A.* The directions also indicate that an item may be used once, more than once, or not at all. Both of these procedures prevent pupils from matching the final pair of items on the basis of elimination.

Two other factors are notable in our example. First, the items in the list of premises in *Column A* are homogeneous. They are all concerned with important space events. Such homogeneity is necessary if a matching exercise is to function properly. Second, for each premise in *Column A* there are several plausible responses in *Column B.* Thus, the incorrect responses serve as attractive choices for those pupils who are in doubt about the correct answers. Both this homogeneity of the material and this plausibility of responses tend to minimize the opportunity for successful guessing.

Uses of Matching Exercises

The typical matching exercise is limited to the measurement of factual information based on simple associations. Wherever learning outcomes emphasize the *ability to identify the relationship between two things,* and a sufficient number of homogeneous premises and responses can be obtained, a matching exercise seems most appropriate. It is a compact and efficient method of measuring such simple knowledge outcomes. Examples of relationships considered important by teachers, in a variety of fields, include the following:

Men	Achievements
Dates	Historical Events
Terms	Definitions
Rules	Examples
Symbols	Concepts
Authors	Titles of Books
Foreign Words	English Equivalents
Machines	Uses
Plants or Animals	Classification
Principles	Illustrations
Objects	Names of Objects
Parts	Functions

The matching exercise has also been used with pictorial materials in relating pictures and words and in identifying positions on maps, charts, and diagrams. Regardless of the form of presentation, however, the pupil's task is essentially that of relating two things which have some logical basis for association. This restricts the use of the matching exercise to a relatively small area of pupil achievement.

Advantages and Limitations of Matching Exercises

The major advantage of the matching exercise is its compact form, which makes it possible to measure a large amount of related factual material in a relatively short time. This is a mixed blessing, however, since it frequently leads to the excessive use of matching exercises and a corresponding overemphasis on the memorization of simple relationships.

Another advantage frequently cited for the matching exercise is ease of construction. As with the alternative-response item, poor items can be rapidly constructed, but good items require a high degree of skill. Much of the difficulty arises from the fact that the correct response for each premise must also serve as a plausible response for the other premises. Any lack of plausibility will reduce the number of possible choices and provide clues to the correct answer. The matching exercise tends to have more such irrelevant clues than any other item type, with the possible exception of the true-false item.

The main limitations of the matching exercise have already been indicated. It is restricted to the measurement of factual information based on rote memorization, and it is highly susceptible to the presence of irrelevant clues. Another factor, somewhat related, should also be mentioned. This is the difficulty of finding homogeneous material which is significant from the viewpoint of our objectives and learning outcomes. For example, we might start out with a few great scientists and their achievements, which we feel all pupils should know. In order to construct a matching item, it becomes necessary to add the names and achievements of other, lesser known, scientists. Thus we find ourselves measuring factual information which was not included in our original test plan and which is far less important than other aspects of knowledge we had intended to include. In short, less significant material is introduced into the test because significant material of a homogeneous nature is unavailable. This is a common problem in constructing matching exercises and one not easily avoided. One solution is to begin with multiple-choice items, where each item can be directly related to a particular outcome, and switch to the matching form only when homogeneous material makes the matching exercise a more efficient method of measuring the same achievement.

Suggestions for Constructing Matching Exercises

Although the matching exercise has limited usefulness in classroom tests, whenever it is used special efforts should be made to remove irrelevant clues and to arrange it in such a manner that the pupil can respond quickly and without confusion. The following suggestions are designed to guide such efforts:

1. *Use only homogeneous material in a single matching exercise.* This has been mentioned before and is repeated here for emphasis. It is without a doubt the most important rule of construction and yet the one most commonly violated. One reason for this is that homogeneity is a matter of degree and what is homogeneous to one group may be heterogeneous to another. For example, let us assume that we are following the usual suggestion for obtaining homogeneity and develop a matching exercise which includes *only* men and their achievements. We might end up with a test exercise similar to the following one:

EXAMPLES

Directions: On the line to the left of each achievement listed in *Column A*, write the letter of the man's name in *Column B* who is noted for that achievement. Each name in *Column B* may be used once, more than once, or not at all.

	Column A		*Column B*
(A)	1. Invented the telephone	A	Alexander Graham Bell
(B)	2. Discovered America	B	Christopher Columbus
		C	John Glenn
(C)	3. First United States astronaut to orbit the earth	D	Abraham Lincoln
		E	Ferdinand Magellan
		F	George Washington
(F)	4. First President of the United States	G	Eli Whitney

Although the matching exercise in our example may be homogeneous for most pupils in the primary grades, the discriminations called for are so gross that pupils above that level see it as a heterogeneous collection of inventors, explorers, and presidents. Thus, to obtain homogeneity at higher grade levels, it would be necessary to have only inventors and their inventions in one matching exercise, explorers and their discoveries in another, and presidents and their achievements in another. At a still higher level, it might be necessary to limit matching exercises still further, such as to inventors whose inventions are in the same specific area, in order to keep the material homogeneous and free from irrelevant clues. It should be noted that as we increase the level of discrimination called for in a matching exercise, homogeneous material of a significant nature becomes increasingly difficult to obtain. Take the inventors for example. How many significant inventions are there in any one specific area?

2. *Include an unequal number of responses and premises, and instruct the pupil that responses may be used once, more than once, or not at all.* This will make all of the responses eligible for selection for each premise and will decrease the likelihood of successful guessing. When an equal number of responses and premises are used and each response is used only once, the probability for guessing the remaining responses correctly is increased each time a correct answer is selected. Odds for correct guessing increase as the list of available responses decreases, and the final response, of course, can be selected entirely on the basis of this process of elimination.

With the typical matching exercise, imperfect matching can be obtained by including a few more, or a few less, responses than premises. In either case, the directions should instruct the pupil that each response may be used once, more than once, or not at all.

3. *Keep the list of items to be matched brief and place the shorter responses on the right.* A brief list of items is advantageous to both the teacher and the pupil. From the teacher's standpoint, it is easier to maintain homogeneity in a brief list. In addition, there is a greater likelihood that the various learning outcomes and subject-matter topics will be measured in a balanced manner. Since each matching exercise must be based on homogeneous material, a long list requires excessive concentration in one area. From the pupil's viewpoint, a brief list enables him to read the response rapidly and without confusion. Approximately four to seven items in each column seems preferable. There certainly should be no more than ten in either column.

Placing the shorter items on the right, as responses, also contributes to more efficient test taking. This enables the pupil to read the longer premise first and then to scan rapidly the list of responses.

4. *Arrange the list of responses in logical order.* Place words in alphabetical order and numbers in sequence. This will contribute to the ease with which the pupil can scan the responses in searching for the correct

answers. It will also prevent the pupil from detecting possible clues due to the arrangement of the responses.

EXAMPLES

Directions: On the line to the left of each historical event in *Column A,* write the letter from *Column B* which identifies the time period during which the event occurred. Each date in *Column B* may be used once, more than once, or not at all.

Column A		*Column B*	
(B)	1. Boston Tea Party	A	1765–1769
(A)	2. Repeal of the Stamp Act	B	1770–1774
(E)	3. Enactment of the Northwest Ordinance	C	1775–1779
(C)	4. Battle of Lexington	D	1780–1784
(A)	5. Enactment of Townshend Acts	E	1785–1789
(B)	6. First Continental Congress		
(E)	7. United States Constitution drawn up		

This matching exercise also illustrates the use of *fewer* responses than premises and the desirability of placing the shortest items on the right.

5. *Indicate in the directions the basis for matching the responses and premises.* Although the basis for matching is rather obvious in most matching exercises, there are advantages in clearly stating the intended basis. For one thing, ambiguity and confusion will be avoided. For another, testing time will be saved, since the pupil will not need to read through the entire list of premises and responses and then "reason out" the basis for matching.

Special care must be taken when stating directions for matching items. Directions which precisely indicate the basis for matching frequently become long and involved, placing a premium on reading comprehension. For younger pupils, it may be desirable to give oral directions, put an example on the blackboard, and have pupils draw lines between the matched items rather than transfer letters.

6. *Place all of the items for one matching exercise on the same page.* This will prevent the disturbance created by thirty or so pupils switching the pages of the test back and forth. It also prevents pupils from overlooking the responses appearing on another page and generally adds to the speed and efficiency of test administration.

SUMMARY

The construction of classroom tests, like other phases of teaching, is an art which must be learned. It is not automatically derived from a knowledge of subject matter, a formulation of the learning outcomes to be achieved, or a psychological understanding of the mental processes of pupils, although all of these are basic prerequisites. The ability to construct high quality test items requires, in addition, a knowledge of the principles and techniques of test construction and skill in their application.

In this chapter techniques for constructing short-answer items, true-false or alternative-response items, and matching exercises have been considered. These simple forms of objective test items are restricted, almost entirely, to the measurement of knowledge outcomes. They are generally unsuitable for measuring understandings, thinking skills, and other complex types of achievement.

The short-answer item requires pupils to supply the appropriate word, number, or symbol to a direct question or incomplete statement. It can be used for measuring a variety of simple knowledge outcomes but it is especially useful for measuring problem-solving ability in science and mathematics. The ease with which short-answer items can be constructed and their relative freedom from guessing favors their use. However, the areas in which they can be effectively used are restricted by the relatively simple learning outcomes measured and by the fact that the scoring is contaminated by spelling errors of varying degrees of magnitude. Where short-answer items are used, the question must be stated clearly and concisely, be free from irrelevant clues, and require an answer which is both brief and definite. Problems requiring only a number or a symbol for an answer are particularly adaptable to the short-answer form.

The alternative-response item requires the pupil to select one of two possible answers. The most common form is the true-false item but there are numerous variations. This item type is used for measuring simple knowledge outcomes where only two alternatives are possible, or where the ability to identify the correctness of statements of fact is important. It is also adaptable to measuring the ability to distinguish fact from opinion and the ability to recognize cause-and-effect relationships. The difficulty of constructing items free from clues, which measure significant learning outcomes; the susceptibility of this type to guessing; the low reliability of each item; and the general lack of diagnostic value severely limits its use. It might well be restricted to those areas where other item types are inappropriate. When used, special efforts must be made to formulate statements which are free from ambiguity, specific determiners, and clues of various types.

The matching exercises consists of two parallel columns of phrases, words, numbers, or symbols which must be matched on some basis. Examples of items included in matching exercises are men and achievements, dates and historical events, terms and definitions, and the like. The nature of the matching exercise limits it to measuring the ability to identify the relationship between two things. For this restricted use, it is a compact item type which can be used to measure a large number of relationships in a short time. Its limitations include the difficulty of removing irrelevant clues and the difficulty of finding homogeneous material of a significant nature. Where homogeneous material is available, including more items in one column than the other, arranging the shorter responses on the right and in logical order, and indicating clearly the basis for matching will all contribute to the effectiveness of the matching exercise.

LEARNING EXERCISES

1. Defend the statement, "Short-answer items should *not* be classified as objective items."
2. Criticize each of the following short-answer items. How would you improve each item?
   a. When you fly from Chicago to New York, you see _____, _____, and _____.
   b. Gravity causes water to flow _____.
   c. The largest city in California is _____ and its population is _____.
   d. _____ exists at room temperature as a _____ substance.
   e. The reliability of test results can be indicated by a coefficient of _____.
3. Criticize each of the following true-false items. How would you improve each statement?
   a. There are three reasons for buying life insurance.
   b. Alcoholics are persons who drink excessively.
   c. Camping is fun for the whole family.
   d. Parasites may provide a useful function.
   e. Correction-for-guessing on an objective test is not a procedure that should never be used.
   f. True-false statements are frequently ambiguous.
4. Why should asking pupils to mark the following statement true or false be poor testing practice? "All trees are plants because they are large."
5. Under what conditions would it be preferable to use a matching exercise, rather than some other item type? What are some of the common errors in constructing matching items?
6. In an area in which you are teaching or plan to teach, construct one short-answer item for each of the following:
   a. Knowledge of a specific term.
   b. Knowledge of a specific fact.
   c. Knowledge of a principle.
   d. Knowledge of a method or procedure.
7. Construct one true-false item for each of the outcomes listed in the previous item.
8. Construct a matching item in which all of the responses are plausible choices for each premise, and all responses are used more than once.

SUGGESTIONS FOR FURTHER READING

EBEL, R. L. *Essentials of Educational Measurement.* Englewood Cliffs, N.J.: Prentice-Hall, Inc., 1972. Chapter 7, "True-False Items." This author thinks more highly of true-false items than most other test specialists. He makes a strong case for true-false items and describes and illustrates how to construct them.

STANLEY, J. C., and K. D. HOPKINS. *Educational and Psychological Measurement and Evaluation.* Englewood Cliffs, N.J.: Prentice-Hall, Inc., 1972. Chapter 10, "Constructing Specific Types of Objective Tests." Presents practical suggestions for the construction of all of the various item types.

STOREY, A. G. *The Measurement of Classroom Learning.* Chicago: Science Research Associates, Inc., 1970. Chapter 5, "Objective Item Types." Describes the construction of the various item types and makes a strong case against the use of true-false items.

WESMAN, A. G. "Writing the Test Item," Chapter 4 in R. L. Thorndike (ed.), *Educational Measurement.* Washington, D.C.: American Council on Education, 1971. Provides general suggestions for item writing and specific rules for constructing each of the item types. A comprehensive treatment.

CHAPTER 8
Contsructing Objective Test Items: Multiple-Choice Form

Objective test items are *not* limited to the measurement of simple learning outcomes. . . . The multiple-choice item can measure at both the knowledge and understanding levels. . . . It is also free of many of the limitations of other forms of objective items.

The multiple-choice item is generally recognized as the most widely applicable and useful type of objective test item. It can more effectively measure many of the simple learning outcomes measured by the short-answer item, the alternative-response item, and the matching exercise. In addition, it can measure a variety of the more complex outcomes in the knowledge, understanding and application areas. This flexibility, plus the higher quality of the items usually attained with the multiple-choice form, has led to its extensive use in achievement testing.

CHARACTERISTICS OF MULTIPLE-CHOICE ITEMS

A multiple-choice item consists of a problem and a list of suggested solutions. The problem may be stated in the form of a direct question or an incomplete statement and is called the *stem* of the item. The list of suggested solutions may include words, numbers, symbols, or phrases and are called *alternatives*. The pupil is typically requested to read the stem and the list of alternatives and to select the one correct, or best, alternative. The correct alternative in each item is called merely the *answer*, while the remaining alternatives are called *distracters*. These incorrect alternatives receive their name from their intended function—to distract those pupils who are in doubt about the correct answer.

Whether to use a direct question or incomplete statement in the stem depends on several factors. The direct-question form is easier to write, is more natural for younger pupils, and is more likely to present a clearly formulated problem. On the other hand, the incomplete statement is more concise, and if skillfully phrased, it too can present a well-defined problem. A common procedure is to start each stem as a direct question, shifting to the incomplete statement form *only* when the clarity of the problem can be retained and greater conciseness achieved.

EXAMPLES

Direct-question form:
In which one of the following cities is the capital of California located?
    A   Los Angeles
    Ⓑ   Sacramento
    C   San Diego
    D   San Francisco
Incomplete-statement form:
The capital of California is located in
    A   Los Angeles.
    Ⓑ   Sacramento.
    C   San Diego.
    D   San Francisco.

In these examples, there is one absolutely correct answer. The capital of California is located in Sacramento and nowhere else. All other alternatives are clearly wrong. For obvious reasons, this is known as the *correct-answer* type of multiple-choice item.

Not all knowledge can be stated in such precise terms that there is only one absolutely correct response. In fact, when we get beyond the simple aspects of knowledge, represented by questions of the who, what, when, and where variety, answers of varying degrees of acceptability are the rule rather than the exception. Questions of the *why* variety, for example, tend to reveal a number of possible reasons, some of which are clearly better than the others. Likewise, questions of the *how* variety usually reveal several possible procedures, some of which are clearly more desirable than the others. Measures of achievement in these areas, then, become a matter of selecting the *best answer,* as the following illustrates:

EXAMPLES

Best-answer type:
Which one of the following factors contributed most to the selection of Sacramento as the capital of California?
    Ⓐ   Central location
    B   Good climate
    C   Good highways
    D   Large population

(or)

Which one of the following factors is given most consideration, when selecting a city for a state capital?

   (A) Location
   B   Climate
   C   Highways
   D   Population

What is the most important purpose of city zoning laws?

   A   Attract industry
   B   Encourage the building of apartments
   (C) Protect property values
   D   Provide school "safety zones"

The *best-answer* type of multiple-choice item tends to be more difficult than the *correct-answer* type. This is due partly to the finer discriminations called for and partly to the fact that such items are used to measure learning outcomes of a more complex nature. The best-answer type is especially useful for measuring learning outcomes that require the understanding, application, or interpretation of factual information.

USES OF MULTIPLE-CHOICE ITEMS

The multiple-choice item is the most versatile type of test item available. It can measure a variety of learning outcomes from the simple to the complex and it is adaptable to most types of subject-matter content.[1] It has such wide applicability and so many specific uses that many standardized tests use multiple-choice items exclusively.[2] It is obvious that all of the specific uses of the multiple-choice item cannot be illustrated. We shall confine ourselves, here, to its use in measuring some of the more typical learning outcomes in the knowledge, understanding, and application areas. The measurement of more complex outcomes, using modified forms of the multiple-choice item, will be considered in the following chapter.

Measuring Knowledge Outcomes

Learning outcomes in the knowledge area are so prominent in all school subjects and multiple-choice items can measure such a variety of these outcomes that illustrative examples are endless. Here, we shall present some of the more typical uses of the multiple-choice form in measuring knowledge outcomes common to most school subjects.

---

[1] N. E. Gronlund, *Constructing Achievement Tests* (Englewood Cliffs, N.J.: Prentice-Hall, 1968).

[2] This practice is not recommended for classroom testing. Despite the wide applicability of the multiple-choice item there are learning outcomes, such as the ability to organize and present ideas, that cannot be measured with any form of selection item.

Knowledge of Terminology. A simple but basic learning outcome measured by the multiple-choice item is that of knowledge of terminology. For this purpose, the pupil can be requested to show his knowledge of a particular term by selecting a word which has the same meaning as the given term or by selecting a definition of the term. Special uses of a term can also be measured, by having the pupil identify the meaning of the term when used in context.

EXAMPLES

Which one of the following words has the same meaning as the word *egress?*
    A   Depress
    B   Enter
    Ⓒ   Exit
    D   Regress
Which one of the following statements best defines the word *egress?*
    A   An expression of disapproval
    Ⓑ   An act of leaving an enclosed place
    C   Proceeding to a higher level
    D   Proceeding to a lower level
What is meant by the word *egress* in the following sentence: "The astronaut hopes he can now make a safe *egress*"?
    A   Separation from the rocket
    B   Reentry into the earth's atmosphere
    C   Landing on the water
    Ⓓ   Escape from the space capsule

Knowledge of Specific Facts. Another learning outcome basic to all school subjects is the knowledge of specific facts. It is important in its own right, and it provides a necessary basis for developing understandings, thinking skills, and other complex learning outcomes. Multiple-choice items designed to measure specific facts can take many different forms but questions of the *who, what, when,* and *where* variety are typical.

EXAMPLES

Who was the first United States astronaut to orbit the earth in space?
    A   Scott Carpenter
    Ⓑ   John Glenn
    C   Virgil Grissom
    D   Alan Shepard
What was the name of the missile which launched the first United States astronaut into orbital flight around the earth?
    Ⓐ   Atlas
    B   Mars
    C   Midas
    D   Polaris

When did a United States astronaut first orbit the earth in space?
    A   1960
    B   1961
    Ⓒ   1962
    D   1963

Where did the Friendship Seven capsule land after the first United States orbital flight around the earth?
    Ⓐ   Atlantic Ocean
    B   Caribbean Sea
    C   Gulf of Mexico
    D   Pacific Ocean

Knowledge of Principles. Knowledge of principles is also an important learning outcome in most school subjects. Multiple-choice items can be constructed to measure knowledge of principles as easily as those designed to measure knowledge of specific facts. The items appear a bit more difficult but this is because principles are more complex than isolated facts.

EXAMPLES

The principle of capillary action helps explain how fluids
    A   enter solutions of lower concentration.
    B   escape through small openings.
    C   pass through semipermeable membranes.
    Ⓓ   rise in fine tubes.

Which one of the following principles of taxation is characteristic of the federal income tax?
    A   The benefits received by an individual should determine the amount of his tax.
    Ⓑ   A tax should be based on an individual's ability to pay.
    C   All citizens should be required to pay the same amount of tax.
    D   The amount of tax an individual pays should be determined by the size of the federal budget.

Knowledge of Methods and Procedures. Another common learning outcome readily adaptable to the multiple-choice form is knowledge of methods and procedures. This includes such diverse areas as knowledge of laboratory procedures; knowledge of methods underlying communication, computational, and performance skills; knowledge of methods used in problem solving; knowledge of governmental procedures; and knowledge of common social practices. In some cases we might want to measure knowledge of procedures before we permit pupils to obtain practice in a particular area (e.g., laboratory procedures). In other cases, knowledge of methods and procedures may be important learning outcomes in their own right (e.g., knowledge of governmental procedures). The following test items illustrate a few of these uses in different school subjects:

EXAMPLES

Which one of the following methods of locating a specimen under the microscope is most desirable?

A   Start with coarse adjustment up and with eye at eyepiece turn down coarse adjustment.

(B)   Start with coarse adjustment down and with eye at eyepiece turn up coarse adjustment.

C   Start with coarse adjustment in center and with eye at eyepiece turn up and down until specimen is located.

To make treaties, the President of the United States must have the consent of the

A   Cabinet.

B   House of Representatives.

(C)   Senate.

D   Supreme Court.

Alternating electric current is changed to direct current by means of a

A   condenser.

B   generator.

(C)   rectifier.

D   transformer.

If you were making a scientific study of a problem, your first step should be the

(A)   collection of information about the problem.

B   development of hypotheses to be tested.

C   design of the experiment to be conducted.

D   selection of scientific equipment.

We have merely scratched the surface with our illustrative uses of multiple-choice items in the measurement of knowledge outcomes. As you develop items in the particular school subjects you teach, many other uses will occur to you.

Measuring Outcomes at the Understanding and Application Levels

Many teachers limit the use of multiple-choice items to the knowledge area because they believe that all objective-type items are restricted to the measurement of relatively simple learning outcomes. Although this is true of most of the other types of objective items, the multiple-choice item is especially adaptable to the measurement of more complex learning outcomes. The examples that follow illustrate its use in the measurement of various aspects of understanding and application.

In reviewing the following illustrative items, it is important to keep in mind that such items measure learning outcomes beyond that of factual knowledge *only if* the applications and interpretations are new to the pupils. Any specific applications or interpretations of knowledge can, of course, be taught directly to pupils as any other specific fact is taught. Where this is done and the test items contain the same problem situations and solutions used in teaching, it is obvious that the pupils can be given credit for no more than the mere retention of factual knowledge. To measure understanding and application an element of novelty must be included in the test items. For illustrative purposes, it is necessary to assume that such novelty exists in the examples that follow.

Ability to Apply Facts and Principles. A common method of determining if pupils' learning has gone beyond the mere memorization of a fact or principle is to ask them to identify its correct application in a situation which is new to the pupil.

EXAMPLES

Which one of the following is an example of a chemical *element?*
    A   Acid
    B   Sodium Chloride
    Ⓒ   Oxygen
    D   Water

Directions: In each of the following sentences circle the word that makes the sentence correct.

1. This is the boy ⟨who⟩ asked the question.
(that / who / whom)

2. This is the dog who he asked about.
(that / who / whom)

Which one of the following best illustrates the principle of capillarity?
    Ⓐ   Fluid is carried through the stems of plants.
    B   Food is manufactured in the leaves of plants.
    C   The leaves of deciduous plants lose their green color in winter.
    D   Plants give off moisture through their stomata.

Pascal's law can be used to explain the operation of
    A   electric fans.
    Ⓑ   hydraulic brakes.
    C   levers.
    D   syringes.

Which one of the following best illustrates the law of diminishing returns?
    A   The demand for a farm product increased faster than the supply of the product.
    B   The population of a country increased faster than the means of subsistence.
    C   A machine decreased in utility as its parts became worn.
    Ⓓ   A factory doubled its labor force and increased production 50 per cent.

Ability to Interpret Cause-and-Effect Relationships. Understanding can frequently be measured by asking pupils to interpret various relationships between facts. One of the most important relationships in this regard, and one common to most subject-matter areas, is the cause-and-effect relationship. Understanding of such relationships can be measured by presenting the pupil with a specific cause-and-effect relationship and asking him to identify the reason which best accounts for it.

Bread will not become moldy as rapidly if placed in a refrigerator because
   Ⓐ cooling retards the growth of fungi.
   B darkness retards the growth of mold.
   C cooling prevents the bread from drying out so rapidly.
   D mold requires both heat and light for best growth.
There is an increased quantity of carbon monoxide produced when fuel is burned in a limited supply of oxygen because
   A carbon reacts with carbon monoxide.
   Ⓑ carbon reacts with carbon dioxide.
   C carbon monoxide is an effective reducing agent.
   D greater oxidation takes place.
Investing money in common stock provides protection against loss of assets during inflation because common stock
   A pays higher rates of interest during inflation.
   B provides a steady but dependable income despite economic conditions.
   C is protected by the Federal Reserve System.
   Ⓓ increases in value as the value of a business increases.

Ability to Justify Methods and Procedures. Another phase of understanding that is important in various subject-matter areas is that concerned with methods and procedures. A pupil might know the correct method or the correct sequence of steps in carrying out a procedure, without being able to explain *why* it is the best method or sequence of steps. At the understanding level we are interested in the pupil's ability to justify the use of a particular method or procedure. This can be measured with multiple-choice items by presenting the pupil with several possible explanations of a method or procedure and asking him to select the best one.

Why is adequate lighting necessary in a balanced aquarium?
   A Fish need light to see their food.
   B Fish take in oxygen in the dark.
   Ⓒ Plants expel carbon dioxide in the dark.
   D Plants grow too rapidly in the dark.
Why do farmers rotate their crops?
   Ⓐ To conserve the soil
   B To make marketing easier
   C To provide for strip cropping
   D To provide more uniform working conditions throughout the year

Why is nickel used in the process of changing cottonseed oil to a solid fat?
  A It improves the texture and firmness.
  B It removes the nutlike odor.
  C It removes the brownish-yellow color.
  Ⓓ It speeds up the process.

Although various aspects of understanding and application can be measured by single multiple-choice items, as illustrated in the previous examples, a series of multiple-choice items based on a common set of data is even more adaptable to the measurement of complex achievement. Such items will be illustrated in the following chapter.

ADVANTAGES AND LIMITATIONS OF MULTIPLE-CHOICE ITEMS

The major advantage of the multiple-choice item has already been mentioned and illustrated. It is one of the most widely applicable test items for measuring achievement. While it can measure various types of knowledge effectively, it can also measure a variety of complex learning outcomes. In addition to this greater flexibility, it is free from some of the common shortcomings characteristic of the other item types. The ambiguity and vagueness which frequently are present in the short-answer item are avoided because the alternatives provide greater structure to the situation. In the following examples, taken from a test in driver education, note how the vague short-answer item becomes a clear-cut problem when put in multiple-choice form. The short-answer item could be answered in many different ways but the multiple-choice item restricts the pupil's response to a specific area.

EXAMPLES

Poor: Drinking alcohol generally results in increased _____.
Better: Drinking alcohol generally results in increased
        A alertness.
        B attention.
        Ⓒ confidence.
        D self-consciousness.

The need for homogeneous material which includes a series of related ideas, a factor causing the greatest difficulty in constructing matching items, is likewise avoided with the multiple-choice item. Since each item measures a single idea, it is possible to measure one or many relationships in any given area. Use of the best-answer type multiple-choice item also circumvents one of the main difficulties associated with the true-false item—that of obtaining statements which are true or false without qualification. This makes it possible to measure learning outcomes in the numerous subject-matter areas where solutions to problems are not clearly true or false but vary in degree of appropriateness. Another advantage of the multiple-choice item over the true-false item is the greater reliability per item. Because the number of alternatives is increased from two to four or five the opportunity for guessing the correct answer is reduced, and reliability is correspondingly increased.[3]

Two other desirable characteristics of the multiple-choice item are worthy of mention. First, it is relatively free from response sets.[4] That is, pupils generally do not have a tendency to favor a particular alternative when they don't know the answer. Second, the use of a number of plausible alternatives makes the results amenable to diagnosis. The nature of the incorrect alternatives selected by pupils provides clues to factual errors and misunderstandings that need correction.

The wide applicability of the multiple-choice item, plus its unique advantages, makes it easier to construct high quality test items in this form than in any of the other objective forms. This does not mean that good multiple-choice items can be constructed without effort. But for a given amount of effort, multiple-choice items will tend to be of a higher quality than short-answer, true-false, or matching-type items in the same area.

Despite its superiority, the multiple-choice item does have limitations. First, it shares certain limitations with all other paper-and-pencil tests. It is limited to learning outcomes at the verbal level. The problems presented to pupils are verbal problems, free from many of the irrelevant factors present in natural situations. The alternative solutions to problems pupils are asked to consider are verbal alternatives, free from the emotional concomitants of alternative solutions in natural situations. The applications pupils are asked to make are verbal applications, free from the personal commitment necessary for application in natural situations. In short, the multiple-choice item, like other paper-and-pencil tests, measures whether the pupil *knows* or *understands* what to do when confronted with a problem situation, but it cannot determine how the pupil *will* perform in an actual situation. Second, the multiple-choice item shares a basic limitation with other types of selection items. Since it requires selection of the correct answer, it is not well adapted to the measurement of some problem-solving skills in mathematics and science, and it is inappropriate for measuring the ability to organize and present ideas. Third, the multiple-choice item has a limitation not common to other item types, that is, the difficulty of locating a sufficient number of incorrect but

---

[3] See R. L. Ebel, "Expected Reliability as a Function of Choices Per Item," *Educational and Psychological Measurement*, **29**, 565–570, 1969.
[4] L. J. Cronbach, *Essentials of Psychological Testing*, 3rd ed. (New York: Harper and Row, 1970).

plausible distracters. This difficulty diminishes considerably, however, as experience is obtained in constructing such items.

SUGGESTIONS FOR CONSTRUCTING MULTIPLE-CHOICE ITEMS

The general applicability and the superior qualities of multiple-choice test items are realized most fully, obviously, when care is taken in their construction. This involves the formulation of a clearly stated problem, the identification of plausible alternatives, and special efforts to remove irrelevant clues to the answer. The following suggestions provide more specific maxims for this purpose.

1. *The stem of the item should be meaningful by itself and should present a definite problem.* All too frequently the stems of test items placed in multiple-choice form are incomplete statements which make little sense until all of the alternatives have been read. These are *not* multiple-choice items but rather a collection of true-false statements placed in multiple-choice form. A properly constructed multiple-choice item presents a definite problem in the stem, which is meaningful without the alternatives. Compare the stems in the two versions of the test item in the following examples:

EXAMPLES

Poor: South America
          A   is a flat, arid country.
          B   imports coffee from the United States.
          C   has a larger population than the United States.
          Ⓓ   was settled mainly by colonists from Spain.
Better: Most of South America was settled by colonists from
          A   England.
          B   France.
          C   Holland.
          Ⓓ   Spain.

Formulating a definite problem in the stem not only improves the stem of the item but it also has a desirable effect on the alternatives. In the above example, note that the alternatives in the first version are concerned with widely dissimilar ideas. This heterogeneity is possible because of the lack of structure provided by the stem. In the second version, the clearly formulated problem in the stem forces the alternatives to be more homogeneous.

A good check on the adequacy of the problem statement is to cover the alternatives and read the stem by itself. It should be complete enough to serve as a short-answer item. Starting each item stem as a direct question, and shifting to the incomplete statement form only when greater conciseness is possible, provides the most effective method for obtaining a clearly formulated problem.

2. *The item stem should include as much of the item as possible and should be free of irrelevant material.* This will increase the probability of a clearly stated problem in the stem and will reduce the reading time required. The following examples illustrate how the conciseness of an item is increased by removing irrelevant material and by including in the stem those words repeated in the alternatives. It should also be noted that to obtain the conciseness of the final version, it was necessary to shift to the incomplete-statement form.

EXAMPLES

Poor: Most of South America was settled by colonists from Spain. How would you account for the large number of Spanish colonists settling there?
    A   They were adventurous.
    Ⓑ   They were in search of wealth.
    C   They wanted lower taxes.
    D   They were seeking religious freedom.
Better: Why did Spanish colonists settle most of South America?
    A   They were adventurous.
    Ⓑ   They were in search of wealth.
    C   They wanted lower taxes.
    D   They were seeking religious freedom.
Best: Spanish colonists settled most of South America in search of
    A   adventure.
    Ⓑ   wealth.
    C   lower taxes.
    D   religious freedom.

There are a few notable exceptions to this rule. In testing problem-solving ability, irrelevant material might be included in the stem of an item to determine if pupils are capable of identifying and selecting that material which is relevant to the solution of the problem. Similarly, repeating common words in the alternatives is sometimes necessary for grammatical consistency or greater clarity.

3. *Use a negatively stated item stem only when significant learning outcomes require it.* Most problems can and should be stated in positive terms. This avoids the possibility of pupils' overlooking the *no, not, least,* and similar words used in negative statements. In most instances, it also avoids the measurement of relatively insignificant learning outcomes. Knowing the *least* important method, the principle which does *not* apply, or the *poorest* reason is seldom related to important learning outcomes. We are usually interested in pupils learning the *most* important method, the principle which *does* apply, and the *best* reason.

Teachers sometimes go to ridiculous extremes to use negatively stated items because they appear more difficult. The difficulty of such items, however, resides in lack of sentence clarity rather than the greater difficulty of the concept being measured.

EXAMPLES

Poor: Which one of the following states is not located north of the Mason-Dixon line?

      A   Maine
      B   New York
      C   Pennsylvania
      Ⓓ   Virginia

Better: Which one of the following states is located south of the Mason-Dixon line?

      A   Maine
      B   New York
      C   Pennsylvania
      Ⓓ   Virginia

Both versions of this item measure the same specific knowledge. However, some pupils who can answer the second version correctly will select an incorrect alternative on the first version merely because the negative phrasing confuses them. Such items thereby introduce factors which contribute to the invalidity of the test.

Although negatively stated items are generally to be avoided, there are occasions where they are useful. These are mainly in areas where the wrong information, or wrong procedure, can have dire consequences. In the health area, for example, there are practices to be avoided because of their harmful nature. In shop and laboratory work, there are procedures which can damage equipment and result in bodily injury. In driver training there are a number of unsafe practices to be emphasized. Where the avoidance of such potentially harmful practices is emphasized in teaching, it might well receive a corresponding emphasis in testing through the use of negatively stated items. When used, the negative aspects of the item should be made obvious to the pupil.

EXAMPLES

Poor: Which one of the following is not a safe driving practice on icy roads?

      A   Accelerating slowly
      Ⓑ   Jamming on the brakes
      C   Holding the wheel firmly
      D   Slowing down gradually

Better: All of the following are safe driving practices on icy roads EXCEPT

      A   accelerating slowly.
      Ⓑ   jamming on the brakes.

C   holding the wheel firmly.
D   slowing down gradually.

In the first version of the item the "not" is easily overlooked, in which case pupils would tend to select the first alternative and read no further. In the second version, it is improbable that the negative element would be overlooked by any pupil because it is placed at the end of the statement and is capitalized.

4. *All of the alternatives should be grammatically consistent with the stem of the item.* In the illustrative items in the following examples, note how the better version results from a change in the alternatives in order to obtain grammatical consistency. This rule is not presented merely to perpetuate proper grammar usage, however. Its main function is to prevent irrelevant clues from creeping into the item. All too frequently the grammatical consistency of the correct answer is given attention while that of the distracters is neglected. As a result, some of the alternatives are grammatically inconsistent with the stem and are thereby obviously incorrect answers.

EXAMPLES

Poor: An electric transformer can be used
          A   for storing up electricity.
          Ⓑ   to increase the voltage of alternating current.
          C   it converts electrical energy into mechanical energy.
          D   alternating current is changed to direct current.
Better: An electric transformer can be used to
          A   store up electricity.
          Ⓑ   increase the voltage of alternating current.
          C   convert electrical energy into mechanical energy.
          D   change alternating current to direct current.

Similar difficulties arise from lack of attention to the tense of verbs, to the proper use of the articles "a" or "an," and to other common sources of grammatical inconsistency. Since most of these errors are the result of carelessness, they can be detected easily by a careful reading of each item before assembling the items into a test.

5. *An item should contain only one correct or clearly best answer.* Including more than one correct answer in a test item and asking pupils to select all of the correct alternatives has two major shortcomings. First, such items are usually no more than a collection of true-false items presented in multiple-choice form. They do not present a definite problem in the stem, and the selection of answers requires a mental response of true or false to each alternative rather than a comparison and selection of alternatives. Second, since the number of alternatives selected as correct answers varies from one pupil to another there is no satisfactory method of scoring.

Poor: The state of Michigan borders on
        (A) Lake Huron.
        B Lake Ontario.
        (C) Indiana.
        D Illinois.

Better: The state of Michigan borders on
        A Lake Huron.   (T) F
        B Lake Ontario.   T (F)
        C Indiana.   (T) F
        D Illinois.   T (F)

The second version of this item makes clear to the pupil the type of response expected. He is to read each alternative and decide whether it is true or false. Thus, this is *not* a four-alternative multiple-choice item. It is a series of four statements each of which has two alternatives—true or false. This second version, which is called a cluster-type true-false item, not only clarifies the nature of the mental process involved but it also simplifies the scoring. Each statement in the cluster can be considered one point and scored as any other true-false item is scored. In contrast, how would you score a pupil who selected alternatives. A, B, and C in the first version? Would you give him two points because he correctly identified the two answers; would you give him only one point because he also selected one incorrect alternative; or would you give him no points because he responded incorrectly to the item as a whole? How would you evaluate his response to alternative D? Assume that he knew Illinois did not border on Michigan and therefore did not select it, or assume that he was uncertain and left it blank. There is no method of scoring which will satisfactorily handle these problems. Multiple-choice items, like the one in the first version, should be avoided or converted to the true-false form.

There is another important facet of this rule concerning single-answer multiple-choice items, that is, the answer must be one that can be agreed upon by authorities in the area. The best-answer type item is especially subject to variations of interpretation and disagreement concerning the correct answer. Care must be taken to be certain that the answer is clearly the best answer. Frequently a rewording of the problem in the stem will correct an otherwise faulty item.

Poor: Which one of the following is the best source of heat for home use?
        A Coal
        B Electricity
        C Gas
        D Oil

Better: In the midwestern part of the United States, which one of the following
is the most economical source of heat for home use?

    Ⓐ Coal
    B   Electricity
    C   Gas
    D   Oil

In the first version of the item, several different alternatives could be
defended as correct depending on whether the "best" refers to cost, efficiency, cleanliness, or accessibility. The second version avoids this problem
by making the criterion of "best" explicit.

6. *Items used to measure understanding should contain some novelty
but beware of too much novelty.* The construction of multiple-choice items
which measure learning outcomes at the understanding level requires a
careful choice of situations and skillful phrasing. The situations must be new
to the pupils but not too far removed from the illustrative examples used
in class. If the test items contain problem situations identical to those used
in class, pupils can, of course, respond on the basis of memorized answers.
On the other hand, if the problem situations contain too much novelty, some
pupils may respond incorrectly merely because they lack necessary factual
information concerning the situations used. Asking a pupil to apply the
law of supply and demand to some phase of banking, for example, would
be grossly unfair, if he had not had a previous opportunity to study banking policies and practices. He may have a good understanding of the law
of supply and demand but be unable to demonstrate his understanding
because of his unfamiliarity with the particular situation selected.

The problem of too much novelty can usually be avoided by selecting
situations from the everyday experiences of the pupils, by including in the
stem of the item any unique factual information needed, and by phrasing
the item so that the type of application or interpretation called for is
clearly understood.

7. *All distracters should be plausible.* The purpose of a distracter is to
distract the uninformed away from the correct answer. To the pupil
who has not achieved the learning outcome being tested, the distracters
should be at least as attractive as the correct answer and preferably more
so. In a properly constructed multiple-choice item, each distracter will
be selected by some pupils. If a distracter is not selected by anyone, it
makes no contribution to the functioning of the item and should be eliminated or revised.

One factor contributing to the plausibility of distracters is their homogeneity. If all of the alternatives are homogeneous with regard to the
knowledge being measured, there is much greater likelihood that the distracters will function as intended. Whether alternatives appear homogeneous and distracters plausible, however, also depends on the age level
of the pupils. Note the difference in homogeneity in the following two
items:

Poor: Who discovered the North Pole?
       A   Christopher Columbus
       B   Ferdinand Magellan
       Ⓒ   Robert Peary
       D   Marco Polo
Better: Who discovered the North Pole?
       A   Roald Amundsen
       B   Richard Byrd
       Ⓒ   Robert Peary
       D   Robert Scott

    The first version would probably appear homogeneous to pupils at the primary level because all four choices are the names of well-known explorers. However, pupils in higher grades would eliminate alternatives A, B, and D as possible answers because they would know these men were not Polar explorers. They might also recall that these men lived several hundred years before the North Pole was discovered. In either case, they could quickly obtain the correct answer by the process of elimination. The second version includes only the names of Polar explorers, all of whom were active in Polar explorations at approximately the same time. This homogeneity makes each alternative much more plausible and the elimination process much less effective. It, of course, also increases the level of difficulty of the item.

    In selecting plausible distracters, the learning experiences of the pupils must not be ignored. In the foregoing illustrative item, for example, the distracters in the second version would not be plausible to pupils if Robert Peary was the only Polar explorer they had studied. Obviously, distracters must be familiar to pupils before they can serve as reasonable alternatives. Less obvious is the rich source of plausible distracters provided by the pupils' learning experiences. Common misconceptions, errors of judgment, and faulty reasoning that occur during the teaching-learning process provide the most plausible and educationally sound distracters available. One way to tap this supply is to keep a running record of such errors. A quicker method is to administer a short-answer test to pupils and tabulate the errors which occur most frequently. This provides a series of incorrect responses which are especially plausible because they are in the language of the pupil.

    8. *Verbal associations between the stem and the correct answer should be avoided.* Frequently a word in the correct answer will provide an irrelevant clue because it looks or sounds like a word in the stem of the item. Such verbal associations should never permit the pupil who lacks the necessary achievement to select the correct answer. However, words similar to those in the stem might be included in the distracters to increase their plausibility. Pupils who depend on rote memory and verbal associations will then be led away from, rather than to, the correct answer. The following item, taken from a fifth-grade test on a weather unit, illustrates the incorrect and correct use of verbal associations between the stem and the alternatives:

EXAMPLES

Poor: Which one of the following agencies should you contact to find out about a tornado warning in your locality?

    A   State Farm Bureau
    Ⓑ   Local Radio Station
    C   United States Post Office
    D   United States Weather Bureau

Better: Which one of the following agencies should you contact to find out about a tornado warning in your locality?

    A   Local Farm Bureau
    Ⓑ   Nearest Radio Station
    C   Local Post Office
    D   United States Weather Bureau

In the first version of the item, the association between "locality" and "local" provides an unnecesary clue. In the second version, this verbal association is used in two distracters to make them more attractive choices. It should be noted that if this use of irrelevant verbal associations in the distracters is overdone, pupils will soon get wise and avoid alternatives with pat verbal associations.

9. *The relative length of the alternatives should not provide a clue to the answer.* Since the correct answer usually needs to be qualified, it tends to be longer than the distracters unless a special effort is made to control the relative length of the alternatives. Where the correct answer cannot be shortened, the distracters can be expanded to the desired length. Lengthening the distracters is desirable for another reason also. The added qualifiers and increased specificity frequently contribute to their plausibility. The best we can hope for in equalizing the length of the alternatives for a given test item is to make them approximately equal. Consequently, we still have the problem of the length of the correct answer. Although it should not be consistently longer than the other alternatives, neither should it be consistently shorter nor consistently of median length.

EXAMPLES

Poor: What is the major purpose of the United Nations?

    Ⓐ   To maintain peace among the peoples of the world
    B   To establish international law
    C   To provide military control
    D   To form new governments

Better: What is the major purpose of the United Nations?

      (A)   To maintain peace among the peoples of the world
      B   To develop a new system of international law
      C   To provide military control of nations which have recently attained their independence
      D   To establish and maintain democratic forms of government in newly formed nations

The relative length of the correct answer should vary from one item to another in such a manner that no discernible pattern is available to provide a clue to the answer. This means, of course, that it will be longest a portion of the time.

10. *The correct answer should appear in each of the alternative positions approximately an equal number of times, but in random order.* Some teachers seem to have a tendency to bury the correct answer in the middle of the list of alternatives. As a consequence, the correct answer appears in the first and last positions far less than it does in the middle positions. This, of course, provides an irrelevant clue to the alert pupil.

In placing the correct answer in each position, approximately an equal number of times, care must be taken to avoid a regular pattern of responses. A random placement of correct answers can be attained with the use of any book. For each test item, open the book at an arbitrary position, note the number on the right-hand page, and place the correct answer for that test item as follows:

If page number ends in	*Place correct answer*
1	First
3	Second
5	Third
7	Fourth
9	Fifth

An even simpler method for obtaining a random placement of the correct answer is to place all verbal alternatives in alphabetical order and all numerical answers in numerical order.

11. *Use special alternatives such as "none of the above" or "all of the above" sparingly.* The phrase "none of the above" or "all of the above" is sometimes added as the last alternative in multiple-choice items. This is done to force the pupil to consider all of the alternatives carefully and to increase the difficulty of the items. All too frequently, however, these special alternatives are used inappropriately. In fact, their limitations are such that there are relatively few situations where their use is appropriate.

The use of "none of the above" is restricted to the correct-answer type multiple-choice item and consequently to the measurement of factual knowledge where absolute standards of correctness can be applied. It is clearly inappropriate in best-answer type items, since the pupil is told to select the *best* of several alternatives of varying degrees of correctness.

Use of "none of the above" is frequently recommended for items measuring computational skill in mathematics, and spelling ability. These learning outcomes should generally not be measured by multiple-choice items, however, they can be measured much more effectively by short-answer items. Where "none of the above" *is used* in such situations, the item may be measuring nothing more than a pupil's ability to recognize incorrect answers. This is a rather inadequate basis for judging his computational skill or spelling ability.

The alternative "none of the above" should be used only when the measurement of significant learning outcomes requires it. As with negatively stated item stems, these are situations where procedures or practices are to be clearly avoided for safety, health, or other reasons. Where knowing what *not* to do is important, "none of the above" might be appropriately applied. When used for this purpose, it must, of course, also be used as an incorrect answer a proportionate number of times.

The use of "all of the above" is fraught with such difficulties that it might better be discarded as a possible alternative. When used, some pupils will note that the first alternative is correct and select it without reading further. Other pupils will note that at least two of the alternatives are correct and thereby know that "all of the above" must be the answer. In the first instance, pupils mark the item incorrectly because they did not read all of the alternatives. In the second instance, pupils obtain the correct answer on the basis of partial knowledge. Both types of response prevent the item from functioning as intended.

12. *Do not use multiple-choice items where other item types are more appropriate.* Where various item types can serve a purpose equally well, the multiple-choice item should definitely be favored because of its many superior qualities. There are situations, however, where the multiple-choice form is inappropriate or at least less suitable than other item types. In certain problem-solving situations in mathematics and science, for example, supply-type short-answer items are clearly superior. Where there are only two possible responses (e.g., fact or opinion), the alternative-response item is more appropriate. Where there is a sufficient number of homogeneous items but few plausible distracters for each, a matching exercise might be more suitable. Although we should take full advantage of the wide applicability of the multiple-choice form, we should not lose sight of a basic principle of test construction cited earlier—that is, *select the item type which measures a learning outcome most directly and most effectively.*

SUMMARY

The multiple-choice item consists of a problem and list of alternative solutions. The pupil responds by selecting the alternative which provides the correct or best solution to the problem. The incorrect alternatives are called distracters, since their purpose is to distract the uninformed pupil from the correct response. The problem can be stated as a direct question or an incomplete statement. In either case, it should be a clearly formulated problem which is meaningful without reference to the list of alternatives.

The multiple-choice form is extremely flexible. It can be used to measure a variety of learning outcomes at the knowledge and understanding levels. Knowledge outcomes concerned with vocabulary, specific facts, principles, and methods and procedures can all be measured with the multiple-choice item. Aspects of understanding, such as the application and interpretation of facts, principles, and methods, can also be measured with this item type. Many other, more specific, uses occur in particular school subjects.

The main advantage of the multiple-choice item is its wide applicability in the measurement of various phases of achievement. It is also free of many of the limitations of other forms of objective items. It tends to present a more well-defined problem than the short-answer item, it avoids the need for homogeneous material required by the matching item, and it reduces the clues and susceptibility to guessing which are characteristic of the true-false item. In addition, the multiple-choice item is relatively free from response sets and is useful in diagnosis.

Its limitations derive mainly from the fact that it is a selection-type paper-and-pencil test. It measures problem-solving behavior at the verbal level only. Since it requires selection of the correct answer, it is inappropriate for measuring learning outcomes requiring the ability to recall, organize, or present ideas.

The construction of multiple-choice items involves the formulation of a well-defined problem in the stem of the item, the selection of one correct or clearly best solution, the identification of several plausible distracters, and the avoidance of irrelevant clues to the answer. Items used to measure learning outcomes at the understanding level must also include some (but beware of too much) novelty.

LEARNING EXERCISES

1. In an area in which you are teaching or plan to teach, construct one multiple-choice item for each of the following:
   a. Knowledge of a specific term.
   b. Knowledge of a specific fact.
   c. Knowledge of a principle.
   d. Knowledge of a method or procedure.
   e. Understanding of a fact or principle.
   f. Application of a fact or principle.
2. Criticize each of the following multiple-choice items. How would you improve each item?
   a. Illinois
      (1) borders on five states.

      (2) is north of Indiana.

      (3) has a larger population than other states.

      (4) is best known for its dairy products.

  b. Illinois' important resources are

      (1) coal.

      (2) fertile soil.

      (3) petroleum.

      (4) all of the above.

  c. Illinois' population has been

      (1) increasing.

      (2) decreasing.

      (3) staying the same.

      (4) none of the above.

  d. Illinois is not known for

      (1) coal production.

      (2) fertile soil.

      (3) meat packing.

      (4) automobile manufacturing.

  e. In terms of size, Illinois is

      (1) larger than Arizona.

      (2) larger than California.

      (3) larger than Indiana.

      (4) larger than Texas.

3. How does a multiple-choice item designed to measure knowledge outcomes differ from one designed to measure understanding?

4. Describe the relative merits of using the "correct-answer" type and the "best-answer" type of multiple-choice items. What types of learning outcomes are best measured by each?

SUGGESTIONS FOR FURTHER READING

Bloom, B. S., J. T. Hastings, and G. F. Madaus. *Handbook on Formative and Summative Evaluation of Student Learning.* New York: McGraw-Hill Book Company, 1971. See Part Two for series of chapters on the evaluation of learning in each of the major curriculum areas. Numerous illustrations of multiple-choice items, designed to measure a variety of learning outcomes, are presented in each chapter.

Ebel, R. L. *Essentials of Educational Measurement.* Englewood Cliffs, N.J.: Prentice-Hall, Inc., 1972. Chapter 8, "How to Write Multiple-Choice Items." Numerous sample test items are used to illustrate desirable and undesirable characteristics of multiple-choice items.

Gronlund, N. E. *Constructing Achievement Tests.* Englewood Cliffs, N.J.: Prentice-Hall, Inc., 1968. Chapter 3, "Constructing Objective Tests of Knowledge." Describes and illustrates the use of multiple-choice items for measuring the various types of knowledge outcomes listed in the taxonomy of educational objectives.

Wesman, A. G. "Writing the Test Item," Chapter 4 in R. L. Thorndike (ed.), *Educational Measurement.* Washington, D.C.: American Council on Education, 1971. An extended treatment of the topic of item writing with specific suggestions for constructing multiple-choice items.

CHAPTER 9
Measuring Complex Achievement: The Interpretive Exercise

Complex achievement includes those learning outcomes based on the higher mental processes, such as . . . understandings . . . thinking skills . . . and various problem-solving abilities. . . . Many aspects of complex achievement can be measured objectively.

We have already had some experience with the measurement of complex achievement, since this category encompasses all those learning outcomes requiring more than mere retention of factual knowledge. The use of the short-answer item to measure problem-solving abilities in mathematics and science, of the true-false item to measure the ability to recognize cause-effect relationships, and of the multiple-choice item to measure various aspects of understanding and application, all illustrated the measurement of complex achievement. These illustrations, however, were limited to the use of single, independent test items of the objective type. Greater range and flexibility in measuring complex achievement can be attained by using more complex forms of objective test items.

A variety of specific learning outcomes are included in complex achievement. Following are some typical examples:

Ability to apply a principle
Ability to interpret relationships
Ability to recognize and state inferences
Ability to recognize the relevance of information
Ability to develop and recognize tenable hypotheses
Ability to formulate and recognize valid conclusions
Ability to recognize assumptions underlying conclusions
Ability to recognize the limitations of data
Ability to recognize and state significant problems
Ability to design experimental procedures

These, and similar learning outcomes, have been variously classified under such general categories as understanding, reasoning, critical thinking, scientific thinking, creative thinking, and problem solving. There is general agreement that these learning outcomes based on the higher mental processes constitute some of the most significant outcomes of education.[1]

In the past, the measurement of complex achievement was relegated almost entirely to the essay test. However, during the Eight-Year Study, a number of objective tests for measuring complex learning outcomes were developed under the direction of R. W. Tyler.[2] Since that time numerous modifications and adaptations have appeared—many of them to meet specific and limited purposes. The most promising form for measuring a variety of complex learning outcomes, in most school subjects, is the interpretive exercise.[3]

NATURE OF THE INTERPRETIVE EXERCISE[4]

An interpretive exercise consists of a series of objective items based on a common set of data. The data may be in the form of written materials, tables, charts, graphs, maps, or pictures. The series of related test items may also take various forms but are most commonly of the multiple-choice or alternative-response variety. Since all pupils are presented with a common set of data, it is possible to measure a variety of complex learning outcomes. Pupils can be asked to identify relationships in data, to recognize valid conclusions, to appraise assumptions and inferences, to detect proper applications of data, and the like.

The common set of materials used in interpretive exercises provides assurance that all pupils are confronted with the same task. It also makes it possible to control the amount of factual information given to the pupils. We can give them as much or as little information as we think desirable in measuring their achievement of a specific learning outcome. In measuring the ability to interpret mathematical data, for example, we can include the formulas needed or require the pupils to supply them. In other areas, we can provide definitions of terms, meaning of symbols, and other specific facts, or we can expect pupils to provide them. This flexibility makes it possible to measure various degrees of proficiency in any particular area.

---

[1] B. S. Bloom, "Higher Mental Processes," *Encyclopedia of Educational Research*, 4th ed (New York: Macmillan, 1969).

[2] E. R. Smith and R. W. Tyler, *Appraising and Recording Student Progress* (New York: Harper and Row, 1942).

[3] A. G. Wesman, "Writing the Test Item," in R. L. Thorndike (ed.), *Educational Measurement* (Washington, D.C.: American Council on Education, 1971).

[4] Variations of this item are also called "the classification exercise," "key-type items," and "master-list items."

FORMS AND USES OF THE INTERPRETIVE EXERCISE

As with other objective items, there are so many forms and specific uses of the interpretive exercise that it is impossible to illustrate all of them. What we shall do here is present representative examples of this item type as applied to the measurement of complex learning outcomes in a variety of school subjects at the elementary and secondary levels. Different types of introductory material and different methods of responding will also be used, to illustrate the great flexibility of the interpretive exercise. The references at the end of this chapter will provide additional illustrative exercises for your guidance.

Ability to Recognize the Relevance of Information

A learning outcome that is important in all subject-matter areas and can be measured at all levels of instruction is the ability to recognize the relevance of information. The illustrative exercise presented here was prepared for third-grade pupils. An example at the high school level may be found in Chapter 3.

EXAMPLES

Bill lost his overshoe on the way to school. He wanted to put a notice on the bulletin board so other children could help him find it. Which of the following sentences tell something that would help children find the overshoe?
Directions: Circle "yes" if it would help. Circle "no" if it would *not* help.

(yes) no   1. The overshoe was black.
yes (no)   2. It was very warm.
(yes) no   3. It was for his right foot.
yes (no)   4. It was a Christmas present.
yes (no)   5. It was nice looking.
(yes) no   6. It had a zipper.
(yes) no   7. It had a gray lining.

Ability to Recognize Warranted and Unwarranted Generalization

The ability to recognize the validity of generalizations is of central importance in the interpretation of data. As a minimum, pupils should be able to determine which conclusions are supported by the data, which are refuted by the data, and which are neither supported nor refuted by the data. The data may be in the form of tables, charts, graphs, maps, or pictures, and the test items may be in the form of alternative-response items or multiple-choice items. The use of the alternative-response format is illustrated in the following example. (See Figure 12.2, Chapter 12, for sample items using the multiple-choice format.)

EXAMPLES

MORTALITY OF WHITE PERSONS FROM MOTOR
VEHICLE ACCIDENTS IN THE UNITED STATES, 1957–58

Age Period (Years)	Death Rate per 100,000	
	Males	Females
All ages	32.9	11.1
1–4	10.5	8.0
5–14	10.4	5.4
15–19	54.2	16.4
20–24	76.3	12.7
25–44	35.6	9.1
45–64	33.1	12.9
65 and over	58.4	22.5

Source of basic data: Statistical Bulletin, Metropolitan
Life Insurance Company, Vol. 42, February, 1961.

Directions: The following statements refer to the data in the above table. Read each statement and mark your answer according to the following key.
Circle: S if the statement is *supported* by the data in the table.
R if the statement is *refuted* by the data in the table.
N if the statement is *neither* supported nor refuted by the data in the table.

Ⓢ R N 1. The death rate from motor vehicle accidents is higher for men than for women.

S R Ⓝ 2. Motor vehicle accidents are a major cause of death among young men between the ages of 20 and 24.

S R Ⓝ 3. Men over 65 years of age drive no more safely than teen age boys between 15 and 19 years of age.

S Ⓡ N 4. The largest number of people killed in motor vehicle accidents are 65 years of age or over.

S Ⓡ N 5. When all ages are combined, only about 11 per cent of female deaths can be attributed to motor vehicle accidents.

Ability to Apply Principles

The application of principles may be shown in many different ways. In the following examples, pupils are asked to identify principles that explain a situation and to recognize illustrations of a principle:

EXAMPLE I

Mary Ann wanted her rose bush to grow faster so she applied twice as much chemical fertilizer as was recommended and watered it every evening. About a month later she noticed that the rose bush was dying.
Directions: Which of the following principles would be necessary in explaining

why the rose bush was dying? If a principle is necessary, circle the "N," if unnecessary, circle the "U."

N Ⓤ 1. A chemical compound is changed into other compounds by taking up the elements of water.

Ⓝ U 2. Semipermeable membranes permit the passage of fluid.

N Ⓤ 3. Water condenses when cooled.

Ⓝ U 4. When two solutions of different concentration are separated by a porous partition their concentration tends to equalize.

EXAMPLE II

Directions: Read the principle and the statements following it. If a statement describes a condition which illustrates the principle, place a check (X) in the space to the left of the statement.

  Principle: If the demand for a commodity or service is relatively constant, decrease in its supply will increase its market value.

( )   1. The stock market has shown a general upward trend in the price of stocks since World War II.

(X)   2. Fresh fruits and vegetables cost more when *not* in season.

( )   3. Medical costs are higher now than they were ten years ago.

Ability to Recognize Assumptions

Another learning outcome pertinent to the interpretation of various types of data is the ability to identify unstated assumptions which are necessary to a conclusion or course of action.

EXAMPLE I[5]

Statement of Facts: The following table represents the relationship between the yearly income of certain families and the medical attention they receive.

Family Income	Per Cent of Family Members Who Received No Medical Attention During the Year
Under $1,200	47
$1,200 to $3,000	40
$3,000 to $5,000	33
$5,000 to $10,000	24
Over $10,000	14

Conclusion: Members of families with small incomes are healthier than members of families with large incomes.

---

[5] Louis M. Heil, Paul E. Kambly, Marcus Mainardi, and Leah Weisman. "The Measurement of Understanding in Science," Chapter VI in *The Measurement of Understanding*, page 127, National Society for the Study of Education, 45th Yearbook, Part I. Copyright, 1946, by Nelson B. Henry, Secretary of the Society. Used by permission of the publisher, University of Chicago Press.

Assumption: Which one of the following must be assumed to make the above conclusion true? Check one.

            1. Wealthy families had more money to spend for medical care.

   X   2. All members of families who needed medical attention received it.

            3. Many members of families with low incomes were not able to pay their doctor bills.

            4. Members of families with low incomes often did not receive medical attention.

EXAMPLE II[6]

Items 37–43 are concerned with the following situation.

One of the methods formerly used by geologists to determine the age of the earth was a calculation based on the amount of salt (NaCl) in the ocean, and the amount added to ocean waters each year by the rivers that empty into the ocean. If this method of age determination is used, certain assumptions must be made. Items 37–43 consist of a number of assumptions. The assumption in each item is

   KEY: 1. *Necessary* for the calculation and is *probably true.*

            2. *Necessary* for the calculation but is *probably false.*

            3. *Not necessary* for the calculation but is *probably true.*

            4. *Not necessary* for the calculation and is *probably false.*

37. The salt concentrations of the oceans is gradually increasing.   (1)
38. Oceans have been on the earth since our planet was formed.   (2)
39. Ever since its origin, the earth has revolved around the sun.   (3)
40. The oceans now contain all the salt that has ever been added to them. (2)
41. The salts which rivers have carried to the oceans have all occurred in mineral form in the rocks before they were dissolved by the river water.   (4)
42. The proportion of the lithosphere existing above the ocean waters has been constant throughout the geologic ages.   (2)
43. The continental masses have existed in essentially their present outline since the formation of the earth.   (2)

Ability to Recognize Inferences

In interpreting written material it is frequently necessary to draw inferences from the facts given. The following exercise measures the extent to which pupils are able to recognize warranted and unwarranted inferences drawn from a passage:

EXAMPLES[7]

Directions: Assuming that the information below is true, it is possible to establish other facts using the ones in this paragraph as a basis for reasoning. This is

---

[6] Clarence H. Nelson, *Let's Build Quality Into Our Science Tests,* page 9, Copyright © 1958 by the National Science Teachers Association (Washington, D.C.: National Education Association). Used by permission of the publisher.
[7] Horace T. Morse and George H. McCune, *Selected Items for the Testing of Study Skills and Critical Thinking,* page 66, Bulletin No. 15, Fifth Edition. Copyright © 1971 by National Council for the Social Studies (Washington, D.C.: National Education Association). Used by permission of the publisher.

called drawing inferences. There is, of course, a limit to the number of kinds of facts which may be properly inferred from any statement.

By writing the proper symbol in the space provided, indicate that a statement is TRUE, if it may be properly inferred from the information given in the paragraph. Indicate that it is UNTRUE, if the information given in the paragraph implies that it is false. Indicate that NO INFERENCE can be drawn if the statement cannot be inferred one way or the other. Use only the information given in the paragraph as a basis for your responses. . . .
Use the following symbols in writing your answers:

  T—if the statement may be inferred as TRUE.
  F—if the statement may be inferred as UNTRUE.
  N—if no inference can be drawn about it from the paragraph.

Paragraph A

By the close of the thirteenth century there were several famous universities established in Europe, though of course they were very different from modern ones. One of the earliest to be founded was one of the most widely known. This was the University of Bologna, where students from all countries came who wished to have the best training in studying Roman Law. Students especially interested in philosophy and theology went to the University of Paris. Those who wished to study medicine went to the Universities of Montpellier or Salerno.

Questions on Paragraph A

(T)   1. There were law suits between people occasionally in those days.
(N)   2. The professors were poorly paid.
(F)   3. In the Middle Ages people were not interested in getting education.
(T)   4. There were books in Europe at that time.
(N)   5. Most of the teaching in these medieval universities was very poor.
(N)   6. There was no place where students could go to study.
(F)   7. There were no doctors in Europe at this time.
(F)   8. There was no way to travel during the Middle Ages.
(T)   9. If a student wanted to be a priest, he would probably attend the University of Paris.
(N) 10. There were no universities in Europe before the thirteenth century.
(N) 11. There was only one langauge in Europe at this time.

Ability to Interpret Experimental Findings

To determine the extent to which pupils understand scientific methodology, Nelson has suggested the use of interpretative exercises based on classical experiments.[8] The following example is one he based on Francesco Redi's study of spontaneous generation:

---

[8] C. H. Nelson, *Let's Build Quality into Our Science Tests* (Washington, D.C.: National Science Teachers Association, 1958).

EXAMPLES[9]

Items 20–24 are based upon the following situation.

PROBLEM: How do the simpler living organisms originate?

HYPOTHESIS 1: *Flies may be produced by spontaneous generation from dead organic substances.*

EXPERIMENTAL TEST OF HYPOTHESIS

Redi, an Italian physician and scientist, put pieces of fresh meat inside of one set of jars which he immediately sealed with parchment (represented by Jar A in the Figure below). Inside of another set of jars (represented by Jar B in the Figure below) he also put some pieces of fresh meat, but these jars he left open. Later he observed flies entering and leaving the open jars at will. No flies could enter the closed jars. Some days later the meat in the open jars teemed with maggots, but no maggots developed in the meat inside of the closed jars.

As a refinement in procedure, he repeated the above experiment but instead of covering one set of jars with parchment he now closed them with fine-meshed gauzelike Naples veiling (respresented by Jar C. in the figure below). Flies, attracted by the odor of the flesh inside the jars, frequently alighted on the veiling, occasionally depositing eggs on the veiling. These eggs soon hatched into maggots *on top of the veiling,* but no maggots developed in the meat inside the jars.

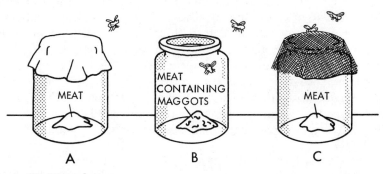

For items 20–23 mark space
   1—if the item is true according to the data and tends to support Hypothesis I;
   2—if the item is true according to the data but tends to refute Hypothesis I;
   3—if the item is irrelevant to Hypothesis I, regardless of its truth or falsity according to the data;
   4—if the item is false according to the data, but if true, would tend to support Hypothesis I;
   5—if the item is false according to the data, but if true, would tend to refute Hypothesis I.

SUGGESTION: It will be easier if you decide first whether each statement is true or false according to the data.

20. Judging on the basis of what happened in all three jars, no maggots were to be seen in the meat in Jar A because they suffocated in this tightly closed jar. (4)

21. Jar B, which was the only jar that the flies could enter, was also the only jar in which maggots appeared in the meat. (2)

22. The maggots which appeared on top of the veiling of Jar C appeared there only because tiny particles of decaying meat that were carried upward through the veiling by the circulating air turned into maggots. (4)

23. Maggots were not found in the meat in Jar C for the same reason that they were not observed in Jar A. (2)

24. On the basis of Redi's data alone, what is the status of Hypothesis I?
    1. It is established as true beyond doubt.
    2. It is probably true—the evidence tends to support it.
    3. It remains as much unsettled as at the outset.
    °4. It is probably false—the evidence tends to refute it.
    5. It is definitely false without any doubt whatsoever.

Use of Pictorial Materials

Pictorial materials can serve two useful purposes in interpretive exercises. (1) They can serve as a medium for measuring a variety of learning outcomes similar to those already discussed. It is simply a matter of replacing the written or tabular data with some pictorial form of presentation. This use is especially desirable with younger pupils and in areas where the ideas can be more clearly conveyed in pictorial form. (2) They can also serve as a direct measure of the ability to interpret graphs, cartoons, maps, and other pictorial materials. In many school subjects, these are important learning outcomes in their own right.

The following examples illustrate the use of pictorial materials:

EXAMPLE I

At the right is a graph of Bill's weekly allowance distribution.

1. What is the ratio of the amount Bill spends for school supplies to the amount he spends for movies?
    A   7:2
    Ⓑ   1:3
    C   2:7
    D   3:1
2. What would be the best title for this graph?
    A   Bill's weekly allowance
    B   Bill's money graph
    Ⓒ   Bill's weekly expenditures
    D   Bill's money planning

EXAMPLE II[10]

1. The cartoon illustrates which of the following characteristics of the party system in the United States?
    - (A) Strong party discipline is often lacking.
    - B   The parties are responsive to the will of the voters.
    - C   The parties are often more concerned with politics than with the national welfare.
    - D   Bipartisanship often exists in name only.

2. The situation shown in the cartoon is *least* likely to occur at which of the following times?
    - A   During the first session of a new Congress
    - B   During a political party convention
    - C   During a primary election campaign
    - (D) During a presidential election campaign

   Cartoons such as this can be obtained from newspapers and news magazines. It is then simply a matter of preparing questions that call forth the desired interpretations. Either alternative-response or multiple-choice items might be used with this type of exercise. The important thing is to select a cartoon that illustrates a concept or principle that is relevant to the learning outcomes to be measured. Interpretive exercises of this type are especially useful in the social studies area.

---

[10] Educational Testing Service, *Making the Classroom Test: A Guide for Teachers,* page 6. Copyright © 1973 by Educational Testing Service (Princeton, New Jersey). Used by permission of the publisher.

EXAMPLE III[11]

In the following questions you are asked to make inferences from the data which are given you on the map of the imaginary country, Serendip. The answers in most instances must be probabilities rather than certainties. The relative size of towns and cities is not shown. To assist you, the map is divided into squares lettered vertically from A to E and numbered horizontally from 1 to 5.

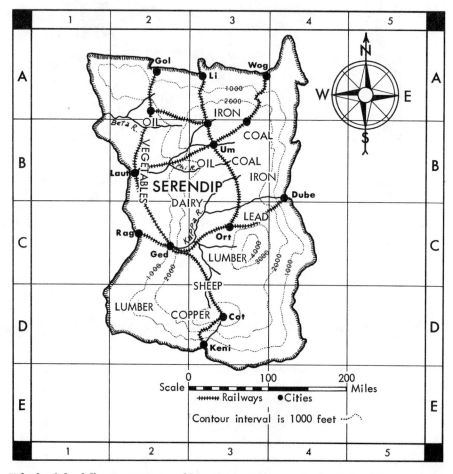

Which of the following cities would be the best location for a steel mill?

A Li   (3A)
Ⓑ Um   (3B)
C Cot   (3D)
D Dube   (4B)

---

[11] Educational Testing Service, *Multiple-Choice Questions: A Close Look*, page 5. Copyright © 1973 by Educational Testing Service (Princeton, New Jersey). Used by permission of the publisher.

EXAMPLE IV[12]

This question is based on the following situation:

A piece of mineral is placed in a bottle half-filled with a colorless liquid. A two-holed rubber stopper is then placed in the bottle. The system is then sealed by inserting a thermometer and connecting a glass tube to the stoppered bottle and a beaker of limewater as shown in the accompanying diagram:

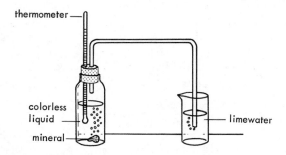

The following series of observations is recorded:

I. Observations during the first few minutes:
1. Bubbles of a colorless gas rise to the top of the stoppered bottle from the mineral.
2. Bubbles of colorless gas begin to come out of the glass tube and rise to the surface of the limewater.
3. The limewater remains colorless throughout this period of time.
4. The thermometer reads 20° C.

II. Observations at the end of thirty minutes:
1. Bubbles of colorless gas continue to rise in the stoppered bottle.
2. The piece of mineral has become noticeably smaller.
3. There is no apparent change in the level of the liquid in the bottle.
4. The colorless liquid in the bottle remains colorless.
5. The thermometer reads 24° C.
6. The limewater is cloudy.

Which one of the following is the best explanation for the appearance of gas bubbles at the end of the tube in the beaker of limewater?

A   The pressure exerted by the colorless liquid is greater than that exerted by the limewater.

Ⓑ   The bubbles coming from the mineral cause an increased gas pressure in the stoppered bottle.

C   The temperature increase at the end of thirty minutes causes an expansion of gas in the stoppered bottle.

D   The decrease in the size of the piece of mineral causes reduced pressure in the stoppered bottle.

---

[12] Educational Testing Service, *Multiple-Choice Questions: A Close Look*, page 15. Copyright © 1973 by Educational Testing Service (Princeton, New Jersey). Used by permission of the publisher.

EXAMPLE V[13]

Distribution of Scientists
by U.S. Geographic Division, 1960

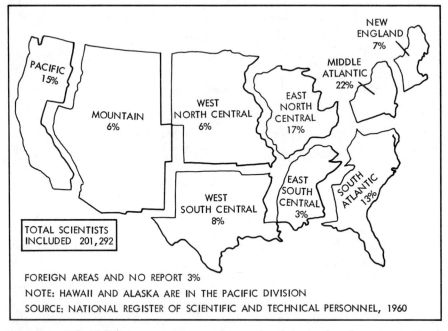

TOTAL SCIENTISTS
INCLUDED 201,292

FOREIGN AREAS AND NO REPORT 3%

NOTE: HAWAII AND ALASKA ARE IN THE PACIFIC DIVISION

SOURCE: NATIONAL REGISTER OF SCIENTIFIC AND TECHNICAL PERSONNEL, 1960

Directions: The following statements refer to the data in the above map. Read each statement and mark your answer according to the following key.

Circle: T—if the data in the map is sufficient to make the statement *true.*

F—if the data in the map is sufficient to make the statement *false.*

I—if the data in the map is *insufficient* to determine whether the statement is true or false.

(T) F I   1. The South Atlantic division has more than twice as many scientists as the West North Central division.

T F (I)   2. More scientists are trained in the Middle Atlantic division than in any other division.

T F (I)   3. The number of scientists is increasing more rapidly in the Eastern divisions than the Western divisions.

(T) F I   4. There are more than 6,000 scientists in the East South Central division.

T (F) I   5. There are fewer scientists per square mile in the New England division than in any other division.

T F (I)   6. There is less need for scientists in the Mountain division than in the Pacific division.

---

[13] The map on which this item is based was reproduced from *Scientific Manpower Bulletin,* No. 17, National Science Foundation (Washington, D.C.: April, 1962). Used by permission of the publisher.

OTHER EXAMPLES OF
INTERPRETIVE EXERCISES

As noted earlier, interpretive exercises take so many different forms that it is impossible to illustrate them all. Thus, it is desirable to consult other sources for examples of exercises in your particular teaching area. In addition to the references at the end of this chapter, standardized tests should also be consulted. Many standardized tests of achievement include some interpretive exercises and some standardized tests; use them as a basic item type. An example of the latter is the *Sequential Tests of Educational Progress*. These tests are discussed in Chapter 12, and sample test items are shown there.

In reviewing standardized tests for examples of interpretive exercises, it is important to keep in mind that the test materials are under copyright and thus cannot be reproduced for classroom use. They provide excellent models, however, and thus can assist in the construction of this item type. Patterning interpretive exercises after existing models aids the beginner.

ADVANTAGES AND LIMITATIONS OF
INTERPRETIVE EXERCISES

The interpretive exercise has several advantages over the single, independent objective test item.[14] *First,* the introductory material makes it possible to measure an ultimate objective of education and one of increasing importance in all school subjects—the ability to interpret written materials, charts, graphs, maps, pictures, and other communication media encountered in everyday situations. The rapid expansion of knowledge in every subject-matter area has made it impossible to learn all of the important factual information in a given field. This has led to greater dependence on libraries, reference materials, self-study techniques, and consequently interpretive skills. *Second,* the interpretive exercise makes it possible to measure more complex learning outcomes than can be measured with the single objective item. Some data, such as those presented in the interpretive exercise are necessary if pupils are to demonstrate thinking and problem-solving skills. The inclusion of such data in individual test items is possible but awkward. In addition, by having a series of related test items based on a common set of data, both greater depth and breadth can be obtained in the measurement of intellectual skills. *Third,* the interpretive exercise minimizes the influence of irrelevant factual information on the measurement of complex learning outcomes. As we noted with the single multiple-choice item, a pupil may be unable to demonstrate his understanding of a

---

[14] A. G. Wesman, "Writing the Test Item," in R. L. Thorndike (ed.), *Educational Measurement* (Washington, D.C.: American Council on Education, 1971).

principle simply because he lacks some of the specific facts concerning the situation in which application is to be made. This blocking of response, caused by a lack of detailed factual information not directly pertinent to the purpose of the measurement, can be largely eliminated with the interpretive exercise. In the introductory material, we can provide pupils with the common background of information needed to demonstrate understandings, thinking skills, and problem-solving abilities.

The main advantage of the interpretive exercise over the essay test, in measuring complex achievement, is derived from the greater structure provided. Pupils are not free to redefine the problem or to demonstrate those thinking skills in which they are most proficient. The series of objective items forces them to demonstrate the specific mental processes called for. This, of course, also makes it possible to measure separate aspects of problem-solving ability and to use objective scoring procedures.

As with all forms of test items, the interpretive exercise has some definite limitations. Probably the greatest limiting factor, and one that may have occurred to you as you reviewed the sample items, is the difficulty of construction. Selecting printed materials which are new to the pupils but which are relevant to the instructional outcomes requires considerable searching. When pertinent material is found, it usually must be edited and reworked to make it more suitable for testing purposes. Then, test items must be constructed which call forth the specific behaviors indicated in the learning outcomes being measured. The final process is most often a circular one, i.e., that of going back and forth between revising the introductory material and revising the test items until a satisfactory product is obtained. This entire procedure is time consuming and requires much greater skill than that needed to construct single objective test items. Three positive comments can be made regarding the difficulty of constructing interpretive exercises. (1) There is an increasingly large number of illustrative items of this type appearing in various subject-matter fields. The references at the end of this chapter contain numerous examples which may serve as guides to test construction. (2) The increased instructional emphasis on complex learning outcomes resulting from the use of interpretive exercises offsets the additional effort required in test construction. (3) The task becomes easier with practice and experience.

A second limitation, especially pertinent where the introductory material is in written form, is the heavy demand on reading skill. The poor reader is handicapped by both the difficulty of the reading material and the length of time it takes him to read each test exercise. The first problem can be controlled somewhat by keeping the reading level low and the second by using brief passages. Both of these are only partial solutions, however, since the poor reader will still be at a decided disadvantage. In the primary grades and in classes which contain a predominance of poor readers, interpretive exercises might better be limited to the use of pictorial materials.

In comparison to the essay test, the interpretive exercise has two short-comings as a measure of complex achievement. First, it cannot measure a pupil's overall approach to problem solving. It is efficient for measuring specific aspects of the problem-solving process but it does not indicate whether the pupil can integrate and use these specific skills when faced with a particular problem. Thus, it provides a diagnostic view of the pupils' problem-solving abilities, in contrast to the holistic view that can be obtained with essay questions. Second, since the interpretive exercise usually uses selection items, it is limited to learning outcomes at the recognition level. To measure the ability to *define* problems, to *formulate* hypotheses, to *organize* data, and to *draw* conclusions, supply procedures such as the essay test must be used.

SUGGESTIONS FOR CONSTRUCTING INTERPRETIVE EXERCISES

There are two major tasks in constructing interpretive exercises: (1) the selection of appropriate introductory material, and (2) the construction of a series of dependent test items. In addition, special care must be taken to construct test items which require an analysis of the introductory material in terms of complex learning outcomes. The following suggestions will aid in constructing interpretive exercises of high quality:

1. *Select introductory material that is in harmony with the objectives of the course.* Interpretive exercises, like other testing procedures, should measure the achievement of specific instructional goals. Success in this regard depends to a large extent on the introductory material, since this provides the common setting on which the specific test items are based. If the introductory material is too simple, the exercise may become a measure of general information or simple reading skill. On the other hand, if the material is too complex, or unrelated to instructional goals, it may become a measure of general reasoning ability. Both extremes must be avoided. Ideally, the introductory material should be pertinent to the course content and complex enough to call forth the mental reactions specified in the course objectives.

The amount of emphasis given to the various interpretive skills in the course objectives is also a factor here. Care must be taken not to overload the test with interpretive items in any particular area. The selection of introductory material should be guided by the general emphasis to be given to the measurement of complex achievement and by the relative emphasis to be given to each specific type of interpretive skill.

2. *Select introductory material that is appropriate to the curricular experience and reading level of the pupils.* Many complex learning outcomes can be measured with different types of introductory material. The ability to recognize the validity of conclusions, for example, can be measured with

written materials, tables, charts, graphs, maps, or pictures. The type used should be familiar to the pupils so that the nature of the material does not prevent them from demonstrating their achievement of the complex learning outcomes. It would be grossly unfair, for example, to ask pupils to recognize the validity of conclusions based on data presented in graph form, if they had not had experience in interpreting graphs similar to those used in the test.

Where various types of introductory material will serve a purpose equally well and where they are all familiar to the pupils, we would tend to favor that material which places the least demand on reading skill. For elementary pupils, pictorial materials would be definitely favored. For higher grade levels, pictorial materials and verbal materials with a low vocabulary load and simple sentences would be given preference. Although general reading skill is a factor in all written tests, it can become an especially prominent factor in interpretive exercises unless special efforts are made to minimize its influence.

3. *Select introductory material that is new to pupils.* In order to measure complex learning outcomes, the content of the introductory material must contain some novelty. Asking pupils to interpret materials identical to those used in instruction provides no assurance that the exercise is measuring anything other than rote memory. Too much novelty, however, must be avoided. Materials similar to those used in class but which vary slightly in content or form are most desirable. Such materials can usually be obtained by modifying selections from textbooks, newspapers, news magazines, and various reference materials pertinent to the course content.

4. *Select introductory material that is brief but meaningful.* Another method of minimizing the influence of general reading skill on the measurement of complex learning outcomes is to keep the introductory material as brief as possible. Digests of articles are frequently available and provide good raw material for interpretive exercises. Where digests are unavailable, the summary of an article or a key passage may provide sufficient material. In some cases, the relevant information is summarized more adequately in a table, diagram, or picture.

In striving for brief introductory material, be careful not to omit elements which are crucial to the interpretive skills being measured. The material should, of course, also be complete enough to be meaningful and interesting to the pupils.

5. *Revise introductory material for clarity, conciseness, and greater interpretive value.* Although some materials (for example, graphs) can be used without revision, most selections require some adaptation for testing purposes. Technical articles frequently contain long, detailed descriptions of events. On the other hand, news reports and digests of articles are brief but frequently present exaggerated reports of events to attract reader interest. While such exaggerated reports provide excellent material for measuring the ability to judge the relevance of arguments, the need for

assumptions, the validity of conclusions, and the like, the material must usually be modified to be used effectively.

Revision of the introductory material and construction of the related test items tend to be interdependent procedures. Rewriting of material frequently suggests questions to be used, and the construction of test questions often necessitates revisions of the material. In revising a description of an experiment, for example, assumptions, hypotheses, or conclusions which are explicitly stated in the description may be deleted and used as a basis for questions. By the same token, a question calling for application of the experimental findings may require the addition of new material to the selection. Thus the revision of the introductory material and the construction of test items proceed in a circular fashion until a clear, concise interpretive exercise evolves.

6. Construct test items which require analysis and interpretation of the introductory material. There are two common errors in the construction of interpretive exercises which invalidate them as a measure of complex achievement. One is to include questions which are answered directly in the introductory material—that is, asking for factual information which is explicitly stated in the selection. Such questions measure simple reading skill. The second is to include questions which can be answered correctly without reading the introductory material—that is, requiring answers based on general information in the area. These questions, of course, merely measure simple knowledge outcomes.

If the interpretive exercise is to function as intended, it should include only those test items which require pupils to read the introductory material and to make the desired interpretations. In some instances, the interpretations will require pupils to supply knowledge beyond that presented in the exercise. In others, the interpretations will be limited to the factual information provided. The relative emphasis on knowledge and interpretive skill will be determined by the specific learning outcomes being measured. Regardless of the emphasis, however, the test items should be dependent on the introductory material, while at the same time calling forth mental reactions of a higher order than those related to simple reading comprehension.

7. Make the number of test items roughly proportional to the length of the introductory material. It is inefficient to have pupils analyze a long, complex selection of material and answer only one or two questions concerning it. Although it is impossible to specify the exact number of questions which should accompany a given amount of material, the items presented earlier in this chapter illustrate a desirable balance. Other things being equal, we shall always favor the interpretive exercise which has brief introductory material and a relatively large number of test items.

8. In constructing test items for an interpretive exercise, observe all pertinent suggestions for constructing objective items. The form of test item used in the interpretive exercise will determine the suggestions for construction which have greatest value. If common forms of the multiple-choice or alternative-response item are used, the specific suggestions for constructing these item types should be observed. Where modified forms are used, suggestions for constructing each of the various types of objective items should be reviewed for their applicability in construction. Freedom from irrelevant clues and technical defects is as important in interpretive exercises as it is in single, independent test items.

9. *In constructing key-type test items, make the categories homogeneous and mutually exclusive.* The key-type item, which is used rather frequently in interpretive exercises, is a modified multiple-choice form which uses a common set of alternatives. In this regard, it is also similar to the matching item. Its construction should be guided by the suggestions for constructing these item types, with special attention devoted to the categories used in the key. All of the categories in any one key should be homogeneous. That is, they should all be concerned with similar types of judgment. At the same time, there should be no overlapping of categories. Each alternative should provide a distinct and separate category so that a clear-cut system of classification is provided and so that each item has only one correct answer.

EXAMPLES

The majority of dental scientists are in general agreement that fluoridated water reduces tooth decay. A number of cities have fluoridated their water supply and reports indicate that fluoridated water is both safe and inexpensive. Despite an intensive educational campaign pointing out the benefits of fluoridated water many cities do not have fluoridated water.
Resolved: In the interests of national health, all cities should be required to fluoridate their water supply.
Directions: Read each of the following statements carefully. In front of each statement mark
    KEY: A—if the statement supports the resolution.
            B—if the statement contradicts the resolution.
            C—if the statement is a fact.
            D—if the statement is an opinion.
———1. The long-range effects of fluoridated water on an individual's health have not been studied.
                    (Similar items complete the exercise.)

In this example note that the key includes two overlapping types of categories. One is concerned with the relationship of each statement to the resolution and the other with the nature of the statement itself. This makes it impossible to have only one correct answer for each statement. Item 1, for example, would have to be marked category B because it contradicts the resolution and category C because it is a statement of fact.

The above key could be improved by limiting the categories to the relevance of the statements to the resolutions, as illustrated in the following key:

KEY: A—if the statement *supports* the resolution.
        B—if the statement *contradicts* the resolution.
        C—if the statement neither supports nor contradicts the resolution.

If judging both the factual nature of a statement and its relevance is significant, these two elements can be combined in such a way that discrete categories are obtained as follows:

KEY: A—if it is a statement of *fact* which *supports* the resolution.
        B—if it is a statement of *opinion* which *supports* the resolution.
        C—if it is a statement of *fact* which *contradicts* the resolution.
        D—if it is a statement of *opinion* which *contradicts* the resolution.

The major drawback to combining two types of judgment in one category is the greater complexity of the key. This would be especially undesirable with younger pupils.

10. *In constructing key-type test items, develop standard key categories where applicable.* Despite the usefulness of the interpretive exercise for measuring complex achievement, it has not been used extensively by classroom teachers. A big factor in restricting its use has been the difficulty of construction. The popularity of the key-type item in interpretive exercises can probably be attributed to the fact that it uses a common set of alternatives. This makes it easier to construct than the regular multiple-choice form which requires a different set of alternatives for each item.

It is frequently possible to simplify further the construction of key-type interpretive exercises by developing key categories that can be reused with different content. For example, a learning outcome such as the ability to recognize assumptions might lead to the following key:

KEY: A—an assumption which is necessary to make the conclusion valid.
        B—an assumption which would invalidate the conclusion.
        C—an assumption which has no bearing on the validity of the conclusion.

This key could be used with a brief description of a situation, a conclusion based on the situation, and a list of assumptions. Both the key and the form of the item could be used repeatedly with only the content varying. Although selecting new content material is still a problem, the framework provided by the standard key categories simplifies the process considerably.

This use of standard key categories is, of course, not applicable in all areas and should not be permitted to determine which learning outcomes receive emphasis. Rather, the time and effort saved by such procedures should free the teacher to explore more creative applications of the interpretive exercise in other areas.

SUMMARY

Complex achievement refers to those learning outcomes based on the higher mental processes. Such outcomes are classified under a number of general headings including understanding, reasoning, thinking, and problem solving. The attainment of goals in these areas can be measured by both objective and subjective means. The most commonly used objective item is the *interpretive exercise.*

The interpretive exercise consists of a series of objective questions based on written materials, tables, charts, graphs, maps, or pictures. The questions require pupils to demonstrate the specific interpretive skill being measured. For example, pupils might be called upon to recognize assumptions, inferences, conclusions, relationships, applications, and the like. The structure provided by the interpretive exercise makes it possible to obtain independent measures of each specific aspect of thinking and problem-solving skill. While it is efficient for measuring such specific learning outcomes, it does not provide evidence concerning the ability of pupils to integrate and use these skills in a global attack on a problem. Thus it is limited to a diagnostic analysis of problem-solving skills.

Probably the major factor in retarding the use of the interpretive exercise has been the difficulty of construction. This process involves (1) the selection of appropriate introductory material, (2) a revision of the material in harmony with the outcomes to be measured, and (3) the construction of a series of dependent test items that call forth the desired behavior. Although these steps are admittedly time consuming, the rewards in terms of improved teaching-learning practices would seem to justify the time and effort required.

LEARNING EXERCISES

1. What are the advantages of the interpretive exercise over the essay test for measuring complex achievement? What are the disadvantages?
2. For which one of the following learning outcomes is the interpretive exercise most likely to be appropriate? Why?
   a. Explains cause-effect relations.
   b. Formulates tenable hypotheses.
   c. Recognizes valid conclusions.
   d. Selects and organizes ideas.
3. Discuss the relative merits of the interpretive exercise and the single-item multiple-choice question. For which situation would each be most useful? What are the limitations of each?

4. Construct one interpretive exercise for each of the following:
   a. A paragraph of written material.
   b. A picture or cartoon.
   c. A chart or graph.
5. What steps would you follow in examining an interpretive exercise to determine whether it had been properly constructed?
6. What are some of the factors to consider when you are deciding whether to use interpretive exercises in a classroom test?

SUGGESTIONS FOR FURTHER READING

GRONLUND, N. E. *Constructing Achievement Tests.* Englewood Cliffs, N.J.: Prentice-Hall, Inc., 1968. Chapter 4, "Constructing Objective Tests of Complex Achievement." Describes and illustrates the use of simple and complex item types for measuring the higher-level outcomes in the taxonomy of educational objectives.

MEHRENS, W. A., and I. J. LEHMANN. *Measurement and Evaluation in Education and Psychology.* New York: Holt, Rinehart & Winston, Inc., 1973. See Chapter 10, "Writing Objective Test Items: The Multiple-Choice and Context-Dependent Items," for sample interpretive exercises and suggestions for writing them.

WESMAN, A. G. "Writing the Test Item," Chapter 4 in R. L. Thorndike (ed.), *Educational Measurement.* Washington, D.C.: American Council on Education, 1971. An extended treatment of the topic of item writing. See pages 120–128 for the construction of interpretive exercises.

Illustrative Test Items

MORSE, H. T., and G. H. McCUNE. *Selected Items for the Testing of Study Skills and Critical Thinking.* Washington, D.C.: National Council for the Social Studies, 1971.

Multiple-Choice Questions: A Close Look. Princeton, N.J.: Educational Testing Service, 1973. Illustrates the use of the multiple-choice item for measuring complex achievement in a variety of fields. Maps, graphs, pictures, diagrams, and written materials are used. Each item is followed by a statistical and logical analysis of its effectiveness.

CHAPTER 10
Measuring Complex Achievement: The Essay Test

Some aspects of complex achievement cannot be measured objectively.
. . . Learning outcomes which indicate pupils are to originate ideas . . .
to organize and express ideas . . . and to integrate ideas in a global attack
on a problem . . . require the greater freedom of response provided
by the essay test.

Up to this point, our main concern has been with objective test items.
We have noted that such items can measure a variety of learning outcomes,
from simple to complex, and that the interpretive exercise is especially useful for measuring complex achievement. Despite this wide applicability of
objective-item types, there remain significant instructional outcomes for
which no satisfactory objective measurements have been devised. These
include such outcomes as the ability to recall, organize, and integrate ideas;
the ability to express oneself in writing; and the ability to supply rather
than merely identify interpretations and applications of data. Such outcomes require less structuring of response than that imposed by objective
test items. It is in the measurement of these outcomes that the essay
question serves its most useful purpose.

FORMS AND USES OF ESSAY QUESTIONS

Our discussion of the essay question will be limited to its use in the
measurement of complex achievement. In doing so, the fact that many
teachers use essay questions to measure knowledge of factual information
is not being disregarded. Unfortunately, this is probably one of the major
uses in classroom testing. It is just that using essay tests to measure factual

knowledge is seldom warranted. The distinctive feature of essay questions is the freedom of response permitted the pupil. He is free to select, relate, and present ideas in his own words. While this freedom enhances the value of essay questions as a measure of complex achievement, it introduces scoring difficulties which makes them inefficient as a measure of factual knowledge. For most purposes, knowledge of factual information can be more efficiently measured by some type of objective item.

Essay questions should be used, primarily, for the measurement of those learning outcomes that cannot be measured by objective test items. The unique features of essay questions can be utilized most fully when their shortcomings are offset by the need for such measurement. Learning outcomes concerned with the abilities to select, organize, integrate, relate, and evaluate ideas, require the freedom of response and the originality provided for by essay questions. In addition, these outcomes are of such great educational significance that the expenditure of energy in the difficult and time-consuming task of evaluating the answers can be easily justified.

The freedom of response provided by essay questions is not an all-or-none affair but rather a matter of degree. At one extreme, the response is almost as restricted as that in the short-answer objective item. Here a sentence or two may be all that is required. At the other extreme, the pupil is given almost complete freedom in making his response, and his answer may require several pages. Although variations in freedom of response tend to fall along a continuum between these extremes, essay questions can be conveniently classified into two types. These are the restricted response type and the extended response type referred to earlier.

Restricted Response Questions

The restricted response question tends to limit both the content and the form of pupil response. The content is usually limited by restricting the scope of the topic to be discussed. Limitations on the form of response are generally indicated in the statement of the question.

EXAMPLES

List, in statement form, the major differences between the Korean War and previous wars in which the United States has participated.
Why is the barometer one of the most useful instruments for forecasting weather? Answer in a brief paragraph.
Describe two situations which illustrate the application of the law of supply and demand. Do not use examples discussed in class.

Another way of restricting responses in essay tests is to base the questions on specific problems. For this purpose, introductory material like that used in interpretive exercises can be presented. Such items differ from objective interpretive exercises only by the fact that essay questions are used instead of multiple-choice or alternative-response items.

The majority of dental scientists are in general agreement that fluoridating a city's water supply is a safe and inexpensive method of preventing tooth decay. However, many cities have not fluoridated their water because the residents voted against it. One of the main arguments against fluoridation is that *fluoridating a city's water supply violates the individual's freedom of choice*.

    (A) Indicate whether you agree or disagree with the italicized part of the last statement.

    (B) List reasons which support your position.

Because of the greater structure imposed by the restricted response question, it is most useful for measuring learning outcomes requiring the interpretation and application of data in a specific area. In fact, any of the learning outcomes measured by an objective interpretive exercise can also be measured by a restricted response essay question. The major difference is that the interpretive exercise measures at the recognition level while the restricted response question requires that the pupil supply the answer. In some instances, the objective interpretive exercise would be favored because of the ease and reliability of scoring. In other situations, the restricted response question might be favored because of its more direct relevance to the learning outcome (e.g., the ability to *formulate* valid conclusions).

Although restricting pupils' responses to essay questions makes it possible to measure learning outcomes of a more specific and clearly defined nature, these same restrictions make them less valuable as a measure of those learning outcomes emphasizing integration, organization, and originality. Restricting the scope of the topic to be discussed and indicating the nature of the response desired limits the pupil's opportunity to demonstrate these behaviors. For such outcomes, greater freedom of response is needed.

Extended Response Questions

The extended response question provides a wide range of latitude. The pupil is generally free to select any factual information which he thinks is pertinent, to organize the answer in accordance with his best judgment, and to integrate and evaluate ideas as he deems appropriate. This freedom makes it possible for the pupil to demonstrate his competence in these particular areas—that is, the ability to select, organize, integrate, and evaluate ideas. On the other hand, this same freedom makes the extended response question inefficient for measuring more specific learning outcomes, and it introduces scoring difficulties which severely restrict its use as a measuring instrument.

EXAMPLES

Compare the administrations of President Eisenhower and President Kennedy in terms of significant developments in international relations. Cite specific illustrations where possible.

Critically evaluate the significance of the sea captain's pursuit of the white whale in *Moby-Dick*.

Describe the influence of Mendel's laws of heredity on the development of biology as a science.

Write a scientific evaluation of the Copernican theory of the solar system. Include scientific observations which support your statements.

The need for a measure of a pupil's global attack on a problem, like that provided by the extended response question, can easily be defended. The specific thinking and problem-solving skills measured by objective interpretive exercises and restricted response essay questions seldom function in isolation. In a natural situation they operate together in a manner which includes more than a sum of the specific skills involved. These skills interact with each other and with the knowledge and understanding called for by the problem. Thus, it is not just the specific skills we are interested in measuring but also how they function as an integrated whole.

There is general agreement among both teachers and test specialists that the extended response question does call forth complex behaviors that cannot be measured by more objective means. Where the disagreement arises is in the extent to which the scoring can provide a satisfactory measure of these complex behaviors. Test specialists point out that the scoring is so unreliable that such questions should not be used for measurement purposes but should be used as teaching devices only. With little regard for the opinions and evidence of test specialists, the majority of teachers continue to use the extended response question in the measurement of pupil achievement. Unfortunately, they all too frequently do so without regard to the learning outcomes being measured or to the complexities involved in the construction and scoring of such questions. Neither the "head in the sand" position of the test specialists nor the "everything is coming up roses" attitude of the teachers seems to be contributing much to the valid measurement of pupil achievement. It would seem more sensible to identify the complex behaviors we want to measure, formulate questions which elicit these behaviors, evaluate the results as reliably as we can, and then use these admittedly inadequate data as the best evidence we have available.

Summary Comparison of Learning Outcomes Measured

As noted earlier, the restricted response question can measure a variety of complex learning outcomes similar to those measured by the objective interpretive exercise. The main difference is that the interpretive exercise requires pupils to *select* the answer, and the restricted response question requires the pupil to *supply* the answer. In comparison, the extended response question measures more general learning outcomes, such as abilities to select, organize, integrate, and evaluate ideas. A summary comparison of the types of complex learning outcomes measured by each of these essay types in comparison to the objective interpretive exercise is presented in Table 10.1.

TABLE 10.1
TYPES OF COMPLEX LEARNING OUTCOMES MEASURED BY ESSAY QUESTIONS AND OBJECTIVE INTERPRETIVE EXERCISES

Type of Test Item	Examples of Complex Learning Outcomes that Can Be Measured

Objective Interpretive Exercises	Ability to—
	     identify cause-effect relationship
	     identify the application of principles
	     identify the relevance of arguments
	     identify tenable hypotheses
	     identify valid conclusions
	     identify unstated assumptions
	     identify the limitations of data
	     identify the adequacy of procedures
	 (and similar outcomes based on the pupil's ability to *select* the answer)

Restricted Response Essay Questions	Ability to—
	     explain cause-effect relationships
	     describe applications of principles
	     present relevant arguments
	     formulate tenable hypotheses
	     formulate valid conclusions
	     state necessary assumptions
	     describe the limitations of data
	     explain methods and procedures
	 (and similar outcomes based on the pupil's ability to *supply* the answer)

Extended Response Essay Questions	Ability to—
	     produce, organize, and express ideas
	     integrate learnings in different areas
	     create original forms (e.g., designing an experiment)
	     evaluate the worth of ideas

The learning outcomes in Table 10.1 are of course *merely suggestive of the types of learning outcomes that can be measured.* With slight modifications in wording an infinite variety of outcomes could be stated in each area. It should also be remembered that the freedom of response provided by the essay question is a matter of degree. Thus, functions of the restricted response question and the extended response question will tend to overlap near the middle of the range.

ADVANTAGES AND LIMITATIONS OF ESSAY QUESTIONS

The main advantage of the essay question has already received considerable emphasis—that is, it provides a measure of complex learning outcomes which cannot be measured by other means. It should be pointed out, however, that the use of essay questions does not guarantee the measurement of complex achievement. To serve such purposes, the construction of essay questions must receive the same careful planning that goes into the construction of objective test items. The course objectives pertinent to complex achievement must be carefully defined in terms of specific learning outcomes and the essay questions must be phrased so as to call forth the desired behavior. Where a table of specifications is used in planning for the test, it is, of course, simply a matter of constructing the questions in accordance with the specifications indicated in the table.

A second advantage confined largely to the extended response question, is the emphasis given to the integration and application of thinking and problem-solving skills. Although objective items, such as the interpretive exercise, can be designed to measure various aspects of complex achievement, the ability to integrate and apply these skills in a general attack on a problem requires the unique features of the essay question. In addition to the importance of measuring these outcomes such questions tend to have a desirable influence on pupils' study habits. The research studies in this area are based on more general uses of the essay question than we are considering here, but they are in general agreement that pupils tend to direct their attention toward the integration and application of larger units of subject matter when essay questions are included in classroom tests.[1] Questions designed specifically to measure complex learning outcomes should have even a greater influence on these desirable pupil learnings.

Since the pupil must present his answer in his own handwriting, the essay test is frequently looked upon as a device for improving writing skills. No one would disclaim that the ability to express oneself in writing is an educational objective of great significance. However, there is some question whether the tensions and pressures of test taking provide a desirable climate for developing writing skills. It would seem that written assignments which could be completed under more favorable conditions would contribute more to the attainment of this objective.

Another commonly cited advantage of the essay question is its ease of construction. This factor, probably more than any other, has led to its

[1] W. E. Coffman, "Essay Examinations," in R. L. Thorndike (ed.), *Educational Measurement* (Washington, D.C.: American Council on Education, 1971).

widespread use by classroom teachers. In a matter of minutes, most teachers can formulate several essay questions. This is an attractive feature to the busy teacher who is caught up in the pell-mell of daily activities. This apparent advantage can be very misleading, however. Constructing essay questions which call forth the specific behaviors emphasized in a particular set of learning outcomes requires considerable time and effort. Where ease of construction is stressed, it usually refers to the all-too-frequent practice of dashing off questions at the last minute with little regard for the course objectives. In such cases there is some question whether ease of construction can be considered an advantage. In addition to the invalidity of the measurement, evaluating the answers to carelessly developed questions tends to be a confusing and time-consuming task.

The limitations of the essay test are so severe that it would probably be discarded entirely as a measuring instrument were it not for the fact that it measures significant learning outcomes which cannot be measured by other means. The most serious limitation is the unreliability of the scoring. A series of studies has shown that answers to essay questions are scored differently by different teachers and that even the same teachers score the answers differently at different times. Variations in scoring the same paper have been shown to range all the way from near perfect scores to those representing dismal failure.[2] Such results hardly foster confidence in the essay test. In all fairness, however, it should be pointed out that in most studies reporting on the reliability of scoring essay questions the learning outcomes being measured were not clearly identified. Evaluating essay questions without adequate attention to the learning outcomes being measured is comparable to the "three blind men appraising the elephant." One teacher stresses factual content, one organization of ideas, and another writing skill. With each teacher evaluating the degree to which different learning outcomes are achieved, it is not surprising that they disagree so widely in their scoring. Even variations in scoring by the same teacher can probably be accounted for to a large extent by inadequate attention to learning outcomes. Where evaluation of answers is not guided by clearly defined outcomes, it tends to be based on less stable intuitive types of judgment. Although the subjective process of scoring essay questions will always include some uncontrollable variations, the scoring reliability can be greatly increased by clearly defining the outcomes to be measured, properly framing the questions, carefully following scoring rules, and obtaining practice in scoring.[3]

A closely related limitation of essay questions is the amount of time required for scoring the answers. If the scoring is done conscientiously and helpful comments are written on the papers, even a small number

---

[2] W. E. Coffman, "Essay Examinations," in R. L. Thorndike (ed.), *Educational Measurement* (Washington, D.C.: American Council on Education, 1971).
[3] W. E. Coffman, "Essay Examinations," in R. L. Thorndike (ed.), *Educational Measurement* (Washington, D.C.: American Council on Education, 1971).

of papers may require several hours of scoring time. Where classes are large and a number of essay questions are used in a test, conscientious scoring becomes practically impossible. Ironically, most of the suggestions for improving the scoring of essay questions require more time, not less as might be hoped for. The only practical solution seems to be to reserve the use of essay questions for those learning outcomes that cannot be measured objectively. With fewer essay questions to score in a given test, more time will be available for a careful reading and evaluation of the answers.

Another shortcoming of essay questions which restricts their efficient use is the limited sampling they provide. So few questions can be included in a given test that some areas are measured intensely while many others are neglected. This inadequate sampling makes essay questions especially inefficient for measuring knowledge of factual information. For such outcomes we can use objective test items, reserving essay questions for measuring complex achievement. This does not eliminate the sampling problem, however, since we would also like an adequate sample of complex behaviors. Here, where we must use essay questions despite their limited sampling, special efforts should be made to obtain as representative a sample as possible. One way of doing this is to accumulate evidence from a series of essay questions administered at different times throughout the school year.

SUGGESTIONS FOR CONSTRUCTING ESSAY QUESTIONS

The improvement of the essay question as a measure of complex learning outcomes requires attention to two basic problems: (1) how to construct essay questions which call forth the desired behavior, and (2) how to score the answers so that a reliable measure of the achievement is attained. Here we shall confine ourselves to suggestions for constructing essay questions. In the next section, we shall consider suggestions for improving scoring. While this provides a convenient organization for discussion purposes, it should be noted that these two procedures are closely interrelated.

1. *Restrict the use of essay questions to those learning outcomes which cannot be satisfactorily measured by objective items.* Other things being equal, we shall always favor objective measurement over subjective measurement. There appears to be little justification for using essay questions to measure learning outcomes which can be satisfactorily measured by more objective means. By the same token, the problems of scoring and the inadequacy of sampling provide ample justification for not using essay questions in those areas. It is where other things are *not* equal, that the use of essay questions is most desirable. Where objective items are inadequate for measuring the learning outcomes, the use of essay questions can be defended despite their limitations. Some of the complex learning out-

comes, such as those pertaining to the organization, integration, and expression of ideas, will be neglected unless essay questions are used. It is by restricting its use to these areas that the essay question's unique contribution to the evaluation of pupil achievement can be most fully realized.

2. *Formulate questions which will call forth the behavior specified in the learning outcomes.* As with objective items, essay questions should measure the achievement of clearly defined instructional objectives. If the ability to apply principles is being measured, for example, the questions should be phrased in such a manner that they call forth that particular behavior. Essay questions should never be hurriedly constructed in the vain hope that they will measure broad, important (but unidentified) educational objectives. Each essay question should be carefully designed to elicit particular aspects of behavior defined in the desired learning outcomes (see list of thought questions and sample item stems in box).

Constructing essay questions in accordance with particular learning outcomes is much easier with restricted response questions than with extended response questions. The limits placed on the scope of the topic and the type of response expected make it possible to relate a question directly to one or more of the specific outcomes. In the case of the extended response question, the extreme freedom makes it difficult to phrase the question so that the pupil's responses will reflect the particular learning outcomes desired. This difficulty can be partially overcome by indicating the bases on which the answer will be evaluated.

EXAMPLES

Write a two-page statement defending the importance of conserving our natural resources. (Your answer will be evaluated in terms of its organization, its comprehensiveness, and the relevance of the arguments presented.)

Informing the pupils that they should pay special attention to organization, comprehensiveness, and the relevance of the arguments adds structure to the task and makes it possible to key the item to a particular set of learning outcomes. These directions alone will not, of course, provide assurance that the appropriate behaviors are exhibited. It is only when the pupils have been specifically taught how to organize ideas, how to treat a topic comprehensively, and how to present relevant arguments that such directions serve their intended purpose.

3. *Phrase each question so that the pupil's task is clearly indicated.* The specific purpose a teacher had in mind when formulating a question is frequently not conveyed to the pupil because of the vague and ambiguous phrasing of the question. As a result pupils interpret the question differently and a hodge-podge of answers is received. Since it is impossible to determine which of the incorrect answers are due to misinterpretation and which to lack of achievement, the results are worse than worthless.

SOME TYPES OF THOUGHT QUESTIONS AND SAMPLE ITEM STEMS

1. *Comparing*
   Describe the similarities and differences between . . .
   Compare the following two methods for . . .

2. *Relating cause and effect*
   What are major causes of . . . ?
   What would be the most likely effects of . . . ?

3. *Justifying*
   Which of the following alternatives would you favor and why?
   Explain why you agree or disagree with the following statement.

4. *Summarizing*
   State the main points included in . . .
   Briefly summarize the contents of . . .

5. *Generalizing*
   Formulate several valid generalizations from the following data.
   State a set of principles that can explain the following events.

6. *Inferring*
   In light of the facts presented, what is most likely to happen, when . . . ?
   How would (Senator X) be likely to react to the following issue?

7. *Classifying*
   Group the following items according to . . .
   What do the following items have in common?

8. *Creating*
   List as many ways as you can think of for . . .
   Make up a story describing what would happen if . . .
   Write a list of questions that should be answered before . . .

9. *Applying*
   Using the principle of . . . as a guide, describe how you would solve the following problem situation.
   Describe a situation that illustrates the principle of . . .

10. *Analyzing*
    Describe the reasoning errors in the following paragraph.
    List and describe the main characteristics of . . .
    Describe the relationship between the following parts of . . .

11. *Synthesizing*
    Describe a plan for proving that . . .
    Write a well-organized report that shows . . .
    Write a set of specifications for building a . . .

12. *Evaluating*
    Criticize or defend each of the following statements.
    Describe the strengths and weaknesses of the following . . .
    Using the criteria developed in class, write a critical evaluation of . . .

They may actually be harmful if used as a measure of pupil progress toward instructional objectives.

One way to clarify the nature of the question is to make it as specific as possible. For the restricted response question, this means limiting and structuring the question until the desired response is clearly defined.

EXAMPLES

Poor: Why do birds migrate?
Better: State three specific hypotheses which might explain why birds migrate south in the fall of the year.

The improved version of the preceding item presents the pupils with a definite task to perform. Although some pupils may not be able to provide the answer, they will all certainly know what type of response is expected. Note also how easy it would be to relate such an item to a specific learning outcome such as "the ability to formulate tenable hypotheses."

Where an extended response question is desired, some limitation of the question may be possible but care must be taken not to destroy its unique function. If it becomes too limited and structured, it will be less effective as a measure of the ability to select, organize, and integrate ideas. The best procedure for clarifying the extended response question seems to be the one suggested earlier, that is, provide the pupil with explicit directions concerning the type of response desired.

EXAMPLES

Poor: Compare the Democratic and Republican parties.
Better: Compare the current policies of the Democratic and Republican parties with regard to the role of government in private business. Support your statements with specific examples, where possible. (Your answer should be confined to two pages. It will be evaluated in terms of the appropriateness of the facts and examples presented, and the skill with which it is organized.)

The first version of the above item provides no common basis for responding and consequently no frame of reference for evaluating the answer. Even if the only learning outcome being measured was the "ability to organize," greater structure would be needed. Where pupils interpret a question differently their answers will be organized differently because organization is partly a function of the content being organized. Also, some pupils would delimit the problem before answering and thereby provide themselves with a much easier task of organization than that of pupils who attempted to treat the broad aspects of the problem.

The improved version provides pupils with a clearly defined task without destroying their freedom to select and organize the answer. This is achieved by both limiting the scope of the question and by including directions concerning the type of answer desired.

4. Indicate an approximate time limit for each question. Most essay questions place a premium on speed of writing because inadequate attention is paid to time limits during the construction of the test. As each question is constructed, the teacher should estimate the approximate time needed for a satisfactory response. In judging the response time to be allotted to a question, it is well to keep in mind the speed of writing of the slower pupils in class. Most errors in judging the amount of time needed are in the direction of too little time. It is better to use fewer questions and more generous time limits than to put some pupils at a distinct disadvantage.

The time limits allotted to each question should be indicated to the pupils, so they can pace their writing on each question and not be caught at the end of the testing time with "just one more question to go." Where the test contains both objective and essay questions, the pupils should, of course, be told approximately how much time to spend on each part of the test. This may be done orally or included on the test form itself. In either case, care must be taken not to create overconcern about the time factor. The *adequacy* of the time limits might very well be emphasized in the introductory remarks to allay any anxiety that might arise.

5. Avoid the use of optional questions. A fairly common practice in the use of essay questions is to provide pupils with more questions than they are expected to answer and to permit them to choose a given number. The teacher, for example, may include six essay questions in a test and direct pupils to write on any three of them. This practice is generally favored by pupils because they can select those questions they know most about. Except for the desirable effect on pupil morale, however, there is little to recommend the use of optional questions.

Where pupils answer different questions, it is obvious that they are taking different tests and the common basis for evaluating their achievement is lost. Each pupil is demonstrating the achievement of different learning outcomes. As noted earlier, even the "ability to organize" cannot be measured adequately without a common set of responses because organization is partly a function of the content being organized.

The use of optional questions might also influence the validity of the test results in still another way. When pupils anticipate the use of optional questions they can prepare answers on several topics in advance, commit them to memory, and then select questions where the answers are most appropriate. During such advance preparation, it is also possible, of course, for them to obtain help from others in selecting and organizing their answers. Needless to say, this provides a distorted measure of the pupil's achievement. It also tends to have an undesirable influence on study habits, since intensive preparation in a relatively few areas is encouraged.

SUGGESTIONS FOR SCORING ESSAY QUESTIONS

Provisions for improving the reliability of scoring answers to essay questions begin long before the test has been administered. The first step is when the learning outcomes are clearly defined in behavioral terms. This is followed by a careful phrasing of the questions in accordance with the learning outcomes and the inclusion of explicit directions concerning the types of answers desired. It is only when both the pupils and the teacher have a clear notion of the task to be performed that reliable scoring can be expected. No degree of proficiency in evaluating answers can compensate for poorly phrased questions.

When the necessary preliminary steps have been taken in constructing essay questions, the following suggestions can be used effectively to increase the reliability of the scoring:

1. *Prepare an outline of the expected answer in advance.* This should contain the major points to be included, the characteristics of the answer (e.g., organization) to be evaluated, and the amount of credit to be allotted to each. For a restricted response question calling for three specific hypotheses, for example, a list of acceptable hypotheses would be prepared and a given number of scoring points would be assigned to each. For an extended response question, the major points would be outlined. In addition, the relative amount of credit to be allowed for such characteristics as the accuracy of the factual information, the pertinence of the illustrative examples, and the skill of the organization would be indicated.

Preparing a scoring key provides a common basis for evaluating the pupils' answers. This increases the likelihood that our standards for each question will remain stable throughout the scoring. If prepared during the construction of the test, such a scoring key also helps us phrase questions which clearly convey to the pupils the types of answers expected.

2. *Use the scoring method which is most appropriate.* There are two common methods of scoring essay questions. One is called the *point method* and the other the *rating method*. With the point method, each answer is compared to the ideal answer in the scoring key and a given number of points assigned in terms of the adequacy of the answer. With the rating method, each paper is placed in one of several piles as the answer is read. These piles represent degrees of quality and determine the credit assigned to each answer. If eight points are allotted to the question, for example, the pile representing the highest quality might be assigned eight points, the next six, the next four, the next two, and the last none. Usually between three and five categories are used with the rating method.

Restricted response questions can generally be satisfactorily scored by the point method. The restricted scope and the limited number of characteristics included in a single answer make it possible to define degrees of quality with sufficient preciseness to assign point values. The extended response question, however, usually requires the rating method. Only gross judgments can be made concerning the relevance of ideas, the organization of the material, and similar qualities evaluated in answers to extended response questions. Classifying such characteristics into five categories is probably as precise as we can expect to be.

Where the rating method is used, it is desirable to make separate ratings for each characteristic evaluated. The answers should be rated separately for organization, comprehensiveness, relevance of ideas, and the like. This provides for greater objectivity and increases the diagnostic value of the results.

3. Decide on provisions for handling factors which are irrelevant to the learning outcomes being measured. There are a number of factors that influence our evaluations of answers to essay questions which are not directly pertinent to the purposes of the measurement. Prominent among these are legibility of handwriting, spelling, sentence structure, punctuation, and neatness. We should make a special effort to keep such factors from influencing our judgment when evaluating the content of the answers. In some instances, such factors may, of course, be evaluated for their own sake. Where this is done, a separate score for written expression or for each of the specific factors should be obtained. As far as possible, however, we should not let such factors contaminate the extent to which our test scores reflect the achievement of other specific learning outcomes.

Another decision concerns the presence of irrelevant and inaccurate factual information in the answer. Should you ignore it and score only that which is pertinent and correct? If you do, some pupils will write everything that occurs to them, knowing that you will sort out and give credit for anything correct. This discourages careful thinking and desirable evaluative abilities. On the other hand, if you take off points for irrelevant and inaccurate material, the question of how much to lower the score on a given paper is a troublesome one. Probably the best procedure is to decide in advance approximately how much the score on each question is to be lowered where the inclusion of irrelevant material is excessive. The pupils should then be warned that such a penalty will be imposed.

4. Evaluate all answers to one question before going on to the next question. One factor which contributes to unreliability in the scoring of essay questions is a shifting of standards from one paper to the next. A paper with average answers appears to be of much higher quality when it follows a failing paper than when it follows one with near perfect answers. One way to minimize this influence is to score all answers to the first question, shuffle the papers, then score all answers to the second question, and so on, until all of the answers have been scored. A more uniform standard can be maintained with this procedure, since it is easier to keep in mind the basis for judging each answer, and answers of various degrees of correctness can be more easily compared. Where the rating method is used and the papers are placed in several piles on the basis of each answer, shifting standards can also be checked by reading each answer a second time and reclassifying where necessary.

Evaluating all answers to one question at a time helps counteract another type of error that creeps into the scoring of essay questions. Where we evaluate all of the answers on a single paper at one time, the first few answers create a general impression of the pupil's achievement which colors our judgment concerning the remaining answers. Thus, if the first answers are of high quality, we tend to overrate the following answers, while if they are of low quality we tend to underrate them. This "halo effect" is less likely to form when the answers for a given pupil are not evaluated in continuous sequence.

5. *Evaluate the answers without looking at the pupil's name.* The general impressions we form about each pupil during our teaching is also a source of bias in evaluating essay questions. It is not uncommon for a teacher to give a high score to a poorly written answer with the rationalization that "the pupil really knows that material even though he didn't express it too clearly." A similar answer by a pupil regarded less favorably will receive a much lower score with the honest conviction that the pupil got everything he deserved. This form of "halo effect" is one of the most serious deterrents to reliable scoring by classroom teachers and is especially difficult to counteract.

Where possible, the identity of the pupils should be concealed until all answers are scored. The simplest procedure for achieving this is to have the pupils put their names on the back of the papers. In some cases, such as where our curiosity cannot be easily controlled, it is better to identify the papers by numbers rather than names. Where the identity of a pupil cannot be concealed because of familiar handwriting, the best we can do is make a conscious effort to eliminate any such bias from our judgment.

6. *If especially important decisions are to be based on the results, obtain two or more independent ratings.* Sometimes essay questions are included in tests used to select pupils for awards, scholarships, special training, and the like. In such cases, two or more competent persons should score the papers independently and their ratings should be compared. After any large discrepancies have been satisfactorily arbitrated, the independent ratings may be averaged for more reliable results.

SUMMARY

The essay question is especially useful for measuring those aspects of complex achievement which cannot be measured by more objective means. These include (1) the ability to supply rather than merely identify interpretations and applications of data, and (2) the ability to select, organize, and integrate ideas in a general attack on a problem. Outcomes of the first type are measured by *restricted response* questions and outcomes of the second type by *extended response* questions.

Although essay questions provide a relevant measure of significant learning outcomes, they have several limitations which severely restrict their use: (1) the scoring tends to be unreliable, (2) the scoring is time consuming, and (3) a limited sampling of achievement is obtained. Because of these shortcomings, it is suggested that essay questions be limited to testing those outcomes that cannot be measured by objective items.

The construction and scoring of essay questions are interrelated processes which require careful attention if a valid and reliable measure of achievement is to be obtained. Questions should be so phrased that they measure the attainment of definite learning outcomes and clearly convey to the pupils the type of response expected. Indicating an approximate time limit for each question and avoiding the use of optional questions also contributes to more valid results. Scoring procedures can be improved by (1) using a scoring key, (2) adapting the scoring method to the type of question used, (3) controlling the influence of irrelevant factors, (4) evaluating all answers to each question at one time, (5) evaluating without looking at the pupils' names, and (6) obtaining two or more independent ratings where important decisions are to be made.

LEARNING EXERCISES

1. In an area in which you are teaching or plan to teach, identify several learning outcomes that can be best measured with essay questions. For each learning outcome construct two essay questions.
2. Criticize the following essay questions and restate them so that they meet the criteria of a good essay question.
   a. Discuss air transportation.
   b. Do you think the government should spend more on moon exploration?
   c. What is your attitude toward socialized medicine?
3. For each of the following, would it be more appropriate to use an extended response question or a restricted response question?
   a. Compare two periods in history.
   b. Describe the procedure for using a dictionary.
   c. Indicate the advantages of one procedure over another.
   d. Evaluate a short story.
4. Essay tests are frequently defended on the grounds that they provide the pupils with an opportunity to learn to write. How would you react to this view?
5. What factors should be considered in deciding whether essay questions are to be included in a classroom test? Which of the factors are most important?
6. Describe how essay tests might be used to facilitate learning. What types of learning are most likely to be enhanced?

SUGGESTIONS FOR FURTHER READING

Coffman, W. E. "Essay Examinations," Chapter 10 in R. L. Thorndike (ed.), *Educational Measurement*. Washington, D.C.: American Council on Education, 1971. A comprehensive discussion of essay testing and the related research.

EBEL, R. L. *Essentials of Educational Measurement*. Englewood Cliffs, N.J.: Prentice-Hall, Inc., 1972. In Chapter 6, "The Characteristics and Uses of Essay Tests," Ebel compares essay and objective tests and provides suggestions for the preparation and grading of essay questions.

MEHRENS, W. A., and I. J. LEHMANN. *Measurement and Evaluation in Education and Psychology*. New York: Holt, Rinehart & Winston, Inc., 1973. Chapter 8, "The Essay Test: Preparing the Questions and Grading the Responses." Presents examples of different types of essay questions, a review of the claims for using essay tests, and suggestions for construction and scoring.

STANLEY, J. C., and K. D. HOPKINS. *Educational and Psychological Measurement and Evaluation*. Englewood Cliffs, N.J.: Prentice-Hall, Inc., 1972. Chapter 10, "Constructing and Using Essay Tests." See especially the sections concerning the reliability and validity of essay tests.

CHAPTER 11
Assembling, Administering, and Appraising Classroom Tests

Classroom tests are most effective when attention is given to the quality of the individual test items . . . the orderly arrangement of the items . . . the clarity of the directions . . . and the procedures for administering and scoring. . . . Classroom tests can also be improved by applying simple methods of item analysis . . . and by building a test-item file.

In the preceding chapters, we have emphasized the importance of planning classroom tests carefully and of constructing test items that are relevant to the learning outcomes specified in the test plan. These steps have received considerable attention because they are crucial to the validity of a test. The only way we can have any certainty that a classroom test will serve its intended purpose is to identify the learning outcomes we wish to measure and then to construct test items which call forth the specific behavior described in the learning outcomes. Our work does not stop here, however. We must also assemble the items into a test, prepare directions, administer the test, score the test, and interpret and appraise the results.

Care in planning a test and in constructing individual test items should be followed by similar care in preparing the test for use, in administering the test, and in scoring and appraising the results. Lack of attention to such factors can have an adverse effect on the validity of the results. In the final analysis, valid achievement testing is the end product of a systematically controlled series of steps beginning with the identification of objectives and ending with the scoring and interpretation of results. Although validity is "built in" during the construction of the test items, systematic procedures of assembly, administration, and scoring are necessary to assure that the test items will function with maximum effectiveness. Appraising test items after a preliminary tryout can also improve the quality of the items by indicating how each item actually does function in measuring pupil achievement.

ASSEMBLING THE CLASSROOM TEST

The preparation of test items for use in a test is greatly facilitated if the items are properly recorded, if they are written at least several days before they are to be used, and if extra items are constructed. This simplifies the task of reviewing, selecting, and arranging the items in final test form. Writing test items early makes it possible to put them aside for a time before reviewing them for defects. Constructing extra items makes it possible to eliminate those items found to be defective. It also provides some latitude in fitting the final draft of the test to the table of specifications.

Recording Test Items

As test items are being constructed it is desirable to write each item on a separate index card. In addition to the test item, the card should contain information concerning the specific learning outcome and subject-matter content measured by the item. A space should also be reserved on the card for item analysis information and comments concerning the effectiveness of the item. An illustrative card containing this information is presented later in this chapter (see Figure 11.2).

Placing each item on a separate card provides the flexibility needed in preparing a test for use. As the items are being reviewed and edited, items can be eliminated, added, or revised with very little difficulty. The same holds true when arranging the items for the test. They can be arranged and rearranged merely by sorting the cards. The flexibility of this recording system also makes it possible to build a card file of effective test items for future use. The specific procedure for building such an item file will be described later in this chapter.

Reviewing and Editing Test Items

No matter how carefully test items have been prepared, defects inadvertently creep in during construction. As we concentrate on the clarity and conciseness of a question, a verbal clue slips in unnoticed. As we attempt to increase the difficulty of an item, we unwittingly introduce some ambiguity. As we rework an item to make the incorrect choices more plausible, the behavior called forth by the item is unintentionally modified. In short, we focus our attention so closely on some aspects of item construction that we overlook others. This results in an accumulation of unwanted errors. Such technical defects can most easily be detected by (1) reviewing the items after they have been set aside for a few days, and (2) asking a fellow teacher to review and criticize the items.

In reviewing test items, it is desirable to put yourself in the role of the pupil taking the test. From this vantage point, each item should be read carefully and a judgment made concerning the type of response called forth by the item. At the same time, the item should be surveyed carefully for technical defects. The following questions will aid in analyzing the quality of each item.

1. *Is the aspect of knowledge, understanding, or thinking skill called forth by the item in harmony with the specific learning outcome and subject-matter content being measured?* Where a table of specifications has been used as a basis for constructing the test items, this is merely a matter of checking to see whether the item still relates to the same cell in the table. If the functioning content of an item has shifted during construction, the item should either be modified so that it serves its original purpose or reclassified in light of the new purpose served by the item. In any case, the response called forth by an item should be in agreement with the purpose for which the item is to be used.

2. *Is the point of the item clear?* A careful review of test items frequently reveals ambiguity, inappropriate vocabulary, and awkward sentence structure which were overlooked during the construction of the items. It seems that returning to test items after they have been set aside for a few days provides a fresh outlook which makes such defects more apparent. The difficulty of the vocabulary and the complexity of the sentence structure must, of course, be judged in terms of the maturity level of the pupils. However, at all levels, special efforts must be directed toward the removal of ambiguity. In its final form, each item should be so clearly worded that all pupils understand the task. Whether a pupil responds correctly should be determined solely by whether he possesses the knowledge or understanding being measured.

3. *Is the item free from irrelevant clues?* As noted earlier, an irrelevant clue is any element which leads the nonachiever to the correct answer and thereby prevents the item from functioning as intended. These include (1) grammatical inconsistencies, (2) verbal associations, (3) specific determiners (i.e., words such as *always* and *never*), and (4) some mechanical features, such as correct statements tending to be longer than incorrect ones. Most of these clues can be removed merely by making a deliberate attempt to detect them during the item review. The suggestions for constructing each of the item types provides an excellent source of specific points to consider in searching out such clues.

Where it is possible to get a fellow teacher to review the test items, he should be asked to read each item, indicate his answer, and note any technical defects in the item. If his answer does not agree with the key, ambiguity may be indicated. Asking him to "think out loud" as he determines the answer will usually reveal his interpretation of the question and the source of the ambiguity. This is the area in which another reviewer can be most useful. He will be less helpful in evaluating the type of response called forth by the item, since this requires a knowledge of what the pupils have been taught. Only the teacher knows for sure whether an item measures understanding or merely the retention of a previously learned answer.

When the test items have been revised and those to be included in the test have been tentatively selected, a final check should be made in terms of the following questions:

1. Do the test items measure a representative sample of the learning outcomes?
2. Do the test items measure a representative sample of the various phases of course content?
3. Are the test items adapted in difficulty to the purpose of the test and to the pupils for whom the test is intended?
4. Are the test items free from overlapping (so that the information in one does not provide a clue to the answer in another)?

The first two questions can be answered by comparing the final selection of items with the table of specifications. Answers to the last two are determined by reviewing the test items as a whole. Affirmative answers to these questions mean the items are ready to be arranged in final test form.

Arranging the Items in the Test

There are various methods of grouping items in an achievement test, and the method will vary somewhat with the use to be made of the results. For most classroom purposes, however, a satisfactory arrangement of items can be obtained by a systematic consideration of the following factors: (1) the types of items used, (2) the learning outcomes measured, (3) the difficulty of the items, and (4) the subject matter measured.

First and foremost, the items should be arranged in sections by item type. That is, all true-false items should be grouped together, then all matching items, then all multiple-choice items, and so on. This arrangement provides for the fewest sets of directions; it is easier for the pupils since they can retain the same mental set throughout each section; and it greatly facilitates scoring. Where two or more item types are included in a test, there is also some advantage in keeping the simpler item types together and placing the more complex item types in the test, as follows:[1]

---

[1] It is, of course, not expected that all item types will appear in the same test. Seldom are more than a few types used, but this is the general order.

1. True-false or alternative-response items.
2. Matching items.
3. Short-answer items.
4. Multiple-choice items.
5. Interpretive exercises.
6. Essay questions.

Arranging the sections of the test in the above order provides a sequence which roughly approximates the complexity of the learning outcomes measured, ranging from the simple to the complex. It is then merely a matter of grouping the items *within* each item type. For this purpose, items which measure similar outcomes should be placed together and then arranged in order of ascending difficulty. For example, the items in the multiple-choice section might be arranged in the following order: (1) knowledge of terms, (2) knowledge of specific facts, (3) knowledge of principles, and (4) application of principles. Keeping the items which measure similar outcomes together is especially helpful in determining the types of learning outcomes causing pupils the greatest difficulty.

If for any reason it is infeasible to group the items by the learning outcomes measured, it is still desirable to arrange the items in order of increasing difficulty. Beginning with the easiest items and proceeding gradually to the most difficult items has a motivating effect on pupils. Also, encountering difficult items early in the test frequently causes pupils to spend a disproportionate amount of time on such items. If the test is long, they may be forced to omit later questions which they could easily have answered.

With the items classified by item type, as has been suggested, an order of increasing difficulty can be obtained by arranging the sections of the test and by arranging the items within each section. The sequence of item types which has been suggested, beginning with true-false items and ending with essay questions, provides a general order of ascending difficulty for arranging the sections of the test. Some shifts in the first four item types may be warranted by the difficulty of the specific items used, but interpretive exercises and essay tests should certainly be last. When the separate sections are arranged in sequence, the items within each section should then be placed in order of increasing difficulty.

In constructing classroom achievement tests, there is little to be gained by grouping test items in terms of subject-matter content. Where it appears desirable to do so, such as in separating historical periods, these divisions should be kept to a minimum.

To summarize, the most effective method for organizing items in the typical classroom test is to (1) form sections by item type, (2) group the items within each section by the learning outcomes measured, (3) arrange both the sections and the items within sections in an ascending order of difficulty. Use subject-matter groupings only where they are needed for some specific purpose.

Preparing Directions for the Test

Teachers frequently devote considerable time and attention to the construction and assembly of test items and then dash off directions with very little thought. In fact, many teachers include no written directions with their tests, assuming either that the items are self-explanatory or that the pupils are conditioned to answering the types of items used in the test. Oral directions are, of course, also used by some teachers, but they all too frequently leave much to be desired. Whether written, oral, or both, the directions are a vital part of the test and should include at least the following points:[2]

1. Purpose of the test.
2. Time allowed for answering.
3. Basis for answering.
4. Procedure for recording the answers.
5. What to do about guessing.

The amount of detail devoted to each of these points depends mainly on the age level of the pupils, comprehensiveness of the test, complexity of the test items, and the experience of the pupils with the testing procedure used. Use of new item types and separate answer sheets, for example, requires much more detailed directions than familiar items requiring pupils merely to circle or underline the answer.

Purpose of the Test. The purpose of the test is usually indicated at the time the test is announced or at the beginning of the semester when the evaluation procedures are described as a part of the general orientation to the course. Should there be any doubt whether the purpose of the test is clear to all pupils, however, it might better be explained again at the time of testing. This is usually done orally. The only time a statement of the purpose of the test needs to be included in the written directions is when the test is to be administered to several sections taught by different teachers. Here a written statement of purpose assures greater uniformity.

Time Allowed for Answering. It is desirable to indicate to the pupils how much time they will have for the total test and how to distribute their time on each of the parts. Where essay questions are included, it is also desirable to indicate approximately how much time should be allotted to each question. This enables the pupils to use their time most effectively and prevents the less able pupils from spending too much time on questions that are particularly difficult for them.

---

[2] N. E. Gronlund, *Constructing Achievement Tests*. (Englewood Cliffs, N.J.: Prentice-Hall, 1968).

Classroom tests of achievement should generally have liberal time allowances. Except for special purposes, such as measuring proficiency in shorthand, typing, and simple computational skills, speed is not an important factor. Our main concern is the level of achievement each pupil has attained. Were it not for practical considerations like the length of class periods and the pressure of other school activities, there would be no need for any time limits with most classroom achievement tests.

Judging the amount of time pupils will need to complete a given test is not a simple matter. It depends on the types of items used, the age and ability of the pupils, and the complexity of the learning outcomes measured. As a rough guide, the average high school pupil should be able to answer two true-false items, one multiple-choice item, *or* one short-answer item per minute of testing time. Interpretive test items would take much more time; the exact amount depends on the length and complexity of the introductory materials. Also, elementary pupils generally require more time per item than high school pupils, and reading skill is an important determiner of the amount of time needed by a specific group. Experienced teachers familiar with the ability and work habits of a given group of pupils are in the best position to judge time allotments. Where such experience is lacking, it is better to err in the direction of allotting too much time than to deprive some of the slower pupils from demonstrating their maximum levels of achievement.

Basis for Answering. The directions for each section of the test should indicate the basis for selecting or supplying the answers. With true-false, matching, and multiple-choice items this part of the directions can be relatively simple. For example, a statement like "select the choice which best completes the statement or answers the question" might be sufficient for multiple-choice items. Where interpretive exercises are used, however, more detailed directions are necessary since the basis for the response is much more complex. The directions must clearly indicate the precise type of interpretation expected. As illustrated in Chapter 9, each interpretive exercise usually requires its own unique directions.

It is sometimes desirable to include sample test items correctly marked so that pupils can check their understanding of the basis for answering. This practice is especially desirable for elementary school pupils, and also for pupils at other levels where complex item types are used.

As noted earlier, essay questions frequently require special directions concerning the type of response expected. If special emphasis is to be on the selection and organization of ideas, for example, this should be indicated to the pupil so that he has a more adequate basis for responding.

Procedure for Recording the Answers. Answers may be recorded on the test form itself or on separate answer sheets. Where the test is short, or the number of pupils taking the test is small, or the pupils are relatively young, answers are generally recorded directly on the test paper. For most other situations, separate answer sheets are preferred because they reduce the time needed for scoring, and they make it possible to use the test papers over again. The latter feature is especially desirable when the test is to be given to pupils in different sections of the same course.

Directions for recording the answer on the test paper itself can be relatively simple. With selection items, it is merely a matter of instructing the pupils to circle, underline, or check the *letter* indicating the correct answer. For pupils in the primary grades, it is usually better to ask them to mark the answer directly by drawing a line under it. With supply items, the directions should indicate where to put the answer, and the units in which it is to be expressed if the answer is numerical.

Separate answer sheets are easily constructed and the directions for their use can be placed on the test paper or on the answer sheet itself. A common type of teacher-made sheet is presented in Figure 11.1. The directions on this sheet are rather general, since they must cover instructions for recording various types of answers. It should also be noted that pupils are instructed to cross out rather than circle the letters indicating the correct answers. This is to facilitate scoring with a stencil key. Circled letters cannot be readily seen through holes in a stencil.

Special answer sheets developed for machine scoring can be used with classroom tests but there is no advantage in using them unless machine scoring facilities are readily available and the number of papers to be scored warrants the expense. Where machine scoring is to be used, special directions should be obtained from the company supplying the scoring service. An example of an answer sheet for machine scoring is presented in Chapter 14 (Figure 14.3).

What to Do About Guessing. Where test items of the selection type are used, the directions should tell pupils what to do when they are uncertain of the answer. Should they guess or should they omit the item? If no instructions are given on this point, the bold pupils will guess freely while others will answer only those items of which they are fairly certain. The bold pupils will select some correct answers just by lucky guesses and thus their scores will be higher than they should be. On the other hand, if the pupils are merely instructed "Do not guess" or "Answer only those items of which you are certain" the more timid pupils will omit many items they could answer correctly. Such pupils aren't very certain about anything and this uncertainty prevents them from responding, even when they are reasonably sure of the answers. With these directions, the bold pupils will continue to guess, although possibly not quite so wildly.

As noted by Cronbach,[3] the tendency to guess or not to guess when in doubt about an item is determined by personality factors and cannot be entirely eliminated by directions which caution against guessing or which promise penalties to those who do guess. The only way to eliminate varia-

---

[3] L. J. Cronbach, *Essentials of Psychological Testing*, 3rd ed. (New York: Harper and Row, 1970).

Course_____	Name_____
Section_____	Date _____
Test_____	Score: Part I_____
	Part II_____
	Total_____

DIRECTIONS: Read all directions on the test paper carefully and follow them exactly. For each test item, indicate your answer on this sheet by crossing out the appropriate letter (x) or filling the appropriate blank. Be sure that the number on the answer sheet is the same as the number of the test item you are answering.

True-False		Multiple-Choice		Short-Answer	
Item	Answer	Item		Item	Answer
1	T F	21	A B C D E	41	_____
2	T F	22	A B C D E	42	_____
3	T F	23	A B C D E	43	_____
4	T F	24	A B C D E	44	_____

FIGURE 11.1. Top portion of a teacher-made answer sheet.

tions in the tendency to guess is to instruct pupils to answer every item. When this is done, no pupil is given a special advantage and it is unnecessary to correct for guessing in the scoring. Directions such as the following are usually sufficient to communicate this to the pupils: "Since your score is the number right, be sure to answer every item."

Some teachers object to such directions on the grounds that encouraging guessing is undesirable from an educational standpoint. Most responses to doubtful items are not wild guesses, however, but guesses guided by some information and understanding. In this respect, they are not too different from the "informed" guesses we make when we predict weather, judge the possible consequences of a decision, or choose one course of action over another. Problem solving always involves a certain amount of this type of "informed" guessing.

A more defensible objection to directions which encourage guessing is that the chance errors introduced into the test scores lower the accuracy of measurement. Although this is certainly objectionable, it probably has less influence on the validity of the results than the systematic advantage given to the "bold" guessers by the "do not guess" directions.

For liberally timed classroom tests, the "answer-every-item" directions are definitely favored. However, for speed tests, and in situations where teachers prefer to discourage guessing, directions such as the following provide a good compromise:

> Answer all items for which you can find some reasonable basis for answering, even though you are not completely sure of the answer. *Do not guess wildly*, however, since there will be a correction for guessing.[4]

There seems to be a trend in standardized testing toward the "make informed guesses but not wild guesses" type of directions. It should be noted, however, that speed is a more significant factor in standardized testing than in ordinary classroom testing and that the test items are not as closely keyed to the learning experiences of the pupils. Where pupils are familiar with the content of the test and have ample opportunity to consider every item, there is generally no need to warn against "wild" guesses or to attempt a correction for it.

Reproducing the Test

In preparing the test materials for reproduction it is important that the test items be spaced and arranged so that they can be read, answered, and scored with the least amount of difficulty. Cramming too many test items on a page is poor economy. What little paper is saved will not make up for the time and confusion which results during the administration and scoring of the test.

All test items should have generous borders. Multiple-choice items should have the alternatives listed in a vertical column beneath the stem of the item, rather than across the page. Items should not be split with parts of the item on two different pages. With interpretive exercises, the introductory materials can sometimes be placed on a facing page or separate sheet with all of the items referring to it on a single page.

Unless a separate answer sheet is used, the space for answering should be down one side of the page, preferably the left. The most convenient method of response is circling the letter of the correct answer. With this

---

[4] The correction-for-guessing formula and the rationale for its use will be discussed under scoring later in this chapter.

arrangement, scoring is simply a matter of placing a strip scoring key beside the column of answers.

Test items should be numbered consecutively throughout the test. Each test item will need to be identified during discussion of the test and for other purposes such as item analysis. Where separate answer sheets are used, consecutive numbering is, of course, indispensable.

The duplication of classroom tests is usually by mimeograph or Ditto machine. Where a large number of copies are desired, the photo-offset method is also used. Regardless of the reproduction process selected, it is desirable to proofread the entire test before it is administered. Charts, graphs, and other pictorial material must be checked especially carefully to be certain that the reproduction has been accurate and the details clear.

ADMINISTERING AND SCORING CLASSROOM TESTS

The same care which has gone into the preparation of the test should be carried over into the administration and scoring. Here we are concerned with (1) providing optimum conditions for obtaining the pupils' responses, and (2) selecting convenient and accurate procedures for scoring the results.

Administering the Test

The guiding principle in administering any classroom test is that *all pupils must be given a fair chance to demonstrate their achievement of the learning outcomes being measured.* This means a physical and psychological environment conducive to their best efforts and the control of factors which might interfere with valid measurement.

Desirable physical conditions such as adequate work space, quiet, proper light and ventilation, and comfortable temperature are sufficiently well-known by teachers to warrant little attention here. Of greater importance, but frequently neglected, are the psychological conditions influencing test results. Pupils will not perform at their best if they are overly tense and anxious during testing. Some of the things which create excessive test anxiety are:

1. Threatening pupils with tests, if they do not behave.
2. Warning pupils to do their best "because this test is important."
3. Telling pupils they must work fast to complete the test on time.
4. Threatening dire consequences if they fail the test.

The antidote to test anxiety is to convey to the pupils, by both word and deed, that the test results are to be used to help them improve their learning. They should also be reassured that the time limits are adequate to allow them to complete the test. This, of course, assumes that the test will be used to improve learning and that adequate time limits have been provided.

The time of testing can also be a factor influencing the results. If tests are administered just before "the big game" or "the big dance," the results may not be representative. Furthermore, in the case of individual pupils, fatigue, the onset of illness, or worry about a particular problem may prevent maximum performance. Arranging the time of testing in terms of such factors and permitting the postponement of the test in individual cases, when appropriate, can enhance the validity of the results.

The actual administration of the test is a relatively simple matter, since a properly prepared classroom test is practically self-administering. Oral directions, if used, should be presented in a clear, concise manner. Any sample problems or illustrations put on the blackboard should be kept brief and simple. Beyond this, suggestions for administering a classroom test consist mainly of things to avoid.

1. *Do not talk unnecessarily before the test.* When a teacher announces that there will be "a full forty minutes" to complete the test and then talks for the first ten minutes, pupils feel that they are being unfairly deprived of testing time. Besides, just before a test is no time to make assignments, admonish the class, or introduce next week's topic. Pupils are mentally set for the test and will consciously ignore anything not pertaining to the test for fear it will hinder the recall of information needed to answer the questions. Thus, the well-intentioned remarks fall on "deaf ears" and merely increase anxiety toward the test and cause hostility toward the teacher.

2. *Keep interruptions during the test to a minimum.* At times a pupil will ask to have an ambiguous item clarified and it will be desirable to explain the item to the entire group at the same time. Such interruptions are necessary but should be kept to a minimum. All other distractions, both from without and within the classroom, should, of course, also be eliminated where possible. It is sometimes desirable to hang a "Do not disturb—TESTING" sign on the outside of the door.

3. *Avoid giving hints to pupils who ask about individual items.* If the item is ambiguous it should be clarified for the entire group, as indicated earlier. If it is not ambiguous, the pupil should be told to answer it as best he can. Refraining from giving hints to pupils who ask for help is especially difficult for beginning teachers. However, providing unfair aid to some pupils (the bold, the apple polishers, and so on) decreases the validity of the results and lowers the morale of the class.

4. *Discourage cheating, if necessary.* Where good teacher-pupil rapport exists and the pupils view tests as helpful rather than harmful, cheating is usually not a problem. Under other conditions, however, it might be necessary to discourage cheating by special seating arrangements and careful supervision. Receiving unauthorized help from other pupils during a test has the same deleterious effect on validity and class morale as receiving special hints from the teacher. We are interested in each pupil doing his very best; but for valid results, his score must be based on his own unaided efforts.

Scoring the Test

Procedures for scoring essay questions were described in the last chapter. Here the discussion will be limited to the scoring of objective items.

If the pupils' answers are recorded on the test paper itself, a scoring key is usually obtained by marking the correct answers on a blank copy of the test. The scoring procedure is then simply a matter of comparing the columns of answers on this master copy with the columns of answers on each pupil's paper. A strip key, which consists merely of strips of paper on which the columns of answers are recorded, may also be used if more convenient. These can be prepared easily by cutting the columns of answers from the master copy of the test and mounting them on strips of cardboard cut from manila folders.

Where separate answer sheets are used, a scoring stencil is most convenient. This is a blank answer sheet with holes punched where the correct answers should appear. The stencil is laid over each answer sheet and the number of answer checks appearing through the holes are counted. When this type of scoring procedure is used, each test paper should also be scanned to make certain that only one answer was marked for each item. Any item containing more than one answer should be eliminated from the scoring.

As each test paper is scored, it is desirable to mark each item that is answered incorrectly. With multiple-choice items, a good practice is to draw a red line through the *correct* answer of the missed items rather than through the pupil's wrong answers. This will indicate to the pupil those items he missed and at the same time will let him know what the correct answers are. Time will be saved and confusion avoided during discussion of the test. Marking the correct answers of missed items is especially simple with a scoring stencil. Where no answer check appears through a hole in the stencil, a red line is drawn across the hole.

In scoring objective tests, each correct answer is usually counted one point. This is done because an arbitrary weighing of items makes little difference in the pupils scores on the test. If some items are counted two points, some one point, and some one-half point, the scoring is more complicated without any accompanying benefits. Scores based on such weightings will be similar to the simpler procedure of counting each item one point.

Where pupils are told to answer every item on the test, a pupil's score is simply the number of items he has answered correctly. There is no need to consider wrong answers or to correct for guessing. When all pupils answer every item on a test, the rank order of the pupils' scores will be the same whether the "number right" is used or a correction for guessing is applied. Some teachers prefer to correct for guessing because they feel the resulting scores provide a more accurate indication of the pupil's actual achievement. As we shall see in the following section, however, this is questionable.

Correcting for Guessing. A correction for guessing is usually applied where pupils do not have sufficient time to complete all items on the test and where they have been instructed that there will be a penalty for guessing. The most common formula used for this purpose is the following:

$$\text{Score} = \text{Right} - \frac{\text{Wrong}}{n-1}$$

In this formula, n is the number of alternatives for an item. Thus, the formula would apply to various selection-type items as follows:

True-false items:
$$S = R - \frac{W}{2-1}$$
$$\text{(or)}$$
$$S = R - W$$

Multiple-choice items:

$$\text{(A) Three alternatives } S = R - \frac{W}{2}$$

$$\text{(B) Four alternatives } S = R - \frac{W}{3}$$

$$\text{(C) Five alternatives } S = R - \frac{W}{4}$$

Use of a correction formula in the scoring makes it necessary to count both right and wrong answers. Items which were omitted by a pupil are *not* counted in the scoring.

These correction-for-guessing formulas assume that when a pupil does not know the answer to an item he guesses blindly among all alternatives and he selects the correct answer a given number of times on the basis of chance alone. Thus, if a pupil has 60 items right and 15 items wrong on a true-false test, it is assumed that he guessed blindly on 30 items on the test and had chance success in guessing (15 right and 15 wrong). The formula merely removes his lucky guesses from his score by subtracting the number wrong from the number right: Correct score $= 60 - 15 = 45$.

The same assumption is made in applying the formula to multiple-choice items but the possibility of selecting the correct answer is less because there are more alternatives from which to choose. For example, where a pupil has 60 items right and 15 items wrong on a four-alternative multiple-choice test, it is assumed that he guessed blindly on 20 items and guessed successfully one-fourth of the time. Thus, his blind guessing resulted in 5 right answers and 15 wrong answers. To remove his lucky guesses from his score, it is simply a matter of subtracting one third of his wrong answers. This is what the correction formula does, as the following illustrates:

$$S = R - \frac{W}{3} \qquad\qquad S = 60 - \frac{15}{3} = 55$$

The correction-for-guessing (or correction-for-chance) formula provides a suitable correction where the basic assumption can be satisfied—that is, that pupils guess blindly when they do not know the answer. Such blind guessing seldom occurs in classroom testing, however. Some correct guesses are informed guesses based on partial information, and some wrong answers are due to misinformation or extremely plausible distracters. Where pupils can eliminate some of the alternatives in items and make informed guesses among those remaining, the formula *undercorrects* for chance success. Where pupils select incorrect alternatives because of misinformation or the plausibility of distracters, the formula *overcorrects* for chance success. Consequently, when the correction formula is used with classroom tests an unknown amount of error is introduced into the scoring. Although it is hoped that the two types of error will cancel each other out, there is no way of determining the amount of distortion in the test scores.

Because of the questionable assumption on which the correction-for-guessing formula is based, it is recommended that it not be used with the ordinary classroom test. The only exception is where the test is speeded to the extent that pupils complete different numbers of items. Here its use is defensible, since pupils could increase their scores appreciably by rapidly (and blindly) guessing at the remaining untried items just before the testing period ended.

APPRAISING CLASSROOM TESTS

After a classroom test has been scored and pupils have discussed the results, the usual practice is to discard the test. Except for the pupil criticism during class discussion, which aids in identifying some of the defective items, the teacher has little evidence concerning the quality of the test he used. In addition, by discarding the test he is wasting much of the careful planning and hard work that went into its preparation. A more desirable procedure would be to appraise the effectiveness of the test items and to build a file of high quality items for future use. In a few years the file of items would be so extensive that items could be reused with a long enough time interval in between to prevent pupils from being familiar with the specific content of the items.

The effectiveness of each test item can be determined by analyzing the pupils' responses to the item. This item analysis is usually designed to answer questions such as the following:

1. Did the item function as intended?
   a. Did *norm-referenced* test items adequately discriminate between high and low achievers?
   b. Did *criterion-referenced* test items adequately measure the effects of the instruction?
2. Were the test items of appropriate difficulty?
3. Were the test items free of defects?
4. Were each of the distracters effective (in multiple-choice items)?

Answers to such questions are of obvious value in selecting or revising items for future use. The benefits of item analysis are not limited to the improvement of individual test items, however. There are a number of fringe benefits of special value to classroom teachers. The most important of these are the following:

1. *Item analysis data provide a basis for efficient class discussion of the test results.* Knowing how effectively each item functioned in measuring achievement makes it possible to confine the discussion to those areas which will be most helpful to pupils. Easy items that were answered correctly by all pupils can be omitted from the discussion, and the concepts in those items causing pupils the greatest difficulty can receive special emphasis. Similarly, misinformation and misunderstandings, reflected in the choice of particular distracters, can be corrected. Of no less significance is the fact that item analysis will expose technical defects in items. During discussion defective items can be pointed out to pupils, saving much time and heated discussion concerning the unfairness of these items. If an item is ambiguous and two answers can be defended equally well, both answers might be counted correct and the scoring adjusted accordingly.

2. *Item analysis data provide a basis for remedial work.* Although discussing the test results in class can clarify and correct many specific points, item analysis frequently brings to light general areas of weakness requiring more extended attention. In an arithmetic test, for example, item analysis may reveal that the pupils are fairly proficient in arithmetic skills but are having difficulty with problems requiring the application of these skills. In other subjects, item analysis may indicate a general weakness in knowledge of technical vocabulary, in an understanding of principles, or in the ability to interpret data. Such information makes it possible to focus remedial work directly on the particular areas of weakness.

3. *Item analysis data provide a basis for the general improvement of classroom instruction.* In addition to the above uses, which by themselves should contribute to improved instruction, item analysis data can assist in evaluating the appropriateness of the specific learning outcomes and the course content for the particular type of pupils being taught. For ex-

ample, material that is consistently too difficult for the pupils might suggest curriculum revisions or shifts in teaching emphasis. Similarly, errors in pupil thinking which persistently appear in item analysis data might direct attention to the need for more effective teaching procedures. In these and similar ways, item analysis data can provide insights into instructional weaknesses and clues for their improvement.

4. *Item analysis procedures lead to increased skill in test construction.* Item analysis reveals ambiguities, clues, ineffective distracters, and other technical defects that were missed during the preparation of the test. This information is used directly in the revision of the test items for future use. In addition to the improvement of the specific items, however, we derive benefits from the procedure itself. As we analyze pupils' responses to items, we become increasingly cognizant of technical defects and the factors causing them. During revision of the items, we obtain experience in rewording statements so that they are unambiguous, rewriting distracters so that they are more plausible, and modifying items so that they are of a more appropriate level of difficulty. As a consequence, our general test construction skills are appreciably increased by the experience.

Item Analysis Procedure for Norm-Referenced Tests

Since norm-referenced and criterion-referenced tests serve different functions, the method for analyzing the effectiveness of the test items differs. Here, we shall consider item analysis procedures used with norm-referenced tests. A discussion of item analysis procedures used with criterion-referenced mastery tests will follow in a later section.

For most norm-referenced classroom tests, a simplified form of item analysis is all that is necessary or warranted. A suitable procedure is to compare the responses of pupils ranking in the upper and lower thirds of the class on the basis of the total test score.[5] The responses of pupils in the middle third are not included in the analysis but are assumed to follow the same trend as those in the upper and lower thirds.

To illustrate the method of item analysis, let us suppose that we have just finished scoring 37 test papers for a sixth-grade science unit on "weather." Our item analysis might then proceed as follows:

1. Rank the papers in order from the highest to the lowest score.
2. Select the 12 papers with the highest scores (approximately one third) and the 12 papers with the lowest scores.
3. For each test item, tabulate the number of pupils in the upper and lower groups who selected each alternative. This tabulation can be made

---

[5] Upper and lower quarters or halves might also be used, if more convenient. For more refined analysis, the upper and lower 27 per cent is frequently recommended and statistical guides are most commonly based on this percentage.

directly on the test paper or on the test item card as shown in Figure 11.2.

4. Estimate the *difficulty* of each item (percentage of pupils who got the item right).
5. Estimate the *discriminating* power of each item (difference between the number of pupils in the upper and lower groups who got the item right).
6. Evaluate the effectiveness of the distracters in each item (attractiveness of the incorrect alternatives).

The first three steps of this procedure merely provide a convenient tabulation of pupils' responses from which we can readily obtain an estimate of item difficulty, item discriminating power, and the effectiveness of

---

Course__Science_____   Dates used_____

Content__Weather Instruments__   _____

Outcome__Knowledge_____   _____

ITEM

Which of the following instruments is most useful in weather forecasting?

     A Anemometer

     B Barometer

     C Thermometer

     D Rain gauge

ITEM ANALYSIS DATA

Alternatives	A	(B)	C	D	Omits
upper 12 pupils	0	12	0	0	0
lower 12 pupils	2	5	3	2	0

Difficulty__71%____   Discriminating Power___.58____

Comment:

FIGURE 11.2. Test item card with item-analysis data recorded.

each distracter. This latter information can frequently be obtained simply by inspecting the item analysis data. Note in Figure 11.2, for example, that 12 pupils in the upper group and 5 pupils in the lower group selected the correct alternative (B). This makes a total of 17 out of the 24 pupils who got the item right, indicating that the item has a moderate *level of difficulty*. Since more pupils in the upper group than in the lower group got the item right, it is *discriminating positively*. That is, it is distinguishing between high and low achievers (as determined by the total test score). Finally, since all of the alternatives were selected by some of the pupils in the lower group, *the distracters (alternatives A, C, and D) appear to be operating effectively.*

Although item analysis by inspection will reveal the general effectiveness of a test item, and is satisfactory for most classroom purposes, it is sometimes desirable to obtain a more precise estimate of item difficulty and discriminating power. This can be done by applying relatively simple formulas to the item analysis data.

Estimating Item Difficulty. The difficulty of a test item is indicated by the *percentage of pupils who get the item right*. Hence, we can estimate item difficulty by means of the following formula, in which R = the number of pupils who got the item right, and T = the total number of pupils who tried the item.

$$\text{Difficulty} = \frac{R}{T} \times 100$$

Applying this formula to the item analysis data in Figure 11.2, our level of item difficulty (P) would be 71 per cent, as follows:

$$P = \frac{17}{24} \times 100 = 71 \text{ per cent}$$

Note that in estimating item difficulty from item analysis data, our calculation is based on the upper and lower thirds of the group only. We assume that the responses of pupils in the middle third of the group would follow essentially the same pattern. This estimate of difficulty is sufficiently accurate for classroom use and is easily obtained since the needed figures can be taken directly from the item analysis data.

Estimating Item Discriminating Power. As we have already noted, an item discriminates in a positive direction if more pupils in the upper group than the lower group get the item right. Positive discrimination indicates that the item is discriminating in the same direction as the total test score. Since we assume that the total test score reflects achievement of desired objectives, we would like all of our test items to show positive discrimination.

The discriminating power of an achievement test item refers to *the degree to which it discriminates between pupils with high and low achieve-ment.* An estimate of item discriminating power can be obtained by sub-tracting the number of pupils in the *lower* group who got the item right (R_L) from the number of pupils in the *upper* group who got the item right (R_U) and dividing by *one half of the total* number of pupils in-cluded in the item analysis $(\frac{1}{2}T)$. Summarized in formula form, it would be:[6]

$$\text{Discriminating Power} = \frac{R_U - R_L}{\frac{1}{2}T}$$

Applying this formula to the item analysis data in Figure 11.2, we would obtain an index of discriminating power (D) of .58, as follows:

$$D = \frac{12 - 5}{12} = .58$$

This indicates approximately average discriminating power. An item with maximum *positive* discriminating power would be one where all pu-pils in the upper group got the item right and all pupils in the lower group got the item wrong. This would result in an index of 1.00, as follows:

$$D = \frac{12 - 0}{12} = 1.00$$

An item with no discriminating power would be one where an equal number of pupils in both the upper and lower groups got the item right. This would result in an index of .00, as follows:

$$D = \frac{12 - 12}{12} = .00$$

With this formula it is also possible to calculate an index of *negative* discriminating power, that is, one where more pupils in the lower group than the upper group get the item right. This is generally wasted effort, however, since we are not interested in using items, which discriminate in the wrong direction. Such items should be revised, so that they dis-criminate positively, or discarded.

Evaluating the Effectiveness of Distracters. How well each distracter is operating can be determined by inspection and there is no need to calcu-late an index of effectiveness, although the formula for discriminating power could be used for this purpose. In general, a good distracter is one that attracts more pupils from the lower group than the upper group. Thus, it should discriminate between the upper and lower groups in a manner opposite to that of the correct alternative. An examination of the following item analysis data will illustrate the ease with which the effectiveness of

---

[6] Item discriminating power can also be expressed by means of a correlation coefficient obtained directly from charts prepared for this purpose. See D. C. Adkins, *Test Con-struction* (Columbus, Ohio: Charles E. Merrill, 1974).

distracters can be determined by inspection. Alternative A is the correct answer.

Alternatives	*A	B	C	D	Omits
Upper 12	5	5	0	2	0
Lower 12	3	4	0	5	0

First note that the item discriminates in a positive direction since 5 in the upper group and 3 in the lower group got the item right. The index of discriminating power is fairly low ($D = .17$), however, and this may be partly due to the ineffectiveness of some of the distracters. Alternative B is a poor distracter because it attracts more pupils from the upper group than the lower group. This is most likely due to some ambiguity in the statement of the item. Alternative C is completely ineffective as a distracter since it attracted no one. Alternative D is functioning as intended for it attracts a larger proportion of pupils from the lower group. Thus, the discriminating power of this item can probably be improved by removing any ambiguity in the statement of the item and revising or replacing alternatives B and C. The specific changes must, of course, be based on an inspection of the test item itself. Item analysis data merely indicate poorly functioning items, not the cause of the poor functioning.

Cautions in Interpreting Item Analysis Data on Norm-Referenced Tests

Item analysis provides a quick, simple technique for appraising the effectiveness of individual test items. The information provided by such an analysis is limited in many ways, however, and must be interpreted accordingly.[7] Following are some of the major cautions to observe:

1. *Item discriminating power does not necessarily indicate item validity.* In our description of item analysis, we used the total test score as a basis for selecting the upper group (high achievers) and the lower group (low achievers). This is the most common procedure, since comparable measures of achievement are usually not available. Ideally, we would examine each test item in relation to some independent measure of achievement. However, the best measure of the particular achievement we are interested in evaluating is usually the total score on the achievement test we have constructed. This is so because each classroom test is uniquely related to specific instructional objectives and course content. Even standardized tests in the same content area are usually inadequate as independent criteria because they are aimed at more general objectives than those measured by a specific classroom test in a particular course.

---

[7] L. J. Cronbach, *Essentials of Psychological Testing*, 3rd ed. (New York: Harper and Row, 1970). E. J. Furst, *Constructing Evaluation Instruments* (New York: Longmans, Green, 1958).

Using the total score from our classroom test as a basis for selecting high and low achievers is perfectly legitimate as long as we keep in mind that we are using an internal criterion. In doing so, our item analysis provides evidence concerning the *internal consistency* of the test rather than its validity. That is, we are determining how effectively each test item is measuring whatever the total test is measuring. Such item analysis data can be interpreted as evidence of *item validity* only where the validity of the total test has been proven, or can be legitimately assumed.

2. *A low index of discriminating power does not necessarily indicate a defective item.* Items which discriminate poorly between high and low achievers should be examined for the possible presence of ambiguity, clues, and other technical defects. If none is found, and the items measure an important learning outcome, they should be retained for future use. Any item that discriminates in a positive direction can make a contribution to the measurement of pupil achievement and low indices of discrimination are frequently obtained for reasons other than technical defects.

Classroom achievement tests are usually designed to measure several different types of learning outcomes (knowledge, understanding, application, and so on). Where this is the case, test items which represent an area receiving relatively little emphasis will tend to have poor discriminating power. For example, if a test has forty items measuring knowledge of specific facts and ten items measuring understanding, the latter items can be expected to have low indices of discrimination. This is because the items measuring understanding have less representation in the total test score and there is typically a low correlation between measures of knowledge and measures of understanding. Low indices of discrimination, here merely indicate that these items are measuring something different from what the major part of the test is measuring. Removing such items from the test would make it a more homogeneous measure of knowledge outcomes, but it would also damage the validity of the test since it would no longer measure learning outcomes in the understanding area. Since most classroom tests measure a variety of types of learning outcomes, low positive indices of discrimination are the rule rather than the exception.

Another factor which influences discriminating power is the difficulty of the item. Those items at the 50 per cent level of difficulty make maximum discriminating power possible, since it is only at this level of difficulty that all pupils in the upper half of the group can get the item right while all pupils in the lower half get it wrong.[8] As we move away from the 50 per cent level of difficulty, toward easier or more difficult items, the index of discriminating power becomes smaller. Thus, items which are very easy

---

[8] It should be noted that the 50 per cent level of difficulty does not guarantee maximum discriminating power but merely makes it possible. If half of the pupils in the upper group and half of the pupils in the lower group got the item right, it would still be at the 50 per cent level of difficulty but the index of discrimination would be zero.

or very difficult have low indices of discriminating power. It is frequently necessary, or desirable, to retain such items, however, in order to measure a representative sample of learning outcomes and course content.

To summarize, a low index of discriminating power should alert us to the possible presence of technical defects in a test item but it should not cause us to discard an otherwise worthwhile item. A well-constructed achievement test will, of necessity, contain items with low discriminating power and to discard them would result in a test which is less, rather than more, valid.

3. *Item analysis data on classroom tests are highly tentative.* Item analysis procedures focus our attention so directly on the difficulty and discriminating power of a test item that we are commonly misled into believing that these are fixed, unchanging characteristics of the item. This, of course, is not true. Item analysis data will vary from one group to another, depending upon the level of ability of the pupils, their educational background, and the type of instruction they have had. Add to this the small number of pupils we have available for analyzing the items in our classroom tests, and the tentative nature of our item analysis data becomes readily apparent. If just a few pupils change their responses, our indices of difficulty and discriminating power can be increased or decreased by a considerable amount.

The tentative nature of item analysis data should discourage us from making fine distinctions between items on the basis of indices of difficulty and discriminating power. If an item is discriminating in a positive direction, all of the alternatives are functioning effectively, and it has no apparent defects, it can be considered satisfactory from a technical standpoint. The important question then becomes, not how high is the index of discriminating power, but rather, does the item measure an important learning outcome? In the final analysis, the worth of an achievement test item must be based on logical rather than statistical considerations.

When used with norm-referenced classroom tests, item analysis provides us with a general appraisal of the functional effectiveness of the test items, a means for detecting technical defects, and a method for identifying instructional weaknesses. For these purposes, the tentative nature of item analysis data is relatively unimportant. Where we record indices of item difficulty or discriminating power on item cards for future use, we should interpret these indices as rough approximations only. As such, they are still superior to our unaided estimates of item difficulty and discriminating power.

Item Analysis and Criterion-Referenced Mastery Tests

The item analysis procedures used with norm-referenced tests are not directly applicable to criterion-referenced mastery tests. Since criterion-referenced tests are designed to describe pupils in terms of the types of learning tasks they can perform, rather than to obtain a reliable ranking of pupils, indices of item difficulty and item discriminating power are less meaningful.

Item Difficulty. The desired level of item difficulty for a criterior-referenced mastery test is not based on the ability of the items to discriminate between high and low achievers, as it is for norm-referenced tests. Instead, the difficulty of each test item is determined by the specific learning outcome it is designed to measure. If the learning task defined by the outcome is easy, the test item should be easy. If the learning task has a moderate level of difficulty, the test item should have a moderate level of difficulty. No attempt is made to arbitrarily alter item difficulty in order to increase discriminating power, or to obtain a spread of test scores. The standard formula for determining item difficulty can be applied to criterion-referenced test items, but the results are not typically used to select test items or to manipulate item difficulty. Most items on a criterion-referenced mastery test will have a large difficulty index (high percentage passing) when the instruction has been effective.

Item Discriminating Power. The ability of test items to discriminate between high and low achievers is not a crucial factor in evaluating the effectiveness of criterion-referenced test items. Some of the best items might have very low, or zero, indices of discrimination. If all pupils answer a test item correctly (i.e., zero discrimination) at the end of instruction, for example, this might indicate that both the instruction and the item have been effective. Although such items would be eliminated from norm-referenced tests, because they fail to discriminate, here they provide useful information concerning which learning tasks all pupils have mastered. Since the purpose of a criterion-referenced test is to describe what pupils can do, rather than to discriminate among them, our traditional indices of discriminating power are of little value for judging the quality of the test items.

Analyzing Criterion-Referenced Mastery Items. A crucial question in evaluating a criterion-referenced mastery test is, "To what extent did the test items measure the effects of the instruction?" To answer this question the same test must be given before instruction (pretest) and after instruction (posttest) and the results compared. A simple item-by-item comparison can be made by means of an item-response chart such as that shown in Table 11.1.

To prepare a chart like Table 11.1, you simply list the numbers of the test items across the top of the chart and the pupils' names down the side of the chart, and then record correct (+) and incorrect (−) responses for each pupil on the pretest (B) and posttest (A). The results in our sample table have been deliberately distorted to illustrate some of the basic patterns of item response. An analysis of the effectiveness of each item as a measure of *instructional effects* is as follows:

TABLE 11.1
A PORTION OF AN ITEM-RESPONSE CHART SHOWING CORRECT $(+)$ AND INCORRECT $(-)$ RESPONSES BEFORE AND AFTER INSTRUCTION[*]

Items ⟶	1		2		3		4		5	
Pretest (B) Posttest (A)	B	A	B	A	B	A	B	A	B	A
Jim Hart	−	+	+	+	−	−	+	−	−	+
Dora Larson	−	+	+	+	−	−	+	−	+	+
Lois Trent	−	+	+	+	−	−	+	−	−	+
Donna Voss	−	+	+	+	−	−	+	−	−	+
Dick Ward	−	+	+	+	−	−	+	−	+	+
Bob West	−	+	+	+	−	−	+	−	−	−

[*] From N. E. Gronlund, *Preparing Criterion-Referenced Tests for Classroom Instruction.* New York: Macmillan, 1973. Used by permission.

Item one.   This is an *ideal* item for a criterion-referenced mastery test. All pupils responded incorrectly before instruction and correctly after instruction. Both the item and the instruction were effective.

Item two.   This item was *too easy* to measure the effects of instruction, since all pupils responded correctly both before and after instruction.

Item three. This item was *too difficult* to measure the effects of instruction, or the instruction was inappropriate.

Item four.   This item indicates an extremely *defective* item, or an easy item followed by incorrect instruction.

Item five.   This item illustrates an *effective* item, with a fairly typical response pattern. Some pupils responded correctly before instruction but a larger proportion did so after instruction.

Where an index of item effectiveness is desired for each item, the following formula can be used to obtain a measure of *Sensitivity to Instructional Effects* (S).[9]

$$S = \frac{R_A - R_B}{T}$$

where

R_A = number of pupils who got the item right *after* instruction.
R_B = number of pupils who got the item right *before* instruction.
T = total number of pupils who tried the item both times.

---

[9] W. J. Kryspin and J. T. Feldhusen, *Developing Classroom Tests* (Minneapolis: Burgess, 1974).

Applying this formula to the five test items in Table 11.1, we would obtain indices of sensitivity to instructional effects (S) as follows:

$$\text{Item one:} \quad S = \frac{6-0}{6} = \quad 1.00$$

$$\text{Item two:} \quad S = \frac{6-6}{6} = \quad .00$$

$$\text{Item three:} \quad S = \frac{0-0}{6} = \quad .00$$

$$\text{Item four:} \quad S = \frac{0-6}{6} = -1.00$$

$$\text{Item five:} \quad S = \frac{5-2}{6} = \quad .50$$

Thus, the ideal item for a criterion-referenced mastery test yields a value of 1.00. Effective items fall between .00 and 1.00, and the higher the positive value the more sensitive the item is to instructional effects. Items with zero and negative values do not reflect the intended effects of instruction.

Since the values used to represent effective criterion-referenced test items (.00 to 1.00) are the same as those used to represent item discriminating power, care must be taken not to confuse the meaning of the two indices. The traditional *index of discriminating power* (D) indicates the degree to which an item discriminates between high and low achievers on a single administration of the test. The *index of sensitivity to instructional effects* (S) indicates the degree to which an item reflects the intended effects of instruction (i.e., learning gains) occurring between the pretest and the posttest.

Effectiveness of Distracters. How well each alternative functions in a multiple-choice item is also important in criterion-referenced tests. Ideally, a pupil should choose one of the incorrect alternatives if he has not achieved the objective that the test item measures. Thus, some check should be made of the frequency with which each distracter is selected by those failing an item. This type of analysis might best be done on the pretest, where a relatively large proportion of pupils can be expected to fail the items. If some items contain distracters that are not selected at all, or only rarely, a need for revision is indicated.

Building a Test Item File

A file of effective items can be built and maintained easily if items are recorded on cards like the one presented in Figure 11.2. By indicating on the item card both the learning outcome and the subject-matter content measured by the item, it is possible to file the cards under both headings. A satisfactory procedure is to use areas of subject-matter content as major categories with the learning outcomes forming the subcategories. For example, our illustrative item in Figure 11.2 measures knowledge of weather instruments so it would be placed in the first category under weather instruments, as follows:

Weather Instruments:
   Knowledge
   Understanding
   Application

This type of filing system makes it possible to select items in accordance with any table of specifications in the particular area covered by the file.

Building a test item file is a little like building a bank account. The first several years are concerned mainly with making deposits. Withdrawals must be delayed until a sufficient reserve is accumulated. Thus, items are recorded on cards as they are constructed; item analysis information is added after the items have been used; and then the effective items are deposited in the file. At first it seems to be additional work with very little return. However, in a few years it is possible to start using some of the items from the file and supplementing these with other newly constructed items. As the file grows, it becomes possible to select the majority of the items from the file for any given test without repeating the items too frequently. To prevent using a specific test item too often, the date an item is used is usually recorded on the card.

A test item file assumes increasing importance as we shift from test items which measure knowledge of specific facts to those which measure understanding, application, and thinking skills. Items in these latter areas are difficult and time consuming to construct. With all of the other demands on our time, it is nigh unto impossible to construct effective test items in these areas each time we prepare a new test. We seem to have two alternatives: either we neglect the measurement of learning outcomes in these areas (which has been the typical practice), or we slowly build a file of effective items in these areas. The choice seems obvious, if the quality of pupil learning is our major concern.

For a test file to be most effective, pupils should not be permitted to keep their test papers after the test has been scored and discussed in class. This disturbs some teachers who feel that the pupils should have their test papers for later study and review. There is no particular advantage in permitting pupils to keep their test papers, however, *if* there has been an adequate discussion of the test results in class and a general review in the particular areas of weakness revealed by the test. After all, our major aim is to help pupils improve their general knowledge and understanding in a given area. The test is merely a sample of this achievement. Although a discussion of test results will contribute to improved learning, extended study of the answers to specific test items may actually detract from our major aim. This certainly would be the case where pupils concentrated on learning the sample of material included in the test to the neglect of the larger area of achievement it represented.

SUMMARY

The same care that goes into the construction of individual test items should be carried over into the final stages of test development and use. Giving careful attention to the procedures for: (1) assembling the test, (2) administering and scoring the test, and (3) appraising the results, will provide increased assurance that valid results are obtained.

The preliminary steps in preparing the test for use are simplified if the items are recorded on cards. This facilitates the task of editing the items and arranging them in the test. The editing process involves a check of each item to be certain it is free from ambiguity and irrelevant clues and that its functioning content is in harmony with the intended purpose. The final group of items selected for the test should also be checked against the table of specifications to make sure that a representative sample of the learning outcomes and course content is being measured. In arranging the items in the test, all items of one type should be placed together in a separate section. The items within each section should be organized by the learning outcome measured and then placed in order of ascending difficulty. The directions for the test should convey clearly to the pupil the purpose of the test, the time allowed for answering, the basis for answering, the procedure for recording the answers, and what to do about guessing.

The procedures for administering the test should provide all pupils with a fair chance to demonstrate their achievement. Both the physical and the psychological atmosphere should be conducive to maximum performance. Unnecessary interruptions and unfair aid from other pupils, or the teacher, should be avoided.

The scoring of the test can be facilitated by a scoring key, or scoring stencil if separate answer sheets are used. Counting each right answer one point is usually satisfactory. A correction for guessing is unnecessary with the typical classroom test where pupils have sufficient time to consider all questions. Because assumptions underlying the use of correction-for-guessing formulas are questionable, it is recommended that they be used only with speeded tests.

After the test has been scored, it is desirable to appraise the effectiveness of each item by means of item analysis. For norm-referenced tests, this involves the use of simple statistical procedures for determining item difficulty (percentage of pupils who got the item right), item discriminating power (difference between the number of high achievers and low achievers who got the item right), and the effectiveness of each distracter (degree to which it attracts more low achievers than high achievers). Since criterion-referenced mastery tests are designed to describe the learning tasks pupils can perform, rather than to discriminate among pupils, the traditional indices of item analysis are not fully appropriate. More meaningful for criterion-referenced tests is a comparison of the pupils' item responses before (pretest) and after (posttest) instruction. This can be accomplished by means of an item-response chart, or by computing an index of sensitivity to instructional effects. This type of information is useful for determining the extent to which criterion-referenced mastery items are measuring the intended effects of instruction. The results of item analysis are valuable in discussing the test with pupils, in planning remedial work, in improving our teaching and testing skills, and in selecting and revising items for future use. For these and other purposes, however, item analysis data must be interpreted cautiously because of their limited and tentative nature.

Building a test file of effective items involves recording the items on index cards, adding item analysis information, and filing the cards by both subject-matter content and learning outcomes measured. Such a test item file is especially valuable in the areas of complex achievement where the construction of test items is difficult and time consuming. When a sufficient file of high quality items has been assembled, the burden of test preparation is considerably lightened.

LEARNING EXERCISES

1. It what ways might poorly arranged items in a test adversely influence the validity of test results? What arrangement is best for valid results? Why?
2. Prepare a set of directions for a fifty-item multpile-choice test, taking into account all of the factors discussed in this chapter.
3. Why is the 50 per cent level of difficulty recommended for norm-referenced test items? What problems might this create in classroom testing? What level of difficulty is best for criterion-referenced test items?
4. What special precautions might be taken to prevent objective test items from becoming ambiguous?
5. Under what conditions should a correction for guessing be used in scoring a test? What are some of the reasons a correction for guessing should *not* be used with the typical classroom test?
6. What are some of the things that can be done to increase the discriminating power of items in a norm-referenced test?
7. If item analysis data showed that an item was answered correctly by 9 out of 10 pupils in the upper group and 5 out of 10 pupils in the lower group, what would the index of item difficulty be? Should the item be considered easy or difficult? What would the index of discriminating power be?
8. What are some of the limitations of using the index of discriminating power? Of using the index of sensitivity to instructional effects?

9. Why is the index of discriminating power of little value in evaluating items on a criterion-referenced mastery test? Could the index of sensitivity to instructional effects be used with norm-referenced tests?
10. What are some advantages and disadvantages of maintaining a test item file?

SUGGESTIONS FOR FURTHER READING

ANASTASI, A. *Psychological Testing*, 4th ed. New York: Macmillan Publishing Co., Inc., 1976. Chapter 8, "Item Analysis." Describes item analysis procedures for norm-referenced tests.

GRONLUND, N. E. *Preparing Criterion-Referenced Tests for Classroom Instruction.* New York: Macmillan Publishing Co., Inc., 1973. See Chapter 6, "Using and Appraising Criterion-Referenced Tests," and Appendix A, "Checklist for Evaluating a Criterion-Referenced Test." Checklist includes criteria that would be useful in evaluating any classroom test.

MEHRENS, W. A. and I. J. LEHMANN. *Measurement and Evaluation in Education and Psychology.* New York: Holt, Rinehart & Winston, Inc., 1973. Chapter 11, "Assembling, Reproducing, Administering, Scoring, and Analyzing Classroom Achievement Tests." Presents a discussion of the topics covered in this chapter, with numerous references to the professional literature.

THORNDIKE, R. L. (ed.). *Educational Measurement.* Washington, D. C.: American Council on Education, 1971. See Chapter 5 by S. Henrysson, "Gathering, Analyzing and Using Data on Test Items"; Chapter 6 by R. L. Thorndike, "Reproducing the Test"; Chapter 7 by W. V. Clemans, "Test Administration"; and Chapter 8 by F. B. Baker, "Automation of Test Scoring, Reporting and Anaylsis." A comprehensive treatment of the preparation, administration, and analysis of tests.

PART III

Using Standardized Tests

CHAPTER 12
Standardized Achievement Tests

Standardized achievement tests play an important role in the school program. . . . They supplement and complement informal classroom tests and serve as the basis for many educational decisions. . . . But, trying to learn the characteristics of the hundreds of tests available is an exercise in futility. . . . Learning the basic principles of standardized achievement testing—and becoming familiar with some typical examples in each testing area—provides the best background for effective test selection and use.

There are three types of published tests that are of major concern to teachers. These may be classified as tests of (1) achievement, (2) aptitude, and (3) personality. The last category includes measures of various aspects of character, adjustment, attitude, and interest. Because the instruments used to measure such personality characteristics are primarily self-report techniques, rather than tests in the strict sense of the term, they will be considered in Chapter 17 along with other methods of evaluating personal-social development. In this chapter, we shall consider standardized achievement tests, and in the following chapter standardized tests of aptitude.

The number of standardized achievement tests has grown to the point where it would now be infeasible to list and describe the many tests available. What we have decided to do in this chapter is to describe how standardized achievement tests are constructed, to indicate the major types of achievement tests used in the schools, to present principles pertinent to their selection and use, and to list typical examples of some of the most widely used tests in each area. Although the tests included in this chapter are of high general quality, there are many other achievement tests of equally high quality. It is hoped that the tests referred to here will simply serve as a starting point for exploring the many good standardized achievement tests available. As a minimum, you should become familiar with some of the better tests in your own teaching area.

The specific procedure for locating, selecting, and using standardized tests will be described in detail in Chapter 14. It should be pointed out here, however, that the selection of standardized achievement tests poses special problems in today's schools. Vast changes are taking place in school programs. New curricula are being adopted, the content of specific courses is being radically modified, and many new instructional techniques are being introduced. These innovations have resulted in increased variability within school programs and greater diversity among school programs. Thus, standardized achievement tests no longer have the same long-range relevance nor the same wide applicability they once had. Curriculum innovations tend to introduce new instructional objectives and new content into the school program, making formerly used tests inappropriate. By the same token, achievement tests that are adequate for measuring the learning outcomes of one school system may be inadequate for measuring the outcomes of another. Thus, there is a continuous need to base the selection of standardized achievement tests on the instructional objectives of the school in which the tests are to be used. This is the only way we can have any assurance that the tests will provide valid information concerning that particular school program.

CONSTRUCTION OF STANDARDIZED ACHIEVEMENT TESTS

The construction of a standardized achievement test is typically based on a recognition of the need for some particular type of educational information. This need may be in the area of the basic skills (reading, language, arithmetic) or in a particular subject-matter area. The need may be to determine the pupils' general level of achievement (survey test) or to diagnose the pupils' particular learning difficulties (diagnostic test). Once the need has been recognized and clarified, the general nature of the test is specified and test development begins.

Although the procedures for constructing standardized tests will vary somewhat with the nature of the test, the following steps are typical for the construction of a survey achievement test (norm-referenced test):

1. Planning the test.
2. Preparing the test items.
3. Experimental tryout and revision.
4. Administering the standardization edition.

The first two steps are essentially the same as those used in constructing an informal classroom test. The main differences are that the standardized achievement test typically covers a broader range of skills and understandings than the classroom test, and the preparation of the items for the standardized test usually involves the combined effort of teachers, curriculum specialists, and test experts.

The last two steps give the standardized test its unique features. The pretesting makes it possible to develop high-quality test items whose difficulty level and discriminating power are known and to establish standard procedures for administering and scoring the test. Finally, the administration of the standardization edition provides for the preparation of tables of norms. These make it possible to compare a pupil's test performance with that of other groups of pupils on a national, regional, or state level.

Planning the Test

The systematic planning of a standardized achievement test includes identifying the instructional objectives and content to be measured, determining the relative emphasis to be given to each objective and each area of content, and building a table of specifications that reflects the desired emphasis. These steps are, of course, the same ones followed in planning for a classroom test. Here, however, it is important that the objectives and content of the test reflect what is typically taught in a wide variety of schools. To provide some assurance that this is the case a careful study is made of the most widely used textbooks, of representative courses of study, of the recommendations of curriculum specialists, and of the research literature pertaining to the area. This analysis is then used in preparing the test plan.

The planning of a standardized achievement test typically includes the cooperative efforts of teachers, curriculum specialists, and test experts. In some cases, committees of teachers participate directly in identifying the learning outcomes to be tested and in building the plan for the test. In other instances, teachers are simply asked to review the plans made by specialists. This provides a check on whether the most important outcomes and content have been included, whether the content is appropriate for the particular grade level, and whether curriculum differences from school to school have been given adequate attention.

It should be noted that the procedure for selecting test content for a standardized achievement test is generally an attempt to build a test that fits the largest number of school programs. In the final analysis, it might fit some programs very well, some only fairly well, and some not at all. It is likely to be in greatest harmony with traditional school programs, unless special efforts have been made to measure the more complex outcomes reflected in modern curriculum approaches. Some test publishers now include a table of specifications in the test manual, so that the relevance of the test content to the school program can be more readily determined. A typical example of such a table is shown in Figure 12.1.

MATHEMATICS BASIC CONCEPTS

	1 Recall Factual Knowledge	2 Perform Mathematical Manipulation	3 Solve Routine Problems	4 Demonstrate Comprehension Math Ideas and Concepts	5 Ingenuity and Insight	6 Higher Mental Processes	Total
1. Number and Operation	Item No. 38, 49	2, 24, 32, 36	1, 25	4, 7, 9, 11, 13, 27, 28	23, 40, 45	3	19
2. Geometry and Measurement			10, 30, 46	17, 18, 21, 22, 34, 35, 39, 48, 50	16, 26, 37, 44	43	17
3. Relations, Functions, and Graphs		12			41		2
4. Proof						42	1
5. Probability and Statistics				6, 19, 20			3
6. Mathematical Sentences		8		15			2
7. Sets, Mathematical Systems	31					33	2
8. Application			47	5, 14, 29			4
TOTAL	3	6	6	23	8	4	50

1. Recall Factual Knowledge is restricted to questions which require only the recall of a definition, fact, theorem, without doing anything with it.

2. Perform Mathematical Manipulation is used for questions, regardless of complexity or level of mathematics, that call for the application of a technique that has been learned--where no decision is required on how to approach the solution.

3. Solve Routine Problems includes questions in which a choice of the technique to be used is necessary or a definition or theorem recalled and applied, but where there is a straightforward technique available which is commonly taught.

4. Demonstrate Comprehension of Mathematical Ideas and Concepts is used for questions which require some understanding of the underlying concepts which will be necessary to do the item and the student must not only decide what to do but how to do it.

5. Solve Nonroutine Problems Requiring Insight or Ingenuity is concerned with questions which require a student to develop his own technique for solving a problem which he has probably not met in a textbook. The solution may be straightforward or simple, but some insight should be needed to find it.

6. Apply "Higher" Mental Processes to Mathematics is used to classify questions testing generalization, evaluation, the nature of proof, induction, logical inference, and decisions about the sufficiency of data.

FIGURE 12.1. Table of specifications and ability classification for the test of Mathematics Basic Concepts, *Sequential Tests of Educational Progress, Series II*, Grades 7 to 9. (Copyright © 1969 by Educational Testing Service. All rights reserved. Used by permission.)

The numbers in the cells refer to the number of each test item that was designed to measure that ability. Items 38 and 49, for example, measure "recall of factual knowledge" regarding "number and operation." Where such a table is not included, it is necessary to analyze the test items, one by one, to determine their relevance to the objectives and content stressed in the particular school program for which the test is being selected.

Preparing the Test Items

When the specifications for a standardized achievement test have been clearly formulated, the writing of the test items begins. As in the planning of the test, this is typically a cooperative venture involving teachers, curriculum specialists, and test experts. The items may be written by teachers and criticized and revised by the specialists, or the teachers may be asked to review a pool of test items written by others. The participation of teachers in item preparation increases the likelihood that the content, vocabulary, and complexity of the items will be appropriate for the particular course and grade level for which the test is intended.

The preparation of test items involves the writing of items that directly measure the instructional objectives and content defined in the table of specifications. If two, or more, equivalent forms of the test are being developed, a relatively large pool of items must be prepared. Typically, this pool of items also includes more items than will ultimately be used, to allow for the replacement of items that must be discarded after the tryout of the experimental edition of the test.

When a sufficient pool of items has been prepared, the items are then edited by trained item writers and assembled into the experimental form of the test. This experimental edition, or pretest, includes directions, test format, time limits, and scoring provisions as similar as possible to those desired in the final edition. Before being printed, copies of the experimental forms of the test may again be submitted to teachers and curriculum specialists for a final review.

Experimental Tryout and Revision

The experimental edition of the test is administered to groups of pupils like those for whom the test is intended. If the test is one designed for nation-wide use, this might involve a relatively large tryout sample representing different geographic regions, different-size schools, and different economic levels. The purpose of the experimental tryout is to obtain data concerning the following:

1. The difficulty of each test item.
2. The discriminating power of each test item.
3. The effectiveness of each distracter for each test item.
4. The equivalence of the items in the various forms of the test.
5. The adequacy of the directions, the time limits, and the test format.

The difficulty, discriminating power, and effectiveness of each test item are determined by item analysis. The procedure used here is essentially the same as that described in Chapter 11, except that for standardized tests the computations are typically done by computer. The teachers administering the tests, of course, also provide helpful information. Their criticisms are especially useful for improving the directions to the pupils and for increasing the effectiveness of the other procedures of test administration.

The item-analysis data, from the experimental tryout, are used to eliminate or revise any test items that prove to be defective. Items that are too easy or too difficult and items that do not discriminate between high and low achievers (as determined by total test score) are typically eliminated from the test. The remaining items are edited and improved, as needed, and the final edition of the test is prepared. In some cases, a second experimental tryout may precede the preparation of the final, or standardization, edition.

The items for the final forms of the test are selected in such a manner that the test content of each form matches the original table of specifications, that the tests are of appropriate difficulty, and that the different forms of the test are equivalent in terms of both content and difficulty. The final edition of the test also, of course, includes standard instructions for administering, standard directions to the pupils, standard time limits, and standard procedures for scoring.

Administering the Standardization Edition

The last step in preparing a standardized achievement test is to administer the final edition of the test to a representative group of pupils for the purpose of establishing norms (reliability and other technical features of the test are, of course, also determined at this time). Test norms will be discussed in detail in Chapter 15. It is sufficient to point out here that norms are merely the scores earned by representative groups of pupils at various age and grade levels. Norms make it possible to compare an individual's test score with those of other individuals whose characteristics are known. Thus, it is possible to compare a pupil's test performance with that of a typical twelve-year-old, a national group of sixth graders, or a select group of pupils attending private schools in New England.

The most important element in the standardization process is that of selecting a group of pupils that is truly representative of the pupils for whom the test is intended. Where national norms are desired, this means a sample of pupils that is representative of the total school population in the United States. Test publishers attempt to attain this ideal by selecting a proportionate number of pupils from all geographic regions of the country, from all of the various-size school systems, and from all socioeconomic levels. Sampling techniques are used that provide a distribution of pupils that is approximately proportional to the most recent census data for the United States. Where regional or state norms are being prepared, the same care must be taken to obtain a representative sample but the task is, of course, much simpler.

Although most of the more widely used tests provide norms based on a carefully selected norm sample, the norms for some standardized tests leave much to be desired. Test norms are sometimes based on a limited and biased selection of pupils or on test results that were sporadically sent in by some users of the test. Such biased norm samples are, of course, of little value in interpreting test scores. Therefore, it is extremely important to study the composition of the norm group when one is selecting a standardized achievement test. Criteria for judging the adequacy of norms are presented in Chapter 15.

The final standardized edition of an achievement test will usually include test booklets for each form of the test, answer sheets, scoring stencils, and a manual. The manual typically contains detailed information concerning the nature of the test, procedures for administering and scoring, norm tables, suggestions for interpreting and using the results, validity and reliability, and a description of the norm sample and the sampling procedures used. For some tests, there is so much technical information to report that both an administrator's manual and a technical manual are provided. Where this is done, it is necessary to consult the technical manual when one is evaluating the quality of the test and the adequacy of the norm group. In such cases, the administrator's manual is likely to contain little more than the directions for administering and scoring the test and the norm tables for interpreting the results.

CHARACTERISTICS OF STANDARDIZED TESTS

As noted in the procedural steps for constructing a standardized achievement test, a standardized test has certain distinctive features. These include a fixed set of test items designed to measure a clearly defined sample of behavior, specific directions for administering and scoring the test, and norms based on representative groups of individuals like those for whom the test was designed. Standard content and procedure make it possible to give an identical test to individuals in different places and at different times. The norms enable us to compare an individual's test score to the scores of known groups who have taken the test. Thus, test norms provide a standard frame of reference for determining an individual's level of performance on a particular test and for comparing his relative level of performance on several different tests (providing all were standardized on the same group of pupils).

Equivalent forms are provided for many standardized tests. These make it possible to repeat the test without fear that individuals will remember the answers from the first testing. Because equivalent forms of a test are built to the same specifications (but independently), they measure the same sample of behavior with different sets of test items. They therefore can be used interchangeably for such purposes as measuring educational growth, checking on questionable test results from an earlier testing, and the like.

Comparable forms are also provided for some standardized tests. These are forms that measure the same aspects of behavior but at different grade levels. For example, one form may cover grades 1 to 3, and other forms cover grades 4 to 6, 7 to 9, and 10 to 12. Such forms are especially useful for maintaining continuity of measurement in a school-wide testing program and for studying long-term trends in educational growth.

In summary, the characteristics of a carefully constructed standardized test include the following:

1. The test items are of high technical quality. They have been developed by educational and test specialists; tried out experimentally (pretested); and selected on the basis of difficulty, discriminating power, and relationship to a clearly defined and rigid set of specifications.
2. Directions for administering and scoring are so precisely stated that the procedures are standard for different users of the test.
3. Norms, based on representative groups of individuals, are provided as aids in interpreting the test scores. These norms are based on various age and grade groups on a national, regional, or state level. Norms for special groups, such as private schools, might also be supplied.
4. Equivalent and comparable forms of the test are typically provided as well as information concerning the degree to which the forms are comparable.
5. A test manual and other accessory materials are provided as guides for administering and scoring the test, for evaluating its technical qualities, and for interpreting and using the results.

Despite the common characteristics of standardized tests, no two tests are exactly alike. Each test measures somewhat unique aspects of behavior and serves a slightly different use. Also, there is wide variation in the completeness and quality of test materials from one test to another. To further complicate test selection, some tests with similar titles measure aspects of behavior that differ markedly, whereas other tests with dissimilar titles measure aspects of behavior that are almost identical. Thus, the intelligent selection of standardized tests, from among the literally hundreds of tests available in each area, involves a careful study of the test content and the test materials in light of the functions to be measured and the uses to be made of the results.

STANDARDIZED VERSUS INFORMAL CLASSROOM TESTS

Standardized achievement tests and carefully constructed classroom tests are similar in many ways. Both are based on a carefully planned table of specifications, both have the same type of test items, and both provide clear directions to the pupils. The main differences between the two types reside in (1) the nature of the learning outcomes and content measured, (2) the quality of the test items, (3) the reliability of the tests, (4) the procedures for administering and scoring, and (5) the interpretation of scores. Comparative advantages of standardized and informal classroom tests of achievement are shown in Table 12.1.

TABLE 12.1

COMPARATIVE ADVANTAGES OF STANDARDIZED AND INFORMAL
CLASSROOM TESTS OF ACHIEVEMENT

	Standardized Achievement Tests	Informal Achievement Tests
Learning outcomes and content measured	Measure outcomes and content common to majority of United States schools. Tests of basic skills and complex outcomes adaptable to many local situations; content-oriented tests seldom reflect emphasis or timeliness of local curriculum.	Well adapted to outcomes and content of local curriculum. Flexibility affords continuous adaptation of measurement to new materials and changes in procedure. Adaptable to various-sized work units. Tend to neglect complex learning outcomes.
Quality of test items	General quality of items high. Written by specialists, pretested, and selected on basis of effectiveness.	Quality of items is unknown unless test item file is used. Quality typically lower than standardized, due to limited time and skill of teacher.
Reliability	Reliability high; commonly between .80 and .95, frequently is above .90.	Reliability usually unknown; can be high if carefully constructed.
Administration and scoring	Procedures *standardized;* specific instructions provided.	Uniform procedures possible but usually flexible.
Interpretation of scores	Scores can be compared to norm groups. Test manual and other guides aid interpretation and use.	Score comparisons and interpretations limited to local school situation.

A review of the comparative advantages of the two types of tests indicate that each is superior for certain purposes and inferior for others. The broader coverage of the standardized test, its more rigidly controlled procedures of administering and scoring, and the availability of norms for evaluating scores make it especially useful for the following instructional purposes:

1. Evaluating the general educational development of pupils in the basic skills and in those learning outcomes common to many courses of study.
2. Evaluating pupil progress during the school year or over a period of years.
3. Grouping pupils for instructional purposes.
4. Diagnosing relative strengths and weaknesses of pupils in terms of broad subject or skill areas.
5. Comparing a pupil's general level of achievement with his scholastic aptitude.

The inflexibility of the standardized test makes it of little value for those purposes for which the informal classroom test is so admirably suited.

1. Evaluating the learning outcomes and content unique to a particular class or school.
2. Evaluating the day-to-day progress of pupils and their achievement on work units of varying sizes.
3. Evaluating knowledge of current developments in such rapidly changing content areas as science and social studies.

The complementary functions of the two types of tests indicate that both are essential to a sound instructional program. Each provides a specific type of information regarding the pupils' educational progress. In both cases, however, the value of the information depends on the extent to which the tests are related to the instructional objectives of the school. Standardized achievement tests, like informal classroom tests, can serve the many worthwhile instructional purposes attributed to them only when they measure the particular learning outcomes and content deemed important by those responsible for the instructional program.

ACHIEVEMENT TEST BATTERIES

Standardized achievement tests are frequently used in the form of test batteries. A battery consists of a series of individual tests all standardized on the same representative group of pupils. This makes it possible to compare test scores on the separate tests and thus determine the relative strengths and weaknesses of pupils in the different areas covered by the test. With an elementary school test battery, for example, it is possible to determine that a pupil is strong in language skills but weak in arithmetic skills, good in reading but less proficient in spelling, and the like. Such comparisons are not possible with separate tests that have been standardized on different groups of pupils, because the base for comparison is not uniform.

A major limitation of test batteries is that all parts of the battery are usually not equally appropriate for measuring the objectives of a particular school. When a test battery is constructed, it is based on the objectives and the content considered important by the specialists building the test. Although the goals of a particular school are apt to be in harmony with some sections of the battery, it is fairly certain that they will not be in harmony with all sections. Variations in subject-matter content from one curriculum to another and differences in grade placement of instructional materials make it very unlikely that the various sections of a test battery will be uniformly applicable to the instructional program of any given school. This limitation is especially pronounced in content-oriented test batteries. It is of less significance in batteries designed to measure basic skills and general educational development.

Elementary School Achievement Batteries

The use of achievement batteries has been especially prominent at the elementary school level. A survey by Goslin has shown that approximately 80 per cent of the schools use an achievement battery in grades three through six, and slightly less than half of these schools also use a battery in grades one and two.[1] This extensive usage is understandable because there is considerable uniformity in the learning outcomes sought, especially in the basic skills.

Tests of Basic Skills. Elementary school batteries that focus on the basic skills typically include sections on reading, language, mathematics, and study skills. To allow for increasing difficulty and for varying emphases from one grade level to another, a series of comparable forms are developed to cover the various grade levels. Each form in the series of batteries typically covers one or two grades at the primary level, and two or more grades beyond grade four.

The basic skills in an achievement battery are measured by a number of subtests. Although the names of the subtests vary somewhat from one test publisher to another, and the batteries at the primary level, typically contain fewer subtests, there is considerable uniformity in the nature of the outcomes measured by the various basic skill batteries. The following subtests are typical of those used in each basic skill area:

    READING
        Vocabulary (meaning of words)
        Comprehension (meaning of paragraphs and other written material)
    LANGUAGE
        Mechanics (capitalization, punctuation)
        Expression (correctness, effectiveness)
        Spelling (from dictation, or identifying misspelled words)

---

[1] D. A. Goslin, *Teachers and Testing* (New York: Russell Sage Foundation, 1967).

MATHEMATICS
    Computation (fundamental operations)
    Concepts (meaning of arithmetic concepts)
    Problem solving (solving story problems)
STUDY SKILLS
    Library and reference skills
    Reading maps, graphs, and tables

In addition to the above skills, some elementary school achievement batteries include tests in the content areas of science and social studies. For these batteries, it is usually possible also to obtain a separate partial battery limited to the measurement of basic skills. Batteries confined to the basic skills are generally preferred because content-oriented tests become quickly outdated and are seldom well suited to the specific objectives of the local instructional program.

The following list contains some of the more widely used achievement batteries for measuring basic skills at the elementary school level. The grade range covered by the tests is given in parentheses. Where a high school edition of the battery is also available, that grade range has been included to make clear that the series of elementary batteries constitute the first part of a more comprehensive achievement-testing program.

California Achievement Tests (Grades 1 to 12)
Comprehensive Tests of Basic Skills (Grades K to 12)
Iowa Tests of Basic Skills (Grades 1 to 8)
Metropolitan Achievement Tests (Grades K to 13)
SRA Achievement Series (Grades 1 to 9)
Stanford Achievement Tests (Grades 1 to 13)

These and most of the other tests referred to in this chapter are briefly described in Appendix D. More detailed descriptions and critical reviews of the tests are available in Buros' *Mental Measurements Yearbooks.*[2]

Although the batteries of tests designed to measure the basic skills are all somewhat similar in terms of the areas of skill covered, they vary considerably in terms of the nature of the test materials used and the specific abilities measured within each skill area. Therefore, in selecting an achievement battery, it is important to appraise carefully the specific test items to be certain that the abilities measured are relevant to the learning outcomes stressed in the school program. Any achievement battery will, of course, measure only some of the important outcomes of an elementary school program. Other tests and evaluation procedures will be needed for a comprehensive coverage of a school's objectives.

As Cronbach[3] has noted, there are times when it may be desirable to

[2] O. K. Buros, *The Seventh Mental Measurements Yearbook* (Highland Park, N.J.: Gryphon Press, 1972).
[3] L. J. Cronbach, "Evaluation in Course Improvement," in N. E. Gronlund (ed.), *Readings in Measurement and Evaluation* (New York: Macmillan, 1968).

use a test battery even though parts of it do not closely match the objectives of the school. Although a program of "modern mathematics" might deemphasize computational skills, for example, it still would be desirable to determine the influence the new program is having on pupil development in that area. We should not, of course, delude ourselves into thinking that the achievement battery is measuring the outcomes of "modern mathematics," but it is legitimate to ask to what extent the more traditional outcomes of mathematics are being sacrificed by the new program.

Tests of General Educational Development. In addition to those batteries that emphasize basic skills, one notable battery has focused more broadly on the measurement of general educational development. This is the *Sequential Tests of Educational Progress (STEP, Series II)*, which covers grades 4 to 14. This battery includes tests in each of the following major areas: Reading, Mechanics of Writing (spelling, capitalization, punctuation), English Expression (correctness and effectiveness of expression), Mathematics-Computation, Mathematics Basic Concepts, Science, and Social Studies. A unique feature of the *STEP II* is that the academic-oriented tests emphasize the measurement of complex learning outcomes. This can be seen by a review of the abilities measured by the Mathematics Basic Concepts Test, shown earlier in Figure 12.1. The science and social studies tests also stress critical understandings and higher level abilities (e.g., application, interpretation, evaluation). Thus, this battery calls for a deeper mastery than the typical tests designed to measure basic skills and knowledge of course content.

Typical test items from the *STEP II* Social Studies Test (Grade 4 to 6) and the Science Test (Grades 7 to 9) are shown in Figure 12.2. Interpretive exercises like these are used throughout the tests. The stimulus materials include quotations, tables, charts, graphs, maps, cartoons, and pictures. Items of this type make it possible to measure complex outcomes that are not dependent upon the specific learning experiences in any particular course. Thus, they provide a fairer measure of achievement for pupils with varying educational backgrounds.

The advantages of tests like *STEP II*, from a teaching standpoint, are (1) they provide for greater flexibility in the selection of course content, (2) they tend to encourage both teachers and students to give more attention to the understanding and application of knowledge, and (3) they provide good models for improving informal classroom tests. With regard to the last point, the *STEP II* illustrates the wide variety of materials that can be used in testing and the wide array of complex learning outcomes that can be measured with objective items. Test items in standardized tests are, of course, copyrighted and cannot be reproduced. The procedures, however, can be adopted and adapted for use in classroom tests.

In summary, there are a number of cautions to consider when one is selecting and using elementary school achievement batteries.

12. "Central America lacks coal and iron, and there is little money for building factories. There are few industries to provide jobs for workers."

From the information above, which of the following statements about Central America is probably true?

(A) Much steel is made there.
(B) There are many large cities there.
(C) Most of its people have modern houses.
(D) Many of its people work on farms.

Questions 8—9 are based on a chart of average pulse rates.

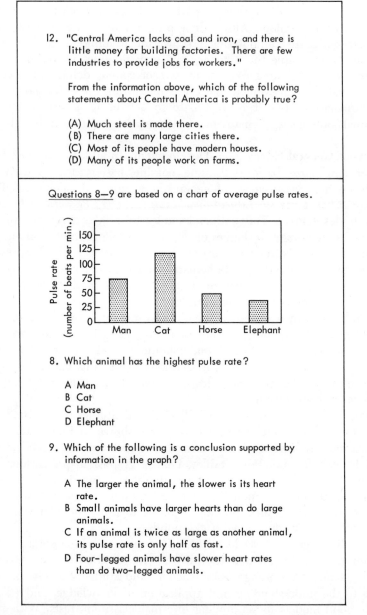

8. Which animal has the highest pulse rate?

A Man
B Cat
C Horse
D Elephant

9. Which of the following is a conclusion supported by information in the graph?

A The larger the animal, the slower is its heart rate.
B Small animals have larger hearts than do large animals.
C If an animal is twice as large as another animal, its pulse rate is only half as fast.
D Four-legged animals have slower heart rates than do two-legged animals.

FIGURE 12.2. Sample items from *Step II*, Social Studies Test (Grades 4 to 6) and Science Test (Grades 7 to 9). (Copyright © 1969 by Educational Testing Service. All rights reserved. Used by permission.)

1. Achievement batteries that focus on the basic skills measure important outcomes of the elementary school program, but these constitute only a portion of the outcomes of a modern curriculum. Other methods of evaluation will be needed to appraise pupil learning adequately.

2. Content-oriented tests in the areas of social studies and science become quickly outdated, measure only a limited sampling of learning outcomes, and seldom match closely the current emphasis of a modern school program. Learning outcomes in content areas are probably best measured by teacher-made tests, supplemented by an achievement battery designed to measure general educational development.

3. Tests of general educational development have a broader orientation than the typical test of basic skills. They include tests in the academic areas, but the items are designed to measure understanding, application, and other complex outcomes. Such tests are probably most useful in schools with a modern curriculum. Because they stress general outcomes, it is desirable to supplement them with more specific measures (teacher-made or standardized) of the particular content that has been covered during instruction.

4. Elementary school achievement batteries differ considerably in the emphasis given to the various areas of basic skills, to the different areas of content, and to the specific types of learning outcomes measured. Thus, it is imperative that the selection of a battery be based on a careful study of the tests, in light of the objectives of the instructional program and the types of educational decisions for which the results are to be used.

The common core of learning at the elementary school level makes the achievement battery especially useful for obtaining evidence of learning progress. As we shall see later, however, the survey battery has only limited value for diagnosing the strengths and weaknesses of low-performing pupils. Therefore, survey achievement testing should be followed up by diagnostic testing whenever learning problems are indicated. These tests will be discussed in a later section.

High School Achievement Batteries

The achievement battery has been less widely used at the high school level. Diversity of course offerings, variations in content among courses in the same subject-matter area, and the greater flexibility pupils have in selecting courses for their programs make it extremely difficult to design a test battery for general high school use. Test publishers have attempted to find a common core on which to base a battery of tests in one of the following ways:

1. By continuing to build the tests around the basic skills of reading, mathematics, language, and study skills. This is the procedure used in such tests as the *Comprehensive Tests of Basic Skills* (*CTBS*). As noted earlier (in the list of achievement batteries), this particular test battery provides a continuous series of tests of basic skills ranging from the primary level through grade 12 in high school.

2. By building tests that emphasize knowledge of course content and skills in the major areas of high school study: mathematics, science, social studies, and English. This approach is used in such batteries as the *Tests of Academic Progress* (*TAP*), designed for grades 9 to 12.
3. By building tests that measure general educational development in intellectual skills and abilities that are not dependent upon any particular series of courses. Typical tests in this category are the *Iowa Tests of Educational Development* (*ITED*) and the *Sequential Tests of Educational Progress* (*STEP, Series II*). The *ITED* is designed for high school use and is commonly used in conjunction with the *SRA Achievement Series* under the title *SRA Assessment Survey* (Grades 1 to 12). The *STEP II* high school battery is one of a continuous series from grade 4 to the college sophomore level.

High school achievement batteries with major emphasis on the basic skills (e.g., *CTBS*) are apt to be more useful for determining whether pupils have the necessary skills to succeed in high school than for measuring the outcomes of a high school program. Although some of the subtests may reflect the outcomes being stressed in the high school curriculum (e.g., language usage), the major emphasis is on skills that are prerequisite to the learning of course content. Pupils who have mastered reading, language, arithmetic, and study skills before entering high school are more likely to benefit fully from the high school program. Those who have not are good candidates for remedial instruction. Thus, tests of basic skills are especially useful for surveying the skills of pupils entering high school, for identifying individuals or groups in need of remedial instruction, and for evaluating the effectiveness of remedial programs. If used to measure the learning outcomes of the high school curriculum, it must be recognized that basic skill batteries measure only a very limited number of such outcomes.

Those batteries that emphasize both knowledge of course content and skills (e.g., *TAP*) pose special problems at the high school level. These tests are intended to measure outcomes of the high school program, but, of necessity, the coverage is so broad that only a relatively small number of items can be included in each area. A science test of 50 or 60 items, for example, is expected to cover the fields of biology, chemistry, physics, geology, astronomy, and weather. Similarly, a test of the same length in social studies is expected to cover American history, world history, government, economics, sociology, and geography. In addition to the limited sampling in each content area, there tends to be considerable emphasis on the recall of factual information. Because it takes several years to construct and standardize an achievement test battery, and its content is obtained from books that also have a writing and publication lag of several years, the test items are not likely to reflect adequately the current content of a modern high school curriculum.

Content-oriented achievement batteries are most useful in schools that have a traditional curriculum. Even here, however, it must be remembered that they provide only a very general survey of *some* of the curriculum outcomes and of *some* of the areas of course content. Choosing among the various achievement batteries of this type would therefore require a very careful analysis of the learning outcomes and content measured by each battery to see which one best measured the objectives of the instructional program. This analysis should go beyond the subtest titles and involve a study of the test items themselves. Questions such as the following should guide the analysis:

1. What proportion of the test items are relevant to the course content of the curriculum?
2. What proportion of the test items measure such outcomes as recall of factual information, understanding, and application?
3. How does the content analysis of the items compare to the objectives of the instructional program? Which objectives are adequately measured and which are not?

Although this type of analysis is important in the selection of any achievement test, it has special significance here. It will not only aid in the choice of the most appropriate test battery, but it will also make clear the relatively large number of instructional objectives that are not measured by the battery that is selected for use. This will aid in the selection of supplementary evaluation procedures. It should also result in more cautious interpretation and use of the test results. After such an analysis, it is unlikely that the selected battery would be used as the sole basis for evaluating the high school curriculum or for judging the effectiveness of the teachers.

Achievement batteries designed to measure general educational development (e.g., *ITED* and *STEP II*) are of special interest because they measure complex learning outcomes that cut across subject-matter lines. The subtests of these batteries cover the basic areas of the high school curriculum, but they emphasize understandings, interpretive skills, and the ability to apply knowledge and skill to new situations. Because these learning outcomes are closely related to the ultimate objectives of education, such achievement batteries are likely to have a desirable influence on the curriculum and teaching methods of the school. As with other achievement batteries, however, the tests should be in harmony with the school's objectives. Batteries that stress complex learning outcomes, rather than the measurement of routine skills and factual information, are apt to be more appropriate for schools with a modern curriculum than for schools favoring a more traditional approach.

Tests of general educational development also have special value as predictive instruments for college-bound students. Because they measure intellectual skills and abilities like those needed for advanced study, they tend to provide a good estimate of potential for college work. Validity coefficients typically range between .60 and .80 when twelfth-grade test results are correlated with freshmen grades in college. This compares favorably with predictions based on scholastic aptitude test scores. An additional benefit derived from the use of the tests of general educational development for determining college readiness is that they can aid in educational planning. Because strengths and weaknesses are reported for each of the major academic areas, the test results can be used to help pupils select a college major and to plan a remedial program for removing any serious deficiencies.

In summary, the following cautions should be kept in mind when one is selecting and using a high school achievement battery:

. Achievement batteries that measure the basic skills are more useful for determining the pupils' readiness for high school courses than for measuring outcomes of the high school curriculum. They, of course, would be especially appropriate for measuring the outcomes of any special programs designed to improve the basic skills.
2. Achievement batteries that include content-oriented tests tend to be better suited for schools with a traditional curriculum. Because the tests tend to have broad coverage but limited sampling in each content area, they must be selected with great care. A detailed analysis of each test item is necessary to determine how relevant the tests are to the objectives of the school's instructional program.
3. Tests of general educational development stress complex learning outcomes that are more in harmony with a modern school curriculum than with a traditional one. For these schools, the tests' emphasis on understanding, interpretation, and application can be expected to have a beneficial effect on the instructional program. For schools that are in the process of changing to a more modern curriculum, the tests can aid in the transition.
4. High school achievement batteries differ not only in their general orientation, but also in the nature of the specific subtests included in the battery and in the particular emphases within each subtest. There is even larger variation here than at the elementary level, because of the greater differentiation in course offerings. Therefore, special care is required in the review and evaluation of the tests and in the comparison of their content with the school's objectives and with the intended uses of the results.

At the high school level, it is frequently necessary to supplement achievement batteries with separate standardized tests in specific content areas. These will be considered in the following section.

ACHIEVEMENT TESTS IN SPECIFIC AREAS

In addition to achievement batteries, there are literally hundreds of separate tests designed to measure achievement in specific areas. The majority of these can be classified as tests of course content or reading tests of the general survey type. A limited number of tests have also been developed for use in determining learning readiness and for diagnosing learning difficulties.

The separate test has certain advantages over a test battery. First, it is easier to select a separate test that fits the instructional objectives of a particular area. The difficulty of relating an entire battery of tests to instructional objectives was pointed out earlier. Second, a separate test is usually longer than the subtests of a battery. This provides a more adequate sample of behavior and more reliable part scores for diagnostic purposes. Third, the flexibility of the separate test makes it easier to adapt to classroom instruction. The teacher can administer the separate test when it best fits his instructional needs, rather than following the rigid schedule of the school testing program.

The major limitation of separate tests is that each test is usually standardized on a different group of pupils. Because norm groups are not comparable, relative achievement of pupils in different areas cannot be compared. For example, it is not possible to determine whether a pupil has achieved more in science than mathematics, or in social studies than English, if the tests were not standardized on the same representative group of pupils. This is an especially serious limitation if the results are to be used for guidance purposes. Knowing a pupil's strengths and weaknesses in the basic areas of achievement is essential for proper educational and vocational planning.

Advantages of both the achievement test battery and separate tests in specific areas are capitalized upon in a comprehensive program. The achievement battery, administered as part of the school-wide testing program, provides a general survey of the pupils' educational development, and separate tests are selected for more specific instructional purposes. Thus, an elementary teacher might follow up a test battery with a more diagnostic test, or a high school teacher might follow it up with a subject-matter test more directly related to the specific learning outcomes he is emphasizing. Where such a comprehensive program is not possible, the achievement test battery is generally favored and teachers must rely much more heavily on their own informal classroom tests as aids to teaching.

Content-Oriented Tests

Achievement tests designed to measure the content of specific courses are numerous at the secondary level. In fact, there are over a hundred separate tests in each of the major content areas of English, mathematics, science, and social studies. There are also separate tests in the areas of foreign language, business, and fine arts, but these are not as numerous as those designed for the basic courses. All of these tests of specific course content are intended as end-of-course tests and thus are used primarily to measure the pupils' final levels of achievement.

One of the most notable collections of tests for measuring specific course content at the secondary school level is that published by the Cooperative Test Division of Educational Testing Service. These are the *Cooperative Achievement Tests,* which consist of a series of separate tests in each of the following areas: English, foreign language, mathematics, science, and social studies. Within each content area, there are tests for most of the school subjects. In the science area, for example, there are separate tests for general science, biology, chemistry, and physics. Probably the most unique series of *Cooperative* tests is in the foreign language area. Here, tests have been designed, in cooperation with the Modern Language Association, to measure competence in five languages: French, German, Spanish, Italian, and Russian. In each language, tests provide separate measures of skill in listening, speaking, reading, and writing at two levels (beginning and advanced). Because there are two equivalent forms for each of the two levels of achievement, the *MLA Cooperative Foreign Language Tests* include a total of sixteen tests for each language. The mathematics tests range from arithmetic to calculus, and include both traditional and modern emphases. The social studies tests cover the various courses in history, civics, and American government. In general, the *Cooperative Achievement Tests* are well designed and measure a variety of learning outcomes from simple to complex.

Two other series of content-oriented tests for use at the secondary level are published by Harcourt Brace Jovanovich, Inc., and by Houghton Mifflin Company. Both series include a number of separate tests in each of the major content areas. Although the tests vary in quality, many of them require students to demonstrate understanding and application as well as knowledge of factual information. For a complete listing of the separate tests included in these and other test series, consult the catalogues of the test publishers in Appendix C. For critical reviews of the tests, see Buros' *Mental Measurements Yearbooks.*[4]

There are several cautions that should be considered when one is selecting and evaluating tests in specific content areas:

1. Because these tests are content oriented, the date of construction is especially important. Developments in some content areas, such as science and social studies, are taking place at such a rapid rate that content-oriented tests are soon out of date.

---

[4] O. K. Buros, *The Seventh Mental Measurements Yearbook* (Highland Park, N.J.: Gryphon Press, 1972).

2. In addition to timeliness of test content, special attention should be directed toward its appropriateness for the particular course in which it is to be used. Because a standardized test includes only the content common to a variety of school systems, it is apt to lack comprehensiveness and at the same time to include questions on material that has not been included in the local curriculum.
3. Many content-oriented tests are limited to the measurement of knowledge outcomes, although there are a number of notable exceptions. Standardized tests of specific knowledge are seldom as pertinent and useful as well-constructed teacher-made tests in the same area.
4. Where a content-oriented test measures a variety of learning outcomes beyond those of specific knowledge, it is important that the learning outcomes measured by the test be in harmony with those emphasized in instructional objectives.

Because of its flexibility and timeliness, the informal teacher-made test is frequently better suited to the measurement of instructional objectives in a particular course than is the standardized achievement test. However, when carefully selected in terms of course content and learning outcomes, the standardized test can serve as a valuable check on the teacher's informal classroom tests.

Reading Tests

One of the most widely used tests at all levels of instruction is the reading test. It plays a prominent role in achievement test batteries and receives special emphasis in tests of general educational development. In addition, there are well over a hundred separate tests of reading ability.

Many reading tests are of the survey type. These are designed to measure a pupil's general level of reading ability. Such tests commonly measure vocabulary, reading comprehension, and rate of reading. The following list of reading skills is typical of those that reading survey tests attempt to measure:[5]

> Identifies the meaning of given words
> Identifies the meaning of words when used in context
> Identifies details that are directly stated in a passage or selection
> Identifies ideas that are implied in a passage or selection
> Identifies relationships (e.g., time, cause-effect) in a passage or selection
> Identifies the main thought or purpose of a passage or selection
> Identifies inferences drawn from a passage or selection

---

[5] For a more comprehensive list of reading abilities, see "Barrett's Taxonomy of Cognitive and Affective Dimensions of Reading Comprehension," in H. M. Robinson (ed.), *Innovation and Change in Reading Instruction*, Sixty-seventh Yearbook of the National Society for the Study of Education, Part II (Chicago: University of Chicago Press, 1968), p. 19.

Identifies conclusions drawn from a passage or selection
Identifies the literary devices used in a passage or selection
Identifies the writer's tone, mood, and intent

Reading tests differ greatly in the extent to which they cover the above skills and in the degree of emphasis given to each skill. Some tests focus on the lower levels of comprehension (e.g., identifying directly stated details), whereas others stress the more complex interpretive skills (e.g., identifying relationships, inferences, and conclusions). Moreover, the last two reading skills in the above list are more likely to be found in high school reading tests than in those designed for the elementary school.

Reading tests also differ widely in the nature of the material to be read by the pupil. Some tests use short passages of a sentence or two, whereas others use extended passages. Some use stories only, whereas others use stories, letters, poems, and scientific articles. Still another source of difference among reading tests lies in the extensiveness with which each type of reading material and each reading skill is sampled. One test, for example, may have a relatively large number of test items measuring the ability to draw conclusions from scientific articles, whereas another test has just a few such items. These differences highlight the importance of carefully defining what reading abilities are to be measured before selecting a test for use.

Typical reading tests of the survey type, at the elementary and high school levels, include the following:

Elementary School Level
  Gates-MacGinitie Reading Tests (Grades 1 to 12)
  Nelson Reading Test (Grades 3 to 9)
  Separate reading tests from achievement batteries
High School Level
  Davis Reading Test (Grades 8 to 13)
  Iowa Silent Reading Test (Grades 6 to 14)
  Nelson-Denny Reading Test (Grades 9 to 16)
  Reading Comprehension: Cooperative English Tests (Grades 9 to 14)
  Separate reading tests from achievement batteries

For information on these reading tests see Appendix D. For detailed descriptions and critical reviews of these and other reading tests, see Buros' guides.[6]

In a school program, reading tests may be selected for any, or all, of the following uses: (1) to evaluate the effectiveness of reading instruction, (2) to identify pupils needing remedial work in reading, (3) to predict success in subject-matter courses, (4) to determine whether poor reading ability can account for low scores on scholastic aptitude tests,

[6] O. K. Buros, *Reading Tests and Reviews* (Highland Park, N.J.: Gryphon Press, 1968). Also, see Buros' latest *Mental Measurements Yearbook*.

and (5) to help locate the causes of underachievement in school subjects. Although a single reading test may not serve all of these uses equally well, the uses to be made of the results are an important consideration in test selection. The ideal reading test for a particular program is the one that best measures the instructional objectives and most effectively fulfills the uses to which the results will be put.

In summary, the following cautions should be kept in mind when one is selecting and using reading survey tests:

1. No two reading tests are exactly alike. Although reading survey tests typically measure vocabulary, reading comprehension, and rate of reading, they differ radically in the nature of the material that the reader is expected to comprehend, in the specific reading skills tested, and in the adequacy with which each skill is measured.
2. Reading survey tests measure only a limited number of the outcomes of reading instruction. The mechanics of reading (e.g., perceptual skills, word analysis, and so on) are typically measured by diagnostic reading tests. Some specialized reading skills (e.g., reading maps, graphs, and charts) are more commonly measured by tests of study skills. Attitude toward reading and interest in reading, both of which are extremely important outcomes of reading instruction, must be determined by observation.
3. Reading tests can serve a variety of purposes in the school program. Thus, in addition to matching the objectives of instruction, test selection should take into account all of the possible uses to be made of the results.

In addition to reading tests of the survey type, there are a number of reading readiness tests and reading diagnostic tests. These will be considered in the following sections.

Readiness Tests

A number of tests have been designed to determine pupil readiness for learning school tasks. At the elementary level, reading readiness tests are probably most familiar, but recently a new type of early school readiness and achievement test has also appeared. At the secondary level, readiness tests (called prognostic or aptitude tests) are available for some school subjects. These are most common in the areas of mathematics and foreign language. Although readiness tests are essentially specialized scholastic aptitude tests, they are considered here because the test items are drawn from specific achievement areas. This has the advantage of providing diagnostic as well as predictive information. Thus, in addition to predicting learning success in a particular achievement area, test performance can provide information concerning the specific skills in which the pupil needs improvement if his learning is to be maximally effective.

Early School Readiness and Achievement Tests. Several tests have been developed to measure those basic concepts and skills considered essential for effective learning in the early school years. The tests are typically designed for preschool use (kindergarten, or sooner) but also can be used in the early primary grades. A typical example is the *Boehm Test of Basic Concepts.* This test is based on a selection of verbal concepts (e.g., biggest, nearest, several, and so on) that are needed to understand oral communication and to profit most from school experiences. The test items are read to the pupils and they mark their answers by placing an X on pictures designed to measure the concepts. See Figure 12.3 for a sample item.

Mark the boat that is <u>farthest</u> from the shore.

FIGURE 12.3. Sample item from the *Boehm Test of Basic Concepts* (Copyright © 1967, 1969 by The Psychological Corporation, New York, N.Y. All rights reserved. Reproduced by permission.)

Somewhat similar in makeup and purpose are the *Cooperative Preschool Inventory, Stanford Early School Achievement Test,* and *Tests of Basic Experience.* These tests emphasize basic concepts, but they also tap other types of preschool learning (e.g., knowledge of environment). Although these tests are broader in scope than the *Boehm Test,* the intended use is the same—to determine the pupils' achievement of important concepts and skills and to detect deficiencies for which appropriate learning experiences might be provided. These tests should be useful in planning for and evaluating preschool instruction, and in designing remedial programs for individual pupils.

Reading Readiness Tests. Tests of reading readiness are used at the kindergarten and first-grade level to help determine whether pupils have the necessary knowledges and skills to begin reading, and to group pupils for beginning reading instruction. The following functions are commonly measured by reading readiness tests:

1. *Visual discrimination.* Identifying similarities and differences in words, letters, numbers, geometric figures, or pictures.
2. *Auditory discrimination.* Identifying similarities and differences in spoken words, or sounds.
3. *Verbal comprehension.* Demonstrating an understanding of the meaning of words, sentences, and directions.
4. *Recognition of letters, words, and numbers.* Identifying letters of the alphabet, words, and numerals.
5. *Recognition of words in sample lessons.* Identifying words that have been taught in sample lessons.
6. *Drawing or copying.* Demonstrating skill in drawing or copying geometric forms, objects, letters, or numbers.

Not all reading readiness tests provide comprehensive coverage of the above areas. Some tests cover only a few readiness skills, whereas others include tasks from four or five of the areas. Thus, as in all types of testing, the first order of business is to decide what, specifically, is to be measured. In this particular case, it means deciding what reading readiness skills are most relevant to the reading program. A clear description of the skills to be measured is a prerequisite to valid test selection and use.

Some of the more widely used reading readiness tests include the following:[7]

> *Gates-MacGinitie Reading Readiness Skills*
> *Lee-Clark Reading Readiness Test*
> *Metropolitan Readiness Test*
> *Murphy-Durrell Reading Readiness Analysis*

Readiness for beginning reading involves more than the skills measured by reading readiness tests. Such factors as mental ability (a mental age of six years to six years and six months is frequently accepted as desirable for beginning reading), physical development, experiential background, social and emotional adjustment, and desire to read must also be considered. The reading readiness test focuses on important prerequisite skills, but test performance must be interpreted in light of the pupil's total readiness for learning.

Prognostic Tests. Aptitude or prognostic tests for high school use are designed to predict success in particular school subjects. These tests are especially useful in decisions concerning course selection and instruction. An algebra aptitude test, for example, may help decide whether a pupil should be encouraged to take algebra or general mathematics. When used in conjunction with other information, the results of an algebra aptitude test may also aid in the planning of course activities and in pro-

---

[7] For descriptions and reviews of reading readiness tests, see Buros' guides listed in footnote 6.

vision for individualized instruction. Although specialized aptitude tests seldom predict success any better than general scholastic aptitude tests, the nature of the test content tends to make them more useful for diagnostic and instructional purposes.

Typical tests in the area of mathematics include the following: *Survey Test of Algebraic Aptitude, Orleans-Hanna Algebra Prognosis Test,* and *Orleans-Hanna Geometry Prognosis Test.* In the foreign language area, the following are typical examples: *Modern Language Aptitude Test* and *Pimsleur Language Aptitude Battery.* In addition to tests in these academic areas, there are also specialized aptitude tests in such areas as art and music. These will be described in the following chapter. For a complete listing of prognostic or aptitude tests, see Buros' *Mental Measurements Yearbooks* (see footnote 4).

The following points provide useful guidelines for selecting and using readiness, or prognostic tests:

1. Because these tests are predictive instruments, evidence should be sought in the test manual concerning the effectiveness with which they predict success in the given area. Validity coefficients should be at least as high as those obtained with general scholastic aptitude tests and preferably higher.
2. In addition to their predictive value, these tests also have some general diagnostic value. Thus, the content of the test should be carefully evaluated in light of the type of readiness information desired and the uses to be made of the results.
3. These tests provide just a fraction of the information needed to determine readiness for learning in a given area. The pupil's social and emotional adjustment, his past achievement in the area, his motivation to learn, and his cultural background also must be taken into account.

In summary, readiness tests are useful to the extent to which they provide valid predictions of achievement, reveal remediable weaknesses in learning readiness, and are supplemented by background information concerning the pupil's total readiness for learning.

Diagnostic Tests

Survey tests provide some diagnostic information by indicating the general areas in which a pupil has performed poorly (e.g., arithmetic), and by further delimiting the nature of the weakness (e.g., computation, concepts, or problem solving). A study of responses to individual test items can provide still further information concerning the particular nature of the learning difficulty. The survey test is limited as a diagnostic tool, however, because of the relatively small number of items that measure each function. Arithmetic items designed to measure addition, for example, would include just a few of the number combinations that pupils might be expected to know. This limited sampling is necessary in a test designed to survey broadly all of the outcomes in a given area. Although this limited sampling of many different aspects of achievement enhances the test as a survey test, it restricts its usefulness for diagnostic purposes. The pupil will not be able to demonstrate his strengths and weaknesses on all types of problems, and the small number of items testing each function makes judgments about specific learning difficulties rather unreliable. Thus, survey tests may provide some clues concerning pupils' learning problems, but pupils with pronounced learning disabilities should be more carefully studied with diagnostic tests.

Tests that have been specifically designed for diagnostic purposes differ from survey tests in three important ways: (1) they have a larger number of part scores and a correspondingly larger number of test items measuring each function; (2) the test items are based on a detailed analysis of the specific skills involved in successful performance and a study of the most common errors made by pupils; (3) test difficulty tends to be lower. The lower difficulty is necessary in order to provide adequate discrimination among those pupils with learning disabilities. In short, a good diagnostic test will permit a pupil to demonstrate all aspects of the skill being measured and will pinpoint the types of errors that he has made.

The two areas in which diagnostic tests are most common are reading and arithmetic. Typical tests in the reading area include the following:

Doren Diagnostic Reading Test (Grades 1 to 4)
Gates-McKillop Reading Diagnostic Tests (Grades 2 to 6)
Stanford Diagnostic Reading Test (Grades 2.5 to 13)

Like other reading tests, diagnostic batteries also differ considerably in the specific aspects of reading that are measured. The *Stanford,* for example, identifies specific strengths and weaknesses in reading comprehension, vocabulary, syllabication, auditory skills, various aspects of phonetic analysis, and rate of reading (see Figure 12.4). There are seven subtest scores at Level I (grades 2.5 to 4.5) and eight subtest scores at Level II (grades 4.5 to 8.5) in this group administered test. In contrast, a comprehensive individually administered test like the *Gates-McKillop* provides over twenty separate scores, including areas (e.g., oral reading, word-attack skills) that cannot be measured by group testing. This variation in the range of skills measured by the different diagnostic tests emphasizes the importance of carefully analyzing a test before it is selected for use.[8]

Diagnostic tests in arithmetic are relatively few in number. Typical tests include *Diagnostic Tests and Self Helps in Arithmetic* (Grades 3 to 12)

---

[8] For descriptions and reviews of reading diagnostic tests, see Buros' guides listed in footnote 6.

Test I: READING COMPREHENSION. Find the one word
that belongs in each space and make a cross in the
circle in front of that word.

Several times a day Judy wants to practice her
piano lesson. She must like to__1__the piano.
Maybe she wants to become a _2__.

1 ◯clean ◯break ◯move ◯play
2 ◯musician   ◯mechanic
◯physician   ◯singer

Test 2:   VOCABULARY. Make a cross in the circle beside
the word that best completes the sentence
that the teacher reads.

"A book about a person's life is his"

1 ◯bibliography ◯autograph ◯biography

Test 3:   SYLLABICATION. Find the first syllable of the
word and make a cross in front of it (at the right).

1 conclude   ◯co ◯con ◯conc

Test 4:   SOUND DISCRIMINATION. Make a cross in the
circle beside the word that has the same sound.

1 she ◯feet ◯set ◯rope

Test 5:   BLENDING. Find the three sounds that make a
word and then make a cross in the circle next to
each sound in the word.

1 ◯c ◯a ◯s
◯d ◯e ◯t

Test 6:   RATE OF READING. Make a cross in the circle next
to the word in every third line that best fits in with the
sentence.

1 Many years ago people thought that when
2 North America was discovered by
3 ◯Columbus ◯Edison ◯Washington

FIGURE 12.4. Sample item from *Stanford Diagnostic Reading Test,* Level II. (Copyright 1966 by Harcourt, Brace & Jovanovich, Inc. All rights reserved. Reproduced by permission.)

and the *Stanford Diagnostic Arithmetic Test* (Grades 2.5 to 8.5). The
following list of subtests, from Level II (Grades 4.5 to 8.5) of the *Stanford,*
illustrates the types of part scores that are obtained from a diagnostic
arithmetic test:

1. Concepts of Numbers and Numerals
    Part A. Number Systems and Operations
    Part B. Decimal Place Value
2. Computation with Whole Numbers
    Part A. Addition and Subtraction
    Part B. Multiplication
    Part C. Division
3. Common Fractions
    Part A. Understanding
    Part B. Computation
4. Decimal Fractions and Percent
5. Number Facts
    Part A. Addition
    Part B. Subtraction
    Part C. Multiplication
    Part D. Division
    Part E. Carrying

The items in the *Stanford* require the pupils to supply, rather than select, the answers. All of the problems are presented in the test booklet except the tests of number facts. These number facts (e.g., $7 + 9$) are dictated to the pupils at a pace of one every 5 to 7 seconds to measure quick recall. This makes it possible to determine the areas in which the number facts have been mastered (e.g., addition) and the specific combinations (e.g., 8×9) that are still causing difficulty. In addition to analyzing the pupil's errors on the *Stanford*, the teacher is encouraged to identify further the nature of the difficulty by asking the pupil to explain what he did in arriving at each of the incorrect solutions to the problems he missed.[9]

Several reservations should be kept in mind when one is selecting and using diagnostic tests.

1. Each diagnostic test reflects the author's viewpoint toward diagnosis. When one is selecting a test, the diagnostic procedures should be evaluated in light of the specific type of information desired.
2. Diagnostic tests are designed for pupils of below-average performance. Thus, they are good for identifying weaknesses in learning but not for indicating the level of proficiency. A high score on a subtest simply means this is *not* an area of weakness.
3. Diagnostic tests indicate the typical errors a pupil makes, but they do not indicate the causes of the errors. Although some causes can be easily inferred from the type of error made, or from a pupil's explanation of how he arrived at the answer, causes of a particular deficiency are frequently multiple and interrelated in a complex manner.

---

[9] For descriptions and reviews of arithmetic diagnostic tests, see O. K. Buros, *The Seventh Mental Measurements Yearbook* (Highland Park, N.J.: Gryphon Press, 1972).

4. Related to the previous point is the fact that diagnostic tests provide only partial information for diagnosing a pupil's difficulty. In the reading area, for example, intelligence, vision, hearing, physical condition, emotional factors, and cultural deprivation must also be considered.
5. Results from diagnostic tests, concerning specific learning difficulties, tend to have a low reliability because of the relatively few items measuring each type of error. Thus, the findings regarding specific strengths and weaknesses for any particular pupil should be regarded as clues to be verified by other objective evidence and by regular classroom observation.

In summary, a diagnostic test is a useful tool for analyzing learning difficulties, but it is simply a starting point. Supplementary information concerning the physical, intellectual, social, and emotional development of the pupil is also needed before an effective remedial program can be initiated.

CRITERION-REFERENCED TESTS

Until the early 1970s, test publishers had been concerned almost exclusively with standardized tests. A common feature of these tests, as noted earlier, is that they provide norm groups for test interpretation. Thus, a pupil's performance on a standardized achievement test is given meaning by noting his relative standing in the norm group. This *norm-referenced* interpretation is a distinctive characteristic of standardized tests.

To fulfill instructional needs that were not being met by these norm-referenced tests (e.g., individualized instruction, mastery learning programs), some test publishers are now making available *criterion-referenced* tests. These tests typically contain sets of test items designed to measure each of a series of behaviorally stated instructional objectives. A sufficient number of items is used for each objective to make it possible to describe test performance in terms of a pupil's mastery of each objective. Thus, a pupil's performance can be described without comparing his test performance to that of other pupils (making test norms unnecessary).

The following typical comment by a test publisher reflects this new emphasis on criterion-referenced testing:

> Educators have needed and will continue to need comparative information on student performance in broad curricular areas, information that is now provided by standardized tests commonly called "norm-referenced" tests. There is, however, an increasing need for information that tells the educator specifically what the student has learned and still needs to learn. Criterion-referenced tests were developed to satisfy this increasing need; rather than comparing a student's performance with that of a norm

group, a criterion-referenced test evaluates a student's mastery or non-mastery of educational objectives. (CTB/McGraw-Hill 1974 Catalog)

In some cases entire systems of criterion-referenced tests have been developed. Typical examples of such systems are the following:[10]

Individual Pupil Monitoring System: Mathematics (Grades 1 to 8) [7]
Individual Pupil Monitoring System: Reading (Grades 1 to 6) [7]
Mastery: An Evaluation Tool (Reading, Mathematics) (Grades 3 to 8) [10]
Prescriptive Mathematics Inventory (Grades 4 to 8) [3]
Prescriptive Reading Inventory (Grades 1.5 to 6) [3]

Test results from such criterion-referenced systems indicate pupil progress in terms of mastery of a set of specified behavioral objectives. A typical individual report form, based on three test items for each objective, is shown in Figure 12.5. These systems also typically include guides for prescribing learning activities to overcome pupil weaknesses on non-mastered objectives, as indicated by the "aid probe number" in Figure 12.5. Although these criterion-referenced testing programs were first developed for reading and mathematics, where the skills are more easily identified and sequenced, this type of testing can be expected to spread to other areas of the curriculum as the demand warrants it.

Custom-made Criterion-Referenced Tests

In addition to providing criterion-referenced tests that have been pre-designed for school use, some test publishers maintain banks of objectives and related test items and will prepare custom-made criterion-referenced tests to fit a particular school program. The test user typically selects the objectives to be measured from an objectives catalogue and specifies the number of items to be used for measuring each objective. The test publisher then assembles the test by taking from the item banks those items that measure the selected set of objectives. Scoring and reporting services are also typically provided for these custom-made tests. Information concerning custom-made tests can be obtained from test publishers' catalogues.[11]

SUMMARY

Standardized achievement tests measure the common objectives of a wide variety of schools, have standard procedures for administration and scoring, and provide norms for interpreting the scores. A test manual and other

---

[10] The numbers in brackets refer to the publishers listed in Appendix C.
[11] See Appendix C for a list of test publishers and for addresses of other objective-item pools.

mastery: an evaluation tool
Individual Student Report

Student name ─
School and group name ─

Testing date ─
Subject tested ─
Grade tested ─
Test number ─

mastery: an evaluation tool

SRA CRITERION-REFERENCED MEASUREMENT PROGRAM

REPORT FOR THOMAS ANDERSON
GROUP MS. JONES CLASS / LINCOLN SCHOOL

SUBJECT SOBAR READING
GROUP I.D. 50 BURTO
GRADE 6
DATE 10-31-74
TEST # 440121
CODE 01

OBJECTIVE: (LEARNER WILL IDENTIFY . . .)
OBJ CATALOG NO   DIA PROBE NOS

#	Objective / Catalog No / Dia Probe Nos	OBJ MST	ITEM RIGHT
1	SYLLABICATION OF WRITTEN WORD — WAI7 RA17 RB8	Y	+ +
2	SINGULAR FORM OF IRREGULAR VERB — V15 RA15 RB6	N	+ - 0
3	IF WORD ENDING IN S IS PLUR. POSSES OR VERB — V32 RA15 RB6	Y	+ +
4	TENSE OF SENTENCE — V35 RA15 RB6	Y	+ +
5	IF WORD WITH ER IS NOUN, VERB, OR ADJECTIVE — V4 RA15 RB6	Y	+ +
6	MEANING OF OBSCURE PREFIXED WORD, ROOT GIVEN — V21 RB7	Y	+ +
7	MEANING OF OBSCURE SUFFICED WORD, ROOT GIVEN — V25 RA16 RB7	Y	+ +
8	BEST DEFINITION OF SINGLE-MEANING WORD — V44	N	+ 0 +
9	IF WORDS ARE SYNONYMS, ANTONYMS OR NEITHER — V53 RA30 RA27 RB21 RB22	N	- +
10	MEANING OF A HOMOGRAPH — V4 RA30 RB21	Y	+ +
11	MEANING OF A SYMBOL — V55	N	- - 0
12	MEANING OF TERMS—POETRY — V62	N	- -
13	MEANING OF TERMS—GOVERNMENT — V73	Y	+ +
14	MEANING OF TERMS—CHEMISTRY — V68	Y	+ +
15	WORD MEANING USING CONTEXT CLUES — C6 RA31 RB19	N	0
16	MEANING OF NON-LITERAL LANGUAGE — C11 RA31 RB20	N	- +
17	PHRASE ANSWERING KEY WORD (WHAT, HOW) QUEST — C21	Y	+ +
18	EXPLICIT MAIN IDEA OF STORY — C22 RA23 RB14	Y	+ +
19	SIGNIFICANT DETAIL OF STORY — C24 RA23 RB13	Y	+ +
20	SEQUENCE OF MAIN EVENTS IN STORY — C25 RA26 RB17	N	- +

OBJECTIVE: (LEARNER WILL IDENTIFY . . .)
OBJ CATALOG NO   DIA PROBE NOS

#	Objective / Catalog No / Dia Probe Nos	OBJ MST	ITEM RIGHT
21	IMPLIED MAIN IDEA OF STORY — 6C27 RA20 RB14	N	+ + -
22	ANSWER TO QUESTION INVOLVING INFERENCE — 6C29 RA20 RB15	Y	+ + +
23	CHARACTERS' FEELINGS AND REACTIONS — 6C30 RA20 RB15	Y	+ + +
24	COMPARISONS OF STORY MATERIAL — 6C32 RA20 RB15	Y	+ + +
25	IMPLIED CAUSE OF EXPLICIT EFFECT — 6C33 RB11	N	0 - -
26	IMPLIED EFFECT OF EXPLICIT CAUSE — 6C34 RB16	N	- - 0
27	CONCLUSIONS OR GENERALIZATION — 6C35 RA25 RB15	Y	+ +
28	DIFFERENCES IN POINT OF VIEW — 6C38 RB11	Y	+ +
29	AUTHOR'S PURPOSE — 6C41 RB9	N	- +
30	ILLOGICAL THINKING — 6C43	Y	+ +
31	LOCATION OF FRONT MATTER IN BOOKLET — SS1	Y	+ +
32	LOCATION OF BACK MATTER IN BOOKLET — SS5	Y	+ +
33	WORD TO LOOK UP IN INDEX TO SOLVE PROBLEM — SS7	N	- 0
34	ANSWERS TO FACTUAL QUEST., USING BOOKLET PARTS — SS8	N	+ -
35	ANSWERS TO QUEST., USING BOOK'S LEARNING AIDS — SS11	Y	+ +
36	CORRECT ALPHABETIZATION BY 2ND AND 3RD LETTERS — SS17 RA32 RB25	Y	+ +
37	DEF. SYN., OR ANT., USING DICTIONARY ENTRY — SS19 RB25	Y	+ +
38	INFORMATION FOUND ON LIBRARY CATALOG CARD — SS25 RB24	N	- - 0
39	USE OF MAP READING DEVICE — SS37 RB26	Y	+ +
40	BEST SUMMARY OF INFORM. IN GRAPHIC MATERIAL — SS35 RB26	Y	+ +

diagnosis®: an instructional aid Probe number
Objective tested
Objective catalog number
Mastery of objective
Non-mastery of objective
Item answered correctly
Item answered incorrectly
Item not answered
Number of local items answered correctly if local norms included

SRA SCIENCE RESEARCH ASSOCIATES INC

NO OF OBJ TESTED **40**
NO OF SRA OBJ MASTERED **25**
% OF SRA OBJ MASTERED **62.5**
LOCAL TEST SCORE

N = NO, DID NOT MASTER OBJ.
Y = YES, MASTERED
NO OF SRA OBJ **40**
+ = RIGHT ANSWER
- = WRONG ANSWER
0 = OMISSION

accessory materials are typically provided to aid in the administration of the test and the use of the results. The test items are generally of high quality because they have been prepared by specialists, pretested, and selected on the basis of their effectiveness and their relevance to a rigid set of specifications.

Despite their high technical quality, standardized achievement tests complement rather than replace teachers' informal classroom tests. They are especially useful for measuring general educational development, determining pupil progress from one year to the next, grouping pupils, diagnosing learning difficulties, and comparing achievement with scholastic aptitude. They are of little value for measuring learning outcomes unique to a particular course, the day-to-day progress of pupils, and knowledge of current developments in rapidly changing fields. These latter purposes are more effectively served by informal classroom tests.

Achievement test batteries are widely used at the elementary school level. They cover the basic skills (i.e., reading, language, mathematics, and study skills), and some batteries also include sections on science and social studies. Test batteries are less widely used at the high school level because of the difficulty of identifying a common core of content. Batteries at this level are confined to the basic skills, to content included in the basic high school subjects, or to measures of general educational development. The main advantage of a test battery is that a pupil's strengths and weaknesses in different areas can be determined. The complete test battery seldom fits all of the instructional objectives of the school, however, and this must be taken into account when one is interpreting the results.

In addition to achievement test batteries, there are many separate standardized tests designed to measure achievement in specific areas. These include tests on course content, reading tests, readiness tests, and diagnostic tests. Although these can be more readily adapted to the instructional program than complete batteries, the following cautions should be kept in mind during their selection and use: (1) standardized tests with similar titles may differ radically in terms of the type of test content and in terms of the emphasis given to the various skills measured; (2) standardized tests measure only a portion of the knowledge, skills, and developmental abilities needed to evaluate, predict, or diagnose learning progress; (3) standardized tests are effective to the extent that they measure the instructional objectives and serve the intended uses of the particular school program in which they are administered.

To fulfill instructional needs that were not being met by standardized achievement tests (i.e., norm-referenced tests), some test publishers are now making available ready-made and custom-made criterion-referenced tests. These tests measure pupil mastery of instructional objectives and,

FIGURE 12.5. Individual report form showing objectives tested on the reading section of *Mastery: An Evaluation Tool.* (Copyright © 1974 by Science Research Associates, Inc. All rights reserved. Reproduced by permission.)

thus, describe what learning tasks a pupil can and cannot perform in a particular instructional area.

LEARNING EXERCISES

1. To what does the term *standardized* refer in a standardized test?
2. What are the similarities and differences in construction of a classroom test and a standardized test of achievement? How are the learning outcomes measured by each apt to differ?
3. State as many ways as you can think of that the various batteries of basic skills tests might differ from one another.
4. What effect would you expect on classroom instruction if a test of general educational development were given annually to all pupils in grades four, five, and six? What influence, if any, might this have on the nature of the classroom tests used by the teacher?
5. If possible, study the manual of an achievement test battery. Review the information on how it was constructed. How complete is the information?
6. Examine two standardized achievement tests in an area you are teaching or plan to teach. How do the tests differ in terms of the learning outcomes and content each measures?
7. What effect would you expect on the high school science curriculum if standardized tests of specific course content were given annually to all pupils? In what ways might the effect be beneficial? In what ways harmful?
8. Readiness tests generally provide no better prediction of school success than scholastic aptitude tests. What then would be the advantage of using readiness tests?
9. What are the advantages and limitations of diagnosing a pupil's learning difficulties by analyzing his responses to individual test items on a general survey test of achievement. Why would a diagnostic test be more useful?
10. What are some possible advantages of using a criterion-referenced achievement test instead of a standardized (norm-referenced) achievement test? What are some possible disadvantages?

SUGGESTIONS FOR FURTHER READING

ANASTASI, A. *Psychological Testing*, 4th ed. New York: Macmillan Publishing Co., Inc., 1976. Chapter 14, "Educational Testing." Describes common types of tests used in education.

BLANTON, W. E., R. FARR, and J. J. TUINMAN (eds.). *Reading Tests for the Secondary Grades: A Review and Evaluation*. Newark, Delaware: International Reading Association, 1972. Provides reviews of fourteen published reading tests that are available for use with high school students.

HARRIS, T. L. "Reading," *Encyclopedia of Educational Research*, 4th ed. New York: Macmillan Publishing Co., Inc., 1969. Pages 1060–1104. See especially discussions of reading readiness (page 1087) and diagnostic and remedial practices (page 1093).

MEHRENS, W. A., and I. J. LEHMANN. *Standardized Tests in Education,* 2nd ed. New York: Holt, Rinehart & Winston, Inc., 1975. Chapter 3, "Standardized Achievement Tests." Describes numerous diagnostic, readiness, criterion-referenced, and survey achievement tests and their uses in the school.

NOLL, V. H., and D. P. SCANNELL. *Introduction to Educational Measurement,* 3rd ed. Boston: Houghton Mifflin Company, 1972. Chapter 9, "Measuring Achievement in Elementary Grades." Chapter 10, "Measuring Achievement in the Secondary Grades." Describe various achievement tests used in the schools.

Test Bulletin

KATZ, M. *Selecting an Achievement Test: Principles and Procedures.* Princeton, N.J.: Educational Testing Service, 1973.

CHAPTER 13
Standardized Aptitude Tests

Aptitude tests are designed to predict future performance in some activity. . . . Those used in schools range from the traditional scholastic aptitude tests to the more recent differential aptitude tests. Attempts also have been made to develop special tests for creativity . . . art . . . music . . . and the culturally deprived. Typical examples of these tests will be discussed, . . . but the emphasis will be on principles of selection and use.

Because one of the major aims of the school is to assist each pupil to achieve the maximum of which he is capable, it is not surprising that standardized aptitude tests play a prominent role in the school. Some estimate of pupil ability is necessary in determining learning readiness, in individualizing instruction, in organizing classroom groups, in identifying underachievers, in diagnosing learning problems, in placing pupils in special classes, and in assisting pupils with their educational and vocational plans. Although the results of achievement tests are also useful for these purposes, aptitude tests make a unique contribution.

ACHIEVEMENT AND APTITUDE TESTS

Before we proceed with discussions of the various types of aptitude tests, it might be well to consider some basic similarities and differences between achievement tests and aptitude tests. A common distinction is that *achievement* tests measure what a pupil has learned, and *aptitude* tests measure his ability to learn new tasks. Although this appears to be a clear distinction, it oversimplifies the problem and covers up some important similarities and differences. Actually both types measure what a pupil has learned, and both are useful for predicting his success in learning new tasks. The major differences lie in (1) the types of learning measured by each test, and (2) the types of prediction for which each is most useful.

Types of Learning Measured: The Ability Spectrum

The various types of learning measured by achievement and aptitude tests can be most clearly depicted if they are arranged along a continuum, as shown in Table 13.1. In this spectrum of ability tests, achievement tests

TABLE 13.1

SPECTRUM OF ABILITY TESTS IN TERMS OF TYPES OF LEARNING MEASURED*

Level	General Test Type	Types of Learning Measured
A	Content-oriented achievement tests (e.g., *Tests of Academic Progress*)	Knowledge of subject matter in particular courses such as social studies, English, mathematics, and science.
B	Tests of general educational development (e.g., *Iowa Tests of Educational Development, STEP II*)	Basic skills and complex learning outcomes common to many courses, such as application of principles and interpretation of data.
C	School-oriented aptitude tests (e.g., *Cooperative School and College Ability Tests*)	Verbal, numerical, and general problem-solving abilities similar to those learned in *school*, such as vocabulary, reading, and arithmetic reasoning.
D	Culture-oriented verbal aptitude tests (e.g., *Cognitive Abilities Test, Verbal Battery and Quantitative Battery*)	Verbal, numerical and general problem-solving abilities derived more from the *general culture* than from common *school experiences*.
E	Culture-oriented nonverbal aptitude tests (e.g., *Cognitive Abilities Test, Nonverbal Battery*)	Abstract reasoning abilities based on figure analogies, figure series, picture classification and other nonverbal tasks.

* Adapted from L. J. Cronbach, *Essentials of Psychological Testing* (New York: Harper and Row, Publishers, 2nd ed., 1960, 3rd ed., 1970).

fall at Levels A and B and aptitude tests fall at Levels C, D, and E. The spectrum classifies the various types of tests in terms of the degree to which the test content is dependent upon specific learning experiences. At one extreme (Level A) is the content-oriented achievement test that measures knowledge of specific course content. At the other extreme (Level E) is the culture-oriented nonverbal aptitude test that measures a type of learning little influenced by direct training. Thus, as we move through the different levels of the spectrum, from A to E, the test content becomes less dependent upon any particular set of learning experiences.

The closer two tests are to each other in the spectrum, the more nearly alike are the types of learning measured. Achievement tests designed to measure general educational development (Level B) and scholastic aptitude tests based on school-learned abilities (Level C), for example, both measure somewhat similar abilities, and thus they can be expected to correlate rather highly. By the same token, the farther apart two tests are in the spectrum, the less they have in common and consequently the lower the correlations between them. This information is useful in selecting and using aptitude tests. For instance, we can expect aptitude tests at Level C and D to provide a better prediction of school achievement than those at Level E. On the other hand, if we are primarily interested in identifying pupils with undeveloped learning *potential*, tests at Level E would be more useful. In the use of this spectrum, however, it must be remembered that these are merely convenient categories for classifying the different types of ability tests and that some tests will overlap two or more categories. There are a number of wide-spectrum scholastic aptitude tests, for example, that include a range of test content covering Levels C, D, and E in a single test score.

Types of Predictions Made with Achievement and Aptitude Tests

Achievement and aptitude tests can also be distinguished in terms of the types of predictions for which each is most useful. Because past achievement is frequently the best predictor of future achievement, both types of achievement test are useful in predicting future learning. In general, the content-oriented achievement test (Level A) can predict how well a pupil will learn new knowledge in the same content area but it is of less value in predicting future learning in other areas. For example, a test of first-semester English will be a good predictor of second-semester English but not of second-semester mathematics, science, or social studies. In other words, its value as a predictor of future learning depends largely on the relationship between the content being measured and the content in the future learning situation. Tests measuring general educational development (Level B) are much more effective predictors of future achievement than content-oriented tests because they measure intellectual skills and abilities common to a variety of content areas. In fact, tests of educational development have been shown to be as good predictors of general school achievement as the best aptitude tests.[1]

---

[1] J. C. Merwin and E. F. Gardner, "Development and Application of Tests of Educational Achievement," *Review of Educational Research*, 32, 40–50, Feb. 1962.

If achievement tests are such good predictors of future learning, why do we use aptitude tests (Levels C to E) in schools? There are at least several good reasons. (1) An aptitude test can be administered in a relatively short time (some as short as 20 minutes), whereas a comprehensive battery of achievement tests would take several hours. (2) In addition to time saved, aptitude tests can be used with pupils of more widely varying educational backgrounds. Because the type of learning measured is that common to most pupils, an individual is less apt to be penalized because of specific weaknesses in his past training. (3) Aptitude tests can be used before a pupil has had any training in a particular area. For example, success in a French course cannot be predicted by an achievement test in French until the person has had some training in it. (4) There is an additional reason that applies more specifically to the culture-oriented aptitude test (Levels D and E). Because these are measures of aptitude least influenced by school-learned abilities, they can be used to distinguish low achievers working up to their ability from those with potential for higher achievement. Identifying such underachievers with aptitude tests that depend heavily on school-learned abilities (Level C) is possible but less effective, because the achievement skills required to respond to the test are the very ones in which the underachiever is most apt to be weak.

In summary, both achievement tests and aptitude tests measure learned abilities, but achievement tests measure those that are more directly dependent upon specific school experiences, whereas aptitude tests measure those based on a wide range of both in-school and out-of-school experiences. This is a matter of degree, however, and it is possible to arrange both types of test on a continuum, ranging from the measurement of specific course content (Level A) to the measurement of culturally learned abilities (Levels D and E). Achievement tests and aptitude tests become very much alike near the center of the continuum (Levels B and C). Achievement and aptitude tests are also similar in that they are both useful for predicting future achievement. In general, aptitude tests provide a more convenient measure and one that predicts over a wider range of future experiences. As with types of learning outcomes measured, these differences are less pronounced near the center of the continuum.

INTELLIGENCE, SCHOLASTIC APTITUDE, AND LEARNING POTENTIAL

Tests designed to measure learning ability have traditionally been called *intelligence tests*. This terminology is still used for many individually administered tests and for some group tests, but its use is declining. There are a number of reasons for this: (1) Many people have come to associate the concept "intelligence" with inherited capacity. (2) There is increasing controversy over the meaning of "intelligence" and the nature of the factors that should be included in the concept. (3) Tests in this area have been increasingly used for predictive rather than descriptive purposes. If we are mainly interested in predicting achievement, for example, a mixture of school-learned abilities is apt to be more useful than a more pure measure of "intelligence." In place of the term *intelligence test* have come such terms as *tests of mental ability, tests of general ability, tests of academic aptitude,* and *tests of scholastic aptitude.* The latter term has probably been used more widely in school settings than have any of the others.

It is important to recognize that scholastic aptitude tests do *not* measure native capacity or learning potential directly. Like all other tests used in school, *a scholastic aptitude test measures performance based on learned abilities.* In this sense, it is a specific type of achievement test. *Any conclusion concerning capacity or potential for learning must be inferred from the results* and such inference can be validly made only when the following conditions (or assumptions) have been met:

1. All pupils have had an equal opportunity to learn the types of tasks presented in the test.
2. All pupils have been motivated to do their best on the test.
3. All pupils have the "enabling behaviors" (such as reading skill) necessary for maximum performance on the test.
4. None of the pupils is hampered by test panic, emotional problems, or other "disabling behaviors," which can prevent maximum performance on the test.

These conditions are seldom fully met, of course, and the extent to which they are *not* met determines how much we err in estimating learning potential from scholastic aptitude test scores. Many of the misinterpretations and misuses of scholastic aptitude tests arise from failure to recognize the influence these conditions have on test results and consequently on the inferences that can be drawn from them.

The safest procedure is to interpret a pupil's scores on a scholastic aptitude test as a measure of his present learning ability. Undoubtedly the test performance reflects inherited characteristics to some (unknown) degree, but it also reflects the individual's experiential background, motivation, test-taking skills, persistence, self-confidence, and emotional adjustment. These factors are all a part of the individual's present ability to perform and as such affect both his test scores and his school achievement. It should be noted, however, that many of these factors can be modified by training, and therefore both learning ability and school achievement can be improved. It is when we interpret scholastic aptitude scores as direct and unmodifiable measures of learning potential that we are apt to misuse the results.

GROUP TESTS OF SCHOLASTIC APTITUDE

The majority of scholastic aptitude tests administered in the schools are group tests. These are tests that, like standardized achievement tests, can be administered to a large number of pupils at one time by persons with relatively little training in test administration. Some group tests provide a single score, whereas others provide two or more scores based on measures of separate aspects of mental ability. Here we shall briefly describe and illustrate the various types of group tests. More detailed information on the tests discussed in this chapter may be found in Appendix D. Critical reviews of these and other scholastic aptitude tests may be found in Buros' *Mental Measurements Yearbooks*.[2]

Single-Score Tests

Scholastic aptitude tests that yield a single score are designed to measure the general mental ability of pupils. Typically, such a variety of types of items is included in the test that no particular ability or skill receives undue emphasis in the total score. Thus the specific aspects of mental ability (such as verbal, numerical, and abstract reasoning) are blended together into one global measure of scholastic aptitude. These are sometimes called wide-spectrum tests and would cover Levels C through E in the spectrum of abilities described earlier (see Table 13.1).

A common format for the single-score test is to arrange the items in a spiral-omnibus pattern, that is, to mix together items of different types and arrange them in increasing order of difficulty. This makes it possible to have one set of directions and a relatively short testing time (30 to 40 minutes), because there are no separate subtests. Examples of widely used tests of this type are the *Henmon-Nelson Tests of Mental Ability* (Grades K to 12) and the *Otis-Lennon Mental Ability Test* (Grades K to 16). See Figure 13.1 for sample test items from the *Otis-Lennon* test.

Single-score tests are typically used to measure readiness for school learning and to predict success in future schoolwork. They are highly verbal in nature and this, of course, contributes to their predictive value because school learning is largely verbal. By the same token, they do not provide a good estimate of undeveloped learning *potential* for pupils from culturally deprived homes or for pupils with poor reading skill. Neither do they provide for differential prediction for various types of schoolwork. They were not designed for these purposes. They are intended only as a general measure of current readiness for schoolwork. Thus, a low score will indicate lack of readiness to perform well on school tasks, but the low score

---

[2] O. K. Buros, *The Seventh Mental Measurements Yearbook* (Highland Park, N.J.: Gryphon Press, 1972).

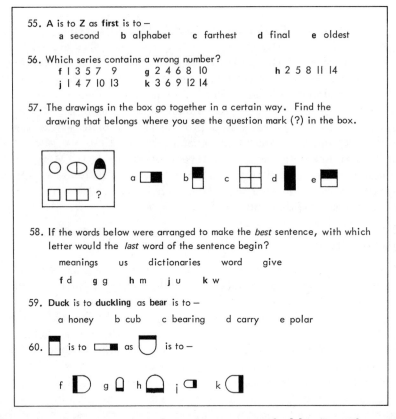

FIGURE 13.1. Sample items from the *Otis-Lennon Mental Ability Test*, Elementary II Level, Grades 4–6.9. (Copyright 1967 by Harcourt Brace Jovanovich, Inc. All rights reserved. Reproduced by permission.)

will reveal neither the nature nor the cause of the poor performance. To determine this, it would be necessary to check on the extent to which the basic assumptions cited earlier had been met (i.e., equal opportunity to learn the tasks, maximum motivation, and so on), and to make a more comprehensive study of the pupil receiving the low score. Single-score scholastic aptitude tests provide a quick, effective, general measure of present learning ability. Inferences concerning a pupil's undeveloped learning potential are likely to be especially hazardous with this omnibus-type test.

Tests with Verbal and Nonverbal Scores

A number of group tests have been designed to yield verbal and nonverbal or language and nonlanguage scores. A typical example of this type test is the *Short-Form Test of Academic Aptitude* (Grades 1.5 to 12). This test, a successor to the *California Short-Form Test of Mental Maturity*, contains four separately-timed subtests: Vocabulary, Analogies (picture analogies), Sequences (number and figure series), and Memory (delayed recall). The Vocabulary and Memory subtests provide a language score (verbal) and Analogies and Sequences provide a nonlanguage score (nonverbal). A total score, based on all subtests, is also provided.

The obvious advantage of using tests with both verbal and nonverbal scores is that one can identify learning ability at two different levels. The verbal score generally provides the best prediction of school success because verbal ability plays such a prominent role in learning school tasks. Thus, high verbal scores indicate the presence of those abilities needed for immediate success in schoolwork. In a sense this is developed learning potential supported by all of the functional skills necessary for effective performance. The nonverbal score, on the other hand, provides a more satisfactory estimate of a pupil's undeveloped learning potential. For example, a pupil with above-average mental ability who is deficient in reading is apt to have a low verbal score but an above-average nonverbal score. Although his chances of immediate success in schoolwork are poor because of his reading deficiency, his chances of future success are good if he is given appropriate remedial work. Thus the nonverbal score serves as a check on the undeveloped learning potential of those with low verbal scores.

The differences between verbal and nonverbal scores must be relatively large before they can be used for diagnostic purposes. The separate scores usually correlate quite highly with each other because of the general mental ability factor common to both sets of scores. A safe procedure is to ignore the differences between verbal and nonverbal scores unless they are at least one standard deviation (15 or 16 IQ points) apart. Differences smaller than this can usually be accounted for by random errors of measurement. The test manual will typically provide information concerning the interpretable differences between verbal and nonverbal scores, but where this is lacking the use of one standard deviation difference provides a practical conservative estimate.

Tests with Verbal and Quantitative Scores

Some group tests of scholastic aptitude provide separate verbal (V) and quantitative (Q) scores. These tests are designed to provide differential prediction of school success. They are based on the principle that tests of verbal ability are best for predicting achievement in courses in which verbal concepts are emphasized, and tests of quantitative ability are best for predicting success in courses stressing mathematical concepts. Widely used tests of this type include the *Cooperative School and College Ability Tests* (*SCAT, SCAT Series II,* Grades 4 to 14) and the *Kuhlmann-Anderson Measure of Academic Potential* (Grades K to 12). The *SCAT* tests provide verbal, quantitative, and total scores at all grade levels in which the test is used. The *Kuhlmann-Anderson* test yields a total score, only, from kindergarten to grade 6, and separate verbal, quantitative, and total scores for grades 7 to 12. Sample items from the *SCAT Series II* are shown in Figure 13.2.

Part I – Verbal Ability

Find the lettered pair of words that go together in the same way as the first pair of words.

comma : period ::

A begin : cease
B cut : sever
C delay : deter
D pause : stop

Answer

[A] [B] [C] ■

Part II – Mathematical Ability

Mark

A if the part in Column A is Greater,
B if the part in Column B is greater,
C if the two parts are equal,
D if not enough information is given for you to decide.

Column A	Column B	Answer
100%	$\frac{16}{17}$	■ [B] [C] [D]

FIGURE 13.2. Sample items from the *Cooperative School and College Ability Test* (*SCAT, Series II*), Level 2, Grades 10–12. (Copyright © 1966 by Educational Testing Service. All rights reserved. Used by permission.)

Group tests providing separate verbal and quantitative scores are also widely used for predicting success in college. Typical tests of this type include a special series of the *SCAT*, entitled *Cooperative Academic Ability Test* (Grade 12) and the college edition of *Henmon-Nelson Tests of Mental Ability* (Grades 13 to 17). Tests that are specifically designed to predict success in college have a relatively high level of difficulty, to provide adequate ceiling for the above-average ability groups for whom the tests are intended.

The value of using a test with separate verbal and quantitative scores rests largely on the extent to which they provide differential prediction. For example, do verbal scores correlate more highly with English and social studies grades and quantitative scores correlate more highly with mathematics and science grades? The results of predictive studies are contradictory and not especially encouraging. The technical manual of the *Kuhlmann-Anderson Test*, for example, reports the following correlations for grade ten.

	V Score	Q Score
Average English and social studies grades	.57	.45
Average mathematics and science grades	.52	.49

These results are fairly typical, although in some cases mathematics and science grades have shown a slightly higher correlation with quantitative than with verbal scores. The fairly consistent correlations between verbal scores and grades in courses of all types may simply reflect the highly verbal nature of the instruction and the classroom testing on which the course grades are based. Despite the cause of the correlations, however, such results indicate the uncertainty surrounding differential prediction and the need to study carefully the evidence presented in the test manual.

Although the usefulness of V and Q scores for general differential prediction may be somewhat limited, the separate scores can still be helpful in individual cases. A pupil with an extremely low quantitative score, for example, is likely to have difficulty in mathematics courses and in those sections of other courses that stress mathematical concepts. Knowing this beforehand can alert the teacher to an area where special help may be needed. As with verbal and nonverbal scores, however, there must be a relatively large difference between V and Q scores before they can be used for such diagnostic purposes. A difference of one standard deviation (15 or 16 IQ points) provides a good conservative estimate of differences that are likely to be significant. Smaller differences should be ignored, unless the test manual presents evidence to the contrary.

Multiscore Tests

Group tests have also been developed that measure several mental abilities. One notable test of this type is the multilevel edition of the *Cognitive Abilities Test* (Grades 3 to 12). This test, a successor to the widely used *Lorge-Thorndike Intelligence Tests*, contains three separate test batteries: Verbal Battery, Quantitative Battery, and Nonverbal Battery. The several subtests included in each battery are shown in Figures 13.3 (Verbal), 13.4 (Quantitative), and 13.5 (Nonverbal). The sample items shown in these figures illustrate the variety of item types used in group tests of mental ability.

The items in each subtest of this edition of the *Cognitive Abilities Test* are arranged in a "multilevel" format. In other words, the items for all grade levels (3 to 12) are arranged in each subtest from easy to difficult, and pupils at different grade levels simply start and stop at different points. This item arrangement makes it possible to test pupils at all of the grade levels with the same test booklets. Moreover, if the assigned level is inappropriate for a particular group (above average or below average), it is

VOCABULARY (Pick the word that has most nearly the same meaning as the word in dark type.)

wish   A agree   B bone   C over   D want   E waste

SENTENCE COMPLETION (Pick the one word that makes the truest and most sensible complete sentence.)

John likes to _____ a ball game.

F watch   G eat   H help   J read   K talk

VERBAL CLASSIFICATION (Pick the word that belongs with the three words in dark type.)

eye   ear   mouth

L nose   M smell   N head   P boy   Q speak

VERBAL ANALOGIES (Pick the word that is related to the third word in the same way that the second word is related to the first.)

fire ⟶ hot : ice ⟶

F cream   G melt   H box   J cold   K mice

FIGURE 13.3. Sample items from the Verbal Battery of the *Cognitive Abilities Test,* Multi-Level Edition. (Copyright 1972 by Houghton Mifflin Company. All rights reserved. Reproduced by permission.)

simply a matter of shifting to a higher or lower level within the test. All subtests may be obtained in a single all-in-one booklet, or separate multi-level booklets may be obtained for each battery in the test (Verbal, Quantitative, and Nonverbal).

The Primary Battery of the *Cognitive Abilities Test* (Grades K to 3) is a group test using pictorial materials and oral instructions. There are four short subtests: oral vocabulary, relational concepts, multimental concepts, and quantitative concepts. This nonreading test is, of course, not a multiscore test, but it serves as part of the continuous series of the *Cognitive Abilities Test,* covering grades kindergarten through twelve.

Another well-known multiscore scholastic aptitude test is the *Academic Promise Test* (APT) (Grades 6 to 9). This test measures the following abilities:

V—VERBAL: The ability to understand word meanings and to reason with words.
N—NUMERICAL: The ability to use numerical skills and to think in quantitative terms.

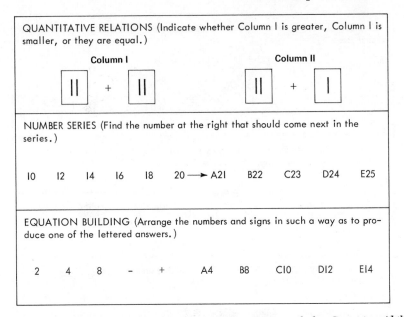

QUANTITATIVE RELATIONS (Indicate whether Column I is greater, Column I is smaller, or they are equal.)

Column I   **Column II**

NUMBER SERIES (Find the number at the right that should come next in the series.)

10   12   14   16   18   20 ──▶ A21   B22   C23   D24   E25

EQUATION BUILDING (Arrange the numbers and signs in such a way as to produce one of the lettered answers.)

2   4   8   —   +   A4   B8   C10   D12   E14

FIGURE 13.4. Sample items from the Quantitative Battery of the *Cognitive Abilities Test,* Multi-Level Edition. (Copyright 1972 by Houghton Mifflin Company. All rights reserved. Reproduced by permission.)

> AR—ABSTRACT REASONING: The ability to reason and form concepts from nonverbal figures.
> LU—LANGUAGE USAGE: The ability to identify the correctness of grammar, spelling, punctuation and word usage.

Sample items representing each of these areas are shown, later, in Figure 13.9. Although those illustrative items were taken from the *Differential Aptitude Test (DAT)* they are similar, because the *APT* is a junior high school version of the *DAT.* The major difference between the two tests is that the *DAT* also includes a series of vocationally oriented tests that are useful for vocational planning at the high school level. Those tests were not considered necessary in the *APT,* because vocational planning is usually delayed until high school.

In addition to separate scores for each of the abilities measured by the *APT,* the V and LU scores are combined to form a verbal ability score and the AR and N scores are combined to form a nonverbal score. Thus, the various individual scores and combinations of scores provide estimates of the several aspects of scholastic aptitude measured by the various two-score tests (verbal, nonverbal, and quantitative), plus a measure of the language skills considered necessary for effective communication.

The results of multiscore tests are typically presented on profile charts. As with two-score tests, care must be taken to be certain that the differences between scores represent real differences in abilities. The

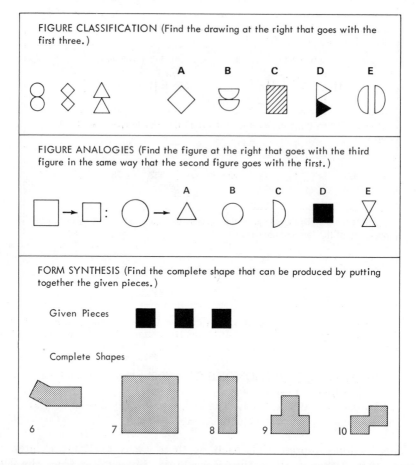

FIGURE 13.5. Sample items from the Nonverbal Battery of the *Cognitive Abilities Test,* Multi-Level Edition. (Copyright 1972 by Houghton Mifflin Company. All rights reserved. Reproduced by permission.)

safest procedure for making significant differences readily discernible is to plot score bands on the profile chart that take into account the amount of error present in each score. This is illustrated on a profile chart for the *APT* in Figure 15.3 (Chapter 15).

Summary Comparison of Group Tests

The variety of group tests of scholastic aptitude that we have been discussing can be illustrated by circles, as shown in Figure 13.6. The single-score test provides a general measure of mental ability, and thus is represented by a single circle with the letter G in it. The verbal (V)-nonverbal (NV) and verbal (V)-quantitative (Q) tests are both illustrated by two overlapping circles. The overlap in the circles (approximately

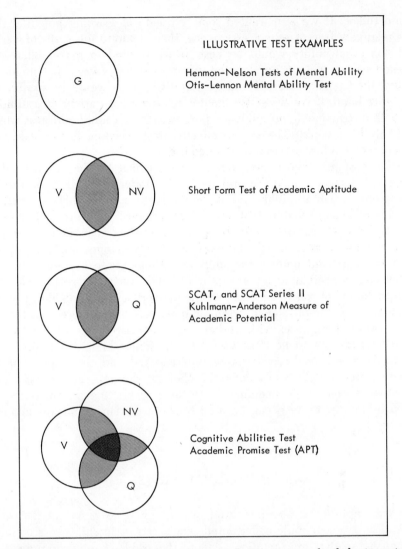

ILLUSTRATIVE TEST EXAMPLES

Henmon–Nelson Tests of Mental Ability
Otis–Lennon Mental Ability Test

Short Form Test of Academic Aptitude

SCAT, and SCAT Series II
Kuhlmann–Anderson Measure of
Academic Potential

Cognitive Abilities Test
Academic Promise Test (APT)

FIGURE 13.6. Summary comparison of types of group tests of scholastic aptitude.

50 per cent) represents the presence of a general mental ability factor common to both scores. The other portions of the circles represent the specific abilities (verbal, nonverbal, or quantitative) that are measured by each battery of subtests. The multiscore batteries of subtests also overlap each other, to show that they reflect a general mental ability as well as the specific abilities they were designed to measure.

Choosing the Appropriate Test. The decision as to which type of test to select depends upon both the use for which the test is intended and the grade level at which the test is to be used. If we are interested only in an overall prediction of school success, a general measure of mental ability would suffice. If we also wanted some estimate of learning potential that was relatively free of school experience, then separate measures of verbal and nonverbal ability would be best. If we wanted to make differential predictions, or detect pupils who were extremely weak in numerical ability, then separate verbal and quantitative scores would be useful. On the other hand, if we wanted estimates concerning a variety of aptitudes, for both instructional and guidance purposes, then a multiscore test would probably be favored. The key to effective test selection is to choose the type of test that best serves the intended use.

Choice of test type is also influenced somewhat by the grade level at which it is to be used. At the primary level (kindergarten to grade three), representing mental ability by a single score is probably all that is warranted. The test material, of necessity, is primarily nonverbal (pictorial) and separate scores are apt to be more misleading than helpful. A test with separate scores can still be used, of course, if one simply interprets the total score and ignores the subscores. From grade four on, separate verbal and nonverbal scores are desirable. The verbal score provides the best prediction of school success, but the nonverbal score provides a useful estimate of the undeveloped learning potential of pupils, especially the poor reader. Both tests with verbal and quantitative scores and multiscore tests are apt to be most useful at the junior high and high school levels. As education becomes more differentiated and the pupil is faced with an increasingly wide range of choices, the separate measures of aptitude become more meaningful. At these levels, the information provided by multiscore tests can be used for both guidance and instructional purposes.

INDIVIDUAL TESTS

Scholastic aptitude is also measured by individual tests. As noted earlier, these tests are commonly called intelligence tests or intelligence scales, although a broader interpretation is more defensible. Cronbach prefers to call them measures of "general ability," because responses to the tests are influenced by knowledge, skills, attitudes, and other factors, many of which are not included in the concept "intelligence."[3] Because our major concern with these tests is in school situations, we are primarily interested in their use as tests of scholastic aptitude. As with group tests, it is important to keep in mind that, regardless of title, these tests measure learned abilities only. Under no circumstances should they be interpreted as measures of inborn mental capacity or innate learning potential. Although the test scores will reflect innate potential to some degree, performance on

---

[3] L. J. Cronbach, *Essentials of Psychological Testing*, 3rd ed. (New York: Harper and Row, 1970).

these tests is so dependent on past home and school experiences that inferences concerning *undeveloped potential* are apt to be misleading. These individual tests are best interpreted as measures of present ability that are helpful in learning school tasks.

Individual tests are administered to one pupil at a time in a face-to-face situation. The problems are presented orally by the examiner and the pupil responds by pointing, giving an oral answer, or performing some manipulative task. The administration of individual tests requires extensive training. Typically this is obtained in a special course in individual testing. An integral part of the course is extensive practice in test administration under supervision. Both the time required for individual testing and the need for specially trained examiners place severe restrictions on the use of individual tests in the schools.

For the majority of pupils, group tests provide a satisfactory estimate of scholastic aptitude. In certain instances, however, it is desirable to obtain scores from an individual test. Because the individual test is administered to one pupil at a time, it is possible to control more carefully such factors as motivation and to assess more accurately the extent to which disabling behaviors are influencing the score. The influence of reading skill is deemphasized because the tasks are presented orally to the pupil. In addition, clinical insights concerning the pupil's method of attacking problems and his persistence in solving them are more readily obtained with individual testing. These advantages make the individual test especially useful for testing young children and for retesting pupils whose scores on group tests are questionable. These include, as a minimum, all of those with extremely low scores and those whose scores differ considerably from the teacher's estimate of ability. Where educational decisions are to have far-reaching influences, such as the placement of pupils in special classes for the mentally handicapped, the more dependable individual measure of mental ability is also preferred.

The two most highly regarded individual tests for use with school children are the *Revised Stanford-Binet Intelligence Scale* and the *Wechsler Intelligence Scales*. Each of these will be briefly described. Although teachers would not be expected to administer such tests, some familiarity with the testing procedures should contribute to more effective interpretation and use of the test scores.

Stanford-Binet Scale

The *Stanford-Binet Scale* was extensively revised in 1960 and renormed in 1972. This revision is called *Form L-M* because it incorporates the best items from the *L* and *M* forms of the earlier 1937 edition. The revision consists of a series of tests arranged by age levels. The tests begin at the two-year-old level and continue up through the superior adult level. At the lowest age levels the test requires the child to identify objects, identify parts of the body, repeat digits, obey simple commands, and the like. At age six, a vocabulary test is introduced. This test is also used at the remaining age levels along with a variety of other tasks. The following types of test items, at the six- and eight-year levels, illustrate the nature of the expected test behavior. The standard for receiving credit on each task is also indicated.

Year Six

1. *Vocabulary.* Tells the correct meaning of six or more words from a master list of 45, arranged in order of increasing difficulty.
2. *Differences.* Explains the differences between a series of two things named by the examiner (e.g., bird and dog). Needs two out of three correct for credit.
3. *Mutilated Pictures.* Tells what part is missing in incomplete pictures. Needs four out of five correct for credit.
4. *Number Concepts.* Gives examiner number of blocks asked for (out of 12 blocks). Needs four out of five different combinations correct for credit.
5. *Opposite Analogies.* Completes three out of four verbal analogies for credit (e.g., "A table is made of wood; a window of . . .").
6. *Maze Tracing.* With pencil, traces shortest distance between starting and stopping points marked on mazes. Needs two out of three correct for credit.

Year Eight

1. *Vocabulary.* Tells the correct meaning of eight or more words from the same master list of 45 used at earlier levels.
2. *Memory for Stories.* Answers factual questions concerning a story read aloud by the examiner. Needs five out of six correct for credit.
3. *Verbal Absurdities.* Explains what is foolish about a set of absurd statements. Needs three out of four correct for credit.
4. *Similarities and Differences.* Explains in what ways a series of two things are alike and different (e.g., baseball and orange). Needs three out of five for credit.
5. *Comprehension.* Answers questions asked by examiner (e.g., "What makes a sailboat move?"). Needs four out of six correct for credit.
6. *Naming the days of the Week.* Names the days of the week. Credit is given for correct order.

In addition to the six tests at each age level, there is also one alternate test. This can be administered in place of any of the other tests at that level. It might be used where an error in administration occurs or where a particular test is inappropriate for some reason (e.g., Maze Tracing for a physically handicapped pupil).

As can be noted in the sample test items, the tasks vary from one level to another and include both verbal and nonverbal performance. Below age six there is approximately an even balance between verbal and nonverbal content, but from age six on an increasingly heavy emphasis is placed on verbal abilities.[4] Thus, although the responses on the *Stanford-Binet* do not depend directly on reading skill, verbal development is an important factor. The performance of pupils whose verbal development has been handicapped (e.g., poor readers, culturally deprived children, bilingual children) will tend to receive lower scores on this test than on a nonverbal test of mental ability.

The administration of the *Stanford-Binet,* like that of other individual tests, requires a specially trained examiner, who meets with the child in a counseling-type setting. After establishing rapport with the child, the examiner begins at the level at which the child can pass all of the tests. From there, he continues to administer tests at successively higher levels until he reaches a level at which the child fails all tests. The *mental age* of the child is then determined by adding to the basal age (age level at which he passes all tests) two months' credit for each test he passes at the higher levels (credit is one month below age six and four months at superior adult levels). The following illustrates the computation of mental age for a nine-year-old pupil.

Passed all tests at year eight	= 8 years (basal age)
Passed 4 tests at year nine	= 8 months (2 × 4)
Passed 2 tests at year ten	= 4 months (2 × 2)
Passed 1 test at year eleven	= 2 months (2 × 1)
Failed all tests at year twelve	= No credit

Total mental age (sum of credits) = 9 years, 2 months

When mental age has been computed, it is converted to an IQ by means of tables presented in the test manual. This is a deviation IQ with a mean of 100 and a standard deviation of 16 (see discussion of IQ later in this chapter).

In summary, the *Stanford-Binet Scale* consists of a variety of mental tasks arranged by age level. A child's mental age and IQ are determined by the summing of credits for the successful completion of tasks at each level. Test performance is expressed by a single score, which represents a highly verbal measure of general mental ability.

Wechsler Scales

The *Wechsler Scales* include three tests that collectively cover all ages, from age four through adult. The three tests are as follows:

---

[4] J. M. Sattler, "Analysis of the Functions of the 1960 *Stanford-Binet Intelligence Scale, Form L-M," Journal of Clinical Psychology,* **21,** 173–179, 1965.

Wechsler Preschool and Primary Scale of Intelligence (WPPSI) (Ages 4 to 6.5)

Wechsler Intelligence Scale for Children (WISC-R) (Ages 6.5 to 16.5)

Wechsler Adult Intelligence Scale (WAIS) (Ages 16 to adult)

The *Wechsler* tests are organized by subtests rather than by age level. Each test consists of a Verbal Scale made up of five or six subtests and a Performance Scale made up of five subtests. Although the subtests vary slightly from one level to another, the following subtests from the *WISC-R* illustrate the nature of the test content in the *Wechsler* tests. The sample questions, in parentheses, were not taken from the *WISC-R* but are nevertheless similar.

Verbal Scale

1. *Information.* Answers questions based on general information (e.g., "How many legs does a cat have?").
2. *Similarities.* Explains in what way a series of paired things are alike (e.g., apple and orange).
3. *Arithmetic.* Solves problems similar to those used in school (e.g., "If pencils cost two for a nickel, how many could you buy for a quarter?").
4. *Vocabulary.* Tells the meaning of words from a master list of 32, arranged in order of increasing difficulty.
5. *Comprehension.* Answers questions requiring common-sense comprehension (e.g., "Why should people tell the truth?").
   Digit Span (alternate test). Repeats series of digits forward and backward after hearing them once (e.g., 493). This test may substitute for any of the others in the Verbal Scale.

Performance Scale

6. *Picture Completion.* Tells what part is missing in incomplete pictures.
7. *Picture Arrangement.* Arranges sets of cartoon panels in proper sequence so they tell a story.
8. *Block Design.* Arranges sets of blocks (colored red and white) so that they match pictures of designs on examiner's cards.
9. *Object Assembly.* Puts together jigsaw puzzles based on parts of objects (e.g., car).
10. *Coding.* Matches numbers and symbols by referring to a simple code that the examinee keeps in front of him.
    Mazes (alternate for the coding test). Traces on a paper maze, as in the *Stanford-Binet* Maze Tracing.

Each subtest, in the *Wechsler Scales,* is administered and scored separately.[5] The scores are then combined to provide a verbal IQ, a performance IQ, and a total IQ. Like the *Stanford-Binet,* the *Wechsler*

---

[5] The *WISC-R* (revised in 1974) is administered by alternating between the Verbal and Performance Scales (test order is 1, 6, 2, 7, and so on).

uses a deviation IQ with a mean of 100, but here the standard deviation is 15 rather than 16.

The total IQ on the *WISC-R* correlates highly with the *Stanford-Binet* IQ (approximately .80) indicating that the two measure somewhat similar abilities. Also, both tests provide highly reliable results (.90+) when administered by competent examiners. From the viewpoint of the teacher, who will use the test results rather than obtain them, the most important difference between the scales is in the types of scores provided. The *Stanford-Binet* provides a single, highly verbal IQ score that is useful for straightforward prediction of school success. The *Wechsler Scales*, on the other hand, provide more diagnostic information because of the separate verbal and performance scores. When a pupil has a higher performance IQ than verbal IQ, for example, it alerts us to the possibility of poor verbal development (e.g., poor reader, culturally deprived child) or a language handicap (e.g., bilingual child). When the performance IQ is lower, it might indicate the presence of an emotional problem. As Cronbach has noted, the greater opportunity for frustration on the performance tasks and the tendency of emotionally distraught children to use an overcautious approach both tend to lower the performance score.[6] Such differences between scores are meaningful, of course, only when they are sufficiently large. As with group tests, a difference between verbal and performance scores should be at least one standard deviation (15 IQ points) before it is considered significant.

CAUTIONS IN INTERPRETING SCHOLASTIC APTITUDE SCORES

Before pointing out some of the cautions to be observed in interpreting the scores derived from scholastic aptitude tests, we must describe the most frequently used scores. This description will be brief, however, because Chapter 15 is devoted to the various types of derived scores used in standardized testing.

Mental Age and Intelligence Quotient

Two of the most common types of scores used with scholastic aptitude tests are the *mental age* (MA) score and the *intelligence quotient* (IQ). The mental age score indicates a pupil's *level* of mental development. A pupil with a mental age of 12, for example, has a mental ability score equivalent to the average score for twelve-year-olds. The intelligence quotient refers to a pupil's *rate* of mental development. The conventional *ratio* IQ, used in most of the older intelligence tests, was calculated by

---

[6] L. J. Cronbach, *Essentials of Psychological Testing*, 3rd ed. (New York: Harper and Row, 1970).

dividing mental age (MA) by chronological age (CA) and multiplying by 100. Thus, if a pupil had a MA of 12 and a CA of 10 his IQ would be 120. This would indicate that his mental development was proceeding at a faster rate than that of the average child. It will be noted from the formula that when a pupil's MA and CA are equal his IQ will be 100, and if his MA is lower than his CA his IQ will be less than 100. The IQ has been highly regarded as an index of intelligence because it supposedly indicates the same relative ability at different age levels and remains fairly constant for any given individual.

Although the *ratio* IQ, based on the above formula, might still be used in some mental ability tests, it has been replaced in most tests by the *deviation* IQ. This is an IQ based on standard scores with a mean (average score) of 100 and a standard deviation of 15 or 16. The deviation IQ can be interpreted in much the same way as the ratio IQ, but it has some definite advantages. These will be considered in Chapter 15, where the relative merits of standard scores are discussed.

Cautions in Interpreting IQ Scores

Many of the misinterpretations and misuses of IQ scores have been due to the false belief that a person's IQ, like his blood type, is a fixed quantity that does not vary. Because the IQ is a score derived from tests that include a variety of types of mental tasks, which have less than perfect reliability, and which measure such a variable quality as human performance, this expectation is extremely unrealistic. Variations in IQ from one time to another can be expected, even under the most ideal testing conditions. Proper use of the IQ score requires that this variation be recognized and taken into account rather than ignored.

Assuming that the basic conditions of testing, such as equal opportunity for development and maximum motivation, have been met, we can still expect the following types and amounts of variation in the IQ score:

1. An IQ from the same test can be expected to vary from 5 to 10 points on the basis of the standard error alone. Thus, an IQ of 105 can be most safely interpreted as a band of IQ scores ranging from 100 to 110.
2. When IQ scores from different tests are compared, the IQ can be expected to show some variation from one test to another. A comparative study has indicated that differences as large as 8 points in verbal IQ can be expected among widely used group tests. Nonverbal IQs differed by only a few points.[7] Because each test measures slightly different aspects of mental ability and each is standardized on a different population, the IQs are not directly comparable. In interpreting IQ scores, we should know the test from which it was derived.

---

[7] A. N. Hieronymus, and J. B. Stroud, "Comparability of IQ Scores on Five Widely Used Intelligence Tests," *Measurement and Evaluation in Guidance,* **2**, 135–140, 1969.

3. Greater variation in IQ scores can be expected for elementary school pupils than for high school pupils. This can be accounted for largely by the fact that abilities tend to be less stable during their formation. Where group tests are used, variation is still greater because the control of conditions necessary for maximum performance is seldom possible.

The variations in IQ discussed above are normal variations that can be expected under ideal testing conditions. Although such variation might be disturbing to those who expect the IQ to be perfectly constant, it should not be upsetting to teachers who want to use IQ scores for practical purposes. Knowing a pupil's IQ is somewhere between 85 and 95 or between 115 and 125 is accurate enough to provide an extremely useful appraisal of his ability to learn.

The greatest problems in interpreting and using IQ scores are not caused by normal variations in the IQ. These we can estimate fairly accurately and make allowances for. The major problems arise when IQ scores contain an indeterminate amount of error because the basic conditions of aptitude testing have not been met. In general, IQ scores are less dependable for the following types of pupils:

1. Those whose home environment is barren enough to prevent full opportunity to learn the types of tasks included in the test (e.g., culturally deprived).
2. Those who are little motivated by school-type tasks.
3. Those who are weak in reading skills or have a language handicap.
4. Those who have poor emotional adjustment.

Radical changes in IQ have been noted where environmental deprivation was removed, where remedial work overcame deficiencies in educational skills, and where emotional problems were remedied. Although such changes can be interpreted in terms of fulfilling the necessary conditions for adequate testing, the extent to which an individual IQ score has been influenced by such factors can seldom be fully determined. Consequently, the only safe procedure is to consider a single IQ score as a highly tentative estimate that needs verification by other test results and by classroom observation. As the results of several IQ tests accumulate and other evidence of ability is added, a fairly dependable estimate of scholastic aptitude will emerge.

CULTURE-FAIR TESTING

Because all tests are measures of learned abilities, special problems arise in testing the aptitudes of individuals from different cultures, or different subcultures. There are a number of cultural differences that are likely to influence test performance. In addition to the more obvious one of language, there are such differences as motivation, attitude toward testing, competitiveness, speed, practice in test taking, and opportunity to learn the knowledges and skills measured by the test. Culture-fair testing is an attempt to obtain a measure of ability that is relatively free of all, or most, of these differences. Although various approaches have been used to accomplish this, the following procedures are typical: (1) The test materials are primarily nonverbal and include diagrams or pictures familiar to the various cultural groups for whom the test is intended. At times, translated verbal tests are used. (2) Attempts are made to use materials and methods that are interesting to the examinees, to encourage motivation. (3) Liberal time limits are typically provided, to de-emphasize speed as a factor. (4) The test procedures are kept simple, to rule out differences in test-taking experience. (5) Test content is based on those intellectual skills that are common to the cultural groups being tested. It must be recognized, of course, that culture-fair testing is more an ideal than a reality. Most attempts to remove cultural bias from tests have fallen short of their goal.

One of the best-known tests in this area is the *Culture-Fair Intelligence Tests* (Grades 4 to 16) by R. B. Cattel. These are short nonverbal tests that use pictures and diagrams common to a wide variety of cultures. Responses on the several tests include (1) selecting the item that comes next in a series, (2) selecting the item that does not belong with the others, (3) selecting the item that completes a matrix, and (4) matching a sample design, by placing a dot in the appropriate place on one of several alternate designs. The tests have been given to individuals in a number of different countries with mixed results. In general, test performance tended to differ most where the cultural differences were greatest. When used in schools within the American culture, the Cattell tests can be expected to provide essentially the same results as the Nonverbal Battery of the *Cognitive Abilities Test*.

The use of pictorial content in an attempt to build a test that is culturally fair to all subcultures within our American society is best illustrated by the *Davis Eells Games*. This test was designed to measure general problem-solving ability free from social-class bias. The test items consist of pictures portraying problem situations familiar to children from all urban cultural groups (see Figure 13.7). The instructions, which are read to the pupils, are also based on vocabulary common to all American urban children. Thus, reading skill is eliminated, and the tasks are designed to permit pupils from all social classes an equal opportunity to demonstrate their reasoning ability in situations familiar to them. Although the test appeared to be more fair to culturally deprived pupils than the conventional test of mental ability, studies did not bear this out. Lower-class pupils performed no better on this test than they did on conventional tests. This, plus the fact that the test was a poor predictor of school achievement, led to its being discontinued.

The pupil sees:

The teacher reads:

Now look at this top row of pictures. Look at the boys and the gate. Each picture has a number on it—No. 1, No. 2, and No. 3. Which boy is starting the best way to get over the gate? No. 1, or No. 2 boy, or No. 3 boy? Draw a line on the right box.

Now look at the next picture; it is beside the one you just did. It shows a boy and a girl waving their hands. Hold your finger on that picture—a boy and a girl waving their hands. Look at the picture while I tell you about it. Which number is right? Mark the right box.

No. 1 Box: They are waving at a boy.
No. 2 Box: They are waving at a girl.
No. 3 Box: We cannot tell from this picture whom they are waving to.

Be sure to mark a box.

FIGURE 13.7. Sample item from the *Davis-Eells Games* by Allison Davis and Kenneth Eells. (Copyright 1952 by Harcourt Brace Jovanovich, Inc. All rights reserved. Reproduced by permission.)

A third approach to culture-fair testing is one developed by the Educational Testing Service (ETS) for the New York City schools. This project is broad in scope and combines both teaching and evaluation procedures. It evolved in the early 1960s, after the New York City school board banned mental ability testing on the grounds that it was culturally biased. The approach developed by ETS, entitled *Let's Look at Children,* involves the use of common sets of material for both instruction and assessment. The materials and procedures are designed to help first-grade teachers better understand, assess, and increase the intellectual development of pupils.

The ETS materials are of three types: (1) A guidebook designed to aid teachers in the identifying and developing the intellectual skills of their pupils during regular classroom instruction. Suggestions are also given for the use of different types of learning materials and games for fostering intellectual development. (2) A set of instructional materials and assessment tasks designed to elicit and develop specific aspects of intellectual behavior that are not apt to arise spontaneously in the behavior of children. (3) A set of thirty written exercises designed to tap intellectual abilities in the following six areas: Shapes and Forms, Spatial Relations, Time Concepts, Mathematics, Communication Skills, and Logical Reasoning. These exercises may be used for instruction, practice, or assessment. A pupil's performance on these exercises is used to describe his level of intellectual development in each of the areas.

From an evaluation standpoint, the most unique feature of the ETS approach is that pupils are given instruction and practice on a variety of tasks similar to those on which they are later to be evaluated. This tends to provide increased assurance that the assumption of "equal opportunity to learn" has been more adequately fulfilled. Also, practice on paper-and-pencil exercises similar to those used in assessment tends to standardize test-taking behavior and thus to rule it out as a source of difficulty. Finally, because the materials and procedures are interesting to children, motivation tends to be more adequately controlled.

From an instructional standpoint, the ETS approach has a twofold advantage: (1) the materials and methods can be used directly to improve specific aspects of intellectual performance; and (2) the assessments of intellectual skills can be used to plan future classroom learning experiences for individual pupils.

Testing the Culturally Deprived with Conventional Tests

The majority of pupils from culturally deprived homes are tested with conventional scholastic aptitude tests, that is, with the types of group and individual tests discussed earlier in this chapter. There are two reasons for this practice. First, there is a scarcity of tests that can be truly described as culture fair. Second, the culture-fair tests that are available tend to be poor predictors of school success. A possible reason for the poor prediction is described by Anastasi, as follows:[8] "A test constructed entirely from elements that are equally familiar in many cultures might measure trivial functions and possess little theoretical or practical validity in *any* culture." In another section of the same book, she defends the use of conventional tests with the culturally deprived primarily on the basis of their value in making predictions. Note these comments:[9]

> To criticize tests because they reveal cultural influences is to miss the essential nature of tests. Every psychological test measures a behavior sample. Insofar as culture affects behavior, its influence will and should be reflected in the test. Moreover, if we rule out cultural differentials from a test, we might thereby lower its validity against the criterion we are trying to predict. The same cultural differentials that impair an individual's test performance are likely to handicap him in school work, job performance, or any other activity we are trying to predict.

---

[8] A. Anastasi, *Psychological Testing*, 3rd ed. (New York: Macmillan, 1968), p. 253.
[9] Ibid., p. 558.

In another of her writings, Anastasi elaborates on the above idea by stating the following:[10]

> The purpose of tests is to show what the individual is able to do at the time of testing. Tests are not designed to show the causes of behavior or the origins of individual differences in performance. To identify causal factors, we need to investigate the experiential backgrounds of the individuals or groups tested. Nor can tests be used as instruments of social reform. To compensate for a cultural handicap, we need remedial programs directed toward the individual as well as toward society. Masking the handicap by the use of a culture-fair test is no solution.

The attitude Anastasi holds toward testing is shared by many test experts. They see the problem not as one of replacing present tests with culture-fair tests, but rather as one of improving testing practices.

Regardless of whether conventional tests are used with the culturally deprived out of necessity or of choice, special precautions must be taken to assure valid results. Much of the difficulty that arises from testing such pupils resides in the failure to take into account their cultural handicap during test administration and interpretation. Some of the culturally determined factors that might influence test performance are language handicap, low achievement motivation, poor verbal development, inadequate experiential background, lack of test-taking skills, unfavorable attitude toward testing, anxiety, and lack of self-confidence. These and similar factors provide the basis for the following suggestions for testing the culturally deprived with conventional group aptitude tests:[11]

1. *Provide adequate orientation to the test to be given.* Adequate orientation to a test should include an explanation of why the test is being given, how the results are to be used, and the nature of the test procedures (e.g., directions, types of items, and so on). The explanation must, of course, be adapted to the age level of the pupils. At higher age levels, written materials might be handed out. Some test publishers provide materials that are useful for this purpose.

2. *Provide preliminary practice in test taking.* Practice in test taking may be given with specially prepared materials, or with an alternate form of the test that is to be given. The latter is to be preferred with young children, because it provides them with the best opportunity to become familiar with the specific directions and types of test materials to be used during regular testing. Under no circumstances, of course, should the pupils

---

[10] A. Anastasi, "Culture-Fair Testing," in N. E. Gronlund (ed.), *Readings in Measurement and Evaluation* (New York: Macmillan, 1968), p. 285.

[11] For a more detailed discussion of the problems involved in testing the culturally deprived, see M. Deutsch, J. A. Fishman, L. S. Kogan, R. D. North, and M. Whitman, "Guidelines for Testing Minority Group Children," *Journal of Social Issues*, 20, 127–145, 1964.

be allowed to see the particular test form that is to be used during the regular testing period.

3. *Administer the tests under normal conditions.* In most cases, to provide "normal conditions," tests should be administered by the pupils' classroom teacher in the regular classroom. When other examiners must be used, special efforts need to be made to establish good rapport with the pupils.

4. *Carefully observe the pupils' behavior during testing.* Watch pupils for any apparent difficulty in understanding directions; any signs of lack of motivation, of nervousness, or of anxiety; any evidence of lingering, skipping of items, or random marking of answers. If behavior like this does occur, make a record of it so that it can be used when a pupil's test performance is being interpreted.

5. *Retest low-scoring pupils with a lower form of the test.* Retesting with a lower form of the test will provide a greater spread of scores and consequently a more reliable estimate of the pupils' ability. The multilevel format, like that used in the *Cognitive Abilities Test,* is especially good for this purpose because pupils can move to a lower level simply by starting and stopping at different points (an alternate form must, of course, be used).

6. *Whenever possible, obtain both verbal and nonverbal measures of ability.* One means of checking on the extent to which a language handicap or experiential deprivation may have depressed a pupil's verbal ability scores is to obtain his nonverbal scores as well. A multiscore test may provide diagnostic information that is even more useful in special cases.

7. *Interpret the test scores as measures of present performance only.* Interpreting test scores in terms of present performance only means avoiding inferences concerning inherited ability. The scores should be examined in light of the nature of the cultural handicap, the conditions of testing, and the personal characteristics that might distort test performance. Low scores should stimulate a search for the causes of the poor performance. *Under no circumstance* should the scores be interpreted as representing innate potential or fixed abilities.

8. *Verify the test results by comparing them with other information.* More intelligent interpretation of aptitude scores is likely to result when test performance is checked against teachers' observations, achievement test scores, grades, and various other types of data concerning the pupils' total development. Discrepancies between the test scores and other information may suggest retesting or may simply clarify the nature of the factors influencing test performance.

Although the above suggestions would be appropriate for testing any group of pupils, they are especially crucial when one is testing the culturally deprived. Probably even more important, however, is what is done with the test results. We can legitimately speak of "culture-fair testing" only when the test performance of culturally deprived pupils is used (1) to plan remedial programs for improving their academic abilities, and (2) to develop new curricula for increasing their educational opportunities.

DIFFERENTIAL APTITUDE TESTING

The work of Guilford has been a major influence in moving testing from the measurement of a limited number of general mental abilities to the measurement of numerous specific abilities. On the basis of years of research, using the method of factor analysis, he has proposed a three-dimensional model to provide a complete "structure of intellect."[12] His theoretical model is shown in Figure 13.8. Note that the model contains 120 cells ($5 \times 6 \times 4$) and that each cell represents an ability that can be described by (1) what the person does (operation), (2) the nature of the material on which he performs the operation (content), and (3) the type of outcome or product involved (product). For example, a test based on figure analogies, like that in the Nonverbal Battery of the *Cognitive Abilities Test* (see Figure 13.5), would be classified in the Cognition-Figural-Relations cell because it calls for the recognition of figure relations. Similarly, a test using verbal analogies, such as those in the Verbal Battery of the *Cognitive Abilities Test* (see Figure 13.3), would be classified in the Cognition-Semantic-Relations cell because it calls for recognition of the relations between word meanings.[13]

Tests have not been developed for each of the cells in the "structure of intellect," but the model has served as a guide to Guilford and his co-workers, in their search for specific abilities. It is assumed that someday tests will exist for all 120 cells, but this is not likely to happen without the model being modified in the process. From the standpoint of differential testing, the model emphasizes the potentially large number of relatively independent factors that might be used to describe the various dimensions of human ability.

The experimental search for specific abilities by Guilford and others, combined with the increasing emphasis on educational and vocational guidance since the Second World War, has resulted in a number of multi-aptitude batteries. Although such batteries are intended primarily for guidance purposes, they can also be useful in individualizing instruction and in the planning of courses that utilize a broader range of human abilities. As noted earlier, school learning is largely verbal learning, regardless of the name of the course. The differential testing of abilities provides an opportunity to develop learning experiences that take advantage of each individual's total pattern of aptitudes.

---

[12] J. P. Guilford, *The Nature of Human Intelligence* (New York: McGraw-Hill, 1967).
[13] For a brief, clear description of the Guilford model, illustrated with numerous specific test items, see J. P. Guilford, "Three Faces of Intellect" in N. E. Gronlund (ed.), *Readings in Measurement and Evaluation* (New York: Macmillan, 1968).

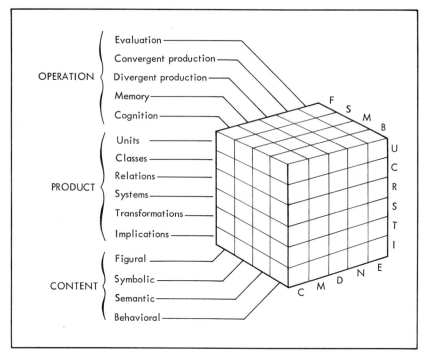

FIGURE 13.8. Guilford's structure of intellect model. (From J. P. Guilford, *The Nature of Human Intelligence.* New York: McGraw Hill, 1967. Reproduced by permission.)

Multiaptitude batteries that measure both educational and vocational aptitudes have been designed primarily for the high school level, and beyond. One of the most widely used tests of this type is the *Differential Aptitude Tests (DAT)* (Grades 8 to 12). As noted earlier, the *Academic Promise Test (APT)* provides a junior high school version (Grades 6 to 9), but uses only those tests measuring educational aptitudes. Another widely used aptitude battery is the *General Aptitude Test Battery (GATB)*. The *GATB* was developed by the Federal Government for use in offices of the United States Employment Service (USES). It can be given in high schools, however, by special arrangement with USES. The *GATB* contains a larger number of vocationally oriented tests than the *DAT* and is therefore especially well-suited to the guidance of persons not going to college.

Here we shall describe the *DAT*, to illustrate the nature and content of multiaptitude batteries. Information concerning other batteries available for use in the schools can be obtained from Buros' *Mental Measurements Yearbooks* (see footnote 2).

Differential Aptitude Tests

The *DAT* battery includes eight tests, each measuring a separate set of abilities. Although some of the tests measure abilities specific enough to fit a particular cell in Guilford's model (see Figure 13.8), others measure a composite of abilities that have been found useful in educational and vocational guidance. The eight tests are: Verbal Reasoning (VR), Numerical Ability (NA), Abstract Reasoning (AR), Clerical Speed and Accuracy (CSA), Mechanical Reasoning (MR), Space Relations (SR), Spelling (S), and Language Usage (LU). In addition to separate scores on each of these tests, a combined verbal and numerical score (VR + NA) provides an index of scholastic aptitude similar to that obtained with group tests of mental ability. Sample items from the eight tests are shown in Figures 13.9 and 13.10. Those in Figure 13.9 also represent the four tests that are included in the *Academic Promise Test* (*APT*), a downward extension (Grades 6 to 9) of the *DAT*.

Using a battery of aptitude tests, like the *DAT*, has several advantages over using a series of separate tests covering the same areas. First, because all tests have been standardized on the same population, it is possible to compare a pupil's strengths and weaknesses on the various measures of aptitude. Second, because all tests are built for the same population of users, they are matched in difficulty and appropriateness for the grade levels for which they are intended. Separate tests covering the same areas are apt to range widely in difficulty, especially the vocational tests. Third, using a common test format and uniform testing procedures for all tests simplifies test administration.

The scores for the *DAT* are plotted on a profile chart similar to that used for the *APT* (see Figure 15.3, Chapter 15). The profile chart is arranged so that differences between scores of *one inch or greater* are interpreted as significant differences. The use of *one inch* score bands, like those illustrated for the *APT* in Figure 15.3, provides the simplest method of profiling and lends itself to quick interpretation. Where the bands do *not* overlap, the difference is significant; where they do overlap, the difference is not significant.

The tests in the *DAT* tend to be internally consistent (split-half reliabilities average about .90), and the intercorrelations between tests are low enough to indicate that each test is measuring a relatively independent ability. The evidence of differential prediction, however, is rather disappointing. One might expect the Verbal Reasoning scores to best predict English achievement, the Numerical Ability scores to best predict mathematics and science achievement, the Spatial Relations scores to best predict achievement in mechanical drawing, and so on. A review of the extensive data presented in the test manual, however, reveals only slight differences in prediction from one area to another. The best predictor of school marks in all courses turns out to be the general mental ability measure (VR + NA).

The disappointing performance of the *DAT* in providing differential prediction of school marks is shared by other multiscore aptitude tests. Cronbach suspects that the difficulty resides more in the measures of

ABSTRACT REASONING

Which "answer figure" is next in the series?

PROBLEM FIGURES   ANSWER FIGURES

                                                A   B   C   D   E

NUMERICAL ABILITY

Select the correct answer for each problem.

Add	13	A	14
	12	B	25
		C	16
		D	59
		E	none of these

VERBAL REASONING

Fill the blanks with the pair of words which make the sentence true or sensible

. . . . . . is to night as breakfast is to . . . . . .

A.   supper —— corner   Supper is to night as breakfast is to morning.
B.   gentle —— morning   Pair E has both supper and morning; supper fits
C.   door —— corner   in the blank at the beginning of the sentence
D.   flow —— enjoy   and morning fits in the blank at the end. On
E.   supper —— morning   the sample Answer Sheet, the space under E
                             has been blackened on line Y to show that
                             pair E is the right one.

LANGUAGE USAGE

Which of the lettered parts of each sentence contains errors in grammar, punctuation, or spelling?

SAMPLES OF ANSWER SHEETS

Ain't we / going to / the office / next week?
     A   B   C   D

	A	B	C	D	E
X.					
Y.					

FIGURE 13.9. Sample items from the *Differential Aptitude Tests* (*DAT*). (Reproduced by permission. Copyright 1947, © 1961, 1962, 1972, The Psychological Corporation, New York, N.Y. All rights reserved.)

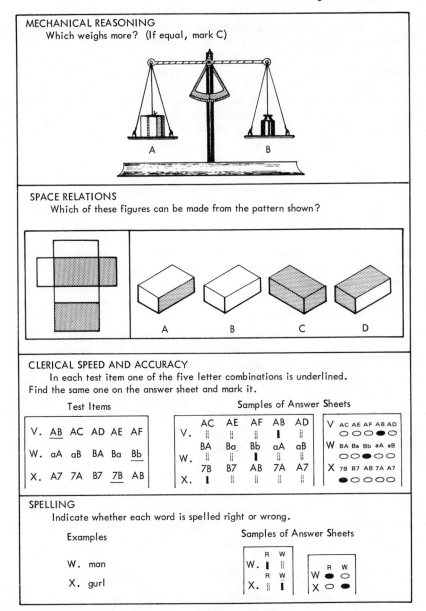

FIGURE 13.10. Sample items from the *Differential Aptitude Tests* (*DAT*). (Reproduced by permission. Copyright 1947, © 1961, 1962, 1972, The Psychological Corporation, New York, N.Y. All rights reserved.)

school performance than in the tests of aptitude. He states his position as follows:[14]

[14] L. J. Cronbach, *Essentials of Psychological Testing*, 3rd ed. (New York: Harper and Row, 1970), p. 373.

The failure of differential prediction of marks is probably not due to weaknesses in the predictors so much as to the fact that examining and marking methods in all academic instruction depend on about the same complex of abilities. Reading, verbal understanding, motivation, and work habits put the same students ahead in most courses. If the criterion in geometry or science were broken down in terms of subskills, each measured independently and objectively, perhaps different combinations (of VR, NA, AR, etc.) would predict each subskill . . . Differential prediction of this kind would not tell the student's chances for success, but it might help him and his teacher know where his weaknesses within the course will appear. Once he and his teachers know this, they ought to make special changes in the teaching method to spoil the prediction!

In addition to clarifying a possible reason for poor differential prediction, Cronbach's quote highlights a very important distinction between guidance and instructional uses of aptitude scores. For guidance purposes, we are mainly interested in highly stable test scores that provide good predictions. From an instructional standpoint, we are more interested in diagnosing a pupil's strengths and weaknesses so that his learning can be improved. This might involve planning special learning experiences to compensate for a deficiency, or it may mean providing a remedial program to help overcome a deficiency. Performance on such *DAT* tests as Numerical Ability, Spelling, and Language Usage, for example, is subject to improvement through direct training. Brinkmann has shown that even the Space Relations scores on the *DAT* can be raised significantly by a brief training program.[15] Thus, as teachers, we might attempt to upset predictions of poor performance by both modifying the abilities themselves (to the extent possible), and by using the pupils' patterns of abilities in planning for individualized instruction.

The case of Frank F., taken from his actual school records, provides an illustration of how *DAT* scores might be used for instructional purposes.[16] Frank was an underachiever in school, although all of his teachers remarked that he was a hard worker and apparently had high ability. His percentile scores on the *DAT*, in grade nine, were as follows:

VR	NA	AR	SR	MR	LU	Spelling
90	90	65	70	60	25	30

Standardized achievement test batteries supported the above scores, indicating that he was high in all areas of achievement except language skills.

---

[15] E. H. Brinkmann, "Programmed Instruction as a Means of Improving Spatial Visualization," *Journal of Applied Psychology*, **50**, 179–184, 1966.
[16] For further details see F. B. Womer and W. B. Frick, "Personalizing Test Use: Selected Cases" in N. E. Gronlund (ed.), *Readings in Measurement and Evaluation* (New York: Macmillan, 1968).

He continually received low school marks, however, because of his poor performance on classroom tests and written assignments. Thus, despite his high verbal and numerical aptitude scores, his consistent attempts to do well, and his high achievement on standardized (objective) tests, he apparently was unable to communicate his knowledge through writing because of his weaknesses in language skills. With the difficulty pinpointed, his English teacher provided remedial help in self-expression, language usage, and writing effectiveness. These efforts were supported by his other teachers, who helped Frank overcome his writing problems in their respective subject areas.

In terms of their wider implications, scores on multiaptitude batteries like the *DAT* can also aid in curriculum planning. By noting the strengths and weaknesses of our particular pupil population in each of the various aptitude areas, we should be able to plan more intelligently the types of course offerings and special programs that will be most useful. Differential aptitudes are especially helpful in planning for pupils with low verbal and numerical ability. Examining their higher scores in other areas (mechanical, spatial, and so on), can provide clues concerning the types of course experiences that might best meet their needs.

There is no reason why all school courses need to be so highly verbal. It would appear that various areas of study (e.g., industrial education, home economics, and so on) could include more courses that place major emphasis on mechanical, spatial, and other practical types of reasoning ability. We could also examine the courses in academic areas to determine how the various types of aptitude might be more fully utilized there.

In summary, it appears that differential aptitude testing has helped to identify a wide range of abilities that can be used to describe individual differences, but schools have been slow to incorporate the information into the instructional program. Perhaps as learning research further clarifies the various ways that individuals learn, instructional materials and methods can be more specifically adapted to pupils with different patterns of ability and different modes of learning.[17]

TESTING IN SPECIAL AREAS

There are a number of tests designed to measure aptitudes and abilities in special areas. Here we shall briefly discuss only those that might be of general interest to teachers, i.e., tests of creativity, artistic aptitude, and musical aptitude. More detailed information concerning tests in these

---

[17] See L. J. Cronbach, "How Can Instruction Be Adapted to Individual Differences?" Chapter 2 in R. M. Gagné (ed.), *Learning and Individual Differences* (Columbus, Ohio: Charles E. Merrill, 1967).

areas may be obtained from Buros' *Mental Measurements Yearbooks* (see footnote 2).

Tests of Creativity

A major contribution of Guilford's "structure of intellect" model, discussed earlier (Figure 13.8), was his distinction between convergent and divergent thinking. In *convergent thinking* there is only one correct or best answer to a problem (e.g., "What is the shape of a brick?"). The aptitude tests discussed earlier in this chapter use test items that call for convergent thinking. In *divergent thinking* there are many possible answers to a problem and the examinee is required to provide as many as he can (e.g., "List all of the uses you can think of for a common brick."). Guilford and his coworkers have developed a number of different types of test items for measuring divergent thinking (see footnote 13), and they have stimulated others to prepare similar test materials. The most highly developed creativity tests designed for school use are those in the *Torrance Tests of Creative Thinking* (Grades K to adult).

The *Torrance* tests include a Verbal section and a Figural section. The verbal tests include a variety of items, such as listing all of the possible causes and consequences of an action depicted in a picture, suggesting ways to improve toys, listing unusual uses of a common object, presenting unusual questions about a common object, and suggesting all the things that would happen if an improbable situation were true. The figural tests require the pupils to construct and complete pictures. Both the verbal and figural tests are scored for fluency (number of responses), flexibility (variety of responses), originality, and elaboration. The scoring, as might be expected, is fairly difficult and time consuming.[18]

Tests of creativity, like the *Torrance* tests, are relatively new and designed primarily for research use. Studies have already shown, however, that they possess several promising features: (1) the scores have a relatively low relationship with conventional tests of mental ability, indicating that they are probably measuring separate aspects of behavior; (2) the scores are fairly stable over both time intervals and alternate forms of the same test; (3) examinees find the tasks interesting and motivating. The major shortcomings, at present, appear to be the complexity of the test procedures (especially the scoring) and the scarcity of evidence concerning the relationship of the scores to either creative achievement or school achievement. What evidence there is indicates that the relationships are low. Hopefully, future studies will lead to further refinements in the tests,

---

[18] For a more detailed description of creativity tests and related research, see S. B. Crockenberg, "Creativity Tests: A Boon or Boondoggle for Education," *Review of Educational Research*, 42, 27–45, 1972.

to further clarification of the concept of creativity being measured, and to further evidence of the practical utility of the results. Until then, it is not expected that tests of creativity will find widespread use in the classroom.

Tests of Artistic Aptitude

A number of tests of artistic aptitude have been developed. Typically these tests have been concerned with only limited aspects of the behavior needed for success in artistic pursuits. Some of the tests have been confined to judgment and perceptual skills, whereas others have been concerned with artistic production.

Probably the most widely used test in this area is the *Meier Art Judgment Test* (Grades 7 to 16). It consists of a series of pairs of pictures. One picture is a reproduction of a work of art known to have high artistic merit. The other is the same picture but it has been altered in such a way that it violates some artistic principle. The examinee is presented with each pair of pictures and asked to choose the one that is more pleasing.

A second artistic aptitude test has also been developed by Meier. This test was not intended to replace his earlier test but to measure another important element of artistic ability. It is called the *Meier Aesthetic Perception Test*. In this test the examinee is presented with four versions of an art work, and he is required to rank them in order of preference.

Artistic aptitude tests that focus on aesthetic judgment and perceptual skills, like the *Meier* tests, are best considered as measures of artistic appreciation. They provide measures of abilities that may be prerequisites to artistic achievement, but individuals scoring high on such tests may lack the manual skills or creative abilities required for artistic performance.

Tests of artistic production have also been devised. These are based on standardized work samples. A typical test of this type is the *Horn Art Aptitude Inventory* (Grades 12 to 16). This test requires the examinee to make original drawings of common objects and simple designs, and to sketch pictures from a given set of lines. The individual's drawings are evaluated by comparison to a product scale (set of drawings graded by merit). It is obvious that scores on tests like the *Horn* test will be influenced by art training, so the amount of previous training must be considered when one is interpreting the results.

There are two common criticisms of artistic aptitude tests: (1) they tend to measure only limited aspects of the many complex abilities that make up artistic aptitude; (2) the scoring is based on traditional standards of acceptable performance and therefore may penalize the more creative individual. If these limitations are kept in mind and test performance is verified by other evidence of artistic ability, the tests should provide useful information in an area where adequate aptitude measures are extremely difficult to obtain.

Tests of Musical Aptitude

Specialized aptitude tests have also been developed in the area of music. Probably the best-known and most widely used of these tests is the *Seashore Measures of Musical Talents* (Grades 4 to 16). These tests can be presented by phonograph or tape recorder and measure six aspects of auditory discrimination: pitch, loudness, time, timbre, rhythm, and tonal memory. The items in the tests consist primarily of pairs of tones, and the examinee is asked to select the appropriate tone (e.g., higher, louder, more pleasing). The discriminations are made increasingly difficult during the testing by decreasing the differences between the tones.

More recent tests of musical aptitude have given greater emphasis to the use of musical materials in the testing. A typical test of this type is the *Musical Aptitude Profile* (Grades 4 to 12), by E. Gordon, which measures musical expression, aural perception, and kinesthetic musical feeling. Formal music training is not required for taking this test and it provides fairly good predictions of success in musical activities.

As with tests of artistic aptitude, musical aptitude tests measure only a limited number of the factors that are required for effective performance. Such things as mechanical skill, voice quality, creative ability, desire to perform, and persistence in maintaining daily practice also need to be considered. Musical aptitude tests are best viewed as measures of skills and abilities that may be necessary, but certainly are not sufficient, for successful musical performance.

SUMMARY

Standardized aptitude tests are designed to predict future performance in some activity, such as school learning. Like achievement tests, aptitude tests measure learned abilities. They differ from achievement tests, however, in that the test content is broader in scope, and test performance is less dependent upon any specific set of learning experiences. This makes it possible to use the tests with pupils of varying educational backgrounds and to predict performance over a wide range of learning activities.

Group tests of scholastic aptitude may yield a single score, separate verbal and nonverbal scores, separate verbal and quantitative scores, or multiple scores based on a series of specific aptitudes. The single-score test is designed to measure general mental ability only. In tests using verbal and nonverbal scores, the nonverbal score serves as a check on the mental ability of the poor reader. Tests with separate verbal and quantitative scores and multiscore tests are used primarily for differential prediction. Which type of test to choose depends largely on the type of information desired and the use for which it is intended. For straightforward prediction of school success a single-score test may suffice, but for detecting underachievers or helping pupils with educational choices tests with two or more scores would be desirable.

Individual tests of scholastic aptitude deemphasize reading skill and provide more carefully controlled testing conditions. Thus the individual test is especially valuable for testing young children and for checking on questionable scores obtained with group tests. Although extensive training and experience is required to administer individual tests, classroom teachers will likely encounter the scores on school records. It is therefore desirable to know the nature of the test content and the types of scores that are commonly used.

Most group and individual tests of scholastic aptitude report test performance in terms of the deviation IQ. These scores typically have a mean of 100 and a standard deviation of 15 or 16. In interpreting IQs, it is important to recognize that a normal amount of variation in the scores is to be expected and that certain conditions may cause extreme variation. The safest procedure is to view the scores as highly tentative estimates of learning ability that must be verified by other evidence.

Various attempts have been made to develop culture-fair tests but in general the instruments have not lived up to expectations. Efforts in this area, however, have clarified many of the problems involved in testing the culturally deprived and thus have contributed to the trend toward a more "culture-fair use" of conventional aptitude tests.

Comprehensive aptitude batteries also have been developed for school use. These include a series of specific aptitude tests all standardized on the same population. The tests measure a broad range of educational and vocational aptitudes that are useful in both guidance and instruction.

Tests in such special areas as creativity, art, and music are not as highly developed as those in the academic and vocational areas. They are also typically more difficult to administer and score. When carefully used, however, they do provide objective information in areas where such information is at a premium. The main thing is to treat the test scores as tentative and to supplement and complement them with all other relevant data concerning a pupil's development.

LEARNING EXERCISES

1. What are the similarities and differences between achievement tests and aptitude tests?
2. What are the relative advantages and disadvantages of using group scholastic aptitude tests rather than individual tests?
3. Examine a group scholastic aptitude test of each of the following types: (a) single score, (b) verbal-nonverbal, (c) verbal-quantitative, (d) multiscore. What levels of the ability spectrum (see Table 13.1) would each test and subtest cover?

4. John was given two different scholastic aptitude tests at the beginning of ninth grade. His total IQ scores were as follows:

Test A = 120
Test B = 112

What are the factors that might account for this difference in scores?

5. What are the similarities and differences between the *Stanford-Binet Scales* and the *Wechsler Scales?*
6. What are the advantages of informing pupils ahead of time of the exact date they are to be tested and the nature of the test to be given? What are some possible disadvantages?
7. A pupil from a culturally deprived home received an IQ score of 85 on the *Otis-Lennon Mental Ability Test*. What additional information would help you interpret the score? If you could have him take another test, what type of test would you want him to take? Why?
8. Examine Cattell's *Culture-Fair Intelligence Test*. How do the items compare with those in the *Cognitive Abilities Test*, Nonverbal Battery (see Figure 13.5)? For what types of groups, if any, would you expect the two tests to give different results?
9. What are the advantages of using the *Differential Aptitude Tests* instead of a group scholastic aptitude test? What are the disadvantages?

SUGGESTIONS FOR FURTHER READING

Anastasi, A. *Psychological Testing*, 4th ed. New York: Macmillan Publishing Co., Inc., 1976. Chapters 9–13. Includes descriptions of widely used individual, group, and multiple aptitude tests.

Cronbach, L. J. *Essentials of Psychological Testing*, 3rd ed. New York: Harper and Row, Publishers, 1970. Chapter 7, "General Ability: Appraisal Methods"; Chapter 9, "General Ability: Group Tests and Their Use"; and Chapter 11, "Ability Profiles in Guidance." These three chapters cover individual, group, and differential aptitude tests.

Edwards, A. J. *Individual Mental Testing, Part II: Measurement*. Scranton, Penn.: Intext, 1972. Describes the development and characteristics of the *Stanford-Binet* and the *Wechsler Scales*.

Getzels, J., and G. F. Madaus. "Creativity," *Encyclopedia of Educational Research*, 4th ed. New York: Macmillan Publishing Co., Inc., 1969, pages 267–275. Creativity is discussed in relation to intelligence, school behavior, individual development, personal characteristics, and educational facilitation.

Karmel, L. J. *Measurement and Evaluation in the Schools*. New York: Macmillan Publishing Co., Inc., 1970. In Chapter 2, "Contemporary Issues and Problems," see the sections on cultural bias in testing (pages 26–28) and test score differences between races and social classes (pages 41–47). A comprehensive review of research findings.

Mehrens, W. A., and I. J. Lehmann. *Standardized Tests in Education*, 2nd ed. New York: Holt, Rinehart & Winston, Inc., 1975. Chapter 3, "Standardized Aptitude Measures." Describes a number of widely used aptitude tests and their uses in the school.

SAMUDA, R. J. *Psychological Testing of American Minorities: Issues and Conse-quences.* New York: Dodd, Mead & Co., 1975. A comprehensive treatment of the problems of using standardized tests with minorities and suggestions for alternative approaches. Includes a compendium of tests for use with minority groups and an extensive bibliography.

TYLER, R. W., and R. M. WOLF (eds.). *Crucial Issues in Testing.* Berkeley, Calif.: McCutchan (for National Society for the Study of Education), 1974. Part One, "Testing and Minority Groups." Contains several articles on culture fairness and appropriateness of conventional ability tests for minority group members.

CHAPTER 14

Selecting and Using Standardized Tests

There are numerous standardized tests from which to choose. . . . Your task is to locate, evaluate, and select those tests that best suit your specific needs. . . . A systematic procedure facilitates this process. . . . Careful administration and scoring are needed for valid results. . . . There are many uses of standardized tests. . . . These are best served by a school-wide testing program.

As discussed earlier, standardized tests are tests that have been prepared by measurement experts and published for general use. These tests typically contain a carefully developed and fixed set of test items, uniform procedures for administering and scoring, and norms based on some clearly defined reference group. The standard content and procedure provide for uniformity of testing conditions; the norms provide for a meaningful interpretation of test scores. This provision for comparing an individual's test performance with that of others in some well-defined group (norm-referenced interpretation) is a distinctive feature of standardized testing.

The use of standardized tests in schools has increased rapidly over the past few decades. It has been estimated that at least 200 million standardized achievement tests are being administered annually in the United States.[1] This figure does not include aptitude testing, nor any of the other types of standardized tests used in the schools. With such a proliferation in the use of standardized tests, it would seem only sensible to devote great care to their selection and use. Although various school personnel may be involved in test selection, the classroom teacher should play a key role.

Some standardized tests are selected by individual teachers, but more

---

[1] M. G. Holmen and R. F. Docter, *Educational and Psychological Testing: A Study of the Industry and Its Practices* (New York: Russell Sage Foundation, 1972).

commonly the tests are selected in accordance with the school testing program. In either case, the teacher is usually active in the selection process since most testing programs are cooperatively planned by teachers, guidance workers, and administrators. In large school systems where it is necessary to use special committees for this purpose, the individual teacher still has a voice in the process through departmental and general staff meetings.

Although standardized tests can serve a variety of administrative and guidance functions, of central concern to any testing program is the effective use of test results in evaluating and improving the educational development of pupils. It is for this reason important that teachers participate in the selection of standardized tests. Their doing so provides greater assurance that tests are in harmony with the instructional objectives of the school, and that the results will serve the various instructional uses for which they are intended.

Teachers must also know the procedures for administering and scoring standardized tests. In some schools they participate directly in these functions while in others special personnel is used. In either case, however, teacher understanding of the procedures contributes to more effective interpretation and use of test results.

SOURCES OF INFORMATION
ABOUT SPECIFIC TESTS

There are a number of sources of information concerning specific standardized tests. These will be presented in the approximate order in which they should be consulted when searching for information to facilitate the selection of tests.

Buros' Guides

One useful guide for locating the published tests available in a particular area is Buros' *Tests in Print*.[2] The second edition of this guide (*Tests in Print II*) includes a bibliographic entry for all known tests printed in the English language as of March, 1974. The number and percentage of tests published in each major area of measurement are presented in Table 14.1. Of the 2,467 tests listed in this table, approximately 90 per cent are published in the United States.

The large number of tests available in any given area makes the selection of the proper test seem an almost insurmountable task. However, many of the possible tests can be quickly discarded because they are recommended for experimental or research purposes only, or the publication

---

[2] O. K. Buros, *Tests in Print II* (Highland Park, N.J.: Gryphon Press, 1974). O. K. Buros, *Tests in Print I* (Highland Park, N.J.: Gryphon Press, 1961). *Tests in Print III* should appear in the late 1970s.

TABLE 14.1

Classification	Number	Percentage
Personality	441	17.9
Vocations	375	15.2
Miscellaneous	291	11.8
Intelligence	274	11.1
Reading	248	10.1
Mathematics	168	6.8
English	131	5.3
Foreign languages	105	4.3
Science	97	3.9
Social studies	85	3.4
Speech and hearing	79	3.2
Sensory-Motor	62	2.5
Achievement batteries	50	2.0
Fine arts	35	1.4
Multiaptitude batteries	26	1.1
Total	2,467	100.0

[*] Adapted from Buros, Oscar K., *Tests in Print II*, page xxix, copyright © 1974 by Oscar Krisen Buros, published by The Gryphon Press (Highland Park, New Jersey). Used by permission of the publisher.

dates indicate they are too old to be very useful, or the bibliographic information makes clear that they are inappropriate for a particular use.

Each test entry in *Tests in Print II* includes the following information, where relevant, to aid the screening process:

1. Test title.
2. Grade or age levels covered.
3. Publication dates.
4. Special comments on test.
5. Number and type of scores provided.
6. Authors.
7. Publisher.
8. Reference to test reviews in Buros' *Mental Measurements Yearbooks*.[3]
9. Comprehensive bibliographies for some specific tests.

---

[3] O. K. Buros, *The Seventh Mental Measurements Yearbook* (Highland Park, N.J.: Gryphon Press, 1972), O. K. Buros, *The Sixth Mental Measurements Yearbook* (Highland Park, N.J.: Gryphon Press, 1965). O. K. Buros, *The Fifth Mental Measurements Yearbook* (Highland Park, N.J.: Gryphon Press, 1959). O. K. Buros, *The Fourth Mental Measurements Yearbook* (Highland Park, N.J.: Gryphon Press, 1953). O. K. Buros, *The Third Mental Measurements Yearbook* (New Brunswick, N.J.: Rutgers University Press, 1949). O. K. Buros, *The 1940 Mental Measurements Yearbook* (Highland Park, N.J.: Gryphon Press, 1941). O. K. Buros, *The 1938 Mental Measurements Yearbook* (New Brunswick, N.J.: Rutgers University Press, 1938).

Since the entries in *Tests in Print II* contain nonevaluative descriptive information concerning each test, the reference to the *Mental Measurements Yearbooks* is especially valuable. In addition to further descriptive information, the *Yearbooks* provide critical reviews of the tests. Each test is typically reviewed by two or more specialists qualified by training and experience to evaluate the test. Since the reviewers are professional persons with (it is hoped) no "ax to grind," they do not hesitate to point out test weaknesses as well as any exaggerated claims made by test publishers. In addition, of course, they indicate the strengths of a test and the uses for which it is best suited. A typical page from a recent *Mental Measurements Yearbook* is shown in Figure 14.1.

In the past Buros' guides have been published periodically but on no definite schedule. Present plans, however, are to publish *Tests in Print III* in the late 1970s, followed by a new edition every few years, and to put the *Mental Measurements Yearbooks* on a more regular schedule. This would be a boon to test users. These two guides make the screening process involved in test selection a simple two-step matter, for the most recent edition of *Tests in Print* is an excellent source of available tests, and the *Mental Measurements Yearbooks* provide critical reviews that aid in evaluating the tests from technical and practical standpoints.

Test Publishers' Catalogues

The most recent information concerning tests available for school use can be obtained from test publishers' catalogues. These usually contain brief descriptions of each test, including its possible uses, cost, administration time, and similar information. If a publisher's claims for his tests are checked by independent reviews such as those presented in the *Mental Measurements Yearbooks* and professional journal articles, test catalogues can be a helpful source of information. They are especially useful for locating new tests and recent editions of earlier tests. A brief list of test publishers, who will send catalogues upon request, is included in Appendix C.

Using the Test Standards

An extremely useful aid in evaluating and using standardized tests is the *Standards for Educational and Psychological Tests*.[4] This set of standards was prepared by a joint committee of the American Psychological Association, the American Educational Research Association, and the National Council on Measurement in Education. The *Standards* includes recommendations for test publishers and test users under the following headings:

---

[4] American Psychological Association, *Standards for Educational and Psychological Tests* (Washington, D.C.: APA, 1974).

diate application does not seem to be in testing, but rather in examining relationships between chunking and the transfer of meaning. As a research technique, the idea of chunking could lead to substantial discoveries about the nature of communication; this information might then be applied to writing a test to measure differences in how readers handle chunks of information. Such a test would indicate *how* different readers read differently, not simply that they do.

In summary, examiners will wish to thoroughly familiarize themselves with the construction of this test before attempting to administer it. While the data presented indicate that the test discriminates between subjects who read the essays and those who did not read the essays before answering the test questions, there is some question about what skills the test measures. This test quantifies the amount of information which a reader can identify, but it fails to identify the more important relationships between chunking and meaning. Without a consistent theoretical basis for dividing the sentences into chunks, the test does not provide information about the nature of the reading act.

[685]

★**Comprehensive Tests of Basic Skills: Reading.** Grades 2.5–4, 4–6, 6–8, 8–12; 1968–70; 3 scores: vocabulary, comprehension, total; 2 forms; 4 levels; for battery manuals and accessories, see 9; separate answer sheets (CompuScan [NCS], Digitek, IBM 1230, Scoreze) must be used for levels 2–4; postage extra; $1.75 per specimen set of any one level, postpaid; CTB/McGraw-Hill. *
a) LEVEL 1. Grades 2.5–4; Forms Q ('68, 8 pages), R ('69, 8 pages); $5.35 per 35 tests; 49(70) minutes.
b) LEVEL 2. Grades 4–6; Forms Q ('68, 13 pages), R ('69, 13 pages); $5.75 per 35 tests; $2.50 per 50 Digitek or IBM answer sheets; $3 per 50 CompuScan answer sheets; $2.75 per 25 Scoreze answer sheets; $1 per IBM hand scoring stencil; CompuScan scoring service, 17¢ and over per test; 52(75) minutes.
c) LEVEL 3. Grades 6–8; Forms Q ('68, 13 pages), R ('69, 13 pages); prices same as for level 2; 46(65) minutes.
d) LEVEL 4. Grades 8–12; Forms Q ('68, 13 pages), R ('69, 13 pages); prices same as for level 2; 41(60) minutes.

EARL F. RANKIN, *Professor of Education, University of Kentucky, Lexington, Kentucky.*

The reading test of the *Comprehensive Tests of Basic Skills* is a group survey test yielding conventional scores for vocabulary, comprehension, and total reading, like many similar tests. As such, its greatest value lies in evaluating total groups with respect to general level of reading skill and in selecting cases of reading disability which are in need of more intensive diagnosis. Its value as a selecting device for cases of read-

ing disability is considerably enhanced by its joint use with the *California Short-Form Test of Mental Maturity* to measure the gap between anticipated achievement and actual achievement in reading. The administration of both of these tests to a large number of individuals in the standardization sample made it possible to derive valid anticipated achievement scores for the reading test from the intelligence test scores. In the writer's opinion, this is a highly desirable feature.

As its title implies, the test is designed to measure basic skills as distinct from "higher mental processes." One might wonder about the validity of a reading test which is intentionally constructed to exclude the "higher mental processes." However, this would be an unwarranted criticism. The intellectual processes measured are "recognition and/or application, translation, interpretation, and analysis." This classification system was adapted from Bloom's *Taxonomy of Educational Objectives.* These processes are commonly measured by many reading tests. In fact, a number of higher order cognitive processes (as defined by Bloom) are not usually measured in tests of reading. The very high correlations reported in the Technical Report between this reading test and the reading subtest of the *California Achievement Tests* and also with the CTMM-SF indicate that the CTBS reading test is certainly not measuring merely low level skills. Indeed, the correlation coefficients ranging from .82 to .92 between the total reading scores of the CTBS and the CAT suggest that despite the alleged differences in rationale and emphasis claimed by the publisher of these two tests, they are measuring essentially the same thing.

The classification of each test item in the CTBS reading test in terms of the presumed intellectual process is supposedly one of the distinctive features of the test. In the writer's opinion, this feature is not of much diagnostic value to the teacher. The precision of the classification is subject to question. The Test Coordinator's Handbook indicates that the process by which items were classified was somewhat loose and simplified. More importantly, the number of test items designed as measuring one particular intellectual process may be as few as only three or four in the test as a whole. Hence, little reliability could be expected from such a measurement. The main value, then, of the intellectual process classification is that it aided in con-

FIGURE 14.1. Sample page from *The Seventh Mental Measurements Yearbook.* (Copyright 1972 by Oscar Krisen Buros, published by The Gryphon Press, Highland Park, New Jersey. Used by permission.)

Standards for Tests, Manuals, and Reports
    A. Dissemination of Information
    B. Aids to Interpretation
    C. Directions for Administration and Scoring
    D. Norms and Scales
    E. Validity
    F. Reliability and Measurement Error
Standards for the Use of Tests
    G. Qualifications and Concerns of Users
    H. Choice or Development of Test or Method
    I. Administration and Scoring
    J. Interpretation of Scores

Each recommendation in the *Standards* is classified as "essential," "very desirable," or "desirable," depending on its importance and the feasibility of attaining it. A typical page from the *Standards* is shown in Figure 14.2. A review of the complete set of standards provides a good background for evaluating test manuals and other test materials. In addition, the specific recommendations provide a type of checklist of factors to consider when selecting, administering, scoring, and interpreting standardized tests.

Professional Journals

Up-to-date information on testing can also be obtained from professional journals devoted to testing problems. Two of the most useful are the *Journal of Educational Measurement* and *Educational and Psychological Measurement*. These journals include test reviews, reviews of new books in measurement, and articles on the development and use of tests. Other journals providing test reviews are the *Journal of Consulting Psychology* and *Measurement and Evaluation in Guidance*. Numerous other professional journals also include articles on testing that contain information of an evaluative nature. These articles can be most easily located through the use of such bibliographic sources as the *Current Index to Journals in Education*, the *Education Index*, and *Psychological Abstracts*. Pertinent references to testing may be located in these guides by looking under such headings as achievement testing, educational measurement, evaluation, intelligence tests, psychological tests, testing programs, and tests and scales.

STEPS IN SELECTING STANDARDIZED TESTS

Standardized tests play such a vital role in the school program that they should be selected with the utmost of care. Tests which are selected hastily or casually seldom provide adequate or appropriate information on which to base educational decisions. In addition, such tests frequently have an undesirable influence on the school curriculum because they usually are

362   Using Standardized Tests

B. Aids to Interpretation

The responsibility for making inferences about the meaning and legitimate uses of test results rests primarily with the user. In making such judgments, however, he must depend in part on information about the test made available by its developer.

The manual or report form from a scoring service cannot fully prepare the user for interpreting the test. He will sometimes have to make judgments that have not been substantiated by published evidence. Thus, the vocational counselor cannot expect to have validity data available for each job about which he makes tentative predictions from test scores. The counselor or employment interviewer will have examinees who do not fit into any group for which normative or validity data are available. The teacher will have to evaluate the content of an achievement test in terms of his instructional goals and emphasis. The clinician must bring general data and theory into his interpretation of data from a personality inventory. The degree to which the manual can be expected to prepare the user for accurate interpretation and effective use of the test varies with the type of test and the purpose for which it is used. It is the test developer's responsibility to provide the information necessary for good judgment; in fact, developers should make tests as difficult to misuse and to misinterpret as they can.

B1. The test, the manual, the record forms, and other accompanying material should help users make correct interpretations of the test results and should warn against common misuses. Essential

B1.1. Names given to published tests, and to parts within tests, should be chosen to minimize the risk of misinterpretation by test purchasers and subjects. Essential

[Comment: It is desirable that names carry no unwarranted suggestion as to the characteristics measured. Such descriptions as "culture-free," "intelligence," "introversion," "creativity," "primary mental abilities," or "productivity quotients" are questionable for published tests, unless there is appropriate evidence of construct validity, since they may suggest interpretations going beyond the demonstrable meaning of the scores.]

B1.1.1. Devices for identifying interests and personality traits through self-report should be entitled "inventories," "questionnaires," or "checklists" rather than "tests." Very Desirable

[Comment: In referring to such instruments in textual material, however, as in these standards, the word "test" may be used to simplify the language even where it is properly avoided in the title.]

B1.2. The manual should draw the user's attention to data that especially need to be taken into account in the interpretation of test scores. Very Desirable

[Comment: Many test manuals point out variables that should be considered in the interpretation of a test score, such as information about school record, recommendations, or clinically relevant history.

FIGURE 14.2. Sample page from *Standards for Educational and Psychological Tests* (Copyright 1974 by American Psychological Association, Washington, D.C. Used by permission.)

not in complete harmony with the instructional program of the school. These and other pitfalls can be avoided by using a systematic selection procedure which takes into account the educational objectives of the school, the role of standardized tests in the total evaluation program, and the technical qualities most desired in educational tests. The following sequence of steps provides such a systematic procedure.

Defining Needs

Before an intelligent selection can be made from among the great variety of standardized tests available in a particular area, it is necessry to define specifically the type of information being sought through testing. In selecting achievement tests, for example, it is insufficient to search for a test to "evaluate achievement in social studies," to "measure reading development," or to "diagnose strengths and weaknesses in arithmetic." All standardized achievement tests measure somewhat different subject-matter content and different aspects of knowledge, skill, and understanding. To select the most appropriate ones, we must first identify the objectives and specific learning outcomes we are striving for in our teaching. This holds true whether we are selecting a single test for a particular course or a battery of tests for a school-wide testing program.

Clarifying the type of information needed is equally necessary in selecting aptitude tests. It makes a difference whether we are going to use the results for determining reading readiness, for grouping pupils, for vocational planning, or for predicting success in science and mathematics courses. Each function requires different information and consequently a different type of aptitude measure. Thus, selection must be preceded by careful analysis of the intended uses of the results and of the type of test data most appropriate for each use.

Narrowing the Choice

The need for standardized tests is seldom considered apart from a more general evaluation plan. The usual procedure is to develop a comprehensive list of objectives for a total evaluation program and then to identify those specific objectives and purposes which can best be served by means of standardized tests. This approach is especially helpful since the need for standardized tests can be appraised in accordance with other types of information available. This frequently helps to clarify further the nature of the standardized tests to be selected. It would be desirable to choose a test of general educational development, for example, if specific learning outcomes in the knowledge area were already being adequately measured by informal classroom tests. Similarly, if a scholastic aptitude test is to be used at a particular grade level for grouping purposes only, it might be desirable to group pupils on the basis of achievement test results and to replace the aptitude test with a diagnostic reading test. These and similar decisions can be made only when the need for standardized testing is viewed in terms of the general evaluation program.

Other factors in the school situation also help narrow the choice. If, for instance, the school lacks a person with the training and experience required to administer individual tests, only group tests need be considered. If the tests are to be administered by teachers who are relatively inexperienced in test administration, those with simple directions are to be favored. If the same type achievement battery is desired for both the elementary and high school levels, only those batteries with tests at all grade levels need be examined. Considerations such as these provide additional criteria concerning the types of tests to seek.

Locating Suitable Tests

With a general outline of the types of standardized tests desired, a list of possible tests can be compiled from Buros' *Tests in Print* and test publishers' catalogues. Though both sources will provide sufficient information to determine which tests should be considered further, neither provides the type of information needed to evaluate the quality of the test.

The list of possible tests to consider can be reduced to relatively few in each area by consulting critical reviews, described earlier, in Buros' *Mental Measurements Yearbooks*. These reviews are sufficiently detailed to weed out those tests which are clearly inappropriate or which have glaring technical weaknesses. Further information of an evaluative nature can, of course, be obtained from other sources such as those also described in an earlier section.

Obtaining Specimen Sets

The next step of the selection procedure is to obtain specimen sets so that test manuals and test items themselves can be carefully evaluated. Test publishers generally provide specimen sets for each test they publish. These can be purchased at relatively low cost and include a test manual, a test booklet, and scoring keys. A majority of universities, colleges, and large school systems maintain a file of such specimen sets. If such a file is unavailable, however, the sets can be ordered from test publishers' catalogues.

Reviewing the Test Materials

The test manual (sometimes accompanied by a technical manual and related aids) usually provides the most complete information for judging the appropriateness and the technical qualities of a test. A good test manual includes the following types of information:

1. Uses for which the test is recommended.
2. Qualifications needed to administer and interpret the test.
3. Validity: Evidence of validity for each recommended use.
4. Reliability: Evidence of reliability for recommended uses and an indication of the equivalence of any equivalent forms provided.
5. Clear directions for administering and scoring the test.
6. Adequate norms, including a description of the procedures used in obtaining them.

In addition, some test manuals (or supplements to the manuals) provide suggestions and guides for interpreting and using the results. These are especially helpful for determining the functions for which the test is best suited.

In reviewing test manuals in the above areas, the main thing to look for is *evidence*. General statements about validity, reliability, or the adequacy of norms should be disregarded unless they are supported by more detailed descriptions of the procedures used and by statistical evidence of the type discussed in Chapters 4 and 5. In fact, unsupported claims in these areas may be sufficient cause to eliminate a test from further consideration.

Before making a final selection, it is also highly desirable to study the individual test items carefully. The best method of doing this is to attempt to answer each item, as if taking the test. In the case of achievement tests, it is also helpful to classify the items by means of a previously prepared table of specifications. Although time consuming, there is no better means of determining the extent to which a test is appropriate for measuring those knowledges, skills, and understandings emphasized in the instructional program.

Making the Final Selection

The final choice of tests requires a careful appraisal of the strengths and weaknesses of each test in view of the intended uses of the results. This is a professional judgment which depends as much upon the goals of the school in which the tests will be used and the types of decisions for which information is needed, as upon the technical qualities of the tests themselves. Turning, at this juncture, to test publishers, test experts, or anyone else who is unfamiliar with the particular testing needs of the school is no longer helpful. The final decision must be made by persons intimately familiar with the local school situation.

Some teachers attempt to put the final selection on an objective basis by assigning a given number of points to validity, reliability, ease of scoring, and each of the other desired test characteristics. This practice is not recommended since the value of any given characteristic depends on the presence or absence of other qualities. For example, if a test is inappropriate for a given use, its reliability and ease of scoring are of no particular importance. Likewise, if two tests appear equally appropriate but one has very low reliability, the other qualities of the test become relatively insignificant. Rather than a numerical comparison of test qualities, what is needed is a logical analysis and comparison of the tests in light of the particular needs of the school program. Although this is much more demanding, it provides greater assurance that the most appropriate tests will be selected.

Using a Test Evaluation Form

The entire process of test selection will be simplified if a standard form is used when gathering information about specific tests. The use of such a form provides a convenient method of recording data, it increases the likelihood that pertinent information is not overlooked, and it makes possible a summary comparison of the advantages and limitations of each test. Although minor adaptations may be desirable to fit a particular situation, the following types of information are typically included in a test evaluation form:

Identifying Data:
1. Title of test.
2. Authors.
3. Publisher.
4. Date of publication.

General Information:
5. Nature and purpose of test.
6. Grade or age levels covered.
7. Scores available.
8. Method of scoring (hand or machine).
9. Administration time.
10. Forms available.
11. Cost (booklet and answer sheet).

Technical Features:
12. Validity: Type of validity and nature of evidence (content, construct, and criterion-related).
13. Reliability: Type of reliability and nature of evidence (stability, internal consistency, and equivalence of forms).
14. Norms: Type, adequacy, and appropriateness to local situation.

Practical Features:
15. Ease of administration (procedure and timing).
16. Ease of scoring.

17. Ease of interpretation.
18. Adequacy of test manual and accessory materials.

General Evaluation:

19. Comments of reviewers.
20. Summary of advantages and limitations for local use.

Although the test evaluation form provides a useful summary of information concerning tests, it must be reemphasized that no test should be selected on the basis of this information alone. How well a test fits the particular uses for which it is being considered is always the main consideration, and there is no substitute for studying the actual test materials to determine this relevance.

ADMINISTERING STANDARDIZED TESTS

The procedures for administering group tests of achievement and scholastic aptitude are such that the tests can be successfully administered by any conscientious teacher. The main requirement is that the teacher rigorously adhere to the testing procedures prescribed in the test manual. To do this, the teacher must shift roles from that of teacher and helper to that of an impartial test examiner who will not deviate from the test directions.

Teachers sometimes wonder why it is important to follow the test procedures so exactly. What harm is there in helping a pupil if he does not understand the question? Why not give the pupils a little more time if they are almost finished? Are not some of these directions a bit picayunish, anyway? The answer is that *a standardized test must be administered under standard conditions if the results are to be meaningful.* When a standardized test is administered to representative groups of pupils for the purpose of establishing norms and for determining reliability and validity, it is administered in exact accordance with the procedures prescribed in the test manual. Unless we adhere strictly to the same procedures, the standard conditions of measurement are broken and we cannot use the test norms to interpret our scores. Similarly, the information on reliability and validity provided in the test manual does not apply unless standard conditions of administration are maintained. In short, when the procedures for administering a standardized test are altered, the test becomes no more than a well-constructed informal test and the basis for interpreting the test scores is lost.

Steps in Preparing for Test Administration

The following steps assume that the regular classroom teacher will administer the tests. Although in some schools a test specialist carries out this function, there are advantages in using the classroom teacher. In administering the test, he becomes more familiar with the test content, and he has an opportunity to observe the pupils' responses to the testing situation. With this type of information, he is more apt to interpret and use the test scores intelligently.

Order and Check the Testing Materials Well in Advance. Test materials should be ordered so that they will arrive a week or more before the test date. This allows time for correcting any errors in the order and for the teachers to study the test materials and obtain practice in administering the test.

When the test materials arrive, they should be opened and checked to make certain that the correct form of the test has been sent, that there are a sufficient number of tests and answer sheets, and that all other ordered materials have been included. This is also a good time to assemble all other materials needed for the administration of the test. Extra pencils, a stop watch, scratch paper, and other necessary materials can be placed with the tests so that they will be available at the time of testing. Most test examiners use a checklist of needed materials to provide assurance that nothing is overlooked in preparing for the test.

Select a Suitable Location for Testing. The room which provides the most favorable physical and psychological conditions for testing should be used. In most instances this is the regular classroom. The lighting and ventilation are generally good, and pupils are accustomed to taking tests in their own classroom. If there are disturbing street noises, or other distracting influences that cannot be controlled, it would, of course, be desirable to move the pupils to a more quiet classroom.

At times it may be necessary, or desirable, to combine classes and administer the test in an auditorium or some other large room. When this is done, special attention must be given to the writing space afforded each pupil. Inadequate space and an inconvenient place to write can have an adverse affect on test scores. Also, seating should be arranged so that the pupils can see and hear the test examiner and the proctors can move freely among the pupils. If possible, teachers should proctor their own pupils. This provides pupils with a greater feeling of security, removes any hesitancy they might have about asking questions concerning mechanics or unclear directions, and enables the teacher to observe their test behavior.

Make Provisions to Prevent Distractions. There should be no interruptions or distractions of any kind during testing. These can usually be prevented by (1) posting a sign on the door notifying visitors that testing is in progress, (2) making certain that all test materials, including extra pencils and erasers, are available at the time of testing, and (3) making arrangements to terminate temporarily announcements over the loud speaker, the ringing of school bells, and other sources of distraction.

There is another type of distraction that has to be considered. This is the mental distraction that occurs just before and just after an important athletic contest, school dance, school election, and the like. These distractions can best be avoided by proper scheduling of the test. Since major school events are scheduled well in advance, they can easily be avoided when determining the date of testing.

Study the Test Materials and Practice Administering the Test. No matter how simple the administration of a particular test may appear, it is always wise to read the test manual, take the test yourself, and administer it to some other person before administering it to a group of pupils. This familiarity with the test materials makes it possible to anticipate questions and to know the types of answers that can and cannot be given in clarifying directions. The understanding of the test obtained with these procedures will, of course, also increase the effectiveness with which to test results are used. Test scores become much more meaningful when the test procedures are intimately known.

If more than one teacher is giving the same test, practice in administering the test can be obtained by testing each other. When this is done the directions, timing, and other aspects of administration should be followed in the same precise manner that is to be used in testing pupils. This procedure affords the greatest likelihood of detecting and correcting weaknesses in reading directions and keeping time accurately.

Test Administration Procedures

When proper preparations have been made, the administration of group standardized tests is a relatively simple procedure. Basically, it involves the following four tasks: (1) motivating the pupils to do their best, (2) adhering strictly to directions, (3) keeping time accurately, and (4) recording any significant events which might influence test scores.

Motivating Pupils. The goal of all standardized testing is to obtain maximum performance within the standard conditions set forth in the testing procedures. We want each person to earn the highest score he is capable of achieving. This obviously means that each person must be motivated to put forth his best effort. Although some persons will respond to any test as a challenge to their ability, others will not work seriously at the task unless they are convinced that the test results will be beneficial to them.

In school testing, we can stimulate pupils to put forth their best effort by convincing them that the test results will be used primarily to help them improve their learning. We can also make clear to them the value of standardized test results for understanding themselves better and for planning their future. These need to be more than hollow promises made at the time of testing, however. Test results must be used in the school in such a manner that these benefits to the pupils are clearly evident.

Before administering a particular test, the teacher should indicate to the pupils the purpose of the test and the specific uses to be made of the results. At this time, the advantages of obtaining a score which represents the pupils' best efforts should be emphasized, but care should be taken not to make the pupils overly anxious. Verbal reassurance that the size of the score is not as important as the fact that it represents his best effort is usually helpful. The judicious use of humor can also offset test anxiety to a degree. The most effective antidote, however, is a positive attitude toward test results. When the pupils are convinced that valid test scores are beneficial to their own welfare, both test anxiety and motivation tend to become problems of minor concern.

Adhering Strictly to Directions. The importance of following the directions given in the test manual cannot be overemphasized. Unless the test is administered in exact accordance with the standard directions, the test results will contain an indeterminate amount of error and thereby be uninterpretable in terms of the test norms provided.

The printed directions should be read *word for word* in a loud, clear voice. They should never be paraphrased, recited from memory, or modified in any way. The oral reading of directions will usually be vastly improved if the directions have been mastered beforehand, and they have been read several times in practice administrations.

After the directions have been read, and during the testing period, some pupils are likely to ask questions. It is usually permissible to clarify directions and answer questions concerning mechanics (for example, how to record the answer), but the test manual must be your guide in answering pupils' questions. If the manual states that the pupils should be referred back to the directions, for example, this should be followed exactly. In some scholastic aptitude tests, the ability to follow directions is a part of the test and to clarify the directions is to give unfair aid to the pupils. Where it is permissible to clarify directions, care must be taken not to change or modify the directions in any way during the explanation.

Teachers find it extremely difficult to refrain from helping pupils who are having difficulty in answering items on a standardized test. When questioned about a particular test item, there is a considerable temptation to say: "You remember, we discussed that last week," or to give some similar hints to the pupils. This, of course, merely distorts the results. When asked about a particular test item, during testing, the teacher should quietly tell the pupil: "I'm sorry but I cannot help you. Do the best you can."

Keeping Time Accurately. If the test contains a series of short subtests which must be timed separately, it is desirable to use a stop watch when giving the test. For most other purposes, a watch with a second hand is satisfactory. To insure accurate timing, a written record of the starting and stopping times should be made. This should be in terms of the exact hour, minute, and second as follows:

	Hour	*Minute*	*Second*
Starting time	2	10	0
Time allowed		12	
Stopping time	2	22	0

As with the written directions, the time limits must be adhered to rigidly. Any deviation from the time limits given in the test manual will violate the standard conditions of administration and invalidate the test results.

Recording Significant Events. During testing, the pupils should be carefully observed, and a record made of any unusual behavior or event which might have an influence on the test scores. If, for example, a pupil appears overly tense and anxious, sits staring out of the window for a time, or seems to be marking his answers in a random manner without reading the questions, a description of the behavior should be recorded. Similarly, if there are interruptions during the testing (despite your careful planning), a record should be made of the type and length of the interruption and in what manner, if any, it altered the administration of the test.

A record of unusual pupil behavior and significant events provides valuable information for determining whether test scores are representative of the pupils' best efforts and whether standard conditions have been maintained during testing. Questionable test scores should, of course, be rechecked—by administering a second form of the test.

SCORING STANDARDIZED TESTS

The aim in scoring standardized tests is to obtain *accurate* results as rapidly and economically as possible. Where a relatively small number of pupils are being tested, this aim can usually be satisfactorily achieved by hand-scoring methods. For larger groups, however, and especially for a school-wide testing program, the use of a scoring machine is generally more effective.

Hand Scoring

The scoring of standardized tests by hand is a routine clerical task. The procedure consists mainly of comparing the pupils' answers on the test booklet, or separate answer sheet, with the correct answers listed on a scoring key and counting the number correct. In some cases, such as where a correction formula is used, simple arithmetic skills are also involved. Despite the simplicity of hand-scoring procedures, the task is fraught with possibilities for error. Untrained scorers make frequent errors in counting answers, following instructions, using scoring guides, and the like. Such scoring errors can be reduced to a minimum by taking the following precautions:

1. Provide supervised practice in scoring the test. Have each person score several sample papers under supervision, check his scoring accuracy, and give instruction as needed.

2. During the regular scoring of test papers, have each paper rescored by a second person. If this is impractical, rescore a representative sample of the papers, such as every fifth paper, to determine if further rescoring is needed.
3. Have each person initial the papers he scores. Where the scorer can be identified, he is more apt to make a special effort to avoid errors.
4. Rescore any paper which has scores that appear questionable, such as exceptionally high or low scores, scores which deviate widely from the teacher's judgment, and the like.

Accuracy cannot be overemphasized in the scoring of standardized tests. Even small scoring errors have a detrimental influence on the reliability and validity of the test results. Large errors may lead to educational decisions which are injurious to individuals or groups.

Should Teachers Do the Scoring? Many schools still rely on the classroom teacher to score the standardized tests administered to his pupils. This is usually defended on the following grounds: (1) it is fast, accurate, and economical; (2) teachers will obtain insight into the types of errors most frequently made by their pupils; and (3) it stimulates more active interest in the use of the test results. These reasons are seldom valid, however. In the first place, trained clerks can generally score standardized tests faster, more accurately, and at lower cost than classroom teachers. It is false economy to have professionally trained personnel perform routine clerical tasks. Secondly, scoring objective answers on standardized tests is a mechanical procedure which provides no insight into the nature of the test items missed by pupils. Finally, teachers view the scoring of standardized tests as an onerous task. Whether participation in such a distasteful activity contributes to greater interest in the use of the test results is highly questionable. It is more apt to result in unfavorable attitudes toward the entire testing program.

Where hand scoring is necessary, the most desirable procedure is to select and train clerical workers for the task. If they are unavailable and teachers must be used for the scoring, it is imperative that they be given training and supervised practice. It should not be assumed that teachers are efficient at routine clerical tasks merely because they are good teachers.

Machine Scoring

The most effective method of relieving teachers of the burdensome task of scoring standardized tests is to use machine scoring. A number of electrical and electronic scoring machines are available for this purpose and their services can be obtained directly from most test publishers.

The earliest scoring machines were developed by International Business Machines Corporation (IBM). These machines use special answer sheets like the one presented in the top half of Figure 14.3. Answers are recorded on the sheet by blackening the answer space with a special soft pencil. Some large school systems have their own IBM scoring machines, but IBM scoring services are also available through test publishers.

Electronic test processing equipment developed at the University of Iowa combines a test scoring machine with an electronic computer and a fast output printer. This equipment automatically scores the answer sheets, converts the raw scores to various types of derived scores, and provides printed reports of the results. Answer sheets can be processed at a rate of more than 9,000 an hour. The use of this equipment is controlled by the Measurement Research Center, Iowa City, Iowa. The services of MRC are available to schools through test publishers. A typical MRC answer sheet is shown in the lower half of Figure 14.3.

The main advantage of machine scoring over hand scoring is that it is more accurate. In addition, machine scoring is inexpensive. Test scores can be obtained from test publishers at a relatively small cost, and supplementary statistical and reporting services are usually available for an additional moderate service charge. The major disadvantage is that, despite the speed of the machine, it may take a week or more to obtain the results from test publishers. This is not a serious limitation, however, and one that can be offset by careful scheduling of the testing dates.

REPORTING AND RECORDING TEST RESULTS

When standardized tests have been scored, a copy of the results should be sent to the teachers concerned as rapidly as possible. Unless test results are made available to teachers quickly, much of their instructional value is lost. This is an especially significant factor where fall testing is used, and the results are needed for instructional planning.

In addition to reporting the test results directly to teachers, test scores should be entered on the cumulative record form of each pupil. This should include all of the necessary information, for interpreting and using the test results effectively. As a minimum, the following information should be indicated: (1) date the test was given; (2) grade in which the test was given; (3) test title and form used; (4) total and part scores, expressed in appropriate units; and (5) nature of norm group, where percentile or standard scores are used.

For effective use of test results and other evaluative data, it is essential that the pupils' cumulative records be kept up to date and easily accessible. Test scores soon gather dust where school policy, or the record system itself, provides barriers to their use. All teachers should have free and ready access to the pupils' records and should be encouraged to use them as needed.

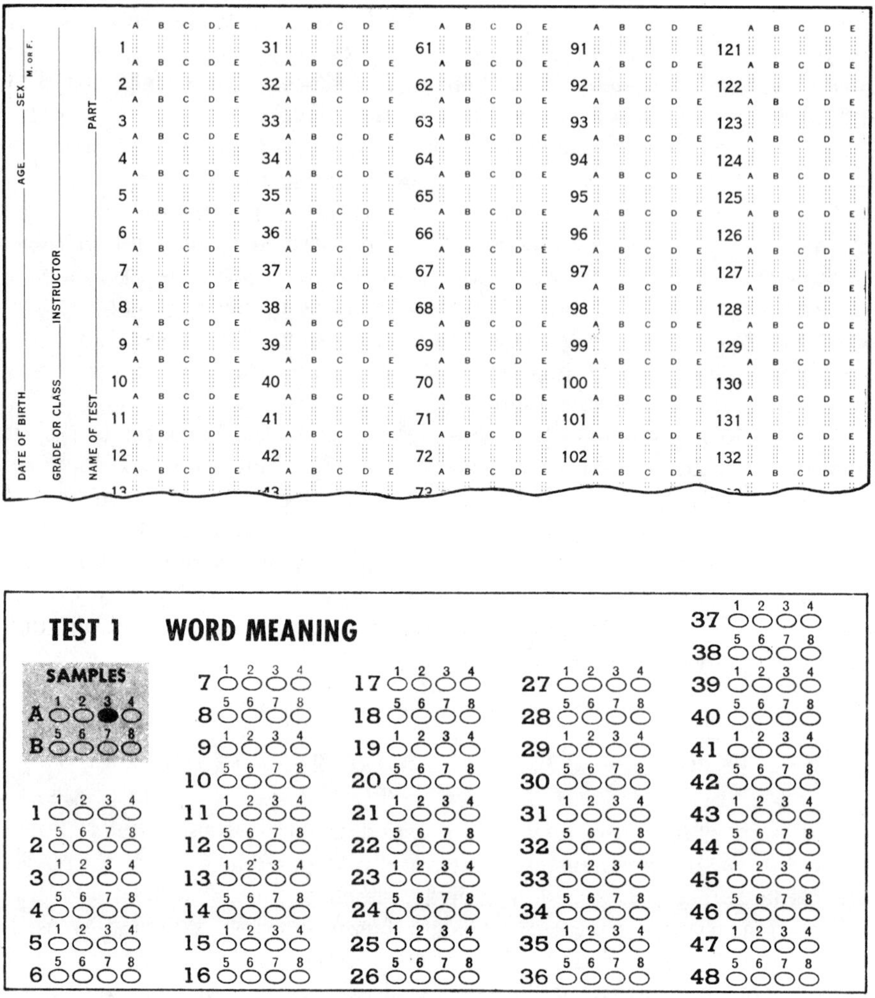

FIGURE 14.3. Machine-scoring answer forms. (IBM answer sheet courtesy of International Business Machines Corporation. MRC answer sheet from *Stanford Achievement Test*. © 1964 by Harcourt Brace Jovanovich, Inc. All rights reserved. Used by permission.)

USING THE RESULTS OF STANDARDIZED TESTS

The administration and scoring of group standardized tests are rather mechanical procedures requiring rigid adherence to fixed rules and directions. Interpretation and use of test results, however, cannot be reduced to any such rigid set of rules. These functions require sound professional judgment based on broad training and experience. In the following chapter, we shall present the technical considerations in interpreting test scores and norms. Here the discussion will be limited to some of the possible uses and misuses of standardized test results.

Possible Uses of Standardized Tests

If they are carefully selected and used with discretion, standardized tests of achievement and scholastic aptitude can play an important role in the evaluation program of the school. As noted earlier, they should be selected in accordance with the purposes for which the results are to be used. Effective use requires the recognition that standardized tests provide only partial information in a comprehensive evaluation program. This information must be supplemented by the results of classroom tests, teacher observations, performance evaluations, and other types of evaluative data.

All too frequently, standardized tests are permitted to dominate and modify the educational program of the school undesirably. This is most apt to occur where little attention is paid to objectives and where there is a feeling that standardized tests must—somehow—measure the important outcomes of education. The result, of course, is that the school curriculum is shaped by test publishers rather than by local school personnel. Proper use of standardized tests demands that we view them as tools which contribute to the achievement of *our* educational objectives by providing us with the information we desire concerning our pupils. When viewed in this manner, they can contribute to more effective educational decisions in a number of areas.

Curriculum Planning. Standardized tests of achievement and scholastic aptitude can aid curriculum planning in a particular school or course in the following ways:

1. *Identifying the level and range of ability among pupils.* Among other things, curriculum plans must take into account the learning ability of the pupils and their present levels of achievement. Standardized tests provide objective evidence on both of these points.

2. *Identifying areas of instruction needing greater emphasis.* If the standardized tests have been carefully selected in terms of the objectives of the school, instructional weaknesses will be revealed by those areas of the test in which the pupils do poorly. Standardized tests are especially helpful in appraising instructional weaknesses in the area of basic skills. In this as well as other areas, however, the results of standardized tests should be verified by other evidence of achievement.

3. *Evaluating experimental programs of instruction.* Where changes in curriculum content or instructional procedures are being introduced on an experimental basis, standardized tests of scholastic aptitude can be used to equate groups on learning ability, and standardized tests of achievement can contribute to a more objective comparison of the new and old methods. The limited objectives measured by standardized tests must, of course, be taken into account in interpreting the results.

4. *Clarifying and selecting instructional objectives.* Standardized testing aids in the clarification and selection of objectives in several ways. First, the process of selecting standardized tests forces us to identify and state

our objectives as clearly as possible. Second, an examination of the items in standardized tests clarifies to us how different objectives function in testing. As we go back and forth (during test selection) between our objectives and the items in the tests under consideration, our notion of what a particular objective looks like in operational terms becomes increasingly clear. Third, results of standardized tests provide evidence which helps in selecting objectives at a particular grade level or in a particular course. If fall test results indicate that pupils in the sixth grade are weak in study skills, for example, the teacher may want to include an objective in this area even though he had not originally planned to devote much attention to study skills. Similarly, standardized test results might indicate that a particular objective is unnecessary because it has been satisfactorily achieved at an earlier grade level.

In using the results of standardized tests in curriculum planning we should not lean on them too heavily. Even the most comprehensive battery of achievement tests measures only a portion of the objectives of a well-balanced curriculum.

Sectioning and Grouping Pupils. One of the most common uses of standardized test results is that of organizing groups of pupils who are similar in terms of learning ability. This ability grouping is frequently used in large schools when it is necessary to form several classes at each grade level or several sections of the same course. It is also used widely by teachers in forming instructional groups within classes. Elementary teachers, for example, commonly form reading groups and arithmetic groups on the basis of pupil ability.

Forming school or classroom groups according to ability is frequently referred to as homogeneous grouping. This is somewhat of a misnomer, however, since pupils grouped in terms of one type of ability are apt to vary considerably in other abilities, in interests, in attitudes, and in other characteristics significant from a learning standpoint. Ability grouping is a much more suitable term but even here there is the danger of assuming that the pupils in a given group will be identical in ability. All we can hope for is that the range of ability in the group will be smaller than it would be without such grouping.

Although ability grouping is practiced widely, there is still considerable criticism of its use. Two of the most common objections are: (1) it does not adequately provide for individual differences, and (2) a stigma is attached to pupils in the slowest groups. The first objection is a valid one which has helped clarify the role of ability grouping. It is becoming increasingly clear that ability grouping, by itself, is inadequate in coping with individual differences. It merely reduces the range of ability in a group so that individualized instruction can be applied more effectively. The second objection describes a real danger that is difficult to avoid. Separate grouping in each subject has helped. Where a pupil can be in a slow group in English, an average group in social studies and science, and an accelerated group in mathematics, there is less apt to be a stigma attached to those in the slow group. Flexible grouping which permits pupils to shift from one group to another, as performance improves, also helps in counteracting undesirable attitudes toward pupils in the slow group.

Ability groups can be formed on the basis of scholastic aptitude or achievement test scores. A more desirable practice is to use both. Borderline cases are more effectively placed when both types of test scores are used. If a pupil's achievement test score is near the cutoff point for the accelerated group, for example, he could be placed in the regular or accelerated group on the basis of how his scholastic aptitude test score compares with those of the pupils to be placed in each group. Using both types of test results will generally result in groups that are more alike in learning ability. In forming instructional groups within the classroom, standardized test results are generally used for preliminary grouping only. Later adjustments in grouping depend heavily on the teacher's day-to-day evaluations of his pupils' learning process.

Individualizing Instruction. Regardless of the method of sectioning classes or grouping pupils within classes, individual differences in aptitude and achievement will still exist among the pupils in any given group. Thus it is necessary to study the strengths and weaknesses of each pupil in class so that instruction can be adapted, as much as possible, to their individual learning needs. For this purpose (1) scholastic aptitude tests provide clues concerning learning ability, (2) reading tests indicate the difficulty of material the pupil can read with comprehension, (3) achievement tests point out general areas of strength and weakness, and (4) diagnostic tests pinpoint the particular errors of learning that are handicapping the pupil.

The use of tests to diagnose in order to remedy learning difficulties is one of the most common ways of using test results to individualize instruction.[5] At the elementary school level, a large fraction of teaching time is devoted to helping individual pupils identify and correct their errors in reading, arithmetic, spelling, and writing. At the high school level, considerable time is also devoted to the specific learning difficulties of individual pupils, both in general skill areas, like that of reading, and in the understanding of specific subject-matter content. Published diagnostic tests are especially useful in diagnosis because they provide a systematic approach to the identification of learning errors. Since these tests are limited almost entirely to the areas of reading and arithmetic, however, it is frequently necessary to use general achievement tests for diagnostic purposes. When this is done, an analysis of a pupil's responses to the individual test items will provide clues to his learning difficulties.

---

[5] See D. A. Goslin, *Teachers and Testing* (New York: Russell Sage Foundation, 1967), p. 22.

Identifying Pupils Needing Special Help. Some pupils deviate so markedly from the normal group of pupils at their grade or age level that special treatment, beyond that which can be provided by the classroom teacher, is needed. The extremely gifted, the mentally retarded, the very poor reader, the emotionally disturbed, and similar exceptional children fall into this category. For this type of pupil, standardized testing serves as a screening process; it identifies those pupils requiring further study so that special provisions can be made for meeting their exceptional needs.

Evaluating the Educational Development of Pupils. Standardized tests are especially useful in measuring the learning progress of pupils over extended periods of time. Equivalent forms of the same test can be used in the fall and spring to measure progress during the school year. Where achievement test batteries are administered annually, a long-range picture of the pupils' educational development can be obtained. Standardized tests are better suited to this type of measurement than teacher-made tests because the measurements are more comparable from one time to the next.

In using standardized tests as one basis for determining the educational development of pupils, care must be taken not to overgeneralize from the results. Tests which provide somewhat comparable measures of general educational development throughout the school years must, of necessity, be confined to those learnings which are in the process of continuous development and which are common to diverse curricula. In the main, this means the basic skills and those critical abilities used in the interpretation and application of ideas which cut across subject-matter lines. Although these are extremely significant educational outcomes, they provide only a partial picture of total educational development. Knowledge and understanding of specific subject-matter content, skills which are unique to each subject field, attitudes and appreciations, and similar learning outcomes that cannot be measured by standardized tests of educational development, are equally important.

Helping Pupils Make Educational and Vocational Choices. At the high school level, standardized test results can contribute to more intelligent educational and vocational decisions. In deciding which curriculum to pursue, which specific courses to take, whether to plan for college, or which occupations to consider, the pupil can be aided greatly by knowledge of his aptitudes and his strengths and weaknesses in achievement. Standardized tests are especially useful in educational and vocational planning because they indicate to the pupil how he compares with persons beyond the local school situation. This is important because these are the persons with whom he will be competing when he leaves high school, whether he goes to college or directly into an occupation.

Supplementary Uses. In addition to the above uses of standardized tests, all of which are directly concerned with improving the instruction and guidance of pupils, there are a number of supplementary uses to which they can be put. These include such things as: (1) appraising the general effectiveness of the school program in developing basic skills, (2) identifying areas in the educational program where supervisory aid can be used most effectively, (3) providing evidence for accountability programs and for interpreting the school program to the public, and (4) providing information for use by other schools, colleges, and prospective employers. When standardized test results are presented to individuals and groups outside the school, it should be emphasized that these tests measure only a limited number of the objectives of the school program.

Misuse of Standardized Tests

As noted earlier, standardized tests can be misused in any of the areas discussed above, if: (1) there is inadequate attention to the educational objectives being measured, (2) there is a failure to recognize the limited role the tests play in the total evaluation program, (3) there is unquestioning faith in the test results, or (4) the group tested is markedly different from the norm group. These factors contribute to the misapplication and misinterpretation of standardized test results in any situation. In addition, there are two specific misuses that warrant special attention.

Assigning Course Grades. Some teachers use standardized test scores as a basis for assigning course grades. This is undesirable for at least two reasons: (1) standardized tests are seldom closely related to the instructional objectives of a particular course, and (2) they measure only a portion of the desired learning outcomes emphasized in instruction. The practice of using standardized tests for grading purposes tends to place too much emphasis on a limited number of ill-fitting objectives. In addition to the unfairness to the pupil, this encourages both teachers and pupils to neglect those objectives which are not measured by the tests.

In borderline cases, especially where promotion or retention is being decided, standardized test results can serve a valuable supplementary function. Knowing a pupil's scholastic aptitude and his general level of educational development contributes to a more intelligent decision concerning his best grade placement. Except for such special uses, however, standardized tests should play a minor role in determining course grades.

Evaluating Teaching Effectiveness. In some schools a teacher's effectiveness is judged by the scores his pupils make on a standardized test. This is an extremely unfair practice since there are so many factors, other than teaching effectiveness, which influence test scores. Many of these, such as the level of ability of the class, cultural background of the pupils, previous educational experiences of the pupils, and the relative difficulty of learning different course materials, cannot be controlled or equated with sufficient accuracy to justify inferring that the results derived solely from the teacher's efforts. Even if such factors could be controlled, standardized tests would serve as a poor criterion of teaching success because of the two factors mentioned earlier—they are not closely related to the instructional objectives of particular courses, and they measure only a portion of the learning outcomes teachers strive for in their instruction.

THE SCHOOL-WIDE TESTING PROGRAM

The contribution of standardized testing to the total educational program of the school is substantially increased when the tests are selected and used in conjunction with a testing program organized on a school-wide basis. There are several advantages to a carefully planned, systematic program. First, planning the program requires reviewing the instructional goals of the entire school to determine the need for evaluation instruments in general and for standardized tests in particular. This process clarifies the role of standardized testing in the instructional and evaluation programs of the school and leads to more effective interpretation and use of the results. Second, a planned program provides for selection of tests that serve a variety of uses. Although as teachers we are primarily interested in using standardized tests to improve pupil learning, carefully selected tests can also serve administrative and guidance functions in the school. An organized program increases the likelihood that these needs will also be considered during test selection. Third, a planned program provides results that are comparable from one year to the next. This obviously gives us a clearer picture of the pupils' educational development than that obtained by sporadic testing with a variety of different tests. Fourth, a planned program makes it possible to accumulate test results and other evaluative data systematically. A systematic record contributes to more meaningful and rational interpretation of test scores since it encourages examination of results in relation to previous test scores and other pertinent accumulated data.

A Minimum Program

Since the testing program in any particular school must be developed in terms of instructional goals of the school and the specific uses to be made of the results, it is impossible to present a detailed testing program that would have general application. Each program should be tailor-made to the needs of the school; this requires cooperative study and planning by teachers, guidance personnel, and administrators. About the only contribution we can make to this undertaking is to suggest tests and procedures which should be considered in planning a minimum program.

Scholastic Aptitude Testing. Periodic measures of scholastic aptitude play a significant role in any testing program. The first test is generally given at the end of the first grade or the beginning of the second grade. This should be followed up by a test every several years. Selection of the specific grades in which scholastic aptitude tests are to be given must take into account (1) the way the school is organized, (2) whether the tests are to be given in the fall or spring, and (3) the use to be made of the results. Key points in scheduling the tests are those where the pupil moves from one educational level to another. Thus, in a school organized on a 6-3-3 plan, where spring testing is used, scholastic aptitude tests might be given in the first, third, sixth, ninth, and eleventh grades. If fall testing is used, a sequence like the second, fourth, seventh, tenth, and twelfth grades would provide similar results.

For most schools it would probably be desirable to use a reading-readiness test at the first-grade level and a differential aptitude test at the eighth-grade level. Decisions like this must, of course, depend on the use to be made of the results. There is little advantage in using a reading-readiness test unless reading instruction is individualized, or in using a differential aptitude test unless arrangements are made for interpreting and using the results in the guidance of pupils.

Group tests of scholastic aptitude are satisfactory for the minimum program but low scores and those which deviate considerably from teachers' judgments should be checked by an individual test. If no one in the school is qualified to administer individual tests, doubtful scores can be checked by administering another form of the same group test. When used for this purpose, the group test should be administered to a relatively small number of pupils at one time and the pupils carefully observed during the testing.

Achievement Testing. As a bare minimum, standardized achievement tests should be administered at the same time that scholastic aptitude tests are administered. This will provide evidence of both aptitude and achievement at each of the major transitional points in the pupils' school life. There is an additional advantage to administering scholastic aptitude tests and achievement tests in the same grades and at the same time of the year. Through the use of comparable national or local norms, it is possible to compare the test results and determine the extent to which pupils are achieving up to their expected levels of performance.

A typical minimum testing program which takes into account our suggestions for testing at transitional points is presented in Table 14.2. It should be noted that it is based on a school using a 6-3-3 organizational plan and fall testing. A school organized differently would, of course, have different transitional points and the program would be modified accordingly. As noted earlier, spring testing would also cause a shift in the schedule. In general, all tests would be given one year earlier.

Achievement test batteries used in a minimum testing program should generally be limited to the basic skills at the elementary school level and to measures of general educational development at the high school level. This provides a standard measure of those outcomes which form the common core of a curriculum. More specific instructional outcomes in such

TABLE 14.2
A TYPICAL MINIMUM TESTING PROGRAM*

	Type of Test			
Grade	Reading Readiness	Scholastic Aptitude	Differential Aptitude	Achievement Battery
1	X			
2		X		X
3				
4		X		X
5				
6				
7		X		X
8			X	
9				
10		X	X†	X
11				
12		X		X

* For school using 6-3-3 plan and fall testing.
† Could substitute for scholastic aptitude test at that grade level.

content areas as science, social studies, and literature can usually be measured more effectively with locally constructed achievement tests.

Where possible, it is desirable to go beyond the minimum program and administer achievement tests annually. This provides all teachers with an up-to-date measure of each pupil's strengths and weaknesses. In addition to improving the immediate instructional value of the results, annual testing provides a more comprehensive and meaningful picture of the pupils' general educational progress.

Diagnostic Testing. It is not expected that diagnostic tests will be routinely and regularly administered as are other tests in the testing program. However, a good minimum program will provide for the use of diagnostic tests by individual teachers, as needed. Where general achievement tests uncover weaknesses in the learning of basic skills, for example, a teacher should feel free to request the use of a diagnostic test with those pupils having the learning difficulty. During the planning of a minimum program, this type of testing must be considered in order to assure that the necessary funds are available and that diagnostic testing is included in the in-service training program for teachers.

Self-Report Techniques. If adequate guidance facilities are available in the school, so that the results can be interpreted and used effectively, interest inventories might be added to the minimum program. A general interest inventory administered once or twice at the high school level is useful in educational and vocational planning. If used, interest measures should be scheduled at the grade level where the results are most useful in pupil guidance. Since the tenth and twelfth grades are critical points in educational and vocational planning, the interest inventory could be administered at the beginning of these grade levels.

Selecting the Time of Year for Testing

In addition to the other considerations in planning a school testing program, a decision must be made concerning the best time of the year to give the tests. Spring testing is most frequently favored where the emphasis is on evaluating the effectiveness of the school program and where the results are to be used in sectioning classes for the following year. For most instructional purposes, however, spring testing leaves much to be desired. The results are obtained too late in the school year for classroom planning and too late to correct learning weaknesses revealed by the tests. Fall testing provides teachers with up-to-date information for planning the year's work, for grouping within the class, and for guiding and directing the work of individual pupils. Fall testing also avoids the two most common misuses of standardized testing—grading pupils and evaluating teachers. A survey of state testing programs has shown that fall testing is favored by a majority of schools.[6]

A Note of Caution

The school-wide program of standardized testing constitutes only a small part of the total evaluation program of the school. To measure adequately the diverse instructional goals and to serve the many uses for which objective information is needed in the school, a variety of evaluation methods is required. Teacher-made achievement tests, anecdotal records, performance ratings, sociometric techniques, and similar informal methods of appraisal both supplement and complement standardized test results. Ideally, the school-wide testing program should be planned in conjunction with the total evaluation program of the school so that the role of standardized testing is viewed in proper perspective.

SUMMARY

Teachers should be intimately familiar with the procedures for locating, selecting, administering, scoring, and using standardized tests. This enables them to participate in the school testing program more effectively, to select tests for particular uses more wisely, and to apply test results to instructional problems more intelligently.

The two basic guides for locating information about specific tests are

---

[6] Educational Testing Service, *State Testing Programs: 1973 Revision* (Princeton, N.J.: Evaluation and Advisory Service, ETS, 1973).

Buros' *Tests in Print* and his *Mental Measurements Yearbooks.* Supplementary information may be obtained from test publishers' catalogues and various professional journals containing articles on testing. The use of the test *Standards* helps determine the type of information to seek in evaluating a test.

To provide greater assurance that the most appropriate tests are selected, a systematic selection procedure should be followed. This includes: (1) defining the specific needs for evaluation data, (2) appraising the role of standardized testing in relation to other evaluation procedures and to the practical limitations of the school situation, (3) locating suitable tests through Buros' guides and test publishers' catalogues, (4) obtaining specimen sets of those tests which seem most appropriate, (5) reviewing the test materials in light of their intended uses, and (6) summarizing the data and making a final selection. A summary of data concerning each test under consideration is simplified if a standard evaluation form is used during the information gathering period of the selection process.

Administration of standardized tests involves careful preparation beforehand and strict adherence to standard procedures during testing. In preparing for testing, the materials should be ordered and checked well in advance, a suitable location for testing should be selected, provisions should be made to prevent distractions, and practice should be obtained in administering the test. During administration, the directions and time limits must be rigidly followed. Within the limits of the standard conditions, the pupils should be motivated to do their best. Also, a record should be made of any event during the testing period which might have an influence on the test scores. Questionable scores should be checked by administering a second form of the test.

Scoring of standardized tests is a mechanical procedure which places a premium on accuracy, speed, and economy. Hand scoring is satisfactory where a relatively small number of pupils is involved. Where hand scoring is necessary or desired, trained clerks should be used rather than teachers. When a large number of tests is to be scored, there is no substitute for machine scoring; it is accurate, fast, and relatively inexpensive. Machine scoring services can be obtained directly from most test publishers.

When tests have been scored, results should be made immediately available to the teachers concerned. They should also be recorded in the pupils' cumulative records for future use by all school personnel.

Standardized test results can serve a number of useful purposes in the school. They can aid in curriculum planning, sectioning and grouping of pupils, individualizing instruction, identifying pupils needing special help, evaluating the educational development of pupils, educational and vocational planning, and appraising and reporting on the effectiveness of the school program. In general they should not be used as a basis for assigning course grades or evaluating teacher effectiveness. Standardized tests are not closely enough related to the goals of particular courses and they measure too limited a sampling of instructional objectives to be useful for these purposes.

A formal school-wide testing program provides for more effective use of standardized tests through improved planning, better test selection, greater comparability of test results, and more systematic procedures for recording results. A minimum program should include measures of scholastic aptitude and achievement at transitional points in the school life of pupils and supplementary testing as needed.

LEARNING EXERCISES

1. Consult a test publisher's catalogue and read the descriptions of one achievement test and one scholastic aptitude test. What type of information is provided? Look up the same two tests in the latest Buros' *Mental Measurements Yearbook* (see footnote 3 of this chapter) and compare the reviewers' comments with the test publisher's descriptions. How do they differ?
2. Consult the latest *Mental Measurements Yearbook* and study the reviews for one achievement battery, one reading test, and one scholastic aptitude test. What strengths and weaknesses do the reviewers emphasize?
3. Consult the latest *Mental Measurements Yearbook* and study the reviews of several diagnostic tests. What are some of the types of questions reviewers consider when reviewing this type of test?
4. Consult the *Standards for Educational and Psychological Tests* (see suggested readings at end of this chapter) and review the types of information that test manuals should contain. Compare a recent test manual against the *Standards* and evaluate its strengths and weaknesses.
5. Select one of the best standardized achievement tests (or scholastic aptitude tests) in your teaching area and make a critical evaluation of it, using the evaluation form presented in this chapter. Include reviewers' comments from Buros' *Mental Measurements Yearbooks*.
6. If a student asks you any of the following questions during the administration of a standardized test, and the manual does not provide a definite answer, what would you tell the student?
   a. "Should I include my middle name on the answer sheet?"
   b. "Is there a penalty for guessing?"
   c. "Is there a time limit?"
   d. Should *all* the answers be marked on the separate answer sheet?"
7. The school testing program in Midville, U.S.A., includes an annual aptitude test given in the fall of the year and an annual achievement test given in the spring of the year. The same series of aptitude tests and achievement batteries are used at all grade levels (grades 1 through 12). What are the advantages and disadvantages of this testing program? How would you change it?
8. Describe the advantages and limitations of administering standardized tests at the beginning of the school year.
9. For the testing program in Table 14.2 (or for any other one you might develop), give the names of the specific tests that you would use at each grade level. Explain why each particular test was selected.

SUGGESTIONS FOR FURTHER READING

AMERICAN PSYCHOLOGICAL ASSOCIATION. *Standards for Educational and Psychological Tests.* Washington, D.C.: APA, 1974. Presents recommendations for (1) the preparation of tests, manuals and reports, and (2) the selection and use of standardized tests. An excellent guide for evaluating test materials.

BAUERNFEIND, R. H. *Building a School Testing Program,* 2nd ed. Boston: Houghton Mifflin Company, 1969. Chapter 14, "Planning the Master Testing Program." Describes steps for planning and improving school testing programs.

BUROS, O. K. *Tests in Print II.* Highland Park, N.J.: Gryphon Press, 1974. Provides a brief description of 2,467 tests published in the English language. Test entries are cross-referenced to Buros' *Mental Measurements Yearbooks* (see footnote 3). The 1974 APA *Standards,* listed earlier, is reprinted in full in this volume.

CRONBACH, L. J. *Essentials of Psychological Testing,* 3rd ed. New York: Harper and Row, Publishers, 1970. Chapter 3, "Administering Tests." Describes the principles and procedures of test administration. Good discussion of factors influencing test performance.

GOSLIN, D. A. *Teachers and Testing.* New York: Russell Sage Foundation, 1967. Chapter 2, "The Uses of Standardized Tests in Schools." Chapter 5, "The Role of Teacher as Test User." Reports on a survey of the frequency with which various types of tests were used at different grade levels, the uses made of the results, and the types of test information given to pupils and parents.

HOLMEN, M. G., and R. F. Docter. *Educational and Psychological Testing: A Study of the Industry and Its Practices.* New York: Russell Sage Foundation, 1972. Describes the various test publishers and test scoring organizations, large-scale testing programs, and some of the major uses and criticisms of testing. The appendix provides the addresses and brief descriptions of a large number of testing and scoring companies and their activities.

MEHRENS, W. A., and I. J. LEHMANN. *Standardized Tests in Education,* 2nd ed. New York: Holt, Rinehart & Winston, Inc., 1975. See material on planning and administering a school testing program, and the role of testing in the educational accountability movement.

NOLL, V. H., and D. P. SCANNELL. *Introduction to Educational Measurement,* 3rd ed. Boston: Houghton Mifflin Company, 1972. Chapter 15, "The Measurement Program." Describes the planning of a measurement program and steps for selecting, administering, and scoring the tests. Illustrative programs are presented.

THORNDIKE, R. L. (ed.). *Educational Measurement.* Washington, D.C.: American Council on Education, 1971. See Chapter 18 by J. A. Davis, "Use of Measurement in Student Planning and Guidance"; Chapter 19 by J. R. Hills, "Use of Measurement in Selection and Placement"; Chapter 20 by A. Astin and R. J. Panos, "Evaluation of Educational Programs" for extended discussions of the various uses of measurement results.

CHAPTER 15

Interpreting Test Scores and Norms

Test results can be interpreted in terms of (1) the types of tasks that can be performed (criterion reference), or (2) the relative position held in some reference groups (norm reference). . . . Both types of interpretation are useful. . . . The first describes what a person can do, and the second describes how his performance compares to that of others. . . . Standardized tests typically emphasize norm-referenced interpretation. . . . Interpreting test scores with the aid of norms requires (1) an understanding of the various methods of expressing test scores, and (2) a clear grasp of the nature of the norm group.

Test interpretation would be greatly simplified if we could express test scores on scales like those used in physical measurement. We know, for example, that 5 feet means the same height whether we are talking about the height of a boy or a picket fence; that a 200-pound football player weighs exactly twice as much as a 100-pound cheerleader, and that 8 minutes is exactly one third as long as 24 minutes whether we are timing a standardized test or a basketball game. This ability to compare measurements from one situation to another, and to speak in terms of "twice as much as" or "one third as long as," is made possible by the fact that these physical measures are based on scales which have a true zero point and equal units. The true zero point (e.g., the point at which there is "no height at all" or "no weight at all") indicates precisely where measurement begins and the equal units (e.g., feet, pounds, and minutes) provide uniform meaning from one situation to another and from one part of the scale to another. Ten pounds indicates the same weight to the doctor, the grocer, the farmer, and the housewife. Also, the difference between 15 and 25 pounds represents exactly the same difference as that between 160 and 170 pounds.

Unfortunately, the properties of physical measuring scales, with which we are all so familiar, are generally lacking in educational measurement. A pupil who receives a score of zero on a history test does not have zero knowledge of history. There are probably many simple questions he could have answered correctly which were not included in the test. A true zero point in achievement, where there is "no achievement at all," cannot be clearly established. Even if it could, it would be impractical to start from that point each time we tested. What we do in actual practice is to assume a certain amount of basic knowledge and measure from there. This arbitrary starting point, however, prevents us from saying that a zero score indicates "no achievement at all," or that a score of 100 represents twice the achievement of a score of 50. Since we are never certain how far the zero score on our test is from the true zero point (i.e., the point of "no achievement at all"), test scores cannot be interpreted like physical measurements. We can speak of "more" or "less" of a given characteristic but not "twice as much as" or "half as much as."

The interpretation of test results is additionally handicapped by the inequality of our units of measurement. Sixty items correct on a simple vocabulary test does not have the same meaning as sixty items correct on a more difficult one; nor do either of the scores represent the same level of achievement as sixty items correct on a test of arithmetic, science, or study skills. Our test items simply do not represent equal units like those of feet, pounds, and minutes.

To overcome this lack of a definite frame of reference in educational measurement, a variety of methods of expressing test scores have been devised. As we shall see shortly, the methods vary considerably in the extent to which they provide satisfactory units of measurement. Much of our difficulty in the interpretation and use of test results arises from the fact that we have so many different scoring systems—each with its own peculiar characteristics and limitations.

METHODS OF INTERPRETING TEST SCORES

Raw Scores

If a pupil responds correctly to 65 items on an objective test in which each correct item counts one point, his *raw score* will be 65. Thus, a *raw score* is simply the number of points received on a test when the test has been scored according to the directions. It does not make any difference whether each item is counted one point, or the items are weighted in some way, or a correction for guessing is applied, the resulting point score is known as a raw score. We are all familiar with raw scores from our many years of taking classroom tests.

Although a raw score provides a numerical summary of a pupil's test performance, it is not very meaningful without further information. In general, we can provide meaning to a raw score either by converting it into a description of the specific tasks that the pupil can perform (*criterion-referenced* interpretation), or by converting it into some type of derived score that indicates the pupil's relative position in a clearly defined reference group (*norm-referenced* interpretation).

Criterion-Referenced Interpretation

Criterion-referenced test interpretation permits us to describe an individual's test performance without reference to the performance of others. Thus, we might describe pupil performance in terms of the speed with which a task is performed (e.g., types 40 words per minute without error), the precision with which a task is performed (e.g., measures the length of a line within one sixteenth of an inch), or the percentage of items correct on some clearly defined set of learning tasks (e.g., identifies the meaning of 80 per cent of the terms used to describe fractions). The *percentage-correct score* is widely used in criterion-referenced test interpretation. Standards for judging whether a pupil has mastered each of the instructional objectives measured by a criterion-referenced test are frequently set in these terms.

Criterion-referenced interpretation of test results is most meaningful when the test has been specifically designed for this purpose (see Figure 12.5 in Chapter 12). This typically involves designing a test that measures a specified set of behaviorally stated instructional objectives. Enough items are used for each objective to make it possible to describe test performance in terms of a pupil's mastery or nonmastery of each objective. The value of these descriptions of test performance are enhanced by the fact that the domain of measured objectives is delimited and clearly specified, the test items are selected on the basis of their relevance to the objectives being measured, and there is a sufficient number of test items to make dependable judgments concerning the types of tasks a pupil can and cannot perform.

Criterion-Referenced Interpretation of Standardized Tests. Although standardized tests have been typically designed for norm-referenced interpretations, it is possible to attach criterion-referenced meaning to the test results. This would simply involve analyzing each pupil's test responses item by item and summarizing the results with descriptive statements (e.g., He solved all of the addition problems involving no carrying, but solved only two of the four problems requiring carrying). Some test publishers aid this type of interpretation by (1) providing the list of objectives measured by the test, with each item keyed to the appropriate objective, and (2) arranging the items into homogeneous groupings for easy analysis.

Just because it is possible to make criterion-referenced interpretations of standardized achievement tests does not mean that it is sensible to do so. Since these tests were designed for norm-referenced interpretation, they have built-in characteristics that are likely to make criterion-referenced interpretations inadequate. However, if such criterion-referenced inter-pretations are attempted, the following cautions should be borne in mind:

1. Standardized achievement tests typically contain a conglomerate of learning tasks with relatively few items representing each specific type of task. This, of course, makes it difficult to obtain dependable descrip-tions of the tasks a pupil can and cannot perform.
2. The aim in constructing these norm-referenced tests is to prepare items near the 50 per cent level of difficulty so that maximum discrimination among individuals is obtained. Since the easy items are omitted from the test during test construction, descriptions of the tasks a pupil can per-form will be incomplete. This effect is especially pronounced for low achievers since most of the tasks that they are able to perform have been eliminated from the test.
3. Most standardized tests use selection-type items only. Thus, the de-scriptions of test performance are distorted to an unknown degree by the fact that some correct answers may be due to guessing. This dis-tortion is, of course, especially serious where just a few items are used to measure each particular learning task.

Thus, although standardized achievement tests may serve their intended function well (i.e., provide a dependable ranking of pupils), they typically do not provide a satisfactory basis for describing the specific learning tasks that pupils can and cannot perform. In the future, standardized achieve-ment tests may, of course, be modified in ways that provide more depend-able criterion-referenced interpretations of the results.

Expectancy Tables. The use of expectancy tables, as described and illus-trated in Chapter 4, also falls within the province of criterion-referenced interpretation. The expectancy table makes it possible to interpret raw scores in terms of expected performance on some measure other than the test itself. As illustrated in Chapter 4, for example, the scores on an aptitude test can be used to predict the probability of earning a particular letter grade (A, B, C, D, E) in a course. Similarly, expectancy tables can be used to predict the probability of success in a training program, on a job, or in any other situation of interest. The use of an expectancy table makes it possible to interpret a raw score in a simple and direct manner, without the aid of test norms.

Norm-Referenced Interpretation

Norm-referenced test interpretation tells us how an individual compares to other persons who have taken the same test. The simplest type of com-parison is to rank the scores from highest to lowest and to note where an individual's score falls in the set of ranked scores. This procedure is commonly used in reporting the results of an informal classroom test. Noting whether a particular score is third from the top, about average, or one of the lowest scores in class, provides a meaningful report to teacher and pupil alike. If a pupil's test score is third from the top in a classroom group of thirty pupils, it is a high score whether it represents 90 per cent of the items correct or 60 per cent correct. The fact that a test is relatively easy or difficult for the pupils does not alter our interpretation of test scores in terms of *relative* performance. All that is required is a sufficient spread of test scores to provide a reliable ranking.

Derived Scores. While the simple ranking of raw scores may be useful for reporting the results of a classroom test, such ranking is of limited value beyond the immediate situation because the meaning of a given rank depends on the number of group members. To obtain a more general framework for norm-referenced interpretation, raw scores are typically converted into some type of derived score. A *derived score is a numerical report of test performance on a score scale that has well-defined characteristics and yields normative meaning.* The most common types of derived scores are grade equivalents, age equivalents, percentile ranks, and standard scores. The first two describe test performance in terms of the grade or age group in which an individual's raw score is just average. The last two indicate an individual's relative standing in some particular group (See Table 15.1). Converting raw scores to derived scores is simple with standardized tests. All we need to do is consult the table of norms in the test manual and select the derived score that corresponds to the individual's raw score. Some derived scores are so easily computed that we can also develop local norms, if desired.

Norms. Tables of norms in test manuals merely present scores earned by pupils in clearly defined reference groups. The raw scores and derived scores are presented in parallel columns so that the conversion to derived scores is easily made. These scores do not represent especially good or desirable performance, but rather "normal" or "typical" performance. They were obtained at the time the test was standardized by administering the test to representative groups of pupils for whom the test was constructed. Thus, they indicate the typical performance of pupils in these standardization groups and nothing more. They should not be viewed as standards, or goals, to be achieved by other pupils.

Test norms enable us to answer questions such as the following:

1. How does a pupil's test performance compare with that of other pupils with whom we wish to compare him?
2. How does a pupil's performance on one test (or subtest) compare with his performance on another test (or subtest)?
3. How does a pupil's performance on one form of a test compare with his performance on another form of the test, administered at an earlier date?

These comparisons of test scores make it possible to *predict* a pupil's probable success in various areas, to *diagnose* his strengths and weaknesses, to measure his educational *growth,* and to use the test results for various other instructional and guidance purposes. Such functions of test scores would be severely curtailed without the use of the derived scores provided by test norms.

A summary of the most common types of test norms[1] is presented in Table 15.1. To interpret and use test results effectively, we need a good grasp of the characteristics, advantages, and limitations of each of these types of norms. Therefore each is described in considerable detail in the following pages.

TABLE 15.1
MOST COMMON TYPES OF TEST NORMS

Type of Test Norm	Name of Derived Score	Meaning in Terms of Test Performance
Grade norms	Grade equivalents	Grade group in which pupil's raw score is average.
Age norms	Age equivalents	Age group in which pupil's raw score is average.
Percentile norms	Percentile ranks (or percentile scores)	Percentage of pupils in the reference group who fall below pupil's raw score.
Standard score norms	Standard scores	Distance of pupil's raw score above or below the mean of the reference group in terms of standard deviation units.

GRADE NORMS

Grade norms have been widely used with standardized achievement tests, especially at the elementary school level. They are based on the average scores earned by pupils in each of a series of grades and are interpreted in terms of grade equivalents. For example, if pupils in the standardization group who are beginning the fifth grade earn an average raw score of 24, this score is assigned a grade equivalent of 5.0. Tables of grade norms are made up of such pairs of raw scores and their corresponding grade equivalents.

Grade equivalents are expressed in two numbers; the first indicates the year and the second the month. Grade equivalents for the fifth grade, for example, range from 5.0 to 5.9. This division of the calendar year into tenths assumes little or no change in test performance during the summer

[1] R. L. Thorndike and E. Hagen, *Measurement and Evaluation in Psychology and Education,* 3rd ed. (New York: John Wiley & Sons, 1969).

vacation months. To convert to grade equivalents with a table of grade norms, all one needs to do is locate in the table the pupils' raw scores and read off the corresponding grade equivalents.

It should be especially noted that grade equivalents indicate the *average performance* of pupils at various grade levels. For any particular grade equivalent, 50 per cent of the pupils in the standardization group are above this norm and 50 per cent are below. Consequently, we should not interpret a particular grade norm as something all of our pupils should attain. If half of our pupils are above norm and half are below, we may conclude that our pupils compare favorably with the pupils in the norm group. Whether this is good or bad depends on a number of factors, such as the ability of our pupils, the extent to which the learning outcomes measured by the test reflect our curriculum emphasis, and the quality of the educational facilities at our disposal. If we are teaching pupils with above-average ability under conditions comparable to those of schools in the norm group, merely matching the norm would be cause for concern. On the other hand, if our pupils or educational facilities are inferior to those in the norm group, reaching the norm might call forth considerable pride. In any case, it is well to remember that the norm is merely an average score made by pupils in the standardization group. As such, it represents the typical performance of average pupils in average schools and should not be considered a standard of excellence to be achieved by others.

The popularity of grade norms is largely due to the fact that test performance is expressed in units that are apparently easy to understand and interpret. To illustrate, assume that we obtained the following grade equivalents for John, who is in the *middle of the fifth grade:*

Arithmetic	5.5
Language	6.5
Reading	9.0

In examining these scores, teachers, parents, and pupils alike would recognize that John is exactly average in arithmetic, one year advanced in language, and three and a half years advanced in reading. Grade equivalents provide a common unit with which we are all familiar. The only difficulty is that this familiarity leads those who are unaware of the numerous limitations of grade norms to interpretations which are misleading or inaccurate. In fact, the limitations are so severe that over the years test specialists have made a concerted effort to have them replaced by more suitable scores.

The most serious drawback of grade norms is that the units are not equal on different parts of the scale, or from one test to another. A year of growth in arithmetic achievement from grade 4.0 to 5.0, for example, might represent a much greater improvement than an increase from grade 2.0 to 3.0 or grade 8.0 to 9.0. Thus, being advanced or retarded in terms of grade units has a different meaning on different parts of the grade scale.

A pupil who earns a grade equivalent several grades above his grade placement might be demonstrating vastly superior achievement, or performance just slightly above average.

One reason that grade norms provide unequal units is that growth in school subjects is uneven. At grade levels where educational growth is rapid, grade units indicate large differences in achievement, and where growth slows down grade units correspond to very small differences. This disparity is further complicated by the fact that patterns of growth vary from subject to subject so that our grade units stretch and contract at different points of the scale for different subjects. In general, grade equivalents provide units which are *most* comparable when used at the elementary level in those areas receiving relatively consistent instructional emphasis— arithmetic, language skills, and reading.

A further limitation of grade norms is that high and low grade equivalents have dubious meaning. Raw scores corresponding to grade equivalents below grade 3 and above grade 9 are usually estimated (by extrapolation) rather than determined by measurement. This results in artificial units which do not correspond to the achievement of pupils in any particular group. Estimating these grade equivalents is frequently necessary because the younger pupils do not have the needed skills to take the test and because growth in the basic skills tends to level off in the eighth and ninth grades. In interpreting grade equivalents at the extremes, therefore, it is well to keep in mind that they do not represent the actual performance of pupils at these levels.

The lack of equal units and the questionable value of extreme scores are especially troublesome when comparing a pupil's relative performance in different subjects. This can be illustrated with the test data presented in Table 15.2. These are actual distributions of test scores based on an achievement battery administered to a classroom group of thirty beginning sixth graders. First, note that the reading scores range from a grade equivalent of 3.0 to 10.4, and that the language and arithmetic scores cover a much more restricted range of grade equivalents. This is a typical finding with achievement batteries which measure the basic skills. Now look at the *circled number* near the top of each distribution of scores. This marks the grade equivalent earned by Walt Smith on each of the tests. Note that he is at or near the top of each distribution. His grade equivalent scores and the percentage of the group which obtained scores lower than his are shown in the following summary. In each case the center of the class interval was taken to represent his grade equivalent score.

	Walt Smith's Grade Equivalents	Percentage Below Walt Smith's Grade Equivalents
Reading	10.2	97
Language	8.2	95
Arithmetic	7.2	97

TABLE 15.2

DISTRIBUTION OF GRADE EQUIVALENTS IN READING, ARITHMETIC,
AND LANGUAGE FOR THIRTY SIXTH-GRADE PUPILS

Grade Equivalents	Frequencies		
	Reading	Language	Arithmetic
10.0–10.4	(1°)		
9.5–9.9	2		
9.0–9.4			
8.5–8.9	1	1	
8.0–8.4	2	(1)	
7.5–7.9	3	1	
7.0–7.4	2	5	(1)
6.5–6.9	1	6	9
6.0–6.4	7	7	7
5.5–5.9	2	6	5
5.0–5.4	3	2	3
4.5–4.9	2		4
4.0–4.4	2	1	1
3.5–3.9			
3.0–3.4	2		

° Circled numbers indicate the grade equivalent earned by Walt Smith.

If you inspect Walt Smith's grade equivalents *only,* it is hard to resist the conclusion that he is far more advanced in reading than he is in arithmetic. After all, he is only one year above his grade level in arithmetic, but four years advanced in reading. These differences are quite impressive. They are also misleading, however, since they are largely due to the inequality of grade units from one test to another. When Walt Smith's performance on the tests is compared in terms of the percentage of the group falling below him (percentile rank), it is apparent that his performance is identical on these two tests. In other words, when compared to a group of sixth-grade pupils, he holds the same relative position in arithmetic and reading. Although test scores based on thirty pupils do not represent very impressive evidence, these scores are typical of those obtained from larger samples of pupils. The range of grade equivalent scores characteristically varies from one type of test to another, resulting in unequal units and distorted comparisons between tests.

Another common misinterpretation of grade norms, although not due to weaknesses in the scoring system itself, is to assume that if a pupil earns a certain grade equivalent score in a subject he is ready to do work at that level. For example, we might conclude that a fourth-grade pupil should be doing sixth-grade work in language skills if he earns a grade equivalent of 6.0 on a language skills test. This assumption overlooks the fact that he can obtain a grade equivalent score well above his grade level by doing the less difficult test items more rapidly and accurately than the average fourth-grade pupil. The grade equivalent score of 6.0 may represent nothing more than a thorough mastery of language skills taught in the first four grades. Thus, grade equivalents should never be interpreted literally. At best, they are only rough guides to level of test performance. Pupils at different grade levels who earn the same grade equivalent score are apt to be ready for quite different types of instruction.

In summary, grade norms are based on the average performance of pupils at various grade levels. They are widely used at the elementary school level, largely because of the *apparent* ease with which they can be interpreted. Grade equivalents scores are based on units which are typically unequal. This can lead to misinterpretations and tends to limit the usefulness of the test results. In general, grade norms are most useful for reporting growth in the basic skills during the elementary school period. They are least useful for comparing a pupil's performances on different tests. For whatever purpose grade norms are used, however, inequality of grade units must be considered during interpretation of the results.

AGE NORMS

Age norms are based on the average scores earned by pupils at different ages and are interpreted in terms of age equivalents. Thus, if pupils who are ten years and two months of age earn an average raw score of 24, this score is assigned an age equivalent of 10–2. Tables of age norms in test manuals present parallel columns of such raw scores and their corresponding age equivalents.

Age norms have essentially the same characteristics and limitations as grade norms. The major differences are that (1) test performance is expressed in terms of age level rather than grade level, and (2) age equivalents divide the calendar year into twelve parts rather than ten. Age equivalents for ten-year-olds, for example, range from 10–0 to 10–11.

The use of age norms is probably most common with reading tests (reading age) and mental ability tests (mental age), although they can be used in any achievement area (e.g., arithmetic age). Despite the variations in terminology, all age norms are interpreted in the same way. A pupil with a reading age of 12–6 and a mental age of 13–0, for example, has earned a score on the reading test equal to that of the average twelve-and-a-half-year-old and a score on the mental ability test equal to that of the average thirteen-year-old.

As with grade norms, age norms present test performance in units that are *apparently* easy to understand but which are characteristically unequal. Variations in patterns of growth at different age levels cause age units to lack uniform meaning. They are likely to be most meaningful at the elementary school level where growth in abilities tends to be continuous and somewhat regular. Their interpretation is especially hazardous at the high school level where growth in many abilities tends to level off.

Literal interpretations should be as assiduously avoided with age norms as with grade norms. An eight-year-old child with a mental age of 10–0 has superior mental ability but he is not necessarily ready to cope with the same mental tasks as the average ten-year-old child. His performance might be largely due to rapid and accurate work on the more simple items and exceptional success on the number problems, or it might reflect some other combination of work skills and special ability. The mental age of 10–0 merely tells us that his raw score is equal to the raw score of the average ten-year-old child. It does not tell us what combination of factors went into earning that score.

In summary, age norms are based on the average performance of pupils at various age levels. Age units are characteristically unequal and especially subject to misinterpretation at the high school level. Age norms are most appropriate at the elementary school level and in such areas as mental ability and reading ability, where growth patterns tend to be fairly consistent. As with grade norms, age norms should never be interpreted literally.

The Future of Grade and Age Norms

Because of the possibility of misinterpreting grade and age equivalents, there has been considerable sentiment toward replacing them with more meaningful scores. Here are some typical comments:

> This is as good a place as any to mention—and condemn—a popular but archaic conversion known as "age equivalents" and "grade equivalents." . . . In the writer's opinion, grade conversions should never be used in reporting on a pupil or a class, or in research. Standard scores or percentiles or raw scores serve better. Age conversions are also likely to be misinterpreted. . . . On the whole, however, age equivalents cause less trouble than grade equivalents, if only because the former are not used for policy decisions in education.[2]

> Interpretive scores that lend themselves to gross misinterpretation, such as mental age or grade equivalent scores, should be abandoned or their use discouraged. Very desirable.[3]

Although grade and age equivalents are losing the popularity they once had, they are still widely used in the schools. This is probably partly because of tradition and partly because they provide for a measure of growth

---

[2] L. J. Cronbach, *Essentials of Psychological Testing*, 3rd ed. (New York: Harper and Row, 1970).

[3] American Psychological Association, *Standards for Educational and Psychological Tests*. (Washington, D.C.: APA, 1974).

from one year to the next. Such growth cannot be shown by percentile ranks or the typical standard score since these scores indicate a pupil's relative position in his own grade or age group. If a pupil makes normal progress from year to year, he will tend to maintain the same relative position in the group and thus be assigned the same percentile rank or standard score.

To meet the need for a measure of growth, some test publishers are providing systems of scaled scores. These are a type of standard score that provides a single continuous scale over all grade levels. Scaled scores, like grade and age equivalents, can be used to show educational growth, but they have the advantage of providing approximately equal units throughout the scale. As scaled scores become more widely used and understood, grade and age equivalents are likely to decline in use.

The Use of Quotients

Until recently, quotients were widely used with age equivalents to indicate *rate* of development. The best known of these is the ratio *intelligence quotient* (IQ) which is determined by dividing mental age by chronological age and multiplying by 100. Another is the *educational quotient* (EQ) which uses a similar formula but substitutes a subject age or general achievement age for mental age. Still another is the *accomplishment quotient* (AQ), determined by dividing an educational age by mental age and multiplying by 100. Although some of these are still in use, they are rapidly being discarded and are generally not recommended. The major shortcomings of such quotients are that they assume an equality of age units and a continuity of growth which simply do not exist.

The old *ratio* IQ is being replaced by a *deviation* IQ. This is not a quotient based on the relationship between mental age and chronological age, but a type of standard score. It is obtained directly from tables of norms in test manuals and interpreted like any other standard score. Its properties will be considered in more detail later in this chapter, when standard scores are considered. For now, the significant thing to note is that the *ratio* IQ and the educational quotients patterned after it are obsolete and soon will disappear from the educational scene.

PERCENTILE NORMS

One of the most widely used and easily comprehended methods of describing test performance is that of percentile rank. A percentile rank (or percentile score) indicates a pupil's relative position in a group in terms of the percentage of pupils scoring *below* him. Thus, if we consult a table of norms and find that a pupil's raw score of 39 equals a percentile rank of 75, we know that 75 per cent of the pupils in the reference group obtained a raw score lower than 39. Stating it another way, this pupil's performance surpasses that of 75 per cent of the group.[4]

One method of presenting percentile norms is shown in Table 15.3. These norms are for the *Academic Promise Tests*. The raw scores for each subtest, and for combined subtests, are listed in columns across the table. The procedure for obtaining the percentile rank for any given raw score is to locate the score in the proper column and then to read the corre-

TABLE 15.3

PERCENTILE NORMS FOR ACADEMIC PROMISE TESTS[*]

ACADEMIC PROMISE TESTS—NORMS

FORMS A OR B—BOYS AND GIRLS

	Raw Scores							GRADE
N = 8140	*Abstract Reason-*	*Numeri-*		*Language*			*APT*	**6**
Percentile	*ing*	*cal*	*Verbal*	*Usage*	*AR + N*	*V + LU*	*Total*	**Percentile**
99	49+	40+	45+	48+	86+	89+	168+	99
97	47–48	37–39	42–44	45–47	80–85	82–88	156–167	97
95	45–46	33–36	39–41	40–44	74–79	76–81	144–155	95
90	42–44	30–32	36–38	36–39	68–73	70–75	134–143	90
85	39–41	28–29	34–35	33–35	63–67	66–69	125–133	85
80	36–38	26–27	32–33	31–32	59–62	62–65	117–124	80
75	33–35	24–25	31	29–30	55–58	59–61	111–116	75
70	30–32	23	30	27–28	51–54	56–58	105–110	70
65	27–29	22	28–29	26	47–50	54–55	100–104	65
60	24–26	21	26–27	25	44–46	51–53	95–99	60
55	22–23	20	25	24	42–43	48–50	91–94	55
50	21	19	24	22–23	40–41	46–47	87–90	50
45	20	18	23	20–21	38–39	44–45	83–86	45
40	19	17	22	19	36–37	42–43	80–82	40
35	18	16	21	18	35	40–41	76–79	35
30	17	15	20	17	34	38–39	73–75	30
25	16	14	19	16	32–33	36–37	69–72	25
20	15	13	17–18	15	30–31	33–35	65–68	20
15	14	12	15–16	14	28–29	30–32	61–64	15
10	13	11	13–14	12–13	26–27	27–29	56–60	10
5	12	9–10	11–12	10–11	23–25	23–26	50–55	5
3	10–11	7–8	8–10	8–9	21–22	20–22	44–49	3
1	0–9	0–6	0–7	0–7	0–20	0–19	0–43	1
Mean	25.0	20.1	25.1	23.5	45.1	48.6	93.7	**Mean**
SD	11.3	7.8	8.7	9.7	16.7	17.0	30.9	**SD**

---

[4] Percentile rank is sometimes interpreted as the percentage of individuals receiving scores *equal to or lower than* a given score. The specific interpretation depends on the method of computation used, but for all practical purposes the meaning is essentially the same.

sponding percentile rank at the side of the table. For example, a raw score of 37 on the Abstract Reasoning test is equivalent to a percentile rank of 80, and a raw score of 19 on the Numerical test is equivalent to a percentile rank of 50. Only selected percentile ranks are given in the norm table, and it is suggested that these be considered as midpoints of a band of values. Thus, a percentile rank of 80 is interpreted as a percentile band ranging from 78 to 82. This is to allow for error in the measurement.

A distinctive feature of percentile norms is that we can interpret a pupil's performance in terms of any group in which he is a member, or desires to become a member. Most commonly, performance is reported in terms of the pupil's relative standing in his own grade or age group. In some instances, however, we are more interested in how a pupil compares to those who have completed second-year French, are majoring in home economics, or are enrolled in the college-preparatory program. Such comparisons are possible with percentile norms. The interpretations we can give to a particular score are only limited by the types of decisions we desire to make and the availability of the appropriate sets of norms.

The wide applicability of percentile norms is not without its drawbacks. When interpreting a percentile rank, we must always refer to the norm group on which it is based. A pupil does not have a percentile rank of 86. He has a percentile rank of 86 *in some particular group.* A raw score on a scholastic aptitude test, for example, may be equivalent to a percentile rank of 86 in a general group of high school seniors, 63 in a group of college-bound seniors, and 25 in a group of college freshmen in a highly selective college. Relative standing varies with the ability of the reference group used for comparison.

A related inconvenience with percentile norms is that numerous sets of norms are usually required. We need a set of norms for each group to which we wish to compare a pupil. This is not especially troublesome at the elementary school level where a pupil's own grade- and age-mates provide a suitable basis for comparison. At the high school level, however, where the curriculum becomes diversified and pupils pursue different courses, it becomes a rather acute problem. Here we need sets of norms for pupils who have completed varying numbers of courses in each subject area. For guidance purposes, we should also like norms based on the various educational and vocational groups in which our pupils plan to seek admission. The difficulty of producing such a diverse collection of norms for any particular test is quite obvious. Test publishers usually make available norms within grades and within courses, but norms for special purposes frequently must be developed locally.

The major limitation of percentile norms is that percentile units are not equal on all parts of the scale. A percentile difference of ten near the middle of the scale (e.g., 45 to 55) represents a much smaller difference in test performance than the same percentile difference at the ends (e.g., 85 to 95). This is so because a large number of pupils tend to obtain scores near the middle, while relatively few pupils have extremely high or low scores. Thus, a pupil whose raw score is near average can surpass another 10 per cent of the group by increasing his raw score just a few points. On the other hand, a pupil with a relatively high score will need to increase his raw score by a large number of points to surpass another 10 per cent, simply because there are so few pupils at that level.

The inequality of units requires special caution when using percentile ranks. First, a difference of several percentile points should be given greater weight at the extremes of the distribution than near the middle. In fact, small differences near the middle of the distribution generally can be disregarded. Second, percentile ranks should not be averaged arithmetically. The appropriate average when using percentile norms is the 50th percentile. This is the midpoint of the distribution and is called the *median*, or counting average.

In summary, percentile norms are widely applicable, easily determined, and readily understood. A percentile rank describes a pupil's performance in terms of the percentage of pupils he surpasses in some clearly defined group. This might be his own grade or age group, or any group in which he desires to become a member (e.g., college freshmen). More than one set of norms is usually required and percentile ranks must be interpreted in terms of the specific norm group on which they are based. The most severe limitation of percentile ranks is that the units are unequal. This can be offset somewhat by careful interpretation, however, since the inequality of units follows a predictable pattern.

STANDARD SCORE NORMS

Another method of indicating a pupil's relative position in a group is by showing how far his raw score is above or below average. This is the approach used with standard scores. Basically, standard scores express test performance in terms of standard deviation units from the mean. The *mean* (M) is the arithmetical average, which is determined by adding all scores and dividing by the number of scores. The *standard deviation* (SD) is a measure of the spread of scores in a group. Since the method of computing the standard deviation is not especially helpful in understanding it, the procedure will not be presented here (see Appendix A for computation). The meaning of standard deviation, and the standard scores based on this unit, can best be explained in terms of the normal probability curve (also called the normal distribution curve or simply the normal curve).

The Normal Curve and the Standard Deviation Unit

The normal curve is a symmetrical bell-shaped curve which has many useful mathematical properties. One of the most useful from the viewpoint of test interpretation is that when it is divided into standard deviation units each portion under the curve contains a fixed percentage of cases. This is shown in the idealized normal curve presented in Figure 15.1 (for the moment, disregard the raw scores beneath the figure). Note that 34 per cent of the cases fall between the mean and +1 SD, 14 per cent between +1 SD and +2 SD, and 2 per cent between +2 SD, and +3 SD. The same proportions, of course, apply to the standard deviation intervals below the mean. Only 0.13 per cent of the cases fall below −3 SD or above +3 SD. Thus, for all practical purposes a normal distribution of scores falls between −3 and +3 standard deviations from the mean.

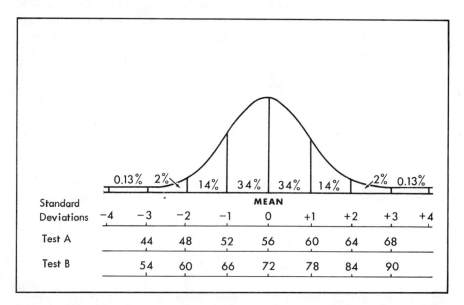

FIGURE 15.1. Normal curve, indicating the approximate percentage of cases falling within each standard deviation interval.

To illustrate the value of standard deviation units for expressing relative position in a group, raw scores from two different tests have been placed beneath the row of deviations along the baseline of the curve in Figure 15.1. The tests have the following means and standard deviations:

	Test A	Test B
M	56	72
SD	4	6

Note in Figure 15.1 that the mean raw scores of both tests have been placed at the zero point on the baseline of the curve. Thus, they have been arbitrarily equated to zero. Next, note that +1 SD is equivalent to 60 (56 + 4) on *Test A* and 78 (72 + 6) on *Test B*; and that −1 SD is equivalent to 52 (56 − 4) on *Test A* and 66 (72 − 6) on *Test B*. If we convert all of the raw scores on the two tests to the standard deviation units in this manner, it is possible to compare directly performance on the tests. For example, a raw score of 62 on *Test A* and 81 on *Test B* are equal because both are +1.5 standard deviation units above the mean. When this conversion to standard deviation units has been made, the raw scores are, of course, no longer needed. A +2.5 *SD* on *Test A* is superior to a +2.0 *SD* on *Test B*, regardless of the size of the raw scores from which they were derived. The only restriction for such comparisons is that the conversion to standard deviation units must be based on a common group.

As can be gleaned from this discussion, the utility of the standard deviation is that it permits us to convert raw scores to a common scale which has equal units and which can be readily interpreted in terms of the normal curve. At this point, it should be helpful to review a few of the characteristics of the normal curve which makes it so useful in test interpretation.

Referring to Figure 15.1 again, note that 68 per cent (approximately two thirds) of the cases fall between −1 and +1 standards deviations from the mean. This provides a handy bench mark for interpreting standard scores and the standard error of measurement, since both are based on standard deviation units. Note also that the fixed percentages in each interval make it possible to convert standard deviation units to percentile ranks. For example, −2 *SD* equals a percentile rank of 2, since 2 per cent of the cases fall below that point. Starting from the left of the figure, it can be seen that each point on the base line of the curve can be equated to the following percentile ranks:

$$-2\,SD \;=\; 2\%$$
$$-1\,SD \;=\; 16\% \;(\; 2 + 14\,)$$
$$0\,(M) = 50\% \;(16 + 34\,)$$
$$+\,1\,SD = 84\% \;(50 + 34\,)$$
$$+2\,SD \;= 98\% \;(84 + 14\,)$$

This relationship between standard deviation units and percentile ranks enables us to interpret standard scores in simple and familiar terms. When used for this purpose, we must, of course, be able to assume a normal distribution. This is not a serious restriction in using standard score norms, however, since the distribution of scores on which they are based usually closely approximates the normal curve. In many instances the standard scores are *normalized*, that is, the distribution of scores is made normal by the process of computing percentiles and converting directly to their standard score equivalents. While it is generally safe to assume a normal distribution when using standard scores from tables of norms in test manuals, it is usually unwise to make such an assumption for standard scores computed directly from a relatively small number of cases, such as a classroom group.

Types of Standard Scores

There are numerous types of standard scores used in testing. Since they are all based on the same principle and interpreted in somewhat the same manner, only the most common types will be discussed here.

z-Score. The simplest of the standard scores, and the one on which others are based, is the z-score. This score expresses test performance simply and directly in terms of the number of standard deviation units a raw score is above or below the mean. In the previous section, we discussed z-scores but did not identify them as such. The formula for computing z-scores is

$$z\text{-score} = \frac{X - M}{SD}$$

where

$$X = \text{any raw score}$$
$$M = \text{arithmetic mean of raw scores}$$
$$SD = \text{standard deviation of raw scores}$$

You can quickly become familiar with this formula by applying it to various raw scores in *Test A* or *Test B* of Figure 15.1, and then visually checking your answer along the base line of the curve. For example, z-scores for the raw scores of 58 and 50 on *Test A* ($M = 56$, $SD = 4$) would be computed as follows:

$$z = \frac{58 - 56}{4} = .5 \qquad z = \frac{50 - 56}{4} = -1.5$$

It should be noted that a z-score is always minus when the raw score is smaller than the mean. Forgetting the minus sign can cause serious errors in test interpretation. It is for this reason that z-scores are seldom used directly in test norms. They are usually transformed into a standard score system which uses only positive numbers.

T-Score. The term *T-score* was originally applied to a specific type of normalized score based on a group of unselected twelve-year-old children. In recent years, however, it has come to refer to any set of normally distributed standard scores which has a mean of 50 and a standard deviation of 10. T-scores (*linear* conversion) can be obtained by multiplying the z-score by 10 and adding the product to 50. Thus,

$$T\text{-score} = 50 + 10\,(z)$$

This formula will provide T-scores only when the original distribution of raw scores is normal, because with this type of conversion (linear) the distribution of standard scores retains the same shape as the original raw score distribution.[5] Applying this formula to the two z-scores computed earlier ($z = .5$, $z = -1.5$), we would obtain the following results:

$$T = 50 + 10\,(.5) = 55 \qquad T = 50 + 10\,(-1.5) = 35$$

Since T-scores always have a mean of 50 and a standard deviation of 10, any single T-score is directly interpretable. A T-score of 55, for example, always indicates one-half standard deviation above the mean, and so on. Once the concept of T-scores is grasped, interpretation is relatively simple.

Normalized T-scores are obtained by (1) converting the distribution of raw scores into percentile ranks, (2) looking up the z-score each percentile rank would have in a normal distribution and assigning these z-scores to the corresponding raw scores, and (3) converting the z-scores to T-scores, using the formula presented earlier. The procedure of going from raw score to percentile to the corresponding z-score in a normal distribution is called an *area* conversion, and provides normalized z-scores that are then transformed directly into normalized T-scores. This process results in a normally distributed set of standard scores, regardless of the shape of the original distribution of raw scores. Normalizing is used by test publishers to remove minor irregularities in the raw score distributions.

Many other normalized standard scores are computed in the same way that normalized T-scores are determined, but different values are used for the mean and standard deviation. For example, standard scores with a mean of 500 and a standard deviation of 100 are used with the tests of the College Entrance Examination Board. Consequently, on these tests a score of 550 means one-half standard deviation above the mean in the same manner as a T-score of 55. Standard scores can be assigned any arbitrarily selected mean and standard deviation and the interpretation is the same, since the basic frame of reference is the standard deviation unit.

Deviation IQ. Another widely used standard score is the deviation IQ. Here the mean is set at 100 and the standard deviation at 16 (15 on some tests). Thus, a pupil with an IQ of 84 has scored one standard deviation below the mean (T-score $= 40$), and a pupil with an IQ of 116 has scored one standard deviation above the mean (T-score $= 60$). Scores on intelligence tests could just as easily be expressed in terms of standard scores with a mean of 50 and a standard deviation of 10. However, the IQ concept is so deeply inbedded in our culture that a mean and standard deviation were selected which closely approximate the distribution of scores obtained with the old ratio IQ.

Expressing IQs in terms of standard scores gives them the advantage, over ratio IQs, of equal units and a common meaning at all age levels. They can also be readily converted to percentile ranks and to other types of standard scores, as we shall see shortly.

---

[5] Some persons call any set of scores derived from this formula *T-scores*, whereas others call them *linear T-scores* or *Z-scores*, to distinguish them from *normalized T-scores*.

Stanines. Some test norms are expressed in terms of single-digit standard scores called stanines (pronounced *stay-nines*). This system of scores receives its name from the fact that the distribution of raw scores is divided into nine parts (*standard nines*). Stanine 5 is located precisely in the center of the distribution and includes all cases within one fourth of a standard deviation on either side of the mean. The remaining stanines are evenly distributed above and below stanine 5. Each stanine, with the exception of 1 and 9 which cover the tails of the distribution, includes a band of raw scores the width of one half of a standard deviation unit. Thus, for all practical purposes, stanines present test norms on a 9-point scale of equal units. These standard scores have a mean of 5 and a standard deviation of 2. The distribution of stanines in relation to the normal curve and the per cent of cases in each stanine are shown in Figure 15.2.

Comparison of Score Systems

The equivalence of scores in various standard score systems and their relation to percentiles and to the normal curve is presented in Figure 15.2. This figure illustrates the interrelated nature of the various scales for reporting relative position in a normally distributed group. A raw score one standard deviation below the mean, for example, can be expressed as a

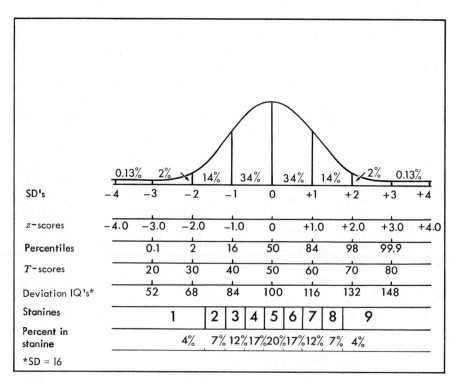

FIGURE 15.2. Corresponding standard scores and percentiles in a normal distribution.

z-score of -1.0, a percentile rank of 16, a T-score of 40, a deviation IQ of 84, or a stanine of 3. Thus, the various scoring systems are merely different ways of saying the same thing, and we can readily convert back and forth from one scale to another (providing, of course, that we can assume a normal distribution and comparable norm groups).

The relations among the scoring system shown in Figure 15.2 are especially helpful in learning to understand a particular standard score scale. Until we fully understand T-scores, for example, it is helpful to convert them, mentally, into percentile ranks. A T-score of 60 becomes meaningful when we note that it is equivalent to a percentile rank of 84. This conversion to percentile ranks, which are more easily understood, is also useful for interpreting standard scores to parents and pupils. Still another value of knowing the relations among the scales is in comparing a pupil's performance on tests using different scoring systems. An IQ of 110 can be compared to a percentile rank of 16 (or a T-score of 40) on an achievement test, for example, in order to determine the *degree of under-achievement*. It should be noted that this type of comparison assumes that the norms for the different tests are comparable.

In summary, standard scores indicate a pupil's relative position in a group in terms of standard deviation units above or below the mean. In a normal distribution, the various standard score scales and the percentile scale are interrelated, making it possible to convert from one to another. Standard scores have the special advantage of providing equal units. Thus, unlike percentiles, ten standard score points represents the same difference in test performance anywhere along the scale. In addition, standard scores can be averaged arithmetically. One drawback of standard scores is that they are not readily understood by pupils and parents. A more serious limitation is that interpretation is difficult unless the scores are normally distributed. This is not a problem in using standard score norms, however, since norm tables are generally based on normalized standard scores.

PROFILES

One of the major advantages of converting raw scores to derived scores is that a pupil's performance on different tests can be compared directly. This is usually done by means of a test profile, like the one presented in Figure 15.3. Such a graphic representation of test data makes it easy to identify a pupil's relative strengths and weaknesses. Most standardized tests have provisions for plotting test profiles.

The student profile shown in Figure 15.3 illustrates a desirable trend in profile construction. Instead of plotting test scores as specific points on the scale, test performance is recorded in the form of bands which extend one standard error of measurement above and below the pupil's obtained scores. It will be recalled from our discussion of reliability, that there are approximately two chances out of three that a pupil's true score falls within

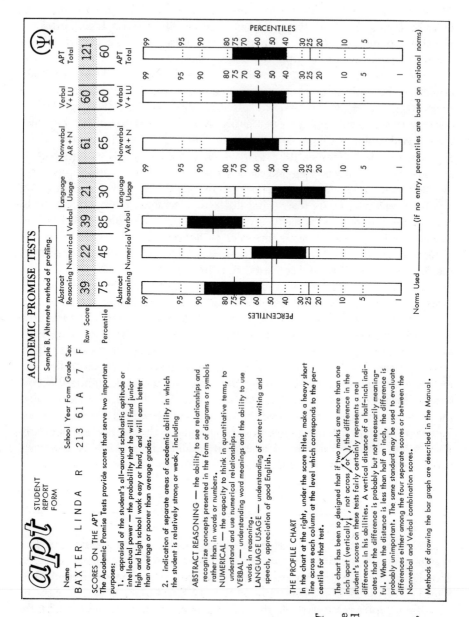

FIGURE 15.3. *APT* Student Profile, showing use of score bands. (Reproduced by permission. Copyright © 1959, 1960, 1961, The Psychological Corporation, New York, N.Y. All rights reserved.)

one standard error of his obtained score. Thus, these bands indicate the ranges of scores within which we can be reasonably certain of finding the pupil's true standings. Plotting them on the profile enables us to take into account the inaccuracy of the test scores when comparing performance on different tests. Interpreting differences between tests is simple with these score bands. If the bands for two tests overlap, we can assume that performance on the two tests does not differ significantly. If the bands do *not* overlap, we can assume that there is probably a real difference in performance.

The score bands used with the *Differential Aptitude Tests* and the *Academic Promise Tests,* are plotted by drawing a short cross line for the percentile score and then making a band which extends one-half inch above and one-half inch below that score. Thus, the profile chart is designed so that one inch between scores is significant (see Figure 15.3).

The individual profile chart for the *Metropolitan Achievement Tests* is arranged in such a manner that the score bands can be expressed in terms of stanines. As shown in Figure 15.4 each score is plotted as a band two stanines wide. The plotting is simply a matter of making a dot to represent the stanine score and then drawing a line one stanine distance long to the right and to the left of the dot.

All test publishers do not make provisions for plotting score bands, but we can expect more of them to follow this practice in the future. There is no need to wait for special provisions, however. It is possible to plot these bands for any test for which we have a standard error of measurement. All we need to do is determine the error band in raw score points and refer to the norm table with these figures. For example, if a pupil has earned a raw score of 74 and the standard error of measurement is 3, his error band in raw score points ranges from 71 to 77. By locating these two numbers in the norm table we can obtain the corresponding range in percentiles, standard scores, or in whatever derived score is being used, and plot the results directly on the profile. The use of such bands minimizes the tendency of test profiles to present a misleading picture. Without the bands, we are apt to attribute significance to differences in test performance which can be accounted for by chance alone.

When using profiles to compare test performance, it is essential that the norms for all tests be comparable. Many test publishers provide for this by standardizing a battery of achievement tests and a scholastic aptitude test on the same population.

JUDGING THE ADEQUACY OF NORMS

With the tables of norms provided in test manuals, we can easily and quickly convert raw scores into derived scores. As noted earlier, these derived scores may be expressed in terms of grade equivalents, age equiva-

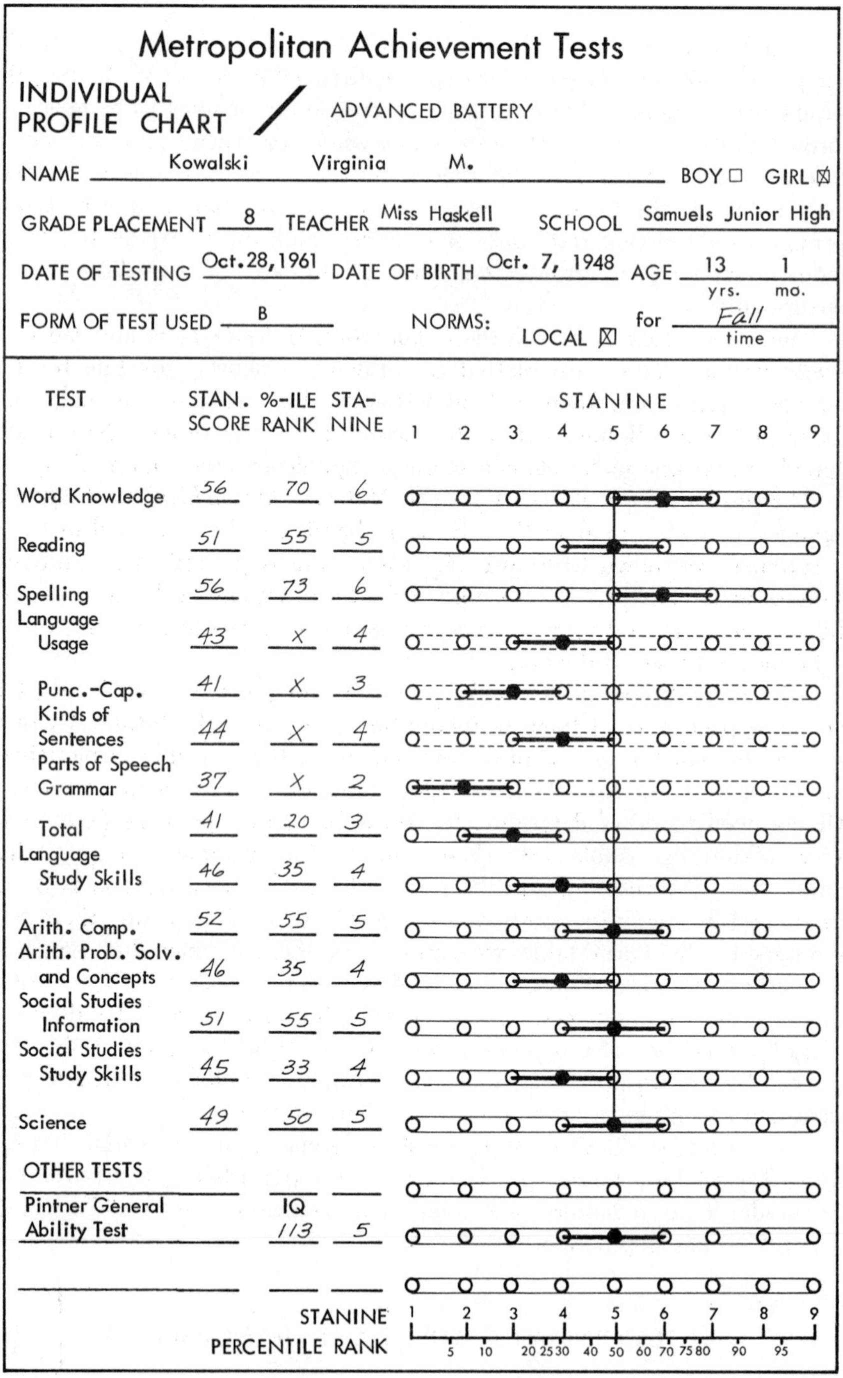

Metropolitan Achievement Tests

INDIVIDUAL PROFILE CHART / ADVANCED BATTERY

NAME ___Kowalski___ ___Virginia___ ___M.___ BOY ☐ GIRL ☒

GRADE PLACEMENT ___8___ TEACHER ___Miss Haskell___ SCHOOL ___Samuels Junior High___

DATE OF TESTING ___Oct. 28, 1961___ DATE OF BIRTH ___Oct. 7, 1948___ AGE ___13___ ___1___
                                                      yrs.   mo.

FORM OF TEST USED ___B___ NORMS: LOCAL ☒ for ___Fall___ time

TEST	STAN. SCORE	%-ILE RANK	STA-NINE
Word Knowledge	56	70	6
Reading	51	55	5
Spelling	56	73	6
Language Usage	43	X	4
Punc.-Cap.	41	X	3
Kinds of Sentences	44	X	4
Parts of Speech Grammar	37	X	2
Total	41	20	3
Language Study Skills	46	35	4
Arith. Comp.	52	55	5
Arith. Prob. Solv. and Concepts	46	35	4
Social Studies Information	51	55	5
Social Studies Study Skills	45	33	4
Science	49	50	5

OTHER TESTS

	IQ	
Pintner General Ability Test	113	5

STANINE: 1 2 3 4 5 6 7 8 9
PERCENTILE RANK: 5 10 20 25 30 40 50 60 70 75 80 90 95

FIGURE 15.4. Student profile of *Metropolitan Achievement Tests*. (From *Manual for Interpreting Metropolitan Achievement Tests*, Grades 1–9, by Walter M. Durost. Copyright 1962 by Harcourt Brace Jovanovich, Inc. All rights reserved. Reproduced by permission.)

410

lents, percentiles, or some form of standard score. Regardless of the type of derived score used, the major purpose is to make possible interpretation of pupils' test performance in terms of a clearly defined reference group. This should not be just any reference group, however, but one which provides a meaningful basis for comparison.

The adequacy of test norms is a basic consideration during test selection and a factor to be reckoned with during the interpretation of test scores. The following criteria indicate the qualities most desired in norms:

1. *Test norms should be relevant.* Test norms are based on various types of groups. Some represent a national sample of all pupils at certain grade or age levels while others are limited to samples from a given region or state. For special purposes, the norms might also be confined to a limted group such as high school pupils in independent schools, girls who have completed secretarial training in a commercial high school, or college freshmen in engineering. The variety of types of groups available for comparison makes it necessary to study the nature of the norm sample before using any table of norms. We should ask ourselves: Are these norms appropriate for the pupils being tested and for the decisions to be made with the results?

If we merely want to compare our pupils with a general reference group in order to diagnose strengths and weaknesses in different areas, national norms may be satisfactory. Here our main concern is with the extent to which our pupils are similar to those in the norm population on such characteristics as scholastic aptitude, educational experience, and cultural background. The more closely our pupils approximate those in the norm group, the greater is our certainty that the national norms provide a meaningful basis for comparison.

Where we are trying to decide such things as which pupils should be placed in an accelerated group, who should be encouraged to select the college preparatory curriculum, or whether a particular pupil should pursue a career in engineering, national norms are much less useful. For such decisions, we need norms on each of the specific groups involved. A pupil can have above average aptitude and achievement when compared with pupils in general and still fall short of the ability needed to succeed in highly select groups. Where decisions involve predictions of future success in a particular area, comparing a pupil with his potential competitors is more meaningful than comparisons with his present grade- or age-mates.

2. *Test norms should be representative.* Once we have satisfied ourselves that a set of test norms is based on a group with which comparisons are desired, it is appropriate to ask whether the norms are truly representative of that group. Ideally, we would like the norms to be based on a random sample of the population they represent. This is extremely difficult and expensive, however, so we must usually settle for something less. As a minimum, we should demand that all significant subgroups of the population be adequately represented. For national norms, it is desirable to have

a proper proportion of pupils from such subgroups as the following: boys and girls, geographic regions, rural and urban areas, socio-economic levels, racial groups, and schools of varying size. The most adequate representation in these areas is obtained when the norm sample closely approximates the population distribution reported by the United States Census Bureau.

In evaluating test norms, it is easy to be misled by the size of the norm sample. Some descriptions in test manuals place great emphasis on the large number of pupils tested, with little attention to the sampling procedure used. As noted in these comments by a leading test publisher, size of the norm sample provides an insufficient criterion for judging the adequacy of norms.[6]

> Unfortunately, many alleged general norms reported in test manuals are not backed even by an honest effort to secure representative samples of people-in-general. Even tens of hundreds of thousands of cases can fall woefully short of defining people-in-general. Inspection of test manuals will show (or would show if information about the norms were given completely) that many such massed norms are merely collections of all the scores that opportunity has permitted the author or publisher to gather easily. Lumping together all the samples secured more by chance than by plan makes for impressively large numbers; but while seeming to simplify interpretation, the norms may dim or actually distort the significance of a score.

Whether appraising national or special-group norms, we should always favor the carefully chosen, representative sample over the larger, but biased, sample based on availability of results. This requires going beyond the titles on the norm tables and making a careful study of the procedures used in obtaining the norm sample. If this information is unavailable, it is safe to conclude that the norms are probably *not* representative.

3. *Test norms should be up to date.* One factor that is commonly neglected in judging the adequacy of norms is whether they are currently applicable. With the rapid changes that are taking place in education, we can expect test norms to become out of date much sooner than they did when the curriculum was more stable and there was less emphasis on accelerated programs. These changes can be expected to have the greatest influence on achievement test norms but their effect on those of scholastic aptitude tests should not be overlooked. Note these remarks by Cronbach.[7]

> Test norms become obsolete. On general mental tests, for example, adults score higher on the average than adults did a decade ago. These changes may be attributed to an increasing level of education or other social changes.

[6] H. G. Seashore and J. H. Ricks, *Norms Must be Relevant,* Test Service Bulletin No. 39 (New York: The Psychological Corporation, 1950).

[7] L. J. Cronbach, *Essentials of Psychological Testing,* 3rd ed. (New York: Harper and Row, 1970), p. 112.

It is generally unsafe to use the copyright date on the test manual as an indication of when the norms were obtained, since this date may be changed whenever the manual is altered (no matter how slightly). The description of the procedures used in establishing norms should be consulted for the year in which the norm groups were tested. Where a test has been revised, it is also desirable to make certain that the norms are based on the new edition.

4. *Test norms should be comparable.* It is frequently necessary, or desirable, to compare directly scores from different tests. This is the case when we make profile comparisons of test results to diagnose a pupil's strengths and weaknesses, or compare aptitude and achievement test scores to detect underachievers. Such comparisons can be made precisely only if the norms for the different tests are comparable. Our best assurance of comparability is obtained when all tests have been normed on the same population. This is routinely done with the tests in an achievement battery, and some test publishers also administer a scholastic aptitude test to the same norm group. Whenever the scores from different tests are to be compared directly, the test manuals should be checked to determine whether the norms are based on the same group, or if not, whether they have been made comparable by other means.

5. *Test norms should be adequately described.* It is difficult to determine if test norms provide a meaningful basis of comparison unless we know something about the norm group and the norming procedures used. The type of information we might expect to find in a test manual includes the following: (1) method of sampling; (2) number and distribution of cases included in the norm sample; (3) characteristics of the norm group with regard to such factors as age, sex, race, scholastic aptitude, educational level, socio-economic status, types of schools represented, and geographic location; (4) extent to which standard conditions of administration and motivation were maintained during the testing; and (5) date of the testing, including whether it was done in the fall or the spring. Other things being equal, we should always favor the test for which we have detailed descriptions of these and other relevant factors. Such information is needed if we are to judge the appropriateness of test norms for our particular purposes.

THE USE OF LOCAL NORMS

For many purposes, local norms are more useful than the norms provided in test manuals. If our pupils deviate markedly from those in the published norms on such characteristics as scholastic aptitude, educational experience, or cultural background, for example, comparison to a local group may be more meaningful. Local norms are also desirable when we are selecting pupils for a specific group, such as an accelerated program in mathematics or a retarded class in reading. Where it is desired to make profile comparisons of scores obtained from tests standardized on different populations, local norms can also be used to obtain comparable scores by administering all tests to a common local group.[8] In general, the more emphasis we give to instructional uses of test results, the greater will be our need for local norms.

Local Percentile Norms

Some test manuals provide detailed directions for preparing local norms. These are most commonly based on percentile ranks because of the ease with which such norms can be computed. A typical procedure is illustrated in Figure 15.5. This is a completed worksheet which was used to construct local norms on one of the *Cooperative English Tests*. The directions given in the test manual may be summarized as follows:

1. The scores are grouped by intervals of two (Column 1).
2. A tally is made of the number of students earning scores falling in each group (Column 2).
3. The tallies are added and placed in the frequency column (Column 3).
4. The frequencies in Column 3 are added from the bottom up (e.g., $1 + 3 = 4$, $4 + 7 = 11$, and so on) to determine the cumulative frequency (Column 4).
5. The percentile rank (Column 5) for each score group is computed as follows (using the score interval of 128–129 to illustrate):
   (a) Find one half the *frequency* of the score group ($\frac{1}{2} \times 10 = 5$).
   (b) Add the result of (a) to the *cumulative frequency* for the score group just below it ($5 + 11 = 16$).
   (c) Divide the result of (b) by the *total number of students* in the norm group, and multiply by 100 ($16 \div 300 = .05$ $.05 \times 100 = 5$).
6. The percentile bands (Column 6) are obtained by consulting special tables in the manual. These bands take into account the error present in the scores and are interpreted in the same manner as those shown in the profiles presented earlier.

It should be noted that, with the exception of the percentile bands, this procedure can be used to construct local percentile norms for any test.

Local Stanine Norms

Stanine scores are also widely used for local norms. In addition to being easily computed, they have the following desirable qualities:

[8] R. L. Thorndike and E. Hagen, *Measurement and Evaluation in Psychology and Education*, 3rd ed. (New York: John Wiley & Sons, 1969).

For use with
School and College Ability Tests (SCAT)
Sequential Tests of Educational Progress (STEP)
and all other Cooperative Tests

**Score
Distribution
Sheet**

Name of Test _Cooperative English Expression-Form 2A_   Time of Testing _Spring 1962_
School, College, or Group _Newport City Schools_   **Fall or Spring**   Grade or Class _11_
Other Characteristics of Local Norms Group _139 boys and 161 girls_

Score Group	Tally	Frequency	Cumulative Frequency	Percentile Rank	Percentile Band
170 - 171	/	1	300	99	99 - 100
168 - 169		0	299	99	99 - 100
166 - 167	/	1	299	99	98 - 99
164 - 165	//	2	298	99	97 - 99
162 - 163	///	3	296	98	95 - 99
160 - 161	++++	5	293	97	91 - 99
158 - 159	++++ ///	8	288	95	86 - 98
156 - 157	++++ ++++ ///	13	280	91	81 - 97
154 - 155	++++ ++++ ++++ /	16	267	86	74 - 95
152 - 153	++++ ++++ ++++ ////	19	251	81	67 - 91
150 - 151	++++ ++++ ++++ ++++ /	21	232	74	59 - 86
148 - 149	++++ ++++ ++++ ++++ //	22	211	67	52 - 81
146 - 147	++++ ++++ ++++ ++++ ///	23	189	59	44 - 74
144 - 145	++++ ++++ ++++ ++++ ///	23	166	52	37 - 67
142 - 143	++++ ++++ ++++ ++++ //	22	143	44	30 - 59
140 - 141	++++ ++++ ++++ ++++ /	21	121	37	24 - 52
138 - 139	++++ ++++ ++++ ////	19	100	30	18 - 44
136 - 137	++++ ++++ ++++ ///	18	81	24	13 - 37
134 - 135	++++ ++++ ++++ /	16	63	18	9 - 30
132 - 133	++++ ++++ ////	14	47	13	5 - 24
130 - 131	++++ ++++ //	12	33	9	3 - 18
128 - 129	++++ ++++	10	21	5	1 - 13
126 - 127	++++ //	7	11	3	1 - 9
124 - 125	///	3	4	1	0 - 5
122 - 123	/	1	1	1	0 - 3

Total Number of Students . . . . _300_

This form is a worksheet for preparing local norms. Directions for recording information
and computations for SCAT, STEP, and 1960 or later editions of other Cooperative tests
are given in the MANUAL FOR INTERPRETING SCORES for each test used.

Cooperative Test Division   Educational Testing Service Princeton,
© Copyright 1957, All rights reserved   (E|T|S)   New Jersey Los angeles 27, California

FIGURE 15.5. Example of how local percentile norms are computed. (From _Manual
for Interpreting Scores. Cooperative English Tests._ Copyright 1960 by Cooperative Test
Division, Educational Testing Service. Used by permission.)

1. The stanine system uses a nine-point scale that is readily understood by
   pupils and parents. Simply stating that "the scores range from a high of
   9 to a low of 1, with an average of 5" is sufficient to communicate the
   essential meaning of the stanine scale.
2. Stanines are normalized standard scores that make it possible to compare
   a pupil's performance on different tests (providing, of course, that all
   tests were administered to a common group). Typically a difference of

two stanines represents a significant difference in test performance between tests (assuming test reliability is satisfactory). Thus, a pupil with a stanine of 7 in arithmetic and 5 in spelling is probably demonstrating superior performance in arithmetic.

3. The stanine system makes it possible to readily combine diverse types of data (e.g., test scores, ratings, ranked data) because stanines are computed like percentile ranks but are expressed in standard score form. Thus, the conversion to stanines is simple, and the standard score feature makes it possible to add together stanine scores from various measures to obtain a composite score. A simple summing of stanines will give equal weight to each measure in the composite.

4. Since the stanine system uses a single-digit score, it is easily recorded and takes less space than other scores. (It was originally developed to fit into a single column on an IBM card.)

The main limitation of stanine scores is that growth cannot be shown from one year to the next. If a pupil's progress matches that of the norm group he will retain the same position in the group and thus be assigned the same stanine. This shortcoming is, of course, also characteristic of percentile ranks and of other standard scores used to indicate relative position in a particular group. To determine growth, we would need to examine the increase in his raw scores.

Stanines are sometimes criticized on the grounds that they are rather crude units, because they divide a distribution of scores into only nine parts. On the plus side, however, these crude units prevent the overinterpretation of test scores. Although greater refinement might be desirable for some special purposes (e.g., identifying gifted pupils), stanines provide satisfactory discriminations in test performance for most educational uses of test results. With a more refined scoring system, there is always the danger that minor chance differences in scores will be interpreted as significant differences.

Assigning Stanines to Raw Scores. The transforming of raw scores into stanines is relatively simple if the scores are ranked from high to low and there are no ties in rank. The top 4 per cent of the raw scores are assigned a stanine score of 9; the next 7 per cent of the raw scores are assigned a stanine score of 8; the next 12 per cent a stanine score of 7, and so on. The percentage of cases falling at each stanine level, and the number of pupils to be assigned each stanine score for any size group from 20 to 100, is shown in Table 15.4. These figures, showing the number of pupils that should receive each stanine score, are determined by multiplying the number of cases in the group by the percentage of cases at each stanine level and rounding off the results.

Distributions of test scores typically have a number of pupils with the same raw score. Consequently, we have ties in rank that prevent us from obtaining a perfect match with the theoretical distributions shown in

Table 15.4. Because *all pupils with the same raw score must be assigned the same stanine score,* all we can reasonably expect to do is approximate the distribution shown in Table 15.4 as closely as possible. The step-by-step procedure for assigning stanines to test scores is described and illustrated in Table 15.5.

CAUTIONS IN INTERPRETING TEST SCORES

Interpreting test scores with the aid of norms requires an understanding of the type of derived score used and a willingness to study carefully the characteristics of the norm group. In addition, however, we need to keep in mind the following general cautions which apply to the interpretation of any test score:

1. *A test score should be interpreted in terms of the specific test from which it was derived.* No two scholastic aptitude tests nor achievement tests measure exactly the same thing. Achievement tests are especially prone to wide variation and the differences are seldom reflected in the test title. For example, one arithmetic test might be limited to simple computational skills while another contains a large number of reasoning problems. Similarly, one science test may be confined largely to items measuring knowledge of terminology while another with the same title stresses the application of scientific principles. With such variation it is misleading to interpret a pupil's test score as representing general achievement in any particular area. We need to look beyond test titles and to evaluate the pupil's performance in terms of what the test *actually* does measure.

2. *A test score should be interpreted in light of all relevant characteristics of the pupil.* Test performance is influenced by the pupil's aptitudes, educational experiences, cultural background, emotional adjustment, health, and the like. Consequently, when a pupil performs poorly on a test, it is desirable to first consider the possibility of cultural deprivation, a language handicap, improper motivation, or similar factors which might have interfered with the pupil's response to the test. If the test is an achievement test, we must, of course, also take into account the pupil's scholastic aptitude. A low ability pupil performing below average might be progressing at a rate satisfactory for him. On the other hand, a bright pupil performing well above average might be achieving far short of his potential.

3. *A test score should be interpreted in terms of the type of decision to be made.* The meaningfulness of a test score is determined to a considerable extent by the use to be made of it. For example, an IQ score of 100 would have different meanings if we were selecting pupils for a mentally retarded class, attempting to predict achievement in high school, or trying to decide whether a pupil should be encouraged to go to college. We shall find test scores much more useful when we stop considering them as high or low

TABLE 15.4

STANINE TABLE SHOWING THE NUMBER OF PUPILS TO BE ASSIGNED EACH STANINE FOR GROUPS CONTAINING 20 TO 100 CASES*

No. of Cases	Stanine Scores									No. of Cases	Stanine Scores								
	1	2	3	4	5	6	7	8	9		1	2	3	4	5	6	7	8	9
	Percentage of Cases										Percentage of Cases								
	4	7	12	17	20	17	12	7	4		4	7	12	17	20	17	12	7	4
20	1	1	2	4	4	4	2	1	1	61	3	4	7	10	13	10	7	4	3
21	1	1	2	4	5	4	2	1	1	62	3	4	7	11	12	11	7	4	3
22	1	2	2	4	4	4	2	2	1	63	3	4	7	11	13	11	7	4	3
23	1	2	2	4	5	4	2	2	1	64	3	4	8	11	12	11	8	4	3
24	1	2	3	4	4	4	3	2	1	65	3	4	8	11	13	11	8	4	3
25	1	2	3	4	5	4	3	2	1	66	3	4	8	11	14	11	8	4	3
26	1	2	3	4	6	4	3	2	1	67	3	5	8	11	13	11	8	5	3
27	1	2	3	5	5	5	3	2	1	68	3	5	8	11	14	11	8	5	3
28	1	2	3	5	6	5	3	2	1	69	3	5	8	12	13	12	8	5	3
29	1	2	4	5	5	5	4	2	1	70	3	5	8	12	14	12	8	5	3
30	1	2	4	5	6	5	4	2	1	71	3	5	8	12	15	12	8	5	3
31	1	2	4	5	7	5	4	2	1	72	3	5	9	12	14	12	9	5	3
32	1	2	4	6	6	6	4	2	1	73	3	5	9	12	15	12	9	5	3
33	1	2	4	6	7	6	4	2	1	74	3	5	9	13	14	13	9	5	3
34	1	3	4	6	6	6	4	3	1	75	3	5	9	13	15	13	9	5	3
35	1	3	4	6	7	6	4	3	1	76	3	5	9	13	16	13	9	5	3
36	1	3	4	6	8	6	4	3	1	77	3	6	9	13	15	13	9	6	3
37	2	3	4	6	7	6	4	3	2	78	3	6	9	13	16	13	9	6	3
38	1	3	5	6	8	6	5	3	1	79	3	6	10	13	15	13	10	6	3
39	1	3	5	7	7	7	5	3	1	80	3	6	9	14	16	14	9	6	3
40	1	3	5	7	8	7	5	3	1	81	3	6	9	14	17	14	9	6	3
41	1	3	5	7	9	7	5	3	1	82	3	6	10	14	16	14	10	6	3
42	2	3	5	7	8	7	5	3	2	83	3	6	10	14	17	14	10	6	3
43	2	3	5	7	9	7	5	3	2	84	4	6	10	14	16	14	10	6	4
44	2	3	5	8	8	8	5	3	2	85	3	6	10	15	17	15	10	6	3
45	2	3	5	8	9	8	5	3	2	86	3	6	10	15	18	15	10	6	3
46	2	3	5	8	10	8	5	3	2	87	4	6	10	15	17	15	10	6	4
47	2	3	6	8	9	8	6	3	2	88	3	6	11	15	18	15	11	6	3
48	2	3	6	8	10	8	6	3	2	89	4	6	11	15	17	15	11	6	4
49	2	4	6	8	9	8	6	4	2	90	4	6	11	15	18	15	11	6	4
50	2	3	6	9	10	9	6	3	2	91	4	6	11	15	19	15	11	6	4
51	2	3	6	9	11	9	6	3	2	92	4	6	11	16	18	16	11	6	4
52	2	4	6	9	10	9	6	4	2	93	4	6	11	16	19	16	11	6	4
53	2	4	6	9	11	9	6	4	2	94	4	7	11	16	18	16	11	7	4
54	2	4	7	9	10	9	7	4	2	95	4	7	11	16	19	16	11	7	4
55	2	4	7	9	11	9	7	4	2	96	4	7	11	16	20	16	11	7	4
56	2	4	7	9	12	9	7	4	2	97	4	7	12	16	19	16	12	7	4
57	2	4	7	10	11	10	7	4	2	98	4	7	12	16	20	16	12	7	4
58	2	4	7	10	12	10	7	4	2	99	4	7	12	17	19	17	12	7	4
59	3	4	7	10	11	10	7	4	3	100	4	7	12	17	20	17	12	7	4
60	3	4	7	10	12	10	7	4	3										

* Adapted from W. N. Durost, *The Characteristics, Use, and Computation of Stanines.* Copyright 1961 by Harcourt Brace Jovanovich, Inc. Used by permission.

TABLE 15.5

PROCEDURE FOR TRANSFORMING RAW SCORES TO STANINES[*]

Stanine	Score Interval (A)	Tallies (B)	Frequencies (C)	Grouping Actual	Grouping Theoretical
9	58	|	1		
	57		–	4	4
	56	|	1		
	55	||	2		
8	54		–		
	53		–		
	52		–		
	51	|	1	7	6
	50	|	1		
	49	||	2		
	48		–		
	47	|||	3		
7	46	|	1		
	45	|||	3		
	44	||	2	12	11
	43		–		
	42	|||| |	6		
6	41	||	2		
	40	||	2		
	39	||	2	12	15
	38	|	1		
	37	||||	5		
5	36	||||	5		
	35 (E)	||	2		
	34	|||| ||	7	20	18
	33	|||	3		
	32	|||	3		
4	31	||||	5		
	30	|	1		
	29	|||	3	14	15
	28	|||	3		
	27	||	2		
3	26	||||	4		
	25	|||| |	6	13	11
	24	|||	3		
2	23	|	1		
	22	|	1	4	6
	21	||	2		
1	20	|	1		
	19		–	4	4
	18	|	1		
	17	||	2		
			90 (D)		

Directions For Illustration 1

1. Arrange test papers or answer sheets in rank order from high to low. On a separate piece of paper list every score in a column from the highest obtained score to the lowest, column (A). Opposite each score write the number of individuals who obtained that score. This may be done by counting the papers or answer sheets having the same score, or it may be done by tallying the scores in the manner shown in column (B).

2. Add the frequencies (C) and write the total at the bottom of the column (D). This is shown to be 90.

3. Beginning at the bottom, count up (cumulate) to one-half the total number of scores, in this case 45 (one-half of 90). This falls opposite the score of 34 (E), which is the median to the nearest whole number.

4. In the column at the extreme left of the Stanine Table (Table 15.4), look up the total number of cases (90). In this row are the theoretical frequencies of cases at each stanine level for 90 cases. In the middle of this row you will find the number of cases (18) to which a stanine of 5 should be assigned. Starting with median (in Illustration 1), lay off as nearly this number (18) of scores as you can. Here it is 20.

5. Working upward and downward from scores falling in stanine 5, assign scores to stanine levels so as to give the closest approximation possible to the theoretical values. It is helpful to bracket these scores in the manner shown in column (A).

After having made a tentative assignment, make any adjustments necessary to bring the actual frequencies at each level into the closest possible agreement with the theoretical values. Remember, however, that all equal scores must be assigned the same stanines.

Illustration 1. Tally sheet for distribution of scores.

* Adapted from W. N. Durost, *The Characteristics, Use, and Computation of Stanines.* Copyright 1961 by Harcort Brace Jovanovich, Inc. Used by permission.

"in general," and begin evaluating their significance in relation to the specific decision to be made.

4. A test score should be interpreted as a band of scores rather than a specific value. Every test score is subject to error and this error must be allowed for during test interpretation. One of the best means of doing this is to consider a pupil's test performance as a band of scores one standard error of measurement above and below his obtained score. For example, if a pupil earns a score of 56 and the standard error is 3, his test performance should be interpreted as a band ranging from score 53 to score 59. Such bands were illustrated in the profiles presented earlier. Even where they are not plotted, however, we should make allowances for these error bands surrounding each score. This will prevent us from making interpretations which are more precise than the test results warrant. Treating small chance differences between test scores as though they were significant can only lead to erroneous decisions.

5. A test score should be verified by supplementary evidence. When interpreting test scores, it is impossible to determine fully the extent to which the basic assumptions of testing have been met (i.e., maximum motivation, equal educational opportunity, and so on), or to which the conditions of testing have been precisely controlled (i.e., administration, scoring, and so on). Consequently, in addition to the predictable error of measurement, which can be taken into account with standard error bands, a test score may contain an indeterminate amount of error due to unmet assumptions or uncontrolled conditions. Our only protection against such errors is to place little reliance on a single test score. As Cronbach[9] has noted:

> The most helpful single principle in all testing is that test scores are data on which to base further study. They must be coordinated with background facts, and they must be verified by constant comparison with other available data.

The misinterpretation and misuse of test scores would be substantially reduced if this simple principle were more widely recognized.

In passing, it is wise to note that this caution should not be restricted to test scores. It is merely a specific application of the more general rule that no important decision should ever be based on one limited sample of behavior.

SUMMARY

Test interpretation is complicated by the fact that the raw scores obtained for a test lack a true zero point (point where there is "no achievement at

---

[9] L. J. Cronbach, *Essentials of Psychological Testing,* 3rd ed. (New York: Harper and Row, 1970), p. 381.

all") and equal units (such as feet, pounds, and minutes). In an attempt to compensate for the lack of these properties and to make test scores more readily interpretable, various methods of expressing test scores have been devised. In general, we can give meaning to a raw score either by converting it into a description of the specific tasks that the pupil can perform (*criterion-referenced* interpretation), or by converting it into some type of derived score that indicates the pupil's relative position in a clearly defined reference group (*norm-referenced* interpretation).

Criterion-referenced test interpretation permits us to describe an individual's test performance without reference to the performance of others. This is typically done in terms of some universally understood measure of proficiency (e.g., speed, precision) or the percentage of items correct in some clearly defined domain of learning tasks. The *percentage-correct score* is widely used in criterion-referenced test interpretation, but it is primarily useful in mastery testing where a clearly defined and delimited domain of learning tasks can be most readily obtained.

Although criterion-referenced interpretation is possible with standardized tests, such interpretations are likely to be inadequate because these tests were designed to discriminate among individuals rather than to describe them. In the future test publishers can be expected to produce tests that are more amenable to criterion-referenced interpretation.

Expectancy tables also provide a type of criterion-referenced interpretation. Instead of describing an individual's performance on the test tasks, it describes his expected performance in some situation beyond the test (e.g., success in college). Expectancy tables provide a simple and direct means of interpreting test results without the aid of test norms.

Standardized tests have typically been designed for norm-referenced interpretation. This involves converting the raw scores to derived scores by means of tables of norms. These derived scores indicate a pupil's relative position in a clearly defined reference group. They have the advantage over raw scores of providing more uniform meaning from one test to another and from one situation to another.

Test norms merely represent the typical performance of pupils in the reference groups on which the test was standardized and consequently should not be viewed as desired goals or standards. The most common types of norms are grade norms, age norms, percentile norms, and standard score norms. Each type has its own unique characteristics, advantages, and limitations, which must be taken into account during test interpretation.

Grade norms and age norms describe test performance in terms of the particular grade or age group in which a pupil's raw score is just average. These norms are widely used at the elementary school level, largely due to the apparent ease with which they can be interpreted. Describing test performance in terms of grade and age equivalents can frequently lead to unsound decisions, however, because of the inequality of the units and the invalid assumptions on which they are based.

Percentile norms and standard score norms describe test performance in terms of the pupil's relative standing in a group in which he is a member or desires to become a member. A percentile rank indicates the percentage of pupils falling below a particular raw score. Percentile units are unequal, but the scores are readily understood by persons without special training. A standard score indicates the number of standard deviation units a raw score falls above or below the group mean. It has the advantage of providing equal units which can be treated arithmetically, but persons untrained in statistics find it difficult to interpret such scores. Some of the more common types of standard scores are z-scores, T-scores, deviation IQs, and stanines.

With a normal distribution of scores, we can readily convert back and forth between standard scores and percentiles. This makes it possible to utilize the special advantages of each. Standard scores can be used to obtain the benefits of equal units, and we can convert to percentile equivalents when interpreting test performance to pupils, parents, and others who lack statistical training.

A pupil's performance on several tests which have comparable norms may be presented in the form of a profile. This makes it possible to identify readily areas of strength and weakness. Profile interpretation is more apt to be accurate when standard error bands are plotted on the profile.

The adequacy of test norms can be judged by determining the extent to which they are (1) relevant, (2) representative, (3) up to date, (4) comparable, and (5) adequately described. In some instances, it is more appropriate to use local norms than published norms. When local norms are desired, percentile and stanine norms can be readily computed.

In addition to a knowledge of derived scores and norms, the proper interpretation of test scores requires an acute awareness of (1) what the test measures, (2) characteristics and background of the pupil, (3) type of decision to be made, (4) amount of error in the score, and (5) extent to which the score is in harmony with other available data. No important educational decision should ever be based on test scores alone.

LEARNING EXERCISES

1. Describe the problems that might be encountered in making criterion-referenced interpretations of standardized achievement tests.
2. In Midtown, U.S.A., test results showed that the three fourth-grade classes had the following average grade equivalent scores on a standardized achievement battery:

    School A   4.8
    School B   4.7
    School C   3.2

    What type of information would you need to interpret properly the low performance in School C?

3. A fifth-grade boy received an average grade equivalent score of 6.8 on a standardized achievement battery administered in the fall of the year. What arguments might be presented for and against moving him ahead to the sixth grade?

4. What advantages do stanines have over T-scores? What disadvantages?

5. Explain each of the following statements:
   a. Standard scores provide *equal* units.
   b. Percentile scores provide *systematically unequal* units.
   c. Grade equivalent scores provide *unequal* units that vary in an unpredictable manner.

6. Assuming that all of the following test scores were obtained from the same normally distributed group, which score indicates highest performance? Which lowest?
   a. z-score = .65.
   b. T-score = 65.
   c. Percentile score = 65.

7. Consult the section on norms and scales in *Standards for Educational and Psychological Tests* and review the types of information that test manuals should contain. Compare a recent test manual against the *Standards*. (See reference in "Suggestions for Further Reading.")

8. Why shouldn't test *norms* be used as *standards* of good performance? What is the difference between a norm and a standard?

9. What is the value of using national norms? Under what conditions would it be desirable to use local norms?

10. What would be the relative advantages and disadvantages of using local norms for pupils in a culturally deprived area? For what purposes would more general norms (e.g., national) be useful with these pupils?

SUGGESTIONS FOR FURTHER READING

AMERICAN PSYCHOLOGICAL ASSOCIATION. *Standards for Educational and Psychological Tests*. Washington, D.C.: APA, 1974. See the sections on "Norms and Scales" (pages 19–24) and "Standards for the Use of Tests" (pages 56–75). The first section indicates what to look for in test manuals and the second describes criteria for the effective interpretation and use of tests.

ANASTASI, A. *Psychological Testing*, 4th ed. New York: Macmillan Publishing Co., Inc., 1976. Chapter 4, "Norms and the Interpretation of Test Scores." Describes the various types of norms; computer interpretation of test scores; and criterion-referenced testing.

CRONBACH, L. J. *Essentials of Psychological Testing*, 3rd ed. New York: Harper and Row, Publishers, 1970. Chapter 4, "Scoring." Cronbach discusses the common types of test scores and norms.

LENNON, R. T. "Scores and Norms," *Encyclopedia of Educational Research*, 4th ed. New York: Macmillan Publishing Co., Inc., 1969, pages 1206–1211. Discusses the common types of test scores and norms and the problems of obtaining representative norm groups.

LYMAN, H. B. *Test Scores and What They Mean*. Englewood Cliffs, N.J.: Prentice-Hall, Inc., 1971. A simple, lucid extension of the material presented in this chapter.

THORNDIKE, R. L. (ed.). *Educational Measurement*. Washington, D.C.: American Council on Education, 1971. Chapter 12 by L. V. Jones, "The Nature of Measurement," and Chapter 15 by W. H. Angoff, "Scales, Norms and Equivalent Scores." Comprehensive and advanced treatments of the topics.

Test Bulletins

RICKS, J. H. *Local Norms—When and Why*, Test Service Bulletin, No. 58. New York: The Psychological Corporation, 1971.

SEASHORE, H. G. *Methods of Expressing Test Scores*, Test Service Bulletin, No. 48. New York: The Psychological Corporation, 1955.

PART IV

Evaluating Procedures, Products, and Typical Behavior

CHAPTER 16

Evaluating Learning and Development: Observational Techniques

---

Direct observation provides the only means we have for evaluating some aspects of learning and development, . . . and it provides supplementary information concerning others. The problem is . . . how to get an objective record of the most meaningful behavior? This can be greatly facilitated through the use of such techniques as: (1) anecdotal records, (2) rating scales, and (3) checklists.

As we have noted in previous chapters, a large number of learning outcomes can be measured by paper-and-pencil tests. This is especially true of outcomes in the cognitive domain, such as those pertaining to knowledge, understanding, and thinking skills. The significance of these areas in all subject-matter fields has placed paper-and-pencil testing in a prominent and central role in educational evaluation. This is as it should be, but we must be careful not to become solely dependent on paper-and-pencil testing. There are a number of important behavioral changes that require the use of other procedures.

Learning outcomes in skill areas and behavioral changes in personal-social development are especially difficult to evaluate with the usual paper-and-pencil test. A list of such outcomes, with representative types of pupil behavior, is presented in Table 16.1. This list is by no means complete but it is comprehensive enough to illustrate the great need to supplement paper-and-pencil testing with other methods of evaluation.

Learning outcomes and aspects of development like those in Table 16.1 can generally be evaluated by one of the following procedures: (1) observing the pupil as he performs and describing or judging his behavior (evaluating a speech), (2) observing and judging the quality of the product resulting from his performance (evaluating handwriting), (3) asking his peers about him (evaluating social relationships), and (4)

TABLE 16.1
OUTCOMES REQUIRING EVALUATION PROCEDURES BEYOND
THE TYPICAL PAPER-AND-PENCIL TEST

Outcome	Representative Behaviors
Skills	Speaking, writing, listening, oral reading, performing laboratory experiments, drawing, playing a musical instrument, dancing, gymnastics, work skills, study skills, and social skills.
Work habits	Effectiveness in planning, use of time, use of equipment, use of resources; the demonstration of such traits as initiative, creativity, persistence, dependability.
Social attitudes	Concern for the welfare of others, respect for laws, respect for the property of others, sensitivity to social issues, concern for social institutions, desire to work toward social improvement.
Scientific attitudes	Open-mindedness, willingness to suspend judgment, sensitivity to cause-effect relations, an inquiring mind.
Interests	Expressed feelings toward various educational, mechanical, aesthetic, scientific, social, recreational, vocational activities.
Appreciations	Feeling of satisfaction and enjoyment expressed toward nature, music, art, literature, physical skill, outstanding social contributions.
Adjustments	Relationship to peers, reaction to praise and criticism, reaction to authority, emotional stability, social adaptability.

questioning him directly (evaluating expressed interests). Although these *observational techniques, peer-appraisals,* and *self-report methods* are more subjective than we would like, and their use frequently requires more time and effort than the typical testing procedure, they provide the best means available for evaluating a variety of important behaviors. Our choice is simple: either we use these techniques in an attempt to evaluate each learning outcome and aspect of development as directly and validly as possible, or we neglect those that cannot be measured by paper-and-pencil tests. From an educational standpoint, the choice seems obvious.

In this chapter, we shall describe those observational techniques found especially useful by teachers. These include:

- Anecdotal records.
- Rating scales.
- Checklists.

The following chapter will be devoted to peer appraisals and self-report techniques.

ANECDOTAL RECORDS

Teachers' daily observations provide them with a wealth of information concerning the learning and development of their pupils. For example, a third-grade teacher notices during oral reading that Mary mispronounces several simple words, that George sits staring out the window, and that Jane keeps interrupting the reading with irrelevant questions. Similarly, a high school chemistry teacher notices during a laboratory period that Bill is slow and inefficient in setting up his equipment, that John finishes his experiments early and helps others, and that Betty handles the chemicals in a careless and dangerous manner despite repeated warnings. Such daily incidents and events have special evaluative significance. They enable us to determine how a pupil typically performs or behaves in a variety of situations. In some instances, this information merely supplements and verifies data obtained by more objective methods. In other cases, it provides the only means we have for evaluating desired behavioral changes.

Impressions gained through observation are apt to provide an incomplete and biased picture, however, unless we keep an accurate record of our observations. A simple and convenient method of doing this is provided by *anecdotal records*.

Anecdotal records are factual descriptions of the meaningful incidents and events which the teacher has observed in the lives of his pupils. Each incident is described shortly after it happens. The descriptions may be recorded on separate cards like the one shown in Figure 16.1, or running accounts, one for each pupil, may be kept on separate pages in a notebook. A good anecdotal record keeps the objective description of an incident separate from any interpretation of the meaning of the behavior. For some purposes, it is also desirable to provide an additional space for recommendations concerning ways to improve the pupil's learning or adjustment. Such recommendations are seldom made, however, until a series of anecdotes have been accumulated.

Uses of Anecdotal Records

The use of anecdotal records has frequently been limited to the area of social adjustment. While they are especially appropriate for this type of reporting, this is a needless limitation. Anecdotal records can be used for obtaining data pertinent to a variety of learning outcomes and to many aspects of personal and social development. The potential usefulness of the anecdotal method can be revealed by reviewing the various areas of learning outcomes presented earlier in this chapter (see Table 16.1); you will note that many of the behaviors listed there can be appraised by means of direct observation.

The problem in using anecdotal records is not so much what *can* be

---

Class **4th Grade**   Pupil **Bill Johnson**

Date **4/25/63**   Place **Classroom**   Observer **M. G.**

INCIDENT

As class was about to start, Bill asked if he could read a poem to the class— one he had written himself—about "spring." He read the poem in a low voice, constantly looked down at the paper, moved his right foot back and forth, and pulled on his shirt collar. When he finished, Jack (in the back row) said "I couldn't hear it. Will you read it again—louder?" Bill said "no" and sat down.

INTERPRETATION

Bill enjoys writing stories and poems and they reflect considerable creative ability. However, he seems very shy and nervous in performing before a group. His refusal to read the poem again seemed to be due to his nervousness.

FIGURE 16.1. Anecdotal record form.

evaluated, but rather what *should* be evaluated, with this method. It is obvious that we cannot observe and report on all aspects of pupil behavior, no matter how useful such records might be. Thus, the time-consuming nature of the task requires that we be *selective* in our observations.

Deciding What Behaviors to Observe and Record

In general, our objectives and desired outcomes will guide us in determining what behaviors are most worth noting. In addition, we must also be alert to those unusual and exceptional incidents which contribute to a better understanding of each pupil's unique pattern of behavior. Within this general framework, there are several steps we can take to limit and control our observations so that a realistic system of recording can be developed. They are:

1. Confining our observations to those areas of behavior that cannot be evaluated by other means.
2. Limiting our observations of all pupils at any given time to just a few types of behavior.
3. Restricting the use of extensive observations of behavior to those few pupils who are most in need of special help.

There is no advantage in using anecdotal records to obtain evidence of learning in areas where more objective and practical methods are available. Knowledge, understanding, and various aspects of thinking skill can usually be evaluated by paper-and-pencil tests. Many learning outcomes of other types, such as the ability to give a speech, operate a microscope, or write a theme, are most effectively evaluated by rating methods or by product evaluation. Records of actual behavior are best used to evaluate how a pupil typically behaves in a natural setting. How does he approach a problem? How persistent is he in carrying out a task? How willing is he to listen to the ideas of others? What activities seem to attract his interest? What contributions does he make to class activities? How effectively does he work with others? How does he respond to praise and criticism? Noting a pupil's verbal comments and actions in various natural situations provides certain clues to his attitudes, interests, appreciations, habits, and adjustment patterns that cannot be obtained by any other means. These are the types of behavior toward which we should focus our attention when keeping anecdotal records.

The best we can hope for with anecdotal records is a fairly representative sample of pupil behavior in the different areas in which we desire information. This usually can be obtained more easily if we concentrate our observations on a few areas at a time. For example, an elementary teacher might pay particular attention to reading interests during the free reading period, to signs of appreciation during music and art, and to patterns of social relations during recess. Similarly, a high school science teacher might concentrate on incidents reflecting scientific attitude during certain class discussions and laboratory periods, and on work habits and laboratory skills during others. In some cases the activity itself will indicate the types of observation most fruitful to focus on, while in others the emphasis at any given time may need to be determined in an arbitrary manner. Despite the concentration of attention on certain areas at a particular time, however, we should always be alert to other incidents and events which have special significance for understanding the pupil's learning and development.

In addition to recording some information on all pupils, there are times when we need more comprehensive information regarding a relative few. The severely retarded reader, the socially rejected child, and the gifted underachiever are typical of those needing special attention. More extensive observations of such pupils are helpful in understanding their difficulties and in providing clues for remedial action. The most complete and useful information is obtained when we concentrate our observations on one or two pupils at a time. During such observations it may also be necessary to restrict further our record keeping on other pupils.

Some teachers become discouraged when they first use anecdotal records because they attempt to do too much. Limiting observations and reports to specific types of behavior, to specific pupils, or both, is frequently necessary to make the procedure feasible. It is much better to have a clearly delimited and workable observational plan than to end up with an incomplete and atypical collection of unrelated incidents.

Advantages and Limitations of Anecdotal Records

Probably the most important advantage of anecdotal records is that they provide a description of actual behavior in natural situations. The old adage that "actions speak louder than words" has direct application here. A pupil may show good knowledge of health practices, but not use a handkerchief when he sneezes or coughs; he may profess great interest in science but approach his laboratory work in a haphazard and uninterested fashion; or he may express great concern for the welfare of others but behave in a selfish manner. Records of actual behavior provide a check on other evaluation methods and also enable us to determine the extent of change in the pupil's typical patterns of behavior.

In addition to compiling descriptions of the most characteristic behavior of a pupil, anecdotal records make possible gathering evidence on events that are exceptional but significant. Typical examples are the quiet pupil who speaks in class for the first time, the hostile pupil who makes a friendly gesture, the extreme conformist who shows a sign of originality, and the apathetic pupil who shows a spark of interest. These individually significant behaviors are apt to be excluded by other evaluation techniques. They are also likely to be overlooked by teachers unless a concerted effort is made to observe such incidents. Keeping anecdotal records makes us more diligent in observation and increases our awareness of these unique behaviors.

A special advantage to the elementary teacher is that anecdotal records can be used with very young pupils and with others who are retarded in basic communication skills. They are especially valuable here because paper-and-pencil tests, self-report techniques, and peer appraisals are likely to be impracticable or of limited use. Observational records of younger pupils are of special value for still another reason. Since young children tend to be more spontaneous and uninhibited in their actions, their behavior is easier to observe and interpret.

The major limitation of anecdotal records is the amount of time required in maintaining an adequate system of records. Though this can be offset somewhat by limiting observations and reports as suggested earlier, it is still a time-consuming task. If a teacher keeps anecdotal records for his own use only, he can work out a realistic plan by starting with a few anecdotes each day and gradually increasing it to a reasonable number. If the entire staff is to begin using anecdotal records, it is desirable to have all teachers record as many anecdotes as is practicable for a period of a few weeks, and then hold a staff meeting to discuss the recorded anecdotes and to decide what constitutes a reasonable number. It is generally unwise to set a specific number that must be recorded each week, but an approximate minimum can serve as a useful general guide. When anecdotal records are used on a school-wide basis, the most time-consuming aspect is the summarizing of anecdotes and the recording of the summaries in the pupil's cumulative records. Of course, much of this work can be handled by the clerical staff.

Another serious limitation of anecdotal records is the difficulty of being *objective* when observing and reporting pupil behavior. Ideally, we would like a series of verbal "snapshots" which accurately represent the pupil's actual behavior. This goal is seldom attained, however, for the teacher's own biases, hopes, and preconceived notions inevitably enter into his observations and reports. For example, he will tend to notice more desirable qualities in those pupils he likes best and more undesirable qualities in those he likes least. If he is evaluating the effectiveness of a new teaching technique in which he has great faith, there will be a tendency to note positive results and to ignore the negative. If he believes that boys are less well coordinated than girls, he will tend to perceive their performance skills as being of lower quality. Training in observation and reporting can reduce such distortions to a minimum, but they cannot be eradicated entirely. When anecdotal records are accumulated from a number of teachers, however, the biases of any particular teacher become less influential in the total pattern.

A related difficulty is that of obtaining an adequate sample of behavior. When a pupil is participating in class discussion, he may be so tense and anxious that he apears cold and unfriendly toward others and his ideas seem disorganized. When observed in less formal settings, such as in the laboratory or on the playground, his behavior might be quite different. Similarly, a pupil may appear highly motivated and interested in mathematics class but bored and uninterested during English literature, or he may be attentive and inquisitive in science one day and apathetic the next. Everyone's behavior fluctuates somewhat from situation to situation and from one time to another. Therefore, to obtain a reliable picture of a pupil's typical pattern of behavior we need to observe him over a period of time and in a variety of situations. This also implies that general interpretations and recommendations concerning a pupil's adjustment should be delayed until a fairly adequate sample of behavior is obtained.

Improving the Effectiveness of Anecdotal Records

In the previous sections, we have stated or implied a number of ways to improve procedures for observing and reporting pupil behavior. These and other points are listed here in a series of suggestions for the effective use of anecdotal records.

1. *Determine in advance what to observe, but be alert for unusual behavior.* We are more apt to select and record meaningful incidents if we re-

view objectives and outcomes and decide which behaviors require evaluation by direct observation—that is, those that cannot be effectively evaluated by other means. We can further focus our observations by looking for just a few specific types of behavior at any given time. While such directed observations are highly desirable for obtaining evidence of pupil learning, there is always the danger that unique incidents which have special value for understanding a pupil's development will be overlooked. Consequently, we must be sufficiently flexible to note and report any unusual behavior in the event that it may be significant.

2. *Observe and record enough of the situation to make the behavior meaningful.* It is difficult to interpret behavior apart from the situation in which it occurred. An aggressive action, such as pushing another child, for example, might reflect good-natured fun, an attempt to get attention, a response to direct provocation, or a sign of extreme hostility. Clues to the meaning of behavior frequently can be obtained by directing attention to the actions of the other pupils involved and the particular setting in which the behavior took place. The record, therefore, should contain those situational conditions which seem necessary for understanding the pupil's behavior.

3. *Make a record of the incident as soon after the observation as possible.* In most cases it is infeasible to write a description of an incident at the time it happens. However, the longer we delay in recording observations, the greater the likelihood that important details will be forgotten. Making a few brief notes at opportune times following behavioral incidents and completing the records after school generally provides a feasible and satisfactory procedure.

4. *Limit each anecdote to a brief description of a single specific incident.* Brief and concise descriptions take less time to write, less time to read, and are more easily summarized. Just enough detail should be included to make the description meaningful and accurate. Limiting each description to a single specific incident also simplifies the task of writing, using, and interpreting the records.

5. *Keep the factual description of the incident and your interpretation of it separate.* The description of an incident should be as accurate and objective as you can make it. This means stating exactly what happened in clear and nonjudgmental words. Avoid such terms as *lazy, unhappy, shy, hostile, sad, ambitious, persistent,* and the like. If used at all, reserve such words for the separate section in which you give your tentative interpretations of the incident. There is no need to intepret each incident, but when interpretations are given they should be kept separate and clearly labelled as such.

6. *Record both positive and negative behavioral incidents.* There is a general tendency for teachers to note more readily those behaviors which disturb them personally and which interfere with the on-going process in the classroom. The result is that anecdotal records frequently contain a disproportionate number of incidents which indicate the *lack* of learning

or development. For evaluation purposes, it is equally important to record the less dramatic incidents which provide clues concerning the growth that *is* taking place. Thus, a conscious effort should be made to observe and record these often more subtle positive behaviors as well as the more obvious negative reactions.

7. Collect a number of anecdotes on a pupil before drawing inferences concerning typical behavior. A single behavioral incident is seldom very meaningful in understanding a pupil's behavior. We all have our moments of "peak performance" and "extreme error-proneness," elation and despair, confidence and self-doubt. It is only after observing a pupil a number of times in a variety of settings that his basic pattern of behavior begins to emerge. Consequently, we should generally delay making any judgments concerning his learning or development until we have a sufficient sample of behavior to provide a reliable picture of how the pupil typically behaves in different situations.

8. Obtain practice in writing anecdotal records. At first, most teachers have considerable difficulty in selecting significant incidents, in observing them accurately, and in describing them objectively. Some training and practice is therefore desirable before embarking on the use of anecdotal records. If the entire school staff is involved, a regular in-service training program should be provided. Where an individual teacher wants to explore their use in his own classroom, the aid of a supervisor or fellow teacher can be helpful in appraising the quality of the records. It might be wise to start by observing pupils' study habits during a study period, as this will provide sufficient time to observe and record significant behavior.

RATING SCALES

In contrast to the unstructured descriptions of behavior obtained with anecdotal records, rating scales provide a systematic procedure for obtaining and reporting the judgments of observers. Typically, a rating scale consists of a set of characteristics or qualities to be judged and some type of scale for indicating the degree to which each attribute is present. The rating form itself is merely a reporting device. Its value in appraising the learning and development of pupils depends largely upon the care with which it is prepared and the appropriateness with which it is used. As with other evaluation instruments, it should be constructed in accordance with the learning outcomes to be evaluated, and its use should be confined to those areas where there is a sufficient opportunity to make the necessary observations. If these two principles are properly applied, a rating scale serves several important evaluative functions: (1) it directs observation toward specific and clearly defined aspects of behavior, (2) it provides a common frame of reference for comparing all pupils on the same set of characteristics, and (3) it provides a convenient method for recording judgments of the observers.

Types of Rating Scales

Rating scales may take many specific forms, but the majority of them can be identified as belonging to one of the types described in the following discussion. Each type will be illustrated by using two dimensions from a scale for rating "contributions to class discussion."

Numerical Rating Scale. One of the simplest types of rating scales is that where the rater checks or circles a number to indicate the degree to which a characteristic is present. Typically, each of a series of numbers is given a verbal description which remains constant from one characteristic to another. In some cases, the rater is merely told that the largest number is high, 1 is low, and the other numbers represent intermediate values.

EXAMPLES

Directions: Indicate the degree to which this pupil contributes to class discussions by encircling the appropriate number. The numbers represent the following values: 5—*outstanding,* 4—*above average,* 3—*average,* 2—*below average,* and 1—*unsatisfactory.*

1. To what extent does the pupil participate in discussions?
     1   2   3   4   5
2. To what extent are the comments related to the topic under discussion?
     1   2   3   4   5

The numerical rating scale is useful when the characteristics or qualities to be rated can be classified into a limited number of categories and when there is general agreement concerning the category represented by each number. As commonly used, however, the numbers are only vaguely defined, so that considerable variation in the interpretation and use of the scale occurs.

Graphic Rating Scale. The distinguishing feature of the graphic rating scale is that each characteristic is followed by a horizontal line. The rating is made by placing a check on the line. Typically a set of categories identifies specific positions along the line, but the rater is free to check between these points if he desires.

EXAMPLES

Directions: Indicate the degree to which this pupil contributes to class discussions by placing an *x* anywhere along the horizontal line under each item.

1. To what extent does the pupil participate in discussion?

      never   seldom   occasionally   frequently   always

2. To what extent are the comments related to the topic under discussion?

      never   seldom   occasionally   frequently   always

The scale shown in this example uses the same set of categories for each characteristic and is commonly referred to as a *constant-alternatives* scale. Where these categories vary from one characteristic to another the scale is called, quite logically, a *changing-alternatives* scale.

Although the line in the graphic rating scale makes it possible to rate at intermediate points, the use of single words to identify the categories has no great advantage over the use of numbers. There is little agreement among raters concerning the meaning of such terms as *seldom, occasionally,* and *frequently.* What is needed are behavior descriptions which indicate more specifically what pupils are like who possess various degrees of the characteristic being rated.

Descriptive Graphic Rating Scale. This rating form uses descriptive phrases to identify the points on a graphic scale. The descriptions are thumbnail sketches which convey in behavioral terms what pupils are like at different steps along the scale. In some scales, only the center and end positions are described. In others, a descriptive phrase is placed beneath each designated point. A space for comments is also frequently provided, to enable the rater to clarify his rating or to record behavioral incidents pertinent to the characteristics being rated.

EXAMPLES

Directions: Make your ratings on each of the following characteristics by placing an *x* anywhere along the horizontal line, under each item. In the space for comments, include anything that helps clarify your rating.

1. To what extent does the pupil participate in discussions?

⌐———————┬———————┬———————┬———————⌐

| Never participates; quite, passive | Participates as much as other group members | Participates more than any other group member |

Comment:

2. To what extent are the comments related to the topic under discussion?

⌐———————┬———————┬———————┬———————⌐

| Comments ramble, distract from topic | Comments usually pertinent, occasionally wanders from topic | Comments are always related to topic |

Comment:

The descriptive graphic rating scale is generally the most satisfactory for school use. It clarifies to both the teacher and the pupil the types of behavior that represent different degrees of progress toward desired learning outcomes. The more specific behavior descriptions also contribute to greater objectivity and accuracy during the rating process.

Ranking Methods. some rating procedures do not require a printed scale. Probably the most applicable and best known of these is the simple *rank-order method*. With this approach, the pupils (or products) being rated are merely ranked in the order in which the rater estimates they posess the characteristic being judged. Typically, the rater will rank from both ends toward the middle. For example, a teacher may rank all of his pupils in order of their "participation in class discussion," by indicating the one who is highest in participation, then the one who is lowest, then the one who is next highest, next lowest, and so on, until a complete ranking is obtained. Ranking from the ends toward the middle simplifies the procedure and increases the likelihood that the pupils will be properly ranked. Even with this refinement, however, ranking is a cumbersome procedure if the number to be ranked is large.

A practical modification of the usual ranking method requires the rater to sort the pupils (or products) into a given number of groups. This is essentially the procedure followed when essay questions, English themes, and various types of class projects are divided into groups, on the basis of overall quality, for the purpose of assigning letter grades (i.e., A, B, C, D, and E). This division into groups is also frequently used as a first step in complete ranking. The pupils (or products) are sorted into a series of graded groups and then ranked within each group.

A more precise, though time-consuming, procedure for obtaining a ranking of pupils (or products) is by means of the *paired-comparison method*. With this approach, each pupil is paired with every other pupil and the rater indicates which one of each pair is superior in the characteristic being rated. A simple tally of the number of times each pupil is checked as superior provides the basis for ranking. Since the rater is required to judge whether each pupil is better or worse than each of the other pupils in the group, the results tend to be more reliable than those obtained by the usual ranking procedure. The number of comparisons required, however, severely curtails the use of this procedure. It is most useful where there is a relatively small number of pupils (or products) to be rated, and in those research situations where reliability is given a much higher priority than the practicality of the procedures.

In comparison to rating scales, ranking methods have one important advantage. They force the rater to differentiate among the pupils being rated. He cannot rate them all high or all average as is possible on a rating scale. With ranking, the pupils (or products) must be placed in relative order from high to low. The two major limitations of ranking procedures are: (1) they do not provide behavioral descriptions of the pupils, and (2) the meaning of a rank depends on the size and nature of the group. Ranking tenth in a group of ten is quite different from ranking tenth in a group of forty. Also, a pupil who ranks tenth in a gifted group might be superior to a pupil who ranks first in a regular classroom group.

Uses of Rating Scales

Rating scales can be used in the evaluation of a wide variety of learning outcomes and aspects of development. As a matter of convenience these uses may be classified into three major evaluation areas: (1) procedure, (2) product, and (3) personal-social development.

Procedure Evaluation. In many areas, achievement is expressed specifically through the performance of the pupil. Typical examples include the ability to give a speech, manipulate laboratory equipment, work effectively in a group, sing, play a musical instrument, and perform various physical feats. Such activities do not result in a product that can be evaluated, and paper-and-pencil tests are generally inadequate. Consequently, the procedures used in the performance itself must be observed and judged.

Rating scales are especially useful in evaluating procedures because they direct our attention to the same aspects of performance in all pupils, and they provide a common scale on which to record our judgments. If the rating form has been carefully prepared in terms of specific learning outcomes, it also serves as an excellent teaching device. The dimensions and behavior descriptions used in the scale make clear to the pupil the type of performance desired.

Two items from a typical rating scale for evaluating a speech are presented in Figure 16.2. The first part of the form is devoted to the content of the speech and how well it is organized. The second part is concerned with aspects of delivery such as gestures, posture, appearance, eye contact, voice, and enunciation. In developing such a scale, a teacher must, of course, include those characteristics which are most appropriate for the type of speaking ability to be evaluated and for the age level of the pupil to be judged.

Product Evaluation. Where pupil performance results in some type of product, it is frequently more desirable to judge the product rather than the procedures. The ability to write a theme, for example, is best evaluated by judging the quality of the theme itself. Little is to be learned by observing the pupil as he writes the theme. In some areas, however, such as typing, cooking, and woodworking, it might be most desirable to rate *procedures* during the early phases of learning and *products* later, after the basic skills have been mastered. In any event, product rating provides desirable evaluative information in many areas. In addition to those already mentioned, it is useful in evaluating such things as handwriting, drawings, maps, graphs, notebooks, term papers, book reports, and objects made in vocational courses.

A rating scale serves somewhat the same purposes in product evaluation that it does in procedure evaluation. It helps us to judge the products of all pupils in terms of the same characteristics, and it emphasizes to the pupils those qualities desired in a superior product.

In some instances, it is necessary or desirable to judge a product in

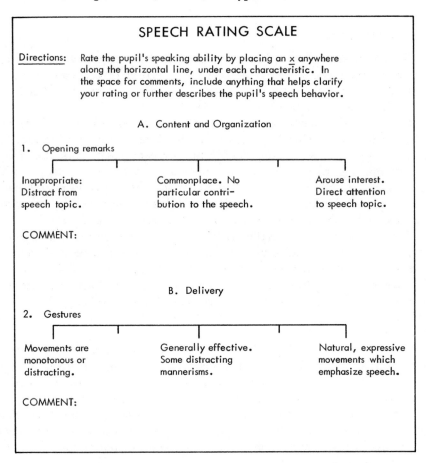

FIGURE 16.2. Sample items from speech rating scale.

terms of its overall quality rather than its separate features. Where this is the case, the products may be simply placed in rank order, or they may be compared to a product scale. A *product scale* is a series of samples of the product which have been carefully graded to represent different degrees of quality. An example of such a scale, for evaluating handwriting, is presented in Figure 16.3. The scale is used by moving a sample of the pupil's handwriting along the scale until the quality of the writing matches. The pupil's handwriting is then assigned the value indicated on the scale.

Product scales can be used in judging the quality of any product, but in most areas teachers will need to develop their own scales. This can be readily done by selecting samples of pupil work which represent from five to seven levels of quality and arranging them in order of merit. The levels can then be assigned a value from one to seven and each of the remaining pupil products can be compared to the scale and rated in terms of the quality level it matches most closely. Such a scale might be developed

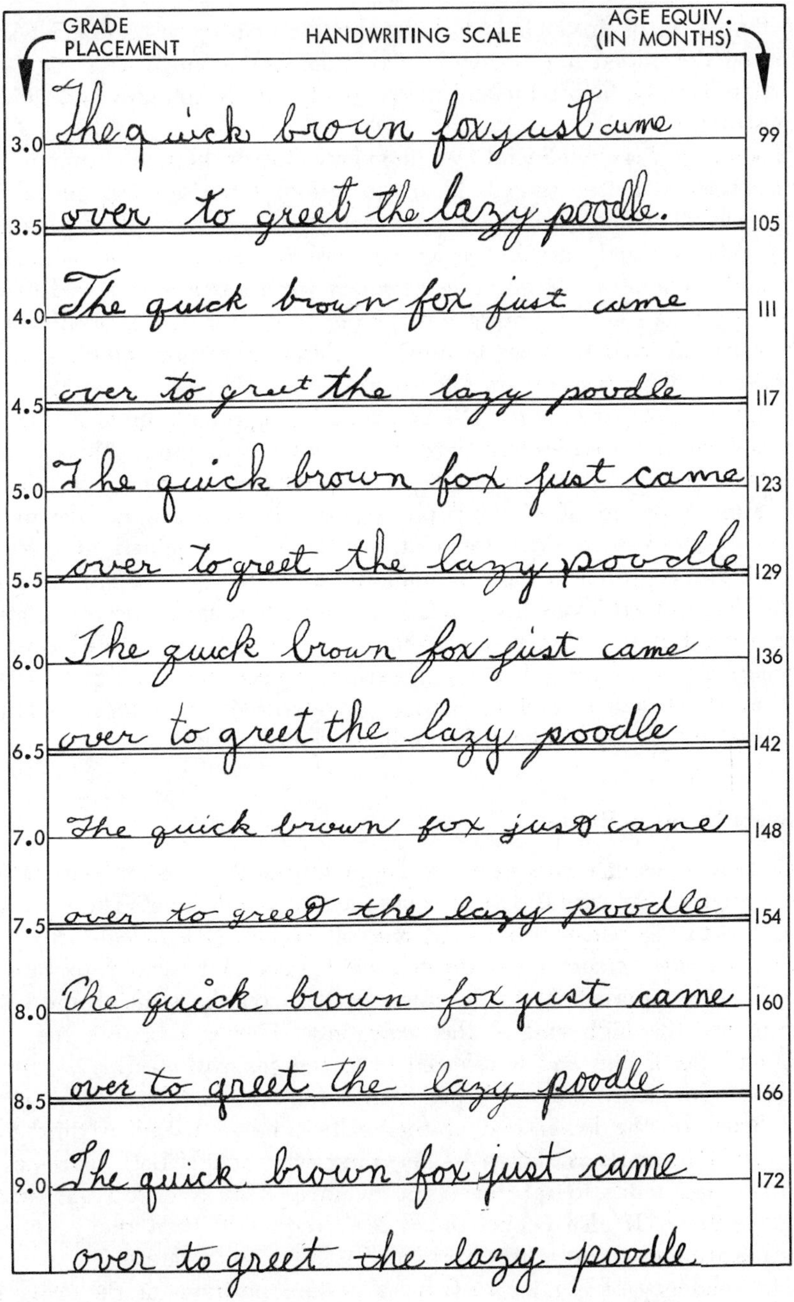

FIGURE 16.3. Handwriting scale used in the *California Achievement Tests*. (Copyright 1957 by California Test Bureau. Used by permission.)

each time a set of products is to be evaluated, or a more permanent scale might be developed and made available for pupil guidance. The latter procedure is to be favored where the product is fairly complex and difficult to construct.

Evaluating Personal-Social Development. One of the most common uses of rating scales in the schools is in the rating of various aspects of personal-social development. Most report cards have a special place for rating the pupils on such attributes as citizenship, interest, classroom conduct, and cooperation. In addition, teachers are frequently required to rate each pupil on a standard rating form at periodic intervals. Typically, these ratings are on such traits as leadership, initiative, responsibility, honesty, ability to get along with others, and emotional stability.

The rating of personal-social characteristics represents quite a different process from that used in procedure and product evaluation. When judging procedures and products, the ratings are usually made during or immediately after a period of directed observation. In contrast, ratings in the area of personal-social development are typically obtained at periodic intervals and represent a kind of summing up of the general impressions a teacher has formed about his pupils. The ratings are based on observation, to be sure, but the observations tend to be casual and spread over an extended period of time. We can generally expect such ratings to reflect more of the teacher's feelings and personal biases than those obtained at the end of a period of planned and directed observation.

Common Errors in Rating

Certain types of errors occur so frequently and persistently in ratings that special efforts are needed to counteract their influence. These include errors due to (1) personal bias, (2) halo effect, and (3) logical error.

Personal bias errors are indicated by a general tendency to rate all individuals at approximately the same position on the scale. Some raters tend to use the high end of the scale only. This is probably the most common type of bias and is referred to as the *generosity error*. Occurring much less frequently but with persistence for some raters is the *severity error*, whereby the lower end of the scale is favored. Still a third type of constant response is shown by the rater who avoids both extremes of the scale and tends to rate everyone average. This is called the *central tendency error*. It also occurs much less frequently than the generosity error but it tends to be a fixed response style for some raters.

The tendency of a rater to favor a certain position on the scale has two undesirable results. First, it makes a single rating of an individual of dubious value. A high or low rating might reflect the personal outlook of the rater rather than the personal characteristics of the person rated. This is not quite so serious if the ratings are used only in the local school setting. In a local school situation, we are apt to know the rating habits of individual teachers and are thus able to discount their tendencies to overrate or underrate. Second, favoring a certain position on the scale limits the range of any given individual's ratings. Therefore, even if we make allowances for a teacher's general tendency to rate pupils high, the ratings for different pupils may be so close together that they fail to provide reliable discriminations.

The *halo effect* is an error that occurs when a rater's general impression of a person influences how he rates him on individual characteristics. If the rater has a favorable attitude toward the person being rated he will tend to rate him high on all traits; if his attitude is unfavorable he will tend to rate him low. This differs from the generosity and severity errors where the rater tends to rate everyone high or everyone low.

Since the halo effect causes a pupil to receive similar ratings on all characteristics, it tends to obscure his strengths and weaknesses on different traits. This obviously limits the value of the ratings, even though the general impression the pupil has created might be a valid indication of how he influences others.

A *logical error* results when two characteristics are rated as more alike, or less alike, than they actually are because of the rater's beliefs concerning their relationship. In rating intelligence, for example, teachers tend to overrate the intelligence of pupils with high achievement because they logically expect the two characteristics to go together. Similarly, teachers who hold the common, but false, belief that gifted pupils have poor social adjustment will tend to underrate them on social characteristics. The errors, here, do not result from biases toward certain pupils on certain positions on the rating scale, but rather from the rater's preconceived notions concerning human nature. He assumes a more direct relationship among traits than actually exists and errs accordingly.

The various types of errors which appear in ratings are rather disconcerting to the classroom teacher who must depend on rating scales for evaluating certain aspects of learning and development. Fortunately, however, the errors can be markedly reduced by proper design and proper use.

Principles of Effective Rating

The improvement of ratings requires careful attention to selection of the characteristics to be rated, design of the rating form, and conditions under which the ratings are obtained. The following principles summarize the most important considerations in these areas. Since the descriptive graphic rating scale is the most generally useful form for school purposes, the principles are directed specifically toward the construction and use of this type of rating scale.

1. *Characteristics should be educationally significant.* Rating scales, like other evaluation instruments, must be in harmony with the objectives and

desired learning outcomes of the school. Thus, when constructing or selecting a rating scale the best guide for determining what characteristics are most significant is our list of specific learning outcomes. Where these have been clearly stated in behavioral terms, it is often simply a matter of selecting those that can be most effectively evaluated by ratings and then modifying the statements to fit the rating format.

2. *Characteristics should be directly observable.* There are two considerations involved in direct observation. First, the characteristics should be limited to those that occur in school situations so that the teacher has an opportunity to observe them. Second, they should be characteristics that are clearly visible to an observer. Overt behaviors like participation in classroom discussion, clear enunciation, and skill in social relations can be readily observed and reliably rated. However, less tangible types of behavior, such as *interest* in the opposite sex, *feeling* of inferiority, and *attitude* toward minority groups, tend to be unreliably rated because their presence must be inferred from outward signs which are indefinite, variable, and easily faked. Whenever possible, we should confine our ratings to those characteristics which can be observed and judged directly.

3. *Characteristics and points on the scale should be clearly defined.* Many of the errors in rating arise from the use of general, vague trait characterizations and inadequate identification of the scale points. The brief descriptions used with the descriptive graphic rating scale help overcome this weakness. They not only clarify the meaning of the points on the scale but they also contribute to a fuller understanding of each characteristic being rated. Where it is infeasible or inconvenient to use a descriptive scale, as on the back of a school report card, a separate sheet of instructions can be used to provide the desired behavioral descriptions.

4. *Between three and seven rating positions should be provided and raters should be permitted to mark at intermediate points.* The exact number of points to be designated on a particular scale is determined largely by the nature of the judgments to be made. In areas permitting only crude judgments, fewer scale positions are needed. There is usually no advantage in going beyond the seven-point scale, however. Only rarely can we make finer discriminations than this, and we provide for those few situations by allowing the rater to mark between points if he so desires.

5. *Raters should be instructed to omit ratings where they feel unqualified to judge.* Rating scales to evaluate personal-social adjustment are apt to contain some characteristics which the teacher has had little or no opportunity to observe. To require ratings on such traits merely introduces error into the descriptions of the pupil. It is far better to permit the rater to omit these ratings. Some rating forms provide a place to check "unable to judge" or "insufficient opportunity to observe" for each characteristic. Others provide a space for comments after each characteristic, where it is possible either to justify the rating given or to note the reason for not making a rating.

6. Ratings from several observers should be combined, wherever possible. The pooled ratings of several teachers will generally provide a more reliable description of pupil behavior than that obtained from any one teacher. In averaging ratings, the personal biases of individual raters tend to cancel each other out. Combined ratings are especially applicable at the high school level, where specific teacher-pupil contact is limited but each pupil has classes with a number of teachers. They are less feasible at the elementary school level, since here we are apt to have only the ratings of the pupil's one regular teacher. The lack of additional raters at this level, however, is at least partially offset by the greater opportunity for the teacher to observe his pupils in a variety of situations. Furthermore, the smaller number of elementary teachers in a school makes it easier to detect and allow for common biases, such as the tendency to overrate or underrate pupils.

CHECKLISTS

A checklist is similar in appearance and use to the rating scale. The basic differences between them is in the type of judgment called for. A rating scale provides an opportunity to indicate the *degree* to which a characteristic is present or the *frequency* with which a behavior occurs. The checklist, on the other hand, calls for a simple "yes-no" judgment. It is basically a method of recording whether a characteristic is present or absent, or whether an action was taken or not taken. Obviously, a checklist should not be used where degree or frequency of occurrence are important aspects of the appraisal.

Checklists are especially useful in evaluating those performance skills that can be divided into a series of clearly defined, specific actions. A typical example of such a checklist is shown in Figure 16.4. This instrument makes it possible to record the actions of a pupil as he attempts to locate an object under the miscroscope. On the first part of the form, the teacher is to indicate the pupil's sequence of actions by numbering them in the order in which they occur. In other places, he is to check phrases which characterize the pupil's skill in using the microscope. This procedure requires the teacher to observe one pupil at a time and to record the actions as they occur.

The form in Figure 16.4 illustrates the major points to consider in developing a checklist for procedure evaluation. These may be summarized as follows:

1. Identify and describe clearly each of the specific actions desired in the performance.
2. Add to the list those actions which represent common errors, if they are

STUDENT'S ACTIONS	Sequence of Actions		STUDENT'S ACTIONS (Continued)	Sequence of Actions
a. Takes slide	1	ah.	Turns up fine adjustment screw a great distance	
b. Wipes slide with lens paper	2	ai.	Turns fine adjustment screw a few turns	
c. Wipes slide with cloth		aj.	Removes slide from stage	16
d. Wipes slide with finger		ak.	Wipes objective with lens paper	
e. Moves bottle of culture along the table		al.	Wipes objective with cloth	
f. Places drop or two of culture on slide	3	am.	Wipes objective with finger	17
g. Adds more culture		an.	Wipes eyepiece with lens paper	
h. Adds few drops of water		ao.	Wipes eyepiece with cloth	
i. Hunts for cover glasses	4	ap.	Wipes eyepiece with finger	18
j. Wipes cover glass with lens paper	5	aq.	Makes another mount	
k. Wipes cover glass with cloth		ar.	Takes another microscope	
l. Wipes cover with finger		as.	Finds object	
m. Adjusts cover with finger		at.	Pauses for an interval	
n. Wipes off surplus fluid		au.	Asks, "What do you want me to do?"	
o. Places slide on stage	6	av.	Asks whether to use high power	
p. Looks thru eyepiece with right eye		aw.	Says, "I'm satisfied"	
q. Looks thru eyepice with left eye	7	ax.	Says that the mount is all right for his eye	
r. Turns to objective of lowest power	9	ay.	Says he cannot do it	19,24
s. Turns to low-power objective	21	az.	Told to start a new mount	
t. Turns to high-power objective		aaa.	Directed to find object under low power	20
u. Holds one eye closed	8	aab.	Directed to find object under high power	
v. Looks for light				
w. Adjusts concave mirror				
x. Adjusts plane mirror		**NOTICEABLE CHARACTERISTICS OF STUDENT'S BEHAVIOR**		
y. Adjusts diaphragm				
z. Does not touch diaphragm	10	a.	Awkward in movements	
aa. With eye at eyepiece turns down coarse adjustment	11	b.	Obviously dexterous in movements	
ab. Breaks cover glass	12	c.	Slow and deliberate	✓
ac. Breaks slide		d.	Very rapid	
ad. With eye away from eyepiece turns down coarse adjustment		e.	Fingers tremble	
ae. Turns up coarse adjustment a great distance	13,22	f.	Obviously perturbed	
af. With eye at eyepiece turns down fine adjustment a great distance	14,23	g.	Obviously angry	
ag. With eye away from eyepiece turns down fine adjustment a great distance	15	h.	Does not take work seriously	
		i.	Unable to work without specific directions	✓
		j.	Obviously satisfied with his unsuccessful efforts	✓

SKILLS IN WHICH STUDENT NEEDS FURTHER TRAINING	Sequence of Actions		CHARACTERIZATION OF THE STUDENT'S MOUNT	Sequence of Actions
		a.	Poor light	✓
a. In cleaning objective	✓	b.	Poor focus	
b. In cleaning eyepiece	✓	c.	Excellent mount	
c. In focusing low power	✓	d.	Good mount	
d. In focusing high power	✓	e.	Fair mount	
e. In adjusting mirror	✓	f.	Poor mount	
f. In using diaphragm	✓	g.	Very poor mount	
g. In keeping both eyes open	✓	h.	Nothing in view but a thread in his eyepiece	
h. In protecting slide and objective from breaking by careless focusing	✓	i.	Something on objective	
		j.	Smeared lens	✓
		k.	Unable to find object	✓

FIGURE 16.4. Checklist for evaluating skill in the use of the microscope. (From Ralph W. Tyler, "A Test of Skill in Using a Microscope," *Educational Research Bulletin,* 9:493–96, 1930. Bureau of Educational Research and Service, Ohio State University. Used by permission.)

limited in number and can be clearly identified (for example, actions *c* and *d* in Figure 16.4).

3. Arrange the desired actions and likely errors in the approximate order in which they are expected to occur.
4. Provide a simple procedure for numbering the actions in sequence or for checking each action as it occurs.

In addition to its use in procedure evaluation, the checklist can also be used in evaluating products. For this purpose, the form usually consists of a list of characteristics which the finished product should possess. In evaluating the product, the teacher simply checks whether each characteristic is present or absent. Before using a checklist for product evaluation, it should be decided that the quality of the product can be adequately described by merely noting the presence or absence of certain characteristics. If quality is more precisely indicated by noting the *degree* to which each characteristic is present, a rating scale should be used instead of a checklist.

In the area of personal-social development, the checklist can serve as a convenient method of recording evidence of growth toward specific learning outcomes. Typically, the form lists the behaviors which have been identified as representative of the outcomes to be evaluated. An illustrative form for evaluating pupils' "concern for others" is shown in Figure 16.5. With this form, the teacher writes a pupil's name at the top of each column and periodically checks those behaviors in which growth has been noted. A more detailed account can also be kept on this form by dating each particular behavior observed in a pupil.

The checklist is probably *least* useful in summarizing a teacher's general impressions concerning the personality and adjustment of pupils. In evaluating such characteristics as initiative, social maturity, and emotional stability, for example, it is seldom sufficient to note merely whether the trait is present or absent. Here, we are largely concerned with the degree to which a characteristic is present or the frequency with which certain behaviors occur. Since these finer discriminations are almost always possible, we should generally favor the rating scale in this area. Only where our appraisal is so rough that we are limited to a simple "present-absent" judgment should we resort to the use of a checklist.

PUPIL PARTICIPATION IN RATING

In this chapter, we have limited our discussion to observational methods used by the teacher. We purposely omitted those checklists and rating scales used as self-report techniques by pupils since these will be considered in the following chapter. Before closing our discussion here, however, it should be pointed out that most of the devices used for recording the teacher's observations can also be used by the pupil to judge his own

	Concern for Others

Note: Check each child two or three times during the term to determine if growth has taken place.

School _____

Date _____

Behavior to be observed	Names of Children									
Is sensitive to needs and problems of others										
Helps others meet needs and solve problems										
Willingly shares ideas and materials										
Accepts suggestions and help										
Makes constructive suggestions										
Sticks to group plans and decisions										
Works courteously and happily with others										
Gives encouragement to others										
Respects the property of others										
Enjoys group work										
Thanks others for help										
Commends others for contributions										

FIGURE 16.5. Checklist for evaluating pupil's "Concern for Others." (From John U. Michaelis, *Social Studies for Children in a Democracy.* Copyright 1968, by Prentice-Hall, Inc., Englewood Cliffs, New Jersey. Used by permission.)

progress. From an instructional standpoint, it is frequently useful to have a pupil rate himself (or his product) and then compare his rating with that of the teacher. If this comparison is made during an individual conference, the pupil and teacher can explore the reasons for each rating and discuss any marked discrepancies between the two sets of ratings.

Self-rating by the pupil and a follow-up conference with the teacher have a number of potential benefits. It should help the pupil to (1) understand better the objectives of the course, (2) recognize more clearly the progress he is making toward the objectives, (3) diagnose more effectively his own particular strengths and weaknesses, and (4) develop increased skill in self-evaluation. Of special value to the teacher is the additional insight gained. He has an opportunity to see how each pupil views his own learning and development in relation to the goals of the course.

Pupil participation need not be limited to the *use* of the evaluation instruments. It is frequently desirable also to have pupils take an active part in the *development* of the instruments. Through class discussion, for example, they can help identify the qualities desired in a "good speech" or a "well-written report," or the particular behaviors that characterize "good citizenship." A combined list of these suggestions can then be used as a basis for constructing a rating scale or checklist. Involving pupils in the development of evaluation devices has special instructional values. First, it directs learning by causing the pupils to think more carefully about the qualities to strive for in a performance or product. Second, it has a motivating effect, since pupils tend to put forth most effort when working toward goals they have helped to define.

SUMMARY

Observational techniques are especially useful in evaluating performance skills and certain aspects of personal-social development. In addition, the results of observation supplement and complement paper-and-pencil testing by indicating how pupils typically behave in natural situations.

The least structured of the observational techniques is the anecdotal record. This is simply a method of recording factual descriptions of pupil behavior. To make anecdotal record keeping feasible, it is desirable to restrict observations at any given time to a few types of behavior or to a few pupils. Anecdotal records possess the advantages of (1) providing a description of behavior in natural settings, (2) highlighting evidence of exceptional behavior which is apt to be overlooked by other techniques, and (3) being usable with the very young and the retarded. Their limitations are (1) the time and effort required to maintain an adequate record system, (2) the difficulty of writing objective descriptions of behavior, and (3) the problem of obtaining an adequate sample of behavior. These limitations can be minimized by following specific procedures for observing and recording the behavioral incidents. Suggestions for improving anecdotal records include: (1) determining in advance what to observe, (2) describing the setting in which the behavior occurred, (3) making the record as soon as possible after observing the behavior, (4) limiting each anecdote to a single incident, (5) separating factual description from interpretation, (6) recording both positive and negative incidents, (7) collecting a number of anecdotes before drawing inferences, and (8) obtaining practice in observing and recording pupil behavior.

Rating methods provide a systematic procedure for obtaining and recording the judgments of observers. Of the several types of rating scales available, the descriptive graphic scale seems to be the most satisfactory for school use. For some purposes, ranking methods also are useful. In the rating of procedures, products, and various aspects of personal-social development certain types of errors commonly occur. These include: (1) personal bias, (2) halo effect, and (3) logical errors. The control of such errors is a major consideration in constructing and using rating scales. Effective ratings result when we (1) select characteristics which are educationally significant, (2) limit ratings to directly observable behavior, (3) define clearly the characteristics and the points on the scale, (4) limit the number of points on the scale, (5) permit raters to omit ratings where they feel unable to judge, and (6) combine ratings from several raters, wherever possible.

Checklists perform somewhat the same functions as rating scales. They are used in evaluating procedures, products, and aspects of personal-social development where an evaluation of the characteristics is limited to a simple "present-absent" judgment.

Involving pupils in the construction and use of rating devices has special values from the standpoint of learning and aids in the development of self-evaluation skills.

LEARNING EXERCISES

1. Select one of the following and construct a rating scale that would be useful for evaluating the effectiveness of the *performance*.
   a. Giving an oral report.
   b. Working in the laboratory.
   c. Participating in group work.
   d. Playing some type of game.
   e. Demonstrating some skill.
2. Select one of the following and construct a rating scale or checklist that would be useful for evaluating the product.
   a. Constructing a map, chart, or graph.
   b. Writing a personal or business letter.
   c. Writing a theme, poem, or short story.
   d. Making a drawing or painting.
   e. Making a product in home economics.
   f. Making a product in industrial education.
3. Prepare a checklist for evaluating the ability to drive an automobile. Would a rating scale be better for this purpose? What are the relative advantages of each?
4. On which of the following characteristics would you expect teachers' ratings to be most accurate? Why?
   a. Appearance.
   b. Attitude toward school.
   c. Leadership.
   d. Self-confidence.

5. What are the advantages and disadvantages of using "product scales" in rating?
6. Observe a child at play and write an anecdotal record. Give both your descriptive account of the child's behavior and your interpretation of the behavior, but place these under separate headings.
7. What are the relative advantages and disadvantages of each of the following for evaluating pupils' "creativity"?
   a. Anecdotal records.
   b. Teachers' ratings.
   c. Checklists.
   d. Tests of creativity.
8. List and briefly describe the steps you would follow if you were going to have pupils participate in evaluating the effectiveness of their class discussion.

SUGGESTIONS FOR FURTHER READING

BRANDT, R. M. *Studying Behavior in Natural Settings.* New York: Holt, Rinehart & Winston, Inc., 1972. Good discussion of the problems associated with observational techniques.

CRONBACH, L. J. *Essentials of Psychological Testing,* 3rd ed. New York: Harper & Row Publishers, 1970. Chapter 17, "Judgments and Systematic Observations." Emphasizes use of ratings and means of improving them.

FITZPATRICK, R., and E. J. MORRISON. "Performance and Product Evaluation," Chapter 9 in R. L. Thorndike (ed.), *Educational Measurement.* Washington, D.C.: American Council on Education, 1971. A comprehensive discussion of the principles and procedures involved in evaluating performance and products.

TENBRINK, T. D. *Evaluation: A Practical Guide for Teachers.* New York: McGraw-Hill Book Company, 1974. Chapter 10, "Constructing Checklists and Rating Scales." Provides numerous examples to illustrate the practical suggestions for construction.

THORNDIKE, R. L., and E. HAGEN. *Measurement and Evaluation in Psychology and Education,* 3rd ed. New York: John Wiley & Sons, Inc., 1969. Extensive discussion of rating methods and problems involved in obtaining sound ratings.

CHAPTER 17

Evaluating Learning and Development: Peer Appraisal and Self-Report

Judgments and reports made by pupils themselves provide valuable information in many areas of learning and development. (1) Peer judgments . . . determined by sociometric procedures . . . are especially useful in evaluating personal-social development. . . . (2) Self-report methods provide a fuller understanding of pupils' needs, problems, adjustments, interests, and attitudes . . . aid in assessing learning readiness . . . in curriculum planning . . . in pupil guidance.

A teacher's observations and judgments of pupil behavior are of special value in those areas where the behavior is readily observable and the teacher's training and experience give him special competence to judge. In evaluating the ability to operate a microscope or the quality of handwriting, for example, the teacher is unquestionably in the best position to make the judgment. He can directly observe the procedure, or the product resulting from the procedure, and his knowledge in the area contributes to the validity and reliability of the judgments. There are some areas of pupil development, however, where the teacher's evaluation of behavior is apt to be inadequate unless his observations are supplemented and complemented by the judgments and reports of pupils.

Various aspects of personal-social development can be more effectively evaluated by including peer ratings and other *peer-appraisal* methods in the evaluation program. In the realms of leadership ability, concern for others, effectiveness in group work, and social acceptability, for example, pupils frequently know better than the teacher each other's strengths and weaknesses. The intimate interactions that occur in the give and take of peer relations are seldom fully visible to an outside observer. Some differences between teacher judgment and peer judgment can also be expected to occur because each is using different standards. Children's criteria of social acceptability, for example, are apt to be quite different from the criteria used by adults.

Self-report techniques are also a valuable adjunct to the teacher's observations of behavior. A complete picture of a pupil's adjustments, interests, and attitudes cannot be obtained without a report from the pupil. His own expressed feelings and beliefs in these areas are at least as important as evidence obtained from observing his actual behavior. Although expressed feelings and observable behavior are not always in complete harmony, the self-report provides valuable evidence concerning the pupil's perception of himself and how he wants others to view him. In fact, a discrepancy between reported feelings and actual behavior is, in itself, significant evaluative information.

Though peer appraisal and self-report techniques are useful for understanding pupils better and for guiding their learning, development, and adjustment, the results should *not* be used for marking and reporting, or in any manner that interferes with honest responses. The pupils must be convinced that it is in their own best interests to respond as accurately and frankly as possible. A teacher who has good relations with his pupils and who has consistently emphasized the positive values of the evaluation information should have no difficulty in obtaining the pupils' cooperation in the effective use of these techniques.

PEER APPRAISAL

In some instances it is possible to have pupils rate their peers (fellow pupils) on the same rating device used by the teacher. At the conclusion of a pupil's oral report before the class, for example, the other pupils could rate his performance on a standard rating form. The average of these ratings would provide a good indication of how the group felt about the pupil's performance. Except for oral reports, speeches, demonstrations, and similar situations where one individual performs at a time, however, the usual rating procedures are seldom feasible with pupils. If we ask pupils to rate their classmates on a series of personal-social characteristics, each pupil is required to fill out thirty or more rating forms. This becomes so cumbersome and time consuming that we could hardly expect the ratings to be diligently made. When peer ratings and other methods of peer appraisal are used, we must depend on greatly simplified procedures. Some of the techniques are so simple that they can be used effectively with pupils at the primary school level.

The two most widely used techniques in this area are the (1) "guess who" technique, and (2) sociometric technique. Each of these will be described in turn.

"Guess Who" Technique

One of the simplest methods of obtaining peer judgments is by means of the "guess who" technique. With this procedure, each pupil is presented with a series of brief behavior descriptions and asked to name those pupils who best fit each description. The descriptions may be limited to positive characteristics or they may also include negative behaviors. The following items, taken from a form for evaluating *concern for others,* are typical of the types of positive and negative descriptions used:

1. Here is someone who is *willing* to share ideas and materials with others.
2. Here is someone who does *not* care to share ideas and material with others.

Some teachers prefer to use only the positive behavior descriptions because of the possible harmful effects of negative nominations on group morale. Each individual teacher must make this decision for himself, however, since he is the only one in a position to determine what the effects might be on his pupils. Where good relations have been established among pupils and between teacher and pupils, this is not likely to be a problem. However, if doubt exists, it is usually better to sacrifice part of the evaluative data than to disrupt the morale of the class.

In naming persons for each behavior description, the pupils are usually permitted to name as few or as many as they wish. Typical directions and sample items from a form for evaluating various personal-social characteristics are shown in Figure 17.1. The directions and behavior descriptions must, of course, be adapted to the age level of the pupils. With very young pupils, the technique can be presented as a guessing game with items stated as follows: "Here is someone who talks a lot—guess who?" When the technique is used with older pupils the "guess who" aspect is dropped, and the pupils are merely told to write the names of those who best fit each behavior description.

The "guess who" technique is based on the nomination method of obtaining peer ratings and is scored by simply counting the number of mentions each pupil receives on each description. If both positive and negative descriptions are used, such as friendly and unfriendly, the number of negative mentions on each characteristic are subtracted from the number of positive mentions. For example, 12 mentions as being friendly and 2 mentions of being unfriendly would result in a score of 10 on friendliness. The pattern of scores for each pupil indicates the reputation he holds among his peers. This may not completely agree with the teacher's impressions of the pupil but it is nonetheless significant information concerning personal-social development. In fact, one of the great values of this type of peer appraisal is that it makes the teacher aware of feelings and attitudes among pupils which he had been unable to detect through direct observation.

SOCIAL ANALYSIS OF THE CLASSROOM

Directions

Below are some word pictures of members of your class. Read each statement and write down the names of the persons whom you think the descriptions fit.

REMEMBER: One description may fit several persons. You may write as many names as you think belong under each.

The same person may be nominated for more than one description.

Write "myself" if you think the description fits you.

If you cannot think of anyone to match a particular description, go on to the next one.

You will have as much time as you need to finish. Do not hurry.

NOW YOU ARE READY TO BEGIN.

3. Here is someone who likes to talk a lot, always has something to say.

4. Here is someone who doesn't like to talk much, is very quiet, even when nearly everyone else is talking.

13. This is someone who is always cheerful, jolly, and good-natured, who laughs and smiles a good deal.

14. Here is someone who always seems rather sad, worried, or unhappy, who hardly ever laughs or smiles.

35. Here is someone who is very friendly, who has lots of friends, who is nice to everybody.

36. Here is someone who does not care to make friends or who is bashful about being friendly, or who does not seem to have many friends.

FIGURE 17.1. Sample items from a "Guess Who" form used to evaluate various personal-social characteristics. (From Ruth Cunningham, *Understanding Group Behavior of Boys and Girls*. Copyright 1951 by Bureau of Publications, Teachers College, Columbia University. Used by permission.)

This nominating method can be used to evaluate any aspect of personal-social development for which pupils have had an adequate opportunity to make observations. It is especially valuable for appraising personality characteristics, character traits, and social skills, but it is not limited to these areas. Figure 17.2 contains a list of "guess who" statements which were used to evaluate five different dimensions of creative thinking.[1] The dimension each item attempted to measure is indicated in parentheses following the question. As with other evaluation techniques, the specific items used in any particular "guess who" form should be derived directly from the objectives to be evaluated.

1. Who in your class comes up with the most ideas?   (Fluency)

2. Who has the most original or unusual ideas?   (Originality)

3. If the situation changed or if a solution to a problem wouldn't work, who in your class would be the first to find a new way of meeting the problem?   (Flexibility)

4. Who in your class does the most inventing and developing of new ideas, gadgets, and such?   (Inventiveness)

5. Who in your class is best at thinking of all the details involved in working out a new idea and thinking of all the consequences? (Elaboration)

FIGURE 17.2. Sample "Guess Who" items for evaluating aspects of creative thinking ability. (From E. Paul Torrance, *Guiding Creative Talent.* Copyright 1962 by Prentice-Hall, Inc. Used by permission.)

The main advantage of the "guess who" technique is its usability. It can be administered in a relatively few minutes, to pupils of all age levels, and scoring is a simple matter of counting the number of nominations received. Its main limitation is the lack of information it provides on the shy, withdrawn pupil. Such pupils are frequently overlooked when nomination methods are used. In effect, they have no reputation in the peer group and are simply ignored during the rating process.

Sociometric Techniques

The sociometric technique is a method for evaluating the social acceptance of individual pupils and the social structure of a group. It is also a

---

[1] E. P. Torrance, *Guiding Creative Talent* (Englewood Cliffs, N.J.: Prentice-Hall, 1962).

relatively simple technique, based on pupils' choices of companions for some group situation or activity. A typical sociometric form is shown in Figure 17.3. This form was used to measure pupils' acceptance as seating companions, work companions, and play companions at the later elementary school level. The directions illustrate several important principles of sociometric choosing. (1) The choices should be real choices which are natural parts of the ongoing activities in the classroom. (2) The basis for choice and the restrictions on the choosing should be made clear. (3) All pupils should be equally free to participate in the activity or situation.

Name_____ Date_____

   During the next few weeks we will be changing our seats around, working in small groups and playing some group games. Now that we all know each other by name, you can help me arrange groups that work and play best together. You can do this by writing the names of the children you would like to have sit near you, to have work with you, and to have play with you. You may choose anyone in this room you wish, including those pupils who are absent. Your choices will not be seen by anyone else. Give first name and initial of last name.

   Make your choices carefully so the groups will be the way you really want them. I will try to arrange the groups so that each pupil gets at least two of his choices. Sometimes it is hard to give everyone his first few choices so be sure to make five choices for each question.

Remember!
1. Your choices must be from pupils in this room, including those who are absent.

2. You should give the first name and the initial of the last name.

3. You should make all five choices for each question.

4. You may choose a pupil for more than one group if you wish.

5. Your choices will not be seen by anyone else.

I would choose to sit near these children:

1. _____ 3. _____
2. _____ 4. _____
           5. _____

I would choose to work with these children:

1. _____ 3. _____
2. _____ 4. _____
           5. _____

I would choose to play with these children:

1. _____ 3. _____
2. _____ 4. _____
           5. _____

FIGURE 17.3. Illustrative sociometric form. (From *Sociometry in the Classroom.* Copyright 1959 by Norman E. Gronlund.)

(4) The choices each pupil makes should be kept strictly confidential. (5) The choices should be actually used to organize or rearrange groups. More spontaneous and truthful responses can be expected where the pupils know that their choices will be put into effect.

School activities abound with possibilities for sociometric choosing. Pupils can choose laboratory partners, fellow committee members, companions for group projects, and the like. Although some differences in choice can be expected from one choosing situation to another, a large element of social acceptance runs through all choices. A pupil who is highly chosen for one activity will also tend to be highly chosen for other activities. Greatest variation in the choosing occurs where very specific activities are used and where skill and knowledge play a prominent role in successful performance. Even a relatively unpopular pupil might be highly chosen as a team mate for baseball if he is an exceptionally good player. It is unlikely that he would be chosen as seating companion in the classroom, however, since this is almost a pure measure of social acceptance.

There is some disagreement among sociometric experts concerning the desirability of asking pupils to name also those whom they would *not* want as a companion. The arguments in favor of such negative choices are that rejected pupils can be identified and helped, and that interpersonal friction can be avoided in arranging groups. The counterargument is that such questions make pupils more conscious of their feelings of rejection and that this may disturb both group morale and the emotional development of pupils. The safest procedure seems to be to avoid the use of negative choices unless they are absolutely essential to the purpose for which the technique is being used. Where their use is essential, the approach should be casual and the pupils permitted, rather than required, to make such choices. A statement like the following will ordinarily suffice: "If there are pupils you would rather not have in your group, you may also list their names."

It is usually desirable to restrict the number of choices each pupil makes on a sociometric question. For most purposes, five choices for each activity is a suitable number. Sociometric results have been shown to increase in reliability up to five choices, with no increase beyond that number.[2] Also, five choices makes it easier to arrange sociometric groups since it is sometimes difficult to satisfy the first several choices for all pupils. At the lower elementary grades, it is usually necessary to limit the choices to two or three. Very young children find it difficult to discriminate beyond this number.

Tabulating Sociometric Results. The pupil's sociometric choices must be organized in some fashion, if we are to interpret and use them properly. A simple tally of the number of choices each pupil receives will indicate degree of social acceptance, but it will not provide information concerning

---

[2] N. E. Gronlund, *Sociometry in the Classroom* (New York: Harper and Row, 1959).

who made the choices, whether two pupils chose each other, and what the social structure of the group is like. A complete record of the sociometric results can be obtained by tabulating the choices in a matrix table like the one shown in Figure 17.4. Note that the pupils' names are listed down the side of the table and are numbered from 1 to 20. These same numbers, corresponding to the pupils' names, are then placed across the top of the table so that each pupil's choices can be recorded in the appropriate column. For example, the choices of John A. were as follows:

Chose	*Rejected*
1. Bill H.	X Hendy D.
2. George L.	X Bob F.
3. Mike A.	
4. Betty A.	
5. Pete V.	

These choices were recorded in the table to the right of John A.'s name by placing number 1 in column six to indicate Bill H. as his first choice, number 2 in column seven to indicate George L. as his second choice, and so on. The *X*s represent rejection choices and the circled numbers in the table indicate mutual choices. Note, for example, that Mike A. (number 2) chose Jim B. (number 3), and vice versa. Mutual choices are always an equal number of cells from the diagonal line, in each corresponding column and row.

In this particular tabulation form, the boys and girls are listed separately. This divides the main part of the table into four quarters. The boys' choices of boys fall in the upper left-hand quarter of the table and the girls' choices of girls fall in the lower right-hand quarter. The diagonal line, which goes through the empty cells that are unused because pupils do not choose themselves, cuts through these two quarters. The upper right-hand quarter and the lower left-hand quarter, then, contain only cross-sex choices. This division of the table makes the number of choices given to the same sex and to the opposite sex readily apparent and easy to summarize.

In totalling the number of choices received, in Figure 17.4, each choice was given a value of one regardless of level of choice. Some teachers prefer to weight the choices so that a first choice counts more than a second choice, and so on, but there is no rational basis for assigning such weights. Various arbitrary weighting systems have been tried but none has been shown to be superior to the method used here.[3] While it seems sensible to expect a pupil's first choice to have greater significance than his second, the degree to which choices differ cannot be predicted. One pupil may have a strong first preference, while another is equally attracted

---

[3] N. E. Gronlund, *Sociometry in the Classroom* (New York: Harper and Row, 1959).

Rejections Given		Choices Given				Pupils Chosen																		
SS	OS	SS	OS		Name	1	2	3	4	5	6	7	8	9	10	11	12	13	14	15	16	17	18	19	20
2	0	4	1	1	John A.		3		X	X	1	2	4	③	5		4								
2	0	5	0	2	Mike A.			②	X	X		①		④	5										
0	0	5	0	3	Jim B.		③					②		④	5	③									
0	0	4	1	4	Henry D.					①	2		3		4		5								
0	1	2	1	5	Bob F.						2	3	4				5	⊗							
0	1	2	3	6	Bill H.							②	①										⑤		
2	0	5	0	7	George L.		②	④		X	①		X	③	②	③									
0	0	4	1	8	Dick N.	4			5		①	3			②		5								
1	0	5	0	9	Dale P.		②	③		5	4	①	X												
0	0	4	1	10	Pete V.					5	2		①	3					4						
0	0	3	2	11	Mary A.						⑤		4			①	①	⑤	③				②		
0	0	5	0	12	Betty A.										5	①			②		①		③		④
1	1	4	1	13	Karen B.					⊗						②	②		X			③	4	X	③
1	0	4	1	14	Lois C.								5			1	2	4					④	X	5
1	0	5	0	15	Sharon J.											4	5	②	3						
0	0	3	2	16	Ann K.						3				2	4	5	①				①			
0	0	4	1	17	Margie M.											4	②		③		③				⑤
1	0	4	1	18	Sue R.						④					②	①	3				4	5	X	
0	1	5	0	19	Pat S.						5					2	1	4	②				③	X	③
1	0	4	1	20	Carol W.			3		1	2	4		3		1	①	4							
				SS	Choices Received	1	4	3	2	3	8	7	5	4	5	7	8	6	5	0	2	3	6	0	4
				OS		0	0	0	0	1	4	0	2	0	2	1	4	0	2	0	0	0	1	0	0
				SS	Rejections Received	0	0	0	2	3	0	0	2	0	0	0	0	0	1	0	0	0	0	4	0
				OS		0	0	0	0	1	0	0	0	0	1	0	1	1	0	0	0	0	0	0	0
				SS	Mutual Choices	0	3	3	0	1	2	4	2	3	1	3	5	3	4	0	2	2	4	0	3
				OS		0	0	0	0	0	2	0	0	0	0	1	0	0	0	0	0	0	1	0	0

Central (School)
5A (Class)
F. R. Young (Teacher)

Note: SS = Same Sex   OS = Opposite Sex   X = Rejection

FIGURE 17.4. Matrix table showing choices and rejections of work companions. (From *Sociometry in the Classroom.* Copyright 1959 by Norman E. Gronlund.)

460

to several friends and finds it difficult to discriminate among his first several choices. Until a weighting system is found that handles such discrepancies, the simpler method of counting one for each choice should be used. The level of choice should still be recorded in the matrix table, however, since it is useful when the choices are used to organize groups.

The number of choices a pupil receives on a sociometric question is used as an indication of his social acceptance by peers. Where five choices are used, as in Figure 17.4, pupils who receive nine or more choices are called *stars*. Those who receive no choices are called *isolates*, and those who receive one choice are called *neglectees*. The remaining pupils, who fall somewhere above or below average, are given no special name. If a pupil receives only rejection choices, he is called a *rejectee*. As noted earlier, where pupils choose each other they are called *mutual* choices. This terminology is standard in describing and interpreting sociometric results.

The Sociogram. The matrix table is useful for organizing sociometric data for future use and for determining the social acceptance of individual pupils. It does not provide a clear picture of the social structure of the group, however. Where this is desired, the sociometric results are presented in the form of a sociogram. This is a graphic picture of the social relations existing in a group and it may be plotted directly from the data recorded in the matrix table. A typical sociogram is shown in Figure 17.5. The sociometric data depicted here were taken from Figure 17.4.

Note that the concentric circles form a target-type diagram on which to plot the sociometric data. Pupils in the star category (nine or more choices) are placed in the center of the target; isolates are placed in the outer ring; and the remaining pupils are placed between these extremes in terms of the number of choices received. The boys are represented by triangles and the girls by circles, with the numbers corresponding to each pupil's number in the matrix table (see Figure 17.4.). The uncluttered appearance of this sociogram is due to the fact that the use of lines is confined to mutual choices and rejections. Plotting all choices would result in such a maze of lines that the sociogram would be impossible to interpret.

In constructing a sociogram, it is helpful to start with the most highly chosen pupils and work out from the center of the diagram. Pupils with mutual choices should be placed near each other. The original placement on the chart should be done lightly in pencil since considerable rearrangement is necessary during the plotting to minimize the number of crossed lines. Plotting boys and girls on separate sides of the diagram also simplifies the process since the number of mutual cross-sex choices is usually small. When all pupils have been finally arranged on the diagram, check to be certain that each pupil is still in the proper position between the concentric circles, since this indicates the approximate number of choices he has received.

The sociogram in Figure 17.5 illustrates the common social configurations you can expect in group structure. Girls number 12, 11, 14, 18, and

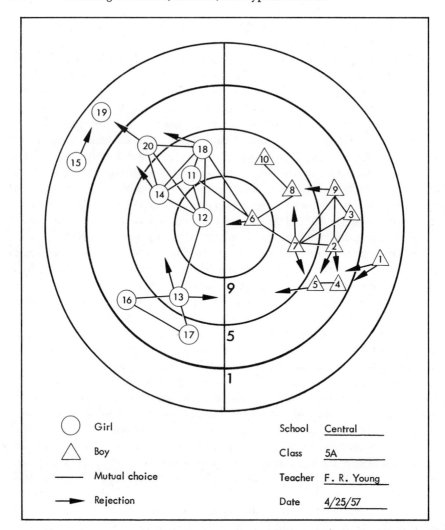

FIGURE 17.5. Sociogram depicting choices and rejections of work companions, based on data in Figure 17.4. (From *Sociometry in the Classroom*. Copyright 1959 by Norman E. Gronlund.)

20 form a very cohesive *clique*. Girls number 13, 16, and 17 form a *triangle*. Boys number 10, 8, and 6 form a *chain* of mutual choices and boys number 4 and 5 form a mutual *pair*. In addition, there seems to be a social *cleavage* between boys and girls, except for the few mutual cross-sex choices of boy number 6. Pupils 1, 15, and 19 are *isolated* from the group and pupil number 19 is actively *rejected* by four of her classmates.

While sociograms depict in graphic form the social relations present in the group, *they do not indicate why* a particular social structure evolved nor *what should be done,* if anything, to change it. The sociogram is merely a starting point. To understand the cliques, cleavages, and social positions of individual pupils, it is necessary to supplement sociometric data with information obtained from observation, "guess who" techniques, and various other evaluation methods.

Uses of Sociometric Results. The sociometric technique has been used for a variety of purposes in the school. Its major uses include: (1) organizing classroom groups, (2) improving the social adjustment of individual pupils, (3) improving the social structure of groups, and (4) evaluating the influence of school practices on pupils' social relations. Each of these uses will be briefly discussed.

The first step in using sociometric results is to put the choices into effect. For example, if committees are to be formed, they should be patterned as closely as possible to the pupils' choices. This can usually be done most effectively by starting with the isolates and working toward the pupils receiving the largest number of choices. With five choices, it is usually possible to satisfy at least two choices for each pupil. By starting with the isolates, you are able to give them their two highest choices. This places them in contact with the pupils with whom they have the best chance for developing social relations. In arranging the groups, the sociometric choices should, of course, not be followed blindly. It may be desirable to place rural and urban pupils together to reduce an undesirable cleavage, or to separate the members of a clique which has been disrupting to the class. These adjustments can and should be made without violating your promise to give all of the pupils some of their choices.

Although sociometric results do not indicate how to improve social adjustment, they do aid in identifying those pupils who are having difficulty in adjusting to the peer group. Isolated and rejected pupils are not apt to improve their social position without special help. If an isolated pupil is new to class, arranging opportunities for social contact may be all that is needed. In other cases, it may be a matter of helping an isolated pupil improve his appearance, social skills, and apparent value to the group. In some instances, the pupil may be so socially withdrawn or aggressive toward others that the assistance of the parents, the school counselor, and other special personnel may be required. Specific remedial procedures should be based on the causes of the pupil's isolation or rejection. The sociometric results merely alert us to the pupils most in need of further study and possible remedial action.

Sociometric measurement can contribute to the improvement of group structure in two ways. First, it helps clarify the cliques, cleavages, and mutual relations present in a group. Second, it provides the basic data for rearranging the group in a manner which is likely to result in a more cohesive social pattern. A disintegrated classroom structure, characterized by an overabundance of cliques, cleavages, and isolated pupils, commonly results in low group morale and a poor climate for learning. It is not expected that a simple rearranging will eliminate cleavages along racial, religious, rural-urban, or socio-economic lines. However, it does provide opportunity for interpersonal contacts and, if accompanied by other efforts to improve relations, these cleavages can be appreciably diminished.[4]

In addition to its more common uses in the classroom, sociometric measurement is also useful in evaluating the effect of particular school practices on pupils' social relations. For example, it can be used to help answer questions like the following: Is our method of ability grouping creating a social cleavage between gifted and regular pupils? Does the competition we have built up between boys and girls in our elementary school result in an extreme sex cleavage? How does our activity program, which prevents bus-transported pupils from participating fully, influence the social relations between town and rural youth? These and similar questions have been studied in schools with the aid of sociometric measures.[5] The simplicity of the technique makes it usable with an entire school population as well as with a single classroom group.

SELF-REPORT TECHNIQUES

In general, there are two types of information that may be profitably obtained by self-report techniques. These are (1) information concerning the pupil's *past behavior*, such as the books he has read, the hobbies he has engaged in, and the experiences he has had in a particular area; (2) information concerning the pupil's *inner life*, such as his worries and concerns, his feelings toward himself and others, his interests, and his opinions. Both types of information are typically inaccessible by other means—the first because it deals with past behavior no longer observable, and the second because it is concerned with behavior not readily discernible to an outside observer.

Of various methods of obtaining information directly from an individual, the oldest and best known is that of the personal interview. The face-to-face contact provided by the interview gives it several advantages as a self-report procedure. First, considerable flexibility is provided. The interviewer can clarify his questions if they are not readily understood, he can pursue promising lines of inquiry, and he can provide the interviewee an opportunity to qualify or expand on his answers, as needed. Second, the interviewer can carefully observe the interviewee during the session, noting the amount of feeling attached to his answers, the topics on which he seems to be evasive, and the areas in which he is most expansive. Third, the interview makes possible not only collecting information from an individual but also sharing information with him and, as in the case of the counseling interview, using the face-to-face contact as a basis for therapy.

The personal interview would provide an almost ideal method of ob-

---

[4] N. E. Gronlund, *Sociometry in the Classroom* (New York: Harper and Row, 1959).
[5] M. E. Bonney, "Sociometric Methods," *Encyclopedia of Educational Research,* 3rd ed. (New York: Macmillan, 1960).

taining self-report information from pupils except for two serious limitations. It is extremely time consuming and the information provided is not standard from one person to another. In the interests of both feasibility and greater comparability of results, the self-report inventory or questionnaire is commonly used in place of the personal interview. An inventory consists of a standard set of questions pertaining to some particular area of behavior, administered and scored under standard conditions. It is a sort of standardized, written interview which makes possible the collection of a large amount of information quickly and an objective summary of the data collected.

The effective use of self-report inventories assumes that the individual is both *willing* and *able* to report accurately. Responses can usually be easily faked if an individual desires to present a distorted picture of himself. Even where he wants to be truthful, there is the possibility that his recollection of past events will be inaccurate and that his self-perceptions will be biased. These limitations can be partly offset by using self-report inventories only in those areas where pupils have little reason for faking, by emphasizing the value of frank responses for self-understanding and self-improvement, and by taking into account the possible presence of distortion when interpreting the results. As we shall see shortly, the problem of obtaining accurate responses varies considerably from one type of self-report inventory to another.

Activity Checklists

Pupils have numerous incidental and informal learning experiences which have implications for classroom instruction. For example, they read books and magazines, watch television, play games, have hobbies, belong to social and special interest clubs, and engage in various scientific, literary, and artistic activities on their own. A survey of such activities is frequently desirable in assessing pupil readiness for new learning experiences and for general curriculum planning. The activities a pupil has engaged in also provide clues to his interests, his creative growth, and his potential for development in various academic and vocational areas. In Project TALENT, one of the most comprehensive studies of high school pupils' aptitudes and abilities ever attempted, information concerning personal experiences was considered so important that 80 minutes of testing time was allotted to the task of obtaining it.[6]

Most activity checklists are constructed by the teacher, or researcher, to fit some specific purpose. A portion of a checklist used by Torrance[7] to study the development of creativity in children is presented in Figure 17.6.

---

[6] J. C. Flanagan, J. T. Dailey, M. F. Shaycoft, D. B. Orr, and I. Goldberg, *Design for a Study of American Youth* (Boston: Houghton Mifflin, 1962).
[7] E. P. Torrance, *Guiding Creative Talent* (Englewood Cliffs, N.J.: Prentice-Hall, 1962).

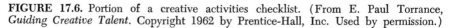

THINGS DONE ON YOUR OWN

Name _____ Grade _____ School _____ Date _____

DIRECTIONS: Below is a list of activities boys and girls sometimes do on their own. Indicate which ones you have done during this school term by checking the blank at the left. Include only the things you have done on your own, not the things you have been assigned or made to do.

( )   1. Wrote a poem
( )   2. Wrote a story
( )   3. Wrote a play
( )   4. Kept a collection of my writings
( )   5. Wrote a song or jingle
( )   6. Produced a puppet show
( )   7. Kept a diary for at least a month
( )   8. Played word games with other boys and girls
( )   9. Used <u>Roget's Thesaurus</u> or some other book in addition to a dictionary
( ) 10. Recorded on a tape recorder an oral reading, dialogue, story, discussion, or the like
( ) 11. Found errors in fact or grammar in newspaper or other printed matter
( ) 12. Acted in play or skit
( ) 13. Directed or organized a play or skit
( ) 14. Made up and sang a song
( ) 15. Made up a musical composition for some instrument
( ) 16. Made up a new game and taught it to someone else

FIGURE 17.6. Portion of a creative activities checklist. (From E. Paul Torrance, *Guiding Creative Talent.* Copyright 1962 by Prentice-Hall, Inc. Used by permission.)

The complete checklist contains 100 items and includes activities related to language arts, science, social studies, art, and other fields.

Another example, a *Things Done* checklist, is shown in Figure 17.7. This is a portion of a 243-item inventory concerned with scientific activities which could have been done or participated in by sixth- and seventh-grade pupils. This particular checklist was designed to aid in the identification of potential scientific and technical talent. It is based on the hypothesis that pupils who have done many things of a scientific nature will continue in these activities and will tend to become scientists. The score on this inventory is simply the number of items checked. The manual also suggests that a tabulation of the number of pupils checking each item is useful in planning science related activities and in discussing science interests with parents.

The contribution of activity checklists to an appraisal of pupil readiness and to curriculum planning is rather self-evident. The more we know about the past learning experiences of pupils the better we can plan their future experiences. Although answers to such checklists can be easily faked, there is little reason for pupils to do so. Emphasizing that the results will be used solely for the planning of future learning activities should be sufficient to elicit honest responses.

( )	1. read book on astronomy	( )	44. used a lightmeter
( )	2. explored a cave	( )	45. held metallic mercury in hand
( )	3. read book on biology	( )	46. tested milk for butterfat
( )	4. visited a zoo	( )	47. made soap
( )	5. read magazine about science	( )	48. seen electroplating being done
( )	6. embedded insects in plastic	( )	49. tested soap
( )	6. used a tuning fork	( )	50. grown crystals
( )	8. embedded flowers in plastic	( )	51. learned the names of geologic eras
( )	9. seen a radar screen	( )	52. collected fossils
( )	10. taken a square root of a number	( )	53. grown plants in a sealed jar
( )	11. used an ammeter	( )	54. read the history of a river or lake
( )	12. seen a star map	( )	55. collected seeds
( )	13. used a voltmeter	( )	56. read about heredity
( )	14. read a star map	( )	57. studied plant growth
( )	15. read a barometer	( )	58. made a collection of different kinds of nuts

FIGURE 17.7. Sample items from *Science Background, IA, Things Done,* checklist. (Copyright 1957 by Science Service, Inc., 1719 North Street, N.W., Washington, D.C. Used by permission.)

Problem Checklists

The most comprehensive and widely used checklists have been in the area of personal-social adjustment. Typically these checklists contain a collection of several hundred problems common to children and youth. The pupil reads through the list and checks those problems which are of concern to him. The marking of the items usually permits the pupil to indicate also which problems he considers most serious. Sample items from the *Mooney Problem Checklists* are shown in Figure 17.8. There are 210 items in the junior high school forms and 330 items in the high school and college forms of these checklists. They cover such areas as health and physical development, school, home and family, money, work, the future, personal concerns, and various types of personal-social relations. The original lists of problems were selected from a master list of over 5,000 items.

First Step: Read the list slowly, and as you come to a problem which troubles you, underline it.

1. Being underweight	56. Frequent headaches
2. Being overweight	57. Weak eyes
3. Not getting enough exercise	58. Often not hungry for my meals
4. Getting sick too often	59. Not eating the right foods
5. Tiring very easily	60. Gradually losing weight
6. Needing to learn how to save money	61. Too few nice clothes
7. Not knowing how to spend my money wisely	62. Too little money for recreation
8. Having less money than my friends have	63. Family worried about money
9. Having to ask parents for money	64. Having to watch every penny I spend
10. Having no regular allowance (or income)	65. Having to quit school to work

FIGURE 17.8. Sample items from the *Mooney Problem Check Lists.* (Reproduced by permission. Copyright © 1950, The Psychological Corporation, New York, N.Y. All rights reserved.)

Problem checklists can be used for several purposes. They can help to (1) identify pupils who are most likely in need of counseling or other personal help; (2) identify the most common problems within a group as a basis for group guidance and curriculum planning; (3) improve the effectiveness of the curricular, extracurricular, and guidance programs of the school in meeting the needs of the pupils. If a tabulation of responses indicates that most pupils are troubled by ineffective study habits, for example, steps can be taken to remedy the situation.

When used to screen individuals for referral to the school counselor, it is, of course, necessary for the pupils to provide their identity. If administered solely as a basis for curriculum planning and for making revisions in the schools' services, however, it may be desirable to obtain anonymous responses. When signatures are used, only those pupils who *want* help with their personal problems can be expected to answer with complete frankness. The protection of anonymity should provide a much more complete and accurate survey of the problems experienced by all pupils.

Personality Inventories

The personality or adjustment inventory is similar to the problem checklist. Instead of a list of problems to be checked, however, the typical personality inventory presents pupils with a series of questions like those used in a psychiatric screening interview. For example, an inventory might include items like the following:

- Do you daydream often?
- Are you frequently depressed?
- Do you have difficulty making friends?
- Do you usually feel tired?

Responses to such questions are commonly indicated by circling "yes," "no," or "?" (for uncertain). In some instances a forced-choice procedure is used, where the items are paired and the respondent must indicate which of the two statements is more characteristic of him.

Personality inventories vary considerably in the type of score provided. Some provide a single adjustment score; other have separate scores for particular adjustment areas (e.g., health, social, emotional, and so on) or for specific personality traits (e.g., self-confidence, sociability, ascendancy, and so on). In general, research has not supported the validity of separate scores for evaluating adjustment by means of inventories. Even the use of the total score for distinguishing between adjusted and maladjusted individuals has been seriously challenged.[8]

All of the limitations of the self-report technique tend to be accentuated

---

[8] L. J. Cronbach, *Essentials of Psychological Testing*, 3rd ed. (New York: Harper and Row, 1970).

in the personality inventory. (1) The replies can be easily faked and the threatening nature of many of the questions provides motivation for presenting a distorted picture. Some inventories provide "control keys" to detect faking and others reduce it by means of the forced-choice procedure, but faking cannot be entirely eliminated. (2) In addition to honesty, accurate responses require good self-insight. This is the very characteristic that poorly adjusted individuals are apt to lack. They are prone to excessive use of adjustment mechanisms which tend to distort their perceptions of themselves and of their relations to others. (3) The ambiguity of the items is also apt to introduce error into the results. Questions like "are you frequently depressed?" do not mean the same thing to different individuals. Besides applying his own interpretation to the word "depressed" a person must also decide what is meant by the word "frequently." Does this mean 60 per cent of the time or 80 per cent of the time? A study by Simpson[9] has shown that words like "frequently" have little common meaning. His results for several words which are widely used in personality inventories are presented in Table 17.1.

The limitations of personality inventories are such that their use should be severely restricted in school situations. They are probably most useful in counseling situations. If scored at all, only the total score should be used. From a counseling standpoint, it may be most helpful to ignore the scoring and use the pupils' responses to individual items as a basis for counseling interviews. Although teachers may assist in the administration of

TABLE 17.1

RANGE OF MEANINGS STUDENTS ATTRIBUTED TO QUANTITATIVE TERMS
COMMONLY USED IN PERSONALITY INVENTORIES*

Portion of Directions →	"Simply indicate how many times out of 100 you think the word indicates an act has happened or is likely to happen."	
Results	25 per cent of students thought the term meant less than this percentage of the time.	25 per cent of students thought the term meant more than this percentage of the time.
Usually	73	87
Often	52	82
Frequently	60	80
Sometimes	15	37
Occasionally	14	33
Seldom	6	17

* Adapted from R. H. Simpson, "Stability in Meanings for Quantitative Terms: A Comparison Over 20 Years," *Quarterly Journal of Speech,* **49,** 146–151, 1963.

[9] R. H. Simpson, "Stability in Meanings for Quantitative Terms: A Comparison Over 20 Years," *Quarterly Journal of Speech,* **49,** 146–151, 1963.

personality inventories, the interpretation and use of the results should be left to the psychologically trained counselor.

Projective Techniques

Projective techniques provide another method of evaluating personal-social adjustment with which the classroom teacher should be familiar. Since they generally require clinical training to administer and interpret, it is not expected that a teacher will use them directly. It is more than likely, however, that he will encounter some clinical reports on pupils which contain interpretations of projective test results.

In contrast to the highly structured personality inventory, projective techniques provide almost complete freedom of response. Typically, the individual is presented with a series of ambiguous forms or pictures and asked to describe what he sees. His responses are then analyzed to determine what conduct and structure he has "projected" onto the ambiguous stimuli.

The two most extensively used projective techniques are the *Rorschach Inkblot Test* and the *Thematic Apperception Test* (*TAT*). The *Rorschach* consists of ten inkblot figures on cards and the *TAT* includes a series of thirty pictures, of which only twenty are used for any particular age or sex group. These tests are typically administered to one individual at a time, and a complete record is made of the individual's responses during the testing. Analysis of the results requires both systematic scoring and impressionistic interpretation with major emphasis on the total personality pattern revealed. Projective techniques are used primarily as an aid to a complete clinical study of those individuals who are experiencing adjustment difficulties.

Interest Inventories

There are several informal methods of obtaining information concerning a pupil's interests. Through direct observation, we can note which areas of study receive his greatest attention, what types of books he reads, and which activities he selects in free-choice situations. By means of activity checklists, we can obtain reports on the things he has done on his own. Through direct questioning, we can have the pupil tell or write about the things he would most like to do. All of these methods provide clues to a pupil's interests, but they also have their shortcomings: our observations are usually restricted to in-school activities, the things done by pupils reflect home environment and opportunity as much as interest, and a pupil's directly expressed interests are limited by his general knowledge and his ability to think of specific activities at the time he is asked. In addition, these informal methods provide no basis for comparing an individual's interests with those of persons in other educational or vocational groups.

Standardized interest inventories overcome many of the limitations of the informal methods. Unfortunately, however, these have been designed primarily for use in educational and vocational guidance. The development of standardized inventories for use in curriculum planning and instruction has been generally neglected.

One of the most widely used interest inventories at the high school and college levels is the *Kuder Preference Record—Vocational.* This inventory contains a number of activities arranged in groups of three. The pupil is forced to decide which one of the three activities he likes most and which one he likes least. An example of the type and arrangement of items used is shown in Figure 17.9. The scoring of the inventory provides a profile of interests in ten areas: Outdoor, Mechanical, Computational, Scientific, Persuasive, Artistic, Literary, Musical, Social Service, and Clerical. It also has a "verification score" to show whether the responses were carefully made. A more recent form of this inventory, the *Kuder General Interest Survey,* uses the same format but simpler vocabulary. It was designed for use in grades 6 to 12.

A number of activities are listed in groups of three. Read over the three activities in each group. Decide which of the three activities you like most. There are two circles on the same line as this activity. Punch a hole with the pin through the left-hand circle following this activity. Then decide which activity you like least and punch a hole through the right-hand circle of the two circles following this activity.

In the examples below, the person answering has indicated for the first group of three activities, that he would usually like to visit a museum most, and browse in a library least. In the second group of three activities he has indicated he would like to collect autographs most and collect butterflies least.

EXAMPLES

Put your answers to these questions in column O.

		O	
P. Visit an art gallery		•P•	
Q. Browse in a library		•Qo	←LEAST
R. Visit a museum	MOST→	oR•	
S. Collect autographs	MOST→	oS•	
T. Collect coins		•T•	
U. Collect butterflies		•Uo	←LEAST

FIGURE 17.9. Sample items from the *Kuder Preference Record-Vocational.* (Copyright 1948 by G. Frederick Kuder. Reprinted by permission of Science Research Associates, Inc.)

In addition to the *Vocational Form* and the *General Form,* there is a *Personal Form* which measures preferences for various personal and social activities and an *Occupational Form* which relates preferences to specific jobs rather than general interest areas. All forms of the *Kuder Preference Record* use the forced-choice technique of responding, are simple to administer, and are relatively easy to interpret to pupils.

Another interest inventory that has been used extensively at the high school and college levels is the *Strong Vocational Interest Blank.* The 1966 form of this inventory consists of 399 items, the majority of which are answered by circling L, I, or D (like, indifferent, or dislike). The items are grouped into the following eight parts: (1) occupations, (2) school subjects, (3) amusements, (4) activities, (5) types of people, (6) order of preference of activities, (7) comparison of interest between two items, and (8) rating of present abilities and characteristics. Sample items, for preferences toward occupations, are shown in Figure 17.10. A new form, entitled the *Strong-Campbell Interest Inventory,* appeared in 1974. It combines the separate forms for men and women, used in the earlier edition, into a single inventory blank that can be used with both sexes.

Part I. Occupations. Indicate after each occupation listed below whether you would like that kind of work or not. Disregard considerations of salary, social standing, future advancement, etc. Consider only whether or not you would like to do what is involved in the occupation. You are not asked if you would take up the occupation permanently, but merely whether or not you would enjoy that kind of work, regardless of any necessary skills, abilities, or training which you may or may not possess.

  · Draw a circle around L if you like that kind of work
   Draw a circle around I if you are indifferent to that kind of work
   Draw a circle around D if you dislike that kind of work
Work rapidly. Your first impressions are desired here. Answer all the items. Many of the seemingly trivial and irrelevant items are very useful in diagnosing your real attitude.

1 Actor (not movie)	L	I	D		46 Jeweler	L	I	D
2 Advertiser	L	I	D		47 Judge	L	I	D
3 Architect.	L	I	D		48 Labor Arbitrator	L	I	D
4 Army Officer	L	I	D		49 Laboratory Technician.	L	I	D
5 Artist	L	I	D		50 Landscape Gardener	L	I	D
6 Astronomer	L	I	D		51 Lawyer, Criminal	L	I	D
7 Athletic Director	L	I	D		52 Lawyer, Corporation	L	I	D
8 Auctioneer	L	I	D		53 Librarian.	L	I	D
9 Author of novel	L	I	D		54 Life Insurance Salesman	L	I	D
10 Author of technical book	L	I	D		55 Locomotive Engineer	L	I	·D

FIGURE 17.10. Sample items from the *Strong Vocational Interest Blank.* (Copyright 1938 by Stanford University. Used by permission.)

The *Strong Blanks* are scored and interpreted in terms of the similarity between an individual's interests and those of persons successfully engaged in particular occupations. The blank must be scored with a different key for each occupation. Electronic scoring machines have simplified the process of scoring an answer sheet for all occupations. Special group keys also make it possible to score the blank for clusters of occupational interest, somewhat similar to those provided by the *Vocational Form* of the *Kuder.*

Relatively few interest inventories have been developed for use at the elementary school level. Typical of the instruments published for use with this age group is the inventory, entitled *What I Like to Do—An Inventory of Children's Interests.* There are 294 items, like those in Figure 17.11, designed to measure interests in art, music, social studies, active play, quiet play, manual arts, home arts, and science. The inventory is recommended for use in grades 4 through 7, and provides norms based on a national sample of pupils. The manual provides suggestions for using the results in curriculum development, guidance, and instruction.

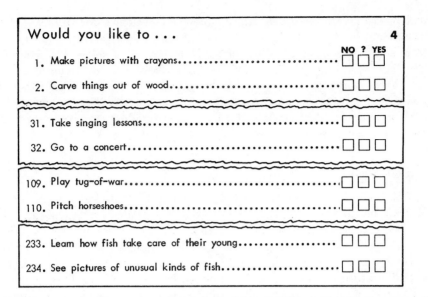

Would you like to ...   4

                                                          NO ? YES
1. Make pictures with crayons.......................... ☐ ☐ ☐

2. Carve things out of wood............................. ☐ ☐ ☐

31. Take singing lessons................................. ☐ ☐ ☐

32. Go to a concert...................................... ☐ ☐ ☐

109. Play tug-of-war.................................... ☐ ☐ ☐

110. Pitch horseshoes................................... ☐ ☐ ☐

233. Learn how fish take care of their young.............. ☐ ☐ ☐

234. See pictures of unusual kinds of fish................ ☐ ☐ ☐

FIGURE 17.11. Sample items reprinted from *What I Like to Do: An Inventory of Children's Interests,* by Louis P. Thorpe, Charles E. Meyers, and Marcella R. Sea. (Copyright 1954, Science Research Associates, Inc.)

Informal interest inventories can, of course, also be developed for use in teaching. Such inventories are especially useful in teaching reading, but could be helpful in any instructional area. Examining instruments like the one in Figure 17.11 will provide guidelines for construction.

As with other self-report techniques, responses to interest inventories can be easily faked. This is seldom a problem, however, where the emphasis is on self-understanding, and educational and vocational planning. Pupils are anxious to find out about their interests and the inventories consist of items which tend to be psychologically nonthreatening.

The instability of pupils' interests during elementary and high school years is a major reason for using interest inventories with extreme caution at these levels. Extensive studies by Strong and others have shown that interests are not very stable until approximately age seventeen.[10] This does not mean that we must wait until this age to measure interests, but rather that our interpretations must be highly tentative. In one sense the instability of interests among children and adolescents is highly encouraging, for it indicates that our efforts to broaden and develop interests through school activities have some chance of succeeding. It is mainly when we are attempting to predict vocational success that stability poses a serious problem. For vocational decisions, we should rely most heavily on interest measures obtained during the last two years of high school, and later.

Another precaution to keep in mind is *not* to confuse interest scores

---

[10] L. J. Cronbach, *Essentials of Psychological Testing,* 3rd ed. (New York: Harper and Row, 1970).

with measures of ability. A strong interest in science, for example, may or may not be accompanied by the verbal and numerical aptitudes needed to pursue successfully a course of study or career in science. A scientific interest may be satisfied by collecting butterflies or by discovering a cure for cancer. Interest measures merely indicate whether an individual is apt to find satisfaction in a particular type of activity. Measures of ability determine the level of activity at which the individual can expect to function effectively.

Attitude Scales

The two chief methods for evaluating pupils' attitudes are (1) direct observation, and (2) attitude scales. When attitudes are specifically developed and evaluated as instructional outcomes, we must rely mainly on observational techniques. Our procedure here is to describe in behavioral terms the attitudes to be evaluated (e.g., concern for others, scientific attitude, and so on) and to gather evidence of these changes by means of anecdotal records, rating scales, and checklists. Self-report methods are generally infeasible for this purpose because responses can be easily faked and because pupils have strong motivation for doing so where course grades might be affected.

Attitude scales are self-report inventories designed to measure the extent to which an individual has favorable or unfavorable feelings toward some person, group, object, institution, or idea. They are primarily useful where the individual has little reason for distorting the results, such as in the development of self-understanding or in research. A common research use is in the study of attitude change resulting from particular experiences (e.g., reading, motion pictures, group discussion, and so on). Group results, based on anonymous responses, can also be used as an aid in evaluating curricular and extracurricular programs, specific educational practices, and teaching effectiveness.

A number of different methods of constructing attitude scales have been developed. Three of the most common are those originated by L. L. Thurstone, H. H. Remmers, and R. A. Likert.[11]

Thurstone's Method. The procedure developed by Thurstone includes the following steps:

1. A series of statements expressing all ranges of opinion toward some attitude object are written or collected. For example, in preparing a scale to measure attitude toward school, a large number of items like the following might be gathered:
   School is exciting.
   School is sometimes interesting.
   School is a waste of time.

---

[11] A. L. Edwards, *Techniques of Attitude Scale Construction* (New York: Appleton-Century-Crofts, 1957).

A good pool of such items for teacher-made scales can be obtained by having pupils write a series of statements representing different degrees of the attitude to be measured.

2. The statements are edited, placed on slips of paper or cards, and sorted into eleven piles by thirty or more judges. Where it is desired to have high scores represent favorable attitudes, the judges are instructed to place the statements expressing the most favorable attitudes in pile 11, those expressing a neutral position in pile 6, those expressing the least favorable attitude in pile 1, and the remainder in one of the intervening piles. In constructing teacher-made scales, any group of teachers or parents can be used as judges, since it is assumed that this sorting process is not influenced by the attitudes of the judges. As noted above, the judges are asked merely to classify the statements, not to indicate their own attitudes.

3. The number of times a statement is placed in each pile provides the basic data for determining the ambiguity and scale value of the item. Where there is considerable disagreement in the placement of an item, it is regarded as too ambiguous and discarded. The scale value of each of the usable statements is based on the median position assigned by the judges.

4. The final form of the attitude scale is constructed by selecting those statements which are most relevant, least ambiguous, and which cover the entire range of scale values. The statements are then arranged in random order, and the subject is simply told to check those statements with which he agrees. His score is obtained by averaging the scale values of the statements he has checked.

Remmers' Method. To avoid the extensive amount of work required in building a separate attitude scale for each specific attitude object, Remmers has developed generalized or master attitude scales. These are designed so that the same statements can be used to measure attitude toward a series of attitude objects in the same general area. For example, statements like the following are included in his scale for measuring attitudes toward any institution:[12]

1. Is perfect in every way.
2. Is the most admirable of institutions.
3. Is necessary to the very existence of civilization.
4. Is the most beloved of institutions.

In responding to the scale, the subject writes in the name of the institution indicated by the examiner and then checks those statements with which he agrees.

Remmers' master scales are constructed and scored in the same manner

---

[12] H. H. Remmers, *Introduction to Opinion and Attitude Measurement* (New York: Harper and Row, 1954).

as the Thurstone-type scale. The major differences are that the attitude statements in the master scales are necessarily more generalized and they are arranged in order of decreasing favorableness, rather than in random order. A number of master attitude scales have been developed under Remmers' direction. These include measures of attitude toward such things as (1) any disciplinary procedure, (2) any school subject, (3) any teacher, (4) any national or racial group, (5) any proposed social action, and (6) any vocation.

Likert's Method. Likert's approach to attitude scale construction is less time consuming than the other two methods, because it does not require the sorting of statements by judges. It also differs in that (1) only clearly favorable or clearly unfavorable attitude statements are used, and (2) the subject is required to respond to each statement on a five-point scale: strongly agree (SA), agree (A), undecided (U), disagree (D), and strongly disagree (SD).

Statements in a Likert-type scale might appear as follows:

SA   A   U   D   SD   School is exciting.
SA   A   U   D   SD   School is a waste of time.

In scoring favorable statements, like the first item above, the alternatives are weighed 5, 4, 3, 2, 1, going from SA to SD. In scoring unfavorable statements, like the second item above, these weights are reversed. Thus, a pupil circling SA on both of the above items would receive five points for the first and one point for the second. An individual's total score on this type scale is the sum of his scores on all items, with the higher score indicating a more favorable attitude.

The Likert-type scale provides results which are comparable to those obtained by the Thurstone and Remmers methods.[13] Its greater simplicity of construction and scoring would seem to favor its use.

A Final Precaution. Attitude scales, like other self-report techniques, provide verbal expressions of feelings and opinions that individuals are willing to make known to others. Their effective use requires a good rapport with the individuals tested and a sincere belief on their part that frank responses are in their own best interests. Even under the most ideal conditions, however, it is desirable to supplement attitudes determined by self-report methods with evidence obtained from direct observation.

SUMMARY

In some areas of learning and development it is desirable to supplement the teacher's observations with information obtained directly from

---

[13] A. L. Edwards, *Techniques of Attitude Scale Construction* (New York: Appleton-Century-Crofts, 1957).

the pupils. We can ask the pupils to rate or judge their peers (their fellow pupils) and to report on their own feelings, thoughts, and past behavior. A variety of (1) peer-appraisal methods, and (2) self-report techniques has been developed for this purpose.

Peer appraisal is especially useful in evaluating personality characteristics, social relations skills, and other forms of typical behavior. The give-and-take of social interaction in the peer group provides pupils with a unique opportunity to observe and judge the behavior of their fellow pupils. Since these peer ratings are based on experiences which are seldom fully visible to adult observers, they provide an important adjunct

Peer-appraisal methods include the "guess who" technique and the sociometric technique. The first of these techniques for obtaining peer ratings requires pupils to name those classmates who best fit each of a series of behavior descriptions. The number of nominations each pupil receives on each characteristic indicates the reputation he holds among his peers. This nominating procedure can be used to evaluate any aspect of behavior which is observable to fellow pupils. The sociometric technique also calls for nominations but here the pupils are to indicate their choice of companions for some group situation or activity. The number of choices a pupil receives serves as an indication of his social acceptance, and the network of choices can be used to plot the social structure of the group. The results can also be used to rearrange groups, to improve the social adjustment of individual pupils, and to evaluate the influence of school practices on pupils' social relations.

Self-report techniques are typically used to obtain information which is inaccessible by other means. This includes reports on the pupil's past experiences and his perceptions of his inner life. Such information can be obtained by personal interview, but a self-report inventory is more commonly used. The inventory is a sort of standardized written interview which provides comparable results from one person to another. Effective use of self-report techniques assumes that the respondent is both willing and able to report accurately. Thus, special efforts must be made to meet these conditions.

Activity checklists provide a survey of the pupil's past experiences which is useful in assessing learning readiness and in curriculum planning. Problem checklists, personality inventories, and projective techniques aid in evaluating the personal-social adjustment of pupils. Of these, the problem checklist is the only one recommended for use by the classroom teacher. Interest inventories contribute to a better understanding of pupils and are especially useful in educational and vocational planning. Attitude scales provide an indication of the feelings and opinions pupils hold toward various groups, institutions, and ideas.

Peer ratings and self-report inventories provide useful information for understanding pupils better and for guiding their learning, development, and adjustment. These purposes will be best served, however, when the information is combined with test results, observational data, and all other available data concerning the pupils.

LEARNING EXERCISES

1. What types of behavior are best evaluated by peer appraisal? What are some of the necessary precautions in using peer-appraisal methods?
2. List several positive and negative statements that might be used on a "guess who" form for evaluating ability to work effectively in a group.
3. List three positive statements and three negative statements that might be used in a sociometric test for evaluating pupils' social acceptance by their peers. What are the advantages and disadvantages of using negative choices?
4. Describe the advantages and limitations of self-report inventories. What can be done to increase the validity of the results?
5. Why have so few interest inventories been developed for use at the elementary school level? How might interest inventories contribute to the instructional program?
6. Write several statements that might be useful in a Likert-type attitude scale for evaluating pupils' attitudes toward a school subject you are teaching or plan to teach.
7. What are the advantages and disadvantages of using each of the following for evaluating pupils' attitudes toward school?
   a. Attitude scale.
   b. Questionnaire.
   c. Teacher observation.
   d. "Guess who" technique.
8. What types of peer-appraisal and self-report methods might be used to determine whether ability grouping is having an undesirable influence on pupil development? How would you proceed to develop each instrument?

SUGGESTIONS FOR FURTHER READING

ANASTASI, A. *Psychological Testing*, 4th ed. New York: Macmillan Publishing Co., Inc., 1976. Chapter 17, "Self-Report Inventories," and Chapter 18, "Measures of Interests, Attitudes and Values." Anastasi discusses factors underlying the development and use of inventories and describes widely used instruments.

CRONBACH, L. J. *Essentials of Psychological Testing*, 3rd ed. New York: Harper and Row, Publishers, 1970. See Chapter 14, "Interest Inventories"; Chapter 15, "General Problems in Studying Personality"; and Chapter 16, "Personality Measurement Through Self-Report" for a comprehensive discussion of self-report measures and their validity.

LINDZEY, G., and D. BYRNE. "Measurement of Social Choice and Interpersonal Attractiveness," in G. Lindzey and E. Aronson (eds.), *Handbook of Social Psychology*, Vol. 2. Reading, Mass.: Addison-Wesley Publishing Co., Inc., 1968. Discusses sociometric techniques and provides a comprehensive review of the related research.

PAYNE, D. A. *The Assessment of Learning: Cognitive and Affective.* Lexington, Mass.: D. C. Heath and Co., 1974. Chapter 8, "The Development of Self-Report Affective Items and Inventories." Describes and illustrates a variety of methods.

SHAW, M. E., and J. M. WRIGHT. *Scales for the Measurement of Attitudes.* New York: McGraw-Hill Book Company, 1967. Describes and illustrates numerous attitude scales covering forty years of attitude measurement. Good source of ideas for attitude scale construction.

SYND, R. B., and A. J. PICARD. *Behavioral Objectives and Evaluation Measures: Science and Mathematics.* Columbus, Ohio: Charles E. Merrill Publishers, 1972. See Chapter 8, "The Use of Self-Evaluation Inventories," for numerous illustrations of self-report instruments designed for classroom use. The illustrations are adaptable to all subject areas.

TENBRINK, T. D. *Evaluation: A Practical Guide for Teachers.* New York: McGraw-Hill Book Company, 1974. See Chapter 11, "Developing Questionnaires, Interview Schedules, and Sociometric Instruments," for practical suggestions in the preparation of self-report and peer-appraisal instruments. Numerous examples illustrate each step in construction.

THORNDIKE, R. L., and E. HAGEN. *Measurement and Evaluation in Psychology and Education,* 3rd ed. New York: John Wiley & Sons, Inc., 1969. Chapter 12, "Questionnaires and Inventories for Self-Appraisal." Includes discussions of the interview, interest inventories, adjustment inventories, and attitude questionnaires.

PART  V

Using Evaluation
Results in Teaching

CHAPTER 18

Improving Learning and Instruction

The main function of evaluation in teaching is the improvement of pupil learning. . . . In this chapter we shall discuss some of the ways evaluation can contribute to this end. . . . A closely related matter—the improvement of instruction—is also considered.

Emphasis throughout this book has been on the need to identify all important objectives of instruction, to define these objectives clearly and specifically in behavioral terms, and to select or develop the evaluation instruments that provide the most valid information for instructional purposes. How much we depend on standardized tests, teacher-made tests, observational techniques, peer-appraisal devices, and self-report methods will vary with the area in which we are teaching and with the age level of the pupils. In areas where performance skills are the major outcomes (such as music, art, physical education), and with younger pupils, we shall need to rely more heavily on anecdotal records, rating scales, checklists, and similar nontest procedures. In other areas, like social studies and mathematics, both standardized tests and teacher-made tests are likely to play a much more prominent role. Despite this shift in emphasis from one situation to another, effective teaching usually requires the use of a variety of evaluation techniques. This is because objectives for any course are complex and varied, and because a comprehensive knowledge of pupils is needed to effectively guide their learning and development.

EVALUATION IN CONVENTIONAL CLASSROOM INSTRUCTION

The evaluation process can facilitate pupil learning in a number of direct and indirect ways. Some of these were described in the section on standardized testing and others were suggested during discussions of various evaluation procedures. Here, we shall summarize and make more explicit some of the direct ways that evaluation can contribute to improved learning and instruction. In general, evaluation can aid in (1) clarifying instructional objectives, (2) preassessing learners' needs, (3) monitoring learning progress, (4) diagnosing and remedying learning difficulties, and (5) appraising course outcomes. We shall consider the specific role of evaluation in each of these areas.

Clarifying Instructional Objectives

One of the major benefits of a systematic approach to classroom evaluation is that it clarifies, for both teacher and pupils, the objectives of instruction. This clarification of intended learning outcomes takes place at several points: (1) during the planning for instruction (where instructional objectives are defined in behavioral terms), (2) during the early stages of instruction (where the general instructional objectives may be shared with pupils), and (3) during testing and classroom evaluation (where the instruments provide pupils with an operational definition of the objectives).

Ideally, plans for classroom evaluation are made at the same time that instructional plans are formulated. This increases the likelihood that the desired learning outcomes will be clearly defined before instruction begins. Although instructional objectives can be specified without special attention to evaluation, they are not likely to be as clear and definite. As noted in Chapter 2, defining objectives for evaluation purposes encourages us to describe in precise terms the behaviors we are willing to accept as evidence of learning.

Instructional objectives that have been explicitly defined in behavioral terms are of obvious value in selecting instructional materials and methods, and in organizing learning activities. They are also useful, however, for guiding pupil learning. The precise descriptions of behavior make signs of learning progress, or lack of progress, more readily apparent during teaching. If we are assisting pupils to think more critically, for example, it is helpful to know that critical thought is represented by such behaviors as "the ability to distinguish fact from opinion" and "the ability to recognize assumptions underlying conclusions." These specific behaviors enable us to provide more meaningful learning experiences and to more readily observe and correct errors in thinking. The same is true in teaching pupils to speak effectively, write effectively, develop understandings, use performance skills, and the like. We are more apt to provide proper direction, if we have clearly and explicitly identified the specific behaviors that represent successful performance.

Sharing Objectives with Pupils. There is conflicting evidence concerning the value of presenting the instructional objectives to pupils. Some studies have shown that it improved learning, and other studies have shown that it did not.[1] These inconsistent findings are difficult to interpret, however, since the studies varied in the specificity of the objectives used, the types of learning involved, and the nature of the pupil population. It may be that knowledge of instructional objectives on the part of pupils is beneficial only under certain learning conditions (still to be determined). The effectiveness of the objectives in facilitating learning may also depend on whether pupils are guided properly in their use. It seems logical to assume that objectives provide direction for pupil learning, but this may result only when we make the relationship between learning activities and intended outcomes explicit to pupils.

If instructional objectives are shared with pupils during conventional classroom instruction, it would seem desirable to provide a list of general instructional objectives only. To include both the general instructional objectives and comprehensive lists of specific learning outcomes may have several undesirable effects. First, the list of intended outcomes may be so long and detailed that it overwhelms the pupils. The slow learner is especially likely to be frustrated by such a detailed listing of expected learning outcomes. Second, presenting pupils with a list of specific learning outcomes for each general instructional objective might encourage pupils to focus on these particular samples of learning outcomes rather than on the total class of behavior that each sample represents. As noted in Chapter 2, the set of specific learning outcomes listed for each general instructional objective is typically a rather limited sample of all of the possible outcomes for that objective. The danger of pupils focusing too narrowly on the specified sample of learning outcomes resides in the fact that at the end of instruction they might be able to perform the specific learning tasks described in the sample without being able to perform the other tasks encompassed by the same general instructional objective. Third, presenting pupils with lists of specific learning outcomes could destroy their usefulness as indicators of complex achievement. At the understanding level, for instance, pupils might memorize examples of a principle if the specific outcome calls for "stating examples of the principle." This, of course, would prevent the pupils' tested responses from serving as a valid indicator of "understanding of principles." Thus, at least for objectives in the more complex areas (e.g., understanding, application, interpretation), presenting pupils with lists of specific learning outcomes might encourage the rote learning of responses, and this would interfere with the teaching and testing of complex achievement. Providing pupils with statements of specific learning outcomes is probably most defensible for objectives at the mastery level (e.g., the learning of basic skills).

Clarification Through Evaluation Instruments. The evaluation instruments used in classroom instruction do more than anything else to convey instructional intent to pupils. We may carefully define our instructional

---

[1] P. C. Duchastel and P. F. Merrill, "The Effects of Behavioral Objectives on Learning: A Review of Empirical Studies," *Review of Educational Research,* **43,** 53–69, 1973.

objectives and share them with pupils, but unless these same objectives are reflected in our evaluation procedures they are likely to have little direct influence on learning. Note this warning by Cronbach.[2]

> What the learner tries depends on his goals. The goals of learning are supposed to be established during planning, but actually the learner's goals depend on what evaluation he anticipates. Goals not reflected in evaluation procedures will be neglected. Progress toward some objectives affects marks; the pupil pays only lip service to other objectives not represented in the evaluation.

In the final analysis, then, it is the evaluation procedures that determine the functional objectives of instruction. If tests require the "application of facts and principles," pupils are less likely to limit their study to the memorization of isolated bits of knowledge. If evaluations of laboratory performance include ratings on "skill in the use of laboratory equipment," pupils are less apt to overlook the significance of this aspect of laboratory work. If the "ability to communicate effectively," is constantly being observed, pupils will tend to direct more attention to spelling, grammar, pronunciation, and other aspects of effective communication. The evaluation procedures indicate to the pupils which objectives are worth working toward and what specific behaviors are needed to attain these outcomes. This highlights the importance of evaluating progress toward all desired learning outcomes. It is only then that we can have any assurance that the objectives of the teacher and the pupils are in accord.

Evaluation instruments will most effectively serve as guides to learning if the nature and purpose of the instruments are communicated to the pupils in the early stages of instruction. This may involve any or all of the following procedures:

1. Use a pretest like the test to be used at the end of instruction and draw pupils' attention to the nature of the test tasks.
2. Administer practice tests during instruction to clarify the types of tasks to be learned.
3. Hand out rating scales, checklists, and other evaluation devices at the beginning of the instructional units in which they are to be used.
4. Have pupils participate in identifying the criteria of successful performance and in developing the evaluation instruments for various classroom activities (e.g., giving an oral report).
5. Provide opportunities for pupils to evaluate their own performance with self-tests, rating scales, and other self-evaluation devices.

Unless procedures like these are used, pupils are not likely to be fully aware of instructional intent until it is too late (i.e., until after they have been tested or evaluated).

---

[2] L. J. Cronbach, *Educational Psychology* (New York: Harcourt Brace Jovanovich, 1962), p. 542.

In summary, the evaluation process can aid in clarifying objectives for both teacher and pupil. For the teacher, the defining of instructional objectives in behavioral terms can contribute to better instructional planning and to more effective guidance of learning activities. For the pupil, the instructional objectives can provide general direction for learning, and the evaluation procedures can provide an operational definition of the tasks to be learned.

Preassessing Learners' Needs

One of the most readily apparent contributions evaluation can make to improved teaching and learning is that of providing more complete information concerning the characteristics and needs of the learners. From the teacher's standpoint this information might be classified into two general types: (1) that which is obtained from the school-wide evaluation program, and (2) that which is obtained from pretesting. The first type provides general background information concerning the level and range of abilities of the pupils we are teaching. The second type provides information concerning the pupils' specific learning needs in relation to the objectives of instruction.

Reviewing School Records. If there is a systematic and comprehensive evaluation program in the school, we can learn a great deal about our pupils before meeting them. A review of each pupil's cumulative record should provide information concerning his scholastic aptitude, record of growth in the basic skills and other areas of achievement, personal-social development, health, home background, and the like. Such information prior to instruction makes it possible to take into account the abilities and needs of pupils during course planning. If some pupils are noted to be deficient in basic skills, for example, review or remedial work can be planned for them. In other instances it might be necessary to modify course goals or instructional plans to rectify common areas of weakness in achievement. Also, the range of individual differences in aptitude and achievement might suggest the need for in-class grouping or for the use of instructional materials of several levels of difficulty.

Some teachers prefer to delay reviewing the school records until they have worked with the pupils for a week or two, to reduce the possible influence of a *Pygmalion effect.* This is a form of self-fulfilling prophecy that supposedly occurs as follows: (1) the teacher reviews the pupils' school records and forms expectations for certain pupils (e.g., high or low achievement), (2) the teacher treats the pupils in accordance with his expectations for them, and (3) the pupils respond by learning at the levels expected of them. In short, pupils achieve in accordance with the teacher's preconceived expectations implanted by school records. There is conflicting evidence as to whether such expectancy effects actually occur,[3] but there is

---

[3] J. D. Elashoff and R. E. Snow, *Pygmalion Reconsidered* (Worthington, Ohio: Charles A. Jones, 1971).

little harm in delaying a review of school records until after a period of personal contact with pupils. In fact, this might serve to counteract the formation of some prejudicial or biased judgments resulting from incorrect or inadequate data in school records.

Pretesting. It is frequently desirable to supplement the general information obtained from school records with the results of a pretest given at the beginning of a course or unit of instruction. This pretesting may serve any of the following uses:

1. To determine the extent to which pupils possess the prerequisite skills needed for effective learning (readiness).
2. To determine the extent to which pupils have already achieved the intended outcomes of instruction (placement).
3. To obtain a base for determining the amount of learning gain during instruction (pretest-posttest design).
4. To provide information that will aid in selecting the most relevant learning activities for pupils (instructional adaptation).

Probably the most common function of pretesting is that of measuring the prerequisite skills needed to begin a course or unit of instruction. This type of pretesting is most useful in highly structured courses where the needed entry behaviors can be clearly defined and where they are considered essential for effective learning progress. For example, a pretest on computational skill might be administered at the beginning of a course in mathematics or science, or a pretest on vocabulary and grammar might be given at the beginning of an intermediate level foreign language course. Similarly, at the unit level, a pretest on addition might be given at the beginning of a unit on multiplication. The results of such pretesting can be used in planning review for the entire class (where common weaknesses exist) and in planning remedial programs for individual pupils. The latter might take the form of programed instruction, self-review units, practice exercises, or some other type of individualized remedial work.

When pretesting is used to determine which of the course outcomes pupils have already achieved or to obtain a base for measuring learning gain during the course, the pretest is simply an alternate form of the final examination (summative test). If certain of the objectives have already been mastered by the majority of pupils, the materials and methods of instruction can be altered accordingly. If a pupil demonstrates that he has already achieved all, or nearly all, of the course objectives, he can be placed in a more advanced course or permitted to complete the unfinished course requirements through independent study. Where the course is organized by units, the items in the pretest might also be arranged by units so that the test results can be used to identify the particular units each pupil has mastered. For some purposes (e.g., measuring learning gain unit by unit), it would be desirable to give pretests at the beginning of each unit rather than at the beginning of the course.

Both pretesting and other preassessments of the pupils' entry behavior can be used in selecting the most relevant learning activities for pupils. A review of the school records and of the pretest item responses of particular pupils (e.g., slow learners), for instance, might indicate that these pupils would profit most from concrete learning tasks presented in a sequential series of small steps with frequent opportunity for positive reinforcement. Similarly, preassessment and classroom observation might suggest that a particular instructional mode (e.g., programed instruction, independent study) might be beneficial for enhancing the learning of certain pupils. Experienced teachers have always been alerted to opportunities for modifying instructional materials and methods to fit the unique needs of particular pupils. Preassessment simply provides additional information on which to base such decisions. How useful this information is depends to a large extent on how well the teacher already knows the pupils. Where a teacher has worked with the pupils for some time, formal preassessment at the beginning of a unit may be unnecessary.

To summarize, preassessing the learners' needs involves reviewing the school records of each pupil and pretesting. These procedures may be used to determine whether pupils possess necessary prerequisite skills, to determine which of the planned instructional objectives pupils have already achieved, to obtain a base for measuring learning gain, and to provide information for selecting the most relevant learning activities for pupils. An understanding of our pupils' abilities and needs early in the instructional process enables us to remedy deficiencies in prerequisite skills and to adapt instruction more closely to group and individual needs.

Monitoring Learning Progresss

The purpose of using tests and other evaluation instruments during the instructional process is to guide and direct pupil learning and to monitor progress toward course objectives. These procedures fall within the province of *formative* evaluation. As noted in Chapter 1, this type of evaluation is seldom used for grading pupils. Instead, it is intended to serve such specific uses as the following: (1) to plan corrective action for overcoming learning deficiencies, (2) to aid in motivating learning, and (3) to increase retention and transfer of learning. Each of these uses will be discussed in turn.

Planning Corrective Action. Periodic testing and evaluation during a course may provide general clues that enable us to better adjust our instruction to the needs of the classroom group. A test at the end of a weather unit, for instance, might reveal inadequate knowledge of weather instruments, thereby suggesting a review, or a trip to the local weather station. Ratings of laboratory performance in science might reveal errors in procedure that would be cleared up by a demonstration to the class. Poorly written answers on an essay test in social studies might indicate the desirability of providing pupils with more practice in organizing and expressing ideas. A test of computational skill in mathematics might suggest review for some pupils and more advanced work for others. Thus, each test and evaluation instrument provides information concerning successes and failures in learning, enabling us to take prompt corrective action and to provide future experiences in closer harmony with the learning needs of the group.

Formative evaluation can also provide more detailed information for correcting learning deficiencies. The pupils' responses to a formative test might be analyzed item by item, for example, to reveal group and individual errors needing correction. A portion of such an item-response chart for a weather unit test is shown in Table 18.1. Note that the test items are grouped by content area and instructional objective, and that a plus sign (+) indicates that the item was answered correctly and a minus sign (−) that it was answered incorrectly. By reading down the chart we can identify items or areas (e.g., "Clouds," "Fronts") where errors should be corrected by group instruction, and by reading across the chart we can identify individual patterns of error (e.g., "Douglas Smith") requiring individualized remedial instruction. Thus, formative evaluation procedures can help us plan corrective action for both individuals and groups.

Motivating Learning. There are two major ways that the evaluation process can facilitate pupil motivation: (1) by providing immediate, attainable goals toward which to work; (2) by providing knowledge of learning progress.

TABLE 18.1

A PORTION OF AN ITEM-RESPONSE CHART SHOWING CORRECT (+) AND INCORRECT (−) RESPONSES ON A WEATHER UNIT TEST[*]

Objectives →	Knows Basic Terms					
Content Areas →	Pressure	Temperature	Humidity	Wind	Clouds	Fronts
Items →	1 2	3 4	5 6	7 8	9 10 11	12 13 14
John Able	+ +	+ +	+ +	+ +	− − −	+ − −
Mary Baker	+ +	+ +	− −	+ −	+ − −	− + +
Henry Charles	+ −	+ +	+ +	− +	− − +	+ − +
Joe Darby	+ +	+ +	+ −	+ +	+ − −	+ + −
Betty Frank	+ +	+ +	+ +	+ +	+ − +	− + −
Bill Jones	+ −	+ +	+ +	− +	− − −	− − −
Louise Kerr	+ +	+ +	+ +	+ +	+ − +	− + +
Kathy Mann	+ +	+ +	+ +	+ +	+ − +	+ + −
Douglas Smith	− −	− +	+ −	+ −	− − +	+ − −
Francis Young	+ +	+ +	+ +	− +	+ − −	+ − −

[*] Reproduced from N. E. Gronlund, *Preparing Criterion-Referenced Tests for Classroom Instruction.* New York: Macmillan, 1973. Reproduced by permission.

Working toward remote goals, without the encouragement of intermediate consequences, has little meaning for children, and adolescents. The teacher who attempts to motivate his class with urgings that "this will be of great value in adult life" has little chance of success. Pupils need short-term goals to serve as guideposts along the way. Tests, ratings, and other formative evaluation procedures serve this purpose.

Both research and personal experience substantiate the fact that the mere expectation that a test will be given tends to stimulate learning activity. There is also considerable evidence that the type of test anticipated will influence how and what pupils study. Older research findings have shown that pupils tend to concentrate on trends, relationships, and the organization of material when preparing for essay tests and on factual details when studying for objective tests.[4] In passing, it should be noted that the objective tests used in these studies emphasized knowledge of factual details rather than understandings, application of facts and principles, and similar complex learning outcomes. Consequently, the results should not be interpreted to mean that objective tests *per se* encourage the memorization of factual information. These findings are simply in harmony with the more general principle that *pupils will tend to emphasize those learning outcomes that are reflected in the evaluation procedures.*

In addition to arousing and directing learning activity toward definite short-term goals, formative evaluation procedures contribute to motivation by letting pupils know how well they are doing. The results from tests, ratings, checklists, and other evaluation devices provide continuous feedback to the learner concerning his successes and failures. Such feedback enhances learning by reinforcing correct responses and by identifying errors that should be eliminated.

A study by E. B. Page[5] has shown that the type of feedback is an important element in motivation. Teachers in 74 classes, in grades seven to twelve, were asked to administer an objective test to their classes, to place the score and grade on each paper, and then to randomly assign the papers to one of three groups. Group 1 papers received no comment beyond the score and grade assigned to all papers. Group 2 papers received general and encouraging comments, like "Good work. Keep at it." Group 3 papers received the specific comment the teacher thought desirable under the circumstance. A later follow-up with a second objective test showed that the highest scores were achieved by the pupils who had received the specific comments (Group 3), the next highest by those given the general comments (Group 2), and the lowest by those receiving no comment on their papers (Group 1). The motivating effect of the comments did not

---

[4] W. W. Cook, "The Functions of Measurement in the Facilitation of Learning," in E. F. Lindquist (ed.), *Educational Measurement* (Washington, D.C.: American Council on Education, 1951).

[5] E. B. Page, "Teacher Comments and Student Performance," in R. G. Kuhlen (ed.), *Studies in Educational Psychology* (Waltham, Mass.: Blaisdell, 1968).

appear to be dependent on the school, grade level, or ability of the pupil.

To be most effective, feedback to the learner should be immediate, as well as specific.[6] This principle of immediacy is carried to the ultimate in the teaching machine, which is simply a device for presenting an orderly sequence of explanations and questions. As the learner responds to each question, he is informed immediately whether his response is correct or incorrect. Although we cannot hope to match this feature of the teaching machine in our routine use of formative evaluation procedures, there are steps that can be taken to implement the principle. First, we can return test papers and all other evaluation results to pupils as soon as possible. Second, we can make specific comments on pupils' papers so that they will have a clear notion of what they did well and where they need improvement. Third, we can help pupils develop self-evaluation skills. When pupils learn the qualities desired in a performance or a product and obtain experience in judging their own work in terms of these criteria, they are better able to provide their own immediate feedback. This type of self-reinforcement and self-correction of errors is basic to learning and an ultimate objective of all education. Unless pupils develop "built-in" standards of performance they are not apt to do much learning on their own, neither during their school years nor after they leave school.

In summary, formative evaluation procedures contribute to pupil motivation by providing short-term goals and by providing feedback concerning learning progress. For maximum results the evaluation procedures should represent all of the important objectives of the course, and the feedback should be specific and prompt.

Increasing Retention and Transfer of Learning. Formative evaluation procedures can contribute to greater retention and transfer of learning by (1) focusing attention on those learning outcomes that are most permanent and most widely applicable, and (2) providing practice in applying previously learned skills and ideas in new situations.

Evidence concerning the relative permanence of various types of learning outcomes is rather sparse. What there is seems to suggest that retention increases as the outcomes become more complex. The results of a classical study in this area are presented in Table 18.2. In this study, tests were given to college students in zoology at the beginning of the course, the end of the course, and again one year later. Note that for the simplest learning outcome, that of naming animal structures, less than a fourth of the course gain was retained a year later. In contrast, all of the gain in the ability to apply principles to new situations was retained, and the ability to interpret new experiments actually increased during the year following instruction. Such findings support the viewpoint that the permanency of learning will be enhanced by using evaluation procedures that emphasize the more complex learning outcomes.

---

[6] G. M. Blair, R. S. Jones, and R. H. Simpson, *Educational Psychology*, 4th ed. (New York: Macmillan, 1975).

TABLE 18.2
THE RELATIVE PERMANENCY OF DIFFERENT LEARNING OUTCOMES IN ZOOLOGY*

	Mean Score			
Type of Examination Exercise	Beginning of Course	End of Course	One Year Later	Percentage of Gain Which Was Retained
1. Naming animal structures pictured in diagrams	22	62	31	23
2. Identifying technical terms	20	83	67	74
3. Recalling information				
a. Structures performing functions in type forms	13	39	34	79
b. Other facts	21	63	54	79
4. Applying principles to new situations	35	65	65	100
5. Interpreting new experiments	30	57	64	125

* Adapted from R. W. Tyler, *Constructing Achievement Tests* (Columbus: Ohio State University, 1934), p. 76.

We are not only interested in pupils retaining what they have learned—we should also like them to be able to apply their learning to new situations. A study of grammar should contribute to better oral and written expression, arithmetic skills should be useful in solving assorted problems, and scientific principles should be helpful in interpreting a variety of scientific phenomena. This positive transfer of learning is a major objective of education. We can expect each new situation the pupil faces to have some element of novelty which requires him to use his old learning in a new way. Unless transfer is possible, learning material has very limited value.

Transfer of learning is most likely to occur where (1) the learning outcomes have wide applicability, (2) the pupils expect transfer to occur, and (3) the pupils recognize the similarity between the new situation and other situations in which the learning had been applicable. The evaluation process can contribute to each of these conditions.

In general, learning outcomes that emphasize the understanding of concepts and principles, the interpretation of materials, thinking skills, and other complex behaviors tend to have the widest applicability and therefore the greatest transfer value. Giving priority to such outcomes when selecting instructional objectives and planning evaluation procedures should increase the likelihood that transfer will take place. The use of formative tests and other evaluation instruments that specifically require the *application* of ideas and skills in new situations can also facilitate transfer. Evaluation of this type teaches pupils to anticipate transfer and to seek out the familiar elements in the new situation. Of course, it also provides practice in making the applications.

Another aspect of formative evaluation that has direct impact on the transfer of learning is that of evaluating typical behavior. When we make day-by-day evaluations of a pupil's typical use of grammar, spelling, study skills, and the like, we are letting him know that we expect new learning in these areas to carry over to, and become a part of, his daily behavior. Helping pupils incorporate their newly acquired understandings and skills into their normal behavior patterns adds greater assurance that the new responses will transfer both to in-school and out-of-school situations.

To summarize, formative evaluation procedures can facilitate retention and transfer of learning by reminding pupils that retention and transfer are expected, by stressing complex learning outcomes, and by providing opportunities to apply newly learned material.

Diagnosing and Remedying Learning Difficulties

There are four major steps in the diagnosis and remediation of learning difficulties: (1) Determining which pupils are having learning difficulty. (2) Determining the specific nature of the learning difficulty. (3) Determining the factors causing the learning difficulty. (4) Applying appropriate remedial procedures. Testing and evaluation can make a significant contribution to each of these steps.

Determining Who Is Having Difficulty. There are a number of methods for identifying those pupils who are experiencing learning difficulty. One of the most common is to compare the results of standardized achievement tests with the results of a scholastic aptitude test. If a pupil's level of achievement is lower than his level of scholastic aptitude, it is assumed that he is not achieving up to potential and that a search for the underlying difficulty is in order. This procedure is useful only if a number of cautions are borne in mind. First, if there is to be a direct comparison of scores, the achievement and scholastic aptitude scores must be expressed in comparable units. Second, the achievement and scholastic aptitude tests must be standardized on the same population. Third, the discrepancies between the achievement and aptitude scores must be relatively large to offset the possibility of the differences arising from measurement errors alone. Fourth, it must be recognized that not all underachievers will be detected by this method because some learning difficulties (e.g., poor reading ability) will tend to lower the scores on both tests and make it appear that aptitude and achievement are in agreement. This is especially likely with scholastic aptitude tests that emphasize school-learned abilities, but it is somewhat applicable to all group tests of mental ability.

Another common method of determining potential learning difficulties is by analyzing pupils' scores on the subtests of achievement batteries. This might be done by the use of profiles (like those presented in Chapter 15) or simply by comparing test scores, as shown in Figure 18.1. These are stanine scores for a group of low achieving pupils. As noted in Chapter 15, the stanine scoring system ranges from 1 to 9, with an average of 5. When comparing performance on two different tests, a difference of two stanines is usually considered a significant difference in performance. Using this as a guide, the scores on the subtests of the achievement battery can be compared to the *Otis-Lennon* scores (measure of scholastic aptitude) to detect areas of underachievement and to the other subtest scores to detect relative strengths and weaknesses. The teachers' comments in Figure 18.1 reflect this type of analysis. Since most test publishers administer a scholastic aptitude test to the same norm group on which the achievement battery is standardized, this type of analysis can be readily made.

In some cases it is desirable to analyze a standardized achievement test item by item and make a tally of those missed by each pupil. Items which are missed by a large number of pupils indicate areas where the class as a whole is doing poorly. This might suggest that either the test has inadequate content validity, or that changes in curriculum and teaching method are needed. The errors of each individual pupil can also be studied for clues to his particular learning difficulties. A major caution in using an analysis of item responses to determine individual learning difficulties pertains to the small number of items representing each area. At best, such an analysis merely provides *clues* which must be followed up by further study and observation.

Informal classroom evaluation procedures can also be used to detect learning difficulties. As noted earlier (see Table 18.1), the same type of item-by-item analysis used with standardized tests can be applied to classroom tests to detect group and individual learning errors. Rating scales, checklists, anecdotal records, and other observational devices also provide clues concerning learning problems. The day-by-day observations and judgments of an experienced teacher are especially valuable; he frequently can spot a pupil's difficulty before it becomes serious.

In determining which pupils are having learning difficulty, we should not confine our efforts to those with problems in the basic skills and the content areas. Pupils who are having difficulty in social relations, emotional adjustment, and other aspects of personal-social development also require attention. Learning problems of this type are significant in their own right, and they have a direct bearing on the pupil's ability to learn in other areas.

Determining the Specific Nature of the Learning Difficulty. The diagnosis of learning difficulties is a matter of degree. In some instances, the general procedures for locating pupils with learning difficulties provide sufficient information for immediate corrective action. In other cases, it may be necessary to supplement this information by further diagnostic study before planning remedial work. In still others, the learning problem may be so persistent and severe that the pupil should be referred to a specialist for intensive diagnosis.

Name	Word Knowl.	Reading	Total Read.	Lang.	Spell.	Math. Comp.	Math. Conc.	Math. Pr. Solv.	Total Math.	Science	Soc. Studies	Otis-Lennon
Jim	5	3	4	2	2	3	4	4	4	6	5	5
Bill	4	5	5	5	5	8	5	6	6	4	5	4
Sue	2	3	3	4	4	4	4	4	4	3	3	3
Bob	6	4	5	4	5	3	3	5	3	4	4	5
Anne	3	4	4	2	4	5	3	4	4	2	2	2
Frank	3	3	3	2	3	1	2	3	1	2	3	2
Judy	2	3	3	3	4	3	2	2	2	4	2	4

Jim — Weaknesses in Spelling and Language are evident. Highest score is in Science. Any special interest there to be built on?

Bill — Highest score in class in Computation. Otherwise, nothing special.

Sue — Reading could probably come up quite a bit. Poor reading is probably affecting performance in all other areas.

Bob — Needs work in math. Perhaps administer some diagnostic tests to further explore difficulties here. Scores in reading and scholastic aptitude suggest he could do much better.

Anne — Doing better than might be expected in terms of last year's grades and aptitude score. Seems to work very hard and enjoy school even though it is not easy for her.

Frank — Check difficulties in computation. Follow up on this at same time as for Bob.

Judy — All scores except Spelling and Science fall below aptitude score. Check attitude toward school, study habits, last year's grades. She should be doing much better generally.

When a pupil's learning difficulty is in the basic skill area, a logical follow-up procedure is the administration of a diagnostic test. Such tests are based on the common errors pupils make and thus provide a systematic method for locating the specific problem, as illustrated in Figure 18.2. Diagnostic tests tend to provide a more reliable sample of a pupil's errors than general achievement tests because they have a large number of items representing each particular aspect of the skill being measured. The test manuals and accessory materials accompanying published diagnostic tests typically provide suggestions for further diagnosis and for use of the test scores in remedial work.

However, because published diagnostic tests are limited almost entirely to the areas of reading and arithmetic, it is frequently necessary to use more informal methods for diagnosing a pupil's learning difficulties. The procedure of analyzing a pupil's responses to each test item, described in the previous section, is one approach to this problem. Another is to administer a general achievement test and ask the pupil to describe aloud the mental process he is following as he answers each question. This "thinking aloud" provides clues to the pupil's weaknesses in knowledge, skill, and method of approaching problems. Since the test is administered on an individual basis, it is also possible to note any emotional factors or undesirable habits which might be interfering with the pupil's responses. Clues concerning the specific nature of a pupil's learning difficulties might also be gleaned from his cumulative record. An examination of past test results, course grades, anecdotal records, and other evaluative data can frequently throw light on the nature of a pupil's present difficulty. This, of course, is also a vital step in searching for the causes of the problem.

Determining the Factors Causing the Learning Difficulty. Some learning difficulties can be attributed to improper teaching methods, unsuitable curricular emphasis, or exceptionally complex course materials. Such instances are fairly easy to detect because a relatively large number of pupils will experience the same difficulty. When this occurs, we should, of course, focus our attention on locating and correcting the shortcomings in our instructional methods and materials. This is one of the major ways that evaluation results can contribute to improved instruction.

Of particular interest to us here, however, are the persistent learning difficulties of individual pupils that cannot be accounted for by faulty instruction. To determine the causes of these problems, we must make a careful study of the pupil and his environment. The major areas to consider are the pupil's scholastic aptitude; reading, arithmetic, and language skills; work-study skills; health and physical condition; emotional adjustment; and home environment. Unfavorable factors in any of these areas might cause or contribute to learning problems.

Figure 18.1. Stanine scores and teachers' comments for pupils in sample class taking *Metropolitan Achievement Tests*—Intermediate Level and *Otis-Lennon Mental Ability Test.* (From *Teacher's Handbook. Metropolitan Achievement Tests.* Copyright 1971 by Harcourt Brace Jovanovich, Inc. Used by permission.)

PUPIL PROFILE FOR ANDY L.

Grade 6. Age: 11 yrs. 5 mos. Tested with SDAT Level II in November of Grade 6. Otis IQ: 115. *Stanford Achievement Test*—Paragraph Meaning: Stanine 7 (taken in Grade 5).

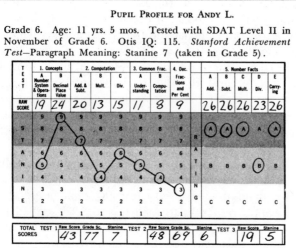

Andy's grade scores for Test 1 Total and Test 2 Total indicate that overall he is performing at an above average level in arithmetic. However, several weaknesses appearing in the profile bear further investigation. He is doing quite well in decimal place value concepts (Test 1B) and in addition and subtraction (Test 2A). His scores in Test 5 indicate practical mastery of the number facts. A pupil of this mental capacity should do better with multiplication (Test 2B), with common fractions (Test 3), and with decimal fractions and per cent (Test 4).

An analysis of the multiplication items in Andy's test booklet shows that he omitted the terminal zero in items 10, 11, 13, and 15. Correction of this error is essential. Except for a careless mistake in one other item, it is the only type of error found in his multiplication. What appears to be a noticeable weakness becomes, upon specific analysis, one persistent error in the multiplication operation.

Andy missed three of eighteen items in division. In one he copied the dividend instead of his correct quotient. In another he brought down the wrong digit, and in another he failed to regroup in subtraction. Actually, he is quite good in division, but a bit careless.

The value of specific analysis of Andy's computation is obvious. He is a better pupil than his test scores indicate, but he does make a few easily remedied mistakes.

Andy's troubles with decimal fractions and per cent, on the other hand, are extensive. Notice his performance on items 7, 8, 13, and 14: $3 \times 2.3 = 6.3$ and $3 \times 4.2 = 12.2$; $12.8 \div 2 = 6.8$ and $39.6 \div 3 = 13.6$.

He operates with the whole number but ignores the decimal fraction part. He finds 50% of 12 to be 6%. It is obvious that Andy has not yet learned decimal fractions and per cent. Other pupils, however, in the same class, do much better with decimal fractions. Thus, a thorough program of instruction in this area must be provided for Andy on an individual basis.

Figure 18.2. Example of a diagnosis of learning errors based on the *Stanford Diagnostic Arithmetic Test —Level II.* (From *Manual. Stanford Diagnostic Arithmetic Test.* Copyright 1966 by Harcourt Brace Jovanovich. Used by permission.)

It should be noted that the causes of learning difficulties are multiple and complex and seldom can be fully determined by the classroom teacher. However, a review of the pupil's cumulative record, special testing and observations (as needed), an interview with the pupil, and possibly a home visit, should provide sufficient information on which to base remedial action. If the pupil's learning problem requires more extended study than can be accomplished within the normal teaching situation, the pupil should be referred to a specialist.

Applying Remedial Procedures. There is no set pattern to be followed in helping pupils overcome learning difficulties. In some instances it may be a simple matter of review and reteaching. In others, an extensive effort to improve motivation, correct emotional difficulties, and overcome deficiencies in work-study skills may be required. The specific remedial procedures used in any given case will depend on the specific nature of the learning difficulty and the factors which have caused and contributed to it.

Testing and evaluation can play a vital role in most remedial programs. The use of periodic testing during remedial teaching might serve any of the following functions: (1) clarify to the pupil the specific types of responses that are expected; (2) provide further diagnostic information about the pupil's difficulties and learning needs; (3) give the pupil a feeling of success through the use of a carefully graded series of test exercises; (4) enhance motivation by providing short-term goals and immediate knowledge of progress; (5) provide information concerning the effectiveness of the remedial procedures. Other evaluation techniques, such as rating scales, checklists, and anecdotal records can, of course, also be used to provide feedback concerning learning progress and the success of the remedial program.

Though the immediate aim of remedial work is the correction of specific learning difficulties, our interest should not stop there. A careful analysis of evaluation results during diagnosis and treatment will reveal learning errors that can be prevented and causal factors that can be modified. The ultimate result of a remedial program should be an improved curriculum and more effective instructional methods.

In summary, evaluation procedures are useful in all phases of diagnostic and remedial work. Although they serve essentially the same functions here as for the general instructional program, attention in diagnosis is focused more directly on the specific responses of individual pupils.

Appraising Course Outcomes

A comprehensive evaluation of pupil achievement at the end of a course, or at some particular summing-up point in the course (e.g., mid-semester), falls within the realm of *summative* evaluation. The purpose here is to obtain a general measure of learning progress that can be used for (1) assigning grades; (2) reporting learning progress to parents, pupils, and school personnel; and (3) improving learning and instruction. The use of evaluation in marking and reporting will be described in the following chapter. Here we shall confine our discussion to the use of summative evaluation in improving learning and instruction.

Pupils should be given feedback from summative tests just as they are from formative tests. Although this is more easily done with a mid-semester examination than with a final examination, some teachers make special provisions for reviewing the final examination results with pupils. In any event, this feedback will most likely be useful if the test is organized in such a way that pupils can readily see their strengths and weaknesses. Arranging the test and answer sheet by objective is helpful for this purpose. An example of a teacher-made answer sheet that was specifically designed for providing feedback on a summative test is shown in Figure 18.3. In reviewing the test results, the pupils would, of course, also have a copy of the test so that they could examine the particular items on which they made errors.

In addition to feedback to pupils, summative evaluation results can be used to check on the attainability of the various instructional objectives and the effectiveness of the instruction. In areas where the majority of class members experience learning difficulties, the fault is likely to reside in the nature of the intended outcomes, or in the materials and methods of instruction. Thus, summative evaluation alerts us to the need for a careful review of those aspects of the teaching-learning process.

Summative evaluation results can also be used to determine the comparative effectiveness of alternate programs for achieving a set of instructional objectives. This type of comparison can be made by following these steps: (1) randomly assign teachers and pupils to two alternate programs, (2) give an equivalent form of the summative test as a common pretest to both groups, (3) provide the instruction as specified for each program, (4) give the common summative posttest to both groups, and (5) analyze and compare the results to determine which program most adequately achieved the intended learning outcomes. Using this systematic procedure, with different materials and methods of instruction, provides a means for continually improving the instructional program.

To summarize, the appraisal of course outcomes at the end of instruction (summative evaluation) can provide some direct feedback to pupils, can aid in evaluating the materials and methods of instruction, and can be used to compare the effectiveness of alternate programs of instruction.

EVALUATION AND MASTERY LEARNING

Mastery learning might be viewed as one aspect of conventional classroom instruction, as was described in Chapter 2. Thus, the intended learning outcomes of a course can be divided into *mastery* outcomes and *de-*

Name			Date

			TERMS
1. ___	26. ___	51. ___	
2. ___	27. ___	52. ___	
3. ___	28. ___	53. ___	___
4. ___	29. ___	54. ___	
5. ___	30. ___	55. ___	Score

			FACTS
6. ___	31. ___	56. ___	
7. ___	32. ___	57. ___	
8. ___	33. ___	58. ___	
9. ___	34. ___	59. ___	
10. ___	35. ___	60. ___	
11. ___	36. ___	61. ___	
12. ___	37. ___	62. ___	
13. ___	38. ___	63. ___	
14. ___	39. ___	64. ___	___
15. ___	40. ___	65. ___	Score

			PRINCIPLES
16. ___	41. ___	66. ___	
17. ___	42. ___	67. ___	
18. ___	43. ___	68. ___	
19. ___	44. ___	69. ___	
20. ___	45. ___	70. ___	
21. ___	46. ___	71. ___	
22. ___	47. ___	72. ___	
23. ___	48. ___	73. ___	
24. ___	49. ___	74. ___	___
25. ___	50. ___	75. ___	Score

KNOWLEDGE	UNDER-STANDING	APPLICATION	
___	___	___	
Score	Score	Score	

FIGURE 18.3. Teacher-made answer sheet for feedback on summative test.

velopmental outcomes. The former are concerned with those minimum essentials of the course (e.g., basic skills) that must be mastered by all pupils, and the latter with the more complex transfer-type objectives (e.g., problem solving, application) toward which pupils can be expected to show varying degrees of progress. Another way of viewing mastery learning in classroom instruction is to consider it a basic strategy to be applied to *all* intended learning outcomes. This is the approach taken by B. S. Bloom, J. H. Block, and others.[7] Here, we shall describe Bloom's mastery learning strategy as an illustration of how mastery learning might be applied to *all* phases of classroom instruction. As will be seen shortly, tests and other evaluation instruments play an equally important role in Bloom's approach to mastery learning.

Bloom's Mastery Learning Strategy[8]

Essentially, Bloom's mastery learning approach is an instructional strategy designed to bring all, or nearly all, pupils to a specified level of mastery on *all* course objectives. It combines regular classroom instruction with feedback-corrective techniques for overcoming individual learning errors. Additional learning time is provided for those pupils who need it. Thus, the Bloom approach uses regular group-based instruction that is supplemented by carefully prescribed corrective study for those pupils who fail to achieve mastery during the group-based instruction.

The following steps outline the essential features of Bloom's mastery learning strategy:

1. The course is subdivided into a series of learning units that include a week or two of learning activity. These units might be chapters in a textbook or some other meaningful segment of course content.
2. The instructional objectives are identified and clearly specified for each learning unit. A wide range of learning outcomes are stressed (e.g., knowledge, comprehension, application) and the objectives are defined in specific terms (as described earlier in Chapter 2).
3. Mastery standards are set for the objectives in each learning unit. This is frequently done in terms of the percentage of test items a pupil is expected to answer correctly. Although the setting of mastery standards is somewhat arbitrary, the performance of pupils who have previously taken the course is typically used as a guide. Mastery is frequently set at 80 to 85 per cent correct for each unit, but this must be adjusted to fit various learning and testing conditions.[9]
4. The learning tasks within each unit are taught using the regular materials and methods of group-based instruction. This phase is similar to conventional classroom instruction.
5. Diagnostic-progress tests (*formative* tests) are given at the end of each

---

[7] J. H. Block (ed.), *Mastery Learning: Theory and Practice* (New York: Holt, Rinehart & Winston, 1971).

[8] The material in this section is adapted from Chapter 2, "Bloom's Mastery Learning Strategy" in N. E. Gronlund *Individualizing Classroom Instruction* (New York: Macmillan, 1974).

[9] N. E. Gronlund, *Preparing Criterion-Referenced Tests for Classroom Instruction* (New York: Macmillan, 1973).

learning unit. The results of these formative tests are used to reinforce the learning of pupils who have mastered the material and to diagnose the learning errors of those who have failed to achieve mastery. They are typically not used for assigning grades.

6. Specific procedures for correcting learning errors and additional learning time are prescribed for those pupils who do not demonstrate unit mastery. These prescriptive-corrective techniques include reading particular pages in an alternate textbook, using programed materials, using audiovisual aids, individual tutoring, and small group study sessions. If one method does not prove successful with a particular learning problem, the pupil is encouraged to use an alternate method. Retesting is typically done after corrective study.

7. Upon completion of all of the course units, an end-of-course test (*summative* test) is administered. The results of this test are used primarily to assign course grades. All grades are assigned on the basis of absolute standards that were set at the beginning of the course. Thus, if all pupils achieve the level of mastery prescribed for an A grade, all will receive that grade.

8. The results of the formative tests (unit tests) and the summative test (final examination) are used as a basis for evaluating and improving the instruction. Typically, the methods, materials, and sequencing of instruction are given close scrutiny wherever a majority of pupils have experienced difficulty in mastering the learning tasks.

In summary, Bloom's mastery learning strategy is a group-based method that uses special techniques for adapting instruction to the needs of individual pupils. It differs from conventional classroom instruction in the following ways: (1) It emphasizes the mastery of *all* objectives in each of a series of learning units. (2) It uses frequent diagnostic-progress tests (formative tests) to identify each pupil's specific learning errors. (3) It uses systematic feedback-corrective procedures and alternate learning resources (e.g., programed material) for helping pupils overcome learning difficulties. (4) It provides additional learning time for those pupils who need it. Thus, instead of holding learning time constant and accepting a wide range of achievement, Bloom's approach provides for variation in learning time and emphasizes a high level of achievement for all pupils. An individual's learning effectiveness and course grade are determined by the level of mastery he achieves, rather than by how his performance compares to that of his classmates.

Role of Testing and Evaluation. As can be gleaned from the description of Bloom's mastery learning strategy, formative tests play a key role in this approach. They are used to improve learning in the following ways: (1) They reinforce the learning of high achievers. (2) They pinpoint the specific learning errors of low achievers. (3) They serve as a basis for the corrective prescriptions given to individual pupils. In short, formative testing provides the diagnostic-feedback-corrective procedures that permits the instruction to be adapted to individual pupils. Since formative test results are not used for grading, their effectiveness as a learning tool is maximized.

In the feedback of formative test results to pupils, Bloom suggests that the feedback-corrective prescriptions be very specific. This might be done by placing the prescriptions on the answer sheet, as shown in Figure 18.4. Although only specific textbook pages are used here, other corrective prescriptions could be added.

As noted earlier, the summative tests are used primarily for assigning course grades. They are typically given at the end of the course to determine how well the pupils have mastered all of the objectives covered by the various units of instruction. Summative test results make only a minor contribution to improved learning, since they are obtained so late in the course. Pupils can be given some feedback of results, but their primary value, other than in grading, is in the contribution they make to the appraisal and improvement of instruction.

Evaluation of attitudes, interests, and other affective outcomes are also considered important in mastery learning. These are typically used for individual development and course improvement, however, and not for assigning grades.

The tests and other evaluation instruments used in Bloom's mastery learning approach are designed primarily for criterion-referenced interpretation (i.e., comparing pupil performance to an absolute standard of mastery), rather than for norm-referenced interpretation (i.e., comparing pupil performance to the performance of others). However, the summative test given at the end of the course typically lends itself to both types of interpretation.

In summary, Bloom's mastery learning approach combines conventional classroom instruction with elements of individualized instruction to bring all pupils to a predetermined level of mastery on *all* course objectives. Formative tests (and other evaluation data) are used to monitor pupil learning progress and to prescribe corrective procedures for overcoming learning difficulties. The results of formative evaluation are *not* used to compare pupils or to assign course grades. Summative evaluation is used for grading purposes.

EVALUATION AND INDIVIDUALIZED INSTRUCTION

Individualized instruction can take many different forms, but it typically involves permitting each pupil to work on a series of individual learning units at his own pace and his own level of achievement. His work on each unit of study is commonly directed by a learning guide called an Individual Study Unit, a Teaching-Learning Unit, a Learning Package, a Self-

CHEMISTRY TEST

Answer sheet

Name _____

Date _____ Test number _2_

CIRCLE your answer for each question. When you score this test, put an R beside each correct answer. Leave your incorrect answers blank.

Alternative learning resources: This test is designed to inform you of your learning difficulties. This test will not count as part of your final grade. Below is a list of learning materials which will explain the ideas you still need to learn. For each item you did not get right, read across to find where the correct answer or idea is explained.

Textbook:

					Right (R)	Chemistry: An Experimental Science	Chemistry: A Science of Matter, Energy, & Change by Choppin and Jaffe	
1.	A	B	C	D	E		Page 21	Page 19	
2.	A	B	C	D	E		Page 21	Page 18	
3.	A	B	C	D	E		Page 28	Page 14	
4.	A	B	C	D	E		Page 28	Page 15	
5.	A	B	C	D	E		Page 31	Page 76	
6.	A	B	C	D	E		Page 31	Page 16	
7.	A	B	C	D	E		Page 33	Page 86	
8.	A	B	C	D	E		Page 32	Page 84	
9.	A	B	C	D	E		Page 33	Page 84	
10.	A	B	C	D	E		Page 33	Page 84	
11.	A	B	C	D	E		Page 31	Page 77	
12.	A	B	C	D	E		Page 17	Page 53	
13.	A	B	C	D	E		Page 21	Page 19	
14.	A	B	C	D	E		Page 25	Page 71	
15.	A	B	C	D	E		Pages 25-26	Pages 69-70	
16.	A	B	C	D	E		Page 28	Page 50	
17.	A	B	C	D	E		Page 33	Page 98	
18.	A	B	C	D	E		Page 34	Page 105	
19.	A	B	C	D	E		Page 31	Page 16	
20.	A	B	C	D	E		Lab manual Pages 14-18	Page 81	
21.	A	B	C	D	E		Page 32	Page 136	
22.	A	B	C	D	E		Page 28	Page 50	
23.	A	B	C	D	E		Page 27	Pages 69-71	
24.	A	B	C	D	E		Page 34	Page 106	
25.	A	B	C	D	E		Page 34	Page 106	
26.	A	B	C	D	E		Pages 25-26	Pages 81-82	
27.	A	B	C	D	E		Page 34	Pages 86-87	
28.	A	B	C	D	E		Page 37	Pages 88-91	
29.	A	B	C	D	E		Page 33	Page 98	
30.	A	B	C	D	E		Page 38	Pages 104-105	

Figure 18.4. Remedial instructional materials keyed to items on a Formative Chemistry Test (From B. S. Bloom, J. T. Hastings, and G. F. Madaus, *Handbook on Formative and Summative Evaluation of Student Learning.* Copyright © 1971 by McGraw-Hill. All rights reserved. Reproduced by permission.)

Instructional Unit, a Student Learning Contract, or some similar name. Despite the variation in titles, learning guides are similar in content and design. They typically include the following key elements:[10]

1. One or more instructional objectives.
2. Pretest (or directions for obtaining it).
3. List of learning activities and materials.
4. Self-tests to aid the pupil in monitoring his learning progress.
5. Posttest (or directions for obtaining it.)

Thus, each learning guide provides a self-contained instructional unit that permits a pupil to work through a program of study, unit by unit, with only a minimum of teacher guidance.

As noted in the learning guide outline, testing plays a prominent role in each individual learning unit. The pretest aids in determining the pupil's readiness for studying the unit and serves as a placement guide. If a pupil does well on the pretest, he may be permitted to skip some of the objectives in the unit or he may be directed to move on to the next unit. The self-tests are designed to measure mastery of each instructional objective within the unit. These tests help the pupil decide when he should move on to the next objective and when he is ready to take the unit posttest. The posttest determines whether the pupil has mastered the objectives in the unit. If a pupil performs satisfactorily on the posttest, he moves on to the next unit of study. If his performance is unsatisfactory, he continues work on the unit and retakes a second form of the posttest at a later date. The flow chart in Figure 18.5 illustrates the use of testing in guiding pupils through units of individualized instruction. To read the chart, start with the UNIT PRE-TEST and simply follow the arrows.

Learning guides for individualized instructional units might be developed locally, or a school might participate in one of the comprehensive individualized instructional programs, such as *Individually Prescribed Instruction* (*IPI*) or *PLAN* (Program for Learning in Accordance with Needs).[11] Regardless of the approach selected for use, there will be heavy emphasis on testing and evaluation. All such programs typically involve (1) pretesting to determine entry behavior and to properly place the pupil in the program, (2) testing during the program to monitor pupil progress, and (3) posttesting to determine the pupil's final mastery of the instructional objectives. Thus, the same types of testing used in conventional classroom instruction are also used in programs for individualizing instruction. Here, however, the testing function is even more crucial because periodic testing is used to guide and direct pupil progress on self-contained learning units that are to be studied on an individual basis.

---

[10] N. E. Gronlund, *Individualizing Classroom Instruction* (New York: Macmillan, 1971).
[11] See N. E. Gronlund, *Individualizing Classroom Instruction* (New York: Macmillan, 1974) for detailed descriptions of these programs and procedures.

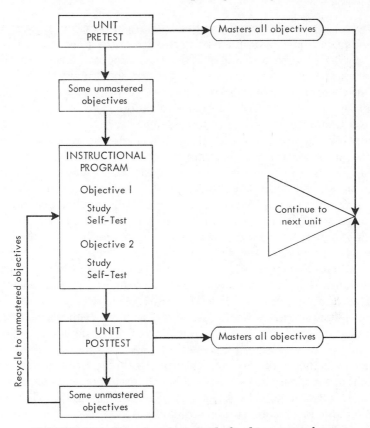

FIGURE 18.5. Flow chart for individualized instructional unit.

Since mastery learning is emphasized in individualized instruction, the tests and other evaluation instruments used are almost exclusively criterion-referenced. Mastery is demonstrated on these measures by attaining a pre-specified level of achievement on each instructional objective. Comparing a pupil's performance to the performance of others is seldom of interest in individualized instruction.

SUMMARY

The primary function of evaluation in classroom teaching is that of improving learning and instruction.

The evaluation process can contribute to improved learning in conventional classroom instruction in a number of ways. (1) It can help clarify the instructional objectives for both teacher and pupil. This aids the teacher in instructional planning and in guiding learning activities. It provides the pupil with a better knowledge of the learning outcomes to be achieved. (2) It can aid in preassessing the pupil's abilities and needs. Such information is useful in determining learning readiness, in properly placing pupils in a learning sequence, and in adapting instruction to group and individual needs. (3) It can assist in monitoring learning progress during instruction. Periodic testing and evaluation during instruction (formative evaluation) can be used to identify learning deficiencies, to plan corrective action, to motivate pupil learning, and to increase retention and transfer of learning. (4) It can help in diagnosing and remedying learning difficulties. Evaluation procedures are useful in identifying which pupils are having learning difficulties, in determining the specific nature of the difficulty, in detecting causes of the difficulty, and in applying appropriate remedial procedures. (5) It can aid in evaluating instructional effectiveness through an appraisal of final course outcomes (summative evaluation). Such evaluation results provide information that can be used in reviewing the methods and materials of instruction, and in comparing alternative programs of instruction.

Evaluation also plays an important role in mastery learning programs. Where a mastery learning approach, such as Bloom's, is used, an attempt is made to bring pupils to a predetermined level of mastery on *all* course objectives. Testing and evaluation serve the same basic functions with this instructional strategy as with conventional classroom instruction, but formative evaluation plays a more prominent role. Here it serves as a diagnostic-feedback-corrective technique for overcoming individual learning errors. The formative evaluation results provide a basis for prescribing corrective study that is adapted to each individual's learning needs. Thus, group instruction is supplemented by individual learning, and the nature of the individual study is determined by formative evaluation. The results of formative evaluation are not used for assigning course grades, but are used strictly for improving pupil learning. Summative evaluation (end-of-course evaluation) is used for grading purposes.

Testing and evaluation in individualized instruction include the same types of procedures used in conventional classroom instruction. Here, however, the procedures are confined to self-contained learning units that are studied on an individual basis. Testing in each individualized study unit typically includes (1) a pretest to determine entry behavior and to properly place the pupil, (2) a self-test to monitor learning progress, and (3) a posttest to measure final mastery of the unit objectives. Thus, the systematic testing and evaluation for each individual learning unit permits the pupil to work through a program of study, unit by unit, with only a minimum of teacher guidance.

LEARNING EXERCISES

1. What types of tests results would be most useful to you in understanding the pupils at the beginning of a course? What types of test results would aid you most in preplanning for the course?

2. After a teacher has scored a *formative* classroom test, what steps might he follow to enhance pupil learning further? How might a *summative* test be used to improve learning?

3. Comment on the statement, "Tests have an undesirable influence on teaching because pupils direct their study toward the tests." What can the teacher do about this?

4. List and briefly describe as many ways as you can think of that a classroom teacher might detect pupils with learning difficulties.

5. Describe how each of the following might be used to facilitate pupil learning.
   a. Scholastic aptitude tests.
   b. Standardized achievement tests.
   c. Objective classroom tests.
   d. Essay tests.
   e. Observational techniques.
   f. Peer-appraisal techniques.
   g. Self-report techniques.

6. What types of tests and evaluation instruments are most likely to encourage transfer of learning?

7. In a course you are teaching, or plan to teach, outline a classroom testing program that includes pretesting, formative testing, diagnostic testing, and summative testing. What types of test content and test items would you use at each stage? Why? How would you use the results?

8. Compare and contrast the use of testing and evaluation in conventional classroom instruction, in a mastery learning program, and in individualized instruction.

SUGGESTIONS FOR FURTHER READING

BLOCK, J. H. "Mastery Learning in the Classroom: An Overview of Recent Research," Chapter 3 in J. H. Block (ed.), *Schools, Society, and Mastery Learning*. New York: Holt, Rinehart & Winston, Inc., 1974. A comprehensive review of research literature concerning the student outcomes obtained with the mastery learning approach.

BLOCK, J. H., and L. W. ANDERSON. *Mastery Learning in Classroom Instruction*. New York: Macmillan Publishing Co., Inc., 1975. A brief book describing how to use mastery learning in group instruction.

BLOOM, B. S., J. T. HASTINGS, and C. F. MADAUS. *Handbook on Formative and Summative Evaluation of Student Learning*. New York: McGraw-Hill Book Company, 1971. See especially Part two. This part contains a series of chapters written by subject-matter specialists who describe the role of teaching and testing in their respective areas.

GAGNÉ, R. M., and L. J. BRIGGS. *Principles of Instructional Design*. New York: Holt, Rinehart & Winston, Inc., 1974. Describes the various steps in systematically designing instruction—from specifying the intended outcomes to assessing student performance.

GLASER, R., and A. J. NITKO. "Measurement in Learning and Instruction," Chapter 17 in R. L. Thorndike (ed.), *Educational Measurement*. Washington, D.C.: American Council on Education, 1971. A comprehensive and systematic treatment of the topic.

GRONLUND, N. E. *Determining Accountability for Classroom Instruction.* New York: Macmillan Publishing Co., Inc., 1974. See Chapter 5, "Evaluating and Improving Classroom Instruction," for practical approaches to the improvement of instruction.

GRONLUND, N. E. *Individualizing Classroom Instruction.* New York: Macmillan Publishing Co., Inc., 1974. A brief book describing several of the leading large-scale programs for individualizing instruction and procedures for developing teacher-made materials.

SMITH, R. M. (ed.). *Teacher Diagnosis of Educational Difficulties.* Columbus, Ohio: Charles E. Merrill Publishers, 1969. Stresses informal methods for diagnosing learning difficulties in reading, written expression, spelling, speech, arithmetic, and personal-social development.

TRAVERS, R. M. W. (ed.). *Second Handbook of Research on Teaching.* Chicago: Rand McNally & Co., 1973. A comprehensive review of research studies on teaching. See especially the ten chapters in Part four, "Research on the Teaching of School Subjects," for research findings in your particular teaching area.

CHAPTER 19
Marking and Reporting

Assigning marks and reporting on pupil progress is a frustrating—but necessary—aspect of classroom instruction. . . . This chapter will remove some of the complexity by . . . describing current marking and reporting practices . . . and by providing guidelines for their effective use.

If instructional objectives have been clearly defined in behavioral terms and evaluation procedures have been effectively applied, the task of reporting pupil progress is greatly simplified. It is still a rather perplexing one, however, since the evaluative data usually must be summarized into a single letter grade, or at best a very brief report form. The process is a highly subjective one for which there are relatively few helpful guidelines. This has led to the use of marks and progress reports which vary widely in composition and meaning.

The greatest confusion exists where an attempt is made to summarize pupil progress in terms of a single letter grade (e.g., A, B, C, D, F). Should the assigned mark represent level of achievement, gain in achievement, or some combination of the two? Should effort be included, or should high achievers be given good marks regardless of effort? Should pupils be marked in terms of their own potential learning ability or in relation to the achievement of their classmates? There are no simple answers to such questions. Practice varies from school to school, and frequently from teacher to teacher within the same school system. Many schools have circumvented such problems by supplementing the single letter grade with more elaborate marking and reporting systems. We shall describe some of these shortly. But first, let us consider some of the functions to be served by marks. This should help identify the qualities desired in a marking and reporting system.

FUNCTIONS OF MARKS AND PROGRESS REPORTS

School marks and other reports of pupil progress serve a variety of specific functions in the school. These can best be described in relation to the users of the reports. They include (1) pupils and parents, (2) teachers and counselors, and (3) administrators.

Reporting to Pupils and Parents

The main reason for reporting to pupils and parents is to facilitate the learning and development of the pupils. Consequently the specific functions to be served are somewhat the same as those of the general evaluation program. The reports should (1) clarify the objectives of the school program, (2) indicate the pupil's strengths and weaknesses in learning, (3) promote greater understanding of the pupil's personal-social development, and (4) contribute to the pupil's motivation.

From the standpoint of pupil learning, most of the functions are probably best served by the day-to-day evaluation and feedback during instruction. However, there also seems to be a need for a periodic summary of progress. Pupils find it difficult to integrate test scores, ratings, and other evaluation results into an overall appraisal of their success in attaining school objectives. The periodic progress report provides this summary appraisal. In addition to giving pupils a general picture of how they are doing, such reports also provide them with a basis for checking the adequacy of their own self-estimates of learning progress.

Questions are frequently raised about the desirability of using school marks and progress reports for motivational purposes. As with other evaluation procedures, it would seem to depend largely on how they are used. If a bad report is held out as a threat to stimulate pupils to work harder, the consequences are apt to be undesirable. However, when the reports are viewed as opportunities to check on learning progress, they are likely to have the same motivational values as properly applied tests, in that they provide short-term goals and knowledge of results. Although the feedback concerning progress is not as immediate as that obtained from testing, properly prepared reports have the advantage of providing a more comprehensive and systematic picture of the pupil's strengths and weaknesses in learning.

Reports to parents should inform them of the objectives of the school and the progress their children are making toward those objectives. This is important from several viewpoints. First, by knowing what the school is attempting to do, parents are better able to cooperate with school personnel in promoting the development of their children. Second, information about the successes, failures, and problems their children are experiencing in school enables parents to give them the emotional support and encouragement that is needed. Third, summary reports of learning progress provide parents with a basis for helping their children make sound educational and vocational plans.[1] To serve these purposes adequately, the reporting system will need to contain as much information and detail as we can reasonably expect parents to comprehend and use.

Uses of Reports by Teachers and Counselors

Marks and progress reports contribute to the instructional and guidance programs of the school by providing increased information about pupils. Such reports supplement and complement test scores and other evaluative data in the cumulative records. If a pupil's past achievements are known, we can better understand his present strengths and weaknesses and can better predict the areas in which he is likely to be successful in the future. The increased information provided by progress reports is especially useful to teachers when they are planning instruction, diagnosing learning difficulties, and coping with special problems of personal-social development. Counselors use the reports, along with other information, to help pupils develop increased self-understanding and make more realistic educational and vocational plans. Many progress reports also provide information which is useful in counseling pupils who have emotional problems.

The instructional and guidance functions of the school would seem to be best served by a reporting system that is both comprehensive and diagnostic. To guide learning effectively, aid in personal-social development, and help with future planning, teachers and counselors need detailed information concerning the pupils' abilities and disabilities in each of the various areas of development.

Use of Reports by Administrators

Marks and progress reports serve a number of administrative functions. They are used for determining promotion and graduation, awarding honors, determining athletic eligibility, and for reporting to other schools and prospective employers. For most administrative purposes, a single letter grade tends to be preferable, largely because such marks are compact and can be easily recorded and averaged. With the increased use of machines for routine clerical work, this advantage will probably assume even greater importance in the future.

There is little doubt that the convenience of the single mark in administrative work has been a major factor in retarding the development of more comprehensive and useful progress reports. This need not be the case, however. Where a new reporting system is being developed, it is possible to retain the use of letter grades for administrative purposes and to

---

[1] R. L. Thorndike and E. Hagen, *Measurement and Evaluation in Psychology and Education,* 3rd ed. (New York: John Wiley & Sons, 1969).

supplement them with the type of information needed by pupils, parents, teachers, and counselors. At the high school level, the retention of letter grades is almost mandatory, since most college admission officers insist on them.

TYPES OF MARKING AND REPORTING SYSTEMS

An effective system of marking and reporting will (1) provide the type of information that is needed by the users of the reports, and (2) present it in a clearly understandable form. These seem like relatively simple criteria to satisfy but most reporting systems fall far short. Much of the difficulty is due to the variety of purposes such reports are expected to serve. As already discussed, for some uses we prefer comprehensive and detailed reports, while for others a single mark may be more desirable. An additional problem arises from variations in the educational backgrounds of the users of the reports. Information that is understandable to teachers and counselors may be confusing to many parents. Most marking and reporting systems represent some type of compromise between the need for detailed information and the need for conciseness and simplicity.

Traditional Marking Systems

The traditional method of reporting pupil progress, which is still in wide use today, consists of assigning a single letter grade (e.g., A, B, C, D, F) or a single number (e.g., 5, 4, 3, 2, 1) to represent a pupil's achievement in each subject. This system is concise and convenient but it has several notable shortcomings: (1) The meaning of such marks is often unclear because they are a conglomerate of such diverse factors as achievement, effort, and good behavior. (2) Even where it is possible to limit the mark to achievement only, interpretation is difficult. A mark of C may mean average work in all areas, or high performance in some areas and low performance in others. An overall summary appraisal in the form of a single mark tells us nothing about the pupil's relative success in achieving the various course objectives. (3) As typically used, letter grades have resulted in an undesirable emphasis on marks as ends in themselves. Many pupils and parents view them as goals to be achieved, rather than as means for understanding and improving pupil learning. While this is not entirely the fault of the marking system, the lack of information provided by a single letter grade probably contributes to this misuse.

Numerous attempts have been made to improve the traditional marking system by changing the number and meaning of the symbols used. One common procedure is to reduce the number of symbols to two or three. Typical reports of this type use letters such as H (honors), S (satisfactory), and U (unsatisfactory), or simply S and U. These variations have been generally unsatisfactory because they provide even less information concerning the pupil's learning progress.

Pass-Fail System

Although a two-category marking system has been used in some elementary schools for many years (e.g., satisfactory-unsatisfactory, pass-fail), it has just recently found widespread use in many high schools and colleges. As typically used at these levels, it is offered as an option to the traditional letter grade (A, B, C, D, F) in a limited number of courses. Students are permitted to take some courses, usually electives, under a *pass-fail* option. Since the pass-fail grade is not included in their grade-point average, this system encourages students to explore new areas of study without the fear of lowering their grade-point average.

As with any two-category system, the pass-fail option provides even less information than the traditional A, B, C, D, F system. In addition, such a system can tend to encourage students to reduce their study efforts in these courses. With one or two courses under a pass-fail option, it is difficult to resist the temptation to shift study time from these courses to those courses in which letter grades are to be assigned. Despite these limitations, the idea of encouraging students to take courses in new areas of study without fear of lowering their grade-point average is a good one. The drawbacks of the system can be minimized, if the courses taken under the pass-fail option are restricted to a limited number of electives.

A special case for the use of a *pass-no grade* marking system can be made for courses taught under a pure mastery learning approach. Here, where pupils are expected to demonstrate mastery of all course objectives before receiving credit for a course, a simple *pass* is all that is needed to indicate mastery. The practice of assigning a letter grade of A to all pupils who complete a course under mastery conditions, as is frequently done, simply adds greater confusion to the meaning of letter grades. When the *pass-no grade* system is used, nothing is recorded on a pupil's school record until mastery of the course work is demonstrated. The mastery learning approach presupposes that each pupil will be given as much time as he needs to attain mastery of the course objectives. Thus, the school record remains blank until the course is successfully completed.

Checklists of Objectives

To provide more informative progress reports, some schools have replaced or supplemented the traditional marking system with a list of behavior descriptions to be checked or rated. These reports, which are most common at the elementary school level, typically include ratings of progress toward the major objectives in each subject-matter area. The following statements for reading and arithmetic illustrate the nature of these reports:

READING
1. Reads with understanding.
2. Works out meaning and use of new words.
3. Reads well to others.
4. Reads independently for pleasure.

ARITHMETIC
1. Uses fundamental processes.
2. Solves problems involving reasoning.
3. Is accurate in work.
4. Works at a satisfactory rate.

The symbols used to rate pupils on each of these major objectives vary considerably. In some schools the traditional A, B, C, D, F lettering system is retained, but more commonly there is a shift to fewer symbols, such as O (outstanding), S (satisfactory), and N (needs improvement).

The checklist form of reporting has the obvious advantage of providing a detailed analysis of the pupil's strengths and weaknesses, so that constructive action can be taken to help him improve his learning. It also provides pupils, parents, and others with a frequent reminder of the objectives of the school. The main difficulties encountered with such reports are in keeping the list of statements down to a workable number and in stating them in such simple and concise terms that they are readily understood by all users of the reports. These difficulties are probably best overcome by obtaining the cooperation of parents and pupils during the development of the report form.

Letters to Parents

To provide for greater flexibility in reporting pupil progress to parents, some schools have turned to the use of informal letters. This makes it possible to report on the unique strengths, weaknesses and learning needs of each pupil, and to suggest specific plans for improvement. In addition, the report can include as much detail as is needed to make clear the pupil's progress in all areas of development.

Although letters to parents might provide a good supplement to other types of reports, their usefulness as the *sole* method of reporting progress is limited by several factors. (1) Comprehensive and thoughtful written reports require an excessive amount of time and skill. (2) Descriptions of a pupil's learning weaknesses are easily misinterpreted by parents. (3) Letters fail to provide a systematic and cumulative record of pupil progress toward the objectives of the school. The flexibility of this method, which is one of its major strengths, limits its usefulness in maintaining systematic records. Since different aspects of development are likely to be stressed from one report to another, the continuity in reporting is lost.

When used in connection with a more formal reporting system, the informal letter can serve a useful role in clarifying specific points in the report and in elaborating upon various aspects of pupil development. It probably should be restricted to this supplementary role, however, and be used only as needed for clarification.

Parent-Teacher Conferences

To overcome the limited information provided by the traditional report card and to establish better cooperation between teachers and parents, some schools have used regularly scheduled parent-teacher conferences. This reporting method has been most widely used at the elementary level, with its greatest use in the primary grades.

The major advantages of the parent-teacher conference derive from the fact that it provides for two-way communication between home and school. Besides receiving a report from the teacher, parents have an opportunity to present information concerning the pupil's out-of-school life. In addition, the conference permits teachers and parents to ask questions, to discuss their common concerns in helping the pupil, and to cooperatively plan a program for improving the pupil's learning and development. The give-and-take in such a conference makes it possible to avoid, or overcome, any misunderstandings concerning the pupil's learning progress.

The parent-teacher conference is an extremely useful tool, but it shares two important limitations with the informal letter: (1) it requires an excessive amount of time and skill, and (2) it does not provide a systematic record of pupil progress. In addition, some parents are *unwilling* to come for conferences, while others are *unable* to come because of work, illness, or other commitments. Thus, like the letter to parents, the parent-teacher conference is probably most useful in conjunction with a more formal report of pupil progress, rather than as a replacement for it.

Current Use of Marking and Reporting Methods

A fairly recent nationwide survey by the National Education Association Research Division has shown the prominent role that the traditional marking system plays in reporting pupil progress.[2] The results, shown in Table 19.1, reveal that letter grades (A, B, C, D, F) were used more frequently than any other system. If the percentages for letter grades (A, B, C, D, F) and number grades (1, 2, 3, 4, 5) are combined, it can be seen that 82 per cent of the elementary teachers and 92 per cent of the secondary teachers used one of these traditional methods of marking pupil progress. Apparently the ease with which such marks can be assigned, averaged, and used for various school purposes contributes to their continued widespread use.

---

[2] National Education Association, "Marking and Reporting Pupil Progress," *Research Summary* 1970S–1 (Washington, D.C.: NEA Research Division, 1970).

TABLE 19.1

PERCENTAGE OF TEACHERS USING EACH METHOD IN REPORTING
STUDENT PROGRESS TO PARENTS*

Method of Reporting	Elementary Teachers	Secondary Teachers
Letter grades (e.g., A, B, C, D, F)	72%	83%†
Parent-teacher conferences	60	20
Written description of performance	24	10
Number grades (e.g., 1, 2, 3, 4, 5)	10	9
Percentage grades	2	10
Pass-fail reports	8	3

* From N. E. Gronlund, *Improving Marking and Reporting in Classroom Instruction.* New York: Macmillan, 1974. (Adapted from NEA Research Division nationwide sample survey of public school teachers, 1970.)

† Percentages were rounded to nearest whole per cent.

The percentages in Table 19.1 total more than 100, indicating that some teachers used more than one method of reporting. This is a healthy sign, because a single reporting method can hardly be expected to serve the varied needs of pupils, parents, teachers, and other school personnel. A multiple marking and reporting system tends to combine the advantages of each reporting method and to overcome some of the limitations resulting from the use of any single reporting method.

MULTIPLE MARKING AND REPORTING SYSTEMS

The use of traditional letter grades (A, B, C, D, F) for reporting pupil progress has persisted in the schools for over fifty years, despite frequent efforts to replace them with a more meaningful report. Their continued use would seem to indicate that they are serving some useful functions in the school (e.g., administrative). In addition, they provide a simple and convenient means of maintaining permanent school records. Thus, rather than attempt to replace letter grades (or number grades), it would seem more sensible to direct efforts toward improving the letter grade system and *supplementing* it with more detailed and meaningful reports of pupil learning progress. Such multiple marking and reporting systems have been developed for use in some schools.

The typical multiple reporting system retains the use of traditional marking (letter grades or numbers) and supplements the marks with checklists of objectives. In some cases, two marks are assigned to each subject: one for achievement and the other for effort, improvement, or growth in terms of potential. A typical example of a high school report form used for multiple marking is shown in Figure 19.1.

PROGRESS REPORT

SOCIAL STUDIES

University of Illinois High School
Urbana, Illinois

_____ 1st quarter – November   _____ 3rd quarter – April

_____ Semester – February   _____ Final Report – June

RATING SCALE: + Outstanding,   S – Satisfactory,   U – Unsatisfactory,   O – Inadequate basis for judgement.

S	U	O	+S	U	O	Respects rights, opinions and abilities of others
S	U	O	+S	U	O	Accepts responsibility for group's progress
S	U	O	+S	U	O	Is careful with property
S	U	O	+S	U	O	Uses time to advantage
S	U	O	+S	U	O	Is attentive
S	U	O	+S	U	O	Follows directions
S	U	O	+S	U	O	Makes regular preparations as directed

+S	U	O	Evidences independent thought and originality
+S	U	O	Seeks more than superficial knowledge
+S	U	O	Evidences growth in orderly and constructive group discussion
+S	U	O	Keeps informed on current affairs
+S	U	O	Discriminates in the selection and use of social studies materials
+S	U	O	Demonstrates growth in the skills of critical thinking
+S	U	O	Places people and events in their chronological and cultural setting
+S	U	O	Demonstrates social responsibility

ACHIEVEMENT

The grade is a measure of achievement with respect to what is expected of a pupil of this class in this school, and in relation to what is expected in the next higher course in this subject.

_____ 5 excellent   _____ 2 passing, but weak

_____ 4 very good   _____ 1 failing

_____ 3 creditable   _____ 0 inadequate basis for judgement

EFFORT

The grade below is an estimate, based on evidence available to the teacher, of the individual student's effort.

_____ 5 excellent   _____ 2 weak

_____ 4 very good   _____ 1 very weak

_____ 3 creditable   _____ 0 inadequate basis for judgement

Teacher: _____

COMMENTS:

Figure 19.1. A comprehensive report form that combines dual marking and checklists of objectives.

Note that the report form in Figure 19.1 provides for a single mark for achievement, a separate mark for effort, and a rating on two lists of objectives. The list of objectives at the upper left are common school objectives appearing on all report forms. The list of objectives at the upper right are those pertaining to the particular subject being marked, in this case social studies. This type of report form makes it possible to assign an achievement grade that is a pure measure of achievement since effort and other personal characteristics are marked separately. It also informs both the pupil and his parents of the progress being made toward the common objectives of the school and the unique objectives of each subject. This report form was developed by committees of pupils, parents, teachers, and other school personnel, and thus reflects the types of information these groups considered most useful.

Guidelines for Developing a Multiple Marking and Reporting System

No marking and reporting system is likely to be equally satisfactory from one school to another. Each school system must develop methods that fit its particular needs and circumstances. The following principles for developing a multiple marking and reporting system provide guidelines for this purpose:

1. *The development of the marking and reporting system should be guided by the functions to be served.* An attempt should be made to provide the type of information most needed by the users of the report. This typically requires a study of the functions for which the reports are to be used by pupils, parents, teachers, counselors, and administrators. Although it is seldom possible to meet all of the needs of these groups, a satisfactory compromise is more likely if their needs are fully known. Typically, it is desirable to supplement letter grades in each subject with separate reports on course objectives, effort, personal and social characteristics, and work habits. The letter grade should be retained as a *pure* measure of achievement and any marks for improvement, effort, or growth in terms of potential, should be made separately.

2. *The marking and reporting system should be developed cooperatively by parents, pupils, and school personnel.* School reports are apt to be most useful when all users of the reports have some voice in their development. This is usually done by organizing a committee consisting of representatives of parent groups, pupil organizations, elementary and secondary school teachers, counselors, and administrators. Ideas and suggestions are fed into the committee through the representatives, and the members carry back to their own respective groups, for modification and final approval, the tentative plans developed by the committee. This cooperative participation not only tends to provide a more adequate reporting system, but it also increases the likelihood that the reports will be fully understood by those for whom they are intended.

3. *The marking and reporting system should be based on a clear statement of educational objectives.* The same objectives that have guided instruction and evaluation should serve as a basis for marking and reporting. Some of these will be general school objectives and others will be unique to particular courses or areas of study. Nevertheless, when developing a reporting system the primary question should be, "How can we best report pupil progress toward these particular objectives?" The final report form will be limited and modified by a number of practical considerations, but the central focus should be on the objectives of the school and course and the behaviors that represent the achievement of these objectives.

4. *The marking and reporting system should be based on adequate evaluation.* Teachers should not be expected to report on aspects of pupil behavior where evidence is lacking or is very unreliable. By the same token, including items in a report form assumes that an attempt will be made to evaluate the behavior in as objective a manner as possible. Ratings on such items as critical thinking, for example, should be the end product of testing and controlled observation, rather than depend on snap judgments based on hazy recollections of incidental happenings. Therefore, in planning a marking and reporting system, it is necessary to take into account the types of evaluation data needed. The items included in the final report form should be those on which we can expect teachers to obtain reasonably reliable and valid information.

5. *The marking and reporting system should be detailed enough to be diagnostic and yet compact enough to be practical.* For the purposes of guiding the learning and development of pupils, we should like as comprehensive a picture of their strengths and weaknesses as possible. This desire for detail, however, must be balanced by such practical demands as the following: (1) the amount of time required to prepare and use the reports must be reasonable; (2) the reports should be clearly understandable to pupils, parents, employers, and school personnel; (3) the reports should be easily summarized for school records. As noted earlier, a compromise between comprehensiveness and practicality is probably best obtained by supplementing the letter grade system with more detailed reports on other aspects of pupil development.

6. *The marking and reporting system should provide for parent-teacher conferences, as needed.* At the elementary school level, regularly scheduled conferences with parents might constitute a basic part of the reporting system. At the high school level, such conferences are typically arranged, as needed, to deal with specific problems. At both levels, however, such conferences should supplement a more formal report form, rather than replace it. A uniform method of reporting pupil progress is needed for school records and this is difficult to obtain from conference notes.

In summary, a multiple marking and reporting system takes into account the varied needs of pupils, parents, teachers, and other school personnel. The letter grade system (A, B, C, D, F) provides a simplified method

of keeping a record of pupil achievement, the checklist of objectives provides a detailed report of pupil strengths and weaknesses in learning
and development, and the parent-teacher conference provides a means of
maintaining cooperation between home and school. When letter grades
are supplemented by other methods of reporting, these grades themselves
become more meaningful. Rather than being a conglomerate of achievement,
effort, improvement, and personal behavior, letter grades can be confined
to a pure measure of achievement. Multiple marking makes this possible
by reporting separately on the other aspects of pupil development.

ASSIGNING LETTER GRADES[3]

Since the A, B, C, D, F marking system is used in the majority of
schools, most teachers will be faced with the problem of assigning letter
grades. This involves questions such as the following:

1. What should be included in a letter grade?
2. How should achievement data be combined in assigning letter grades?
3. What frame of reference should be used in grading?
4. How should the distribution of letter grades be determined?

Each of these issues is important enough to require special attention, so each
will be discussed in turn.

Determining What to Include in a Grade

As noted earlier, letter grades are likely to be most meaningful and
useful when they represent achievement only. If they are contaminated
by such extraneous factors as effort, amount of work completed (rather than
quality of the work), personal conduct, and so on, interpretation becomes
hopelessly confused. When letter grades become a conglomerate of various
aspects of pupil development not only is their meaningfulness as a measure
of achievement lost, but information concerning these other important
aspects of development is also submerged in the process. A letter grade of
B, for example, may represent average achievement with outstanding effort
and excellent conduct, or high achievement with little effort and some
disciplinary infractions. Only by making the letter grade as pure a measure
of achievement as is possible, and reporting on these other aspects separately, can we hope to improve our descriptions of pupil learning and development.

If letter grades are to serve as valid indicators of achievement, they must
be based on valid measures of achievement. This involves the process

---

[3] Much of the material in this section was adapted from N. E. Gronlund, *Improving
Marking and Reporting in Classroom Instruction* (New York: Macmillan, 1974).

described earlier in this book—defining the course objectives as intended learning outcomes, and developing or selecting tests and other evaluation devices that measure these outcomes most directly. How much emphasis should be given to tests, ratings, written reports, and other measures of achievement in the letter grades is determined by the nature of the course and the objectives being stressed. Thus, a grade in English might be determined largely by tests and writing projects, a grade in science by tests and evaluations of laboratory performance, and a grade in music by tests and ratings on performance skills. The types of evaluation data to include in a course grade, and the relative emphasis to be given to each type of evidence, are determined primarily by examining the instructional objectives. Other things being equal, the more important the objective the greater the weight it should receive in the course grade. In the final analysis, letter grades should reflect the extent to which pupils have achieved the learning outcomes specified in the course objectives, and these should be weighted in terms of their relative importance.

Combining Data in Assigning Grades

When it has been decided what aspects of achievement (e.g., tests, written reports, performance ratings) should be included in a letter grade and how much emphasis should be given to each aspect, our next step is to combine the various elements in such a way that each element receives its intended weight. If we decide, for example, that the final examination should count 40 per cent, the midterm 30 per cent, laboratory performance 20 per cent, and written reports 10 per cent, we want our course grades to reflect these emphases. A typical procedure is to combine the elements into a composite score by assigning appropriate weights to each element, and then use these composite scores as a basis for grading.

Combining data into a composite score in such a way that the desired weighting is obtained is not as simple as it might appear at first glance. This can be illustrated by a very simple example. Let us assume that we want to combine scores on a final examination and scores on a term report, and that we want them to be given *equal* weight. Our range of scores on the two measures are as follows:

	Range of Scores
Final Examination	80 to 100
Term Report	10 to 50

Since the two sets of scores are to be given equal weight, we might be inclined to simply add together the final examination score and the term report score for each pupil. We can check on the effectiveness of this procedure by comparing the composite score of a pupil who is highest on the final examination and lowest on the term report ($100 + 10 = 110$) with a pupil who is lowest on the final examination and highest on the term report $(80 + 50 = 130)$. It is obvious from this comparison that simply adding together the two scores will not give them equal representation.

Another common, but erroneous, method of equating scores is to make the maximum possible score the same for both sets of scores. For our illustrative scores, this would involve multiplying the scores on the *term report* by 2, so that the top score on both measures would equal 100. Applying this procedure to the same two extreme cases we considered earlier, our first pupil would have a score of 120 $(100 + 20)$ and our second pupil a score of 180 $(80 + 100)$. It is quite obvious that this procedure does not equate the scores. In fact, there is now an even larger difference between the two composite scores. This is due to the fact that the influence each component has on the composite score depends on the variability, or spread, of scores and not on the total number of points. Thus, to properly weight the components in a composite score, the variability of the scores must be taken into account.

The range of scores in our example provides a measure of score variability, or spread, and this can be used to equate the two sets of scores. We can give the final examination and the term report equal weight in the composite score by using a multiplier that makes the two ranges equal. Since the final examination scores have a range of 20 $(100 - 80)$ and the term report scores a range of 40 $(50 - 10)$, we would need to multiply each *final examination* score by 2 to obtain the desired equal weight.[4] We can check on the effectiveness of this procedure by using the same two cases we considered earlier. The pupil highest on the final examination and lowest on the term report would now have a score of 210 $(200 + 10)$ and the pupil lowest on the final examination and highest on the term report would also have a score of 210 $(160 + 50)$. Our check shows that the procedure gives the two sets of scores equal weight in the composite score. If we wanted our final examination to count twice as much as the term report, it would be necessary, of course, to multiply each final examination score by 4 rather than by 2.

A more refined weighting system can be obtained by using the standard deviation as the measure of variability,[5] but the range is satisfactory for most classroom purposes.

Proper weighting of the components in a composite score can also be obtained by converting all sets of scores to stanines (standard scores, 1 through 9). When all scores have been converted to the stanine system (see Chapter 15), the scores in each set have the same variability. Effective weighting is then obtained by simply multiplying each stanine score by

---

[4] Note that this weighting is the reverse of the incorrect weighting procedure based on making the maximum possible scores equal.

[5] See J. S. Terwilliger, *Assigning Grades to Students* (Glenview, Ill.: Scott, Foresman, 1971).

the desired weight. Thus, a pupil's composite score would be obtained as follows:

	Desired Weight	Pupil's Stanines	Weighted Score
Examination	2	9	18
Laboratory work	1	7	7
Written reports	1	8	8

Composite score = 33

If desired, the composite score can be divided by the sum of the weights (in this case 4) to obtain a composite average (in this case 8.25). Although the composite average is not a stanine, it does indicate a pupil's relative position on a nine-point scale. These composite averages (or the composite scores) can be used to rank pupils in terms of an overall weighted measure of achievement for the purpose of assigning letter grades.

Selecting the Proper Frame of Reference for Grading

Letter grades are typically assigned on the basis of one of the following frames of reference:

1. Performance in relation to other group members (norm referenced).
2. Performance in relation to prespecified standards (criterion referenced).
3. Performance in relation to learning potential or amount of improvement.

Assigning grades on a *norm-referenced* basis involves comparing a pupil's performance with that of a reference group, typically his own classmates. With this system, the grade is determined by the pupil's *relative* ranking in the total group, rather than by some absolute standard of achievement. If his achievement places him high in the group he will receive a high grade, and if his relative achievement is low he will receive a low grade. Since the grading is based on *relative* performance, the pupil's grade is influenced by both his performance and the performance of the group. Thus, he will fare much better, gradewise, in a low achieving group than in a high achieving group.

Although norm-referenced grading has the disadvantage of a shifting frame of reference (i.e., grades depend on the ability of the group), it is widely used in the schools. This is due largely to the fact that most classroom testing and evaluation is norm-referenced. That is, the evaluation is designed to rank pupils in order of achievement, rather than to describe achievement in absolute terms. Although relative position in the group is the key element in a norm-referenced system of grading, the actual grades assigned are also likely to be influenced to some extent by the achievement expectations the teacher has built up from teaching other groups. Thus, a high achieving group of pupils is likely to receive a larger proportion of good grades than a low achieving group.

Assigning grades on a *criterion-referenced* basis involves comparing a pupil's performance to prespecified standards set by the teacher. These standards are typically concerned with the degree of mastery to be achieved by pupils, and might be specified in terms of (1) the specific tasks to be performed (e.g., type 40 words per minute without error), or (2) the percentage of correct answers to be obtained on a test designed to measure a clearly defined set of learning tasks. Thus, with this system, letter grades are assigned on the basis of an *absolute* standard of performance rather than a relative standard. If all pupils demonstrate a high level of mastery, all will receive high grades.

The criterion-referenced system of grading is much more complex than it first appears. To effectively use absolute level of achievement as a basis for grading requires that (1) the domain of learning tasks be clearly defined, (2) the standards of performance be clearly specified and justified, and (3) the measures of pupil achievement be criterion-referenced. These conditions are difficult to meet except in a mastery learning situation. Where complete mastery is the goal, the learning tasks tend to be more limited and easily defined. In addition, percentage-correct scores, which are widely used in setting absolute standards, are most meaningful in mastery learning because they indicate how far a pupil is from complete mastery. All too frequently, schools use absolute grading based on percentage-correct scores (e.g., A = 95–100, B = 85–94, C = 75–84, D = 65–74, F = below 65) where the domain of learning tasks has not been clearly defined and the standards have been set in a completely arbitrary manner. To fit the grading system, teachers attempt to build tests (norm referenced) with scores in the 60 to 100 range. If the test turns out to be too difficult or too easy, the scores are somehow adjusted to fit the absolute grading scale. Such grades are difficult to interpret because they represent an adjusted level of performance on some ill-defined conglomerate of learning tasks.

Although reporting pupil performance in relation to learning potential or amount of improvement shown has been fairly widely used at the elementary school level, this type of grading is fraught with difficulties. Making reliable estimates of learning potential, with or without tests, is a formidible task, since judgments or measurements of potential are likely to be contaminated by achievement to some unknown degree. Similarly, reliable estimates of improvement (i.e., growth in achievement) over short spans of time are extremely difficult to obtain with classroom measures of achievement. Thus, the lack of reliability in judging achievement in relation to potential, and in judging degree of improvement, would result in grades of low dependability. If used at all (e.g., to motivate low ability pupils), such grades should be used in a supplementary role. In dual marking, for example, one letter grade might indicate level of achievement (relative, or absolute) while the second letter grade is used to represent achievement in relation to potential, or the degree of improvement shown since the last marking period.

Determining the Distribution of Grades

As noted in the previous section, there are two basic ways of assigning letter grades as a measure of the level of pupil achievement: the norm-referenced system that is based on relative level of achievement, and the criterion-referenced system that is based on absolute level of achievement. Since the distribution of letter grades is determined differently for these two approaches, each will be discussed in turn.

Norm-Referenced Grading. The assignment of norm-referenced grades is essentially a matter of ranking the pupils in order of overall achievement and assigning letter grades on the basis of each pupil's rank in the group. This ranking might be limited to a single classroom group or might be based on the combined distributions of several classroom groups taking the same course. In any event, before letter grades can be assigned, a decision must be made concerning the proportion of As, Bs, Cs, Ds, and Fs to be used.

One method of grading, that has been widely used in the past, is that of assigning grades on the basis of the normal curve. This procedure would result in a distribution of grades like that shown in Figure 19.2. It will be noted that grading on the normal curve results in an equal percentage

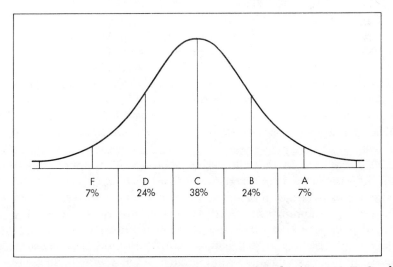

Figure 19.2. Normal curve with a typical distribution of grades (From N. E. Gronlund, *Improving Marking and Reporting in Classroom Instruction.* New York: Macmillan, 1974. Used by permission.)

of As and Fs, and of Bs and Ds. Thus, regardless of the level of ability of the group, the proportion of high grades is to be balanced by an equal proportion of low grades. Such grading is seldom defensible for classroom groups because (1) the groups are typically too small to provide a normal distribution, (2) classroom evaluation instruments are usually not designed to yield normally distributed scores, and (3) the pupil population becomes increasingly more select as it moves through the grades and the less able pupils fail or drop out of school. It is only where a course, or combined courses, have a relatively large and unselected group of pupils that grading on the normal curve might be defended. Even then, however, one might ask whether the decision concerning the proportion of pupils to be failed should be left to a statistical model (i.e., normal curve) or should be made on a more rational basis.

It would seem that the most sensible approach in determining the distributions of letter grades to be used in a school is to have the school staff set general guidelines for the approximate distributions of marks. This might involve separate suggested distributions for introductory and advanced courses, for gifted and slow learning classes, and the like. In any event, the suggested distributions should be flexible enough to allow for variation in the caliber of pupils from one course to another, and from one time to another in the same course. This flexibility can be provided by indicating ranges rather than fixed percentages of pupils who should receive each letter grade. Thus, a suggested distribution for an introductory course might be stated as follows:

A = 10 to 20 per cent of the pupils
B = 20 to 30 per cent of the pupils
C = 30 to 50 per cent of the pupils
D = 10 to 20 per cent of the pupils
F = 0 to 10 per cent of the pupils

These particular percentage ranges are presented for illustrative purposes only. There is no simple or scientific means of determining what these ranges should be for a given situation. The decision must be made by the local school staff, taking into account the philosophy of the school, the nature of the pupil population, and the purposes to be served by the grades. The important thing is that all staff members have a common understanding of the basis for assigning grades and that this basis be clearly communicated to the users of the grades.

In setting an approximate distribtuion of grades for teachers to follow, it is important that the distribution provide for the possibility that there might be no failing grades. Whether pupils pass or fail a course should be based on their absolute level of learning rather than their relative position in some group. If all low ranking pupils have mastered enough of the material to succeed at the next highest level of instruction, they probably all should pass. On the other hand, if some have not mastered the minimum essentials needed at the next highest level, these pupils probably should fail. Whether minimum performance is attained can be determined by reviewing the low ranking pupils' performance on tests and other evaluation instruments, or by administering a special mastery test on the minimum essentials of the course. Thus, even when grading is done on a relative basis (norm referenced), the pass-fail decision must be based on an absolute standard of achievement (criterion referenced) if it is to be educationally sound.

Criterion-Referenced Grading. As indicated earlier, criterion-referenced grading is most useful where a mastery learning approach is used. This is due to the fact that mastery learning places special emphasis on delimiting the domain of learning tasks to be achieved, defining the instructional objectives in behavioral terms, specifying the standards of performance to be attained, and measuring the intended outcomes with criterion-referenced instruments. These procedures provide the necessary conditions for grading on an absolute basis.

If the objectives of a course have been clearly specified and the standards for mastery appropriately set, the letter grades in a criterion-referenced system might be defined in terms of the degree to which the objectives have been attained, as follows:

A = Outstanding. Pupil has mastered all of the major and minor instructional objectives of the course.

B = Very Good. Pupil has mastered all of the major instructional objectives of the course and most of the minor objectives.

C = Satisfactory. Pupil has mastered all of the major instructional objectives but just a few of the minor objectives.

D = Very Weak. Pupil has mastered just a few of the major and minor instructional objectives of the course. He barely has the minimum essentials needed for the next highest level of instruction. Some remedial work would be desirable.

F = Unsatisfactory. Pupil has not mastered any of the major instructional objectives of the course. He lacks the minimum essentials needed for the next highest level of instruction. Considerable remedial work is needed.

If the tests and other evaluation instruments have been designed to yield scores in terms of the percentage of correct answers, criterion-referenced grading then might be defined as follows:

$$A = 95 \text{ to } 100 \text{ per cent correct}$$
$$B = 85 \text{ to } 94 \text{ per cent correct}$$
$$C = 75 \text{ to } 84 \text{ per cent correct}$$
$$D = 65 \text{ to } 74 \text{ per cent correct}$$
$$F = \text{below } 65 \text{ per cent correct}$$

As noted earlier, defining letter grades in this manner is defensible only if the necessary conditions of a criterion-referenced system have been met. Using percentage-correct scores where the measuring instruments are based on some undefined hodgepodge of learning tasks results in grades that are uninterpretable.

With criterion-referenced grading systems such as these, the distribution of grades is not predetermined. If all pupils demonstrate a high level of mastery, all will receive high grades. If some pupils demonstrate a low level of performance, they will receive low grades. Thus, the distribution of grades is determined by the absolute level of performance that each pupil demonstrates, and not by the relative position that each pupil holds in the group.

There are basically two procedures for determining what letter grade a pupil should receive in a criterion-referenced system.[6] The first, called the "one-shot system," provides a single opportunity to achieve the pre-specified standards. The pupil is assigned whatever grade he earns on his first attempt. The second procedure, which is widely used in mastery learning, permits the pupil to make repeated attempts to achieve the prespecified standards. With this approach, the pupil is typically provided with corrective help and enough additional learning time to achieve a satisfactory level of mastery. Thus, the first approach may result in some failing grades, whereas the second approach eliminates pupil failure. Typically, only the letter grades A, B, and C are used, where pupils are permitted to repeat examinations until a satisfactory level of performance is achieved.

The criterion-referenced system for reporting on pupil progress seldom uses letter grades alone. A comprehensive report typically includes a checklist of objectives, to inform both pupil and parent concerning which objectives have been mastered and which have not been mastered by the end of each marking period. In some mastery learning programs, letter grades (or numbers) are assigned to *each* objective to indicate the level of mastery that has been achieved. A typical example of such a report form, designed for use in a junior high school, is shown in Figure 19.3. On this report form, a numerical rating is assigned to each objective as follows:

HAS ACQUIRED

1 = Skill well developed, good proficiency.
2 = Skill developed satisfactorily, proficiency could be improved.
3 = *Basic* skill developed, low proficiency, *needs* additional work.

NOT ACQUIRED

4 = *Basic* skill not acquired.

---

[6] R. G. Williams and H. G. Miller, "Grading Students: A Failure to Communicate," *Clearing House,* **47,** 332–337, 1973.

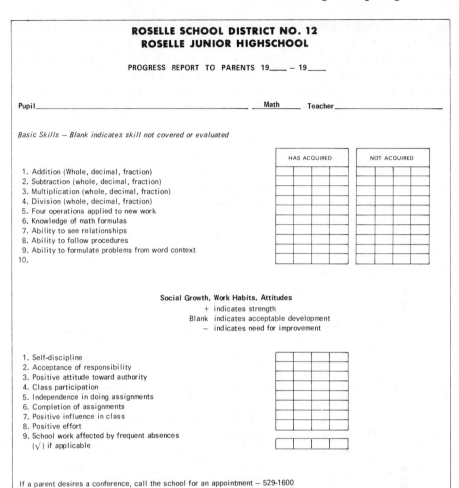

Figure 19.3. Illustrative report form used for Mastery Learning (Reproduced by permission of Roselle School District No. 12, Roselle, Illinois).

As with other types of criterion-referenced grading, the number of 1s, 2s, 3s, and 4s that are to be assigned to each objective is not predetermined, but depends entirely on the absolute level of performance achieved by each pupil. If all pupils achieve good proficiency on a particular objective, all will receive 1s on that objective.

CONDUCTING PARENT-TEACHER CONFERENCES

Regardless of the type of marking and reporting system used in the school, the parent-teacher conference provides an important supplement to the written report of pupil progress. The face-to-face conference makes it possible to share information with parents, to overcome any misunderstandings between home and school, and to cooperatively plan a program of maximum benefit to the pupil. At the elementary school level, where parent-teacher cooperation is most vital, conferences with parents are widely used on a regularly scheduled basis. At the secondary level, the parent-teacher conference is typically used only when some special problem situation arises.

Conferences with parents are most likely to be productive where the conference is preceded by careful planning and where the teacher has developed skill in conducting such conferences. Many schools provide in-service training for teachers to help them develop effective conference techniques. Typically, such training includes knowledge of how to conduct a parent-teacher conference and role playing to provide practice in the use of conference skills. The following guidelines illustrate the types of things that contribute to the effective use of the parent-teacher conference for reporting pupil progress.[7]

Preparing for the Conference:
1. Have a clear grasp of the purpose of the conference.
2. Review the pupil's school records for general background information.
3. Assemble a folder of specific information concerning the pupil's present learning progress.
4. Organize the information to be presented to parents in a systematic manner.
5. Make a tentative list of questions to ask the parents.
6. Anticipate parents' questions.
7. Provide a comfortable, informal setting that is free from interruption.

Establishing and Maintaining Rapport During the Conference:
1. Create a friendly informal atmosphere.
2. Maintain a positive attitude.
3. Use language that is understandable to parents.
4. Be willing to listen to parents.
5. Be honest and sincere with parents and do not betray confidences.

Sharing Information with Parents During the Conference:
1. Begin by describing the pupil's strong points.
2. Describe the areas needing improvement in a positive and tactful manner.
3. Encourage parents to participate in the conference.
4. Be cautious about giving advice.

Planning a Course of Action with Parents During the Conference:
1. Begin the concluding phase of the conference with a brief overall summary.

---

[7] From N. E. Gronlund, *Improving Marking and Reporting in Classroom Instruction* (New York: Macmillan, 1974).

2. Have parents participate in planning a course of action.
3. Review your conference notes with parents.
4. End the conference on a positive note.

In addition to these positive things to do, V. Bailard and R. Strang suggest a list of important "don'ts":[8]

1. Don't put the parent on the defensive about anything.
2. Don't talk about other children or compare this child with other children. It is unprofessional.
3. Don't talk about other teachers to the parents unless the remarks are of a complimentary nature.
4. Don't belittle the administration or make derogatory remarks about the school district.
5. Don't argue with the parent.
6. Don't try to outtalk a parent.
7. Don't interrupt the parent to make your own point.
8. Don't go too far with a parent who is not ready and able to understand your purpose.
9. Don't ask parents questions which might be embarrassing to them. Only information pertinent to the child's welfare is important. Questions asked out of mere curiosity are unforgivable.
10. After the conference, don't repeat any confidential information which the parent may volunteer. It is most unprofessional and can be very damaging to the parent or the child.

Although one cannot expect to conduct an effective conference by simply reading a list of do's and don'ts, such guidelines provide a good framework for in-service training. They also provide a useful reminder of things to do and things to avoid during the process of developing conference skills.

SUMMARY

School marks and progress reports provide information which is helpful to pupils, parents, and school personnel. Pupils find them useful as summary appraisals of learning progress which serve somewhat the same functions as other evaluation results. Parents, teachers, and counselors use the information in guiding learning and development and in helping pupils make realistic future plans. Administrators use the information in determining promotion, athletic eligibility, honors, and graduation. The reports also provide a basis for reporting to other schools and to prospective employers.

The diverse functions that progress reports are expected to serve make

---

[8] V. Bailard and R. Strang, *Parent-Teacher Conferences* (New York: McGraw-Hill, 1964).

it difficult to find a universally satisfactory reporting method. Some of the methods that have been tried include (1) the traditional marking system (e.g., A, B, C, D, F), (2) the pass-fail system, (3) checklists of objectives, (4) informal letters, and (5) parent-teacher conferences. Each method has rather severe limitations when used alone. Probably the best reporting system is one that combines a concise mark for administrative functions with a more detailed report for teaching and guidance purposes. In any event, some combination of methods seems most appropriate.

The letter grade system of marking (A, B, C, D, F) continues to be the most widely used system at both the elementary and secondary levels, despite frequent attempts to replace it with a more meaningful report. This is probably due to the fact that such grades are easily assigned and averaged, and serve many useful administrative functions. Thus, it would seem sensible to retain letter grades, as a pure measure of achievement, and to supplement them with more detailed and meaningful reports of learning progress. Such a multiple marking and reporting system should be developed cooperatively by parents, pupils, teachers, and other school personnel. Special efforts should be made to develop a system that is in harmony with the functions to be served, the objectives of the school, and the nature of the evaluation data available. Ideally, the report form should be as comprehensive and detailed as is practical, and should be supplemented by parent-teacher conferences as needed.

Whether or not a multiple marking and reporting system is used in a school, most teachers will be responsible for assigning letter grades to pupils. This involves such considerations as determining what to include in the letter grade, how to combine the various achievement data into a composite, what frame of reference to use, and what distribution of letter grades to use. The letter grade is most likely to provide a meaningful measure of achievement (1) where it reflects the extent to which pupils have attained the learning outcomes specified in the instructional ob- jectives, (2) where it is based on valid measures of achievement, and (3) where each component of achievement is weighted in terms of its relative importance. Assigning weights to each component requires that the variabil- ity (i.e., spread) of scores be taken into account.

Letter grades may be used to indicate a pupil's *relative* level of achieve- ment (norm-referenced grading) or his *absolute* level of achievement (criterion-referenced grading). When assigning norm-referenced grades, the normal curve is seldom an appropriate model for determining the distribu- tion of grades. A more sensible approach is to have the school staff set up suggested distributions of grades that take into account the philosophy of the school, the nature of the pupil population, and the purposes to be served by the grades. Criterion-referenced grading is most useful where a mastery learning approach is used. Here, the letter grades represent the degree to which the instructional objectives have been mastered. With this system, no predetermined distribution of letter grades is specified. If all pupils achieve a high degree of mastery, all will receive high grades. In some criterion-referenced mastery systems, pupils receive a grade on each objective. Typically, those who fail to achieve mastery on some of the objectives are given remedial help and enough additional learning time to achieve a satisfactory level of mastery.

Even where pupils are assigned grades on a relative basis (norm referenced), the pass-fail decision should be based on a pupil's absolute level of achievement. The important consideration is whether the pupil has the minimum knowledge and skills needed to succeed at the next highest level of instruction, and not his relative standing in the group.

Letter grades are sometimes assigned on the basis of performance in relation to learning potential or amount of improvement. The problems of adequately judging learning potential apart from achievement, and of reliably measuring learning gain over short spans of time, places severe restrictions on the use of these marking methods. If used at all (e.g., for motivation purposes), such grades should supplement grades based on the pupil's relative, or absolute, level of achievement.

Parent-teacher conferences provide an important method of sharing information with parents. Such conferences should supplement the more formal written report of pupil progress, however, rather than replace it. Effective conferences with parents require careful planning and the application of sound conference techniques. Although guidelines are useful in preparing for conferences with parents, in-service training is typically needed to develop adequate conference skills.

LEARNING EXERCISES

1. What are the advantages and limitations of a multiple marking and reporting system?
2. If you were helping set up a multiple marking and reporting system for the grade level you are teaching, or plan to teach, what types of marks and reports would you want included? Why?
3. What are the advantages and limitations of assigning letter grades (A, B, C, D, F) on a *relative* basis (norm-referenced grading)?
4. What are the advantages and limitations of assigning letter grades on the basis of an absolute level of achievement (criterion-referenced grading)? What are the prerequisites for an effective criterion-referenced system?
5. What problems might arise in the interpretation of letter grades that are based on performance in relation to learning potential? What problems are involved in computing such grades?
6. Describe the procedure to be followed in (a) determining what types of evaluation data to use in assigning grades, (b) determining what relative weight should be given to each type of data, and (c) computing composite scores.
7. What would be the limitations of assigning letter grades strictly on the basis of the normal curve? What would be the advantages, if any?

8. Some educators have suggested that letter grades be abolished at the elementary and secondary levels. What would be the advantages and disadvantages of abolishing grades?

9. What factors should be considered when deciding whether to pass or fail a pupil? Do you think it is desirable to have all pupils pass? Explain your answer.

10. What types of information should you have at hand during the parent-teacher conference? How would you explain to a parent that his child was performing poorly in school? Describe the general approach that you would use.

SUGGESTIONS FOR FURTHER READING

BLAIR, G. M., R. S. JONES, and R. H. SIMPSON. *Educational Psychology*, 4th ed. New York: Macmillan Publishing Co., Inc., 1975. See Chapter 19, "Marking, Reporting, and Pupil Placement" for a discussion of factors to consider in marking and reporting.

GRONLUND, N. E. *Improving Marking and Reporting in Classroom Instruction*. New York: Macmillan Publishing Co., Inc., 1974. A brief practical guide (58 pages) describing procedures for both norm-referenced and criterion-referenced marking and reporting. The appendix contains a checklist for evaluating a marking and reporting system, and a sample parent-teacher conference guide.

TERWILLIGER, J. S. *Assigning Grades to Students*. Glenview, Ill.: Scott, Foresman and Company, 1971. A practical guide for assigning norm-referenced grades.

THOMAS, R. M. "Records and Reports," *Encyclopedia of Educational Research*, 4th ed. New York: Macmillan Publishing Co., Inc., 1969, pages 1104–1111. Discusses reporting to parents and others and describes the types of records that are most useful.

THORNDIKE, R. L. "Marks and Marking Systems," *Encyclopedia of Educational Research*, 4th ed. New York: Macmillan Publishing Co., Inc., 1969, pages 759–766. A comprehensive discussion of the procedures and problems of assigning school marks.

Appendices

APPENDIX A
Elementary Statistics

Statistics is concerned with the organization, analysis, and interpretation of test scores and other numerical data. As a minimum, a teacher should know those statistical techniques which enable him to (1) analyze and describe the results of measurement obtained in his own classroom, (2) understand the statistics used in test manuals and research reports, and (3) interpret the various types of derived scores used in testing. Knowing how to make basic statistical computations is probably most directly useful in the first area, but it should also contribute to a greater understanding of statistical descriptions of data.

Many teachers shy away from statistics because they think it involves advanced mathematics. The elementary statistical concepts and skills we shall deal with here involve just three things.

1. *Knowledge of new terms.* This you would expect to encounter in any new area you enter.
2. *Knowledge of statistical symbols.* This is simply a type of shorthand, where symbols represent words or brief descriptions (e.g., M = mean, or arithmetic average).
3. *Simple arithmetic skills.* Statistical computation requires the use of such skills as addition, subtraction, squaring, and the like. Although advanced mathematics would help you understand how the statistical formulas are derived, the practical application of the formulas can be made without this deeper understanding.

The statistical measures we shall be concerned with here are:

1. Measures of central tendency (averages).
2. Measures of variability (spread of scores).
3. Measures of relationship (correlation).

The first two measures provide a convenient means of analyzing and describing a single set of test scores and the last measure can be used to indicate the agreement between two sets of test scores obtained for the same pupils.

ANALYZING UNGROUPED SCORES

When test scores are obtained for a group of pupils they are usually in haphazard order, as shown in Table A.1.

TABLE A.1

SET OF SCORES FOR TWELVE PUPILS

Name	Score	Name	Score
1. John A.	27	7. Henry J.	30
2. Bill B.	33	8. Susan K.	20
3. Mary C.	40	9. Helen M.	33
4. Betty E.	25	10. Dick N.	28
5. George F.	28	11. Jim R.	28
6. Marie G.	36	12. Mike S.	32

Such a set of scores may be analyzed directly, by simply rearranging them in order of size. This procedure is satisfactory where the number of scores is small (less than 20 or 25). With a large number of scores it is more convenient to group the scores into a frequency table before analyzing them. Here we shall describe and illustrate statistical analyses of ungrouped scores. In the following section the same statistical procedures will be illustrated with grouped scores.

Simple Ranking

For some uses, it may be sufficient to arrange a set of scores in order of size and to assign a *rank* to each score. This will indicate the relative position of each score in the group. Ordinarily the largest score is given a rank of 1, the second largest a rank of 2, and so on, until all scores are ranked. The scores from Table A.1 have been rearranged in order of size and assigned ranks to illustrate the procedure. The results are presented in Table A.2.

Special problems arise in ranking when two or more scores are tied for the same rank. Note in Table A.2 for example that the score 33 appears twice and fills the positions ordinarily assigned to rank 3 and rank 4. Since

TABLE A.2

RANKING TEST SCORES

Score	Rank		
40	1		
36	2		
33	3.5	⎫	Score 33 is tied
33	3.5	⎬	for Ranks 3 and 4
32	5		
30	6		
28	8	⎫	
28	8	⎬	Score 28 is tied
28	8	⎭	for Ranks 7, 8, 9.
27	10		
25	11		
20	12		

$N = 12$

the scores are identical the ranks are averaged and each score is assigned a rank of 3.5. The next lowest score (32) is then assigned a rank of 5 because the third and fourth rank positions are occupied. The same procedure of averaging is applied to the three scores of 28. They are tied for ranks 7, 8, and 9, so each is assigned the average rank of 8, and the next lowest score is ranked 10. Note that the rank of the lowest score (12) equals the total number of scores ($N = 12$) being ranked. This provides a good means of checking whether the scores have been ranked correctly.

Measures of Central Tendency

A measure of central tendency is simply an average or typical value in a set of scores. We are all familiar with the "arithmetic average" which is obtained by adding all of the scores in a set and dividing this sum by the number of scores. In statistics this type of average is called the *mean*, and is represented by the letter M (or $\overline{X}$). Two other commonly used measures of central tendency are the *median* (represented by Mdn or P_{50}) and the *mode*. The median is the midpoint of a set of scores. That is, the point on either side of which half the scores occur. The mode ("fashion") is the score which occurs most frequently. Since the mean, median, and mode are different types of averages, the word "average" should be avoided when describing data. Preciseness requires that the specific type of average be indicated.

The method of determining each measure of central tendency will be briefly described below and illustrated in Table A.3.

The Mean (M or $\overline{X}$). The *mean,* or arithmetic average, is the most widely used measure of central tendency. Since it is determined by adding a series of scores and then dividing this sum by the number of scores, the computation from ungrouped data can be represented by the following formula:

$$M = \frac{\text{Number of scores}}{\text{Sum of all scores}} \qquad M = \frac{\Sigma X}{N}$$

in which

Σ = the sum of
X = any score
N = number of scores

Applying this formula to the scores in Table A.3, a mean of 30 is obtained. Note that the mean takes into account the value of each score. One extremely high or low score could have an appreciable effect on the mean.

The Median (Mdn or P_{50}). The *median* is a "counting average." It is determined by arranging the scores in order of size and counting up to (or down to) the midpoint of the set of scores. If the number of scores is *even*

TABLE A.3

MEASURES OF CENTRAL TENDENCY

	Score (X)	
	40	
	36	
50% of	33	
scores	33	
	32	
	30	
Median = 29 →	28	
	28	Mode = 28
50% of	28	
scores	27	
	25	
	20	
	$\Sigma X = 360$	

$$\text{Mean} = \frac{\Sigma X}{N} = \frac{360}{12} = 30$$

(as in Table A.3) the median is halfway between the two middlemost scores. When the number of scores is *odd*, the median is the middle score.

It should be noted that the median is a *point* which divides a set of scores into equal halves. The same number of scores fall above the median as below the median, regardless of the size of the individual scores. Since it is a counting average, an extremely high or low score will not affect its value.

The Mode. The *mode* is simply the most frequent or popular score in the set, and is determined by inspection. In Table A.3 the mode is 28 since the largest number of persons made that score. The mode is the least reliable type of statistical average and is frequently used merely as a preliminary estimate of central tendency. A set of scores sometimes has two modes, and is called *bimodal*.

Measures of Variability

A set of scores can be more adequately described, if we know how much they spread out above and below the measure of central tendency. For example, we might have two groups of pupils with a mean IQ of 110, but in one group the span of IQs is from 100 to 120 and in the other the span is from 80 to 140. These would represent quite different ability groups. We can identify such differences by numbers which indicate how much scores spread out in a group. These are called measures of variability, or dispersion. The three most commonly used measures of variability are the *range*, the *quartile deviation*, and the *standard deviation*.

The Range. The simplest and crudest measure of variability is the *range*. This is obtained by subtracting the lowest score from the highest score. In the example given above, the range of IQs in the first group is 20 points, in the second, 60 points. The range provides a quick estimate of variability but it is undependable, because it is based on the position of the two extreme scores. The addition or subtraction of a single end-score can change the range significantly. In the above example, the ranges of the two groups would become equal, if we added to the first group a pupil with an IQ of 80 and another with an IQ of 140. It is obvious that a more stable measure of variability would be desirable.

The Quartile Deviation (Q). The quartile deviation is based on the range of the middle 50 per cent of the scores, instead of the range of the entire set. The middle 50 per cent of a set of scores is called the *interquartile range* and the *quartile deviation* is simply half of this range. The quartile deviation is also called the *semi-interquartile range*.

The middle 50 per cent of the scores is bounded by the 75th percentile and the 25th percentile. These points are called *quartiles* and are indicated be Q_3 and Q_1, respectively. Quartiles are merely *points* which divide a set of scores into quarters. The middle quartile, or Q_2, is the median.

To compute the quartile deviation, we simply determine the values of Q_3 and Q_1 and apply the following formula:

$$Q = \frac{Q_3 - Q_1}{2}$$

We use the same counting procedure to locate Q_3 and Q_1 that we used to find the median. With the scores arranged in order of size, we start from the lowest score, and count off 25 per cent of the scores to locate Q_1 and 75 per cent of the scores to locate Q_3. This has been done in Table A.4. Note that Q_1 is 27.5 because it falls halfway between 27 and 28, and that Q_3 is 33 because the two scores it falls between are both 33. Note also that when the median (or Q_2) is indicated, the set of scores is divided into *quarters*.

While quartiles are *points* on the scale (like averages and percentiles), the quartile deviation represents a *distance* on the scale. It indicates the distance we need to go *above* and *below* the median to include approximately the middle 50 per cent of the scores.

The Standard Deviation (SD, s, or σ). The most useful measure of variability, or spread of scores, is the *standard deviation*. The computation of the standard deviation does not make its meaning readily apparent, but essentially it is an average of the degree to which a set of scores deviates from the mean. Since it takes into account the amount that each score deviates from the mean, it provides a more stable measure of variability than the range or quartile deviation.

The procedure for computing the SD is illustrated in Table A.4, and it includes the following steps. (1) Subtract the mean from each score to obtain the *deviations* (x) of the scores from the mean. (2) Square each of the deviations to obtain x^2 (note that minus signs are eliminated by squaring). (3) Add these squares to obtain Σx^2. (4) Divide Σx^2 by the number of scores (N) and take the square root.[1] The computation of the standard deviation can be expressed by the following simple formula:

$$SD = \sqrt{\frac{\Sigma x^2}{N}}$$

The standard deviation, like other measures of variability, represents a *distance* on the scale. In a normal distribution, it is equivalent to the distance in score points that we need to go *above* and *below* the mean to include approximately 68 per cent of the scores (call it two thirds). For other interpretations of the standard deviation, and illustrations of its use in computing standard scores, see Chapter 15.

Which Measure of Dispersion to Use. The quartile deviation is used with the median and is satisfactory for analyzing a small number of scores. Since these statistics are obtained by counting, and thus are not affected

1. Appendix B contains a table of square roots which may be used for this purpose.

TABLE A.4

MEASURES OF VARIABILITY

	Score (X)	Deviation (x)	Dev. Squared (x^2)
	40	$+10$	100
	36	$+\ 6$	36
	33	$+\ 3$	9
$Q_3 = 33 \longrightarrow$	33	$+\ 3$	9
	32	$+\ 2$	4
$Mdn = 29 \atop (Q_2)$ $\longrightarrow$	30	0	0
	28	$-\ 2$	4
	28	$-\ 2$	4
	28	$-\ 2$	4
$Q_1 = 27.5 \longrightarrow$	27	$-\ 3$	9
	25	$-\ 5$	25
	20	-10	100

$$M = 30 \qquad\qquad\qquad \Sigma x^2 = 304$$

$$Q = \frac{Q_3 - Q_1}{2} \qquad\qquad SD = \sqrt{\frac{\Sigma x^2}{N}}$$

$$Q = \frac{33 - 27.5}{2} \qquad\qquad SD = \sqrt{\frac{304}{12}}$$

$$Q = \frac{5.5}{2} \qquad\qquad SD = \sqrt{25.33}$$

$$Q = 2.75 \qquad\qquad SD = 5.03$$

by the value of each score, they are especially useful where one or more scores deviate markedly from the others in the set.

The standard deviation is used with the mean. It provides the most reliable measure of variability and is especially useful in testing. In addition to describing the spread of scores in a group, it serves as a basis for computing standard scores, the standard error of measurement, and other statistics used in analyzing and interpreting test scores.

COMPUTING STATISTICS FROM GROUPED DATA

In the previous section we described how to compute statistics from ungrouped data. Such procedures are especially helpful in clarifying the meaning of statistical measures and they are useful where the number of scores to be analyzed is small. When working with twenty-five or more cases, however, it is usually desirable to group the scores into a frequency distribution before making statistical computations.

Grouping Scores into a Frequency Distribution

A frequency distribution is simply a method of organizing test scores to simplify statistical analysis. An example of a frequency distribution is shown in Table A.5. Note that the scores have been grouped by *class intervals,* the number of scores falling in each interval has been tallied, and the tallies have been counted to obtain the *frequency,* or number of scores, in each interval. Thus, there is one score in the interval 18–20, two scores in the interval 21–23, and so on. The total number of scores (N) is the sum of the numbers in the frequency column. In the finished table, the tally column is usually omitted.

TABLE A.5

FREQUENCY DISTRIBUTION OF FORTY TEST SCORES

Class Interval	Tally	Frequency
48–50	/	1
45–47	/	1
42–44	//	2
39–41	7H4	5
36–38	7H4 /	6
33–35	7H4 ///	8
30–32	7H4 //	7
27–29	////	4
24–26	///	3
21–23	//	2
18–20	/	1
		$N = 40$

The frequency distribution in Table A.5 illustrates a number of points that should be observed during construction.

1. A satisfactory number of class intervals is usually somewhere between 10 and 20.
2. The most convenient size to use for the class interval can be determined by dividing the total score *range* by 15 and taking the nearest odd number. An odd number is preferred, so that the *midpoint* of each interval will be a whole number. For example, the range of scores tabulated in Table A.5 was $49 - 18 = 31$. Dividing 31 by 15, we obtain

2.07. The nearest odd number is 3, so that was selected as the size of the interval. Note that the *midpoint* of the lowest interval is 19, the *midpoint* of the next highest interval is 22, and so on. The midpoint of any interval can be determined by adding the score limits of the interval and dividing by 2.

3. All intervals in the same table should be of equal size.
4. The score limits of the intervals should not overlap (e.g., 18–20, 21–23, and so on).
5. The intervals should be arranged in order, with the highest values at the top of the table.
6. The lower score limit of any interval should be a multiple of the size of the interval (e.g., 3 × 6 = 18, 3 × 7 = 21, and so on).
7. To determine the size of the interval that has been used in a frequency distribution, simply subtract the lower score limit of one interval from the lower score limit of the interval just above it (e.g., 21 − 18 = 3, 24 − 21 = 3, and so on). This also provides a good check on the accuracy of the class intervals in a newly constructed frequency table.

Some of the above suggestions may be modified to fit special needs, but they provide useful guidelines for the beginner.

The Limits of a Class Interval. In a frequency distribution, the interval limits are written as scores. For example, the bottom interval in Table A.5 is written 18–20. A test score, however, represents the midpoint of a *distance* extending half a unit below and half a unit above the given score value. Thus, a score of 18 extends from 17.5 to 18.5, and a score of 20 from 19.5 to 20.5. Therefore, the *actual* or *real* limits of the score interval 18–20 extend from 17.5 to 20.5; the *real* limits of the next highest interval extend from 20.5 to 23.5, and so on. The score limits are written for convenience but the *real* limits must be used in certain statistical computations, as we shall see shortly.

Graphic Presentations of Frequency Distributions

A frequency distribution presents test data in a clear, effective manner, and it is satisfactory for most classroom purposes. However, if we desire to study the distribution of scores more carefully, or to report the results to others, a graphic representation may be more useful. The two most commonly used graphs are the *histogram* (or bar graph) and the *frequency polygon* (or line graph). Both graphs are presented in Figure A.1, based on the data in Table A.5. The scores are shown along the baseline, or horizontal axis, and are grouped into the same class intervals used in Table A.5. The vertical axis, to the left of the graphs, indicates the number of pupils earning each score. Thus it corresponds to the frequency column in Table A.5.

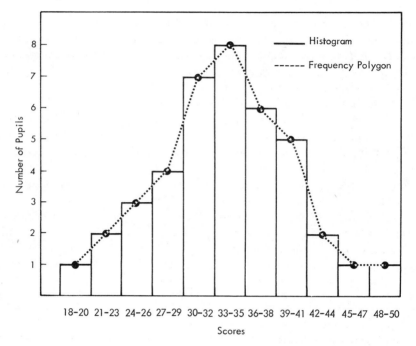

Figure A.1. Histogram and frequency polygon. (Plotted from data in Table A.5.)

Note that the *histogram* presents the data in the form of rectangular columns. The base of each column is the width of the class interval and the height of the column indicates the frequency, or number of pupils falling within that interval. It is as if each pupil earning a score within a given class interval were standing on the shoulders of the pupil beneath him, to form a "human column."

The *frequency polygon* is constructed by plotting a point at the mid-point of each class interval at a height corresponding to the number of pupils, or frequency, within that interval, and then joining these points with straight lines. As can be seen in Figure A.1, the frequency polygon and histogram are simply different ways of presenting the same data. In actual practice we would, of course, use only one of the graphs; the choice being somewhat arbitrary.

Computing the Median and Quartile Deviation

In an earlier section we noted that the median (Mdn) is the 50 per cent point (the point that divides a set of scores exactly in half); that the quartile deviation (Q) is one half the distance between Q_1 (25th percentile) and Q_3 (75th percentile); and that both statistical measures are based on counting. That is, starting from the low end of a set of scores, we count off one fourth of the scores to locate Q_1, one half of the scores to locate the median (Q_2), and three fourths of the scores to locate Q_3. This same counting procedure is used when computing the median and quartile deviation from a frequency distribution but some adjustments are necessary because the scores are grouped into intervals. The basic steps involve counting up to the interval containing the quartile in which we are interested (Q_1, Mdn, or Q_3) and then determining what proportion of the interval must be added to the lower limit of the interval to locate the exact quartile point. The step-by-step procedures for computing the median and quartile deviation are listed below and illustrated in Table A.6.

To compute the *median* (*Mdn*):

1. Divide the total number (N) of scores by 2 ($40 \div 2 = 20$).
2. Starting at the low end of the frequency column, add the scores in each interval until the interval containing the median is reached ($1 + 2 + 3 + 4 + 7 = 17$).
3. Subtract the sum (S) obtained in Step 2 from the number required to reach the median ($20 - 17 = 3$).
4. Find the proportion of the median interval that is to be added to its lower limit by dividing the number obtained in Step 3 by the number of scores in the median interval and multiplying this by the size of the class interval ($\frac{3}{8} \times 3 = 1.13$).
5. Add the amount obtained in Step 4 to the *real* lower limit of the median interval. This sum is the *median* ($32.5 + 1.13 = 33.6$).

These steps can be expressed by the following formula:

$$Mdn = L + \left(\frac{\frac{N}{2} - S}{f} \times i \right)$$

in which

$\quad L =$ *real* lower limit of median interval
$\quad N =$ the total number of scores
$\quad S =$ sum of scores in intervals below L
$\quad f =$ frequency, or number of scores, in median interval
$\quad i =$ size of the class interval

The steps used to compute the median can also be used to locate Q_1 and Q_3, by simply modifying step one to fit the percentage of scores being counted off, and by substituting the word *quartile* for *median* wherever it appears in the procedural steps. The formulas for Q_1 and Q_3, presented below, make clear the changes in Step 1. Note that $N/2$ used in the formula for the median has been changed to $N/4$ in the Q_1 formula and $3N/4$ in the Q_3 formula. The formulas, and procedures, are alike in all other respects.

To compute the *quartile deviation* (Q):

1. Find the value of Q_1 *and* Q_3 by applying the following formulas:

$$Q_1 = L + \left(\frac{(N/4) - S}{f} \times i\right) \qquad Q_3 = L + \left(\frac{(3N/4) - S}{f} \times i\right)$$

The letters in these formulas have the same meaning as those used in the formula for the median but, of course, the letters L and f now refer to the interval in which the particular quartile falls. For the scores in Table A.6, $Q_1 = 29.5$ and $Q_3 = 38.0$.

TABLE A.6

COMPUTATION OF THE MEDIAN AND QUARTILE DEVIATION
FROM A FREQUENCY DISTRIBUTION

Class Interval	Frequency
48–50	1
45–47	1
42–44	2
39–41	5
36–38	6
33–35	8
30–32	7
27–29	4
24–26	3
21–23	2
18–20	1
	$N = 40$

$S = 10$ (Q_1) — $S = 17$ (Mdn) — $S = 25$ (Q_3)

$$Mdn = 32.5 + \left(\frac{\frac{40}{2} - 17}{8} \times 3\right) = 32.5 + 1.13 = 33.63$$

$$Q_1 = 29.5 + \left(\frac{\frac{40}{4} - 10}{7} \times 3\right) = 29.5 + 0 = 29.5$$

$$Q_3 = 35.5 + \left(\frac{\frac{3 \times 40}{4} - 25}{6} \times 3\right) = 35.5 + 2.50 = 38.0$$

$$Q = \frac{38.0 - 29.5}{2} = \frac{8.5}{2} = 4.25$$

2. Subtract Q_1 from Q_3 and divide by 2. This is expressed in the following formula for the quartile deviation.

$$Q = \frac{Q_3 - Q_1}{2}$$

The computation in Table A.6 results in a Q of 4.25.

Note that we can now describe the distribution of scores in Table A.6 by stating that it has a median of 33.63 and a quartile deviation of 4.25. If we remember that the median is the midpoint and that one quartile deviation above and below the median includes approximately the middle 50 per cent of the scores (exactly in a normal distribution), this brief statistical description provides a meaningful substitute for the entire distribution of scores.

Computing the Mean and Standard Deviation

As noted earlier, the mean is the arithmetic average which is determined by dividing the sum of scores by the number of scores, and the standard deviation is a measure of variability or spread of scores around the mean. The formulas used in computing these statistics from ungrouped scores clearly define their meaning but they are inconvenient for computing from a frequency distribution. For these computations the procedures and formulas are modified slightly. The results, of course, have exactly the same meaning, whether computed from ungrouped or grouped scores.

At first glance, the procedure for computing the mean and standard deviation from a frequency table may appear complicated, but it is merely a matter of following a series of simple steps. These are listed below and illustrated in Table A.7.

To compute the *mean* (M) and *standard deviation* (SD)

1. Select any class interval near the middle of the distribution and call this interval zero in the (d) column. The midpoint of this interval is the *assumed mean*, or AM (in Table A.7, the zero interval is 33–35, and the $AM = 34$).
2. Determine the deviation (d) of each interval from the zero interval and enter in the (d) column.
3. In each row, multiply the entry in the f column by the entry in the d column, and enter the result in the fd column.
4. In each row, again, multiply the entry in the fd column by the entry in the d column, and enter the result in the fd^2 column.
5. Add the entries in the fd column to obtain Σfd (in Table A.7, $\Sigma fd = -6$).
6. Add the entries in the fd^2 column to obtain Σfd^2 (in Table A.7, $\Sigma fd^2 = 192$).

TABLE A.7

COMPUTATION OF THE MEAN AND THE STANDARD DEVIATION
FROM A FREQUENCY DISTRIBUTION

Class Interval	Frequency (f)	Deviation* (d)	fd	fd²
48–50	1	5	5	25
45–47	1	4	4	16
42–44	2	3	6	18
39–41	5	2	10	20
36–38	6	1	6	6
33–35	8	0	0	0
30–32	7	−1	−7	7
27–29	4	−2	−8	16
24–26	3	−3	−9	27
21–23	2	−4	−8	32
18–20	1	−5	−5	25
	$N = 40$		$\Sigma fd = -6$	$\Sigma fd^2 = 192$

$$c \text{ (correction)} = \frac{-6}{40} = -.15$$

$$M = 34 + (-.15 \times 3) = 34 - .45 = 33.55$$

$$SD = 3\sqrt{\frac{192}{40} - (-.15)^2} = 3\sqrt{4.80 - .02} = 3\sqrt{4.78}$$

$$SD = 3 \times 2.19 = 6.57$$

* Deviation in interval units is also commonly expressed by x'.

7. Substitute the obtained values in the following formulas:

$$c = \frac{\Sigma fd}{N}$$
$$M = AM + (c \times i)$$
$$SD = i \sqrt{\frac{\Sigma fd^2}{N} - c^2}$$

in which

AM = the assumed mean
c = the correction
i = size of the class interval

The results presented in Table A.7 indicate that this distribution of scores can be described by a mean of 33.55 and a standard deviation of

6.57. Thus we can expect approximately two thirds of the scores to fall between 27 and 40 ($M \pm SD$, rounded to whole numbers). The percentage of cases falling within each standard deviation area under the normal curve and the use of SD in computing standard scores is described in detail in Chapter 15.

COMPUTING THE COEFFICIENT OF CORRELATION

The meaning of *correlation coefficient* and its use in describing the validity and reliability of test scores can be found in Chapters 4 and 5. Basically, a coefficient of correlation expresses the degree of relationship between two sets of scores by numbers ranging from $+1.00$ to -1.00. A perfect positive correlation is indicated by a coefficient of $+1.00$ and a perfect negative correlation by a coefficient of -1.00. A correlation coefficient of .00 lies midway between these extremes and indicates no relationship between the two sets of scores. Obviously, the larger the coefficient (positive or negative), the higher the degree of relationship expressed.

Two of the most common methods of computing the coefficient of correlation are the *rank-difference method* and the *product-moment method*. The rank-difference method, which is described in the computing guide in Chapter 4, is satisfactory if the number of scores to be correlated is small. For most classroom purposes it provides a simple, practical technique. The product-moment method is favored where the number of scores is large. Thus, it is the type of correlation that is most commonly reported in test manuals and research studies. The product-moment coefficient is indicated by the symbol r.

The computation of the product-moment coefficient of correlation will be described and illustrated, here, for ungrouped test scores. The computation with grouped data appears more complicated and requires a much more detailed description. This can be obtained from any standard textbook in statistics. A few such references are listed at the end of this unit.

The following steps will serve as a guide for computing a *product-moment correlation coefficient* (r) from ungrouped data.[2]

1. Begin by writing the pairs of scores to be studied in two columns. Make certain that the pair of scores for each pupil is in the same row. Call one column X and the other Y (see Table A.8).
2. Square each of the entries in the X column and enter the result in the X^2 column.
3. Square each of the entries in the Y column and enter the result in the Y^2 column.

2. Computation is simplified by the use of the table of squares and square roots in Appendix B.

TABLE A.8

PRODUCT-MOMENT CORRELATION FOR UNGROUPED DATA

Score X	Score Y	X^2	Y^2	XY
119	77	14,161	5,929	9,163
118	76	13,924	5,776	8,968
116	72	13,456	5,184	8,352
115	67	13,225	4,489	7,705
112	82	12,544	6,724	9,184
109	63	11,881	3,969	6,867
108	60	11,664	3,600	6,480
106	78	11,236	6,084	8,268
105	69	11,025	4,761	7,245
104	49	10,816	2,401	5,096
102	48	10,404	2,304	4,896
100	58	10,000	3,364	5,800
98	56	9,604	3,136	5,488
97	57	9,409	3,249	5,529
95	74	9,025	5,476	7,030
94	62	8,836	3,844	5,828
93	46	8,649	2,116	4,278
91	65	8,281	4,225	5,915
90	59	8,100	3,481	5,310
89	54	7,921	2,916	4,806
2,061	1,272	214,161	83,028	132,208
(ΣX)	(ΣY)	(ΣX^2)	(ΣY^2)	(ΣXY)

$N = 20$

4. In each row, multiply the entry in the X column by the entry in the Y column, and enter the result in the XY column.
5. Add the entries in each column to find the sum of (Σ) each column. Note the number (N) of pairs of scores. From Table A.8, then:

$$\Sigma X = 2,061 \qquad \Sigma X^2 = 214,161$$
$$\Sigma Y = 1,272 \qquad \Sigma Y^2 = 83,028$$
$$N = 20 \qquad \Sigma XY = 132,208$$

6. Substitute the obtained values in the formula:

$$r = \frac{\dfrac{\Sigma XY}{N} - \left(\dfrac{\Sigma X}{N}\right)\left(\dfrac{\Sigma Y}{N}\right)}{\sqrt{\dfrac{\Sigma X^2}{N} - \left(\dfrac{\Sigma X}{N}\right)^2} \sqrt{\dfrac{\Sigma Y^2}{N} - \left(\dfrac{\Sigma Y}{N}\right)^2}}$$

This formula looks complex, but it involves simple arithmetic. Since the sum of each column is divided by N, this step can be completed before putting the data into the formula. Thus, for the data from Table A.8,

$$\frac{\Sigma X}{N} = \frac{2{,}061}{20} = 103.05$$

$$\frac{\Sigma Y}{N} = \frac{1{,}272}{20} = 63.60$$

$$\frac{\Sigma X^2}{N} = \frac{214{,}161}{20} = 10{,}708.05$$

$$\frac{\Sigma Y^2}{N} = \frac{83{,}028}{20} = 4{,}151.40$$

$$\frac{\Sigma XY}{N} = \frac{132{,}208}{20} = 6{,}610.40$$

Then,

$$r = \frac{6{,}610.40 - (103.05)\,(63.60)}{\sqrt{10{,}708.05 - (103.05)^2}\ \sqrt{4{,}151.40 - (63.60)^2}}$$

$$r = \frac{6{,}610.40 - 6{,}553.98}{\sqrt{10{,}708.05 - 10{,}619.30}\ \sqrt{4{,}151.40 - 4{,}044.96}}$$

$$r = \frac{56.42}{\sqrt{88.75}\ \sqrt{106.44}} = \frac{56.42}{9.42 \times 10.32} = \frac{56.42}{97.21}$$

$$r = .58$$

Although it is not readily apparent from the above formula, the computations involve finding the mean and the standard deviation of each set of scores (X and Y). Thus the formula can also be written

$$r = \frac{\dfrac{\Sigma XY}{N} - (M_x)\,(M_y)}{(SD_x)\,(SD_y)}$$

in which

M_x = mean of scores in X column
M_y = mean of scores in Y column
SD_x = standard deviation of scores in X column
SD_y = standard deviation of scores in Y column

Thus, for the same data

$$r = \frac{6{,}610.40 - (103.05)\,(63.60)}{9.42 \times 10.32} = .58$$

If the means and standard deviations are already available for the two sets of scores, this latter formula is easier to apply. If they are not available, the first formula can be used, and the means and standard deviations of the two sets of scores are computed in the process. (This can be seen by comparing the two formulas.)

It should be noted that the scores in Table A.8 are the same scores used to illustrate rank-difference correlation in Chapter 4. There we obtained a coefficient of .60, compared to the .58 obtained here. Differences this large can be expected from the two methods, but seldom is the difference larger than this (unless there are many ties in rank). Also, for all practical purposes the two types of correlation coefficients can be interpreted in the same manner. For a description of how to interpret and use the coefficient of correlation see Chapter 4.

A Final Caution. Correlation indicates the degree of relationship between two sets of scores, but *not causation*. If X and Y are related, there are several possible explanations: (1) X may cause Y, (2) Y may cause X, or (3) X and Y may be the result of a common cause. For example, the increase in incidence of juvenile delinquency during the past decade has been paralleled by a corresponding increase in teachers' salaries. Thus, the correlation between these two sets of figures would probably be quite high. Obviously, further study is needed to determine the cause of any particular relationship.

REFERENCES

DOWNIE, N. M., and R. W. HEATH. *Basic Statistical Methods*, 4th ed. New York: Harper and Row, Publishers, 1974. An introductory textbook designed for nonmathematics majors.

GELLMAN, E. S. *Statistics for Teachers*. New York: Harper and Row, Publishers, 1973. Uses a nonmathematical approach in describing the statistics needed by teachers.

GUILFORD, J. P., and B. FRUCHTER. *Fundamental Statistics in Psychology and Education*, 5th ed. New York: McGraw-Hill Book Company, 1973. A comprehensive coverage of the techniques of statistical analysis and methods of test development.

TOWNSEND, E. A., and P. J. BURKE. *Using Statistics in Classroom Instruction*. New York: Macmillan Publishing Co., Inc., 1975. A brief book that provides step-by-step directions and practice in using simple descriptive statistics with test scores.

APPENDIX B
Table of Squares and Square Roots

Table of Squares and Square Roots

N	N^2	N	N^2	N	N^2		N	$\sqrt{N}$	N	$\sqrt{N}$	N	$\sqrt{N}$
1	1	51	2601	101	10201		1	1.000	51	7.141	101	10.050
2	4	52	2704	102	10404		2	1.414	52	7.211	102	10.100
3	9	53	2809	103	10609		3	1.732	53	7.280	103	10.149
4	16	54	2916	104	10816		4	2.000	54	7.348	104	10.198
5	25	55	3025	105	11025		5	2.236	55	7.416	105	10.247
6	36	56	3136	106	11236		6	2.449	56	7.483	106	10.296
7	49	57	3249	107	11449		7	2.646	57	7.550	107	10.344
8	64	58	3364	108	11664		8	2.828	58	7.616	108	10.392
9	81	59	3481	109	11881		9	3.000	59	7.681	109	10.440
10	100	60	3600	110	12100		10	3.162	60	7.746	110	10.488
11	121	61	3721	111	12321		11	3.317	61	7.810	111	10.536
12	144	62	3844	112	12544		12	3.464	62	7.874	112	10.583
13	169	63	3969	113	12769		13	3.606	63	7.937	113	10.630
14	196	64	4096	114	12996		14	3.742	64	8.000	114	10.677
15	225	65	4225	115	13225		15	3.873	65	8.062	115	10.724
16	256	66	4356	116	13456		16	4.000	66	8.124	116	10.770
17	289	67	4489	117	13689		17	4.123	67	8.185	117	10.817
18	324	68	4624	118	13924		18	4.243	68	8.246	118	10.863
19	361	69	4761	119	14161		19	4.359	69	8.307	119	10.909
20	400	70	4900	120	14400		20	4.472	70	8.367	120	10.954
21	441	71	5041	121	14641		21	4.583	71	8.426	121	11.000
22	484	72	5184	122	14884		22	4.690	72	8.485	122	11.045
23	529	73	5329	123	15129		23	4.796	73	8.544	123	11.091
24	576	74	5476	124	15376		24	4.899	74	8.602	124	11.136
25	625	75	5625	125	15625		25	5.000	75	8.660	125	11.180
26	676	76	5776	126	15876		26	5.099	76	8.718	126	11.225
27	729	77	5929	127	16129		27	5.196	77	8.775	127	11.269
28	784	78	6084	128	16384		28	5.292	78	8.832	128	11.314
29	841	79	6241	129	16641		29	5.385	79	8.888	129	11.358
30	900	80	6400	130	16900		30	5.477	80	8.944	130	11.402
31	961	81	6561	131	17161		31	5.568	81	9.000	131	11.446
32	1024	82	6724	132	17424		32	5.657	82	9.055	132	11.489
33	1089	83	6889	133	17689		33	5.745	83	9.110	133	11.533
34	1156	84	7056	134	17956		34	5.831	84	9.165	134	11.576
35	1225	85	7225	135	18225		35	5.916	85	9.220	135	11.619
36	1296	86	7396	136	18496		36	6.000	86	9.274	136	11.662
37	1369	87	7569	137	18769		37	6.083	87	9.327	137	11.705
38	1444	88	7744	138	19044		38	6.164	88	9.381	138	11.747
39	1521	89	7921	139	19321		39	6.245	89	9.434	139	11.790
40	1600	90	8100	140	19600		40	6.325	90	9.487	140	11.832
41	1681	91	8281	141	19881		41	6.403	91	9.539	141	11.874
42	1764	92	8464	142	20164		42	6.481	92	9.592	142	11.916
43	1849	93	8649	143	20449		43	6.557	93	9.644	143	11.958
44	1936	94	8836	144	20736		44	6.633	94	9.695	144	12.000
45	2025	95	9025	145	21025		45	6.708	95	9.747	145	12.042
46	2116	96	9216	146	21316		46	6.782	96	9.798	146	12.083
47	2209	97	9409	147	21609		47	6.856	97	9.849	147	12.124
48	2304	98	9604	148	21904		48	6.928	98	9.899	148	12.166
49	2401	99	9801	149	22201		49	7.000	99	9.950	149	12.207
50	2500	100	10000	150	22500		50	7.071	100	10.000	150	12.247

Table of Square Roots

N	$\sqrt{N}$	N	$\sqrt{N}$	N	$\sqrt{N}$	N	$\sqrt{N}$	N	$\sqrt{N}$	N	$\sqrt{N}$
151	12.288	201	14.177	251	15.843	301	17.349	351	18.735	401	20.025
152	12.329	202	14.213	252	15.875	302	17.378	352	18.762	402	20.050
153	12.369	203	14.248	253	15.906	303	17.407	353	18.788	403	20.075
154	12.410	204	14.283	254	15.937	304	17.436	354	18.815	404	20.100
155	12.450	205	14.318	255	15.969	305	17.464	355	18.841	405	20.125
156	12.490	206	14.353	256	16.000	306	17.493	356	18.868	406	20.149
157	12.530	207	14.387	257	16.031	307	17.521	357	18.894	407	20.174
158	12.570	208	14.422	258	16.062	308	17.550	358	18.921	408	20.199
159	12.610	209	14.457	259	16.093	309	17.578	359	18.947	409	20.224
160	12.649	210	14.491	260	16.125	310	17.607	360	18.974	410	20.248
161	12.689	211	14.526	261	16.155	311	17.635	361	19.000	411	20.273
162	12.728	212	14.560	262	16.186	312	17.664	362	19.026	412	20.298
163	12.767	213	14.595	263	16.217	313	17.692	363	19.053	413	20.322
164	12.806	214	14.629	264	16.248	314	17.720	364	19.079	414	20.347
165	12.845	215	14.663	265	16.279	315	17.748	365	19.105	415	20.372
166	12.884	216	14.697	266	16.310	316	17.776	366	19.131	416	20.396
167	12.923	217	14.731	267	16.340	317	17.804	367	19.157	417	20.421
168	12.961	218	14.765	268	16.371	318	17.833	368	19.183	418	20.445
169	13.000	219	14.799	269	16.401	319	17.861	369	19.209	419	20.469
170	13.038	220	14.832	270	16.432	320	17.889	370	19.235	420	20.494
171	13.077	221	14.866	271	16.462	321	17.916	371	19.261	421	20.518
172	13.115	222	14.900	272	16.492	322	17.944	372	19.287	422	20.543
173	13.153	223	14.933	273	16.523	323	17.972	373	19.313	423	20.567
174	13.191	224	14.967	274	16.553	324	18.000	374	19.339	424	20.591
175	13.229	225	15.000	275	16.583	325	18.028	375	19.365	425	20.616
176	13.266	226	15.033	276	16.613	326	18.055	376	19.391	426	20.640
177	13.304	227	15.067	277	16.643	327	18.083	377	19.416	427	20.664
178	13.342	228	15.100	278	16.673	328	18.111	378	19.442	428	20.688
179	13.379	229	15.133	279	16.703	329	18.138	379	19.468	429	20.712
180	13.416	230	15.166	280	16.733	330	18.166	380	19.494	430	20.736
181	13.454	231	15.199	281	16.763	331	18.193	381	19.519	431	20.761
182	13.491	232	15.232	282	16.793	332	18.221	382	19.545	432	20.785
183	13.528	233	15.264	283	16.823	333	18.248	383	19.570	433	20.809
184	13.565	234	15.297	284	16.852	334	18.276	384	19.596	434	20.833
185	13.601	235	15.330	285	16.882	335	18.303	385	19.621	435	20.857
186	13.638	236	15.362	286	16.912	336	18.330	386	19.647	436	20.881
187	13.675	237	15.395	287	16.941	337	18.358	387	19.672	437	20.905
188	13.711	238	15.427	288	16.971	338	18.385	388	19.698	438	20.928
189	13.748	239	15.460	289	17.000	339	18.412	389	19.723	439	20.952
190	13.784	240	15.492	290	17.029	340	18.439	390	19.748	440	20.976
191	13.820	241	15.524	291	17.059	341	18.466	391	19.774	441	21.000
192	13.856	242	15.556	292	17.088	342	18.493	392	19.799	442	21.024
193	13.892	243	15.588	293	17.117	343	18.520	393	19.824	443	21.048
194	13.928	244	15.620	294	17.146	344	18.547	394	19.849	444	21.071
195	13.964	245	15.652	295	17.176	345	18.574	395	19.875	445	21.095
196	14.000	246	15.684	296	17.205	346	18.601	396	19.900	446	21.119
197	14.036	247	15.716	297	17.234	347	18.628	397	19.925	447	21.142
198	14.071	248	15.748	298	17.263	348	18.655	398	19.950	448	21.166
199	14.107	249	15.780	299	17.292	349	18.682	399	19.975	449	21.190
200	14.142	250	15.811	300	17.321	350	18.708	400	20.000	450	21.213

Table of Square Roots

N	$\sqrt{N}$	N	$\sqrt{N}$	N	$\sqrt{N}$	N	$\sqrt{N}$	N	$\sqrt{N}$	N	$\sqrt{N}$
451	21.237	501	22.383	551	23.473	601	24.515	651	25.515	701	26.476
452	21.260	502	22.405	552	23.495	602	24.536	652	25.534	702	26.495
453	21.284	503	22.428	553	23.516	603	24.556	653	25.554	703	26.514
454	21.307	504	22.450	554	23.537	604	24.576	654	25.573	704	26.533
455	21.331	505	22.472	555	23.558	605	24.597	655	25.593	705	26.552
456	21.354	506	22.494	556	23.580	606	24.617	656	25.612	706	26.571
457	21.378	507	22.517	557	23.601	607	24.637	657	25.632	707	26.589
458	21.401	508	22.539	558	23.622	608	24.658	658	25.652	708	26.608
459	21.424	509	22.561	559	23.643	609	24.678	659	25.671	709	26.627
460	21.448	510	22.583	560	23.664	610	24.698	660	25.690	710	26.646
461	21.471	511	22.605	561	23.685	611	24.718	661	25.710	711	26.665
462	21.494	512	22.627	562	23.707	612	24.739	662	25.729	712	26.683
463	21.517	513	22.650	563	23.728	613	24.759	663	25.749	713	26.702
464	21.541	514	22.672	564	23.749	614	24.779	664	25.768	714	26.721
465	21.564	515	22.694	565	23.770	615	24.799	665	25.788	715	26.739
466	21.587	516	22.716	566	23.791	616	24.819	666	25.807	716	26.758
467	21.610	517	22.738	567	23.812	617	24.839	667	25.826	717	26.777
468	21.633	518	22.760	568	23.833	618	24.860	668	25.846	718	26.796
469	21.656	519	22.782	569	23.854	619	24.880	669	25.865	719	26.814
470	21.679	520	22.804	570	23.875	620	24.900	670	25.884	720	26.833
471	21.703	521	22.825	571	23.896	621	24.920	671	25.904	721	26.851
472	21.726	522	22.847	572	23.917	622	24.940	672	25.923	722	26.870
473	21.749	523	22.869	573	23.937	623	24.960	673	25.942	723	26.889
474	21.772	524	22.891	574	23.958	624	24.980	674	25.962	724	26.907
475	21.794	525	22.913	575	23.979	625	25.000	675	25.981	725	26.926
476	21.817	526	22.935	576	24.000	626	25.020	676	26.000	726	26.944
477	21.840	527	22.956	577	24.021	627	25.040	677	26.019	727	26.963
478	21.863	528	22.978	578	24.042	628	25.060	678	26.038	728	26.981
479	21.886	529	23.000	579	24.062	629	25.080	679	26.058	729	27.000
480	21.909	530	23.022	580	24.083	630	25.100	680	26.077	730	27.019
481	21.932	531	23.043	581	24.104	631	25.120	681	26.096	731	27.037
482	21.954	532	23.065	582	24.125	632	25.140	682	26.115	732	27.055
483	21.977	533	23.087	583	24.145	633	25.159	683	26.134	733	27.074
484	22.000	534	23.108	584	24.166	634	25.179	684	26.153	734	27.092
485	22.023	535	23.130	585	24.187	635	25.199	685	26.173	735	27.111
486	22.045	536	23.152	586	24.207	636	25.219	686	26.192	736	27.129
487	22.068	537	23.173	587	24.228	637	25.239	687	26.211	737	27.148
488	22.091	538	23.195	588	24.249	638	25.259	688	26.230	738	27.166
489	22.113	539	23.216	589	24.269	639	25.278	689	26.249	739	27.185
490	22.136	540	23.238	590	24.290	640	25.298	690	26.268	740	27.203
491	22.159	541	23.259	591	24.310	641	25.318	691	26.287	741	27.221
492	22.181	542	23.281	592	24.331	642	25.338	692	26.306	742	27.240
493	22.204	543	23.302	593	24.352	643	25.357	693	26.325	743	27.258
494	22.226	544	23.324	594	24.372	644	25.377	694	26.344	744	27.276
495	22.249	545	23.345	595	24.393	645	25.397	695	26.363	745	27.295
496	22.271	546	23.367	596	24.413	646	25.417	696	26.382	746	27.313
497	22.293	547	23.388	597	24.434	647	25.436	697	26.401	747	27.331
498	22.316	548	23.409	598	24.454	648	25.456	698	26.420	748	27.350
499	22.338	549	23.431	599	24.474	649	25.475	699	26.439	749	27.368
500	22.361	550	23.452	600	24.495	650	25.495	700	26.458	750	27.386

Table of Square Roots

N	$\sqrt{N}$	N	$\sqrt{N}$	N	$\sqrt{N}$	N	$\sqrt{N}$	N	$\sqrt{N}$	N	$\sqrt{N}$
751	27.404	801	28.302	851	29.172	901	30.017	951	30.838	1001	31.639
752	27.423	802	28.320	852	29.189	902	30.033	952	30.854	1002	31.654
753	27.441	803	28.337	853	29.206	903	30.050	953	30.871	1003	31.670
754	27.459	804	28.355	854	29.223	904	30.067	954	30.887	1004	31.686
755	27.477	805	28.373	855	29.240	905	30.083	955	30.903	1005	31.702
756	27.495	806	28.390	856	29.257	906	30.100	956	30.919	1006	31.718
757	27.514	807	28.408	857	29.275	907	30.116	957	30.935	1007	31.733
758	27.532	808	28.425	858	29.292	908	30.133	958	30.952	1008	31.749
759	27.550	809	28.443	859	29.309	909	30.150	959	30.968	1009	31.765
760	27.568	810	28.460	860	29.326	910	30.166	960	30.984	1010	31.780
761	27.586	811	28.478	861	29.343	911	30.183	961	31.000	1011	31.796
762	27.604	812	28.496	862	29.360	912	30.199	962	31.016	1012	31.812
763	27.622	813	28.513	863	29.377	913	30.216	963	31.032	1013	31.828
764	27.641	814	28.531	864	29.394	914	30.232	964	31.048	1014	31.843
765	27.659	815	28.548	865	29.411	915	30.249	965	31.064	1015	31.859
766	27.677	816	28.566	866	29.428	916	30.265	966	31.081	1016	31.875
767	27.695	817	28.583	867	29.445	917	30.282	967	31.097	1017	31.890
768	27.713	818	28.601	868	29.462	918	30.299	968	31.113	1018	31.906
769	27.731	819	28.618	869	29.479	919	30.315	969	31.129	1019	31.922
770	27.749	820	28.636	870	29.496	920	30.332	970	31.145	1020	31.937
771	27.767	821	28.653	871	29.513	921	30.348	971	31.161	1021	31.953
772	27.785	822	28.671	872	29.530	922	30.364	972	31.177	1022	31.969
773	27.803	823	28.688	873	29.547	923	30.381	973	31.193	1023	31.984
774	27.821	824	28.705	874	29.563	924	30.397	974	31.209	1024	32.000
775	27.839	825	28.723	875	29.580	925	30.414	975	31.225	1025	32.016
776	27.857	826	28.740	876	29.597	926	30.430	976	31.241	1026	32.031
777	27.875	827	28.758	877	29.614	927	30.447	977	31.257	1027	32.047
778	27.893	828	28.775	878	29.631	928	30.463	978	31.273	1028	32.062
779	27.911	829	28.792	879	29.648	929	30.480	979	31.289	1029	32.078
780	27.928	830	28.810	880	29.665	930	30.496	980	31.305	1030	32.094
781	27.946	831	28.827	881	29.682	931	30.512	981	31.321	1031	32.109
782	27.964	832	28.844	882	29.698	932	30.529	982	31.337	1032	32.125
783	27.982	833	28.862	883	29.715	933	30.545	983	31.353	1033	32.140
784	28.000	834	28.879	884	29.732	934	30.561	984	31.369	1034	32.156
785	28.018	835	28.896	885	29.749	935	30.578	985	31.385	1035	32.171
786	28.036	836	28.914	886	29.766	936	30.594	986	31.401	1036	32.187
787	28.054	837	28.931	887	29.783	937	30.610	987	31.417	1037	32.202
788	28.071	838	28.948	888	29.799	938	30.627	988	31.432	1038	32.218
789	28.089	839	28.965	889	29.816	939	30.643	989	31.448	1039	32.234
790	28.107	840	28.983	890	29.833	940	30.659	990	31.464	1040	32.249
791	28.125	841	29.000	891	29.850	941	30.676	991	31.480	1041	32.265
792	28.142	842	29.017	892	29.866	942	30.692	992	31.496	1042	32.280
793	28.160	843	29.034	893	29.883	943	30.708	993	31.512	1043	32.296
794	28.178	844	29.052	894	29.900	944	30.725	994	31.528	1044	32.311
795	28.196	845	29.069	895	29.916	945	30.741	995	31.544	1045	32.326
796	28.213	846	29.086	896	29.933	946	30.757	996	31.559	1046	32.342
797	28.231	847	29.103	897	29.950	947	30.773	997	31.575	1047	32.357
798	28.249	848	29.120	898	29.967	948	30.790	998	31.591	1048	32.373
799	28.267	849	29.138	899	29.983	949	30.806	999	31.607	1049	32.388
800	28.284	850	29.155	900	30.000	950	30.822	1000	31.623	1050	32.404

APPENDIX C
A List of
Test Publishers and
Objective-Item Pools

TEST PUBLISHERS

Following is a list of the test publishers and distributors whose tests were referred to earlier in this book (the tests are briefly described in Appendix D). An asterisk (*) after the name indicates that the company provides bulletins on testing and the use of test results. All publishers will provide catalogues of their current tests.

The names and addresses of other test publishers and distributors can be obtained from the latest volume of Buros' *Mental Measurements Yearbook*.

1. American Guidance Service, Inc.
   Publishers Building
   Circle Pines, Minnesota 55014

2. Bureau of Publications
   Teachers College, Columbia University
   New York, New York 10027

3. California Test Bureau/McGraw-Hill*
   Del Monte Research Park
   Monterey, California 93940

4. Consulting Psychologists Press, Inc.
   577 College Avenue
   Palo Alto, California 94306

5. Cooperative Test Division*
   Educational Testing Service
   Princeton, New Jersey 08540

6. Harcourt Brace Jovanovich, Inc.*
   757 Third Avenue
   New York, New York 10017

7. Houghton Mifflin Company*
   One Beacon Street
   Boston, Massachusetts 02107

8. Personnel Press
   191 Spring Street
   Lexington, Massachusetts 02173

9. Psychological Corporation*
   304 East 45th Street
   New York, New York 10017

10. Science Research Associates, Inc.
    259 East Erie Street
    Chicago, Illinois 60611

OBJECTIVE-ITEM POOLS

Collections of instructional objectives and related test items are maintained by some of the test publishers. In addition, information concerning objective-item pools may be obtained from the following sources:

Institute for Educational Research
1400 West Maple Avenue
Downer's Grove, Illionis 60515

Instructional Objectives Exchange
Box 24095
Los Angeles, California 90024

Objectives and Items CO-OP
School of Education
University of Massachusetts
Amherst, Massachusetts 01002

Westinghouse Learning Corporation
P.O. Box 30
Iowa City, Iowa 52240

APPENDIX D
A Selected List of Standardized Tests

A SELECTED LIST OF STANDARDIZED TESTS

Test Name (Publisher's No.) *	Grade† Levels Covered	Testing‡ Time (Minutes)	Major Areas Measured**	MMY†† Review or Date
Achievement Batteries				
California Achievement Tests (3)	1–12	114–153	Reading, mathematics, language	7–5
Comprehensive Tests of Basic Skills (3)	K–12	144–260	Reading, mathematics, language, study skills, science, social studies	1975
Iowa Tests of Basic Skills (7)	1–8	212–279	Reading, mathematics, language, work-study skills	1972
Iowa Tests of Educational Development (10)	9–12	195	Reading, language, mathematics, science, social studies, use of sources	1972
Metropolitan Achievement Tests (6)	K–13	70–315	Reading, mathematics, language, science, social studies, study skills	7–14
SRA Achievement Series (10)	1–9	150–270	Reading, mathematics, language, science, social studies, use of sources	1972
Sequential Tests of Educational Progress—STEP Series II (5)	4–14	305	Reading, writing, English expression, mathematics, science, social studies	1969
Stanford Achievement Tests (6)	1–13	170–320	Reading, mathematics, language, science, social studies, work-study skills	1973
Tests of Academic Progress (7)	9–12	270	Social studies, composition, science, reading, mathematics, literature	1970
Reading Tests				
Davis Reading Test (9)	8–13	40	Level and speed of comprehension	6–786
Doren Diagnostic Reading Test (1)	1–4	60–180	Word recognition skills	1973
Gates-MacGinitie Reading Tests (2)	1–12	40–60	Speed, vocabulary, comprehension	7–689
Gates-McKillop Reading Diagnostic Tests (2)	2–6		Numerous separate skills	6–824

Test Name (Publisher's No.)*	Grade Levels Covered	Testing‡ Time (Minutes)	Major Areas Measured**	MMY†† Review or Date
Iowa Silent Reading Test (6)	6–14	56–91	Vocabulary, comprehension, speed	1973
Nelson Reading Test (7)	3–9	30	Vocabulary, comprehension	6–802
Nelson-Denny Reading Test (7)	9–16, A	30	Vocabulary, comprehension, rate	1973
Reading Comprehension: Coop. English Test (5)	9–14	40	Vocabulary, comprehension	6–806
Stanford Diagnostic Reading Test (6)	2–13	110–160	Vocabulary, reading comprehension, word recognition	7–725
(Also see reading tests in achievement batteries, listed earlier.)				
Scholastic Aptitude Tests				
California Short-Form Test of Mental Maturity (3)	K–16, A	34–43	Language, nonlanguage, and total score	7–337
California Test of Mental Maturity (3)	K–16, A	48–83	Language, nonlanguage, and total score	7–338
Cognitive Abilities Test (7)	K–12	50–105	Verbal, quantitative, nonverbal	7–343
Cooperative Academic Ability Tests (5)	12	45	Verbal, quantitative, and total score	7–346
Cooperative School and College Ability Tests— SCAT Series II (5)	4–14	70	Verbal, quantitative, and total score	7–347
Culture Fair Intelligence Test	4–16, A	30	Nonverbal	6–453
Davis-Eells Games (6)	1–6	60–120	Problem solving ability (pictorial form)	5–326
Henmon-Nelson Tests of Mental Ability (7)	K–12	30	Single score (highly verbal)	1973
College level	13–17	30–40	Verbal, quantitative, and total score	6–462
Kuhlmann-Anderson Measure of Academic Potential, seventh edition (8)	K–12	25–60	Verbal, quantitative, and total score	6–466

Test Name (Publisher's No.)*	Grade† Levels Covered	Testing‡ Time (Minutes)	Major Areas Measured**	MMY†† Review or Date
Lorge-Thorndike Intelligence Tests (7)	K–12	35–50	Verbal and nonverbal scores	7–360
Otis-Lennon Mental Ability Tests (6)	K–16	30–50	Single score (highly verbal)	7–370
Short Form Test of Academic Aptitude (3)	K–12	40–50	Language, nonlanguage, and total score	7–387
SRA Short Test of Educational Ability (10)	K–12	30	Single score (verbal, quantitative)	7–382
Multiaptitude Batteries				
Academic Promise Tests (9)	6–9	90	Verbal, numerical, abstract reasoning, language usage	7–672
Differential Aptitude Tests (9)	8–13, A	181	Verbal reasoning, numerical ability, abstract reasoning, space relations, mechanical reasoning, clerical, spelling, language usage	1973
Early School Readiness and Achievement Tests				
Boehm Test of Basic Concepts (9)	K–2	30	Basic concepts	7–335
Cooperative Preschool Inventory (5)	K	15	Preschool knowledge and concepts	7–404
Stanford Early School Achievement Test (6)	K–1	90	Preschool knowledge and concepts	7–28
Tests of Basic Experience (3)	K–1	125	Preschool knowledge and concepts	1970
Reading Readiness Tests				
Gates-MacGinitie Reading Readiness Skills (2)	1	120	Reading readiness skills	7–749
Lee-Clark Reading Readiness Test (3)	K–1	20	Reading readiness skills	7–752
Metropolitan Readiness Test (6)	K–1	60	Reading readiness and number readiness	1976
Murphy-Durrell Reading Readiness Analysis (6)	K–1	100	Reading readiness skills	7–758
Problem Checklists				
Mooney Problem Check Lists (9)	7–16, A	20–40	Problems in home, school, personal, and social areas	6–145

Interest Inventories

Test Name (Publisher's No.)*	Grade† Levels Covered	Testing‡ Time (Minutes)	Major Areas Measured**	MMY†† Review or Date
Kuder General Interest Survey (10)	6–12	45–60	Ten general vocational interest areas	7–1024
Kuder Preference Record—Vocational (10)	9–16, A	40–50	Ten general vocational interest areas	6–1063
Kuder Preference Record—Personal (10)	9–16, A	40–50	Five types of social relations	6–132
Kuder Preference Record—Occupational (10)	9–16, A	20–30	Scores for fifty occupations	7–1025
Strong Vocational Interest Blank for Men (4)	11–12, A	40	Scores for occupations, and special areas	7–1036
Strong Vocational Interest Blank for Women (4)	11–12, A	40	Scores for occupations, and special areas	7–1037
Strong-Campbell Interest Inventory	11–12, A	40	Scores for occupations (both sexes)	1974
What I Like to Do (10)	4–7	60	Various in-school and out-of-school activities	5–122

* The publishers' numbers (in parentheses) refer to the list in Appendix C.
† Gives total span only—not the number of separate levels available (K = kindergarten, A = adult).
‡ Ranges in time are mainly due to different forms used at different grade levels.
** Indicates the general areas measured but not the specific scores available.
†† Refers to Mental Measurements Yearbook and entry (e.g., 7–2 = second entry in Seventh Yearbook). The date is given for recent editions not reviewed in the Seventh MMY (1972).

APPENDIX E
Taxonomy of Educational Objectives (Major Categories and Illustrative Objectives)

TABLE E.1

MAJOR CATEGORIES IN THE COGNITIVE DOMAIN OF THE TAXONOMY
OF EDUCATIONAL OBJECTIVES (BLOOM, 1956)

Descriptions of the Major Categories in the Cognitive Domain

---

1. **Knowledge.** Knowledge is defined as the remembering of previously learned material. This may involve the recall of a wide range of material, from specific facts to complete theories, but all that is required is the bringing to mind of the appropriate information. Knowledge represents the lowest level of learning outcomes in the cognitive domain.

2. **Comprehenson.** Comprehension is defined as the ability to grasp the meaning of material. This may be shown by translating material from one form to another (words to numbers), by interpreting material (explaining or summarizing), and by estimating future trends (predicting consequences or effects). These learning outcomes go one step beyond the simple remembering of material, and represent the lowest level of understanding.

---

3. **Application.** Application refers to the ability to use learned material in new and concrete situations. This may include the application of such things as rules, methods, concepts, principles, laws, and theories. Learning outcomes in this area require a higher level of understanding than those under comprehension.

---

4. **Analysis.** Analysis refers to the ability to break down material into its component parts so that its organizational structure may be understood. This may include the identification of the parts, analysis of the relationships between parts, and recognition of the organizational principles involved. Learning outcomes here represent a higher intellectual level than comprehension and application because they require an understanding of both the content and the structural form of the material.

5. **Synthesis.** Synthesis refers to the ability to put parts together to form a new whole. This may involve the production of a unique communication (theme or speech), a plan of operations (research proposal), or a set of abstract relations (scheme for classifying information). Learning outcomes in this area stress creative behaviors, with major emphasis on the formulation of *new* patterns or structures.

---

6. **Evaluation.** Evaluation is concerned with the ability to judge the value of material (statement, novel, poem, research report) for a given purpose. The judgments are to be based on definite criteria. These may be internal criteria (organization) or external criteria (relevance to the purpose) and the student may determine the criteria or be given them. Learning outcomes in this area are highest in the cognitive hierarchy because they contain elements of all of the other categories, plus conscious value judgments based on clearly defined criteria.

TABLE E.2

EXAMPLES OF GENERAL INSTRUCTIONAL OBJECTIVES AND BEHAVIORAL TERMS
FOR THE COGNITIVE DOMAIN OF THE TAXONOMY

Illustrative General Instructional Objectives	*Illustrative Behavioral Terms for Stating Specific Learning Outcomes*
Knows common terms Knows specific facts Knows methods and procedures Knows basic concepts Knows principles	Defines, describes, identifies, labels, lists, matches, names, outlines, reproduces, selects, states
Understands facts and principles Interprets verbal material Interprets charts and graphs Translates verbal material to mathematical formulas Estimates future consequences implied in data Justifies methods and procedures	Converts, defends, distinguishes, estimates, explains, extends, generalizes, gives examples, infers, paraphrases, predicts, rewrites, summarizes
Applies concepts and principles to new situations Applies laws and theories to practical situations Solves mathematical problems Constructs charts and graphs Demonstrates correct usage of a method or procedure	Changes, computes, demonstrates, discovers, manipulates, modifies, operates, predicts, prepares, produces, relates, shows, solves, uses
Recognizes unstated assumptions Recognizes logical fallacies in reasoning Distinguishes between facts and inferences Evaluates the relevancy of data Analyzes the organizational structure of a work (art, music, writing)	Breaks down, diagrams, differentiates, discriminates, distinguishes, identifies, illustrates, infers, outlines, points out, relates, selects, separates, subdivides
Writes a well organized theme Gives a well organized speech Writes a creative short story (or poem, or music) Proposes a plan for an experiment Integrates learning from different areas into a plan for solving a problem Formulates a new scheme for classifying objects (or events, or ideas)	Categorizes, combines, compiles, composes, creates, devises, designs, explains, generates, modifies, organizes, plans, rearranges, reconstructs, relates, reorganizes, revises, rewrites, summarizes, tells, writes
Judges the logical consistency of written material Judges the adequacy with which conclusions are supported by data Judges the value of a work (art, music, writing) by use of internal criteria Judges the value of a work (art, music, writing) by use of external standards of excellence	Appraises, compares, concludes, contrasts, criticizes, describes, discriminates, explains, justifies, interprets, relates, summarizes, supports

TABLE E.3

MAJOR CATEGORIES IN THE AFFECTIVE DOMAIN OF THE TAXONOMY
OF EDUCATIONAL OBJECTIVES (KRATHWOHL, 1964)

Descriptions of the Major Categories in the Affective Domain

---

1. **Receiving.**   Receiving refers to the student's willingness to attend to particular phenomena or stimuli (classroom activities, textbook, music, etc.). From a teaching standpoint, it is concerned with getting, holding, and directing the student's attention. Learning outcomes in this area range from the simple awareness that a thing exists to selective attention on the part of the learner. Receiving represents the lowest level of learning outcomes in the affective domain.

2. **Responding.**   Responding refers to active participation on the part of the student. At this level he not only attends to a particular phenomenon but also reacts to it in some way. Learning outcomes in this area may emphasize acquiescence in responding (reads assigned material), willingness to respond (voluntarily reads beyond assignment), or satisfaction in responding (reads for pleasure or enjoyment). The higher levels of this category include those instructional objectives that are commonly classified under "interest"; that is, those that stress the seeking out and enjoyment of particular activities.

3. **Valuing.**   Valuing is concerned with the worth or value a student attaches to a particular object, phenomenon, or behavior. This ranges in degree from the more simple acceptance of a value (desires to improve group skills) to the more complex level of commitment (assumes responsibility for the effective functioning of the group). Valuing is based on the internalization of a set of specified values, but clues to these values are expressed in the student's overt behavior. Learning outcomes in this area are concerned with behavior that is consistent and stable enough to make the value clearly identifiable. Instructional objectives that are commonly classified under "attitudes" and "appreciation" would fall into this category.

4. **Organization.**   Organization is concerned with bringing together different values, resolving conflicts between them, and beginning the building of an internally consistent value system. Thus the emphasis is on comparing, relating, and synthesizing values. Learning outcomes may be concerned with the conceptualization of a value (recognizes the responsibility of each individual for improving human relations) or with the organization of a value system (develops a vocational plan that satisfies his need for both economic security and social service). Instructional objectives relating to the development of a philosophy of life would fall into this category.

---

5. **Characterization by a Value or Value Complex.**   At this level of the affective domain, the individual has a value system that has controlled his behavior for a sufficiently long time for him to have developed a characteristic "life style." Thus the behavior is pervasive, consistent, and predictable. Learning outcomes at this level cover a broad range of activities, but the major emphasis is on the fact that the behavior is typical or characteristic of the student. Instructional objectives that are concerned with the student's general patterns of adjustment (personal, social, emotional) would be appropriate here.

TABLE E.4

**EXAMPLES OF GENERAL INSTRUCTIONAL OBJECTIVES AND BEHAVIORAL TERMS
FOR THE AFFECTIVE DOMAIN OF THE TAXONOMY**

Illustrative General Instructional Objectives	*Illustrative Behavioral Terms for Stating Specific Learning Outcomes*
Listens attentively Shows awareness of the importance of learning Shows sensitivity to human needs and social problems Accepts differences of race and culture Attends closely to the classroom activities	Asks, chooses, describes, follows, gives, holds, identifies, locates, names, points to, selects, sits erect, replies, uses
Completes assigned homework Obeys school rules Participates in class discussion Completes laboratory work Volunteers for special tasks Shows interest in subject Enjoys helping others	Answers, assists, complies, conforms, discusses, greets, helps, labels, performs, practices, presents, reads, recites, reports, selects, tells, writes
Demonstrates belief in the democratic process Appreciates good literature (art or music) Appreciates the role of science (or other subjects) in everyday life Shows concern for the welfare of others Demonstrates problem-solving attitude Demonstrates commitment to social improvement	Completes, describes, differentiates, explains, follows, forms, initiates, invites, joins, justifies, proposes, reads, reports, selects, shares, studies, works
Recognizes the need for balance between freedom and responsibility in a democracy Recognizes the role of systematic planning in solving problems Accepts responsibility for his own behavior Understands and accepts his own strengths and limitations Formulates a life plan in harmony with his abilities, interests, and beliefs	Adheres, alters, arranges, combines, compares, completes, defends, explains, generalizes, identifies, integrates, modifies, orders, organizes, prepares, relates, synthesizes
Displays safety consciousness Demonstrates self-reliance in working independently Practices cooperation in group activities Uses objective approach in problem solving Demonstrates industry, punctuality and self-discipline Maintains good health habits	Acts, discriminates, displays, influences, listens, modifies, performs, practices, proposes, qualifies, questions, revises, serves, solves, uses, verifies

TABLE E.5

EXAMPLES OF GENERAL INSTRUCTIONAL OBJECTIVES AND BEHAVIORAL TERMS
FOR THE PSYCHOMOTOR DOMAIN OF THE TAXONOMY*

Taxonomy Categories	Illustrative General Instructional Objectives	Illustrative Behavioral Terms for Stating Specific Learning Outcomes
(See Harrow, A. J. (1972) for one method of classifying psychomotor behaviors)	Writes smoothly and legibly Draws accurate reproduction of a picture (or map, biology specimen, etc.) Sets up laboratory equipment quickly and correctly Types with speed and accuracy Operates a sewing machine skillfully Operates a power saw safely and skillfully Performs skillfully on the violin Performs a dance step correctly Demonstrates correct form in swimming Demonstrates skill in driving an automobile Repairs an electric motor quickly and effectively Creates new ways of performing (creative dance, etc.)	Assembles, builds, calibrates, changes, cleans, composes, connects, constructs, corrects, creates, designs, dismantles, drills, fastens, fixes, follows, grinds, grips, hammers, heats, hooks, identifies, locates, makes, manipulates, mends, mixes, nails, paints, sands, saws, sharpens, sets, sews, sketches, starts, stirs, uses, weighs, wraps

* Tables E.1–E.5 are from N. E. Gronlund, *Stating Behavioral Objectives for Classroom Instruction* (New York: Macmillan, 1970).

REFERENCES

BLOOM, B. S. (ed.). *Taxonomy of Educational Objectives: Handbook I, Cognitive Domain.* New York: David McKay Co., Inc., 1956.

HARROW, A. J. *A Taxonomy of the Psychomotor Domain.* New York: David McKay Co., Inc., 1972.

KRATHWOHL, D. R., B. S. BLOOM, and B. B. MASIA. *Taxonomy of Educational Objectives, Handbook II: Affective Domain.* New York: David McKay Co., Inc., 1964.

Author Index

Subject Index